SEA

C
A

N

SEA

K E Y

SYRIA

Damascus

R. Tigris

Mosul

Kirkuk

IRAQ

R. Euphrates

Baghdad

PERSIA

Amman

em

TRANSJORDAN

Basra

PERSIAN GULF

SAUDI

ARABIA

RED

Port Sudan

N

Atbara

S E A

rtoum

Scale of Miles

0   100   200   300   400   500

WAVELL
SCHOLAR AND
SOLDIER

Field-Marshal Lord Wavell

WAVELL
SCHOLAR AND SOLDIER

To June 1941

JOHN
CONNELL

COLLINS
St James's Place, London
1964

LORD WAVELL

Mars and Minerva to his cradle came
  Bringing him sword and lyre. And had the time
  Permitted, he had uttered noble rhyme
And to Parnassus left a lasting name
Which, as it was, he made amidst the flame.

Lord Dunsany

Contents

Maps

Illustrations

Acknowledgements

During the last year before he was killed in action in Kenya, Major Lord Wavell spent many months collating and indexing his father's papers and talking to and corresponding with a great number of the men and women, from all walks of life, who had known and worked with the Field-Marshal. It is obvious that this book could not possibly have been written but for these devoted preliminary labours. I can only hope it goes some way towards fulfilling the hopes which sustained Archie John Wavell in his task.

Field-Marshal Lord Wavell's papers are as voluminous as they are historically significant. They consist of, first, folders and bound volumes of almost all the letters and telegrams he wrote and received in the course of his duties after his promotion to Major-General; second, a wide and varied range of his private correspondence over many years; and third, his "Recollections," forming a detailed narrative account of his life, from his earliest childhood until 1941, compiled for his family's sake and dictated during such short leisure hours as he could snatch while he was Viceroy of India from 1943 to 1946. I have drawn freely on all these sources: all quotations of his writings in the text, other than from his published works, are from the Wavell Papers. The source of all those quotations which are set to the full text width inside quotation marks is Wavell's "Recollections" unless otherwise indicated.

I must express my thanks to the Countess Wavell, and to Lady Pamela Humphrys, Lady Felicity Longmore and Lady Joan Gordon, who from 1961 to 1964 gave me access to these papers. I am grateful, too, for all their advice and help; and I must thank the Misses Wavell, the Field-Marshal's sisters, for the loan of letters and for their interest and help.

For advice, assistance and permission to publish hitherto unpublished documents (letters, signals, diaries and reports) my gratitude goes, with apologies in advance to any whose names I may have

ACKNOWLEDGEMENTS

inadvertently omitted, to: Lord and Lady Aldington, Major-General R. H. Allen, Mr. Julian Amery, Colonel R. H. Andrew, Mrs. Joan Astley, Field-Marshal Sir Claude Auchinleck, the Earl of Avon, Major-General D. R. Bateman, Mr. J. Blakiston, Sir Arthur Bryant, Group-Captain G. M. Bryer, Major-General Kenneth Buchanan, Major F. J. Burnaby-Atkins, Lieutenant-Colonel G. S. M. Burton, Major-General Sir Walter Cawthorn, Captain George Spencer Churchill, Mr. Randolph Churchill, Mr. Peter Coats, Mr. and Mrs. Michael Crichton-Stuart, Admiral of the Fleet Lord Cunningham of Hyndhope, Sir George Cunningham, Lady Dill, Major-General E. Dorman O'Gowan, Mr. J. A. Drysdale, Mrs. Duddington, Lieutenant-General Sir John Evetts, Brigadier Sir Bernard Fergusson, Field-Marshal Sir Francis Festing, Colonel Peter Fleming, General the Lord Freyberg, Lieutenant-General Sir Alexander Galloway, Mr. David Garnett, Air Vice-Marshal K. V. Garside, Sir James Grigg, Mr. N. D. Grundy, Field-Marshal Lord Harding of Petherton, Mr. Rupert Hart-Davis, Miss Frances Hendry, Lieutenant-General Sir Brian Horrocks, Mr. Owen Humphrys, Lieutenant-General Sir Balfour Hutchison, Field-Marshal Lord Ironside, General the Lord Ismay, General Sir Henry Jackson, Lord Killanin, Rear-Admiral I. G. L. Van der Kun, of the Royal Netherlands Navy, Professor A. W. Lawrence, Captain B. H. Liddell Hart, Sir Robert Bruce Lockhart, Air Chief Marshal Sir Arthur Longmore, Mrs. A. W. S. Mallaby, Sir George Mallaby, the Rev. J. H. McKew, Major-General Neil McMicking, Lieutenant-Colonel Nigel Noble and other officers of The Black Watch, Mr. Walter Oakeshott, General Sir Richard O'Connor, Air Marshal Sir Lawrence Pendred, Mr. Stewart Perowne, General Sir Frederick Pile, Lieutenant-Colonel Robin and Mrs. Anne Ridgway, Captain S. W. Roskill, R.N., the Earl of Scarbrough, General Sir John Shea, Brigadier E. J. Shearer, Lord Simonds, Lieutenant-General Sir Arthur Smith, Marshal of the Royal Air Force Lord Tedder, Lieutenant-General Sir Francis Tuker, General Sir Ivo Vesey, Mr. David Walker, Field-Marshal Lord Wilson of Libya and Brigadier Desmond Young.

I am indebted to the following publishers and authors for permission to quote extracts from the books named: Cassell & Co., *The Second World War* by Winston S. Churchill and *The Tanks* by Captain B. H. Liddell Hart; Jonathan Cape, *Seven Pillars of Wisdom* by T. E. Lawrence; Hodder & Stoughton, *Lord Wavell* by Major-General R. J. Collins; and Her Majesty's Stationery Office, *History of the Second World War*: *The Mediterranean and Middle East* by Major-General I. S. O. Playfair.

I have also to thank all those who have made their photographs available to me for the illustration of this book, and, in particular, Lady Wavell, her daughters and the Misses Wavell, who have kindly allowed me to reproduce the portrait by Augustus John and the photographs which appear opposite pages 64, 65, 160, 161, 176, 177 and 304 (top). The other pictures are reproduced by courtesy of the Imperial War Museum, with the exception of the last, which comes from the Rommel Family Trust. To all those who have helped in the collection of these illustrations I would like to express my gratitude.

The endpapers and the maps of Ethiopia, Greece and Crete, and Syria and Iraq, are based on those by the Cabinet Office Mapping Section in Major-General I. S. O. Playfair's book mentioned above. I am grateful to Her Majesty's Stationery Office for permission to make use of these, and to Messrs. Longmans for the map of the Western Front in World War I, which comes from Captain Cyril Falls's *The First World War*. The map of Palestine is based on that which appears in Wavell's *Allenby*, and is reproduced by courtesy of Messrs. Harrap. Captain B. H. Liddell Hart has kindly given me permission to base my map of the "Compass" operation on that which appears in *The Tanks* (Cassell, 1959).

To the Council and staff of the Royal United Service Institution, and in particular to the Director and Chief Librarian, Brigadier John Stephenson, I owe a very big debt of thanks. For three years Lord Wavell's papers were in the R.U.S.I.'s vigilant custody; I had a room at my disposal; and whenever and however I asked for help or advice it was always and swiftly forthcoming. Since it was at the R.U.S.I. that Wavell made some of his own first steps in authorship, I take a special pleasure in acknowledging the continuity and tenacity of this association.

I am very grateful to Lt.-Colonel Lord Dunsany for permission to quote two poems by his father.

I must thank Mr. Mark Bonham Carter for the skill, the patience and the good temper which have constantly marked his side of the publisher-author relationship over these years.

Finally, my gratitude to my wife for her share in the work is quite immeasurable.

Preface

Wavell's body lies buried in the cloisters of the College at Winchester, of which he was a scholar. It is a green and quiet place, the air of which is steeped in a profound, cool peace and a mysterious sense of sustained and merited joy. Hither in the afternoon sunlight of 7th June, 1950, Wavell was brought to his rest, after a stately, ceremonial funeral service in Westminster Abbey.

In the years that have elapsed—he was the first to die of the principal commanders on the Allied side in the Second World War—his reputation has stood consistently high. His name has loomed above the political and military controversies that have swirled around others. His achievements as a soldier, with which this volume of his biography is chiefly concerned, though near enough in time to be clear in memory to men now only just entering middle age, yet belong to an epoch of military techniques as remote as Wellington's. There seems only the most tenuous, temporal connection between the world of the Matilda tank and the Stuka and that of the Polaris submarine and the concept of overkill.

Across the gulf of this swift scientific and technological revolution, of what interest are Wavell's strategy and tactics? Since the means of making war have changed so vastly, has not the effect on the nature of war itself been equally radical? And are the ideas and the achievements of a soldier—however eminent and admired in his own time—who had passed his peak before the revolution had accelerated to its present pace, of any particular relevance? Wavell was greatly loved, and about his name there is now a legendary quality, which one writer has described as "Arthurian"—in its context a well-chosen epithet. Is it necessary, is it seemly, to try to look deeper than the legend? As time recedes, as men grow old and their memories blur, will not the legend be of greater, more lasting significance than the factual, appropriately documented account and analysis of his career?

15

These are some of the questions with which, as the first biographer with access to Lord Wavell's private papers, I have been
faced; and with them one other, which touches my conscience
directly: if Wavell had lived longer, would he have given—as other
generals and proconsuls have hastened to give—his own account of
his service and his stewardship? His friend, John Dill, in a moment of
grave crisis in both their lives, when Churchill, about to relieve Wavell
of his command, needed assurance that the dismissed general would
not suggest, or encourage others to suggest, that he had been badly
treated, told the Prime Minister: "After the war he may write—
he writes well—and goodness knows what he may say, but who
cares?"

It is the responsibility of historians to care. The practice of
biography over the past eighteen years has toughened in me the
resolution to strive, so far as I can, to set forth the truth. Because I
had the honour of serving as a subordinate and temporary officer
under Wavell, in the Middle East and in India, I knew enough to
realise that, while the affectionate legend about him was remarkably
accurate, there had never been a full or fair assessment of what he
achieved as a fighting commander in the first two years of the Second
World War, and that Sir Winston Churchill's account of their relationship during those two years was, to put it mildly, less than
complete or just to Wavell. The truth so far as it can be discovered, I
have always believed, will do Wavell justice.

Wavell was a conscientious, dutiful man. He had in him a strong
streak of humility, which led him all his life to rate some of his own
finest qualities lower than others did. He early discovered that he
had an excellent brain, but he thought always that he was lazy. Recalling his own boyhood and young manhood, he accused himself
more than once of taking the easier course; few who knew him in his
maturity would have agreed with this self-criticism. He had great
powers of concentration, and his intelligence moved very quickly. He
had no particular patience with bores, fools or shallow show-offs; and
of this characteristic his famous and formidable silences were a
manifestation.

His mental processes were as clear as they were rapid. On paper
he was extremely articulate; his prose was simple and muscular.
With the possible exception of Alan Brooke, he was the best educated
soldier of his time ; but his outlook was not as severely professional
as Brooke's. His education was excellent, within the classical and

humanist tradition of Winchester; but like the great majority of men of his background, class and generation, he had been taught no science and no technology. His poetic sense, to which he gave increasing rein in later life, was of great if long and carefully concealed significance in his character. His intellect had depth as well as flexibility. He had the imaginative capacity, as a trainer of troops in peacetime and their commander in war, not merely to put himself into his opponent's mind—which is a necessary attribute of successful generalship—but to discern, with startling accuracy, the ideas and the feelings of the private soldiers and subaltern officers who went into battle under his orders. Although he was little of an orator and made few speeches, and flamboyant gestures were eminently distasteful to him, troops were conscious of this personal, poetic sympathy, and gave him unstinted confidence across the barriers of nationality, race, class and creed.

His professional philosophy was strictly empirical. He saw the study, preparation for and practice of his calling as the accumulation of understanding not of abstractions but of human beings, and not of humanity in general but of individuals. In his writings—no other British general to reach high command has written more about his profession and less about himself—he recurred frequently to this theme. In chapter v I have quoted at greater length a lecture he gave in the nineteen-thirties to officers about to enter the Staff College. One passage contains, I believe, the essence of his thinking:

I do advise you to study the human side of military history, which is not a matter of cold-blooded formulas or diagrams, or nursery-book principles, such as:
Be good and you will be happy.
Be mobile and you will be victorious.
Interior lines at night are the general's delight.
Exterior lines in the morning are the general's warning, and so on.
To learn that Napoleon in 1796 with 20,000 men beat combined forces of 30,000 by something called "economy of force" or "operating on interior lines" is a mere waste of time. If you can understand how a young, unknown man inspired a half-starved, ragged, rather Bolshie crowd; how he filled their bellies; how he out-marched, outwitted, out-bluffed and defeated men who had studied war all their lives and waged it according to the

text-books of the time, you will have learnt something worth knowing. But you won't get it from crammers' books.

When Wavell's own testing time came, he was neither young nor unknown; and he had lately defined, in his Lees-Knowles lectures at Cambridge, with singular clarity and candour, the standards by which he believed a general should be judged in his exercise of independent command. Measured by those standards, did he succeed or fail? In Book Two of this volume I have tried to give a narrative account of what Wavell did and how he did it in the two years during which he was Commander-in-Chief, Middle East. I hope that I have not committed the sins either of distortion or of concealment. But it would be foolish, in this Preface, to deny that I have a certain bias. It is not, I think, generally appreciated that Wavell was the last British general to have the privilege and the responsibility of independent command—and then only fortuitously, and during a few crucial months in 1940. Whether the system of close and detailed War Cabinet control, which Churchill imposed, was right or wrong will long be argued by historians; but as contributions to that argument I would offer two conclusions of my own: first, that it was not a system that brought out the best in Wavell; and second, that his victories in the Western Desert were the product of such independence as he secured, and his reverses were sustained when the control from London was rigid. This is the tragedy that lies at the core of Book Two: the trust and confidence which Wavell was given so fully by his subordinates he could never get from Churchill. For war, and for his task in war, Wavell had prepared himself long and diligently; but although as a young man he had been close to, and deeply influenced by, Allenby and Robertson, his relationship with Churchill was a hazard outside his experience. Dill, when breaking-point had come, summed it up in a single, lapidary sentence: " I maintain that in war you must either trust your general or sack him." And Churchill, incapable of trusting, was deeply reluctant to sack. I believe that, had a relationship of trust been established between these two, the course of British campaigns in the Middle East, and thereafter in other theatres of war, would have been profoundly different.

But the biographer's main concern is not with what might have been, however persuasive the case for it, but with what was. Does Wavell's name deserve, on the grounds of what he did, to be added to that list of very great commanders which he himself compiled? Did he possess those natural gifts—the power of quick decision, judgment, boldness and considerable toughness—which he laid down as essential qualifications? And did he deploy them in his campaigns? I believe that the answer to these three questions is Yes. He fought all his campaigns against odds, and in adverse circumstances such as few could have surmounted. I believe that this book offers ample proof of his skill and boldness as strategist and tactician, of his judgment, statesmanship, magnanimity and patience in his dealings with all sorts of men. As he said of Belisarius, he was not only a great man-at-arms himself, but he had the ability to impart his skill, allied to a high degree of resourcefulness in finding novel expedients to meet unusual emergencies.

I am convinced that Wavell is worthy of his place in history as one of the greatest soldiers and noblest characters of his age.

Yet when that is said, there remains an unexplored tract of his mind and spirit, something in him that was elusive, enigmatic even. Wavell drew—and he drew more and more as he grew older and his burden of responsibility increased—on hidden resources in himself, and displayed in the company of his family and close friends qualities which had nothing whatever to do with glory: intellectual and physical zest, laughter, and a tender, vernal romanticism in matters of the heart which mingled, oddly yet beautifully, with the tough sagacity of his practical judgments. There were Cavaliers and Roundheads in his ancestry; and though his outward appearance was as rugged as that of a Cromwellian general, in his spirit the Cavalier predominated. This part of his character found expression in private letters, in conversation, in hunting and the games he played, and in poetry.

None of these was mere relaxation from his professional cares. They all mattered greatly to him for themselves, and not as a means to any end. Those who criticised him for his determination, while he was in high command, to play his round of golf, to have his morning ride, run or swim, could not understand that these were an essential factor in his way of life; without them he would have been less than himself, and by contrast with those long, nocturnal sessions which were part of Churchill's life, they made no exigent demands on anybody else.

In 1943, when Wavell was in England, Churchill, it is said, asked him as one author to another what he was then writing. Wavell answered, "An anthology of poetry," and Churchill was strangely

19

shocked at the idea that a field-marshal, the Commander-in-Chief of a great army, in the middle of a bitterly contested war, could engage in so remote, so donnish and so unsoldierly a pursuit. But poetry without doubt was Wavell's strongest and most lasting solace. The Calvinist faith of his fathers to which Haig returned in the First World War, the love of nature which sustained Allenby and Alan Brooke, music, the painting and drawing which helped Alexander and Tedder—none had for Wavell the fortifying and revivifying significance of the ample array of verse which he had by heart. *Other Men's Flowers* is of the utmost interest, not only for the joy which, during the war and afterwards, it gave to many thousands of readers, but for what those many remembered lines meant to Wavell himself. As his son made clear in his introduction to the Memorial Edition, it was first compiled in the later months of 1941, and was intended to have been "just a family folio"; the family made their suggestions, and reminded him of poems they knew he loved but had forgotten to include; Peter Fleming, on his staff in Delhi, and Rupert Hart-Davis in England arranged for its publication.

Nearly all the poems themselves are part of our rich general heritage; their uniqueness in this setting lies in Wavell's choice of them and the reasons for his choice which he gave in his prefaces and his notes. To quote his son again, this is "an anthology of poems about people, of men and women in their loves and in their sorrows, voyaging, fighting, laughing in all the human situations of the mystery of life and death"; but it is also an anthology about Wavell. I learned more about Wavell from reading and re-reading those poems and his thoughts on them than from months of close and careful study of his official papers. I have always come back to *Other Men's Flowers* with, I venture to think, a joy and a sense of refreshment very like Wavell's own when he remembered the poems he put in it. Here was and is the Wavell who won a tribute beyond professional trust, beyond respect, admiration and all the outward forms of honour, a tribute of spontaneous and simple human affection. He gave much and, self-contained as he had made himself, asked little or nothing in return.

With a good deal of diffidence he allowed one poem of his own to be included, "outside the gate," as he said, at the end of *Other Men's Flowers*. In September, 1944, the first Viceroy's Verse Competition for members of the forces serving in India and SEAC was announced in a magazine called *Army Digest*, published by GHQ

(India); many of the entries for this competition were included in an anthology, *Poems from India*, which the Oxford University Press published the following year. Wavell allowed his sonnet to be reproduced in this volume, and it was printed on the same page as the poem which was his winning selection. By Corporal Keith Watson, of the R.A.F., this was called "To England":

> I shall come back,
> Find you bescarred, and yet more holy,
> Laid low in dust,
> More proud than lowly.
> I shall come back,
> And see again the clover and the rose
> Blooming anew, and bending to each summer wind that blows,
> And, being back, shall find again,
> When war is over,
> The gates of heaven are but the cliffs of Dover.

That Wavell chose this poem out of the many hundreds submitted was as clear and as quietly emphatic a statement of his feelings and thoughts as his own sonnet.

My own favourite example of his humour, which is an equally important and lasting part of the legend, occurs in *Other Men's Flowers*. In the prefatory note to the book's final section, headed "Last Post," he draws attention to the economy of words with which most of Shakespeare's characters got their dying done: "Hamlet ('The rest is silence'); Romeo and Juliet; Antony and Cleopatra; Arthur ('Heaven take my soul and England keep my bones'—a precocious last line for a young one!); Caesar, Cassius and Brutus: the principal exception is, I regret to say, a Commander-in-Chief, Othello—but he was an Oriental."

There was a wholeness about Wavell's character which refreshed and cheered those who knew him. Here was indeed a man for all seasons. It is not easy, therefore, to isolate any one trait as predominant. He had almost all those attributes which Alfred de Vigny perceived in the eternal soldier, "whose lines are as fine and clean as those of an antique medal": a fundamental simplicity, patience, reserve and selflessness, though he lacked (mercifully) the melancholy gravity of de Vigny's Napoleonic War veterans. Of all the burdens which high command imposed, he most disliked the withdrawal into loneliness;

and in the most sombre hours he found it impossible to be completely solemn.

For he was not, in the sense that Haig was, or Rommel or Montgomery, a dedicated soldier, despite all his talent and all his devotion—
a fact which puzzled and exasperated some of his serious-minded
contemporaries, and will have the same effect on military historians,
who treat war with prodigious solemnity. He once wrote:

> The main ethical objection to war for intelligent people is that
> it is so deplorably dull and usually so inefficiently run. "I see no
> reason why the human race, so inefficient in matters of peace,
> should suddenly become efficient in time of war." I've forgotten
> where I saw that but it has always seemed to me that most people
> seeing the muddles of war forget the muddles of peace and the
> general inefficiency of the human race in ordering its affairs.
> War is a wasteful, boring, muddled affair; and people of fine
> intelligence either resign themselves to it or fret badly, especially
> if they are near the heart of things and can see matters which
> ought to be done, or done better, and cannot contrive to get them
> set right.

The lightheartedness of these observations should blind no one to
their wholesome wisdom. They were a rejection of the passionate
plea of a staff officer in the War Office who, in a very dark phase of
the Second World War, wrote to Wavell begging him to go home and
assume dictatorial powers. A general in high command who fought
his campaigns with intelligence, skill and tenacity, but who at the same
time clearly perceived the futility of war and steeled himself to bear its
inefficiency and boredom, is a startling phenomenon for zealous
academic strategists, but perhaps not so rare as they believe.

Wavell's ideas on his profession and the setting in which he had
to pursue it were undoubtedly moulded by his experiences in the
First World War. It taught him a great deal about war from the standpoint of the ordinary infantryman; and these lessons, like almost all
his contemporaries who commanded great formations in the Second
World War, he never forgot. In 1935 he wrote to Liddell Hart:

> If I had time and anything like your ability and industry to study
> war, I think I should concentrate almost entirely on the "actual-
> ities" of war—the effects of tiredness, hunger, fear, lack of sleep,
> weather, inaccurate information, the time factor, and so forth.

The principles of strategy and tactics, and the logistics of war are really absurdly simple; it is the actualities that make war so complicated and so difficult, and are usually so neglected by historians.

The Ypres Salient in 1915 was a harsh school, in which Wavell quickly and grimly learned that the great headquarters where he was to spend much of his career were apt to be dismally remote from the soldier on the firing-step or crawling towards the barbed wire on an offensive patrol. He witnessed and vividly recorded, long afterwards, several glaring examples of the practical inefficiency and waste that resulted from this remoteness. But more searing and quite ineffaceable was the impression he retained of the spiritual and mental gulf which yawned between those who thought they directed the war and those who had to fight it. This was a fact of his time the comprehension of which linked him, intellectually though not emotionally, with men like Siegfried Sassoon, Robert Graves and Wilfred Owen. He had no illusions whatever about war. As a trainer of troops in the nineteen-thirties—in many ways the most creative, happiest and most rewarding period of his life—and later in high command, he strove incessantly to bridge that gulf, not only because of its psychological effects but because he was convinced that it contributed lavishly to the clumsiness with which war was conducted.

Of all the aspects of Wavell's character which I have pondered, his humility is to me—if as his biographer I were to have my back against the wall in his defence—the most important. He ended the letter to the London staff officer which I have already quoted with these words:

> Myself (since you have mentioned me as a White Hope): quite small light table beer, I am afraid; a good journeyman soldier who knows his job reasonably well, not afraid of responsibility but not seeking it; quite intelligent for one of the Unintelligentsia; confident enough in his normal judgment of things military, but no divine fire for leadership of the people. So that's that.

I have no doubts at all about Wavell's greatness as a man. To have served under his command in war and to have spent many days, to have known many dawns and sunsets, in close and concentrated meditation on what he was and what he did, are experiences for which I am

23

for ever grateful. "No great man lives in vain. The history of the world is but the biography of great men"—the latter part of Carlyle's somewhat pedagogic assertion is fiercely questioned nowadays, but I hold tenaciously to the truth of that first sentence.

Inevitably, since as the years go on a writer's mind is an ever-expanding ragbag, I have sought for others with whom to compare him. Abraham Lincoln, whom he himself once described as "wise, simple, with far-reaching vision, great faith and enduring courage"? Belisarius, whom he so greatly admired? Montrose, taking to battle and to the scaffold the certainty of the thinker and the enthusiasm of the boy? Or Malory's Sir Launcelot, "that were never matched of earthly knight's hand"? The quest, though far from vain, is endless. Wavell remains staunchly and cheerfully himself. I should do him less than honour if I strove to depict him other than as he really was.

James Boswell said in his " Introductory" to what I believe to be the best biography ever written:

I profess to write not his panegyrick, which must be all praise, but his Life; which, great and good as he was, must not be supposed to be entirely perfect. To be as he was, is indeed subject of panegyrick enough to any man in this state of being; but in every picture there should be shade as well as light, and when I delineate him without reserve, I do what he himself recommended, both by his precept and his example.

That is the example I have tried to follow. A biographer should intrude himself and his own sentiments once only in a book thus designed. Well aware of Wavell's example in this field, and obedient to my own rule, I stand aside and fling open the door. Perhaps I have been rather longer-winded than Wavell would have liked, but once the reader has turned this page he will not find me using the pronoun "I" again.

24

BOOK ONE

I

Son of the Regiment

Archibald Percival Wavell, the only son and second child of Major Archibald Graham Wavell, was born on 5th May, 1883, at Colchester, where his father was an officer in the Norfolk Regiment. His own service in and deep and abiding connections with The Black Watch were to mould his outlook and his character, but there was hardly a drop of Scots blood in his veins: his mother was a Percival, of Springfield, near Bradwell in Cheshire; and the Wavells had been settled for centuries in Hampshire.

They were originally of Norman stock, from the bay of Vauville at the north-west tip of the Cherbourg peninsula; and in the thirteenth century a Sir Richard de Vauville, who remained loyal to the ill-starred King John when he lost the Duchy of Normandy, emigrated to England and settled in Sussex. Thereafter the name in one form or another—de Vauville, Wauville and de Wavell—is to be found in land registers in the south and west of England. In 1606 a David Wavell, the direct ancestor of Field-Marshal Lord Wavell, was recorded as a freeholder in the Isle of Wight. In the Civil War a son of his was a major in the Royalist army, but a grandson—the major's younger son—was a Puritan pastor in the city of London.

There was always a strong Wavell connection with Winchester, both the city and the school. Wavells were mayors of Winchester again and again in the seventeenth and eighteenth centuries. For thirty-eight years, from 1741 to 1779, a Wavell was rector of St. Maurice, Winchester, and is buried in the church. Between 1478 and 1930 eleven Wavells were educated at the College.

Wavell's great-grandfather, William, was a surgeon, a geologist and a botanist, who discovered the mineral called Wavellite and was a Fellow of the Royal Society. His second son, Arthur Goodall, the Field-Marshal's grandfather, was an enterprising and successful soldier of fortune. From Winchester he went, at the age of nineteen

27

in 1804, into the East India Company's Bengal Army, which, with the French wars convulsing the world, he found dull and far too peaceful. On furlough in Europe he enlisted without the Company's permission in the Spanish Army, rose to be a full colonel within seven years, fought in the sieges of Cadiz and Tarragona, was wounded, acted as a liaison officer between the Regent of Spain and the Duke of Wellington, and was awarded the Order of Knighthood of Ferdinand VII.

Thereafter he had an eventful career as a mercenary in Chile and Mexico, reorganised the Mexican Army (in which he became a general), was given a vast but worthless grant of land in Texas, and led a mission to Britain to ask for formal recognition of Mexico's independence. In 1825, at the age of forty, he married Anne, the youngest daughter of Sir William Paxton, of Middleton Hall, Carmarthen, of a family originally sprung from Paxton in Berwickshire but long settled in the south. A few years later General Wavell retired and made his home at Somborne House, Little Somborne, in the Test valley between Stourbridge and Romsey. The Field-Marshal's father, born in 1843, was the ninth of the General's ten children.

He too was a professional soldier, but of a more orthodox kind than his father. He was commissioned at the age of twenty into the Norfolk Regiment, in which he served for twenty-eight years. He married in 1880, and his three children were born in quick succession: Anne in March, 1882; Archibald Percival, the subject of this biography, in May, 1883, and Lillian Mary in June, 1884.

The Norfolk Regiment was overseas from 1888 onwards, in Gibraltar and India; Archie Wavell thus spent some of the most impressionable years of his early life in an army cantonment in India. But when the battalion moved to Burma in 1891, his father, who was about to be promoted to its command, seized the opportunity of an exchange with an officer in the 2nd Battalion The Black Watch who, for financial reasons, wished to serve abroad. It was a step of the greatest importance in his own life and his son's.

Colonel Wavell took up his appointment at Limerick, but a year later The Black Watch was transferred to Maryhill Barracks in Glasgow. His tenure of command was a happy one; he loved The Black Watch and the regiment returned his affection. Archie meanwhile was nearing ten, and such teaching as he had had was at the hands of his sisters' governess. It was high time for him to go to school.

In the summer of 1893 he was sent to Summer Fields, a big and well-known preparatory school at Oxford. He was sturdily built, a little under height for his age, a quiet, composed and resolute boy. He had never been separated from his family before, but felt no home-sickness. There was a family legend that, as soon as he arrived at Summer Fields, he was introduced to a few boys, began playing with them, and after a few minutes went up to his father and mother, who had brought him, and said, "You can go now. I shall be quite all right." Of his strong spirit of independence there can be no doubt; nor of his intellectual ability; nor of his physical courage.

There were about a hundred boys at Summer Fields. Archie Wavell began in the lowest form, and finished very nearly at the top of the school. The competition was stiffer than in most preparatory schools of the 1890s; the headmaster, the Reverend Dr. C. Eccles Williams, had built up a tradition of scholarships at the big public schools, and it was a lean year in which Summer Fields could not claim eight or more. This record, maintained over many years, was achieved by sound teaching and not by cramming. Monsignor Ronald Knox, who went to the school in 1896, the year that Archie Wavell left, refuted the charge made by his less successful rivals that Williams—the Doctor as he was always called—was a crammer. He was, Knox wrote in 1941: "an amazingly successful educationist with a genius for spotting. . . . But I never persuaded myself that we only got a shop-window education. I believe we had an admirable grounding, that steeping of the mind in the first elements without which education never seems to 'take'."[1]

Education certainly "took" with Wavell. He had powers of detachment and concentration rare in so young a boy. He was a little suspicious of his intellectual capacity, and to a remarkable degree he kept his own counsel. He maintained this reserve all his life, and combined it with a permanent habit of self-depreciation. " I must have been an unattractive boy," he wrote, "very self-centred and rather bumptious, but clever enough to keep out of trouble and on the right side of people."

His surviving contemporaries did not judge him so harshly when, more than fifty years later, they looked back and remembered him as a small boy at Summer Fields. R. H. Dundas[2] wrote in 1952 to Wavell's son:

Your father was a year or two senior to me . . . I'm glad to think that, when I was ten, he was my first and greatest schoolboy hero:

a very solid little boy, with resolution and a low centre of gravity, and very hard to knock over at Soccer . . . I thought him terrific, and am pleased to think how right I was. He went to Winchester (but would have had a wider, if worse, field at Eton); and came down a term or two after he had left Summer Fields. I stood at the door of the Fifth Form room and gazed at him in mute adoration; and he observed, quite kindly, "Young Dundas, I'm not a peepshow." I retired a trifle dashed, but still mute and still adoring.

While Archie was at Summer Fields a considerable part of his holidays was spent, if not on the barrack square, inevitably within the regimental ambience. His father, who had charm as well as strength of character, was now accepted within the close-knit circle of The Black Watch. The son grew up within that circle. In 1894 Colonel Wavell handed the battalion over to Lieutenant-Colonel Wauchope; he had a few months in a staff appointment, and then went to command the regimental depot and recruiting centre at Perth for three and a half years—the years in which his son was most susceptible to influence and atmosphere.

In 1896 twelve Summer Fields' boys won open scholarships to public schools, four of them, including Wavell, to Winchester. He ranked seventh on the Winchester roll. The Doctor wrote to Colonel Wavell: ". . . I fully trust that, please God, he is going to make a good —perhaps great—man. There are not many boys who get Winchester Scholarships on 13 terms' work!"

Wavell himself wrote: "I have always taken examinations easily and they have never worried me, and I have therefore probably gained places above my real merit."

In his summing-up of his own career at Winchester, as at Summer Fields, Wavell underrated not only his intellectual ability but his qualities of character: "I was not popular with my contemporaries and rather lonely, for the same reason as at Summer Fields: there was too much ego in my cosmos."

There was great consistency about Archie Wavell's character. His spirit was like a prism, strong, durable and clear, with its own inner light, and on its surfaces reflecting the light of others. He perceived the flaws in it, and since he was without illusion and without self-deceit, he endowed them with more significance than they merited. Most of his own contemporaries, at Winchester as well as at

30

his private school, were (as their lives afterwards demonstrated) boys of virtue as well as of high intelligence, and they were not prigs. They were quite capable of recognising, even if they did not fully comprehend, Wavell's true quality. He on his side was more than responsive to theirs. He wrote in 1943:

"The three most brilliant and attractive men I can remember of my time in College at Winchester all fell in France—Raymond Asquith, Geoffrey Smith, and my own particular friend, Geoffrey Clarke. No wonder we lacked leadership in the postwar years." He added that for a half (a term) he was Raymond Asquith's "junior" or fag. "He told me that I was not a very good junior, which was true, but he was very kind and tolerant."[3]

Canon Adam Fox, who was another contemporary in College, wrote to Wavell's son: ". . . I think I was right in what I said about his friends—he didn't at all repulse them, but I don't believe he needed them. I have seen it said somewhere that Geoffrey Clarke was his great friend—I don't remember this, and I knew Clarke very well— but it may be your father liked him best, and I dare say he wouldn't have showed it if he did."

This apparently self-confident, composed and resolute boy had at this time serious, though hidden, doubts about his own powers of leadership and—should he decide to follow his father's calling—his ability to become a suitable officer. "I mistrusted my personal courage and toughness. Though I passed as plucky enough a football player, I knew how often I was tempted to funk."

He disguised and he fought the temptations to funk, and he overcame them. Many years, however, were to pass before he was able fully to prove his powers of leadership to himself.

His first surviving schoolboy letter must have been written in his first half; it described with a vividness and a wry detachment which, although characteristic of Wavell throughout his life, were surprising in a boy of thirteen, the idiosyncratic Winchester version of football in which he was being initiated.

A. P. Wavell to Miss Anne Wavell   *Winchester, 1896*

I am playing our footer or trying to. If you have never seen a game of footer, as played at present, you have missed something. However if you want a fairly good idea of it take a bit of ground and water it well and thoroughly till it is a cake of mud and there are little pools here and there and a big one in the middle.

Sprinkle a little sawdust over and dress up in cutshorts (a sort of compromise between knickerbockers and bathing-drawers) and a thin white or white and striped vest and footer boots; take two medium thick ropes, tar and grease them thoroughly and leaving them wet stick them very tightly about the height of your waist off the ground along the piece of ground you have prepared; now lean over these and get some one to push behind you at either side and endeavour to kick some object placed just within your reach on the other side of the rope, theoretically a football but the shins of the man next you do as well and shout, meanwhile, "Behind your side, confound you" at intervals; occasionally vary this with a hot, i.e. form up the sides 3 deep in the middle of the ground facing one another and when the ball is placed in the middle put your head into the chest of the man opposite you and let other men of your side shove behind you and shove for all you're worth; then return to the ropes game; do this for about 50 mins. and you will emerge what is left of you that is to say, proudly conscious of having done your duty; I forgot to mention that on occasions the ball emerges from under ropes or out of a hot; on such occasions you run violently up and down while the kicks (i.e. backs) kick the ball about. Your object in this is to try and induce the kick to kick the ball violently on to some part of your anatomy and stop thus its progression towards your own goal. When you have been thus "planted" as it is called, the consummation of glory has been achieved. The above all refers to an "up" or forward player but there are also "hot-watches" who when the ball emerges from a hot propels it towards his opponents goal and "kick" or backs who have to stop the hot-watches and kick the ball back again. These have a happier lot, as you may conceive, than an up. When I further state that there are about 6 or 7 rules one of which is sure to be broken every 5 minutes and that when a rule is broken a hot is held you may conceive the state of an up after the game. I have in the last 3 games played in all 3 positions. Such is the glorious game of football as played at Winchester. You must see a game some time.

"I think," the boy added proudly, "this is about the longest letter I have ever written."

He did everything keenly and energetically. "He would just go straight ahead," Canon Fox said nearly sixty years later. He worked and read, as he played football, with his whole being. His field of reading widened rapidly, in both prose and poetry—Carlyle, Thackeray, Dickens, Scott, George Eliot, Kipling, Jane Austen, a good deal of history, all Shakespeare, Tennyson, Browning and other poets— and he developed the discipline of learning poetry by heart.

In later life Wavell had a great love and respect for Winchester; but he believed that he himself did not get the best out of it, although he knew that he owed it much. This estimate was not accepted by those who taught him. M. J. Rendall, the Second Master, wrote to Wavell's father: "I am in all ways satisfied with your boy; both in ability and character; he has a large amount of latent power and all his work is strong. He must be a little more communicative as he grows older."

In spite of his uncommunicativeness—Rendall was himself a brilliant and gregarious extrovert—there could be no doubt about Wavell's intellectual capacity. "I found learning easy," he wrote, "and reached the Headmaster's class with more than two years to go." He was "a sound classic" in the Winchester tradition, with prospects of an excellent career in the Civil Service, in the Church or in education. In a boy with as deep and sensitive a vein of poetry in him it was curious that, as he later recorded, he preferred Latin to Greek.

Perhaps I was unlucky in my teachers or the authors whom I had to study. I read the account of Xenophon and his ten thousand with intense boredom, partly because no-one ever attempted to explain to me what Xenophon was doing or the great historical romance that lay behind the bald record of the number of "parasangs" which marked his daily advance. The plays of Sophocles also failed to interest me: their characters seemed unreal and the language stilted, and my teachers were apparently more interested in the niceties of grammar than in the dramatic or literary qualities of the writer. The composition of a Greek task of prose or iambics was complicated by the fact that I never began to understand the system of accenting Greek and was reduced to haphazard sprinkling, which one of my teachers called "the pepperbox method." Homer . . . was the one exception to the distaste with which I regarded Greek. "The surge and thunder of the Odyssey" attracted me deeply in the one term in which I read it, and I have always regretted my inability to read it in the original. . . .[4]

w.   33   B

Pepperbox method or not, the headmaster, W. A. Fearon, a first-rate classical scholar and an excellent teacher, realised that a remarkable boy was passing through his hands.

Rev. Dr. W. A. Fearon to Col. A. G. Wavell, December 27 (189-?)
I have been very much struck with your son's classical work during the past term. . . . He has a rare gift for scholarship, especially for classical composition; and, if his mind was not set in another direction, he would probably have a brilliant career before him at the University. He is in every way doing thoroughly well.

When Wavell left Winchester he gave his interleaved copy of the Odyssey to Duncan Mackenzie,[5] on whose shelves it was still to be found sixty years later. Wavell also recorded that another Wykehamist, who rose to high rank in the Royal Air Force, once told him that he had taken up a military career simply because joining the Army Class was the only way he could escape having to learn Greek.[6] This was not Wavell's reason; but his cool appraisal of his own motives was no less deflationary:

"I never felt any special inclination to a military career, but it would have taken more independence of character than I possessed at the time to avoid it. Nearly all my relations were in the Army. I had been brought up amongst soldiers; and my father, while professing to give me complete liberty of choice, was determined that I should be a soldier. I had no particular bent towards any other profession, and I took the line of least resistance."

The decision to join the Army Class brought a protest from the headmaster. He wrote to Colonel Wavell, pointing out that there was really no need to take the drastic step of putting his son in the Army, "since I believe he has sufficient brains to make his way in other walks of life." Long afterwards Wavell commented: "Not a very tactful letter, perhaps, to a soldier, the son of a soldier. . . ."

Fearon's advice was disregarded. He told Wavell and another scholar who had made the same decision that henceforth they must decide for themselves how much of his work they did. They came to the accurate conclusion that they knew quite enough Latin and Greek to satisfy the Army examiners; they saw no necessity to learn more of subjects which would be of no further use, and therefore put in only token appearances at the headmaster's classes.

However, it meant for Wavell that he came under the influence of another admirable teacher, H. C. Steel, from whom he had for a time private tuition in mathematics. This ceased when Steel wrote to Colonel Wavell to say that the boy knew quite enough mathematics to pass into Sandhurst, and apparently had no ambition to learn any more; private tuition, he pointed out, was a waste of his own time and the Colonel's money.

"Altogether I had an easy time in my last summer half at Winchester," Wavell wrote. He thought this to be the result of his own laziness—a verdict which must be treated with respect, but some reserve. A more charitable assessment could be that he was practising, even if only instinctively, conservation and economy of effort: laziness was hardly a fault of which, in mature life, Wavell could accuse himself. He played cricket as energetically as ever, and he found another kind of private coaching, given to him in history by the College tutor, H. T. Hardy. Hardy thought so highly of his history notes that he asked for them and thereafter made his other pupils copy them. This was the first evidence not only, as he wrote for his family's amusement, "of literary authorship," but of his lifelong talent for seeing a theme through and stripping it down to its essentials.

Another persistent trait, however, manifested itself during his schooldays, at home rather than at Winchester. This, in his later life, was regarded by his family and his friends as a slightly alarming "accident-proneness." There was a plane of his life on which the workaday rules of trial and error did not always apply. Any tendency to negligence he disciplined out of his own character; he knew fear, as any intelligent man must, and he mastered it completely. But his mixture of bad and good luck was unpredictable and apparently uncontrollable. The streak of bad luck took him again and again into hazardous physical scrapes (in later life he was a Jonah in almost every aircraft in which he flew); his streak of good luck deprived them of the worst and most catastrophic effects.

His mother's sister, Aunt Florry, had married an Irishman, Augustus Longfield. They had two children, Jack and Kathleen, of about the same age as their Wavell cousins, and a house near Mallow in County Cork, where the Wavells were often asked to stay. Not far away there was a pool in the Blackwater river, in which the children used to swim. One afternoon when Archie was on holiday from Winchester the boys found the river in spate. Jack challenged Archie to dive in from the high bank.

"I rather fancied myself at diving then, and was not unwilling to show off," he wrote, "and took a header off the highest part of the bank. Unfortunately I hit a rock just under the water, concealed by the flood, and nearly scalped myself. Luckily I did not lose consciousness, or I might have been drowned. I managed to swim ashore, was stitched up by the local doctor and was all right in a few days." There was a scar, however, which he carried with him for the rest of his life.

At school there was one superficial inconsistency in Wavell's career. There was no O.T.C. or C.C.F. in the 1890s; Winchester's Cadet Corps was, in his own words, "a rather forlorn little band." But there was one enthusiast among the senior men in College, who set out to conscript him into its ranks the moment it became known that he was destined for the Army. Wavell resisted and pointed out equably enough that he would have quite enough drill when he went to Sandhurst. The military zealot was unpersuaded, and so—when appealed to—was Colonel Wavell. Archie joined the Corps and remained a private in it for the whole of his service.

In a not very well-fitting red tunic (it was before khaki became the soldiers' working dress), with a rather weighty old Martini, I toiled my short legs—I was small then—on marches where everyone else always seemed out of step, or skirmished pantingly over Teg Down; and wondered whether I was really going to like soldiering. I can remember one compensating five minutes on a big Public School field day in which a regular battery had condescended to take part. The School Corps had to retire hurriedly, so hurriedly that I and a few other of the smaller or lazier ones were left behind and lay down to rest in a sheltering ditch. Presently the battery drove up and unlimbered majestically alongside us to shell our retreating comrades. After a moment's hurried conversation, we decided it was too good a chance to miss, and poured our blank into the battery at a few yards' range. To our joy an umpire appeared and ordered the battery out of action; and we even earned a paragraph in next day's paper to the effect that our reverses in South Africa were hardly surprising when a handful of Winchester schoolboys lining a ditch could put a regular battery out of action. Perhaps I then first learnt the lesson which I have occasionally put into practice since, that unorthodox methods do sometimes succeed in war.[7]

When the South African War began in October, 1899, Wavell was a schoolboy of sixteen. Its impact on his life was strong and significant. Not only did his father, still a serving soldier, hold a command at the beginning of it; he himself was to be in action in it before the confused and protracted campaign was brought to an end.

Colonel Wavell had finished in July, 1898, a happy and successful tour of duty as commander of the 42nd Regimental District at Perth, and moved to a staff appointment at the War Office. The family took a house at Englefield Green, near Egham in Surrey.

Among the British formations engaged in the earlier and disastrous phases of the war was the Highland Brigade, in which was the battalion of The Black Watch that Colonel Wavell had commanded a few years earlier; in command of the Brigade was Major-General Andrew Wauchope, his former second-in-command and successor. The news of the Battle of Magersfontein, fought on 10th-11th December, 1899, and one of a succession of serious British reversals that came to be known as "Black Week," reached Scotland three days later in the murk of a freezing winter fog. Under foolishly optimistic orders, based on shockingly faulty intelligence, the Highland Brigade, after a long night march in rain and mud, had been launched on a frontal assault, in full daylight at the height of the South African summer, on Magersfontein Hill, which was strongly held by the Boers in well-prepared trenches. Out of a total of 948 casualties suffered by the whole British force, the Highland Brigade accounted for 746: General Wauchope was one of the fifteen officers killed; thirty officers were wounded, 173 other ranks killed and 529 wounded or missing—a negligible casualty list, admittedly, by comparison with the hecatombs of young dead that the new century was to regard as commonplace; but Scotland, that bitter December day, was a land of mourning.[8]

The news came at teatime to Winchester. Andy Wauchope, Colonel Coode, C.O. of The Black Watch, Macfarlan the adjutant, an especially likeable and lively subaltern named Giff Edmonds, and several others whom Wavell, as a boy around the barracks, a son of the regiment, had known and admired: silent and miserable he looked at the list. He stood up abruptly and walked out of the room.

Four weeks later, in the middle of January, 1900, Colonel Wavell—promoted to Major-General at the age of fifty-seven—went out to South Africa to command, not the Highland Brigade, but the Fifteenth Brigade, in succession to a general who had died before he could go into action. Lord Roberts had succeeded the ill-starred Buller; and

37

Wavell's brigade formed part of an Army Corps, consisting of one cavalry and four infantry divisions, with which Roberts proposed to take the offensive against the Boers.

General Wavell, who had had a good deal of previous service in South Africa, distinguished himself in the advance to Bloemfontein and beyond. He went down with enteric fever and was in hospital; he returned to become Military Commander of Johannesburg, but fell foul of Lord Kitchener, and after Lord Roberts's return to England there was little chance of further advancement for him. By mid-October, 1900, he was homeward bound, with several other Stellenbosched generals. Meanwhile his son, at the end of his last agreeable summer half, passed fourth into Sandhurst at the age of seventeen and two months.

The Winchester dons saw Archie depart with mingled respect, affeticon, and slightly rueful bewilderment that he should go so soon and so unfulfilled—he had the brains for an open scholarship but no apparent desire to go to a university; he had not been Prefect of Hall; he had not even stayed long enough to captain the College XI—and that he should go to what they regarded as so unrewarding a profession. Rendall wrote to Mrs. Wavell:

> . . . I congratulate him on his very good place in the Sandhurst list; he has undoubted ability and has worked well. I hope in the future he will come out of his shell more; he was too retiring here; probably the Army will do this for him. I saw less of him than I should have liked, but his work lay on other lines.
>
> Of his character I think very well; I saw nothing that was not honourable and gentlemanly. . . .

Wavell spent two terms at Sandhurst instead of the ordinary eighteen months: the Army's demands for officers in South Africa were exigent.

He said, "The book work gave me no trouble, but I was not good at the drill nor at field sketching, which was at that time considered a necessary qualification for an officer. I had short legs and no sense of music or rhythm so found great difficulty in keeping step, and I was not naturally smart, which was the great military virtue at that time, though I was always well enough turned out to keep out of trouble. We spent a lot of time doing sketches and in drawing to scale diagrams of old-fashioned redoubts, lunettes, etc., which I suspect were unchanged since Crimean days. On the other hand we learnt little tactics. As I had no talent for either map-making or drill, I was never promoted."

Despite this catalogue of deficiencies, Gentleman Cadet Wavell was placed first in the order of merit at the end of his first term, and passed out first at the end of his second; his total of marks in all subjects was over eighty per cent; even in the despised "fortification" his knowledge of redoubts and lunettes was such that he obtained 272 out of a maximum of 300 marks; and his conduct—drill and dress notwithstanding—was described as "exemplary."

His father, home from South Africa, took up an appointment as Staff Officer to the Commander-in-Chief in Ireland, H.R.H. the Duke of Connaught. But his mother and sisters were still living at Englefield Green, and at week-ends he cycled home to see them. As he pedalled back to Sandhurst in the wintry darkness, his lamp often went out. Twice he was caught thus by a policeman along the straight stretch of road between the "Jolly Farmer" and Camberley. The normal fine for this offence was then five shillings; but Gentleman Cadet Wavell had the ill-luck to appear before the Farnborough Petty Sessions, and the chairman of the bench was his uncle and godfather, Colonel Llewellyn Wavell, who took pleasure in fining him ten shillings each time.

Mr. Archibald Percival Wavell was commissioned into The Black Watch on 8th May, 1901, three days after his eighteenth birthday. He had a few weeks' leave, which he spent with his father in Dublin. Both regular battalions of his regiment were serving abroad; therefore early in June Second Lieutenant Wavell joined the Details of The Black Watch at Edinburgh Castle. Here he spent two months on what was to all intents and purposes a recruits' drill course, in the company of several other subalterns including one, C. R. B. Henderson, who had been commissioned straight from Rugby. Henderson was so tall that he was nicknamed Long Man; he was a first-class athlete, keen-witted, but unambitious. Similarities of outlook counted for more than fundamental differences of character and aspiration; Henderson became and was for many years Wavell's chief friend and closest companion in the regiment. Theirs was the era of nicknames which had a habit of lingering on, often cacophonously and inappropriately. Alongside Long Man Henderson the stocky, sturdy Wavell became Podgy; and as Podgy, not Archie, one contemporary asserted, he was known until he returned to the regiment after the First World War.

The newly-joined subalterns were housed in a series of bleak single rooms on the top floor of the very summit of the Castle, a wind-swept region known as "The Rookery." Here they rocked and, as Wavell recorded in the last article he ever wrote, "cawed like young rooks. And as young rooks cast debris from their nests to the occasional annoyance of those on the ground level, so we used sometimes to amuse ourselves by driving old golf balls from the roof in the general direction of Edinburgh City."[9]

There are differences as well as gradations in human greatness. Some who are called great achieve it by being manifestly and persistently extraordinary, and in countless aspects of their outlook and behaviour different from their fellows. Wavell was of another kind: he was one of those who do not openly differ from their fellows in many particulars, but whose quality is a compound of ordinary men's ordinary virtues produced to a higher power, and expressed with a stronger intensity of concentration. The first kind soars into the light and may plummet into the darkness. The spirit of the second glows with a steadily increasing strength and range. In an epoch throughout which the meaner, more unhappy aspects of the ordinary man were squalidly exalted, Wavell's life and deeds stand as a heartening reminder of what is virtuous in ordinary Englishmen—their courage, modesty, lack of self-pity, their fidelity and their streak of poetry.

In nothing was he more ordinary and more English than in the fact that his life was rooted in a succession of deep, interlinked yet expanding loyalties: his home and family, his school, his regiment, the Army, the country. It was completely characteristic of the man that when, as a field-marshal and a peer, he had his coat of arms designed for him, and a heraldically-minded friend drew attention to the six martlets of the long-ago knights of Vauville for the shield, Wavell himself insisted merely that the supporters should be a scholar of Winchester and a private of The Black Watch.

This Black Watch private stood for a deep, durable, humorous and very human affection. He summed it all up in a foreword which he wrote, within a few months of his death, for *The Black Watch and the King's Enemies* by his friend and former A.D.C., Bernard Fergusson:

The Jock of to-day comes from the city as often as from the hills or the fields. But he still inherits the spirit and traditions of his Highland forbears—the clan feeling, the toughness, the

40

fierceness in assault, the independence of character, the boundless self-confidence in his own powers in all circumstances and conditions. He has also the habit of impressing his personality on any comrades of other origins, while retaining his own whatever his surroundings. The story has been told elsewhere of an argument between two Lancashire lads who found themselves in a Highland regiment; it was ended by one of them saying with crushing superiority: " Ahve been a Jock longer than tha."

Above all, this account of the fortunes of The Black Watch in the greatest, most wide-spread of all wars illustrates the value of regimental tradition, which has been the cornerstone of the pride, the fighting spirit, the discipline of the British infantry ever since it began to be fashioned with the first units of our Regular Army nearly 300 years ago. It has sustained us in victory and defeat, in peace and war, in barracks or camp, in billets or bivouac; and has produced units whose fame will live with those of Alexander's hoplites, Rome's legions, Napoleon's battalions. Nowhere is this regimental spirit stronger than in Highland regiments. It is the fashion to-day in some quarters to seek a soulless uniformity in all things, and decry any individual tradition or spirit. It will be a sad day and an evil day for the British infantry if the reformers ever succeed in weakening or destroying the Regimental tradition.

After a short musketry course at Hythe, in Kent, Wavell was warned that he would be going with a draft to South Africa. He had a month's leave and then reported to Edinburgh Castle. On the night of 29th September, 1901, the draft set off for active service. There were 115 N.C.O.s and men—some of them recruits, some of them old sweats who had been invalided home and were now fit for service again. Wavell was one of three subalterns with the draft, which was commanded by his friend, Long Man Henderson. It was a grey, lowering evening, but the streets from the Castle walls to the entrance of Waverley Station were lined with people. Headed by the band, in khaki tunics with their kilts swinging, the draft looked fine, and the folk cheered with the utmost enthusiasm. A good many of the Jocks, however, were already notably drunk. At the foot of Cockburn Street, so dense was the crowd, the police had put up barricades. As the column reached the Waverley Bridge the band played *Auld Lang Syne* and the crowd sang the verses with vast, billowing sentiment.

Relatives were allowed on to the platform to bid farewell to their laddies; there were plenty of tears and plenty of cheers as the train drew out of the station.[10]

The draft—known later in regimental lore as the "Dolly Gray" draft, after the music-hall song—had a leisurely but not very eventful passage to Durban. There they entrained at once for Standerton in the south-eastern Transvaal, where four companies of the 2nd Battalion formed part of Colonel Rimington's column. The war was dragging out a bleak and disagreeable phase. The Boer armies had dissolved into small, mobile, mounted "commandos," which were giving a good deal of trouble to far more numerous British forces in their task of holding and protecting fixed lines of communication. Rimington, an able young soldier, had earlier in the war raised and commanded an irregular corps of Guides; his present column was big and well-organised, but while its mounted contingent ranged the country trying to catch Boers, the infantry had the humdrum job of protecting the transport on the march and the camp at night. The days were long, slogging marches across the veld, alongside the wagons drawn by mules and oxen; and at night there was a chain of pickets around the bivouac. "Not very exciting work," as Wavell remembered it, "but it taught a young officer his job on active service, how to handle and look after his men, and himself."

Throughout February, 1902, Rimington's column was engaged in two long drives, both north-westwards from Harrismith towards the Bloemfontein-Johannesburg railway line, with the intention of hemming the commandos in against lines of blockhouses to the north and south. Wavell's diary recorded on 28th February: "End of drive. 1,100 Boers snaffled."

The next day they were relieved by the 1st Battalion The Black Watch, who had just arrived from India. They then had three months' garrison duty in Harrismith. At the end of May, some three weeks after his nineteenth birthday, Wavell was sent to join a company of his own battalion on a blockhouse line near Retief's Nek, where he arrived on 1st June. "Heard peace was declared," he wrote in his diary that night.

Shortly before, as an officer under instruction, he had attended his first court-martial, the memory of which remained with him all his life. The prisoner was an old reservist, whose endurance had collapsed, after more than two and a half years of war, under the strain and the boredom of the apparently aimless and endless marching of the infantry. Like the offender in the illustration to the Army Act who cried, "I will soldier no more, you may do what you please," he had committed an act of deliberate insubordination. The evidence against him was not disputed. When he was asked if he had anything to say in his own defence, it was obvious to the young officer watching that the man was about to burst into an account of his grievances, his weariness, and probably his family troubles. He glared angrily at the stony, unsympathetic face of the President of the court-martial, and said curtly: "I had a good deal to say, but it's no use my saying it to you."

The President snapped: "I consider that contempt of court. I sentence you to fourteen days' field punishment."

When this summary sentence had been served, the court reassembled. Wavell attended once more, hoping that now he might hear the man's defence. But the President announced: "The defence is closed. The court is closed to consider its sentence."

The technical correctness of the President's attitude could not excuse his lack of sympathy: a singularly unhappy first impression for a young officer, but it taught Wavell a valuable lesson about human beings. There is a limit, not in danger but in boredom, beyond which soldiers ought not to be driven. "Obviously," he wrote in 1944, "one cannot discharge men simply because they get bored with war—almost everyone does—but it is a commander's job to prevent men reaching a breaking-point of discipline."

Peace or no peace, it took some time to unwind the cumbrous and sizeable military machine which had been constructed in South Africa before the war's end. Wavell remained in the blockhouse line for some three weeks. "Not much to do," his diary recorded. "A few partridges to shoot and rode into Bethlehem for polo occasionally." And he wrote to his sister: "I played polo on Monday. I sometimes hit the ball now, which I never used to before."

He was back in Harrismith before the end of June. For the first time in their history the two battalions of The Black Watch were together in the same station. On 7th July Wavell played football for the officers against the sergeants on an improvised ground. Tackling a larger, heavier opponent, he fell on a hard and slippery outcrop of rock, and his left shoulder was badly broken. He was taken straight into hospital—there was no X-ray—and the shoulder was set the following morning. The official title of the Harrismith hospital was Number 19 Stationary Hospital: it was an adjective which, as the weeks

43

passed, irked Wavell more and more. His sick leave in the United Kingdom had been granted. The regiment made its leisurely preparations for departure. Still young Wavell lingered and chafed. There was one of life's vicissitudes to which he never became completely reconciled: boredom.

On 18th September he was transferred to Howick, in Natal, to wait in a convalescent camp there. He was not allowed to go and wait in Durban, but at least he was allowed out of camp. Lack of money was something of an impediment. With another young officer he went to a local bank to cash a cheque. Frostily the cashiers assured them that they had orders to refuse to cash any officer's cheque unless he was known and recommended to them. Wavell and his acquaintance demanded to see the manager. He showed them a drawer full of R.D. cheques, and said that the bank had been let down too often. They tried to argue; but after a few minutes the other officer said, "Oh, come on, Wavell, it's no use." They turned to go. The manager said, " Is your name Wavell? What's the name of the place your father had near Perth ? "

"Glendelvine."

" Aye, and what's the nearest village?"

"Murthly."

"I come from Murthly," said the manager. " I'll cash your cheque, and your friend's too, if you'll just endorse it."

On 1st October, 1902, just a year since he had embarked at Southampton, Wavell set out for home, two days before his battalion sailed for India. The permanent effects of his injury were smaller than they might have been, but for the rest of his life he could not put his left arm straight up over his head, and from time to time he had twinges of pain in it. "I think I should have been a better golfer," he reflected, "and perhaps a quicker shot, with a sound shoulder. I used it twice as an excuse for avoiding courses which I had no wish to do—a gymnastic course for which otherwise I should have been detailed, and a signalling course which did not appeal to me."

His first home leave was wintry. His father, on the verge of retirement, rented a house near Ascot while he looked for a permanent home.

"I remember once this winter going out with the Garth on a chestnut mare called Kitty, of my father's. She was a horrible ride really, a mouth like iron, and a very excitable temperament and no paces between neutral and top gear. My father for some reason loved her. He sent me out on her with a snaffle and a curious contraption called a Spanish martingale, warranted to hold any puller. (It didn't, and I have never seen one since.) My left arm was still of little real use and soon gave out. We were hunting in a large wood, cantering slowly along a rather narrow ride with a deep ditch on either side, when Kitty, who had been pulling hard all the time, finally got away with me. She went down that ride like a train, knocking riders to right and left, until she got to the Master; at that moment hounds checked in a wood, and he pulled his horse across the ride, holding up his hand to check the field but keeping his eyes on hounds. He never heard my frantic cries of warning and Kitty caught him square just behind the saddle. I never quite knew what happened to him. Kitty hardly checked, and I never got a pull at her for the next two miles or so. I then tried to sneak off home, but ran into the whole hunt round a corner. The M.F.H. told me to 'take my circus-horse home before I killed myself or something much more valuable'."

At the end of February, 1903, Wavell sailed for India to rejoin his battalion, then stationed at Ambala, a sizeable military cantonment on the Punjab plain, within sight of the Simla hills.

The five years he spent as a young regimental officer in India had a deeply formative effect on Wavell's life and outlook. It was the kind of experience shared by many men of his class and generation, part of a whole way of life which seemed immutable at the time; but in less than half a century it had vanished completely.

Because he was highly intelligent, and because his imagination was extremely receptive, Wavell turned it to excellent account. Kitchener, lately arrived from South Africa as Commander-in-Chief, at the height of his powers, had set in motion certain radical reforms, not only of the structure of the Indian Army but of the strategic dispositions and tactical training of Indian and British Service formations. But the 2nd Battalion The Black Watch, though it changed its station from the Punjab to the North West Frontier, was singularly untouched by the hand of the reformer. Socially there was a majestic indifference to—indeed total rejection of—any possibility of change. But the elaborate ritual of regimental and official society in a provincial cantonment bored Wavell. "I took practically no part in social activities," he wrote. "I was shy and gauche, and had not the least wish to meet any of the ladies in the station."

He concentrated therefore—and his powers of concentration were developing all the time—on his work and on sport. Soldiering in India was, he candidly admitted, "an easy-going business." Thursday was a holiday, and on most other days work was over before lunch. Each company did a musketry course, which took some three weeks, and a month's field training. "But," he wrote, "I can remember little or no battalion or brigade training, though there was probably an occasional field day. There were certainly no manœuvres on any large scale. I was quite a good subaltern, and probably did more work than most . . . I found my feet with my brother officers, and I think learned to handle men quite reasonably well. But I was never really a leader and was quite content to go with the common opinion and practice."

The C.O. of the 2nd Battalion The Black Watch for the greater part of Wavell's service with it in India was Lieutenant-Colonel the Hon. C. E. Maxwell, D.S.O. Chumpy Maxwell was not the first, but he was certainly one of the most singular, of the "characters" whom Wavell encountered throughout his life, and whose idiosyncrasies he observed with an unmalicious joy.

"Chumpy was a fat, heavy man, barely mobile. He was shrewd, pleasant, witty, no bad judge of men, an able and impartial dispenser of justice, clever with his tongue or pen. But as a trainer of a battalion for war or a tactical leader, he was an anachronism and rather a dangerous one. He intended to command the battalion for his four years, and had no further ambition. He succeeded in his objective, but more by skill of pen in his office than by any capacity for training or command in the field. In those days an officer who aspired to command a battalion had to pass a 'Tactical Fitness' examination. Chumpy never did so, nor was he capable of doing so. He represented originally that owing to the war in South Africa he had had no time to prepare for or pass the examination, and that the fact that he had successfully commanded during the war a detachment of the size of a battalion and gained a D.S.O. showed his capacity for command in the field better than any examination. After some correspondence he was promoted on condition that he passed the examination at the earliest opportunity. He never did and never had any intention of trying. I fancy he had been in command for nearly a year before someone on the staff realised he had not passed. He then blandly ignored all correspondence on the subject until compelled to answer. He then wrote a letter reiterating his former arguments and adding that he had already successfully commanded the battalion for a year and that it would be absurd now to examine him to ascertain his ability to do

46

something he was doing very well—or words to that effect. He kept up these tactics for two or three years, and then the Higher Command gave it up, to the old man's great delight."

Wavell's first request to Chumpy Maxwell was for three months' shooting leave in Kashmir. It was granted. Off the young man went, having arranged that the mess newspaper should be sent on to him, and having purchased two textbooks on shorthand. First he walked up to Baltistan to shoot ibex; then he made his base at Bandipur on the Wular lake, some distance from Srinagar, and went after black bear, leopard and barasingh (the Kashmir stag) until the first snowfalls of the Himalayan winter.

In the early years of the twentieth century the principal anxiety of successive Viceroys and Commanders-in-Chief in India concerned the threat of a Russian invasion from the north-west, across Afghanistan. Generations of officers, in units and on the staff, were taught to look to the north-west, to the exclusion of the whole of the rest of India. In the course of time it became customary to ignore the other, the north-eastern frontier; and it fell to Wavell, first as Commander-in-Chief and then as Viceroy, to wrestle with the difficulties which this concentration of interest, training and combat experience on the N.W. Frontier, over forty years, ultimately created.

By 1904 the effects of Kitchener's reforming zeal were beginning to be felt. At the same time, far-reaching reforms were being initiated in the Army at home. In October, with the Russo-Japanese war in progress, conflict seemed imminent between Britain and Russia, and the N.W. Frontier threat looked like becoming an urgent reality. The garrisons dotted all over India were cut to the minimum compatible with a conception of internal security no longer dominated by memories of the Mutiny. Enough manpower—British and Indian— was thereby saved to form nine field divisions instead of the previous four. These nine divisions were speedily deployed along two main axes which met at Peshawar: a northern axis of five divisions guarding the frontier along a line from Peshawar to Lucknow, and a southern axis of four divisions, with one held forward at Quetta, facing Afghanistan. As a part of these regroupings, a Highland Brigade was formed at Peshawar; The Black Watch moved up from Ambala to join the Gordons in Peshawar itself, while the Seaforths were at Nowshera.

However, the threat of a major war rumbled away into the distance for another decade. The Highland Brigade settled down to enjoy the challenge, the ardours and the fun of what all active soldiers regarded as an ideal station. Many youngsters have lost their hearts to the North West Frontier—to the land itself, to the people and to the life.

Sometimes the assault on the spirit is that of stark ugliness and discomfort—appalling heat, a dust-storm across the Peshawar plain, the eroded foothills of Khaibar or Waziristan; more often it is an impression of beauty indescribable in its clarity and contrast with the barren emptiness that went before. The weft and warp of this tapestry is woven into the souls and bodies of the men who move before it. Much is harsh, but all is drawn in strong tones that catch the breath, and at times bring tears, almost of pain.[11]

Few who have served on the frontier, either as soldiers or as civilians, have failed to respond, in some measure, to this fascination; and Wavell was not one of them. He thought that he had never enjoyed three years more. The influence of the land upon his feelings and his thoughts deepened as time passed. Since he had passed his Lower and Higher Urdu examinations while at Ambala, he was able to communicate with its people. He found the Pathans "attractive, with a sense of humour, and obviously men; though they often justified their reputation for cruelty and treachery"; men not dissimilar, in many ways, from the ancestors of his own comrades in The Black Watch—Highlanders, as they were before the Industrial Revolution, the clearances and other processes of civilisation had had their effect.

The climate of the Frontier is excellent: a sharp and crisp winter; a brief, lyrical, flower-strewn and tingling spring; and an intense but short hot weather. Wavell had all the opportunities he wanted for the physical exercise he loved. There was hunting with the Peshawar Vale Hunt, "which was excellent fun; duck and snipe shooting, not big bags, but quite enough to be well worth while; quite good station polo; a fine cricket ground; much better golf than most places in India; football and hockey with the troops; tennis and racquets."

The military training and atmosphere at Peshawar were a good deal more businesslike than they had been at Ambala—with war, even if only a frontier skirmish, always on the horizon, and with Kitchener in Simla sternly reorganising his great Command—but this went against the grain for Chumpy Maxwell and his second-in-command, who shared the lethargic old warrior's outlook. Chumpy, as Wavell remembered him, was "quite antipathetic to field training." Ordinarily he did not leave the orderly room in the morning, or go back to it in the afternoon. On Saturday morning he made his big effort of the week, which was an inspection of the barracks. He waddled round the course, only just making it if the weather were hot, and then sank into a chair in the mess with a large glass of port.

Kitchener had been appalled by the state of training of the forces under his command, and in the cold weather of 1904-5 he instituted the Kitchener Test in order to discover the level of efficiency of every unit. He made the test competitive (which Wavell in later years thought a mistake) and made the prizes, so far as the infantry were concerned, two cups, one for a British and one for an Indian battalion. At Peshawar the Gordons set busily about training and preparing themselves for the test. The young officers of The Black Watch, who felt that competition was the breath of life to the Gordons, were given no encouragement whatever by Chumpy to pay any serious attention to Army Headquarters' impositions. The idea of practising was airily waved away. Therefore when the test was taken in earnest, the regiment's showing, in phase after phase, was deplorable.

Wavell's account of one test—a night attack—and its sequel is revelatory:

"The battalion marched out of Peshawar one afternoon to a rendezvous some miles outside cantonments. I do not think most of us even knew that we were going to do a night attack. I am certain that we had had no practice of any kind. We halted for some time and had tea. Just as it was getting dark, I was summoned to the C.O. He told me I was to guide the battalion on a night march which was to start very shortly. I was given the general direction and the objective on the map we were to reach—a small stream a mile or two away; no other instructions. I just had time before dark to get a compass bearing on a mosque in the distance which I calculated was on the right line, to measure the distance on the map, and to get hold of James Blair with his scouts to help me. By the time this was done, the battalion had fallen in, in quarter-column of companies. The General (Sir Edmund Barrow) and his staff were there watching us. Chumpy ordered me to take post on the right of the leading company with my compass. I protested the impossiblity of guiding the battalion in this way, since the rifles would affect my compass, it would be quite hopeless to keep a compass steady while marching, and I could not shoulder the battalion off in any required direction. The C.O., obviously upset at having to walk some miles in the dark, told me not to argue, and gave the battalion the order 'Quick March!' I pointed out to the commander of the leading company an object just visible ahead in the required direction, told him to lead on to it, and I would give him another object when he reached it. I then doubled out to the object, took a compass bearing, gave the leading company its new mark, and ran forward again. The next forty minutes were a nightmare; the ground was open plain and there were practically no natural objects as marks, so that I had to use some of the battalion scouts as marks; visibility was less than 100 yards so that I had to take constant bearings, posting marks, and running madly in between to keep ahead of the battalion; and I had meanwhile to keep check of the distance we had marched. James Blair and his scouts gave invaluable assistance. At last we calculated we were close to our objective and I advised the C.O. to halt the battalion and deploy. Up came a staff officer and said we were nowhere near our objective, the stream. He walked forward a short distance to see where we had got to, and fell into the stream!"

Some days later General Barrow held the customary post-mortem on the conduct of the exercise.

"The Black Watch," he commented with some candour, "reached their objective correctly, but I cannot imagine how, since the officer detailed to guide them was placed in an impossible position, on the right of the leading company."

Chumpy, who in the meantime had had the matter of night exercises explained to him, stepped forward.

"I beg your pardon, sir, he was not; he was placed well in front of the battalion with the scouts."

"But, Colonel Maxwell," said the general stiffly, "I was there myself, and I saw where you placed the officer."

Chumpy held stoutly to his version, and the assembled officers prepared themselves for a delightful if hardly edifying wrangle between the general and the colonel.

The general upset their anticipations. " It's easy to settle the matter," he observed. "Lieutenant Wavell is here, I think."

Lieutenant Wavell was called to the front of the room and asked where, in fact, he had been placed. A general meant nothing to him then, but his own C.O. meant a good deal. Without hesitation he supported Chumpy's statement that he had been well in front of the battalion all the time, which because of his own exertions was quite true; except, he added, for a moment at the beginning when he had some instructions to give to the right-hand man of the leading company about a mark on which to march.

The general took his defeat with grace, apologised to Chumpy, and refrained from saying a word to Wavell about what he must have known was a rather disingenuous statement.

Next morning Lieutenant Wavell was bidden to see the C.O. Chumpy was as bland as he was massive. "I was pleased, boy, with the way you spoke out at that conference. Never be afraid of generals, and always tell the truth, and you'll get on. If you should want ten days' shooting leave at Christmas, I'm sure the adjutant will approve it after all your hard work."

Chumpy's physical mobility may have been dubious, but his mind was agile; and his laziness was offset by his wit. After the field firing, which was yet another phase of the Kitchener Test, the battalion were warned that they must march back under service conditions. Chumpy, however, decided that he, for one, was tired of pretending to be at war; he refused to send out an advanced guard or to take any military precautions. An attendant umpire, who knew what was afoot, implored the officers to get their C.O. to protect his column. Chumpy, whose sole aim was to get home as easily and as quickly as possible, could not be budged. The battalion inevitably walked straight into an ambush laid, with zeal, by the Gordons. Wavell was acting transport officer. He got the mules and the wagons under such cover as he could, and galloped off to the adjutant for orders. He encountered, not the adjutant, but Chumpy, enveloped in Buddha-like but far from military calm.

"Orders for the transport, my dear Wavell?" He surveyed the (theoretically) disastrous scene with the utmost composure. " Well, I really don't know. What do you think your mules would like? I've noticed a particularly intelligent grey one you have. I suggest you refer it to him, if you can't find the adjutant."[12]

The periods have been few in human history in which happiness such as Wavell and his contemporaries took for granted in their youth has been the lot of more than a small minority. In how much did the happiness which he had the luck to experience in his twenties give Wavell the moral fibre and the fortitude to sustain adversity, not simply on his own behalf, but for the sake of the country and the cause that he served?

In *Other Men's Flowers*, his note to Charles Kingsley's *Three Fishers*

Went Sailing reads: "I heard this song when I was very young and fell in love that night. It did not last, but the song and its memory have remained."[13]

And beneath Browning's *Childe Roland* he commented:

It is a melancholy poem but it has one stirring stanza:

> I shut my eyes and turned them on my heart.
> As a man calls for wine before he fights,
> I asked one draught of earlier, happier sights,
> Ere fitly I could hope to play my part.
> Think first, fight afterwards—the soldier's art:
> One taste of the old time sets all to rights!

It is my prescription for trying to get asleep when worried, to ask "one draught of earlier, happier sights." Sometimes it works, sometimes it happens as it did to Roland that one only recalls a tragedy.[14]

Whether or not, in the midst of the strains and the complexities of high command, the prescription worked, it is certain that Wavell possessed a copious store of "earlier, happier sights" on which to draw, even in the worst of times, and to that store the India of his youth contributed not a little: the life he led; the friends alongside whom he worked and played; the horses he rode; the dog that for several years was his constant companion.

In his profession, at its beginning as at its end, he shouldered cheerfully and uncomplainingly any duty that came his way. As a result he was "the general utility subaltern of the battalion." If a company commander went off on leave, Wavell took over his company. He was acting-adjutant if the adjutant went away. He was transport officer and he commanded the machine-gun section. One summer the quartermaster went home, and Wavell deputised for him. He was a member of the Officers' Mess Committee, under the chairmanship of a cheerful character who, whenever anybody complained of the food, had a simple, disarming answer: " Yes, old boy, perfectly bloody, isn't it?"

Wavell was neither impenetrable nor grim in these days. A private soldier, who was in his half-company for much of his service in India, recalled half a century later, "He joked and talked a lot, and his memory was very good on soldiers' families." His brother-subalterns—those of them who survived World War I—were his lifelong friends: the

serious-minded and the frivolous, the humble and the scamps. They
were his brethren and his companions. One of them wrote:

My main recollection of him was his silence, his industry, his
modesty, his sense of humour and his inimitable likeableness.
I did not visualise him as a potential top-rank general, and still
less, Viceroy; though one felt, as much as one ever thought on
these matters in those days, that he would go far as a valuable
staff officer. . . . He was a very loyal friend and always interested
in one's family and one's affairs, and always remembered them.
He had a real Christian love for his fellow-men. I have never
known anyone who had more.[15]

Equally revealing are his own memories of his friends. His affection
could not blunt his critical faculty.

"Amyas Borton,"[16] he wrote, "joined us in Peshawar and became
one of my greatest friends. He was witty, light-hearted, full of enterprise and ready for any form of sport but not specially good at any.
He was very self-possessed from the start; shortly after he joined he
committed some breach of regimental etiquette and it fell to me, as
the senior subaltern for the time being, to reprove him. I did so with
pulverising effect, as I thought. At the end of my remarks, he put his
hand on my shoulder: 'Most ably and eloquently put, old boy; it shall
not occur again, let us now have a drink.' It was irresistible, and I
doubt if a harsh word has passed between us since.

"Another friend, of a different type, joined about the same time,
or a little later. He was a pure unprincipled buccaneer, and has I
should think broken all eleven Commandments repeatedly. But whatsoever he has done and whatever has happened to him, he has always
come up smiling. An active, impertinent, impenitent little man, he has
little conscience, no fear, and imperturbable good humour. I have
always had a very soft spot for him because of his indomitable courage,
in spite of all his delinquencies."

There was another brother-officer, Arthur Wauchope, his senior
by several years and with a much wider range of experience and interests than any of his pleasant, coltish contemporaries, whose friendship for and influence on Wavell were of a special quality. He was,
as he himself recognised, particularly fortunate in this association:

"On the intellectual side the friendship Arthur Wauchope gave so
generously to a young, immature subaltern was the potent factor. He
was widely read, interested and knowledgeable about so many things—

art, books, architecture, modern developments in science, history, ancient and modern, politics (very mildly) and much else—in which but for him I should probably have taken no interest. I have owed a great deal to him, in those years, and ever since."

In 1906 Wavell branched out into extra-regimental activities. He went on a transport course, and in the autumn had himself attached to the Chitral Relief Column. The Government of India maintained at that time a column, consisting of an infantry battalion (of the Indian Army) and a mountain battery, in this remote, beautiful and strategically sensitive country. Once a year a relief column went up, and to this Wavell had himself attached, in charge of the transport of the mountain battery. His duties were light, because every officer and every man in the battery spent all his working days with mules and was accustomed to loading and handling them.

From Nowshera the column marched over the Malakand, along the Swat valley to Chakdara, and over the Lowari Pass to Kila Drosh, which was the garrison's station. Here there was a week's halt while the relief was completed, and the ponies and mules rested. Kila Drosh is only a morning's ride from Chitral itself, but through wild and precipitous mountain country. With another officer from the Guides, named Campbell, Wavell hired a couple of local ponies and set out to see Chitral.

"The path was narrow with a rock wall on one side and a sheer drop into the river on the other. The ponies would insist on walking or trotting on the extreme edge of the precipice; I realised later that their normal employment was as pack-ponies and that with a bulky pack on each side they had learned the necessity to keep well away from the rock wall. Campbell and I found it rather nerve-testing to be continually on the edge looking over a straight drop and proceeded delicately, till a mile or two short of Chitral we were overtaken by an officer who turned out to be the commander of the Chitral Scouts, named Sawyer. He offered us lunch at Chitral but said we must hurry, and proceeded at a smart canter along the extreme edge of the path. This suited our ponies who followed, but I hated it and so, I am pretty sure, did Campbell. Suddenly round a bend our guide's pony stumbled and both disappeared over the edge. We dismounted and looked over for the corpses; the accident had happened, fortunately for them, where there was only a comparatively short drop of about 15 or 20 feet, but both were lying apparently knocked out. Before we could get down, the pony picked itself up apparently unhurt; Sawyer rose a moment afterwards bleeding from half a dozen deep cuts on his hands, legs and face, but without troubling even to bathe them, he remounted the pony, scrambled back somehow on to the path and went off again at an increased pace, leaving a very definite blood trail. At Chitral he washed and bandaged himself, but treated the affair as hardly worth bothering about."

Without Colonel Sawyer's somewhat exuberant pilotage, Wavell and his companion made their way back to Kila Drosh; the return march to Nowshera was without noticeable excitement; and by the end of October he was back at regimental duty in Peshawar.

In February, 1907, the battalion took part for the first time in organised manœuvres, which proved to be a series of fairly elementary exercises with no continuous theme to link them. They were only at brigade level, and each battalion commander in turn was given command of the brigade. When Chumpy's turn came, the incorrigible old codger told his adjutant, who was acting as brigade major, to issue the appropriate orders, and toddled off by himself to look at his own battalion.

"He arrived where I was lying down in the firing line with my company, poked me in the ribs with his stick and said: 'Well, my boy, do you know I'm in command of the brigade to-day? What do you think of that?' Just then up came General Barrow and his staff, and began to discuss the dispositions of the brigade. 'I see you have put two battalions in the firing line, Colonel Maxwell, and your disposition seems generally sound, but may I ask what your field ambulance is doing in the firing line? It seems hardly the best place for it.' The C.O. turned round and saw for the first time that the bullock-drawn tonga with a native driver which represented the field ambulance was just behind him. The adjutant had forgotten to give it orders and the driver had just driven vaguely on. But Chumpy was seldom nonplussed. 'Oh, that's all right, sir, that's where I told it to be, to take me home when I got tired of this battle, sir; it will be wanted quite soon, quite soon, sir.' The general opened his mouth twice to frame a suitable reply, but could think of nothing to meet the occasion. He turned and walked off without a word. The C.O. prodded me again with his stick: 'That's the way to talk to generals, my boy, and they soon leave you alone.' And off the old man went, chuckling to himself in great glee."

During this same winter Wavell took and passed, with distinction in the written part, his examination for promotion to captain. But actual promotion was nowhere in sight and the simple round of regimental duties, which was his prospect for the next four or five years, began to pall on him. His friend Colonel Mellish, v.c., who had served in Somaliland, had stirred his imagination with the idea of a tour of duty with the King's African Rifles. When Wavell asked for his father's opinion, it was bleakly discouraging. The General wrote that he had been a long time abroad, that he had seen little of his only son, and that he himself was growing old (in fact he lived for another twenty-seven years) and wanted his son to come home. He proposed a tour of duty at the Regimental Depot at Perth, during which he could work for the Staff College.

Father and son were tenacious and strong-willed, but they reached a compromise. Wavell agreed to take long leave at home in 1908 and go up for the Staff College. If he passed, he would be at home for at least two years; if he failed, he would apply for a posting to the K.A.R.

One of his friends, Bob Wallace, had decided that he too would apply for the Staff College. Together they presented themselves in front of Chumpy Maxwell, now in the last weeks of his memorable tour of duty as C.O.

"Sir, we should like to apply for the Staff College."

Chumpy was at his most genial. "Very good idea. Excellent idea. Never went to the Staff College myself, but I'm sure it's a good thing. Certainly send in your applications."

With some diffidence they explained that regulations demanded that, before an officer could make such an application, his name should have been for at least two years on the C.O.'s Staff College list.

"Staff College list?" Chumpy snorted. " Never heard of it. What is it?"

The adjutant was summoned; he had never seen the list. The Orderly Room clerk was called in. There was a slightly uncomfortable pause while he searched some of the dustier shelves. At last he returned, holding in modest triumph a small note-book endorsed "Staff College List, 1903—"

Every page in it was virgin. With majestic urbanity Chumpy wrote on the pages for 1906 and 1907 the names of Wallace and Wavell, and their applications were duly in order, with the appropriate certificates attached.

In February, 1908, Wavell was sent on a month's attachment to the staff at Rawalpindi, in order to qualify for the Staff College examination. His duties were formal to the point of farce: he was merely given a corner in some staff officer's room and a heap of old files to study. However, in the heap he discovered some recent confidential reports, including those on the officers of his own battalion. A dull morning was thereby considerably brightened.

On the following day headquarters was humming with activity: there was trouble on—and beyond—the Frontier. A Pathan sub-tribe, the Zakka Khel, living in the Bazar Valley, south of the Khyber, had become rumbustious, and Simla had ordered a punitive expedition, under the command of General Sir James Willcocks (who subsequently commanded the Indian Corps on the Western Front in 1914-15), to move up the valley. A swirl of telegrams descended on Rawalpindi. An officer from the next room came in and asked Wavell if he could help to decipher the signals. The first telegram he was given asked for an officer to command an ammunition column with the expedition; the only stipulations were that he should be a British Service subaltern who had passed Higher Standard Urdu.

"I had not only done this but had done a transport course and passed H.S. Pushtu. I considered that there could not be a better qualified officer in Northern India. I wrote an answer that Lieutenant Wavell of The Black Watch would be selected to command the ammunition column, enciphered and despatched it, telling the hard-worked staff officer that it was a purely routine matter with which I need not trouble him. It all came out afterwards and there were some rather awkward inquiries as to who had recommended Lieutenant Wavell, but it was decided that I had shown some initiative and was undoubtedly qualified, and I was allowed to go."

The expedition was mounted in Peshawar, where Wavell joined it. He took his ammunition column forward with it, and attached himself to the Seaforths, who fought a stiff little engagement at the north-eastern end of the Bazar Valley and lost some officers. Then a detachment of the Khyber Scouts, Zakka Khel men themselves, under the leadership of the redoubtable Roos-Keppel,[17] came across from the Khyber in a swift outflanking movement, and the fighting was over. The elders came in to Jamrud for a *jirgha*, and made submission. This accomplished, they crowded round Roos-Keppel, a fierce, mousta-chioed dreadnought of a man, and asked him if they had fought well.

"I wouldn't have shaken hands with you," replied Roos-Keppel grimly, "unless you had."

"Willcocks' Week-end War"—as someone uncharitably called it—

was over. Wavell had had his first independent command on active service, and had acquired some useful experience. To his South African medal he could now add another. The ammunition column was disbanded. Wavell finished his staff attachment at Rawalpindi and then went back to the battalion at Sialkot to pack up. He had been granted a year's leave out of India. He and Arthur Wauchope agreed to travel home together. They went to Bombay by way of Agra and Gwalior. On 1st April they sailed for home in the Austrian-Lloyd liner *Afrika*. Wavell was within sight of his twenty-fifth birthday.

The waterfront of the great port dwindled astern, and the surrounding hills took on new contours in the strengthening light. The gulls dipped and swooped in the ship's wake, and as she gathered speed the muddy, grey inshore waters gave way to the deep, sparkling green-blue of the open sea. The liner swung northwards on her course, towards the Red Sea, the Suez Canal and the Mediterranean. Wavell was not to return to India until more than thirty-three years later, and then as Commander-in-Chief at a crucial period in a world war.

II

Efficient Staff Officer

Wavell was back in England before the end of April, 1908. His father had by now settled at Cranborne Lodge in Dorset, an agreeable, medium-sized country house which was to be their home until Mrs. Wavell's death in 1926. Here Wavell spent the summer, working for the Staff College examination. The General, sternly disciplinarian and far more anxious about it than his son showed any sign of being, drove him indoors to work on days when he would far rather have been out of doors.

"I did about a month with a crammer in London, the only time in my life I have ever sought knowledge from a crammer. But the Staff College examination in those days was largely a crammer's exam. There were three mathematical papers, and I had done no mathematics since leaving Winchester, and only simple mathematics then. There were also tricks of topography and military engineering to be learnt, and book French. After a very short time at the crammers I decided that I could learn the military subjects better by myself, and concentrated mainly on mathematics and French, refusing to have anything to do with crammers' military history and very little with their tactics. I learnt their formulæ and tips for military engineering and topography; and there was a useful guide to military geography they produced, with tips for drawing maps of various parts of the world. But they taught very little real useful military knowledge and I did not waste time on their military history, etc. I thought I knew as much or more myself, and I was not going to learn stock answers by heart, as many did. . . .

"The Management did not much like my method of picking and choosing what I would learn instead of doing their normal course; and when my father wrote to ask how they viewed my chances of passing they replied that of course I had no chance whatever this year, since I had been so little with them, but that if I really took a proper course with them next year, I might perhaps get in."

The examination was in early August. Wavell did not let himself be flustered into overwork. He took several weeks' complete holiday in July, and went to Scotland to play golf with Arthur Wauchope. In 1943, in the opening notes to the first section of *Other Men's Flowers*, he wrote:

Music, mystery and magic are the essence of the highest poetry. And surely it should also have meaning. The poems in this section are those that have stayed in my head for these qualities. The first one, *The Hound of Heaven*, has had a special place in my life, as a charm in danger or trouble. Many years ago a friend gave me a copy of Francis Thompson's lyric at St. Andrew's, where I was playing golf. I had it by heart in a very few readings and from that day I have used the magic of its imagery in my times of stress, to distract my mind from peril or disaster. I have re-peated the words of this greatest of all lyrics under fire, on a rough Channel crossing, in pain of body or mind.[1]

When he came to the examination he was fresh, cheerful and relaxed. Nevertheless it was a considerable ordeal. There were eighteen three-hour papers on obligatory and voluntary subjects. One-third of the vacancies were by nomination, the rest by competition. Candidates who hoped to enter the Staff College by nomination only needed to qualify in the obligatory subjects; anyone who hoped to enter by competition had to take, in addition, as many voluntary subjects as he was allowed.

"I naturally was much too young and too undistinguished to have the least hope of a nomination, so I took as voluntary subjects additional mathematics, military history and a language (Hindustani). One language was obligatory and I took French. To the best of my recollection the eighteen papers I did were: three mathematics (two voluntary); three military history (one voluntary); two tactics; two military topography; two military engineering; one military geography; two military organisation; one military law; two languages (one voluntary). It was a strenuous test, and much too academic. For instance, I got quite good marks in the higher mathematical papers, by cramming. I have never since had any occasion to use the formulæ and processes I learnt; I got over 80 per cent in French but am no French scholar; one of the topography papers consisted of a map from which one had to make a panoramic sketch, and a panorama sketch from which one had to reconstruct a map, both useless from any practical point of view."

Wavell took it all with considerable sang-froid. He did not (as some candidates did) scurry off at the end of each paper to cram for the next; he lunched and dined with friends, and between papers refrained, as far as he possibly could, from opening text-books. His father's state of mind was far more anxious. Every night the dutiful son had to send the General the day's examination papers and a report on how he had done, "which," he remembered long after, "I never really knew. Curiously enough, the only paper I really thought I had done very well, military geography, was the one in which I got the worst marks . . . I wonder what went wrong."

Nevertheless, when the list of successful candidates was published, Wavell was first, in front of the half-dozen Sappers and Gunners to whom the top places seemed a natural preserve. On 22nd January, 1909, not yet twenty-six years old and younger by ten years than almost all his fellow-students, he entered the Staff College at Camberley, which was the principal and—in those days, nearly twenty years before the foundation of the Imperial Defence College—the final gateway (or barrier) to extra-regimental promotion in the Army.

Wavell arrived there at a crucial moment. The practical reformers, who shaped the pattern of British defences so that the country survived all the shocks and horrors of World War I, were beginning to see their way, in the field of strategy rather than of tactics, to the fulfilment of some of their aims. Within the Army itself the Esher Committee's radical measures were taking effect. The Committee of Imperial Defence, Arthur Balfour's creation, was now presided over by the equally sagacious and far-sighted Richard Burdon Haldane, the Liberal Secretary of State for War. A modernised and efficient General Staff was growing as rapidly as it could; and for the expansion of this General Staff the Staff College was the recruitment and training ground. Too many of the officers who were Wavell's contemporaries or near-contemporaries at the Staff College were killed in World War I; and the untimely waste of their talents, training and experience was not the least of that war's casualties. But in these years a minority—a minority much diminished by battle—of semi-amateurs were turned into professionals; and they were just enough to prevent the 1914-18 "muddling through" ending in collapse and disaster. Of that minority Wavell was a survivor, and by the felicitous accident of his age both old enough to serve continuously throughout World War I in the rank of major or above, and young enough to exercise high command in World War II.

His mind was a powerful and flexible instrument; it is improbable that it would have become either rigid or rusty had he remained several years more in regimental service; but it is quite certain that at the Staff College—for the first time since he left Winchester—he had to match it, in work, against others as good, and that he was at an age when this experience can be of the utmost value.

During his first eighteen months at the Staff College the Commandant was one of the most brilliant and one of the most controversial soldiers who ever served the British Empire, Major-General (later Field-Marshal Sir) Henry Wilson. Wavell wrote:

"Henry Wilson was tall and lean with a curiously shaped head and face, humorous and ugly. He liked to refer to himself as the ugliest man in the Army. He had a very quick and agile brain, a ready wit, a great fund of humour and geniality. He was a very interesting lecturer. He was much more interested in higher strategy, in the relations between statesmen and soldiers, in the conduct of war at its highest level, than in the details of staff work or tactics. He was happier in dealing with the movement of great continental forces on a map than with the manœuvring of a brigade or division on the ground. His occasional lectures to us were on such matters as the desirability of conscription, the coming struggle with Germany, the size of the British Army in relation to its commitments. One of his favourite dicta was: 'There is no military problem to which the answer is six divisions and one cavalry division' (the then strength of the British Expeditionary Force). He was always interesting and stimulating on these subjects; but I think it would have been better to keep our feet more firmly on the ground."

Wilson embodied, in his powerful personality, the defects as well as the merits of the Staff College in these critical years. Wavell summed them up long afterwards:

"The instruction had, I fancy, greatly improved in quality in the few years before we went there and was more practical. . . . But it was still to my mind too academic and theoretical and aimed too high. Its main object should surely have been to turn out good staff officers and not to train commanders of corps and armies. . . . What seemed to me weak was the administrative side, especially supply and transport. It was never rubbed into us that all operations were entirely dependent on transportation, and it was not till much later in my career that I really realised this truth. . . . Also we did not have enough stress laid on the factor of morale, or how to induce it and maintain it. I think we worked on the theory that the British soldier was naturally brave and there was no need to do anything particular about it. We never considered what differences a national army might have from a regular army or how it would have to be handled. Everard Calthrop[2] was the only one of us who had thought on this, and his ideas were by no means acceptable to the teachers. I remember he suggested that there should be a section of the Intelligence Branch at the War Office, concerned not with any foreign country but with ourselves, with the reactions of the average British civilian to war and the Army. Teachers scoffed at his idea. I am glad to remember that I entirely agreed with him; if such a section had been established in 1910, what a lot of mistakes we should have avoided in 1914-18.

"A good staff officer must be able to produce clear orders or instructions at very short notice. We did not do enough of this. In our first year we did quite an amount of order writing, but not nearly enough under pressure. A paper requiring orders for the move of a brigade or division would be issued, say, on Monday and the answers would not be required till Saturday, whereas in actual practice the order would very likely have had to be written in an hour or two. And in our second year we had very seldom to write a set of orders."

There was a good deal of outdoor work, which the students did on their bicycles. Henry Wilson had introduced a practice, then current at the French Staff College, of having frequent small outdoor exercises with answers given unprepared, on the ground, by the students. At Camberley these were called "*Allez-Allez*" schemes, because (said Wilson) this was the French instructors' constant adjuration to their students; and they were, of course, the ancestors of the Tactical Exercise Without Troops familiar to everyone who held a commission in World War II.

In their second year the students had a series of much bigger exercises, most of them based on centres within reach of Camberley such as Devizes, Aylesbury, Winchester and Guildford, with another on mountain warfare in Wales.

"I think they were on too grand a scale, dealing with armies and corps rather than divisions and brigades, and with command on a high level rather than the machinery of staff work."

Students did two attachments to other arms of the service.

63

Wavell's artillery attachment, in his first year, was not particularly productive; but in his second year, 1910, he found his attachment for a fortnight to the 18th Hussars, in the course of cavalry brigade and divisional training, "interesting and instructive." Allenby, with whom his own life and fortunes were to be linked for many years, was then commanding the Cavalry Division, and was most unpopular. However, Wavell, after watching him take a conference, remarked: "That's the man I should like to go to war under." The officers of the 18th Hussars were all against him; and a fellow-student from Camberley who was his companion in the attachment said, "You only think he's a good soldier because his chin sticks out the same way as yours."

"But," Wavell wrote, "I stuck to my point, as well as my chin."

During Wavell's final year at the Staff College Henry Wilson was succeeded as Commandant by Major-General William Robertson, who was the first soldier in the British Army to rise from private to field-marshal. When he took over the Staff College he was just fifty. His father was a tailor, and he had himself been educated at a village school, whence he went into domestic service. At the age of seventeen he enlisted in the 16th Lancers as a trooper. In manner and speech he was slow and deliberate, and never uttered an opinion unless he had thought it out. In the company of men of vivid imagination and a great degree of articulation he seemed surly and stupid. He was, in fact, neither. He had, as Wavell recalled, "the most charming smile, but did not use it often." His heart was warm, but he did not wear it on his sleeve. He had strong opinions and strong principles. This dual strength made him appear stiff and uncompromising when dealing with other men, particularly politicians (of whom he was indeed profoundly suspicious) and foreigners. The French generals with whom he worked closely in the last two years of World War I nicknamed him *"Général Non-Non."* Wavell said, "Wully died as he had lived, a blunt, commonsense, practical soldier, absolutely straight and honest. . . . I should have liked to have known him better."

Robertson watched over Wavell's career with careful, shrewd interest; but their first encounter did not, at the time, seem particularly auspicious. Wavell was summoned one morning to the Commandant's study. Robertson had in front of him on the desk a paper which Wavell had written for Wilson's eyes. It contained a sentence about the relations between soldiers and statesmen which would have delighted

Major-General A. G. Wavell

Scholar of Winchester

Wilson, but over which Wully had made scrawls with a large blue pencil.

He addressed the young officer sternly: "What do you mean by writing nonsense like this? What have you to do with statesmen and their affairs? Your job is to learn the business of a staff officer, not to meddle with political matters. Never you write nonsense like that again. Do you understand?" Each sentence was punctuated by further heavy scratches at the offending passage.

Wavell promised to bear the Commandant's observations in mind and, not a little crestfallen (for he was proud of his paper), moved to the door. He was half-way out of the room when Robertson spoke again. "Very good otherwise, very good." It took him some time to realise that he had in fact been sent for to be complimented.

One of the principal tasks of the second year at the Staff College was to write what was called a Memoir. This was a long essay on the lessons of all the historical campaigns studied, which instructors and students alike took very seriously: on it an officer's capacity was largely judged, and the Commandant summed up with a long, confidential report. There were four gradings, "A" to "D." In 1910 there were only two "A's" awarded. One went to Ivo Vesey,[3] the other to Wavell. But Wully Robertson had this to say about Wavell's Memoir:

> You have put much good work into this and have evidently devoted to it great care and much labour. I am sorry, however, that your efforts have not been more constantly directed towards military matters, the study of which might have been of real value to you afterwards. The discussion of questions of policy and political matters generally leads to no practical result nor benefit of any kind to the soldier, nor is it his business.

Shortly before Wavell left the Staff College Robertson sent for him, said that he had been told to select a student from the 1909-10 course to go to Russia, and asked him to go. Wavell asked for a day or two to think it over, consulted his friend Cuthbert Fuller,[4] who had already been a language student in Russia, and accepted. His reasoning was straightforward: he was still a subaltern, and after the comparative independence of the Staff College he did not greatly look forward to the routine of regimental life in peacetime; he had the itch to see new places and new things; and, though he himself had no great opinion of his linguistic capacities, he had passed his examinations in

French, Urdu and Pushtu with little difficulty. He made two stipulations: that he should not have to pass the preliminary examination
which the regulations required before a language student was allowed
to go to Russia; and that he should have two months' leave.

These conditions meant, however, that he had to do a great deal
of work in the shortest possible time. He arrived in Moscow on
19th February, 1911, not knowing a word of Russian: he had to sit for
his examination as an interpreter in the following January.

There were several families in Moscow who made a habit of taking
British officers as paying guests throughout their period of study.
Those to whom he might have liked to go were full up for his year; of
others he did not much like what he had heard. He chose to stay with a
family into which no British officer had hitherto penetrated. The head
of the household—who was also his teacher—was a Mme. Ertel, the
widow of a writer whom Wavell described as a friend of Tolstoy.[5] She
presided over a small tribe of women (whose relationship to one another baffled Wavell all the time he was in Russia) in a third-floor
flat in a broad street leading westwards from one of the gates of the
Kremlin.

Wavell had stumbled, by chance, into the heart of Czarist Russia's
bourgeois intelligentsia in the final, forlorn years of its autumnal
flowering. This was the oddest conjunction: they had never met
anyone like Wavell in their lives before; they to him were equally
astonishing. Mme. Ertel had her twenty-year-old daughter, Natalya,
living with her; a sister, who was a teacher in a girls' school; a distant
cousin who had ambitions to become an actress; three elderly great-
aunts, known collectively as the *babushki*, who did most of the housework;[6] and another paying guest, an Armenian student named
Reuben Ivanovitch.

The young Englishman perseveringly charted his way through
this Chekovian maze. Learning the Russian language was the prime
object of his stay in Moscow; but there was much, much more that
he had to and did learn in these first weeks. One of the *babushki* at
dinner, the moment her plate was clean, snatched it up and bustled
out into the kitchen. Another *babushka* snoozed over her knitting.
Professors from the University, students, journalists, artists, doctors,
actors and actresses drifted in every evening after the meal, drank
endless cups of tea from the samovar, ate jam with a teaspoon and
talked incessantly till all hours. Their opinions were liberal and
advanced. They were for progress and against oppressive archaisms,

66

like the Government, the police and the army. In the daytime someone was almost always playing the piano; someone else was almost
always using the telephone—long, ardent, earnest feminine conversations that lasted for twenty minutes or more. Reuben Ivanovitch
ambled moodily in and out of the flat. Breakfast lasted from nine
o'clock to eleven o'clock or later, and if Wavell appeared punctually
between nine and a quarter past, there were only the *babushki* to be
encountered, with long, solicitous, largely incomprehensible questions
about whether the tea or the coffee were to his taste.

The Ertel family tried to address him, in their own fashion, as
Archibald Archibaldovitch, and thought him shy and stand-offish
when he said that he preferred to be known as Mr. Wavell. Their
friends were puzzled that they, of all people, should give hospitality
to an army officer—a member of a caste which, in their own country,
they despised and distrusted. As one by one they came into the flat
of an evening, it would be explained to them in a whispered aside
(whose meaning Archibald Archibaldovitch came to understand sooner
than they realised), "Yes, he *is* an officer, but you needn't be afraid to
meet him. *British* officers are quite respectable people—not like
ours. . . ."

Among the students who were regular callers was one agreeable
and likeable lad, whom Wavell met one day in the street, dressed as a
private soldier, during his period of compulsory military service. The
boy tried to slither past unrecognised. Wavell, who had served his
soldiering apprenticeship with Jocks, on the veld and on the Frontier,
stopped him and greeted him cheerfully. Blushing, deeply embarrassed,
the boy stammered out, "I am ashamed to be seen by you in the uniform of the worst army in the world."

Wavell told his mother, " I am in a thoroughly intellectual circle
here." The social habits of this circle were a good deal more be-
wildering than their opinions or the height of their brows. First,
nobody, so far as he could discover, ever took any physical exercise.
Second, everybody ate a great deal of highly unsuitable food at peculiar
hours. The first fortnight of his stay in Moscow immediately preceded
Lent; and a large lunch every afternoon was ushered in by relays of
indigestible pancakes, served piping hot from the kitchen, with melted
butter, sour cream, egg, salt fish or caviare or any combination of
these oddities. Each of the family tucked in to seven or eight of these
blini at a time; Reuben Ivanovitch, an undersized youth, managed
fifteen or sixteen at a sitting, and a student friend consumed, under

Wavell's fascinated gaze, twenty-four. "I," he wrote to his mother, "can eat about six if I get plenty of exercise afterwards."

Mme. Ertel "was a very good teacher, liked teaching and worked me very hard. . . . She thought me very lazy—Russians when they do work, work incessantly, and by their standards I was idle. But I worked pretty hard by mine."

Life settled into a routine. He worked every morning with Mme. Ertel, muttered apologies for his small appetite at the gargantuan lunch which the *babushki* pressed upon him, withdrew to his room, and worked on his own. Then he trudged the streets for an hour or two, and perhaps had tea at Muir and Merrilies, which he described to his family as "the Moscow equivalent of Harrods." Back at the flat he worked again until supper. His only relaxation at the outset was to go to the theatre; but the first week in Lent, throughout which all the theatres were closed, was grim.

When the spring came he found some relief from the monotony of a highly unfamiliar existence, and some chance of exercise. The Russians had, in the previous year or so, discovered football.[7] Wavell joined a team formed by a Russian doctor who had become a devoted fan of the game and consisting mainly of students and schoolboys. By the end of April he had played several games for them.

The games themselves were fun but (as he told his father) Russian national characteristics kept breaking in. "They are all advertised to begin sharp at 3 p.m.; none begins till about 3.30 and at half-time there is an interval of 15 to 20 minutes, while the players drink tea and smoke a cigarette. When one does think the game is really going to start, a representative of the Moscow sporting paper usually appears with a camera and delays the start for 10 or 15 minutes while the teams are solemnly photographed."

During April his friend Cuthbert Fuller arrived in Moscow, ostensibly to requalify in Russian, but also to pay court to his former teacher, the Princess Sophia Shahovsky (whom he married in the following year). Fuller suggested that they should go off on a tour, to see the Volga, the Caucasus and the Crimea, and Wavell agreed. Ten years to the day after he had been commissioned, he set off with Fuller and another British language student, an Indian Army officer named Churchill.

It was a pleasant holiday, in relaxed and amiable companionship. Travelling by train and ship, they saw a great deal of Russia, from Nijni-Novgorod to Tiflis and Yalta. The climax of the trip was a visit to the battlefield of Balaclava, followed by a night's stay at Sevastopol.

Wavell and Churchill—Fuller had to hurry back to Moscow, having been refused an extension of his leave—reached their hotel tired, hot, covered with dust and much in need of a bath. Opposite each of their bedrooms was a magnificent bathroom; but at the door of each bathroom stood a Cossack orderly on guard, with his master's towel over his arm, soap and sponge in hand, refusing entrance. The officers whom they served were drinking in the hotel lounge; from the little that Wavell and Churchill then knew of Russian officers they were convinced that the drinking would go on for an hour or so and the baths be forgotten.

"We retired to our rooms apparently defeated, undressed, and at a given signal flung open our doors and were into the bathrooms and had closed and locked the doors before the slow-witted orderlies realised what had happened. There was much shouting and banging at doors, but we paid no attention and had a luxurious bath."

A fortnight after Wavell's return to Moscow at the end of May, his teacher's summer visit to the country began. This proved to be a variation on the Chekov theme of the Ertel household in the city, with persistently comic undertones which were sheer Wavell. Mme. Ertel's brother-in-law owned a small estate in the heart of the Russian countryside, forty miles from the nearest railway station. A cipher in the noisy flat in Moscow, he was of hardly more account in his own home. He was a stout, placid and taciturn man, and absented himself on slightly mysterious business for days at a time. For company Wavell had three women—Mme. Ertel and her two sisters—and the Armenian student, Reuben Ivanovitch. The cousin had drifted off to the stage; Natalya was in England, staying with friends at Letchworth.

In England it was Coronation year. Apart from a brief truce in the week of the ceremony itself, one of the fiercest political battles of the century, over the Parliament Act (whose purpose was to clip much of the power of the House of Lords), raged for months. But at Yegorovka in the central Russian province of Tambov the long, sultry summer days had for Wavell more than their fill of *ennui*, mental drudgery and physical discomfort. Mme. Ertel was far from well and she felt the heat acutely. As her temper shortened, she increased the pace of her work with Wavell. His temper, too, was affected by the enormous piles of rich and highly indigestible food pressed on him three times a day by his kind and hospitable hostess.

His one escape was to go for walks through the drowsy, hot countryside. Early in his stay he took Reuben Ivanovitch with him on one of these walks. It was an unhappy experiment: the Armenian returned in such poor shape that he was at once put to bed as if he were seriously ill. Thereafter Wavell walked alone.

With Reuben Ivanovitch sulking, Mme. Ertel irritable, and his hostess forlornly convinced that she was failing to entertain him adequately, he found himself spending more and more time in the company of the third sister—the school-teacher whom hitherto he had hardly seen. She was plump, she was good-natured, and his Russian was now fluent enough for him to understand most of her conversation. But to his dismay she began to make love to him. Passionate little notes were left on his pillow; long, languishing glances were cast at him across the table. This was more than he could stand; he wrote urgently to the British Military Attaché in Petrograd to ask whether he could be given permission to attend Russian Army manœuvres.

While this comedy was being played out at Yegorovka, there occurred a curtain-raiser to the great world drama which had been developing for a decade or more. At the end of June the German Government despatched a gunboat to Agadir, a small port on the coast of Morocco, in order to protect the lives and properties of certain "Hamburg merchants" established in the area.

Someone from Yegorovka happened to drive to the post office, a score or so miles away, and returned with fairly up-to-date newspapers. When Wavell read what they had to say about the Agadir crisis he realised that a European war was an imminent possibility. He determined to return to England at once, or at any rate to report to Petrograd with a view to doing so.

It was inconceivable, the ladies chorused, that war should break out; and anyway, how could he get to it from Yegorovka? There would be no horses for days; how could even he walk, with his baggage, forty miles to the station? Wavell disciplined himself into patience. When the horses finally arrived there was with them a fresh batch of newspapers. The crisis was over—for the time being: there would be no war that year. He went to his room and unpacked his gear.

Mme. Ertel and her relations were delighted, and there followed a long argument. Wavell said that Europe had been driven to the brink of war by the ambitions of Germany. They replied that Russia, at least, would not and could not fight, and that if the Court and the Government tried to declare war there would be an immediate revolution. Wavell took leave to doubt this; he believed, he told them, that they would see all Russia united to defend the country against Germany, and that even the intelligentsia would unite in fervent support of the war effort.

To Wavell's surprise, and to the surprise of the Military Attaché, he was given permission to attend the manœuvres of the Grenadier Corps[8] in September. It was with a distinct sense of relief that he drove away from Yegorovka for the last time in that hot and queasy summer. He found himself attached to the Fifth Kiev Regiment of the Corps for a week's manœuvres not far from Moscow.

"It was my first acquaintance with the Russian Army, and practically the first acquaintance of the Russian Army with a British officer for many years. Except for the formal attendance of the Military Attaché at Petrograd manœuvres, no British officer had been allowed to see Russian training for a very long time. So I was quite a novelty, and when for a formal parade I put on the kilt I created a veritable sensation. I was impressed from the first with the Russian soldier, with his hardihood, physique, marching powers and discipline. But the lack of education of many of the regimental officers was noticeable."

Lack of education was not the officers' only defect. There was also, even among senior officers, a persistent reluctance to take responsibility, of which Wavell had personal experience. At the end of one day's exercise the regimental commander, Colonel von Etter, asked him to act as his orderly and take a message to his four battalions: they were to go to X village where the regimental cookers were, give their men a meal, and then march back to camp.

Wavell found the battalions and delivered the message, but the last battalion commander told him that his cookers were at Y village, and that he would need a further order from the commander before he could take his men there for their meal instead of to X. Nothing Wavell could say would budge him, but suddenly a solution occurred to him.

"Will *you*," he asked Wavell, "order me to go to Y, and take the responsibility?"

Wavell agreed, and the officer went off happily with his men. When Colonel von Etter heard what had happened he laughed, a little bleakly. "You'll now realise," he said, "that this is one great disability from which the Russian Army suffers." A day or two later he introduced Wavell to his divisional commander, who observed in a mildly sardonic voice, "I've heard of you. You're the British subaltern who orders Russian battalions about."

Agreeable and kindly though these Czarist officers were, they seemed to Wavell to be lacking in practical application to some of the routine matters of their profession. During one exercise he encountered a company of infantry halted at a cross-roads while their commander and his second-in-command engaged in an excited argument. When another officer told him that they could not agree on which road to take, Wavell said gently, "They seem to have a compass and a map. Can't they set the map and then decide it?"

"They've done that," replied the young Russian. "Now the question is whether the needle of the compass points north or south."

The Russians knew nothing about the British Army. One illusion Wavell was quite unable to break down was their belief that the British private soldier lived on a diet composed exclusively of chocolate creams.[9] He uncovered another misconception when he was trying to explain his country and its army to a group of officers. A cavalry officer was disconcerted and shaken by the revelation that British officers always wore mufti off duty. When he had digested this curious information he said very politely but a little pityingly, "What you have told me is most interesting, and of course everyone has their own customs; but is it not very strange to go about in civilian dress and a sword?" Wavell agreed that it would be, but explained that British officers did not wear a sword in mufti. At this the cavalryman sprang to his feet and exclaimed, "But people won't be afraid of you!"

"I said we were not out to be feared by our peaceful citizens. 'But what do you do if a civilian insults you?' I explained that we considered ourselves civilians when off duty and should settle any dispute as between civilians. He gave it up then, and obviously formed a low view of the status and spirit of the British officer."

Back in Moscow for the autumn, Wavell took up his football once more. When a German team, calling itself Berlin but consisting almost entirely of players of international status, visited Moscow he played against it in two of the three matches of its tour. In one he represented Russia against Germany; the other—billed as the English in Moscow versus Berlin—was "about the roughest and toughest game of football I have ever played. . . . The Germans won in the end, but we gave them a shaking and the crowd a good thrill."

As the deep winter set in, football stopped; but now Wavell was not reduced to trudging the snowbound streets in solitude, nor to mere skating, which he always thought dull. He had made friends with a couple of university students and the girl cousin of one of them. This young woman, Lydia Arbatskaya, came of a rich merchant family in Moscow; she was attractive, intelligent, highly-strung and a bit of a chatterbox. In this company he was introduced to a new amusement, ice-hilling, an elaborate combination of tobogganing and the motor-cyclists' "wall of death."

The setting was a large ice-rink, at night. In one corner a steep ice-run led down from a tall tower to the floor of the rink. A toboggan, with the momentum of the descent behind it, shot swiftly across the rink to the far side, where there was a sloping, semi-circular wall. The toboggan had then to be steered round the inside of this bowl until it cannoned off a final barrier of ice back to the foot of the tower.

An exhilarating and extremely hazardous variation for skilled ice-hillers involved two linked toboggans, with a pair of passengers on the first steered by a helmsman on the second. One evening, just as three of them—Wavell and Lydia Arbatskaya on the front toboggan, one of the students steering on the second—were about to take off down the ice-run, the other student flung himself on top of his friend. With the weight of four people on them the toboggans went down the run and across the rink at a breathtaking pace. The helmsman lost control, and the two toboggans shot over the top of the ice-wall and crashed on the wooden fence beyond. Lydia Arbatskaya flew through the air to hit the fence; Wavell hit the fence and fell on the girl; and both toboggans and both students fell on top of Wavell. The drop from the rim of the wall was some eight feet. The two younger men were almost unhurt. Wavell had dislocated his thumb in fending off one of the heavy toboggans—thereby probably saving Lydia and himself from death; but she was unconscious and there was a deep cut on her head.

The two young Russians panicked; Lydia, when she came to, was clear-headed and resolute. Her parents disapproved of her ice-hilling and she was determined not to go to a doctor, who would send her home with a bandaged head. Wavell, however, was equally insistent that she must have proper attention. They found a doctor who stitched up the cut and bandaged it so that the girl could arrange her hair over the dressing and conceal it from her parents.

On the following night, knowing that unless she tackled it at once she would never do it again, Lydia persuaded Wavell to take her to the rink once more. "I had been practising by myself for some nights," he said, "and I could get myself safely round the course by this time, but I had never taken a passenger, and to have as my first a young woman with a broken head and highly-strung nerves was not an attractive proposition. However, she insisted. We got round safely in two or three runs, and her nerves were restored."[10]

Memories and reflections he had in plenty after that year in Russia. In less than a decade the world he had known, not merely as a casual student but in a family, was to vanish in war and revolution. But across the gulf of enormous and terrible change, Wavell retained an ineffaceable impression of the quality of the people, the ordinary Russians, "the most interesting and vital people in Europe," as he wrote of them in 1944. "I have always since," he added, "liked the Russians better than any other foreigners I have met, but I have known their weaknesses as well as their strength."

He left Moscow on Christmas Day, 1911, and was home two days later. In January, 1912, after a few days of brushing up with a coach, he sat for the interpretership examination. He took a first class without difficulty, and off he went to Switzerland with his sister Anne to ski.

He was now a man marked out for promotion. During the ten years in which he had held his commission, the Army had changed greatly around him, almost entirely for the better. Since England's anti-militarist tradition ran strong and deep, it was still composed of volunteers, without a conscript to its name. In size, therefore, it could not match the massive arrays of divisions and corps which several European countries were preparing to mobilise. But in quality, as it was soon to prove, it was unrivalled in Europe, or the world. The greatness of that old Regular Army—"the cornerstone which the builders rejected," as its historian described it[11]—was founded on the fortitude, the steadiness, the discipline and the morale of the "other ranks," the private soldier and the N.C.O., whose virtues were those of the nation which bred them, a society lately agricultural, now deeply industrialised yet undebauched. But since there are no bad soldiers but only bad officers, the merits of the officers of the army which went to France in 1914 cannot go unrecognised. There was no "officer corps" in the old British Army. These were in no sense a caste, set apart from civilians; they made no claim to be a social, political or intellectual élite; they were neither arrogant nor exhibitionist. Their principal failing was a cheerful, larky amateurishness—a survival of the Cavalier strain in the English blood—but there were enough natural Cromwellians amongst them to prevent it from getting out of hand. Their virtues were the essential complement of the Army's virtues; and the unifying force was not an Army tradition but a regimental tradition, which N.C.O.s and private soldiers shared to the full with officers. This regimental tradition, however, was not solely, or even in considerable part, a celebration of victory; it was much more a tradition of sacrifice within a brotherhood. The deeds it commemorated were not bloody and vengeful triumphs over a hated enemy, but heroic though hopeless last stands, and the sacrifice of brother for brother, officer for private soldier, private soldier for officer. Wavell carried with him into the staff appointments which, with increasing responsibility in war and peace, he was to hold for the next ten years, a strong and subtle sense of the value of the regimental tradition in which he had been bred and had matured.

Not yet twenty-nine, and by the standards of the time very young to be a G.S.O.3, Acting Captain A. P. Wavell was appointed to the War Office in March, 1912. He worked first in the Russian section, writing a handbook on the Russian Army which, although he laboured far beyond ordinary office hours upon it, earned him no praise and no thanks from his G.S.O.1, "a very grudging sort of fellow."

This task accomplished, he was transferred to the Military Training branch, and joined the section which dealt with the O.T.C. He spent most of the summer of 1912 touring the country inspecting school contingents. This was the life for him: he had an open "runabout" car; he saw a good deal of England, skilfully choosing areas in which he had friends, from each of whose houses he could reach a number of schools; and at the end of the summer term he had a week at the principal O.T.C. camp at Tidworth Pennings.

It was disappointing therefore when autumn came to be ordered back to the Russian section, under the Director of Military Operations and Intelligence, the former Commandant of the Staff College, Henry Wilson. Wavell tried to protest, but was rather frostily reminded that this was the very purpose for which he had been sent to Russia. Desk work it was, but it was one of the most interesting and vitally important of all the departments in the War Office, dealing as it did with both operations and intelligence. The work was reasonably diversified: Wavell's G.S.O.1, for example, dealt with France, as well as with Russia and the Scandinavian countries; and in the Russian section there were only Wavell and a G.S.O.2. Wilson, with his quick, restless and fertile brain, his political interests, his charm and his lack of stuffiness, was an excellent chief; and the directorate was at the centre of the country's defence preparations.

These preparations, in which Wavell as a subordinate staff officer had his part to play, were as extensive as they were careful. One of the most inaccurate of the many myths that have grown up about the First World War is that Britain entered it quite unprepared. It is true that the keynote of the policy followed by the Prime Minister, Herbert Asquith, and the Foreign Secretary, Sir Edward Grey, was peace, and that they both regarded war as something to be avoided by every possible means. But this does not imply that they, or the Government they led, did not make prudent preparations against a war. On the contrary, it was the verdict of the official historian of World War I that "Britain never entered upon any war with anything approaching such forwardness and forethought in the preparation of the scanty military resources at the disposal of the War Office."[12]

Wavell found his own work monotonous at first, since it consisted mainly of indexing and filing information, compiling summaries, answering questions any other branch might want to ask about Russia, and occasionally writing papers about probable Russian action in the event of war with Germany.

He took a furnished flat in Pall Mall, and renewed and strengthened more than one of his old friendships. Everard Calthrop, whom he had first met at the Staff College, also held a War Office appointment. Calthrop was disdainful of convention, and when the two of them lunched together, as they did a good deal, he would lead the way to Soho, to one of the few Chinese restaurants that then existed in London outside Limehouse, or to a pub. Thereafter, Calthrop again in the lead, they would call on some unorthodox or eccentric acquaintance of his, an antique dealer with a shop full of dusty junk, or a second-hand bookseller.

Professionally as well as socially Wavell widened his horizons. Three years after Blériot had flown the Channel and brought his aircraft to land in a hollow of the downs behind Dover Castle, civilians and soldiers were already pioneering in the air. Wavell arranged with Calthrop that they would learn to fly together in early-morning lessons at Brooklands. Wavell had just been accepted for the course by the

Flying Corps authorities when Calthrop announced dolefully that he had told his mother and sister, and they had objected so strongly that he felt he must withdraw.

"I had had no intention of telling my family. I failed to get any other of my friends at the War Office to learn with me, and it seemed rather a dreary business going down alone each morning, so I gave it up—a lack of keenness and enterprise really. I wonder what my fate would have been if I had taken up flying then. . . . I might have become a pioneer of the Royal Air Force, but should quite likely have killed myself, as I am not much of a mechanic and a bit careless."

In the summer of 1912, and again in 1913, Wavell attended military manœuvres in Russia. In 1912 he was accompanied by an elderly lieutenant-general on half pay, who had expected to be sent to formal Guards' exercises near Petrograd but found himself, in the company of a young officer not yet in his thirties, bumping comfortlessly across Russia to Odessa, by sea to Batum and thence to Tiflis, and on to very rough country high up in the Caucasus. Wavell left the general at corps headquarters, out of which the old man did not budge, and attached himself for several days at a time to each of the three arms— infantry, cavalry and artillery. He consolidated and deepened his knowledge of the Russian Army and of the Russian character. The officers of each arm in turn set out to make him drunk. Only once, at an enormous luncheon in honour of the anniversary of the battle of Borodino, at which every one of several hundred officers present insisted on drinking a toast with him, and each professed himself insulted if refused, did the attempt almost succeed. About half-way through the meal he looked up and saw a long, long line of officers at his right hand, each holding his glass. "I said to the officer next to me that I must get out on some pretext, and I managed to get clear while still in full possession of all my faculties. I went to my tent, lay down and slept all evening. Next morning I had not a shadow of a head. The Caucasian wine is good and pure."

He was away on this mission for just over a month, and thoroughly enjoyed the jaunt. He had seen much of the inner life of the Russian Army, he had acquired a considerable insight into the characteristics of all three arms, and he had confirmed his admiration for the Russian soldier and his liking for the Russian people at large.

His experience in 1913 was a good deal less agreeable. The manœuvres he attended, in the Kiev district, were on a bigger scale than any he had previously watched. His observations in the field and his conclusions afterwards followed their earlier pattern. He reported that the Russian soldier was first-class fighting material, that he was adequately led up to battalion level, that the higher command was weak, the General Staff unpractical and academic, with a great addiction to theories and paper plans which never worked out in practice, the equipment in many respects inadequate, the transport and the rear echelon administration almost entirely deficient. History was to demonstrate the soundness of these judgments.

At the end of the manœuvres he stayed for a day or two in Kiev, and got permission (which had never been granted to the Military Attaché) to visit the Russian Army's principal military aviation centre, just outside the city. "I was shown all the aircraft they had," he wrote, "which were very few, and was taken up in one, which incidentally crashed on landing, fortunately with no damage done, except bruises."

This small hazard surmounted, he encountered more serious trouble on his way home. Its origin lay in a piece of bureaucratic fussiness inflicted on him before he left England. Every year, at the beginning of the foreign manœuvres season, all officers going on ob-serving missions were given a printed document, setting out the in-formation which the War Office would like them to acquire. It was customary for each branch to give a list of all the subjects in which it was interested: the Artillery branch wanted to know about Russian gunnery, and all new weapons, including secret designs; the Engineer-ing branch wanted details of Russia's fortifications along her western frontier; Transport would like a full account of the Russian Army's first and second line transport. Wavell always regarded this as a very futile document, and long before he set out in 1913 he had relegated his copy to his Out tray.

Just as he was leaving London on 20th September, a few seconds before the boat-train steamed out, a War Office messenger sprinted along the platform and handed him a sealed envelope. It contained another copy of the questionnaire. In a crowded train he was unable to destroy it. Quietly cursing its unknown sender, he locked it away in an inner compartment of his despatch case, meaning to throw it over-board during the Channel crossing. But the document slipped entirely out of his mind until he saw it three weeks later, in circumstances of considerable drama and danger.

From Kiev he went to Moscow where, after one night at the Metropole Hotel, he stayed with English friends. During his time at the Metropole his room was searched by the secret police. He left Moscow on 10th October. The train reached the frontier about midnight, and there was the usual wait of an hour or more while passports were checked. Wavell left his sleeper to have a cup of tea and a sandwich in the refreshment room. He noticed that there were soldiers with fixed bayonets guarding every carriage on both sides of the line. When he got back to the train a police officer was making his round, returning passports.

Wavell gave his name and held out his hand for his passport. " If you are Captain Wavell," the policeman said heavily, "you are under arrest and must leave the train."

"On what charge am I under arrest?"

"I cannot say."

"Then I refuse to leave."

The altercation became heated. A posse of police, big in stature and bristling with weapons, appeared.

"Do you propose to take me off the train by force?"

"Yes, Captain Wavell."

"All right, I'll come voluntarily, but under protest."

His luggage was taken off the train and impounded; he himself was locked in a cell. The train rumbled and whistled away across the frontier. A cold and extremely angry Wavell was conducted into the presence of another and senior police officer. He renewed his protest in the most energetic terms and demanded to be allowed to send a telegram to the British Ambassador. His baggage was brought in and opened. Every scrap of paper in it was laid on a table in front of the police officer.

"Now to my horror, I suddenly saw that stupid War Office document which had been handed to me just as the train started and which I had entirely forgotten. I was still convinced that my arrest was a blunder on the part of some official but I realised that if they got this paper the authorities might use it as an excuse, and I determined to prevent this if possible."

The police officer sat staring at the mass of paper in front of him. It was obvious that he could not read English and that he was not the most intelligent of his kind. Wavell thought it only fair to help him. There were some Russian hotel bills, there were letters from Russian friends. Wavell took one or two of the most innocuous of these, and asked the officer if he wanted them. He read them, said no, and threw them on the table. Wavell fed him another dose of similar *trivia*.

They too were read and thrown aside. When there was a sizeable pile of these discards Wavell asked, "May I take back those you have already passed?"

The officer agreed. With the pile Wavell managed to abstract the W.O. document, and a little later was able to destroy it, almost under the noses of his guards. The officer put the rest of the papers under seal; and when the Berlin-Warsaw express came into the station Wavell was put on it in charge of two heavily-armed policemen. In the dawn in Warsaw he was marched off to the Citadel, and there he was kept under close arrest until about four in the afternoon. He kept up his own morale, and reduced his bewildered guards to a dither, by abusing them and threatening them with ferocious penalties for this disgraceful treatment of a British officer.

"I was at last taken before a Russian lieutenant-general, dressed as an officer of the General Staff, but really one of their Secret Police branch. He told me that my papers had been examined, that nothing at all incriminating had been found and that I was at liberty. And then he went on: 'And now I require an explanation.' This was a bit too much. I said I was the person who required an explanation; I had been invited to Russian manœuvres as an official guest and then arrested with no justification at all, as he himself admitted, subjected to considerable indignity and treated as a criminal instead of as an officer of a friendly army. He then began to bluster and said I had only myself to blame, since I had been travelling with a Russian secret document. He flourished the printed scheme of manœuvres for the Kiev District which I had been given, containing the general and special ideas which were naturally marked Secret before the manœuvres took place. I told him not to talk nonsense, he must have sufficient military knowledge to know that that was not a secret document after manœuvres and that I had every right to have it. I added that when the secret police searched one's baggage, they might be less clumsy than to mistake that for a secret document. He professed righteous indignation; of course baggage was never searched by the police in Russia. Then how did they know, I inquired, that I had this alleged 'secret' document, which had been inside a locked attaché case inside a locked trunk ever since I left the manœuvre area. Either they knew from the Army authorities that I had been given this document, and had used it as an excuse for arresting me, which I did not believe, or the secret police had seen it when they searched my luggage and had been stupid enough to believe it secret. He changed his tone after this and offered me refreshment. Though I had had nothing to eat or drink for nearly twenty-four hours, I refused; and said that since I was free, if he would return my papers and my baggage and my ticket and book me a sleeper on the express that night, I would return home forthwith, and our Governments could decide what action should be taken against those responsible for such stupid and insulting treatment. That ended the interview and I felt that I had had the better of it."

After some months the Russian Military Attaché in London (who, Wavell knew, was not a soldier at all but a member of the Secret Service Police) asked to see him, and presented him with a gold watch bearing the imperial monogram of Nicholas II, and with it a personal message from the Czar. Ostensibly the presentation was because Wavell, a year or two before, had translated into English a propaganda biography of the Czar—a merely business transaction, which had earned him a fee of £15. In fact it was a clumsy and circuitous way of apologising—Wavell called it an *amende déshonorable*—for his arrest.

The full truth he learned long afterwards. The secret police, searching his room at the Metropole Hotel, were interrupted when he returned unexpectedly. They had had a glimpse of the wretched War Office document, but had not had time to examine it carefully or take a copy. They therefore ordered his arrest, were gravely upset when they failed to find the offending paper, either at the frontier or in Warsaw, and had to invent lame excuses. "It was lucky," Wavell commented "that I managed to get hold of it and prevent their finding it, or I might have had a lot of trouble."

Wavell was thirty in 1913. So far as his regiment was concerned (and therefore his place in the Army List) and despite the fact that he had passed his examination for promotion to captain six years earlier, he was still, after twelve years' service, a subaltern. It was his father's view that it was now high time for him to get married. More than once when Archie came down to Cranborne the old gentleman spoke to him about it—frankly and affectionately. From time to time he introduced his son to a young woman whom he thought eligible. Wavell loved and admired his father, but he had not the slightest intention of marrying to please him; indeed, the idea of marriage did not appeal to him at all at this time. However, in the spring of 1913 he fell in love—briefly, as it turned out, but deeply enough to ask the young woman to marry him. She was Irish, she was a Roman Catholic, she was (as he recalled a lifetime later) "sweetly pretty," and she was

81

years his junior. She refused him. He bore his rejection with fortitude. His was not the kind of heart that would be easily broken.

"Later the same year my cousin Vere Bellairs asked me to go to Ranelagh or Roehampton one afternoon and she said she was taking a very attractive girl. I went with Vere to pick up the young lady at Basil Mansions where she lived. She was a quarter of an hour to half an hour late—not unusual with her, I afterwards discovered. She was a Miss Queenie Quirk, daughter of a Colonel Quirk who commanded the Welch Regiment. She was slim and attractive in a large hat. When we got to Ranelagh we found Vere wanted to look at something dull, so we went off together to watch polo and made friends. We met at intervals up to the outbreak of war in 1914."

In the opening months of 1914 the internal political battle over Home Rule in Ireland convulsed the country far more acutely than did any—as it seemed, comparatively remote—threat of external war. The Liberal Government moved warily and wearily towards the final carrying out of the pledges it had been forced to give to its Irish Nationalist allies in the House of Commons. The Conservative Opposition fought the Home Rule Bill line by line and word by word on its passage to the statute book; and outside the House, the party and its leaders aligned themselves openly in support of the implacable hostility to Home Rule of the Ulster Movement, led by Sir Edward Carson.

The Ulster Unionists had left the Government and the country in no doubt that, if it came to the proof, they would use force to defend their religious and civic liberty, their birthright as citizens of the United Kingdom, and to beat off any attempt to put them, as they passionately believed, under alien rule. They had raised and trained (though not yet armed) a disciplined force called the Ulster Volunteers; they had a complete plan for a provisional administration, a judiciary, a police force and essential services throughout the Six Counties. They refused, however, to be the aggressors, and stood resolutely on the defensive.

It was the Government—or more specifically two members of it, the First Lord of the Admiralty, Mr. Winston Churchill, and the Secretary of State for War, Colonel Seely—who adopted with zest the role of aggressor and thus brought the Army violently, and almost disastrously, into the forefront of national politics.

On 9th March, 1914, the Prime Minister, Mr. Asquith, moved the second reading of the Home Rule Bill in the House of Commons. He offered to exclude the six Ulster counties from its operation for six years. Bonar Law, the Leader of the Opposition, and Carson both demanded that the exclusion be absolute and subject to no time limit. The debate was adjourned indefinitely, without a division.

The Government, in their view, had made a final effort at conciliation, and it had been spurned. The time had therefore come for sterner measures. Ulster's resistance must be suppressed, if necessary by force. It was this decision which inevitably involved the Army.

Many officers of the Regular Army were of Anglo-Irish, Protestant stock and background. Some—not a few—had been born in Ulster and had their homes there. Field Marshal Lord Roberts, v.c., a national hero, was a passionate Ulster Unionist. So was Henry Wilson, who in his position at the War Office was fully aware of, and able deeply to influence, any military planning and preparation for the forceful suppression of Ulster. He was also in frequent and very frank communication with Leopold Amery, one of the ablest of the younger Conservative back-benchers, and with Bonar Law.

Wavell, as a junior officer in Wilson's directorate, was therefore at the heart of the crisis which developed. The decision he reached, in face of considerable pressure, revealed the integrity of his mind and the independence of his judgment.

Intelligence reports had been reaching the Government of plots to raid stores of arms and ammunition in various parts of the Six Counties, and on Saturday, 14th March, the War Office wrote to General Sir Arthur Paget, the G.O.C. in Ireland, telling him of these plots and asking him to take the necessary steps and report immediately. That same evening Churchill, in an excitable and menacing speech at Bradford, hinted that if Ulster persisted in refusing the Government's final offer, as expressed by Asquith in his Commons' speech earlier in the week, the forces of the Crown would have to be employed against her.

In the event, the Navy's part in what came to be known as the "Curragh mutiny" was hardly more than a ritual movement of warships several weeks later. Churchill's opposite number at the War Office, Colonel Seely, lacked the First Lord's capacity for finesse. Impatient for action by Paget, he ordered him to report personally in London, with detailed plans of his intentions, on the morning of Wednesday, 18th March.

For two days Paget, a volatile and very stupid officer, was

engaged in harassing conferences in Whitehall. On the afternoon of his second day in London, orders were posted at the Curragh, the main British military cantonment in Ireland, that ammunition must be served out to every man in barracks. "These sudden orders startled the Curragh garrison from top to bottom."[13]

Meanwhile, Paget was in process of being given his final orders by the Secretary of State and the C.I.G.S., Sir John French. These were verbal, and no written record was preserved. Afterwards there was a great deal of acrimonious controversy about both the content and the purpose of these orders; Paget interpreted them—as he was shortly to make clear to the officers of his Command—in one fashion; the Government, whatever their intentions at the time, subsequently interpreted them quite differently.

Paget took the boat back to Dublin that night, and next morning signalled to Seely that the administrative arrangements for the movement of troops northwards to Ulster were proceeding smoothly. He then summoned his generals and his brigade commanders, outlined in emotional terms the orders he had been given, and said that he had with difficulty extracted two "concessions" from Seely: first, that officers actually domiciled in Ulster would be exempted from taking part in any operations that might occur; they would be "permitted to disappear," and when all was over would be allowed to resume their places without their career or position being affected; second, that while officers who stated that they were unwilling to serve might tender their resignations, these would not be accepted and they would forthwith be dismissed the service.[14]

The principal formations to be committed to the operations were the 5th Division, commanded by Major-General Sir Charles Fergusson,[15] and the 3rd Cavalry Brigade, commanded by Brigadier-General Hubert Gough.[16] They returned each to his headquarters. Fergusson, though gravely upset, decided that it was his and his officers' duty to obey orders, even in circumstances so harsh; there was therefore no crisis, no "mutiny", in his Command. But Gough had other views, other sentiments. In the late afternoon of Friday, 20th March, Paget signalled to the Secretary of State for War: "Regret to report Brigadier and 57 officers, 3rd Cavalry Brigade, prefer to accept dismissal if ordered north."[17]

Whitehall and Fleet Street hummed with rumour that week-end. Journalists, on motor-bicycles with sidecars, sped between Dublin and the Curragh; officers' wives were seen in the main thoroughfare of the cantonment openly in tears.[18]

Captain Wavell, of the Russian section of the Intelligence Department, went to the War Office on Saturday morning.

A. P. Wavell to Maj.-Gen. A. G. Wavell   *21st March, 1914*

Events are moving very quickly in Ulster now and matters have come to a very serious crisis as regards the Army. . . .

What I'm going to say now is *absolutely between ourselves.* Gen. Wilson had all the officers in his department who were in the office this morning down to his room and told us of the situation that had arisen, that he was going to Sir John French and that the matter was being talked over with the Government and it seems that if the Government will not give a pledge that the Army is not to be used against Ulster, Wilson himself and probably a good many others will resign. He certainly will if the Government take any steps to punish Gough and the others. In fact he called us in to ask us, if any of us were thinking of resigning in support of Gough, at least to wait until Monday. Now that is a very serious situation. What has happened is bad enough, but if we are going to have wholesale resignations over what I maintain is still a political matter, it shakes all discipline and drags the Army into politics.

Once it comes to real civil war every man has a right to choose his own side but we haven't got there yet and I hope will still steer clear. The idea of the officers of the Army going on strike, which I think is what it really amounts to, over this business, is to my mind absolutely disastrous. What about the men? They can't resign whatever their opinions are. Of course the Government's ultimatum to the officers, if they put one, was absolutely unfair. It isn't fair to ask a man to make up his mind in a few hours on what he will do in a situation which has not yet arisen, or else lose his commission. I am afraid the Government have trapped the simple, honest officer over this. They can now claim that these resignations are a political move, that the troops were merely being moved as a precautionary measure, and arouse class feeling against the officer. Lloyd George is already busy at Huddersfield doing very much that. But whatever one may think of the Government's tactics, one can't get away from the fact that they are the Government of the country and I think it's up to us to

85

obey still. Of course, one can see the point of view of the officer ordered to Ulster. Once there trouble may break out and one can't very well resign practically in the face of the enemy.

It's difficult to see how the thing is going to end but it's not going to make the Army any more popular. Recruits will be told that they only enlist to shoot their fellow countrymen while Labour speakers will point out how the officer will aid in suppressing stikes but refuse to suppress men of the same political opinion when they go on strike.

What a muddle we've got into over this wretched business, all due to the professional politicians—both sides equally bad. Perhaps I'm pessimistic about it and it may clear up. Anyway, keep all this to yourself.

But there had already been certain dramatic developments in the crisis of which Wavell was still ignorant. Late the previous evening the Army Council had authorised Paget to suspend from duty all senior officers who had tendered their resignations or otherwise disputed his authority, and to take whatever action he thought proper. Gough and two regimental commanders who had also resigned were to be relieved of their commands forthwith and were to report at the War Office as soon as possible. Resignations of all other officers were to be refused.

Gough and the two colonels arrived in London on Sunday and were interviewed individually by Seely and the C.I.G.S. They were given until Monday morning to decide whether they would withdraw their resignations. By that time rumour and counter-rumour had created an explosive situation within the General Staff.

A. P. Wavell to Maj.-Gen. A. G. Wavell   *23rd March, 1914*

. . . When I went to the War Office this morning, a large number of officers apparently had their resignations in their pockets. Apparently what happened to-day was that the three General Staff directors went to French and said that they would resign and that there would be wholesale resignations in the Army, unless Gough and the officers of the 3rd Cavalry Bde. were reinstated and a written pledge given by the Government that the Army would not be used to coerce Ulster. The Government, amazing as it appears to me, gave way. I imagine Sir John French and other members of the Army Council threatened to resign. Anyway at

5 o'clock this evening Wilson had all his directorate in and informed us that Gough and his officers were going back to Ireland with a signed pledge that the Army should not be used against Ulster. He did not read the actual pledge but what he did read us was a statement signed by Gough with regard to the interpretation of the final paragraph of the guarantee, which it seems was obscure. Gough's statement was: "I understand the meaning of the last paragraph to be that the Army will not be used under any circumstances to enforce *the present Home Rule Bill on Ulster.*" This was countersigned by Seely authorising him so to interpret it to his officers on parade.

Well, there you are. The attitude of the majority of officers is that the Army by the action of these officers has saved the situation, won a great victory, etc. I cannot agree. I think they have won a political battle to the ruin or great danger of the Army and the country. For it is a political victory; how can you call it other when the Army refuses to enforce the *present* Home Rule Bill? It seems to me deplorable that those words should be used. And Wilson made no secret of his opinion. He actually said: "The Army have done what the Opposition failed to do" and "will probably cause the fall of the present Government." What right have the Army to be on the side of the Opposition, what have they to do with causing the fall of Governments?

No, to my mind, this has been fought on the wrong issue. The issue on which I too, I think, would have acted as the officers concerned did was the action of the Government in holding a pistol at the officer's head and trying to coerce him by threats at his pocket, saying "You must do this or be *dismissed the Army* losing your livelihood and your pension." It is inconceivable to me how an English Government could have done such a thing. . . .

And the attitude of Sir John French and the Army Council amazes me. Here we have a body of men at the head of the Army who acquiesce in an order like that being framed, fail to see what the effect on the officers will be, and yet submit to *pressure from their subordinates* to get the decision rescinded . . . .

How is the country going to take that state of affairs? And how are you to preserve discipline after this, how are you to use

87

your Army to keep law and order against strikers when once the officers have successfully resisted an attempt to use them to enforce a law which they do not approve?

One lacks perspective at present of course. But I see only disaster from what has happened. We seem to have lost our balance and hard-headedness; this Ulster business should have been settled a year ago, only that it was a good weapon in the political game.

Better destroy this letter, which is written for *you alone*. Perhaps things may turn out better than I expect.

Things did to some extent turn out better than seemed possible on that Monday evening. The worst did not happen in Ulster; there was no civil war, no proclamation of a provisional Government. The worst did not happen to the Army, whose officers were too level-headed to set themselves permanently against the Government, and did not seek to revenge themselves on individual members of it. But the immediate rumpus in Parliament and in the Press was of truly formidable proportions. Asquith refused to endorse the undertakings by which Gough set so much store. Seely resigned; so did the C.I.G.S. and another senior member of the Army Council. Wavell summed up his own view, and his own position, in another letter to his father a week later.

A. P. Wavell to Maj.-Gen. A. G. Wavell   *29th March, 1914*

. . . The majority of my friends applaud Gough's action. They say once the troops had moved civil war could not have been averted. Well I think they should have obeyed orders, whatever they were, that came from the responsible heads of the Army and the Government. But the Army was placed in a most damnable and unfair situation by the Government, and it is hard to blame Gough, especially the way the question was put to him, because he was not asked to obey orders but whether he would serve against Ulster or be dismissed the Army. Of course it was not Gough's action alone that caused the Government to climb down. They were told by the G.S. directors that if they persisted in their plan, nearly the whole of the G.S. at the W.O. would resign. So you see what a position I should have been placed in, if the Government had persisted on Monday. Holding the views I do, I should have thought it wrong to resign, but I should have been in a very small minority, I think, and it would have been a question whether it would have been right to resign against my convictions for the sake of maintaining a show of unanimity among the G.S. It would have been a pretty hard alternative to face. . . .

I don't think there is any danger, as you say, of this thing dividing the Army in any way, if it is settled soon. It will merely increase their contempt for the politicians. But there may be a good many resignations in disgust of the richer men, who will think it simply not worth while to serve when there is a danger of their being placed in such positions. And if "The Army versus the People" becomes an election cry, it will destroy all the work that has been slowly and painfully done to popularise the Army in the last ten years or so, to say the least of it.

The effects of this episode on the Army were not as calamitous as many had feared, and six months later had hardly any meaning at all. There was however a significant phrase in Wavell's third letter to his father: "merely increase their contempt for the politicians." Of the two politicians principally involved one resigned, the other remained in office. Contempt was a strong word, used in a moment of anger and distress; for Wavell, as a consequence of the politicians' irresponsibility, had faced the biggest crisis of his life so far—a crisis of conscience, which had ranged him in opposition to the majority of his friends and brother-officers. It was to his benefit that he discovered that he had resources of independence of mind and integrity of spirit whose existence he had hitherto discounted. But there was a less happy effect. When indignation cooled, contempt was replaced by a suspicion of professional politicians, however talented, however versatile, which deepened and strengthened as the years passed. The source of some misunderstanding and mistrust, a quarter of a century later, between two great servants of the state is perhaps to be found in the reactions of an unknown young staff officer to the behaviour of a powerful and famous Cabinet Minister, nine years his senior, in the days immediately following the second reading of the Irish Home Rule Bill.

Wavell was born in the sunset of the high Victorian era; he had spent his early manhood in its long afterglow, whose apparent serenity had been disturbed by sudden jabs of lightning, by the mutter of thunder, and by clouds massing above the horizon's golden rim. Like many others of his generation, and to a degree that was expressive of his spirit and his intelligence, he had the capacity to enjoy life to the full. More than most, from his special position in the War Office, in these last months before the storm broke, the darkness fell and the old world died, he had reason to know what was coming. He did not allow his knowledge to blur his zest in the slightest. He packed every remaining moment with happiness. Even after the murder of the Archduke Franz Ferdinand at Sarajevo which, as he rightly believed, made a European war inevitable, he took as much leave as he could throughout July. He spent, too, more and more time in the company of the girl he had taken, on a summer afternoon the year before, from Basil Mansions to Ranelagh. It was fun to be in her company; but this was much more than an agreeable acquaintance. She had an array of qualities some of which complemented, some of which contrasted with his own. He had lived in an intensely masculine atmosphere, into which after his return from India he had introduced his sisters. His feelings about his mother were dutiful rather than loving. Cranborne was in essence a Victorian household, with Victorian values and a Victorian rhythm to its existence. Eugénie Quirk's home, temper and outlook were as characteristically Edwardian. Those elements in both of them which were in contrast fascinated and delighted them—and continued to do so all their lives—at least as much as those which were complementary. She was gregarious and sociable; she confessed to being lazy and unpunctual. She was an only child who had grown up surrounded by her parents' cosy and unquestioning affection. Her father, Colonel John Owen Quirk, C.B., D.S.O., was of Manx origin, an athlete, a good shot, physically fearless, affectionate, even-tempered, generous and unambitious. His wife, Eugénie, was an O'Brien, of the Protestant and Unionist branch of that extremely diverse and talented family, the daughter of a distinguished Dublin book collector who was a distant relative of the Napoleonic Marshal MacMahon. She was a beauty, with prematurely white hair (a family trait which descended to her daughter), intelligent, well read, and an excellent mixer. Her daughter, in her turn christened Eugénie but always known in the family as Queenie, said: "She loved music and parties and old furniture." The Quirks were a deeply affectionate couple. Their love spilled over generously to their only child and then to their son-in-law, and he returned it in full. His wooing was cautious and (characteristically) not very demonstrative; It came from a heart that was not cold but had been waiting a long time for the glowing fire, the strength, the passion and the compassion that his marriage was to bring him.

One house-party in Essex was especially memorable. Wavell gave Miss Quirk a lift in his car:

"Somewhere passing through the East End I got into difficulties, not my fault, someone else in a car or on foot did something stupid, and I had to take a quick decision to avoid disaster. The only way out was over a traffic island between two lamp-posts; I took it, got away safely without collision and no policeman happened to be there to question the propriety of my action; so I drove on. I glanced at my passenger; she had remained perfectly calm in the crisis, and made no comment. I gave her good marks for that. The incident was safely over, and I saw no particular reason to comment on it; so we drove on in silence."

Many years later they discussed the episode. She said that his driving over the island had not shaken her: it showed, she thought, an ability to think and act quickly. What did make her a little apprehensive was the complete absence of comment: was a happening of this kind so common in his motoring experience that he took no notice of it at all?

Archie said, "I hoped you hadn't noticed the danger."

"Then," his wife retorted spiritedly, "you must have thought you were courting an imbecile."

His last peacetime leave Wavell spent with friends near Dublin, whence he was summoned urgently back to Whitehall, to find the Army on the verge of mobilisation.

Like hundreds of his contemporaries, he had one dominant thought—to be in the Expeditionary Force and in the fighting in Europe before it was too late; but in the extraordinary chaos which was the War Office in the early days of August, 1914, he was one of the few who—reluctant and resentful—were bidden to stay. He feared that he would never get overseas before it ended. Only the new Secretary of State for War, the majestic, inscrutable titan, Lord Kitchener, foresaw the long, bloody, bitter ordeal that lay ahead. Captain Wavell grumbled, chafed, and worked too hard.

III

Ypres to Tiflis

"Every soldier with any enterprise or ambition," Wavell wrote many years later, "tried to join the B.E.F." The officers at the War Office were, most of them, enterprising and ambitious. A great many of them had been either killed or badly wounded by Christmas. Their valour and their eagerness for battle meant that the whole administration of the War Office was reduced to extreme confusion in a matter of days. Wavell himself made as energetic attempts to get away as any of his colleagues. Twice he nearly succeeded: once, with Henry Wilson's encouragement, as one of the first liaison officers with the British Expeditionary Force, but these posts were plums which senior officers gobbled up; and once as a replacement for a brigade major who was ill on the eve of embarkation, though the man who had the chance was killed at Le Cateau.

From the Military Operations Directorate, General Wilson and at least a third of his officers—and those the most experienced— vanished on or immediately after mobilisation. Wavell, at a few hours' notice, was put in charge of M.O.5, the key section of the whole of this branch of the General Staff. With an officer establishment until 4th August of a G.S.O.1 and two G.S.O.2s (all three of whom subsequently became generals), it took care of security, the secret service, ciphers, and the general network of military intelligence. The ceremony of handing over this vitally important department was reduced to a hurried transfer of the keys of the safe and an introduction to the chief clerk.

By arduous processes of trial and error, Wavell discovered that any task of which every other branch fought shy was inevitably passed to M.O.5. One of these odd jobs was the formation of an Intelligence Corps, "a last-minute improvisation," wrote its founding father with the forbearance of later years, "which produced some curious personalities."

After a time a retired officer, a former member of M.O.5, arrived to take over and Wavell withdrew somewhat glumly to the Russian section. No sooner had he returned to this seeming backwater than the rumour swept all over the country that large numbers of Russian troops, recognisable by the snow on their boots, had landed in the north of Scotland and had been transported to the Western Front. He was overwhelmed by friends and relations with praise for the skill and secrecy with which the whole operation had been arranged. All his disclaimers were met with knowing looks of disbelief.

During these first six eventful weeks of the war such few spare minutes as he had he spent in the company of Eugénie Quirk.

"I had made up my mind some time before that she was the person I should like to marry. I think she made up her mind about now to marry me. But my courtship was peculiar and should have warned her of my egoism, since it consisted mainly in grumbling at having been left out of the Expeditionary Force, and pessimistic forecasts that the war would be over before I got a chance to take part in it. She was very sympathetic, though she probably wanted to slap me. When I got orders to go to France, I decided to try my fortune, and we got engaged somewhere about midnight of 18th/19th September (I had got away late from the War Office). She told me she was lazy and unpunctual—I knew the latter already. I don't think I warned her of any of my failings; I wanted to marry the girl."

And the girl, knowing more about the faults, as well as the virtues, of this strange lover than (perhaps wisely) she ever disclosed, accepted him. "They lived happily ever after"? In many senses, yes. Vicissitudes countless, dangers many, and great shared achievements awaited them; but of the joy that flowed, in thirty-five years of marriage, from the decision made on that September night in London in wartime, there cannot be much doubt. The profound differences between them, the results of heredity and environment, could be reconciled only by the understanding which is constancy's greatest attribute. Theirs was a happy decision, and a happy marriage.

Wavell was in France by 28th September, but he was at G.H.Q., and still a long way from the battle area where he longed to be. This was to take him eight weeks more. Meanwhile his task was to command, as an acting major, the Intelligence Corps, which consisted of thirty or forty officers, distributed singly or in pairs to corps and divisions.

"They had been hurriedly recruited at the outbreak of war from

applicants who claimed to speak languages of which they had sometimes the merest smattering, or to ride a horse or a motor-cycle, which
some of them, I think, mounted for the first time when they were
issued to them by remounts of the R.A.S.C."

Once Wavell had organised the corps and had imposed on it some
measure of control and some understanding of its purpose, he had
barely more than an hour or so of work a day, and inevitably looked
around for other employment. He soon began, as he described it,
wandering. He had reached France at a moment of considerable
historical significance. The first brief phase of open warfare was coming to an end, and there was not to be another until more than four
years had passed. The Allies had held the Germans in the battle of the
Marne, and had driven them back across the river. Advancing in their
turn, they were held in the valley of the Aisne. There followed a
"race to the sea," the Allies and the Germans alternately side-stepping
formations northwards in an effort to outflank each other's exposed,
northern flank. But the defensive power of the machine gun, with its
murderously high rate of casualties, was rapidly immobilising the cavalry, and compelling the infantry to dig in below ground level. The
battle of the Aisne degenerated into trench warfare, and by the time
winter set in there was a sinister stalemate along the whole enormous
front from the borders of Switzerland to the Channel ports. The B.E.F.
was now disposed at the north-west end of the front; G.H.Q., not long
after Wavell joined it, moved from Fère-en-Tardinois to Abbeville,
and thence to St. Omer.

Wavell hated sitting in G.H.Q. in comparative idleness. He went
to see the First Battalion The Black Watch, the 42nd, in their trenches
in the Aisne sector, and they showed him most of the front. Many of
their officers had been wounded, and their ranks were heavily thinned.
This reunion with his own regiment increased his self-distaste. While
G.H.Q. involved itself in the complications of two moves within a few
weeks, he felt specially supererogatory. His jaunts away from its—to
him—frustrating atmosphere were many and frequent, beginning with
one to Ypres, which was then more or less a no-man's-land. This trip
and others he recalled thirty years later.

"I went in an armed but not armoured motor truck with some
Marines, but how I got into this party I have forgotten. We were the
first British, I think, into Ypres, and a German patrol had only left the
town an hour before, according to inhabitants. We went off down the
road to chase it; and were informed by some local people that it was

in some farm buildings a short distance down the road. We dashed down the road and drove into the farm courtyard all keyed up for action. As we tumbled out of the truck, we found ourselves in what would have been a hopeless trap, if the Boche patrol had been there; we were commanded on all four sides by windows. Fortunately for us the patrol had moved on; but we nearly had a casualty from a Marine letting off his rifle in his excitement. We then drove on and eventually established touch with the 7th Division of Rawlinson's force from Ostend, after some doubts as to whether they were friend or foe. . . .

"I don't think G.H.Q. stopped long at Abbeville, my recollection is that it moved very soon to St. Omer. It was there while the battle of Ypres was fought; I was very restless and unhappy during this battle. I think I was more aware than many people at G.H.Q. that a really decisive battle was being fought, and I wanted to take part in it. I motored out to various parts of the front. I was on the Menin Road on the critical day when Gheluvelt was lost and retaken; and I believe I saw Haig start on his ride down the road towards the front which is recorded in the histories, though I never appreciated the significance of the event at the time. I visited a friend in Messines while it was being barely held by our cavalry against repeated German attacks, and was told by the friend that I was a bloody fool to come to a place under shell fire unless I had business there. He was quite right, I had no business at the front; but the trouble was that I had no real business in the rear either. Anyone could have looked after the Intelligence Corps. I knew I was regarded as a G.H.Q. drone by the hard-pressed people I visited at the front, and I felt it. I wanted to get away to more active soldiering.

"I had one or two flights during this period with Amyas Borton, who was now a pilot in the Flying Corps. It was before the days of fighting in the air, but Amyas used to tell me to take my revolver in case we met a Boche. We did on one flight, and Amyas shouted to me to be ready with my revolver and went in pursuit of the enemy. The observer's seat in the back of the plane was wretchedly cold and my fingers were frozen out of all feeling; I was very doubtful whether I could shoot off my revolver when I wanted to; also I had a suspicion that the Boche would probably be armed with a more effective weapon. So I was relieved when it became obvious that we should not catch him.

"These excursions on the ground or in mid-air had no particular

95

object, except that I simply had not enough to do at G.H.Q. and could not sit still and do nothing. I certainly didn't go into danger because I liked it; I have never been a fire-eater of that kind."

During the time at G.H.Q. Wavell had one additional task: as a Russian "expert" he had laid on him the duty of interpreting the Russian communiqués to the Commander-in-Chief, Sir John French. His début in this part was not particularly felicitous. Not long arrived from London, he was sent for late one evening. As he was ushered into the Commander-in-Chief's room, he found himself confronting, besides French, his three Corps Commanders, Haig, Smith-Dorrien and Rawlinson, Henry Wilson and the C.G.S., Archibald Murray.

"We are discussing future plans," said French, "and much depends on the rate of progress of the Russian Army into Germany. Our information is that the Russians will reach Breslau by 15th October. I understand that you have been in the Russian Intelligence Section and know something of the Russian strategical problem, so I sent for you in order to confirm our information. Do you agree that the Russians are likely to reach Breslau by that date?"

"No, sir. I do not."

There was a stir among the generals. So decided and so contrary a view was obviously far from popular in that august company. French himself, clearly not a little put out, asked, "Well then, when *do* you think the Russians will get to Breslau?"

"Not in 1914, sir," Wavell replied with decision, "and I don't think during this winter."

There could now be no discounting the unpleasant sensation he had caused. Heavily, French asked him to explain his reasons for disbelieving the "Russian steamroller" theory, which was then very fashionable.

"Oh yes, sir," said Wavell cheerfully, "it's simply a matter of communications." He then gave a brief account of the lines of supply and movement on either side of the Russo-German frontier. The Russians, he explained, had practically speaking only one line of rail through Poland, and very poor roads, while on the other side there was a network of railways which enabled the Germans to concentrate anywhere on the arc of the frontier, or in East Prussia, and to attack Russian communications as they advanced. (In fact, this was an accurate forecast of the way the winter campaign of 1914-15 was conducted.) Wavell concluded by pointing out that therefore the Russians would have to clear their northern flank—East Prussia—and greatly improve their communications before they could hope to invade Germany with success.

The silence which greeted these highly practical but unwelcome observations was as hostile as it was embarrassed. At last General Rawlinson broke it. "I don't think," he said icily, "that Major Wavell really knows much about it, or is abreast of the latest developments." He pulled a letter from his pocket, written by some panjandrum in London who stated that it was the general opinion of all well-informed persons that the Russians would soon reach Breslau. Everyone cheered up at this optimistic assessment; and Wavell, dismissed from the room as an ill-informed and gloomy prophet, was left to suppose that the generals based their plans on it rather than on his appraisal. By 15th October the Russians had not got to Breslau or anywhere near it.

In the second week of November Wavell was told that he had been appointed G.S.O.2 (Intelligence) at IV Corps H.Q., under Rawlinson. He was not very appreciative: he did not like Intelligence, and regarded a corps as not much better than G.H.Q. Soon after he had heard this news he encountered an old friend, Major C. B. Thomson, looking equally disgruntled. He had just been appointed G.S.O.2 (Operations) at I Corps, under Haig's command; but the appointment for which he hankered was that of G.S.O.2 (Intelligence) in Rawlinson's corps, which he had been assured was vacant.

The opportunity for a little simple, satisfactory horse-trading seemed too good to lose. Wavell and Thomson presented themselves together in the office of the Military Secretary, and asked for permission to exchange appointments. He was perfectly willing, provided that I Corps, to whom the news of Thomson's appointment had already been communicated, would agree. The two friends motored out to I Corps H.Q., the staff of which, since they were engaged in conducting the first battle of Ypres, might have been forgiven a touch of testiness at being presented with a couple of personal problems of relative insignificance. Haig's staff agreed to the exchange nevertheless, but an obstacle was revealed. Direct from the War Office, and even more lately than Wavell, there had arrived to take up the appointment of G.S.O.3 in this headquarters Captain R. J. Collins; and Collins, the elder by two years, was also senior to Wavell in the Army List, despite the fact that Wavell had gone to the Staff College two years ahead of him and had some three years' more experience on the staff.

"Very well," said Wavell, who had never then met Collins, "if we're going to stand on rank, I'll be G.S.O.3 and let Captain Collins be G.S.O.2."[1]

A telephone call was put through to the Military Secretary at G.H.Q., who replied that in no circumstances could Collins, with so little staff experience, be a G.S.O.2. At Haig's headquarters there was little enthusiasm for Thomson, who had been so ill-advised as to express a preference for IV Corps; his behaviour, it was indicated, was inexcusable as well as inexplicable. Leaving his friend to deal as best he could with this situation, Wavell went back to G.H.Q. to see the Military Secretary.

"There will be," he pointed out, "even bigger difficulties about this rank business at IV Corps. They have a G.S.O.3 (Intelligence) who is a major, far older than I am and far senior to me."

"Yes, I see," said the Military Secretary with weary politeness. "Let's cancel that. But what *do* you want?"

The answer was instantaneous and unequivocal. "The first vacancy available as brigade-major of an infantry brigade in the line."

The casualty rate in officers at that time was such that there was little or no delay in fulfilling this requirement. On 16th November, 1914, Major A. P. Wavell (The Black Watch) took up his appointment as Brigade-Major the 9th Infantry Brigade, whose headquarters were at Hooge, on the Menin Road in the Ypres Salient.

To soldiers in the forward area in war, generals, from the brigade level upwards, are a necessary, if remote, element in the mysterious order of nature which has replaced their peacetime existence. Staff officers, on the other hand, are an abomination, perfumed and parasitic, impertinent reminders in their own well-groomed selves that, outside this desert, death's grey land, there is a world where fit, able-bodied men sleep at night between warm, dry sheets, change their shirts and socks regularly, and eat food which is not nauseous with mud or flies or sand. The nearer to the forward area the individual staff officer lives and works, the less is he scorned and despised; a brigade-major in an infantry brigade in action is, it is customarily conceded, a fighting soldier.

In World War II General Wavell, as the Commander-in-Chief in vast and complex theatres of war, was accustomed from time to time to remind his own staff, with benign irony, of the existence of this gulf. It had never been deeper and wider, and it had never had more unfortunate consequences, than in World War I.

There was also prevalent in the aftermath of the war the belief, tinged with contempt and bitterness, that "generals died in bed." It was untrue of the first B.E.F. of 1914-15, the Regular divisions and the few Territorial formations which arrived as reinforcements and held the pass until the first of Kitchener's volunteers could be put in the field.

Ninth Brigade were normally part of 3rd Division, but during the first battle of Ypres they were, for a time, under 1st Divisional H.Q. On the morning of 31st October the commanders of 1st and 2nd Divisions and their staffs had had a conference at Hooge Château; as they were dispersing, two German shells exploded just in front of the house. The 1st Divisional commander was mortally wounded and his G.S.O.1 was killed; the 2nd Divisional commander and his G.S.O.1 were both shell-shocked and a G.S.O.3 was killed. Ninth Brigade headquarters, therefore, had been set up not in the Château but in a small house— originally an *estaminet*—at the roadside near Hooge. But the road itself was under fire and, a few days before Wavell joined, a direct hit on Brigade H.Q. had wounded the brigade commander, the staff captain, the signal officer and the chief clerk; the brigade major had been out at the time, but on the following day a sniper shot him through the arm.

Thus it was a completely new headquarters that assembled on the evening of 16th November. There had been a real urgency about Wavell's appointment. On his way to take it up he called at 3rd Division H.Q. where (since the General, Colin Mackenzie, had been sent home badly wounded) the B.R.A., Brigadier Wing, was in temporary charge until a Major-General, Aylmer Haldane, could come out from England and take over.[2]

Wing, who was proposing to drive up to 9th Infantry Brigade's H.Q., had with him that brigade's new staff captain, none other than Kenneth Buchanan, who had been at Summer Fields with Wavell. The three set off together and reached the *estaminet* near Hooge in the middle of the afternoon. Ninth Brigade, originally from Portsmouth, and consisting of the 1st Bn. Northumberland Fusiliers, the 4th Bn. Royal Fusiliers, the 1st Lincolns and the 1st Royal Scots Fusiliers, was now holding a sector of the Ypres Salient with only a little over a third of its normal complement, the strongest battalion totalling four officers and under 300 men, the weakest only two officers and just over 150 men.

On the evening of Wavell's arrival, the part of the line held by the Northumberland Fusiliers included a small, badly battered château into whose stables the enemy had infiltrated, whence they threatened to make the whole sector untenable. A plan had to be produced at once to put a stop to this attempt. Wavell wrote:

"It was decided to muffle the wheels of an 18-pounder, to man-handle it up the road in the dark to within 100 yards or so of the stables, put a dozen rounds rapid into the stables, and then rush them with 30 or 40 men, the only reserve the battalion could muster. It came off all right, the stables were recaptured without loss, the artillery fire at close range having proved deadly. The gun was safely withdrawn before dawn."

The harsh truth was that the British formations in the Ypres Salient were by now so reduced by casualties, and so lacking in available reinforcements, that they were little more than a screen force; and they were extremely tired. It had been agreed, therefore, that they should be relieved by French troops within a few days. A small detachment arrived on the night of 17th November; only a part of the hard-pressed British brigade could come out. The hand-over was performed after dusk, and an hour or two later Wavell was astonished to hear, on the *pavé* outside Brigade headquarters, a clatter of feet going away from the trenches. All the *poilus* who had just gone into the line were pouring back to the rear. They carried no arms. He seized a couple of them and asked what had happened and where they thought they were going.

"Oh, back to get our suppers," they explained.

"But in the meantime, what about the trenches?"

The *poilus* gesticulated cheerfully. "The Boche won't attack this evening," they assured him.

Forty-eight hours later, on a night of hard frost, the rest of the brigade—indeed most of what remained of the British Army in the Ypres Salient—were relieved by the French. During the preceding day Wavell had taken several French officers on a tour of the trenches they were to take over, and had (he thought) impressed upon them the need for complete silence during the relief. However, when the main French party arrived, it seemed to Wavell that he had never heard such a reckless racket. The *poilus* stood about in groups above and behind the trenches, chattering, smoking and waving lanterns; and officers and N.C.O.s clumped about giving orders and countermanding them at the tops of their voices. All along the line he could hear the same hullabaloo. Yet the Germans, who had a field gun trained down the road by which the British would have to march out, did not fire a single round throughout the night, during which the British infantry and their slow-moving transport went out for a badly needed rest.

A pattern of existence quite unlike the kind of war which even the most far-sighted soldier had ever envisaged now established itself. The First World War was a consequence of gigantic and persistent muddle rather than of conscious, willed evil; and it was waged for a long time in a muddle. The protracted, cruel waste of trench warfare was the product of muddle: nobody planned four years of slaughterous, heroic, futile deadlock. Commanders tumbled their men into the trenches too dazed, too shell-shocked (in the most exact sense) to find them a way out. But it was impossible completely to suppress individuals' independence and adaptibiliy to circumstances, however perverse. The Higher Command on both sides might be completely baffled by the strategic problems which they had been set, but at the lowly tactical level there were intelligent men who, even within the almost paranoiac rigidity of the limits of trench warfare, refused to concede that they were defeated—in their intellect any more than in their spirit.

Wavell was one such officer. His seven months in and out of the line, from November, 1914, to June, 1915, were grimly formative. Kenneth Buchanan watched the process at work. "After a very few weeks on the same staff," he wrote to Wavell's son, "I realised that Archie was the most efficient staff officer I had had anything to do with in my fourteen years' service in the Army." Judicially, Buchanan set out his reasons for this opinion:

a. His example in war. As a Brigade staff officer he insisted on personally visiting every part of the Bde. front. This was by no means normal action of staffs in 1914. This example put all the Bde. staff on their mettle. The more serious a situation, the calmer he became—nothing rattled him.

b. His orders a pattern. As Bde. admin. officer I never made a mistake serious enough to draw a rebuke from him. I take no credit—there was never any ambiguity in his instructions and orders.

c. A capacity for decentralisation. He never interfered with other people's jobs.

d. Power of concentration. He could divorce himself from everything going on around him. In the days of a Bde. mess and office being in one room, back in reserve, he could sit and work out a plan of attack or write orders for a move with a gramophone playing and a proper "din" going on.

e. His meticulous accuracy. In the early days of aeroplane photographs, these were not always accurate. He spent hours of daylight reconnaissance checking the position of trenches on his front at considerable danger to himself, as German trenches were often very close.

f. His physical stamina. I have never served with anyone tougher in war. His great stamina enabled him to be one of those men who never seemed to be physically tired.

g. Great personal courage. He would go anywhere in war, no matter what the situation. . . . As Brigade Major he earned the D.S.O. on many occasions. . . .

Periods in the line, of varying discomfort and danger, alternated with periods of "rest" in billets a short distance behind the line. In his first experience of this system—out from Hooge to the village of Westoutre, back to some trenches on the lower slopes of the Messines Ridge, which the brigade had to hold for the next few months—Wavell discovered its defects.

"A curious tactical paralysis seized on our commanders and staff during the winter of 1914-15—and indeed almost throughout the whole period of trench warfare. It was considered imperative to hang on to every yard of ground, to every trench, however worthless. I never understood this attitude. I think it was partly due to the normal British optimism, to the idea that we should soon be advancing again and that to take up a prolonged defensive position was useless; and partly because the existence of trenches seemed for some reason entirely to destroy the sense of value of the tactical features of ground. Value was assigned to *trenches*, i.e. holes in the ground, because one had once held them, or one's allies had, or the enemy had; though they might be full of water or under enfilade fire or in utterly unsuitable ground. And the natural value of the ground, e.g. high ground or ground covered by an obstacle, or ground concealed from the enemy, was often almost entirely discounted. I could never understand why;

but I was unpopular when I put these questions to commanders or staff. I shudder to think of the number of valuable lives lost by our policy of holding trenches in this winter of 1914-15, and indeed throughout the war. The Boche never made the same mistake. . . .

"Another mistake in this first winter was not sending home a large proportion of our surviving officers to train our new divisions and replacing them with reserve or other officers from home who would have done the trench work quite well—better perhaps, being fresh. We squandered large numbers of our comparatively small remnant of officers of the original B.E.F. on static trench warfare, who would have been invaluable later on. The same applied to senior N.C.O.s."

He discovered that it was not generally regarded as a staff officer's duty to visit the trenches.

"But I did not see how I could do my job without knowing what the trenches were like, and soon started visiting them. It had to be done by night, since there were no communication trenches and all the approaches were under close enemy observation. The trenches were a single line of very poor construction, badly sited, undrained, with very little wire to protect them. In the rain they became knee-deep in mud, and I once found the whole garrison of a trench sitting on the parapet, preferring the risk of enemy bullets to the mud in the trench. It was partly the fault of the Command and staff for not adjusting the trench line to the ground, partly lack of materials and tools, and partly laziness. We started a brigade factory for making appliances to improve the trenches, duck-boards, mud scoops, revetting material, etc. We were the first brigade to do this, and gradually effected some improvement."

On 30th November, exactly a fortnight after he and Wavell had joined, Kenneth Buchanan was wounded in the foot by a sniper, just outside Brigade H.Q. Buchanan's successor, Dorrien-Smith, became very keen on the improvement of the trenches. In Wavell's company he had to introduce to front-line conditions some fresh troops, the Liverpool Scottish, a Territorial battalion who had arrived to replenish the brigade's dangerously reduced numbers. Thus 9th Brigade, on paper, now consisted of five battalions, and the High Command, disregarding the unpalatable fact that they, like every other formation in the Army, were still far below strength, convinced itself that the time had arrived to seize the initiative.

In the middle of December the Allies launched the first of the trench-warfare attacks that were to continue until nearly the end of the war. The British Army's role was to capture the Messines-Wytscharte Ridge, in conjunction with the French Army on the left. The task of the 3rd Division was to attack from the trenches in front of Kemmel eastwards. Ninth Brigade's part was to capture the strongest point in the German line by an attack arranged at two or three hours' notice. Of this last, which he regarded as a piece of utter folly, Wavell wrote:

"We had been in the trenches for 10 or 12 days, and the weather had been vile, cold and wet. We were to hold the line until the attacking brigade (8th Brigade) came along, when we were to thin out and they were to attack through us. About 5.00 p.m. one evening, about two or three days before the attack, the brigadier was called to the telephone by the divisional commander and given the order to capture the Petit Bois before midnight. The Petit Bois, opposite the left of our line, was about the strongest point in the German line, a small square coppice, heavily wired and well entrenched. There was to be no artillery preparation or support—night firing was little practised in those days and anyway ammunition was very short—but we were at liberty to organise support by rifle fire with our own resources! The Brigadier protested vehemently, and the divisional commander agreed that the task was an impossible one; but he said he was helpless, he had direct orders from the Corps. I think the Brigadier would have refused, but the divisional commander implored him to try. Eventually I went along to the H.Q. of the Lincolns, the battalion opposite the Petit Bois, and gave the order to attack and capture it. I felt rather like a murderer. . . . They took it very well and said they would have a try, but had no hope of success. They would attack about 11.00 p.m.

"What actually happened they told me afterwards. They collected the very few fresh men they had in reserve, and proceeded to the front line of trenches. It took them about twenty minutes to get the men out of the trenches, not because they were unwilling, but because they were stuck in the mud and half frozen. Then they started to plod through the heavy mud to the German wire. They were received with violent fire and were quite unable to get through the wire, though they made repeated endeavours to cut it with the few cutters they had. Eventually a German stood up, threw a clod of earth at them, and called out in English: 'Go home, you damned fools!' They took the hint and went, having had 40 casualties out of under 120 who attacked. A stupid affair.

"The actual attack, a day or two later, was also the most complete failure. II Corps had been ordered to attack, and detailed the 3rd Division to do it. The 3rd Division employed one brigade, the 8th. The 8th Brigade decided to use two of its four battalions, the Gordons and the Royal Scots. These two battalions put into the attack, I think, one, or possibly two, companies each. So that the attack of the British Army in this battle dwindled down to two or three companies! The truth is that none of the commanders believed in success and each tried to cut his losses to a minimum. Not the way to win battles; but battles in which no one believes should not be fought . . . .

"Wully Robertson, after watching the attack from behind, summed it up with his usual directness: 'It's no use pissing and farting at these Germans'."

Nine days later Wavell was granted a week's leave. He arrived in England on Christmas morning, and went first to Lady Edward Churchill's house at Windsor[3]; thence he went to Cranborne for three days, to a little enclosed world oddly, unbelievably unchanged by the war; and then for his last three days to the Quirks' flat in Knightsbridge. "It must have been now," he recorded laconically, "that Q.Q. and I decided to get married next time I could get leave."

He was back in France on New Year's Day, and the dismally familiar pattern of trench warfare was resumed. He spent the first six weeks of 1915 either in the trenches in front of Kemmel or "resting" at Loere. One grey, cold, muddy, dangerous or boring day merged into another. Ninth Brigade had come under the orders of 28th Division. This was made up of Regular battalions brought back from garrison duties in India and elsewhere overseas. They had spent some months training in bleak camps in England and, without any rest or leave for acclimatisation, had a high sickness rate; they were then sent to Ypres, in the depths of winter, to take over from the French, who gave them inaccurate maps, which their staff did not trouble to check by personal reconnaissance. The divisional commander, Major-General Bulfin, came to see the brigade once a week, always demanded a trench map, scored it across with a big blue pencil to indicate trenches he wanted dug in impossible places, and hurried off on similar errands to other brigades. The G.S.O.1 never visited 9th Brigade at all during the six weeks they were with the division. "The first G.S.O.2 never came either, but a new one was appointed

W. 105 D2

while we were there, and not knowing the divisional taboo came to brigade headquarters one evening just after he had arrived. I persuaded him to stop till it was dark and took him round half our trench line and pointed out some of the absurd things divisional H.Q. were ordering us to do. He promised to come back next night and go round the other half of the line. But he rang me up next morning and told me he had been given a dressing down by the G.S.O.1 for going to the trenches, and had been told he would lose his appointment if he did it again!''

Of the three great battles that were fought over that small parcel of Flanders and bear the name of the Battles of Ypres, the second, in April and May, 1915, was the most dolorous and unsatisfactory. In the first battle, in 1914, the old army died grimly, confident in its warcraft and giving harder punishment than it received; and in 1917 at Passchendaele, the third battle, our forces had at least the impetus of the offensive, however bloody and unconvincing. But the troops that fought in the Salient in 1915 had neither confidence of skill nor hope of gaining ground. The old army was dead; the new armies and the new equipment were not yet ready. Struggling in a muddy plain, with the enemy holding the advantage of higher ground almost everywhere, they were overlooked, outgunned, outmanœuvred, and not a little bewildered by the new weapons of gas and liquid fire used against them. Only their obstinate courage kept a footing in that cramped semicircle and held the Germans from setting foot on the ramparts of Ypres.[4]

Well-disciplined, well-trained soldiers were killed, maimed or shattered in spirit in attempts to hold on to trench lines which were of no tactical value, because of that mental paralysis and physical inertia in too many generals and their staffs, and that downright failure to fulfil their duty of personal reconnaissance, of which Wavell carried memories for the rest of his life.

K trench had contributed a good deal to the moral ruin of the brigade from whom the 9th Brigade took over. They had been ordered to hold it at all costs. It was just like any other trench at this time, a narrow ditch soggily carpeted with the bodies of the dead, but it was also enfiladed on both sides. Thirty men had been ordered to hold it, and had striven to do so, at the price of a dozen casualties a

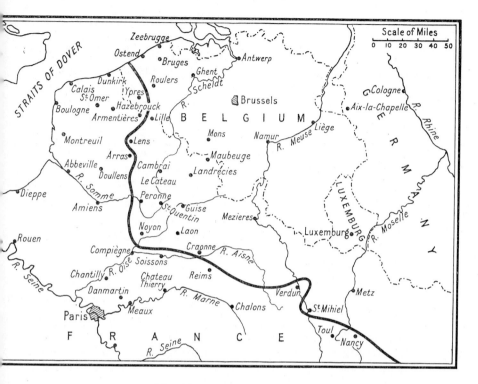

The Western Front, 1915

day. When 9th Brigade's relieving formation marched in, their surviving predecessors crept out weeping. Ninth Brigade realised that
the trench was not worth trying to hold in strength and put in a dozen
men, who suffered half a dozen casualties in twenty-four hours. Then
they decided to fill it in and dig another 150 yards farther back; in the
meantime they put in a token garrison of one stout officer and three
men.

"Not knowing the divisional staff so well in those early days, we
told them what we were doing. Back came the most categorical
order: we were on no account whatever to give up a yard of the
trench and were to put in it the previous garrison of 27 men, and to
report in writing that we had done so. 'What is one to do with these
sort of people?' said the brigadier sadly. 'However, as none of them
obviously come near the trenches, and will never know, we will do as
we intended.' So we dug another K trench in a safer place, filled in the

old one, and reported that K trench was occupied. A week or so later the general asked me, 'How many casualties have you had in K trench in the last ten days?' I replied incautiously with the correct figures, two or three. 'There you are,' he said, 'I knew the trench could be held with a little grit and determination.' And off he went, I expect, to tell the world how he had stiffened up our weak morale and prevented an unnecessary withdrawal."

Going back to the 3rd Division at the beginning of April after these weeks in other company was like going home. Most of April the brigade spent in trenches at St. Eloi, north of their old position, and with brigade headquarters near Dickebusch. The leave for which Wavell had hoped was granted, and he was back in England by 20th April.

His account of the most important happening during this leave was austerely factual:

"Q and I were married at Holy Trinity, Sloane Street, on 22nd April, mainly by the Quirk family bishop, but I think there were other clergy about. Lady Edward Churchill lent us 28, Grosvenor Street for the reception and her house at Windsor for the first days of the honeymoon."

As Wavell and his bride came out of the church into the spring afternoon, they could see the bills of the evening newspaper sellers: "Ypres. Big Battle. Huns Use Gas." They could hear the raucous cockney voices shouting, "Sensation! Gas in big battle! Gas!" Wavell's brigade was near the line of attack: would he be ordered back instantly? "Fortunately," he wrote long afterwards, "this was not necessary." He had his full fortnight's leave. They were at Windsor for three days; they went to Cranborne for four days, and had their last three days at Jules's Hotel in Jermyn Street. She saw him off at Victoria, knowing that he was going back to the most fiercely contested battle of the war so far. It would have been impossible to make a realistic estimate of the chances of their ever seeing each other again. Had they paused to reflect, they would have said that they were luckier than many others of their generation: they had had ten days in the spring.

The 9th Brigade remained in the St. Eloi trenches until nearly the end of May. "During this time the second Battle of Ypres, brought on by the German gas attack, was raging. The smell of chlorine came to brigade H.Q., but never sufficiently strongly to compel us to use our very primitive gas-masks—flannel helmets (with a talc eyepiece) soaked in some chemical. . . .

"I don't remember exactly when we were told that the brigade was to make an attack but I imagine that it was at the end of May or early in June. It was one of those minor attacks on a narrow front that were so often ordered at this period in the war in order to 'support' attacks many miles away. They were supposed to attract enemy reserves, I imagine. They never had the slightest effect on the main attack; and being on a narrow front nearly always failed with heavy loss. This particular attack was made in about the worst possible place, the extreme tip of the Ypres Salient, which was exposed to observation and artillery fire, not merely from the front and both flanks, but from the rear as well, so pronounced was the salient. The objective was to capture three lines of enemy trenches near Bellewarde Lake, close to Hooge.

"I was rather pleased with our plan. It was on the leap-frog system which was a novelty at that time. Two of our five battalions were to capture the first line of trenches; then the other three battalions were to go through them and assault the second trench, which was much larger; and finally the first two battalions, having re-formed, were to go through to the final objective. I believe the plan would have been quite successful so far as capturing enemy trenches went, but for an entirely unforeseen interference; whether we could ever have held them is entirely another story."

The attack was fixed for 16th June, at or just before dawn. Its first phase was a complete success; the first line of enemy trenches was captured with little loss and a number of prisoners were taken. Confusion set in with the second phase, and the whole plan was ruined. In support of 9th Brigade's attack was the 7th Brigade, with two battalions—the Royal Irish Rifles and the H.A.C.—in its front line, with orders to move up gradually and take over the trenches after they had been captured by 9th Brigade. The R.I.R. rose without orders as soon as the attack began and poured forward in a disorderly mob. The H.A.C., a very good Territorial battalion, thought there must have been some change of plan, and went forward with the R.I.R. They entangled themselves with two of 9th Brigade's battalions ahead of them, and within a short time there was a disorganised mass of seven battalions in trenches which would only hold five; and it was impossible to sort them out properly and make a coherent attack since the German artillery fire was coming from all sides of the salient. The situation was not improved by the Corps and Divisional staff behind ordering up more troops in spite of 9th Brigade's protests.

"Some time later, I think it was early in the afternoon, I went out of the dugout to get some fresh air, as there seemed to be a lull in the battle, and to try and see what was happening. About now the adjutant of the 5th Fusiliers came past wounded in the leg and gave me some news of the battle. I think I was about a couple of hundred yards from the dugout when the enemy opened a heavy barrage again. Corps had sent forward another brigade (the 42nd Brigade, I think it was) which came across the open and at once drew the fire of every German gun. It was a stupid order; the brigade had no chance of reaching the trenches under that artillery fire in any fit state to make an attack, and could only have added to the confusion. As a matter of fact few of the brigade got up to the trenches at all. I walked back to the dugout, and just as I got there was hit on the left side of the head by a splinter of H.E. or a shrapnel bullet, or possibly even a machine-gun bullet at long range. It went through my left eye but just missed everything vital. I was bandaged up and sat in the dugout for a bit; but as my right eye also began to close and I could be of no further use, I accepted the brigadier's suggestion that one of the orderlies should take me back to the dressing station near Ypres.

"We started to walk across the fields just north of the Menin Road. It was not a pleasant journey; I was practically blind by this time and could only see by painfully propping open my right eye with one or both hands. The shelling was still heavy, and a good deal of stuff was dropping round us. One shell blew up a party near us, I think it must have been of the advancing 42nd Brigade, another blew myself and my guide into a ditch and covered us with earth. As the fields seemed under just as heavy fire as the road and we could make quicker progress down the road, we did the rest of the journey on the Menin Road, and at last arrived at a dressing station near the Menin Gate. There was an ambulance just about to start back to the casualty clearing station the other side of Ypres, and there was a vacant seat beside the driver. I decided to cut out the dressing station and go straight to the C.C.S., and got up alongside the driver. We drove through Ypres, which was being shelled by very heavy stuff; and I was put on a bed to wait for an ambulance train. . . .

"I had been given a tetanus injection as soon as I got to the C.C.S. Presently a doctor approached me with another needle to inject me. I protested that I had already had a tetanus injection; but he said this one would do no harm, and proceeded to inject me. It must have been a morphia dose, and I remember very little more till I woke up in a base hospital."

In this action the 9th Brigade lost 73 officers out of 96, and more than 2,000 men out of a total strength of about 3,500. Of the five battalion commanders, one was killed and two were severely wounded. These losses were caused by heavy and continuous shelling. One line of trenches was gained. It was, in Wavell's view, "a disastrous waste of a fine and experienced brigade," the result of a mistaken policy of small attacks on narrow fronts, and of persisting after the original assault had failed. This failure was due, he was convinced, entirely to the indiscipline of one battalion.

Wavell was awarded an immediate M.C.—in the first list gazetted after the creation of this decoration for gallantry.

The hospital in which Wavell woke up was the Rawalpindi General Hospital at Wimereux, near Boulogne. Here the remnants of his left eye were removed. His wife came over to be with him, and they returned to England about the end of June.

Altogether he had over four months' sick leave, "a wonderful interlude in the war." He and his wife had a month at Lady Edward Churchill's house, now turned into a convalescent home, at Windsor. Thence they went to Cranborne, later to Northwick, the Cotswold home of Captain George Spencer Churchill, Lady Edward's son; and in the early autumn to the house of another old friend near Dornoch. In the middle of October a medical board passed Wavell as fit, and he was appointed G.S.O.2 to a second-line Territorial division, the 64th Highland, with headquarters at Perth. He tried to get back to France, but he was assured that this division was to be sent thither before long as a formation, and that his experience was required to assist in its preparation.

"I was under three weeks in Perth. I don't think it took me more than twenty-four hours to realise that the division would not go overseas for a very long time, if at all; and I had no intention of spending the rest of the war, or any considerable portion of it, at home. . . . I wrote to friends at G.H.Q. in France and asked them to find me an active job. Some time early in December I got orders to proceed to G.H.Q. in France."

The ten months—15th December, 1915 to 17th October, 1916—which

Wavell spent as a G.S.O.2 in G.H.Q. were his longest period in any appointment during the First World War. He regarded the appointment as dull and the period as uneventful. That he could write this is a curious reflection on the effect of the circumscribed life of G.H.Q. on an intelligent man. This was the year of the aftermath of Loos and the first battle of the Somme—in a wider field, of Jutland, the death of Kitchener and the disintegration of the Asquith Government. But in G.S.O.(B), which Wavell described as the Staff Duties side of the General Staff, *ennui*—his perpetual enemy—was only held at bay by the fact that the head of the branch was Jock Burnett-Stuart, then a brigadier-general. He had, Wavell believed, "probably the best and quickest brain in the Army of his rank." He was forcible and practical; he was, however, somewhat intolerant of all those over him, and his independent nature did not easily brook control from above. "Everyone under him always swore by him. He became a guide and friend to me at once."

Early in 1916 G.H.Q. moved from St. Omer to Montreuil, where it grew to be a portentous organisation. Haig was now C.-in-C., having succeeded French in November, after the battle of Loos. Wavell did not remember seeing him once in all his time on the staff. The weeks slipped into months. Occasionally Wavell could leave the office for a day or two, to go and inspect a training school; but since the schools were naturally in rear areas, he had few chances to go to the front. The world in which he now lived was separated by only a few miles, but by a vast chasm of experience, from that he had known a year before. His father, now aged 73, came out to see him, and Archie took the old gentleman as near the front as visitors were allowed: this was not war as the General had known it, and he had no standards by which to assess it. On 1st July, a few days after the beginning of the battle of the Somme, Wavell went up to see the French sector of the battlefield, in the company of Edward Spears, G.H.Q.'s principal liaison officer with the French High Command. "This," he recorded ruefully, "was the nearest I got to the front."

During this period he managed to increase his home leave by giving lectures at training schools in the United Kingdom. He had a week's leave at the end of March, and was in England again by the end of April. He solved his transport problem by accompanying a friend in the R.F.C. who was flying obsolete or semi-obsolete aircraft back to the manufacturers. Six days after his own thirty-third birthday he wrote to his sister from G.H.Q.

A. P. Wavell to Miss Anne Wavell   *11th May, 1916*
. . . I got a telephone message this morning to say that it was my eldest son's birthday and that both he and Q were very well. I hope Q is quite all right, I haven't heard anything more.

You'll be godmother to him, won't you, and I hope you'll put your foot down about his being called Archibald. I think it's a rotten name.

I'm glad I'm getting home on Sunday for a day to see Q and the infant. I wonder what he'll be like.

The Sunday visit was accomplished by arranging to give a lecture; and again there was a helpful friend who flew him across the Channel. "I can remember well," he wrote, when his son was an officer in The Black Watch, serving with Wingate's Chindits in Burma, "my first sight of him with his proud mother and the thrill it gave me." Defeat had to be conceded over the child's name, but throughout his life he was always known as Archie John.

Wavell had just been promoted major, after fifteen years' service, under a rule lately introduced but for which he would still have been only a very junior captain in his regiment. He was now within reach of being considered for a senior regimental or staff appointment. The Black Watch wanted him to rejoin the 2nd Battalion, then serving in Mesopotamia, with a view to getting command if and when Arthur Wauchope was given a brigade. The fact that he was a Staff College graduate ruled this out, and in October he was told that he was to be sent to Russia, with the temporary rank of lieutenant-colonel, to replace a Colonel Marsh, the British military representative on the staff of the Grand Duke Nicholas, Governor and Commander-in-Chief in the Caucasus. Marsh had been ill and wanted to go home for sick leave. Wavell had some three weeks at home before setting forth. "Q," he recorded, "was anxious to accompany me, but the authorities said no, decisively." The authorities had yet to get the measure of young Mrs. Wavell.

He went to Tiflis by way of Norway, Sweden and Petrograd. In Christiania he met Marsh, accompanied by Mrs. Marsh. So he managed it, said Wavell to himself, and went out and sent a wire to his own wife, telling her to follow him if possible. He was in Tiflis on 21st November, 1916, seventeen days after leaving England.

Apart from the Consul and his wife, and his own cipher officer, there were no other British in Tiflis. Wavell's job was to keep the

General Staff at the War Office informed of the situation on the Caucasus front, and especially of any tactical change in the state of the Turkish troops opposing the Russians. In the winter of 1915-16 the Russians had captured Erzerum, in Turkish Armenia, by a surprise attack; during the summer of 1916 they had passed on into Asia Minor on a broad front and had taken Erzinjan. They had some four corps in the field, to whose supply in winter, with food, munitions and medical services, along one indifferent road, nobody on the Russian General Staff, so far as Wavell could discover, had yet given a thought.

What concerned the War Office was the disposition of the Turkish forces. They knew that any Turkish units or formations which left the Caucasus turned up facing the British forces in Mesopotamia or in Palestine; but the Russian staff would never admit that any Turkish unit had left their front. On the other hand, they were obligingly informative about Turkish deserters, of whom there was a fairly steady stream. Therefore if a Turkish regiment failed to supply a deserter for a week or more, Wavell signalled to the War Office that they could reasonably assume that it had left the Caucasus front, though it would still be shown in the Russian Intelligence reports. This nearly always proved correct. Wavell found that, apart from their refusal to admit Turkish departures, "the Russians were quite good at supplying information about the enemy; they were, however, extremely secretive about their own forces."

His day-to-day dealings with the Grand Duke Nicholas, whom he thought the handsomest and most impressive-looking man he had ever met. He had no great intellect or academic learning, but he was full of common-sense and character. "I believe," Wavell wrote, "that he was very terrible in his wrath, but I never saw him angry. He had charming manners to foreigners. He talked French perfectly but no English, though I think he understood it. He gave me the choice of talking Russian or French with him, and I decided that my Russian was better."

In face of the hostility and secretiveness of his Chief of Staff, General Bolkhovitinov, the Grand Duke insisted that Wavell should have at all times all the information he required, and gave him his private telephone number, known only to a few. Bolkhovitinov, said Wavell, "never actually refused me information, though he often lied. But his lying was crude, and I felt that I could arrive at sufficient information without bothering the Grand Duke." Bolkhovitinov was a big, bulky man with shifty eyes; he was an unscrupulous careerist and time-server. He was also, as his behaviour during and after the Revolution showed, a turncoat. There was a running feud between him and the French liaison officer, Colonel Chardigny. Since France had no direct interest, comparable to Britain's, in the Caucasus campaign—or ought not to have had—Chardigny had little to do, and therefore spent his time discovering scandals (no difficult matter, in Wavell's view) such as the number of typhus casualties in a corps, or the state of transport at the front. He would then call on Wavell and demand that the pair of them should go to the Chief of Staff and make "a combined protest in the name of the Allies."

"Occasionally when the matter was not too controversial I would agree to go and see the Chief of Staff with him. The fact that Chardigny talked very bad Russian sometimes saved the situation. He would break in with some excited condemnation of Russian inefficiency. The Chief of Staff would turn to me and say: 'I can't understand him, what is he saying?' (having of course understood quite well). I would tone down Chardigny's diatribe into a harmless request for information. The Chief of Staff would reply, sometimes in rather scathing terms, and Chardigny would ask me what he had said. I would reply that the Chief of Staff entirely appreciated his view and was taking steps to have the defect remedied, or words to that effect."

In December the first (but by no means the last) of the Quirk-Wavell victories over bureaucracy and bumbledom was registered. Mrs. Wavell made her way to her husband's side, accompanied by her maid, a delicate-looking, red-haired Norfolk girl named Grant. Wavell wrote:

"It was a great performance. Q had first to overcome all the objections of the Foreign Office, who referred her to the War Office, and of the War Office, who referred her to the Foreign Office; and then to accomplish the journey by Norway and Sweden and Finland to Petrograd and then down to the Caucasus. During the last stage she carried out the quite unprecedented feat of getting the window of a Russian railway carriage opened during the winter months, and without knowing a word of Russian!"

They took up their quarters in the Hôtel de l'Orient, whose manager was "almost certainly an agent of the Secret Police, like most hotel managers."

Wavell had a Russian batman, Stepan, a strapping lad from Siberia, cheerful and willing but stupid. Mrs. Wavell's efforts to make him understand anything were seldom successful. Stepan once came rushing up to his master in a great state of dither: "Help me, sir, help me! Her Honour is talking Russian to me!"

There was little or no social activity in Tiflis, but the Wavells lunched or dined from time to time with the Grand Duke or with his staff. There were occasionally operas or entertainments, at the theatre. Grant fell ill of scarlet fever and was whisked off to an isolation hospital. The Wavells' rooms in the hotel were closed for fumigation, and they themselves were technically in quarantine. The manager, when he was not making routine reports on his guests to the secret police, was a kindhearted and considerate fellow. There was not a spare room in the hotel, but he promised to find them accommodation while their rooms were being disinfected. After dinner, under his and his minions' persuasion, the Wavells sat on and on in the dining-room, while a large and noisy party of Russian officers bawled and guffawed on the other side of the room. At last, when they were gone, up came the manager, as suave as if he were in the Ritz in Paris. He hoped they would forgive, he knew they would understand. . . . Beds were being made up for them here, in the dining-room. It seemed, they reflected, a curious place for people in quarantine. Later they learned that there had been several other cases of scarlet fever in the hotel; but those involved, in order not to have to go to the isolation hospital or to have their rooms fumigated, had bribed the doctor and the manager to report it as some other less disturbing disease.

The winter dragged on towards a reluctant, tardy spring. At home, the new Lloyd George Government became increasingly worried about their Russian ally. A powerful military mission, with Henry Wilson at its head, was despatched to Petrograd.

"I got a telegram from Henry Wilson which was a suggestion that I should come up to Petrograd and see him; unfortunately it was sent in a cipher I did not possess. I guessed that it might be an instruction to come up and see him and very nearly got into the train at once. But I didn't quite like leaving my post without orders and wired for a repeat of the telegram in the cipher I had. There was some hold-up of communications and by the time I got the reply it was too late. So I missed seeing the last Imperial ballet and the last Court ball of the Czars."

When Wavell had been in Tiflis some three months his mission moved out of routine military intelligence into politics. General Maude had taken command in Mesopotamia; Wavell was told that

he expected to capture Baghdad within a few weeks, and was instructed to approach the Grand Duke with a proposal that his forces
should advance on Mosul. Chardigny had similar instructions from
his Government. For once, therefore, it looked as if they could speak
together "in the name of Allies." Wavell knew—and Chardigny knew
too—of the existence of the Sykes-Picot agreement, under which
Mosul had been allotted to the French sphere of influence. Chardigny
sought to impress upon Wavell that he must insist to the Grand Duke
or his Chief of Staff that, immediately Mosul was occupied, the French
flag must be hoisted over it. Wavell knew that the very idea would be
fatal to any hopes of inducing the Russians to advance. Pretending
complete ignorance of the Sykes-Picot agreement, he refused to back
Chardigny on this point.

They saw Bolkhovitinov. Wavell made the request, jointly on
behalf of the British and French Governments, that the Russian Army
of the Caucasus should move on Mosul. Chardigny followed at once
with an impassioned oration, demanding that French rights and
responsibilities must be made clear at the outset with the unfurling of
the flag of France over the captured city. Bolkhovitinov feigned not
to understand this tide of Gallic eloquence and growled at Wavell,
"What's he saying about a flag?"

"He is only saying," Wavell replied, "how glorious it will be to see
the flags of the Allies floating over Mosul." Bolkhovitinov muttered
an observation which was far from complimentary to Chardigny and
to France.

"Has he realised the point about the flag, Colonel?" asked Chardigny anxiously.

"Yes, Colonel, I can give you that assurance."

To Wavell's surprise, the Chief of Staff sent for them a day or two
later and told them that the Grand Duke had agreed to make the
advance. In his signal to the War Office reporting this news, Wavell
added his personal opinion that nothing would happen, because the
Russian Army was incapable of moving on Mosul and would in fact
not even attempt to do so. "I was right," he commented long afterwards.

On 15th March, 1917, the revolution began in Petrograd. The
Grand Duke's staff were pessimistic. Wavell held for the time being to
the belief that the Russian Army would continue to fight. The Grand
Duke himself left Tiflis and was succeeded by General Yudenich, who
had been in command at Erzerum. Revolutionary ideas rapidly began

117

to infect the army in the rear areas: less and less work was done in the headquarters. Yudenich did nothing and sought to let matters take their course; but Bolkhovitinov attempted to go over to the revolutionaries. The Soldiers' Councils, which by now were exercising most of the power, gave the Chief of Staff the choice between leaving Tiflis in thirty-six hours or being put under arrest. He left Tiflis.

The revolution at the moment was an internal phenomenon and foreigners were not as yet in danger. Wavell had no tremors, therefore, in leaving his wife in the hotel in Tiflis and going off to visit the front in Asia Minor. He was away from 11th to 21st April. He travelled around under rough conditions, reaching Erzerum and Erzinjan; at the earnest request of one corps commander he gave a rousing address to a big group of semi-mutinous soldiers and restored their morale; and he took a reconnaissance flight in a very unsafe, elderly Russian aircraft over the Turkish lines in the valley of the Euphrates. At Erzinjan three War Office telegrams were delivered to him: they contained the unwelcome news that, instead of letting him go home and thence back to the Western Front, authority wanted him to go to Persia and there continue liaison work with the Russians—a decision against which he protested energetically.

The War Office relented: he was told that he would be allowed to go home, and his posting to Persia was cancelled. Colonel Marsh returned and Wavell, with unfeigned relief, prepared to hand over. The day before he was due to depart, Colonel Marsh (who had in fact already taken over from him) asked him to address a mass meeting of soldiers in the Opera House, at which the attitude of the Caucasus Army to the war was to be debated. Elated at the thought of going home he agreed, and went off to the Opera House to find that the meeting had already begun.

"I was to my consternation led on to the stage itself and placed in a chair alongside the president and principal members of the Soviet, finding myself in a very conspicuous position, as there were only some half dozen persons on the stage facing an audience in which every seat in the large Opera House was occupied by the representatives of every unit in the Army. A civilian, rather a sinister individual in a red tie, was addressing the assembly. The theme of his address, couched in the violent clap-trap of the professional agitator, was to the effect that this war was entirely due to the crimes of the capitalist nations, of whom France and England were, according to him, the most guilty, and that all the woes of the Russian proletariat, and the war itself, were due to these capitalists. His periods were being received with tumultuous applause, and as he grew more violent I measured the distance to the nearest exit in case he ended by denouncing me as a representative of the capitalists. (My French colleague, I noticed, was not present; he had been more prudent and declined the invitation.) As the speaker's vehement peroration was drawing to a close, the president passed me a note: 'Will you speak next?' I hastily wrote an emphatic refusal and passed it back. The speaker ended and was vociferously applauded for several minutes. Then the president got up and said to my consternation that the British representative would now address the meeting. A very nasty, very fast and unexpected one. I stood up and got a very encouraging reception which lasted long enough to enable me to concoct a few sentences. I said: 'The gentleman in the red tie has given you his views of who caused this war. I do not agree with him, but anyway I do not at present care who started this war or how. All I am concerned with is how it is going to finish. I can assure you with absolute faith that as far as the British Army is concerned it will end in one way only, and that is with the total defeat of Germany. The Russian Army has so far fought with us to this end with the utmost gallantry and as a great and loyal ally; I trust that it will continue to do so. But whether it does or not, we are going on to the end, and that end will be the defeat of Germany.' I then sat down. I have seldom made a shorter speech, never a more effective. The whole audience rose to their feet and cheered uninterruptedly for many minutes, for much longer than they had at the previous speech; and I had the pleasure of seeing the gentleman in the red tie (who had glowered at me when I referred to him as such) look at once furious and apprehensive. I then left the meeting before any more fast ones could be bowled."

All the officers of the General Staff with whom Wavell had worked were lined up on the platform of the station in Tiflis to bid him good-bye. One by one—and most of them were bearded—they kissed him warmly on both cheeks. It took the Wavells ten days to reach Petrograd, in conditions of mounting chaos. In the capital they had to wait six days for exit permits, tickets and reservations. Thereafter, except for the normal wartime risks of a sea crossing from Bergen to Aberdeen, their journey was uneventful. They were back in London by the middle of June. Wavell described his mission to Russia as "not an entirely unprofitable interlude from orthodox soldiering."

As soon as he arrived home he was made a brevet lieutenant-colonel, the promotion being back-dated to 3rd June, 1916. This date determined henceforth his position in the extra-regimental list of colonels, into which his name would go automatically four years later. Though his seniority in The Black Watch was unaffected, he was now sure of a much higher place in the Army as a whole, because from the colonels' list, which he would reach at thirty-seven, major-generals were chosen in strict rotation of seniority. What he could not foresee in 1917 was the length to which, after the war, the colonels' list would extend, or how slow—because of this very factor of his youthfulness—his own progress up it would be.

He now hoped and expected to go back to the Western Front, in the appointment of G.S.O.1 to a division for which he had hankered before he was sent to Russia. However, the D.M.O. at the War Office, General Sir Frederick Maurice, sent for him and said that he was to take up a novel appointment, that of liaison between the C.I.G.S., General Sir William Robertson, and General Sir Edmund Allenby, lately commander of the Third Army in France, who had just gone out to succeed General Murray as Commander-in-Chief of the Mediterranean Expeditionary Force in Egypt and Palestine.

"I was not particularly attracted by the appointment. . . . I had hoped for something more active, nearer the front line. However, I couldn't refuse. I had to make the best of it."

IV

With Allenby in Palestine

There are few more difficult or delicate appointments in an army in wartime than that of liaison officer between a commander in the field and the Supreme Command. The liaison officer's responsibility, though indirect, is very real. He cannot take a decision, but on his skilled observation, understanding and advice great decisions must be taken by others. He serves two masters, but must be absolutely loyal to them both. On his truthfulness in reporting, his shrewdness, and the balance of his judgment in assessing what he reports, the success or failure of these decisions must rest.

The War Cabinet and the C.I.G.S. had decided, after the first battle of Gaza, that there was an imperative need for a liaison officer in the Mediterranean theatre of war. In March, 1917, stimulated by General Maude's success in Mesopotamia and aware (from Wavell's reports) that there was no possibility of the Russians taking the offensive in the Caucasus, the C.I.G.S. suggested that he might instruct Murray to go over to the attack. This, according to Lord Hankey,

> fitted in very well with the views of the Prime Minister and the War Cabinet who from a political point of view were particularly keen to win some success, and it was decided to instruct Murray that they were anxious to capture Jerusalem and to obtain from him an estimate of the forces and transport required. On April 17th Murray, who had completed the desert railway to within four miles of Gaza, attacked the gateway of Palestine, but failed to capture it, incurring nearly 3,000 casualties. The War Cabinet then decided to relieve him.[1]

But by whom? After his East African campaign, General Smuts was in London, and in high favour with the Prime Minister, who offered him the command in Palestine. Smuts refused it, however, because Robertson could not, as a consequence of the Russian revolution and the failure of the spring offensive on the Western Front, promise to fulfil all his requirements for a great offensive in Palestine. Meanwhile in France it was clear that there was a real and deepening lack of sympathy between Haig, the C.-in-C., and Allenby, in command of Third Army. From Easter Monday (9th April) on into early May, for a month and more, Third Army, after a brilliant opening offensive—with the greatest gains yet achieved by British troops in a single day—had been unable to consolidate its initial victory, and suffered very heavy casualties. Haig and Allenby had known each other since they were contemporaries at the Staff College in 1896-7; great men both, they were sharply contrasted in character, temperament and outlook. Wavell, Allenby's biographer, wrote:

> Allenby was the more broadminded and the more human; Haig, by virtue of concentration the more technically efficient. . . . The two men never understood each other well, nor were easy in each other's company. Allenby himself once told one of his staff of a meeting between himself and Haig alone. They had important matters to discuss, but from sheer shyness of each other neither uttered a word. They parted with a mutual, but still unspoken, resolve never to meet again without others present.[2]

Early in June, while Third Army was in the process of taking over Fifth Army's front, because Fifth Army had been ordered north for the Flanders offensive, Allenby was summoned home to be asked to take up the task that Smuts had rejected.

> His first reactions were those of dismay. He believed that he was being removed from France and relegated to an unimportant command because of the limited success of the Arras battles. To his successor in the Third Army, Byng, he unburdened himself bitterly; and it was not until after he reached London and had interviews with the Prime Minister that he began to reconcile himself to the change.[3]

Lloyd George told Allenby that Jerusalem was wanted "as a Christmas present for the British nation," and that he was to ask for the reinforcements he found necessary to take it.

Allenby assumed command of what was now called the Egyptian Expeditionary Force at midnight on 28th June, 1917. Three weeks later the C.I.G.S.'s new liaison officer, Brevet Lieutenant-Colonel A. P. Wavell, M.C., arrived at G.H.Q. and reported to the Commander-in-Chief. As he had realised years before, at the Cavalry Division's peace-

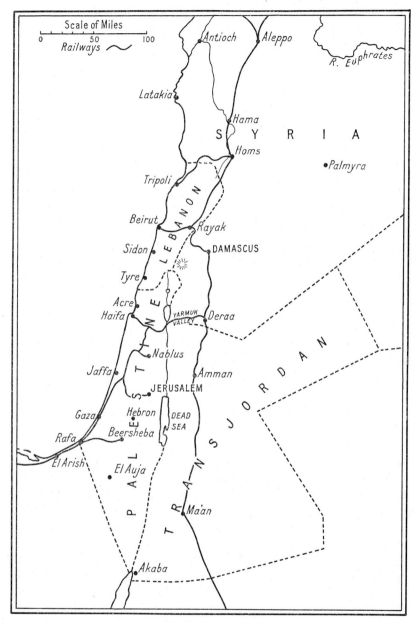

Scale of Miles

0   50   100

Railways ~

Antioch

Aleppo

R. Euphrates

Latakia

Hama

S Y R I A

Homs

Palmyra

Tripoli

L E B A N O N

Beirut

Rayak

Sidon

DAMASCUS

Tyre

Acre

Haifa

YARMUK VALLEY

Deraa

P A L E S T I N E

Nablus

Jaffa

Amman

JERUSALEM

T R A N S J O R D A N

Gaza

Hebron

DEAD SEA

Rafa

Beersheba

El Arish

El Auja

Ma'an

Akaba

Palestine, 1917

123

time manœuvres on the Berkshire Downs, it was indeed a privilege to go to war with Allenby, who at fifty-six was at the peak of his powers but by this, the end of the third year of the war, had had his share of setbacks and ill-luck. A perceptive but puzzled contemporary observer wrote of him at this time: "Opinions vary almost to the very extremes as regards his capacity. His nickname, 'the Bull,' represents one side— the idea that he can simply bang forward in a blind sort of fashion, but won't be turned; the other rates him very much more highly as a scientific soldier. I don't know which is the true estimate, perhaps neither."[4]

After Allenby's Palestine campaign, Wavell argued, there was no more need for bewilderment: he had been vindicated as a skilful soldier and a great leader of men. He wrote: "The British Army has had few leaders with better mental or physical equipment for the rough test of war, less likely to lose heart in the darkest hour, or more remorseless in pressing home an advantage and completing a victory; certainly none with a greater sense of loyalty and duty or more of the truth and straightforwardness that mark a great and generous nature."[5]

Allenby welcomed Wavell—to the latter's deep and abiding relief and gratitude. "No one," he wrote, "could have received me more kindly or openly. A smaller man might have regarded an emissary from the War Office as in some sort a spy and have treated him with suspicion. Allenby from the first took me entirely into his confidence and instructed his staff officers to do the same. I was allowed to see all papers and plans and to have full freedom of movement and access to anyone."

By the time Wavell reached him, Allenby had got a comprehensive and realistic view of his task, and of what his requirements would be, in material and in manpower, to fulfil it. He had been up to the front, he had discovered deficiencies in his command, staff and administrative structure, he had let the C.I.G.S. know—in a forthright signal, despatched while Wavell was on his way—the full extent of his needs, and he was aware of the Cabinet's increasing eagerness that he should achieve a big military victory, for political purposes. On all these issues he was entirely candid with the C.I.G.S.'s liaison officer.

Wavell now had the chance to watch, at close quarters, a strong and able commander at work. He saw the principles of staff work, administration, organisation, planning, intelligence and operational control, in which he had been trained and which had been lost and forgotten in the mud and muddle of Flanders, restored and given meaning and purpose. He saw a whole campaign planned and executed, not without a hitch, but with clean-cut, professional skill and drive, and an attention to detail which henceforth he was never to forget or underrate.

Most important of all, he watched an army that had not been defeated, but was dispirited and distrustful of itself and its High Command, find new life and vigour under dynamic leadership. The decision to take G.H.Q. forward, out of the affluent stewpot of Cairo to Rafa, on the edge of the Sinai Desert and within a few miles of the front, made the troops realise that "at last they had a commander who would live among them and lead them. Within a week of his arrival Allenby had stamped his personality on the mind of every trooper of the horse and every infantryman of the line."[6]

At the end of July, a little over a week after Wavell's arrival, the Chief went on a second trip, to the base establishments at Alexandria and on to the front again. Wavell went with him. They were back in Cairo on 31st July. The General sent for Wavell later that day. He stood at his desk and handed across a personal telegram. In a note beneath Rupert Brooke's sonnet *The Dead*, in the section headed "Last Post" in *Other Men's Flowers*, Wavell wrote: "I can well remember Lord Allenby repeating this poem to me shortly after he had heard the news that his only son, a boy of great promise, had been killed in action."[7]

By the beginning of August Allenby had formulated his plan, and Wavell had it clearly in mind:

The plan itself was simple, as are almost all good plans in war: to concentrate a superior force against the enemy's left flank, while inducing him to believe that his right would again be attacked. The Twentieth Corps and Desert Mounted Corps were to form the striking force against the Turkish left, while the Twenty-first Corps kept the enemy's attention fixed on Gaza. It was in essentials almost exactly the same plan as Roberts had exploited against Cronje in the relief of Kimberley in the Boer War some seventeen years before; and it is certain that Roberts' move had stayed in Allenby's memory, since it was the first big military operation in which he, then a squadron commander, had played a part. . . .

The date for the attack on Beersheba, which was to be the

opening act of the operations, was eventually fixed for October 31. The bombardment of Gaza was to begin some days earlier. The date was the latest possible, and involved some risk of forestalment by weather or by foe; but it enabled all the elaborate administrative preparations to be completed and the troops to come to their starting-places trained, fit, and confident.[8]

Allenby's three principal requirements were the same as Wavell's in his first Western Desert advance in December, 1940: transport, water and secrecy. Of these, and of the ways in which they were to be met, Wavell was fully apprised. He knew too the scale of the reinforcements Allenby wanted. Well briefed, therefore, he left Egypt on 6th August, and was back in London on the evening of the 13th—"quick travelling for those days." On the following morning he saw the C.I.G.S.

"I was shown into his office, an enormous room, covered with maps—I think it was really one of the War Office conference rooms. Wully was sitting at a desk in one corner, writing. When I was shown in and announced, he did not look up but went on writing. After a minute or two he finished, looked up at me and said rather gruffly and abruptly: 'Well, Wavell, what do you want?' I said: 'You sent for me, sir.' 'I sent for you?' he said, apparently incredulously, and seemed to reflect for a moment. 'Oh yes, I remember, it's this Palestine business. I know nothing about Palestine; and I don't know what Allenby is doing, I don't know what he wants. You tell me.' I began my exposition, standing in front of his desk. He looked at me and listened for about a minute, then appeared to get rather bored with the subject, opened the right-hand drawers of his desk one after the other, and finally took a paper from one of them and proceeded to read it. When he had finished it, he put it back in its drawer, rose from his seat, gave me a bored look as if wondering why I was still talking, and walked to the far corner of the room, where he studied a map of France. I was taken aback for a moment but was determined not to be put out. I followed him across the room, stood at his elbow and continued to talk of Palestine, while he seemed absorbed in the map. Presently he again turned his back on me, walked across the room and devoted the same study to a map of Russia, and then to another map. Finally with an impatient shrug as if to say, how can I get rid of this talkative fellow, he returned to his desk, searched the left-hand drawers, found a paper, turned his back on me as far as he could, and read it, marking it with a blue pencil. At last I ended my exposition of the situation and Allenby's plans—it had taken 25 to 30 minutes, I suppose—and said: 'That is all I have to tell you about Palestine, sir.' Dead silence, while he turned another page or two of the paper and marked it in blue pencil. Then he put it back in its drawer and turned to me. 'Now, I've 'eard what you said; and I've got three questions to ask you'; and with that he asked me three questions which showed that not only had he been listening intently but had been thinking hard; the three questions touched the crucial points of Allenby's plan. I answered them as well as I could, and he then said something like this: 'You can go back to Allenby and tell him that I approve his plan; that I can give him most of his requirements, but I can't give him this and that (he specified them and gave reasons); that the sooner he moves the better but that I can't get reinforcements to him quicker than I have indicated. Now is there anything else you want?' I mentioned one or two small points, with which he dealt, and went out with a clear picture of the C.I.G.S.'s mind and of his instructions."

Wavell left London on 21st August, and was back in Egypt—after delays in Rome and Taranto—on 5th September. G.H.Q. had moved up to near Rafa on 15th August. The camp lay midway between Rafa itself and Khan Yunis, just south of the railway. To the north its occupants could just see the Mediterranean; to the east and north-east they looked out over the southern flank of the Judæan highlands and the low, barren hills beyond Beersheba.

The army now comprised three Corps: the Twentieth under General Chetwode, the Twenty-first under General Bulfin, and the Desert Mounted Corps under General Chauvel—in all six British infantry and three cavalry divisions. Another infantry division from Salonika was due to join the Army later.

Motorised transport was only in its beginnings, and the motor vehicles which then existed were not suitable for the tracks across desert and semi-desert land which were to be used in the initial phase of the operation. The striking force was therefore dependent on horses and camels—some 30,000 of the latter. Supplies could be got to it from the railhead at Beersheba and one march beyond; but it could be watered only to Beersheba, and its advance beyond was dependent on getting control of the Beersheba wells, intact if possible. The early capture of Beersheba was therefore a keystone in Allenby's plan; and it could only be ensured by the maximum of secrecy.

His problem was not to conceal—over a dozen or so miles of very open country—all preparations for a move against Beersheba, for that would have been impossible; it was to try to persuade the enemy that this was only a feint, and that the main attack would come, as before, against Gaza. Wavell, in *Allenby*, says that the steps taken to deceive the Turks were varied and ingenious, and that the most spectacular and successful was the famous "haversack ruse." This was devised by Major Richard Meinertzhagen, Allenby's Intelligence Officer. After two unsuccessful attempts to carry it out, Meinertzhagen himself brought it off on 10th October. He rode out into the country to the north-west of Beersheba, contrived to be chased by a Turkish patrol, pretended to be wounded, and dropped his field-glasses, his water-bottle, his rifle and a haversack, freshly stained with his horse's blood, containing papers, letters and money. These he had spent a good deal of time and care in assembling; they included a staff officer's note-book in which he had jotted down "all sorts of nonsense about our plans and difficulties."[9] The "nonsense," in fact, skilfully conveyed the impression that there was a genuine plan for a big attack on Gaza, while the preparations against Beersheba were merely a pretence. Meinertzhagen lingered in sight long enough to watch one of the enemy pick up the haversack and rifle, and then galloped for home. "These papers," Wavell acknowledged, "were one of the principal influences that determined the actions of the Turks before and during the battle."[10]

By the time his offensive was due to begin, Allenby had effected a quiet but striking revolution in his headquarters and throughout his Command, with the minimum of obvious changes. He had with him as his Chief of Staff Major-General Louis Bols, who had served him in a similar capacity in Third Army. He was a buoyantly cheerful extrovert, as straightforward as he was brave, and was on the best of terms with his chief. The detailed planning and the drafting of orders Bols left to the B.G.G.S., Guy Dawnay, who had been in the senior year when Wavell went to the Staff College a decade earlier, and was one of the ablest and most clear-headed staff officers of his generation. The rest of the G.H.Q. staff was small in numbers but efficient. Relations with subordinate formations were excellent. The morale of the troops was high.

The deployment of the forces, between 24th and 30th October, was carried out exactly as arranged; Beersheba fell, at small cost, by midday on 31st October; the feint attack on Gaza was, with a stiffer casualty rate, similarly successful on 1st/2nd November. Thereafter, in the battle's fourth phase, hitches occurred which were overcome by cool and resolute leadership, skilful improvisation and complete understanding between Allenby and his subordinate commanders.[11]

The original plan provided for a swift leftward pivot by Chetwode's Twentieth Corps after the capture of Beersheba, and a north-westerly thrust through the Judæan foothills back to the coast, which would entail en route the destruction of the Turkish strongpoint of Hareira, on the edge of the plain. However, there was what Wavell described as "an awkward and unrehearsed pause before the curtain could rise on the third act" of the drama which he was witnessing. A fierce *khamsin*—a hot, dry wind from the Arabian desert—blew up, and the wells of Beersheba could not meet the increased demands for water. The Turks reacted very strongly to what they thought to be a full-scale drive from Beersheba to Hebron and on to Jerusalem (it was in fact a small but bold raiding party of seventy, mounted on camels, who managed to cut communications on the Beersheba-Hebron road), and there were several days of hard and continuous fighting in the hills to the north of Beersheba.

Chetwode decided that, until he had cleared up this situation, he could not come down into the plain and make the assault on Hareira, which had been planned for 4th November. Allenby at H.Q., Wavell wrote:

knew well the dangers of delay, yet he could do little or nothing to hasten the stroke. For one of his temperament it must have been difficult to remain inactive while the fate of the operation hung in the balance. He must have thought of his initial success at Arras, succeeded by days of stalemate, and have wondered whether a complete success was again to elude him.[12]

On 4th November there was a signal from Chetwode: he must postpone the attack to the 6th. Allenby had remained calm and composed and had refrained from interfering; but now, accompanied by Wavell, he drove up to Twentieth Corps headquarters, quite determined that, if will-power was what was needed to urge the attack forward, he would supply it. He listened quietly to Chetwode's exposition of his administrative difficulties and to his tactical proposals for overcoming them. When he had done, Allenby sat for a moment silent, pondering. He stood up to go; he picked up his cap.

"You can postpone till the 6th," he said. "You'll be all right. I never knew a really well-prepared attack fail yet."

Wavell hearkened, watched, and never forgot. "To listen patiently to all the administrative arguments," he wrote, "to weigh them up quickly, to change his preconceived purpose at once, and having decided to do so, to do it with confidence and cheerful encouragement to his subordinate in spite of the risks he knew it involved, showed him a great man and was a lesson in the art of leadership."

Three divisions made the attack, as Chetwode had planned it, and with great dash, on 6th November, shattered the Turkish left and compelled the hurried retreat of their whole line. On the morning of 7th November, twenty-first Corps found the fortress of Gaza abandoned, and the enemy streaming away along the plain to the north. There followed ten days of relentless and—judged by the standards of the time—very swift pursuit across the ancient, fertile plain of Philistia. Jaffa, more than fifty miles north of Gaza, fell on 16th November; some 10,000 prisoners and a hundred guns were captured. But the enemy, though defeated and in full retreat, was not yet broken: the Turkish Eighth Army withdrew, in fair order, behind the Auja (now the Yarkon) river, and the Seventh Army scrambled up into strong defensive positions in the mountains west of Jerusalem. With Jaffa in their hands, the British now commanded the main road from the coast to Jerusalem and the little branch railway which meandered precariously up from the plain, through the precipitous valleys to a terminus a mile or so south of the city. Wavell wrote:

To the uninitiated pursuit seems the easiest possible form of war. To chase a flying, presumably demoralised enemy must be a simple matter, promising much gain at the expense of some exertion and hardship, but little danger. Yet the successful or sustained pursuits of history have been few, the escapes from a lost battle many. The reasons are partly material, but mainly moral. A force retreating falls back on its depots and reinforcements; unless it is overrun, it is growing stronger all the time. And there are many expedients besides fighting by which it can gain time: bridges or roads may be blown up, defiles blocked, supplies destroyed. The pursuer soon outruns his normal resources. He may possibly be able to feed himself at the expense of his enemies or of the countryside; he is not likely to be able to replenish his ammunition and warlike equipment in the same way. But the chief obstacle he has to overcome is psychological. The pursued has a greater incentive to haste than the pursuer, and, unless he is demoralised, a stronger urge to fight. It is only natural that the soldier who has risked his life and spent his toil in winning a battle should desire relaxation in safety as his meed of victory, and that the general and staff should feel a reaction from the strain. So that, while coolness in disaster is the supreme proof of a commander's courage, energy in pursuit is the surest test of his strength of will. Few have carried out pursuits with such relentless determination as did Allenby in 1917 and 1918.[13]

After 16th November Allenby had a clear choice to make between two alternatives: he could halt for a pause, which would be bound to last several weeks, if not months; or he could press on quickly. The arguments in favour of a pause were many: the difficult nature of the country, the paucity of maps, the bad communications, the fact that the winter rains were due any day, and finally a telegram from the War Office, warning him against involving his army in commitments beyond its strength and hinting that it might become necessary to withdraw troops from him in 1918. After Jaffa's capture Allenby had one day of rest and thought, at the end of which he ordered an immediate advance into the hills.

On the morning of the next day, 18th November, three Divisions—the 75th, West Country Territorials, the Yeomanry, and the 52nd (Lowland)—went forward into the rugged defile of the Bab el Wad, veiled in a thick, soft, wet mist. Within two days the 75th Division, when the clouds lifted, were within sight of Jerusalem and had captured the commanding height of Nebi Samwil to the north-east of the Jaffa-Jerusalem road. And there, in some of the fiercest, most dogged fighting of the war, they stuck in bitter cold, high winds and slashing rain. By 24th November it was obvious that the original attacking formations had been spent to the limit; the enemy tried two counter-attacks and were unable to dislodge them, but fresh troops were essential for the final thrust. Chetwode and Twentieth Corps came up with three Divisions—the 74th, 53rd and 60th—and launched the last, successful attack on 8th December. With first light the next day it became clear that the enemy had gone. After 730 years of Moslem rule, the soldiers of a Christian power entered Jerusalem, not (they believed) as conquerors but as liberators.

The Mayor came out with a white flag and the keys of the holiest city in the Western world, which he was eager to hand over. Major-General Shea, commander of the 60th (London) Division, accepted them on Allenby's behalf; and in the meantime the Turks were being driven off the Mount of Olives in a sharp rearguard action. Allenby decided to make his formal entry into Jerusalem on 11th December, and it was arranged that the Prime Minister would announce the fact in the House of Commons that afternoon.

In the midst of these excitements there arrived at G.H.Q., in the milder air of the plain, a disconsolate little man in Arab dress; he was ushered in rapidly to see Allenby. His name was Major T. E. Lawrence. Just a month before, he had made his gallant and adventurous attack on a Turkish troop train, after blowing up a bridge over the Yarmuk river; he thought it a failure because some of the enemy escaped. Then—according to his own account[14]—he endured unbelievable cruelties and humiliations at the hands of a senior and sodomitical Turkish officer in Deraa, was released, and made his way to Aqaba. He flew to G.H.Q. to report to Allenby, who

> was so full of victories that my short statement that we had failed to carry a Yarmuk bridge was sufficient, and the miserable details could remain concealed. While I was still with him, word came from Chetwode that Jerusalem had fallen; and Allenby made ready to enter in the official manner which the catholic imagination of Mark Sykes had devised. He was good enough, though I had done nothing for the success, to let Clayton take me along as his staff officer for the day. The personal staff tricked me out in their spare clothes till I looked like a major in the British Army. Dalmeny lent me red tabs, Evans his brass hat; so that I had the gauds of my appointment in the ceremony at the Jaffa gate, which for me was the supreme moment of the war.[15]

Like Lawrence, Wavell was one of the twenty officers invited by Allenby to walk in procession behind the Commander-in-Chief to the Jaffa Gate, the main entry to the old walled city of Jerusalem. At the gate there was a guard of honour, representative of the troops who had taken part in the campaign—English, Scottish, Irish, Welsh, Australian, New Zealand, French and Italian—the nearby streets were lined with Timmy Shea's Londoners, and there was a guard of Indian Mohammedan troops over the Haram-es-Sharif (the Temple area), which is one of the most sacred spots in the Islamic world. Austere and humble as it was, the ceremony caught the imagination of the world, and when much else was forgotten about the First World War its memory remained, clear and undefiled.

Wavell had to hurry back to London with his report. The night before he was due to go, he took it in to show Allenby.

"I had written a few sentences of criticism of the failure of the cavalry to cut off the enemy in the pursuit after the Gaza-Beersheba battle. Although Allenby himself had, I know, been critical of the slowness of the mounted troops, he told me in no unmeasured terms that I had no business to criticise them: 'Had I ever commanded mounted troops in a pursuit?' etc. I had the temerity to stick to my guns and say that I maintained my view that the mounted troops should have done better; but that I was his staff officer and if he wished the offending sentence omitted in my report to the W.O. I would of course do so. He was an alarming person when angry, and though I was not afraid of him and argued the point, I found myself at the end of it pouring with perspiration though it was not a warm evening. After A. had finished with me he said, 'Now come along and have a drink,' and I don't think he ever said a harsh word to me again. Incidentally he took my report, less the offending sentence, as the basis of his Despatch on the operations, and hardly altered it."

Wavell was back in England for Christmas and was immediately given a new appointment on the staff of Henry Wilson, who was now permanent British Military Representative on the Supreme War Council at Versailles. Since he wanted either a command or a staff job in the field, Wavell was very reluctant to accept this assignment. Robertson himself took the trouble to explain his choice. "They are talking the most awful nonsense about Palestine at Versailles. I must have someone there who knows about Palestine."

He reported at Versailles early in January, 1918, and found himself at once at the centre of a vital debate on strategic decisions of the highest consequence. The Russians, now under Bolshevik domination, had collapsed militarily and had just signed an armistice with Germany. Very grave questions therefore faced the planners at Versailles: before the Americans (who had entered the war the previous April) brought sufficient forces to France, could the Germans transfer their divisions freed by the Russian collapse, and deliver a last, overwhelming attack on the British and French armies? For how long could the Allies stand on the defensive? And what would be their manpower needs?

Haig, the British C.-in-C. in France, and Robertson, convinced that defeat in France would mean the loss of the war, were determined to make the defensive stand. They knew they would have to muster for it every man they could find, and they were sternly opposed to all diversionary efforts on any other than the Western Front. Lloyd George, however, had always believed that the quickest road to victory lay, not in the carnage of Flanders, but in the elimination, one by one, of Germany's less formidable allies. His principal military supporter in this thesis was Henry Wilson. They wanted an offensive policy in Palestine in 1918, with the object of driving Turkey out of the war altogether. To that end they were willing to let Allenby have enough men and material to enable him to reach Damascus and, if possible, Aleppo. Wavell's appointment was a shrewd attempt by Robertson directly to influence this internal British controversy before it came out into the open in front of the other Allied delegations.

His views, set out in a paper which he put up to Wilson as soon as he reached Versailles, completely accorded with those of Haig and Robertson. From the strong vantage of having just come back from the Eastern theatre, he was a convinced "Westerner." He argued that an advance to Damascus or even Aleppo could have no real effect. Aleppo was 1,500 miles from Constantinople, across the forbidding and almost roadless highlands of Anatolia. To reinforce Allenby's army for an effort of this sort would add seriously to the strain on shipping; the transport of U.S. troops and of food for Britain across the Atlantic was the principal priority; to shift a considerable tonnage to the Mediterranean, where enemy submarines were still very active, would be hazardous. On land, in Asia Minor itself, the Turks' fighting capacity was by no means exhausted. Nor would it be wise to discount Germany's influence over her ally: there were still strong pro-German elements in the Army and the Government, and the guns of the *Goeben* and the *Breslau*, lying at anchor off Constantinople, could be as effective against the city as against the Royal Navy. For all these reasons, Wavell held, all Allied effort must be concentrated on resisting the German attack in the West.

He was summoned to see General Wilson, who was at his most persuasive, his most inventive, painting a verbal picture of the German Ambassador in Turkey and the German Commander-in-Chief standing on the Galata bridge in Constantinople, and one saying to the other, "Mein Gott! I hope Allenby won't take Aleppo!"

Wavell stuck to his opinion, but it was most unwelcome. By the time the Supreme War Council met in full session on 29th January, the British Permanent Military Representative had prepared his own plan for the conduct of the war in 1918. This was that the Allies, while standing on the defensive in France, should "undertake a decisive offensive against Turkey with a view to the annihilation of the Turkish armies and the collapse of Turkish resistance."[16] After two long meetings, it was only accepted on the understanding that the British Government would not divert forces to the Palestine theatre from, or relax its efforts on, the Western Front. Even after Lloyd George had accepted this condition, Robertson entered a formal protest against the recommendation, on the ground that it was impracticable, and that to attempt it would be very dangerous and detrimental to British prospects of winning the war. "I can remember," Wavell wrote, "Wully coming out of the meeting with a face like a thundercloud."

He had made his first involuntary excursion into the realms of High Command. It had had some immediate practical effect, but it had given him a strong dislike for the idea of a Supreme Allied Command, and for the way in which this Command handled its business.

"Once the Palestine operations had been settled, I found little to do. . . . I asked permission to resign my appointment and go to the war. The Supreme War Council was, incidentally, the only place I was at during the whole war which had a pessimistic attitude towards winning it.

"Henry Wilson saw me, expressed his surprise at my wishing to leave an appointment so much at the heart of things, and said he did not see how he could help me to a job in France. I said that if I could be allowed to return to Palestine, I was confident Allenby would give me a job.

"I left Versailles on 25th February, without any regrets. I was ten to twelve days in England and then went off again to Palestine, as a 'pool' officer, with no appointment, trusting to my friends at G.H.Q. in Palestine to find me one.

"An unprofitable interlude, which gave me a poor opinion on the higher direction of international war."

Wavell never had cause to regret his refusal to stay in his Versailles appointment. On 18th April he took over from Brigadier-General Bartholomew in Jerusalem as B.G.G.S. Twenty Corps, under the command of General Chetwode.

"The personality of my Corps Commander, Philip Chetwode, was the primary consideration in my mind. I had seen something of him while I was liaison officer and had stayed several times at his Corps H.Q. Barty, my predecessor, always called him a 'rum 'un.' But I found nothing specially difficult about his personality once one got used to his ways. He had about the best and quickest military brain I have ever known, an extremely good tactical eye for ground and a great gift for expressing a situation clearly and concisely, either by word or on paper. I think he just lacked as a commander the quality of determination and drive, certainly compared with a man like Allenby. He was aristocratic, rather a snob in some ways, and inclined to be satirical at the expense of those not out of the top drawer; otherwise I found him easy to work for; he gave quick and sensible decisions and did not worry about detail. At an early stage I asked him how much of the work that went through my office he liked to see; he answered: 'Just what you think necessary to show me. I shall find out soon enough whether you are doing your job or not.' The one thing I found that it was not safe to do was to bring him work after dinner; he hated it and would be ill-humoured and tiresome. . . . He slept little and woke early but was at his best and brightest in the early morning."

During Wavell's four months' absence much had happened on the Palestine front. After the decision of the Supreme War Council, Smuts was sent out, by the War Cabinet, to consult with Allenby and a representative of the Mesopotamian force and to formulate a plan for a united effort to bring Turkey to her knees. He proposed that the British and Imperial forces in Mesopotamia should stay on the defensive, that Allenby should be given all the troops that could be spared, and that he should advance on a broad front through Palestine and Syria and on the eastern banks of the Jordan, with the capture of Damascus as his objective. The first parts of the plan were carried out during the spring; in the course of hard fighting from the last week of February to the middle of April, the British line had been extended eastwards and northwards from Jerusalem; and Allenby was prepared to slog on with the offensive throughout the summer. But, as Wavell himself wrote,

the difficulty of any planning in war is to arrive at a *true* picture of the situation, i.e. strength and dispositions of the enemy, his intentions, the weather, and many other factors which it is almost impossible to forecast. Given all these, almost anyone could make a good plan; without them there must be a considerable amount of guesswork and risk in planning.[17]

The Palestine campaign of the spring and summer of 1918 is a classic illustration of the truth of this dictum. The offensive had indeed been carefully planned; the dispositions and the intentions

136

of the enemy were well known; yet the plan went awry, because two factors at least were not fully appreciated: the Palestine weather was a great deal less predictable than had been thought, and the effects of the German offensive in France were far more serious than anyone had considered possible.

Allenby's offensive was checked for six months by a force with an effective fighting strength of 33,000—exactly half his own—ragged, sick, half starved, with their lines of communication, already utterly inadequate, subject to increasing harassment by Arab raiding parties, exposed to air reconnaissance as much to espionage. This army, in its stubborn, doomed heroism, owed nothing to its High Command, for Enver Pasha, who had established a virtual dictatorship in Constantinople, was looking for an easy victory in the Caucasus at the expense of reinforcements for Palestine. Jemal Pasha had gone, and a brave Turcophile German, Liman von Sanders, who three years before had held Gallipoli, was Allenby's final and grimly worthy opponent.

At the end of March (with belated rains making the Jordan like a Highland river in spate) and again at the end of April, Allenby made two unsuccessful thrusts across the Jordan into the mountains of Moab. Yet, having failed to capture Amman, or even to establish a salient in the foothills east of the river, he took the risk, justifiably as it proved, of maintaining a considerable force, all summer through, in the southern Jordan valley, two thousand feet below sea-level.[18] Meanwhile, with the now severely retrenched means at his disposal, he prepared quietly for the great decisive attack which was his ultimate intention, from which he had never wavered.

The whole of Twenty Corps did not take part in the attacks across the river, though one of its divisions, the 60th, had been put under Chauvel's command for these operations. Its other two divisions were the 53rd, holding a line from the left flank of the Cavalry Corps in the Jordan valley, through the desolate hills to a point east of the Jerusalem-Nablus road; and the 10th, west of the road, across the mountains to Twenty-first Corps' right flank on the edge of the coastal plain.

"The early part of the summer was occupied by defence reorganisation and training. The E.E.F. was bled white to send troops to France. . . . Further offensive operations were for the time being out of the question; and we had to consider the defence of our very extended front. I learned a good deal from P.C. about this. He had a very good eye for ground. . . . I take a little credit for an appreciation I drew up at this time, that if the Turks did attack they would do so in a certain way and on a certain part of our front. When we advanced in the autumn, amongst captured Turkish documents was found a plan for an attack on our front which almost exactly reproduced that attributed to the enemy in my appreciation.

"One of the defence problems in these hills was a peculiar one. The solidly built stone villages, from which the inhabitants had fled or been evacuated, formed excellent strong points in many places; but it was almost impossible to occupy them owing to the number, size and ferocity of the fleas, so long deprived of their natural fodder. The only solution found was for men preparing the defences to work entirely naked and brush the fleas off one another. The defences, once made, were left to the fleas, to be occupied only in emergency."

The First World War was entering its final phase, though the particip-ants were too weary, too inured to its mixture of bloodshed, muddle, grim hope and deepening disillusion to realise it. In July it became possible, on both the strategic and tactical levels, to plan for a re-newed and final onslaught on Liman von Sanders' dwindled but still aggressive army. When Henry Wilson (now C.I.G.S.) signalled Allenby proposing that in the winter divisions from France should be sent to carry out an offensive in Palestine and then go back to the Western Front in the spring of 1919, the Chief would only offer a limited advance to the line Tiberias-Acre. A month later he outlined to his Corps commanders an even more restricted plan. But a few days later he came back from a morning ride, sent for his Operations staff, and told them that he had decided on an extension of his original plan whose purpose was nothing less than the complete destruction of the Turkish armies. It was to be mobile warfare, on the grand scale and in a manner not practised at all hitherto in World War I. The Cavalry Corps had been sweating out a vile summer in the Jordan valley, with flies, centipedes, giant spiders and the thick, heavy heat their constant companions; they were to be switched to the coastal plain, were to thrust up to and through the central Carmel, near Haifa, and then to break into the great Megiddo-Esdraelon plain, thirty or forty miles in the rear of the Turkish armies and of the railway which served all their forces west of the Jordan, and across their main lines of retreat. Wavell wrote:

It was a daring plan, even against an enemy so inferior in numbers and morale. It would involve a continuous ride of over fifty miles for the majority of the horsemen, and over sixty for some, in the course of which they would have to cross a range of hills in the enemy's possession, passable only by two difficult tracks. There is no parallel in military history to so deep an adventure by such a mass of cavalry against a yet unbroken enemy. But Allenby had not made up his mind lightly, and there was no shaking it by the suggestion of difficulties. He left it to his staff and to his Corps commanders to work out the details of the design, but of the main framework there was to be no alteration. The long Turkish domination of Syria and Palestine, and the military power on which it was founded, were to be given the death-blow in the grand manner.[19]

The plan was a complete reversal of its predecessor, the third battle of Gaza a year earlier. Then Allenby's main blow was delivered against the Turks' left flank, while by secrecy and deception he convinced them that the assault would be up the coast. This time, intending to break through on the coast, he took every possible step to make them fear that the weight of his attack would be in the Judæan hills and through the Jordan Valley. Since Jerusalem and the surrounding countryside were full of Turkish spies, they were given plenty of false information. A hotel was taken over in Jerusalem as a dummy G.H.Q., rooms were allocated, telephones installed, billets were inspected as if for a big staff, tent-lines were marked out, and a bridge was built across the Jordan. Fifteen thousand dummy horses, made of canvas, filled the horse lines. Sleighs, drawn by mules, raised clouds of dust at the times when the canvas horses should have been going to water. Labour battalions, from the West Indies, marched ostentatiously down to the Jordan valley by day, and came back by lorry under cover of darkness.

Meanwhile, on the other flank, the concentration of the great body of troops needed for the real attack was effected with the utmost secrecy. Only a few senior officers knew the details. All movements into the concentration area were made at night. Fires were forbidden at all times. Troops lay up in orange and olive groves. No new tents were pitched. The orange grove irrigation channels provided water for most of the horses under excellent cover. So good were the deception and the concealment that a Turkish Intelligence map dated 17th September—two days before the assault—and captured in the course of the battle showed no suspicion of any concentration in the coastal sector, but a great increase of force in the Jordan valley.

In these great and far-reaching plans of Allenby's, Twenty Corps had a subsidiary role. Wavell, however, was present at the principal conferences. Allenby's confidence—almost overpowering as it seemed at the time—made an ineffaceable impression on him. He recalled that even the staff were alarmed when the Chief promised the cavalry 30,000 prisoners; and that when one defence-minded battalion commander asked what line he should consolidate, Allenby's abrupt answer was "Aleppo."[20] Another memory was of a visit which Allenby and Bols paid Twentieth Corps headquarters not long before the attack was launched. The Chief went into Chetwode's room; Bols talked to Wavell, who had one or two questions about the original offensive which he wanted to ask the C.G.S. They were brushed aside.

"You needn't worry at all," said Bols, "about the initial attack on our first objective in the plain of Esdraelon. What I want to discuss is the subsequent advance to Damascus."

Wavell attributed this to Bols's naturally exuberant optimism, but later Chetwode said that Allenby's conversation with him had been along similar lines. Allenby's outlook had, by then, passed beyond Palestine: under his infectious influence subordinate commanders and staff were equally confident. This, as the history of war repeatedly demonstrates, can be a dangerous infection; but for once optimism was justified.

Chetwode was just as imaginative as Allenby. Shea's 60th Division had joined Twenty-first Corps on the coastal plain, and Chetwode was left with two infantry divisions, the 10th and the 53rd, on a much extended front. He had also handed over a large proportion of his artillery and transport to Twenty-first Corps. His part in the operation was to capture Nablus. He decided, Wavell recalled:

"to concentrate the 53rd Division on the right of the line and the 10th Division on the left, leaving a gap of some seven miles in the centre, where the main road was and the main Turkish strength, to be held by any oddments we could scrape together. The two divisions would then converge on Nablus, keeping to the high ground, by-passing the strongest Turkish defences which guarded the main road. It was a good plan and showed an eye for ground. But I shall not easily forget the consternation of the officer to whom was allotted the task of guarding the centre, with two Pioneer battalions and the Corps Cavalry

Regiment. It was quite logical; the Pioneer battalions would be wanted to work on the main road as soon as the Turks retreated and the Corps Cavalry Regiment to take up the pursuit. As for the chance of the Turks discovering our weakness and attacking, it was practically nil. But the officer concerned was not an imaginative soldier, and that he should be asked to hold many miles of the most vital part of our front, covering the main road to Jerusalem, with so small a force seemed to him sheer madness. I think I had to give him a written absolution for everything that might happen; and even so, I think those few days put years on his life."

This officer's anxieties might have been—though they obviously were not—relieved by a large-scale raid made during the night of 12th August, some five weeks before the main offensive, by the 29th Brigade of the 10th Division on the Turkish defences covering the road to Nablus. The strategic purpose of the raid was to persuade the Turks that this was where Twenty Corps' main attack would be made. Its tactical purpose was to "blood" some of the new Indian units, and to arouse emulation amongst the others. It was a difficult operation, across difficult mountain country. The troops had three weeks' intensive training for it, in a similar landscape south of Jerusalem. They were backed by the artillery of two divisions, nine other batteries and a brigade of mountain artillery. The Turks were entrenched on the top of a ridge nearly five thousand yards in length, some two thousand yards from Twenty Corps' front line and separated from it by a deep, rocky, scrub-covered gully. They were to be attacked from both flanks and from the rear by two Indian battalions and two companies of the 1st Leinster Regiment. The whole operation, which was to take place between 10 p.m. and midnight, was meticulously planned and timed. Special felt-soled boots were issued, bundles of dried grass were laid on the rockiest parts of the gully, a jointed ladder was devised for crossing the enemy's wire, stretcher-bearer posts were manned along the route of withdrawal, a deserted village was illuminated by dummy gun flashes and flares in order to draw the Turkish guns' fire. The raid was entirely successful. For a loss of 107 killed and wounded, 250 prisoners were taken and 14 machine guns, and heavy casualties were inflicted on the dazed and bewildered Turks; and Liman von Sanders claimed to have beaten off "a determined attempt to break through his centre and reach Nablus."[21]

In the planning phase before the main offensive "the administrative factors were the really crucial and difficult ones. I remember that two in particular exercised me, one in our rear and one in our front. In our rear the problem was to build up dumps of ammunition and stores near the front line with the very limited amount of motor transport we had; we could not bring up supplies to these dumps after the offensive began, since practically the whole of our Corps M.T. was being taken for the other Corps, and we should have to rely on the divisional and regimental transport. The D.A.Q.M.G. and I worked out a programme and decided that we could just do it in time, though it would be a close run thing. But Chetwode, for the only time while I was his staff officer, worried me about it; he kept saying that I should never get the gun ammunition up in time. I assured him that it was all right, but his doubts obviously had their effect on my nerves. For three nights running I woke up—or thought I woke, I must have still been half asleep—to hear quite clearly the roar of the opening artillery barrage that preceded our attack, and realised that there was only enough ammunition up for a few minutes' bombardment owing to my failure to get up the ammunition: I then woke up completely and realised that it was a dream. After the third night of this, I went over the calculations again very carefully with the D.A.Q.M.G., and satisfied myself that they were all right. I then decided that as all the orders and instructions for which I was responsible had been issued or drafted, and all was in train, I had better go off for a few days' leave and rid myself of any dreams. So I went down to Egypt and did nothing for three days. . . .

"The problem on our front was that of roads, or rather tracks. There was no known road, except the main Jerusalem-Nablus road, but the Turks must obviously have constructed some behind their lines, as we had done. The difficulty was to discover their trace and the sort of transport they would take. It was not easy since most of the 'roads' were made by clearing the beds of the deep *wadis*; and photographic reconnaissance planes were not easy to come by, nor their results conclusive. I gave my Intelligence as their primary task to produce an accurate or reasonably accurate road map; but their final effort was found during our advance to be very far off the mark."

Allenby's final campaign had been won, in Wavell's view, before a shot was fired; and it was "no soldiers' battle, but the manœuvre of a great master of war."

He himself took an active part only in its first act. Chetwode established his headquarters at Ramallah, an Arab village several miles north of Jerusalem. Wavell wrote: "It was my first experience of running a big H.Q. in battle; on the whole the staff work went all right, but it was a severe test, and I became conscious of a number of things that might have gone wrong if the battle had been difficult or prolonged."

Very little did go wrong. The main contributions to the offensive—Twenty-first Corps' hammer blows, the sweep of the cavalry through the hills and into the Plain of Esdraelon, the Arabs' spectacular diversionary raids from the east—all went according to plan. On the Twenty Corps front the 10th Division, instead of keeping to the hills, drove boldly down the road in the valley and were in reach of Nablus on the evening of 20th September, thirty-six hours after the opening of the attack. There they remained, taking no part in the final phase of the battle. Beisan, at the eastern end of the Plain of Esdraelon, was captured; so was Jenin, some miles north of the point where the Samaria hills debouch on to the plain. The jaws of the trap closed on the hapless Turks. Their resistance crumbled swiftly.

On 26th September, while the cavalry were still rounding up prisoners in all the ravines in the hills of Samaria, Allenby held a conference at Jenin and ordered a rapid advance on Damascus. All Palestine was his: the Turkish Seventh and Eighth Armies had been reduced to a few small, scattered columns, and the Fourth Army was in hasty retreat; some 50,000 prisoners were in his hands, and only about 40,000 Turks and Germans, in grave disarray, lay between the British and Damascus. His forward troops were in Damascus by 1st October. The administrative problems of pursuit began to accumulate. It took him until 26th October, with no serious stand made anywhere by the Turks, to reach Aleppo.

On 23rd September Lord Hankey noted in his diary:

I think the Palestine victory is largely due to the action of the Committee of Prime Ministers last July in refusing to allow the transport of the 54th Division to the Western Front. As the C.I.G.S. said to me in the afternoon, the victories in Palestine and Salonika are most glaring examples of "amateur strategy"—but he is very pleased all the same.[22]

Allenby, his staff, his subordinate commanders, officers, N.C.O.s and men—British, Australian and New Zealand, Indian, Arab and Jew-

143

ish —might be forgiven for disagreeing with the explanation of their victory offered by Hankey and Wilson. Wavell, who thought of soldiering first and politics afterwards, gave a somewhat different assessment:

> In less than six weeks Allenby's army had captured 75,000 prisoners and 360 guns, and had moved its front forward 350 miles. Its own casualty list had been little over 5,000. The most advanced troops, the 5th Cavalry Division, had actually covered some 550 miles in the thirty-eight days from the breaking of the line to the occupation of Aleppo. The greatest exploit in history of horsed cavalry, and possibly their last success on a large scale, had ended within a short distance of the battlefield of Issus (333 B.C.), where Alexander the Great first showed how battles could be won by bold and well-handled horsemen. It had taken just four years to conclude the war with Turkey; it took nearly five more to conclude peace. Which proves the staying power of the pen over the sword.[23]

On 31st October the armistice with Turkey was announced. Brigadier-General Wavell had already applied for leave to the United Kingdom. His wife was shortly due to have their second child. Travel was chaotic, but Wavell knew well enough how to organise his journeys for himself. He passed through Paris on 11th November. He was in London, at the small house, 10 Cliveden Place, which his wife had taken some months before, on the morning of 12th November, about twenty-four hours after the first Armistice Day.

"Such," he wrote, "was the end of the First World War for me. I had had on the whole an interesting and successful war, with varied experience. I had risen from a junior captain to brigadier-general (brevet-lieut.-colonel). Except for the loss of my eye, I had had an easy war and not very much danger or hardship. I had served in three theatres (France, Russia and the Middle East) and had travelled a great many miles. I held in all no fewer than eleven appointments . . . but all except five had been in the nature of stop-gaps. . . . The Western Front was a very dull, unimaginative, heavy-footed business; and I think I learnt more of the art of war in my more unorthodox way-farings."

Implicit in this laconic account was the fact that it was by luck that he was alive when many of the best of his contemporaries were dead. Like every other survivor of World War I he was always conscious of this simple truth, and drew important moral and practical con-clusions from it which deeply influenced his outlook and conduct. Henceforth he put the factor of luck high on the list of essential qualities in a commander.

He had not himself exercised command, but he had been in Allenby's confidence and able to watch him at close quarters. This ex-perience had a profound effect on his own development. When he wrote his biography of Allenby, he called its first volume "a study in greatness." He believed with all his heart that Allenby was a great man, and that he himself had been lucky to serve him. He never forgot the lessons Allenby had taught him, not by precept but by example; and he tried, when he held the same kind of appointment, to put those lessons into practice.

V

Peacetime Soldiering

The Wavells' second child and eldest daughter, Pamela, was born on 3rd December, 1918. Through the twenty years of peace and into the second war, Wavell's family was his private citadel. They never had a permanent home of their own; wherever he was sent, the family followed, after the shortest possible interval. They accustomed themselves to married quarters, hotel rooms, various houses. They brought their own impedimenta of books and toys; there were dogs to be exercised and ponies to be groomed. As the family grew in numbers, moves became costly as well as complicated to organise; but they were made, in the face of every obstacle devised by bureaucrat or banker. A key character in the household was the children's Nannie, Miss Daisy Ribbands, the daughter of a Lowestoft fishing skipper, who had first come to the Wavells when Archie John was born, and remains with them still. She was a skilled and patient organiser who at the end of every move was quickly capable of establishing the essentials of their latest home.

In his home Wavell was neither solitary nor taciturn; here he was at ease and contented. If there was a slightly insecure, gipsyish quality about this way of life—Lady Wavell has described herself as "very tribal"—it was a lovable vagabondage, not shutting others out but welcoming them as guests and friends, over the width of the world. Partings there had to be, as in any other soldier's existence, but there were always reunions. His son summed up this facet of his father's life in a single sentence: "Few soldiers' families can have been so much together and so happy as we have."[1]

Wavell had nearly two months' leave, and at the end of the year was ordered back to Egypt to his appointment with Twenty Corps. He arrived in Cairo on 17th January, 1919, to find the city suffering from the after-effects of the heaviest rainfall for many years, his Corps headquarters at Heliopolis almost inaccessible because the tramway was flooded, and the Corps in the process of dissolution.

He was in Cairo only a day or two and then went up to Haifa to take over the post of B.G.G.S., Advanced H.Q., in place of Bartholomew, who had already gone home. Allenby as Commander-in-Chief had responsibilities, not of combat but of control and administration, extending over a vast area, from Egypt (still under martial law) across Sinai, through Palestine, Transjordan and Syria, into Cilicia and the foothills of the Taurus Mountains. Political and diplomatic problems already abounded. One of the first and most urgent was the refusal of several Turkish generals, of whom the most prominent was Ali Ihsan Pasha, commander of the forces withdrawn from the Mesopotamian front, to disband their armies in accordance with the armistice terms. They were beyond reach by direct action; Allenby had no wish to commit his own exiguous forces any deeper into Turkish territory; he therefore decided to bring pressure on the Turkish Government. Taking Wavell with him, he embarked in the battleship *Temeraire* on 4th February and headed for Constantinople, then under Allied occupation.

"We were only about thirty-six hours in Constantinople. Allenby held a meeting at which the Turkish Ministers of Foreign Affairs and of War represented Turkey; they both looked rather rabbits, but came armed with papers and obviously prepared for discussion. But Allenby simply read out his terms, which included the removal of Ali Ihsan from his command, demanded from the Turks a simple 'yes' or 'no' about their acceptance, and would not allow them to say another word. They accepted meekly, and it was all over in five minutes or little more."

Wavell was concerned not with policy but with administration, whose problems, he wrote, "were diverse and troublesome; they came in in three languages—French and Arabic as well as English. There were four divisions of Occupied Enemy Territory. O.E.T.A. South was Palestine, under an efficient British Administrator, General Money; it gave hardly any trouble. O.E.T.A. East was mostly Syria, Transjordan, etc., under Arab administration, nominally under Feisal, but the administration (such as it wasn't) was run by one Ali Riza Pasha; one used to receive long submissions in Arabic, which were unintelligible before and usually after translation, but nearly always amounted to a request for more money. O.E.T.A. West, the Lebanon and some other parts of Syria, were under French administration. They also always wanted money, and it was just as hard to get from them any information as to how they proposed to spend the money, or had spent it. O.E.T.A. North was Cilicia, also under a French Administrator; he asked for money and submitted no accounts at all. He was a long way off—there was no air travel in those days—and difficult to control . . . I do believe I saved the British taxpayer a million or so by refusing to issue any more money till I got accounts."

At the beginning of March Allenby was in Paris at the Peace Conference, expounding his views on the future of the area over which he ruled. Nationalist riots broke out in Egypt, and he hurried back as High Commissioner as well as Commander-in-Chief. G.H.Q. was re-established in Cairo.

Wavell's family joined him and they shared a house with General Bols. The months passed agreeably. Bols went off to Palestine to be Military Governor, and Wavell became the senior General Staff officer in the whole command, but remained a brigadier-general. The command, however, rapidly lost its strategic importance. Allenby remained as High Commissioner but handed over his military responsibilities to General Sir Walter Congreve, v.c., who assumed the appointment of G.O.C.-in-C. Egypt and Palestine, with Wavell continuing as his B.G.G.S.

These changes had their inevitable effect on Wavell's long-term prospects. Allenby tried to help by urging the Army Council to award him his brevet-colonelcy, but was told coldly that the officer was far too young. Then he attempted to have him appointed to the vacant command of a brigade in Palestine; again the same refusal on the same grounds: too young and much too junior. Early in 1920 came the news from the War Office that Brigadier-General A. P. Wavell, c.m.g., m.c., was to be replaced in his appointment. "The Army," he wrote, "was getting back to normal."

A replacement arrived towards the end of March, an officer some seven or eight years Wavell's senior, but his contemporary at the Staff College. The children were sent back to England and settled in for the summer at Cranborne. Wavell and his wife followed early in April, and he was granted four months' leave—the last long leave he ever had in the Army.

The country was filled with demobilised servicemen spending their gratuities. There was a brief, illusory and inflationary boom. There was open war in Ireland between Sinn Fein and the forces of the British Government. It was a hectic yet sombre time, of painful readjustments and pitiable eagerness to recapture a vanished, pre-war normality. Wavell had come to a turning-point in his life. He had been a brigadier-general for two years; now he had to come down, as a brevet-lieutenant-colonel, to the position of about tenth or twelfth major in his regiment, with no prospect of command of a battalion in it for many years. He had not been at regimental duty for twelve years, but it was to regimental duty that he now returned. With brief intervals—a ski-ing holiday at Gstaad, where he put his knee out badly, and six weeks at a senior officers' course at Woking—he spent almost the whole of 1921 with the regiment in Germany, first in Cologne and later in Silesia. The family were with him for much of the time. His second daughter, Felicity, was born in July. In December he was ordered back to London to take up the appointment of Assistant Adjutant-General at the War Office.

"My appointment meant that I went off the regimental list, was promoted to full colonel, and had to give up any hope of a battalion command. But as things stood I had no prospect of commanding a battalion of The Black Watch for ten or twelve years to come. The prospect of commanding a battalion of another regiment did not particularly attract me. . . . So I might as well take a first-grade staff appointment; it certainly meant better pay, and a settled life for some years. I would rather have gone to G. or Q. than A., but I had a half-promise that I might be transferred to G. later; and A.G.1 was at least the most interesting branch of A."

The door to promotion opened; the door shut on the brotherhood of his youth. He had been an officer of The Black Watch for just over twenty years, and twelve of those he had spent on the staff. "Not a very good regimental record," he wrote, "but I think I can safely say that my heart has always been with the Regiment, and that I have ever since done all that I could to further its interests."

For the next eight years, with an interval on half-pay, Wavell was a staff officer. They were not good years for the Army. The First World War had left its scars but had not taught its lessons. All the Services suffered from retrenchment and economy—in themselves habitual after a long and exhausting war—but they were enforced in an atmosphere that was profoundly hostile to the very existence and purpose of soldiering. A naïve pacifism was preached in schools, universities, cathedral pulpits and the Press; and it was taken for granted by all intellectuals that Regular officers were as bloodthirsty as they were cretinous. A long industrial decline set in, agriculture decayed and society was stagnant. These were the locust years for which a heavy price had later to be paid.

The Wavells established the first home of their own in England. They leased an oddly-shaped house in Hobart Place, near Victoria, which had no back door, a kitchen on the first floor and a twenty-yard-long passage leading from the front door to the stairs; but they found it attractive and the family were very happy in it. Archie John went to his first school and Joan, their fourth and youngest child, was born on St. George's Day, 1923.

The first eighteen months of his time at the War Office Wavell spent in a branch of the Adjutant-General's department which dealt with manpower: the Army's establishments, at home and overseas, terms of service, arrangements of drafts to India and the colonies, statistics, and the Army estimates. He did not find it particularly interesting, since it dealt with men as mere units, and not as human beings.

In July, 1923, he was appointed G.S.O.1 in M.O.1, the main strategic branch of the Operations Directorate in the War Office, dealing with plans for war, home defence, the strategic distribution of the Army and similar matters of fundamental importance. It was a far more interesting branch to a soldier of Wavell's outlook than the Adjutant-General's, but he served in it during what he himself called "a depressing period." Strategic planning was governed by the Cabinet dictum that there need be no preparation for a major war during the succeeding ten years. The economy screws were tightened on the Army, whose main tasks were defined as support of the civil power and imperial policing all over the world. To fulfil them there were 50 battalions, 25 cavalry regiments and 50 batteries of artillery, fewer than there had been in 1914.

In the backstage scramble for such allocations of money as there were, under the stern scrutiny of a Treasury whose presiding Minister was Winston Churchill, inter-Service rivalries and jealousies festered fiercely. No one was specifically responsible for over-all imperial defence. Much therefore depended on the outlook and the personalities of the individual Service Ministers and their Chiefs of Staff—especially the latter. The C.I.G.S., during most of Wavell's time at the War Office, was Field-Marshal the Earl of Cavan, a charming and amiable man, but no match in argument for Lord Beatty at the Admiralty or Lord Trenchard at the Air Ministry. In the constant triangular dog-fights the Army was almost doomed to come off worst.

There were bitter controversies over one major issue after another. With considerable cogency Trenchard argued that the R.A.F. could take over the military control and defence of Iraq and Palestine, of the N.W. Frontier of India, and of the great naval base of Singapore. In Wavell's words, "the R.A.F. claimed to be able to do everything cheaper and more efficiently than the Army. The former quality appealed to the politician, so Iraq and Palestine were handed over to them." Over the N.W. Frontier Trenchard encountered the formidable opposition of the Government of India and of the Indian Army; and though the R.A.F. operated there with notable success, political control remained with the Viceroy, and military control with the C.-in-C. in India.

The inadequacies at the top were not reflected all the way down. The head of Wavell's own directorate was his friend, Jock Burnett-Stuart, under whom he had served in the war and under whom he was to serve again. "Jock was as brilliant as ever, and as caustic, very easy to serve, difficult for his superiors to control. He had little opinion of Cavan's knowledge or intellect, and was at odds with a good deal of H.M.G.'s policy; and as usual he never concealed his views."

From 1924 onwards, with Ramsay MacDonald's first Government and then with Stanley Baldwin's powerful Conservative Administration, the Service chiefs and their subordinates and advisers were involved in a dispute which, however academic it seemed at the time, was to be, less than twenty years later, of crucial importance—to no one more than to Wavell.

In January, 1924, Admiral of the Fleet Earl Beatty wrote to his wife: "Singapore—that infernal place's name will be engraved on my heart. The struggles I have had over it are to be repeated more bitterly than ever and with doubtful results."[2] Nevertheless, after many months of argument, it was on this occasion the Navy's view which, with the Army's support, prevailed over that of the R.A.F., as expounded by Trenchard. The consequences, eighteen years later, of Beatty's departmental victory were momentous and tragic. All the Services suffered with equal severity; but it would be as imprudent as easy to allocate blame. Wavell wrote in 1946:

"The defence of Singapore was a subject on which we spent a good deal of time. I was a member of a committee under Maurice Hankey which dealt with it. There was a hot controversy between the

R.A.F., who claimed to be able to defend Singapore with torpedo-bombers alone, and the Navy and Army, who challenged them to prove their case. The R.A.F. were always very evasive when the calculation of the cost of R.A.F. squadrons as against fixed defences was under consideration; the Navy and Army charged them with trying to make the same squadrons do several roles and defend several places at the same time and thus appear to be much cheaper; they always tried to ride off on the claim of their mobility, while we argued that no amount of mobility could make squadrons available at two or more different places at the same time. In the end, big guns were installed at great cost, and never fired an effective round in the defence of Singapore; while the Air Force which might have saved Singapore by attack on the Japanese transports was not there at the right time, because it had to be elsewhere. So I suppose both sides had some justification for their views. The matter of the defence of the island against attack from the north never arose so far as I remember; the task of the committee was only to plan against seaward attack."

Wavell did a certain amount of work outside the office: he set and corrected Army examination papers, and gave lectures. He began to see his writings in print: articles in *The Army Quarterly*; lectures at the Royal United Service Institution, reproduced in the Journal; and book reviews in *The Times* and *The Times Literary Supplement*. He thought *The Times*'s methods of issuing books for review and of payment were singularly unbusinesslike; but he himself was so innocent that he did not realise that the books were the reviewer's perquisite, and sent his back with the reviews.

His time at the War Office came to an end in December 1925, but he stayed on another month until his successor arrived; he was Colonel William Dobbie, who was to be Governor of Malta at the time when Wavell himself was C.-in-C. in the Middle East. The list of colonels was long; appointments were few and aspirants many. Wavell faced the bleak prospect of going on half-pay, and remaining on half-pay for a long time. There was one post which he would have liked and would have filled excellently—G.S.O.1 at the Staff College—but this went to someone else. Patience and a certain tightening of the belt were necessary. The lease of Hobart Place was sold, and the family withdrew to Cranborne.

There was a marked meanness about the half-pay system (it was abolished just before World War II), for it meant that an officer's income was reduced, not by a half, but by nearly two-thirds. Wavell, in the nine months between January and October, 1926, was being paid less than the pension he would have earned had he retired. It was this facet of the system which he disliked; but pondering its full implications in his quiet, judicial way he concluded: "Six months' or a year's rest or change of employment would be no bad thing in the career of most officers. The ordinary peacetime routine is killing. I should like to see promising officers given a year or so of some civil employment, or travel, at some period in their career."

He himself made good use of his enforced sabbatical to concentrate on writing. Two major projects occupied much of his time. A new edition of the *Encyclopædia Britannica* was in preparation, and Captain B. H. Liddell Hart was its military editor. Wavell, before he left the War Office, had already accepted an invitation to write the article on the operations in Palestine in World War I.

Captain B. H. Liddell Hart to A. P. Wavell   *14th January, 1926*
Just a formal note to say I have read your article on the Egyptian and Palestine campaigns. I simply cannot refrain from a note of congratulation—it combines literary style with clearness and simplicity, perfectly easy to follow and yet of value to military as well as general readers. In fact it is, ideally, what I should like such articles in the E.B. to be—and if only a few more were like it I should feel happier over the general result of the military section. Apart from diffuseness and denseness too many military writers have a tendency to gloss over failures known to all, instead of remembering that for the E.B. they should play the role of the historian not of the apologist. In this respect you hold the balance admirably. . . .

Thereafter for the next two years Wavell wrote frequently for the encyclopædia,[3] earning in all about £100 from the work, and repeated, sincere praise from Liddell Hart. They corresponded copiously until the outbreak of World War II; they argued frequently; and each had a genuine respect for the other's intelligence and powers of lucid exposition.

Wavell's second project was a contribution to a series of full-length studies, called *Campaigns and their Lessons*, which Major-General Sir Charles Callwell was editing for Constable. Callwell asked him to give an account of the Palestine campaigns. Though this book was an undoubted success, laid the foundations of Wavell's reputation as an author, ran into several editions, and was used as a text-book at Sandhurst and elsewhere, he made less than £50 out of it.

In November, 1926, Wavell became G.S.O.1 of the 3rd Division on Salisbury Plain. This was a key appointment in a key formation, of which the commander was Jock Burnett-Stuart. "I could not," he wrote, "have had a chief more to my liking."

The division was dispersed over a large part of south-west England. Headquarters, with its guns and its sappers, was at Bulford on the Plain; the 7th Brigade was at Tidworth, the 8th at Plymouth and the 9th at Portsmouth. Headquarters was a collection of battered wooden huts, and there was not a single modern barrack building within the perimeter. Wavell and his opposite number on the A. & Q. side worked together in one room, with their respective subordinates together in the room next door. The C.R.A. and the C.R.E. were within easy reach. The General's A.D.C. was "a large, untidy but attractive young man," a Wykehamist from the Rifle Brigade named Frank Festing.[4]

Just after Christmas the family moved into Brigmerston Farm House, in the Avon Valley, which was to be their home for three and a half years and, in their wandering lives, one of the happiest. Wavell's recollections of his home in these years were vivid and detailed, but of his work they were vague.

There were reasons for this difference of approach. Jock Burnett-Stuart believed that Wavell, whose great reserves of endurance, energy and concentrated application he fully acknowledged, was resting himself for the future: "aware that he would probably do something big some time, he was storing his powers against that day." The result was that he gave a superficial impression of laziness, of which he himself was perfectly conscious.

"Jack Collins, I know, thinks I was an idle G.S.O.1, and Jock Stuart sometimes used to say that it was always a competition between us who should do the work of setting schemes or exercises and that I always managed to make him do them. But I think I did my job efficiently and really did quite a lot of work."

Burnett-Stuart told Wavell's son:

Our four years on the Plain were your father's happiest, but what difficulty I had to get him to do his work. He wouldn't work if he could get someone else to do it for him—particularly me. Idle is not exactly the word for him—because he was always absorbing something—but he would always put off setting exercises for the divisional manœuvres. The first year he got me so alarmed that they wouldn't be done that I wrote them myself—but he didn't succeed next year.

Far the most significant part of Wavell's work at 3rd Division headquarters was his close association with the birth and early trials of the first mechanised formation in the world, the Experimental Armoured Force of 1927-8, which was the mother of all armoured divisions. In February, 1926, General Milne had succeeded Lord Cavan as C.I.G.S. and at once interested himself in experiments to restore mobility to land warfare. His Military Assistant was Colonel J. F. C. Fuller, a bold and far-sighted theorist on this theme, who sought nothing more than a chance to put his theories into practice. Fuller, without doubt, ought to have commanded the Experimental Armoured Force whose formation Milne authorised. When it was decided that the force should be assembled on Salisbury Plain, and therefore under the command of 3rd Division, Burnett-Stuart wrote to the C.I.G.S. (in August, 1926, before Wavell joined him):

. . . And lastly, what help are you going to give me in organising, launching and guiding this experiment? It is no use just handing it over to an ordinary Divisional Commander like myself. You must connect directly with it as many enthusiastic experts and visionaries as you can; it doesn't matter how wild their views are if only they have a touch of the divine fire. I will supply the common sense of advanced middle age.[5]

Fuller, who in character and outlook would have completely satisfied Burnett-Stuart's requirements, was selected to command the experimental force. Most unfortunately, however, he and Burnett-Stuart differed sharply about the additional responsibilities he would have to carry as a brigade commander in an infantry division. Burnett-Stuart would not compromise, and Fuller then refused the post. "A pity," Wavell commented, "since he would at least have had some stimulating original methods and ideas. The command should really have gone to a cavalry man, but I think that the standard of cavalry brigadiers or colonels was low about this time. I certainly cannot remember a good one. And I don't think that there was a cavalry man in any senior job at the War Office."

On the eve of the training season Colonel R. J. Collins, who was then commanding the 9th Brigade at Portsmouth, was appointed instead of Fuller "to command the Experimental Mechanised Force and the 7th Infantry Brigade." Collins conceived a great liking and a great admiration for Wavell, so great indeed that he undertook the task of writing (while Wavell was still alive) a military biography of him. Wavell reciprocated the liking, but tempered it with an awareness of Collins's limitations as a general. Collins had great energy and enthusiasm, but tactically he was slow and cautious. Wavell said: "Jack worked like a beaver, produced masses of paper and statistics, worked out the amount of petrol required for the force per mile to several places of decimals, and the amount of parking-space to the yard, but never did he handle the Armoured Force with the least conception of the value of speed and mobility and dash."

Collins had some able subordinates, including two who later rose to be general officers,[6] but his force was a scratch collection of primitive and not markedly reliable vehicles, comprising all the units of the different arms that had so far been mechanised and were available for inclusion. The wide variety of vehicles, the wide range of difference in their speed, and the fact that some went quickly on the road and were slow (or useless) in rough country, while others crawled on the road but could move across country, made the task of planning the exercises and the testing of the force extremely difficult. While Collins wrestled with the resulting administrative problems, Burnett-Stuart and Wavell strove to create some idea of the tactical handling of future mobile warfare. Their minds were travelling down unorthodox roads to which Collins had no map. On Burnett-Stuart's orders Wavell devised a tactical exercise without troops (T.E.W.T.) for the Armoured Force.

"I set an exercise on the line of the Avon between Ringwood and Christchurch, the main motive of which was a break-through on a narrow front and the passage of the Armoured Force through this gap to destroy the enemy's rear installations and create confusion and havoc. In view of what happened in France some twelve years later, I think the exercise showed some imagination and foresight, though even Jock considered it a bit over bold. Jack Collins decided that it was harebrained and refused to play at all. . . ."

On 27th November, 1928, the Secretary of State for War announced in the House of Commons that the Armoured Force was to be dispersed, in order that the War Office "might extend the experiment" in a different fashion. In the following January, the lessons of the two-year experience were discussed at the annual Staff Conference at Camberley—"though without the opinion of any Royal Tank Corps officer being directly involved."[7]

Collins opened the discussion with a series of observations which tended to emphasise the drawbacks rather than the potentialities of an armoured force. Wavell followed him, speaking from the viewpoint of the G.S.O.1 of the infantry division which had been pitted against the armoured force. He first stressed the moral effect of such a formation, and the difficulties which a conventional formation was bound to suffer in trying to protect both its troops and all its administrative organisation against such a mobile menace. That moral effect was deepened, he thought, because the infantry could not hit back—since the armoured force could avoid engagement except where it chose. It should aim, therefore, at exploiting its mobility to the full. He pointed out the necessity of incorporating in an armoured formation a small body of men able to fight on foot, in order to enable it to secure a river-crossing or a passage through a defile.

Wavell used the tank generals' analogy of sea warfare, which was to have so strong a bearing on the conduct of the armoured battles in the Western Desert, spoke of the need for a high proportion of light tanks accompanying the medium tanks, and argued that they would be "as necessary as destroyers were at sea for the protection of the battle fleet."

Two sentences impressed themselves deeply on all who heard him: "The requirements of mobility, fire-power and armour must always be to a certain extent conflicting. I suggest, very tentatively, that the respective value of these three might be assessed in the ratio of 3 : 2 : 1."

He ended by urging that the wider the front on which armoured forces could move, the more formidable they would be; hence the importance of developing wireless communications to maintain control over distances hitherto unthinkable.

Two conclusions emerge from a study of this thoughtful speech. First, the whole essence of the tactical problem of the short but momentous phase of land warfare which saw the dominance of the armoured fighting vehicle lay in the efforts to achieve a satisfactory ratio between mobility, fire-power and armour. Second, General Collins was saying no more than the truth when he wrote: "It would be safe to wager that none of the distinguished officers present in the

Rawlinson Hall then pictured on just how wide fronts Wavell's armoured divisions would be called upon to operate little more than a decade ahead."[8]

Wavell said: "The Armoured Force had made people think and it was certainly valuable experience to have been so closely connected with it; but to my mind the tactical handling of the Force had been lamentable."

In the summer of 1929 Archie John, like his father thirty-three years before, went up from Summer Fields to sit for a Winchester scholarship. He did not win one, but he got a Headmaster's Nomination, and went there in the autumn.

"I took him to Winchester for the examination. He was not very bookish in those days, and in fact hardly ever read. When we were waiting outside the Headmaster's house for the oral interview, we heard schoolmasters anxiously coaching their pupils on the books they were to say they had read, giving them a rough sketch of the plot, principal characters, etc. Archie John asked me what he was to say if asked about his reading. I told him to tell the truth and not pretend that he had read books which he had not. When he came out, he said that the Headmaster had asked him what he had read; he had replied that he didn't read much. 'But you must read something,' the Headmaster pressed him. 'Well, the cricket scores in the paper,' conceded Archie John. 'Nothing else at all?' inquired the Headmaster. 'An occasional Edgar Wallace,' admitted Archie John. He said that the Headmaster had laughed and remarked that it was probably the first really honest answer he had had that morning."

Early in 1930 Wavell was told that he had been nominated to command a brigade; at the end of June he left Salisbury Plain for Blackdown, near Aldershot, to take over the 6th Infantry Brigade in the 2nd Division. Except during the ten months he had spent with his old battalion in Germany after the war, he had been a staff officer for twenty years.

"At Aldershot I should have very critical eyes on me, and I knew that the ability to command of one who had been on the staff for so long would be under close test. However, Jock had seemed quite satisfied that I should make good; and a brigade at Aldershot was certainly an opportunity. It was by the way just ten years since I had previously held brigadier's rank!

"I don't think, looking back, that the responsibilities of command

improved my character. Responsibility has never sat lightly on me
and has turned me in on myself too much. And I doubt whether the
exercise of power is really good for anyone. It is certain anyway that
I have never been so carefree or able to enjoy life as much since leaving
Brigmerston."

In June, 1930, Wavell, at forty-seven, was quite unknown to the
public at large; but he had a high reputation in his own profession.
Of the three great soldiers in an earlier generation who had encouraged and influenced him, one—Henry Wilson—had been murdered nine years earlier, on his own doorstep, by an Irish nationalist
fanatic; the other two—Allenby and Robertson—were retired.
Allenby's influence had been the deepest and the most enduring. Lately
he had had three years in close and continuous contact with Jock
Burnett-Stuart's vigorous, critical intelligence. He had also made the
acquaintance and earned the respect of a number of "unorthodox"
military thinkers such as T. E. Lawrence, J. F. C. Fuller and B. H.
Liddell Hart. His own thoughts were beginning to take shape as
fundamental principles and a guide to practice rather than as a body of
doctrine. He was an educated soldier; he was not an academic theorist,
though he was by no means contemptuous of the theorist.

In the 1930s the German Army found its own solution to the great
problem of restoring mobility to land fighting—and the sweeping
victories of 1940-1 were the result. The French Army did not, took
refuge in the defensiveness of the Maginot Line, and paid a terrible
penalty. The British Army found its solution; the foundations of the
desert victories of the British and Commonwealth Armies in 1940-2
(and the explanations of some of the desert reverses) lay in the preparation and training of ten years earlier, and the processes of trial
and error to which it subjected its experiments. The fact that this
solution was achieved within a framework of apparently unbroken
conformity with tradition should not be allowed to mask its revolutionary character. Wavell took a leading part in the tactical and
strategic exploitation of the effects of mechanisation, but the technical
details did not interest him greatly. Details, however essential, were
apt to bore him. His great forte was training. What he wanted to
train—what he was given to train—was infantry. The final paragraph
of the book he had written while on half-pay was significant:

The student of these [Palestine] campaigns who bears away

with him the two lessons that mobility, which gives the power of surprise, should be the chief aim of the organisation of our army, and that training, which gives the ability to manœuvre, will restore to infantry the offensive power on the battlefield which many in France believed it to have lost, will not have read them in vain.[9]

From the moment Wavell assumed command of the 6th Infantry Brigade his main professional aim was to put these two lessons, which staff experience and study had taught him, into practice as a commander. The infantry brigade of those days was a compact formation, not unwieldy to handle, and responsive to the personal leadership of its commander. It was the ideal size for the experiments, the pilot projects, in training and in the recovery of mobility, which Wavell was determined to carry out. He was given a relatively free hand by his divisional and higher commanders, within the very stringent financial limits which the War Office had imposed. He wrote:

"I started without much confidence in my capacity for command, and was not sure that I should make a success of it. I soon found to my relief that I could make up my mind and act quickly in handling my brigade, and could give orders without hesitation, not only in the field but in the various administrative problems; and that the other problems of a commander—administering justice, the confirmation and review of courts-martial, sizing up subordinates and writing confidential reports, etc.—did not worry me unduly."

He now had the opportunity to put some at least of his most important ideas into practice. At this stage in his career he took the staunchness of the trained soldier's courage for granted; but he knew from his own experience that it was a wasting asset. How was it to be best employed? He had seen it extravagantly expended in the carnage of France fifteen years earlier; he was determined that in any formation for which he held responsibility it would henceforth be used economically and prudently. The soldier's mind he did not take for granted. Soldiering, he decided, called for a better, more varied and more lively exercise of the mind than he found prevalent in the British Army midway between the wars. First he pondered the outlook and education of officers. During his four years as a brigadier he made a habit of delivering lectures to officers in the Aldershot Command who were candidates for the Staff College His theme was the study of military history, whose value, if properly undertaken, he did not

Subaltern in India

Wavell before a reconnaissance flight with a Russian
pilot. The Upper Euphrates 1917

question; but examinations in it he detested, and the crammers' methods of preparing officers for promotion examinations he despised.

How, not why, to study military history was what he tried to instil into his hearers. But in his brief exposition of why there was an elegant cogency: "Though the military art is essentially a practical one, the opportunities of practising it are rare. Even the largest scale peace manœuvres are only a feeble shadow of the real thing. So that a soldier desirous of acquiring skill in handling troops is forced to theoretical study of Great Captains—no bad substitute if it is properly done, which it very seldom is. . . ."

His definition of how was no less forceful:

The real way to get value out of the study of military history is to take particular situations, and as far as possible get inside the skin of the man who made a decision, realise the conditions in which the decision was made and then see in what way you could have improved on it.

I would give you a word of warning on the so-called principles of war, as laid down in Field Service Regulations.

For heaven's sake don't treat those as holy writ, like the Ten Commandments, to be learned by heart, and as having by their repetition some magic, like the incantations of savage priests. They are merely a set of common-sense maxims, like "cut your coat according to your cloth," "a rolling stone gathers no moss," "honesty is the best policy," and so forth. Those in F.S.R. are not necessarily complete or the best. They omit for instance the importance of information in war. Clausewitz has a different set, so has Foch, so have other military writers. They are all simply common sense, and are instinctive to the properly trained soldier. Some people tell you that the secret of golf lies in the twist of the hips, or the stiffening of the left leg, or the pronation of the wrists, whatever that may be. The professional dismisses all such things from his mind and hits the ball straight down the middle of the fairway.

Lastly, I do advise you to study the human side of military history, which is not a matter of cold-blooded formulas or diagrams, or nursery-book principles, such as:

Be good and you will be happy.

Be mobile and you will be victorious.

Interior lines at night are the general's delight.

Exterior lines in the morning are the general's warning, and so on.

To learn that Napoleon in 1796 with 20,000 men beat combined forces of 30,000 by something called "economy of force" or "operating on interior lines" is a mere waste of time. If you can understand how a young, unknown man inspired a half-starved, ragged, rather Bolshie crowd; how he filled their bellies; how he out-marched, outwitted, out-bluffed and defeated men who had studied war all their lives and waged it according to the textbooks of the time, you will have learnt something worth knowing. But you won't get it from crammers' books.[10]

In December, 1932, rather more than half-way through his time with 6th Brigade, Wavell spoke to students at the Staff College on the training for war of an infantry brigade. In an altered and shortened form he gave this lecture again at the Royal United Service Institution on 15th February, 1933, under the title "The Training of the Army for War," and in this form it was published in the R.U.S.I. Journal.[11] It received widespread and serious notice, contributed greatly to his developing reputation, and has rightly been regarded as a milestone in the evolution of military thinking between the wars. The draft of the Camberley version, which was preserved in his papers, began:

Your Commandant has asked me to lecture on the training for war of an infantry brigade. I will begin by emphasising the words "for war," not "for a war." We often hear that we are at a disadvantage in our training compared with other nations because we have no definite war problem. I disagree. Problems of organisation and equipment are undoubtedly complicated by our having no definite problem, or rather so many indefinite problems. But in training I hold that it is a positive advantage to have to train simply "for war" and that training for "a war" is a positive danger. Because the war you train for never happens; it certainly did not either for the French or ourselves in 1914. And I believe that most of our training since the war has been dulled and stultified by training for a war—the last war. So I will begin by trying to define for you the essentials of training "for war." What are the qualities of the good soldier, by the development of which we make the man war-worthy—fit for any war? I think most of you will agree that the following four—in whatever order you place them—pretty well cover the field: discipline, physical fitness, technical skill in the use of his weapons, battlecraft. But many will differ on the degree of importance of these qualities. One well-known Brigadier always phrases his requirements of the ideal infantryman as "athlete, stalker, marksman." I always feel a little inclined to put it on a lower plane and to say that the qualities of a successful poacher, cat burglar and gunman would content me. His definition sets discipline and the moral qualities higher; mine is meant to call attention to the value of low cunning in war. Let us leave it at that for the moment. Battle-craft (i.e. common sense or low cunning) is certainly the infantry-man's weak point at the present.

Now for the officer. He must have the knowledge and qualities of a leader, of course, which are defined for you in the text-books and which we all, I think, know well and recognise. But the trouble to my mind is that it is too military and on too narrow and rigid lines. A chief aim should be to improve his general education and his knowledge of civil conditions, and to avoid suppressing the invaluable qualities of originality and imagination. The new system at the Royal Military College and the Royal Military Academy will help, if the child is not "over-laid" in its early military life.

What this little preamble really amounts to is that I am a determined advocate of getting away from "barrack square" training and the barrack square mind as far as possible.

This version of his lecture was filled with what were then new and unpopular ideas ("These adjectives," he remarked in a grim paren-thesis, "are often synonymous"), some of which three decades later the Army has assimilated: the extra-curricular education of officers and N.C.O.s; initiative tests; the problems of umpiring exercises, which are numerous, complex and insoluble; the reorganisation of the training year—then divided into individual and collective training —into three phases, which he called preparation, education and examination; the free and frequent use of T.E.W.T.s; the setting of lively and practicable exercises at all levels; battlefield tours, with a concentration on military realities and not on crammers' clichés. One idea, which he frankly admitted to be Utopian in 1932, was that regimental officers, of the rank of captain and above, who in war would rise to command or senior staff appointments, should be fitted for these employments in peacetime by exchanging jobs for six months with keen Territorial officers, of equivalent age and status, in business firms. This was so breathtaking in its originality that Wavell's critics passed it over in silence, and fastened fiercely on his much more modest proposal that brigades or divisions should hold, for young subalterns, beginners' courses in elementary tactics and administration, to interest them in their profession and set their feet on the right path. He said:

> I know this is an unorthodox view. At a recent conference, where I broached it, the D.M.I. and all my fellow-brigadiers at the Aldershot Command told me I was talking heresy; I consulted my C.O.s for comfort, and they all told me, more politely, that I was wrong. *And I know I am right.*

He reverted to two themes which, in thought, speech and action, in peace and war, had now become, and were to remain, the bases of his professional philosophy:

> May I leave you two last words of advice. The first is that when things go wrong and get into an apparently hopeless muddle on exercises and manœuvres, as they will, it is comforting to remember that war is always a far worse muddle than anything you can produce in peace, and that sorting out muddles is really the chief job of a commander and his staff; and that if you keep your head, and temper, the worst looking muddle has a marvellous way of sorting itself out. But find out afterwards how that particular muddle occurred, and if possible don't let it occur again.
>
> But as a final word, I suggest you put this ideal of the infantry-man before you:
>
> Quick-footed, quick-minded and, as far as possible, light-hearted.

The 6th Brigade's exercises during the training seasons of 1931 and 1932 gave Wavell his first opportunity of working out in practice as a commander the ideas he had evolved as a staff officer and as an increasingly diligent and critical student of his own profession. For much of this time he had the able and enthusiastic assistance of his brigade-major, an officer from the Northumberland Fusiliers named Eric Dorman-Smith,[12] who as a 19-year-old subaltern in the 9th Brigade on the Western Front in 1915 had won an M.C. in the battle in which Wavell had himself been wounded; he was subsequently awarded no fewer than three brevets. One of the most brilliant surviving officers of his generation, he brimmed over with ideas of sharply varying quality. Wavell wrote: "In the two years he was with me he was invaluable, and the right man for an experimental brigade. I could control his ideas and sort out the good from the bad and keep him on practical lines." They inspired each other; together they inspired the brigade; and they set a tactical and logistical revolution in motion.

The exercises which Wavell devised, and Dorman-Smith played his own part in carrying out, were increasingly imaginative, and attracted more and more attention throughout the Army. One primary purpose behind them all was to simulate the conditions of real war in one form or another. They compelled officers, N.C.O.s and men to think and act quickly in a succession of unexpected and surprising circumstances, in conditions of fatigue, bewilderment and incomplete knowledge, and to respond to the experience with zest and quickened intelligence instead of being bored and battered by it. They were presented to all who participated with as much originality as possible—like the programme in an old-fashioned melodrama, for example, or the script for some screen "epic." They were apt to include startling turns of fortune, shifts of loyalty and unexpected interventions. A battalion headquarters would be declared suddenly to have been shelled, and junior officers and W.O.s would have to take over. A river crossing would have to be defended, a night march hastily organised, pitched battles fought between forces of widely differing strengths; and over all these activities Wavell insisted on imposing the confusion and fog which he knew to be inseparable from war.

In setting this series of problems he had one object firmly in view: "If the exercise is subsequently discussed in the officers' mess, it was probably worth while; if there is argument over it in the sergeants' mess, it was a good exercise; while if it should be mentioned in the corporals' room, it was an undoubted success."[13]

Judged by this standard, one exercise deserved more than passing mention. Wavell sent out fifty gunners in civilian clothes and with false identities to act as guerrillas over a tract of difficult and not very familiar country. Prices were set on their heads; the brigade's task was to round them up and to discover their hidden arms dumps. Wavell kept his notes for the conference which ended this exercise;

165

written ten years or so before the beginning of colonial liquidation they were singularly prescient.

This is a common task for soldiers, yet there is little about it in any text-book, and in fact you have to unlearn a good deal of the soldiering you have learnt. It is a poor job for the soldier, dangerous yet dull, very hard work and very thankless. Last night and its results are a typical sort of operation, four battalions and oddments turned out to hunt 40 or 50 scallywags, having a hard day and night, losing perhaps a dozen comrades sniped from ambush, and all there is to show for it is ten or twenty ragged toughs, of whom half will probably be released by the civil authorities in a week or so, and you will perhaps be lucky if you do not have to apologise to some of them.

But we've got to learn to do it, or at least think about it. The advantages are nearly all on the side of the guerrilla in that he is bound by no rules, tied by no transport, hampered by no drill-books, while the soldier is bound by many things, not the least by his expectation of a full meal every so many hours. The soldier usually wins in the long run, but very expensively.

"The captives of our bow and spear are cheap, alas, and we are dear."

In Palestine, in Malaya, Kenya, Cyprus and elsewhere, the sombre truth of those words, spoken at Blackdown on 30th August, 1932, was to be proved again and again.

Technically as well as tactically, 6th Brigade played an important experimental role. It tackled an array of problems which were then new and challenging: the mechanisation of transport, the introduction of mortars into infantry battalions, the close support of infantry by artillery, anti-tank defence, and the carriage of machine guns in armoured carriers. Time and again Wavell's practice disproved the rigid theories of orthodox soldiers; few of his ideas were more bitterly contested than the modernised and forward role which he proposed for the machine gun; yet none, contemplated with the hindsight of history, was more obviously and lastingly valuable.

The machine gun at this time had established a formidable dominance over military thought. It was no longer simply the fact that
. . . we have got
The Maxim gun and they have not,

166

but that, acquired by all "civilised" nations, it had caused the strategic and tactical *impasse*, and the consequent holocaust of Europe's young men, on the Western Front from 1914 to 1918. Until it could be shown to be outmanœuvred and outfought it was supreme. It was easier in peacetime to suggest theoretical ways of "improving" the machine gun, and thus retain the static, defensive brutality of World War I, than to search for methods of restoring mobility to land warfare. It was also a good deal cheaper, in a period of industrial recession and deflation. The Finance Department's natural passion for economy complemented military orthodoxy.

The Machine Gun Corps in World World I was a distinct arm of the service, equal in importance to the artillery or cavalry. Its standard weapon was the heavy Vickers machine gun. The infantry were left with the Lewis gun, inefficient, subject to frequent stoppages and already obsolescent. The Machine Gun Manual laid it down that the heavy machine gun needed a crew of six, and must be mounted and fired from the ground. Wavell—his brigade-major had himself taken a full course at the Machine Gun School—strove to demonstrate that a machine gun was an infantry weapon, and could be fired from a vehicle, by a crew of two, in a much shorter time than, in accordance with the Manual, it took to get the heavy Vickers off its vehicle, mounted on the ground and into action.

Wavell was lucky to have at his disposal a suitable vehicle—the Carden-Loyd Mark VI carrier, the forerunner of the Bren carrier of World War II.[14] General Collins wrote: "Under Wavell's guidance his staff produced a carrier drill for the handling of these new vehicles which formed the basis of the one which the carrier platoons fought in Belgium and France in 1940."[15]

In 1932, however, Collins was Commandant of the Machine Gun School at Netheravon and (in Wavell's view) "as sticky and orthodox as ever." When 6th Brigade gave a demonstration of its commander's ideas at the school, in the presence of the C.I.G.S., Milne, Collins attacked them vehemently, "because they were new and not provided for in the M.G. Manual." Collins called Wavell "an unsound iconoclast."

"But," wrote Wavell, "I remained quite clear on the value of my proposals, even if they were unorthodox; and I claimed that I could get a machine gun into a place where it would do most harm to the enemy in about ten minutes or less, whereas M.G. School methods would take an hour to produce much less effective fire. I admitted taking risks, but said that that was the only way to get results in battle. Jack was genuinely shocked."

Divisional exercises were the climax of the training season in 1932. Wavell had long since realised that the capacity to understand the workings of the other man's mind is an essential element in general-ship; and the flaw in peacetime manœuvres, for a man of his per-ceptiveness, was that he knew his brother-officers too well. In three exercises that autumn he defeated his opponents with an apparently effortless ease. All three were left to meditate ruefully on von Moltke's aphorism, "You will usually find that the enemy has three courses open to him, and of these he will adopt the fourth." Wavell wrote:

"My successes in these exercises had been gained mainly by quite a simple formula. My opponents, and indeed every other commander, kept a large proportion of their available force as a reserve, in attack or defence. I normally deployed the whole of my force in attack, on a wide front. My argument was that a battalion a mile or two away to the flank was just as handy as a reserve as if it was a mile or two behind, and usually much better placed to come in on the enemy's flank. And the enemy was kept guessing where I should concentrate and was likely to become dispersed. It was, I admit, a peace strategem to some extent as I had accurate knowledge of my opponent's strength and a pretty shrewd estimate of his likely reactions. I think I had another advantage, in my methods of controlling a battle. Most commanders remained at their headquarters nearly all the time and attempted con-trol by telephone or despatch-rider. I was on the move most of the time, in a cross-country vehicle, visiting my commanders in turn and learning the situation at first hand. I had also a team of specially trained liaison officers (or rather liaison N.C.O.s). No brigadier, or other commander, so far as I know, had previously used such a team. Liaison officers, if used at all, were detailed for a particular exercise, or possibly for the whole of the brigade training, and were therefore of very limited value. I was determined to have a trained team, and asked my battalion commanders at the beginning of the training season to give me each one officer. When they protested that they could not spare an officer, I took senior N.C.O.s instead, put them on motor cycles and gave them a thorough training in carrying my instructions and intentions, usually verbally, to my C.O.s and reporting back the situation. By the brigade training period they were invaluable, and I believe my C.O.s and myself were thus much better in the picture than in any other brigade.

"I believe a third advantage I gained was by paying more attention to Intelligence arrangements than other commanders, both in the matter of obtaining information and in getting across false information to the enemy.

". . . But I believe it was this season probably that determined my future career, in that I was always afterwards chosen for command and never again for the staff. [The exercises and training] gave me some confidence too as a commander, which I had previously lacked."

These were the years of the Aldershot Tattoo at the height of its fame. Most commanders used to resent what they regarded as its interference with routine training. Wavell, however, saw its value in making commanders and men "use their wits and do something out of the usual run. It was remarkable how dormant imagination, dulled by routine training, would suddenly blossom out."

In one Tattoo staged while he was at Blackdown he was in charge of an item called "A Modern Battle." This opened with a hard-pressed rearguard being driven back over a bridge. At the early rehearsals the subaltern in charge of it executed one variant after another of sealed pattern barrack-square retirement. Wavell tried to make him understand what was supposed to be happening, but to no avail—the section lay down, got up in perfect dressing, walked back a set number of paces and lay down again. Wavell explained once more, and next time the subaltern slightly varied the distances and the intervals. "I was in despair at this woodenness and adjured him to forget all his drill and simply try to imagine that he was in command of a lot of tired, frightened men whom he was trying to keep from running away altogether. Suddenly he tumbled to it, and eventually put up a most realistic 'panic party'; the final retreat of himself and his sergeant over the bridge brought down the house."

Within a decade many a subaltern in a similar plight, but with a real enemy with live ammunition in his pouches, was to re-enact the little drama which Wavell's persistence and persuasiveness had at last brought this youth to comprehend. The impact of his personality on officers and men who served under him at this time was as important as the impact of his ideas on his superiors. His brigade major wrote thirty years later: "He carried confidence about with him. . . . When he was in control of events from the start, he seemed to suggest that everything was going well, however sticky it looked to the victim."[16]

Just after his fiftieth birthday Wavell was promoted to major-general. He could only hold his present appointment until the New Year of 1934; he would then have to go on half-pay unless and until he was given a major-general's appointment. His promotion brought to an end a strenuous and fruitful period in his life.

"I had certainly worked harder than on the Plain, had much less leisure and a great deal more responsibility. I became in fact a much more serious soldier than ever before. I doubt if I have ever had a real let-up since I left Brigmerston. I had made quite a reputation as a commander, and it was this command that put me in the circle of those likely to rise to near the top of my profession. But I think I may have lost some happiness and easiness of life."

In the event he was on half-pay for some fifteen months. During that time the family shared a house at Camberley with an old friend, Ivo Vesey—then Director of Staff Duties at the War Office— and Wavell undertook a number of professional and semi-professional chores. He set and corrected Staff College examination papers, and he rewrote Volume II of Field Service Regulations, the Army's principal training and operational manual. In April, 1934—at the suggestion of Jock Burnett-Stuart, by now G.O.C. in Egypt—he led a reconnaissance party, which included two future generals and a future air marshal,[17] in a survey of the track across the Syrian desert between Haifa and Baghdad, in order to consider and recommend on its possibilities as a military route in wartime. This, Wavell said, "was much better than the eternal writing I had been doing."

In his final confidential report on Wavell's work as a brigadier, the Commander of the 2nd Division, General Jackson, had said that he was in every way fitted to be the Commandant of either Staff College—Camberley or Quetta—Commandant of the Imperial Defence College, Director of Military Operations and Intelligence, Director of Staff Duties, Director of Military Training, Deputy Chief of General Staff in India or Commander of a Regular division, and added that he only needed experience to become qualified for the highest commands or appointments in the Army. This high opinion had been enthusiastically endorsed by the C.-in-C. Aldershot Command, General Sir Charles Harington. Wavell believed himself to have been earmarked for the Imperial Defence College, and had set his heart on it. He was now told that he was to command the 2nd Division instead. He had an interview with the C.I.G.S. and asked why the change had been made. The C.I.G.S. said he was sorry, but everyone had assumed that he would prefer the command of a division.

Wavell made no complaint, but he remarked ruefully that while no one else seemed to rate the I.D.C. very highly, to him it was the equivalent of being chosen for an international match as against being picked for one's county, and (in more professional terms) it was the most important job possible, "because on it depended the best chance of getting the three services to work together in the next war, and to train some men who were likely to hold high command."

The new appointment was not to take effect until March, 1935. He had, therefore, several more months of odd jobs—writing, umpiring exercises and the like—on half-pay. In December, with two officers of similar rank, he attended the *Cycle d'Information des Généraux et des Colonels* held by the French Army at Versailles. Unofficially this course for senior officers was known as the *Ecole des Maréchaux*. The fifty French officers and the three British and five other foreign officers were divided into four syndicates; Wavell was attached to the first. His copy of the list of students and instructions survives, bearing in a neat French hand on its cover "Major-General A. P. Wavell (*armée britannique*)," and pencilled alongside the names of his own syndicate his private identifications of several of them: "Cavalry," "Artillery—bald," "Sapper," "Blue," "Beard," "Fat," "Tall—cavalry—grey."

Wavell's British companions, with both of whom he was later to be closely associated, were remarkable men. Bernard Freyberg, a New Zealander, had a matchless fighting record as a combatant officer in World War I (V.C., D.S.O. and bar, two brevets, wounded five times, and mentioned six times in despatches), joined the Grenadier Guards as a Regular officer after the war and, like Wavell, had just been promoted. James Marshall-Cornwall, a much less extrovert character, was an educated soldier of high linguistic and other attainments; he had won a D.S.O. and an M.C. and had been given two brevets in World War I, was a gunner, four years younger than Wavell, and had just ended a tour of duty as C.R.A. of the 51st (Highland) Division.

Their joint report on the course contained some trenchant criticisms, though not all were destructive. They thought that French officers took their work more seriously than their British counterparts of equivalent rank. They expressed themselves more clearly, more logically and more fluently in speech as well as on paper; they read a map quickly and well, and had a better theoretical knowledge of their profession than most British officers. On the other hand, the French did not give the impression of being as practical or as active physically as their British opposite numbers, and "collectively they would weigh many hundredweights more than the same number of British senior officers." They all came to the conclusion that French officers, from the General Staff downwards, were satisfied that they had nothing to learn from foreign armies. This complacency, amounting almost to arrogance, stemmed, they thought, from the fountain-head. It was made clear throughout the course that officers did not want to encourage initiative or thought in the lower ranks; all that was wanted was that regimental officers should do what they were told; only the machine counted, and given masses of artillery for attack and automatic weapons for defence, all would be well.

> The fruit of their complacent policy is now becoming apparent, in that they are falling behind other armies in many respects without knowing it. They would be greatly surprised at this statement because in all their preliminary lectures before visits to military institutions, they invariably impressed upon us the superiority of their system and of the establishment concerned, only for us to find on inspection that in point of fact they were far behind us in most practical and technical details.
>
> During the three weeks we were living with the French Army, we were never asked a single question about the British Army, our methods or our equipment. If they had asked our opinion at times it would have been of value from their point of view, especially upon all questions affecting the employment of tanks. The French appear to place little practical importance upon the arguments that they use in support of any line of action. In syndicates, they argued wildly in support of a certain course, and then changed round completely for what we would consider quite insufficient reasons. If this could happen in peacetime, as appeared to be their common practice, they will require very careful watching as Allies.[18]

Early in 1935, the Wavells went to stay at old General Wavell's house at Little Somborne. He was now in his ninety-second year. He had seen his son attain his own rank, and his grandson preparing to follow them both to his beloved Black Watch. His brain was still fully active, and he had never lost his interest in life, although he was very deaf and his heart had begun to worry him a little. On the morning of 28th February he got up, began the day as usual with a cold bath, did not feel very well, and went back to bed. He died on 2nd March.

"I think that on the whole he enjoyed his long life, except perhaps towards the end. He was rather an autocrat in family life, as was the tradition of his age... He was a kind and indulgent father to me, and I wish I had been more attentive to him in his old age. As a soldier, I think he might well have gone further than he did, his ideas were rather ahead of his time, he had intelligence and common sense and humanity in his dealings with troops. I think he perhaps lacked ambition and push as a soldier and never put himself forward or caught the eye. . . .

"He always said he wished he had known more of his father's early life, and I have always since wished that I had known more of his; which is the main reason why I have written these notes for my family."

Nine days after his father's death Wavell took over the command of the 2nd Division. His outward appearance of calm, if reticent, confidence in himself was supplemented by the growing belief, among his seniors and contemporaries, that he was the coming man in the Army. Courteous and considerate always; relaxed, efficient and reassuring in his work; utterly devoid of pomposity; at home loving, gay, kind and generous—this least flamboyant of men was also one of the most complex.

There were certain similarities, and certain important differences, between Wavell's position at this time and that of Douglas Haig before the First World War. Like Haig, Wavell was coming to be known, in inner and informed circles, as one of the best soldiers of his generation, educated and thoughtful, as conscientious as he was intelligent. Like Haig, he was making his contribution to the corpus of military thought, and he was proving himself as capable of putting theory into practice, in the field, as of expounding it on paper or in a lecture. But his powers of command, like Haig's, were to some extent offset by a remoteness and taciturnity which for both men were the consequences of increasing isolation rather than fundamentally characteristic. Like Haig, he was serious and contemplative; but he had a copious and unfailing fountain of humour, which Haig lacked.

He was warm all through, but Haig's flame burned beneath layers of icy reserve. Both men had humility; Wavell's was humane, almost earthy, poetic and compassionate; Haig's was religious.

The more responsibility Wavell assumed, the stronger became his confidence, the wider his range of thinking, the bolder and more heterodox his conclusions. He was at the age at which most men's minds are made up, and their views harden on their relationship to their fellows, on their calling and on the world about them; soldiers in particular are believed to be subject to this melancholy process. With Wavell it was reversed: in his fifties he became more malleable, more impressionable. The originality of his mind had a free rein. He was now riding for the heights, not in fulfilment of personal ambition but in service to his country and his time, and the wind sang clear and strong about him.

The Army of the years between the two World Wars was, of set purpose, a refashioning of the pre-1914 Army, with some of its virtues and nearly all its faults. It lived a life apart from that of the outside world, to a degree which a later generation would find incomprehensible and repellent. The anti-militarist tradition in England, of very long standing, had been reinforced by a clamorous, superficially "intellectual" pacifism; the officers were depicted as class-conscious, stupid and tyrannical, the other ranks as their hapless, semi-illiterate, brutal and licentious victims, driven to enlistment only by the capitalists' whip of unemployment. The Army, with a greater realism and a surer sense of history than its critics possessed, was aware of the ancient roots of its unpopularity with those it strove to defend; and it withdrew into a self-conscious isolation. It set out to train recruits and newly-joined young officers solely to be soldiers. Wavell was among the first to recognise that this was a dangerously limiting attitude which would inevitably impair efficiency in time of war. Flexibility, he was convinced, was the primary requirement of the Army of the future, and of the individuals—the leaders and the led —of whom it would be composed. What he had learned in his own life he was now eager to teach in the Army, by example no less than by precept. He was no longer satisfied with the old Army ideal of "the trained soldier," worthy though that had been in many respects: he sought to educate whole men.

However rigid the attitude of higher authority—and it did not change substantially until the outbreak of war and afterwards— Wavell had a few understanding, and often enthusiastic, allies among officers of his own seniority, and he attracted the admiration and the loyalty of a number of his juniors. With these his influence increased steadily.

While he commanded the 2nd Division, among his brigade commanders were Arthur Smith, who was from 1940 to 1942 his and Auchinleck's C.G.S. in Cairo, Maitland Wilson and Victor Fortune. His first G.S.O.1 was George Giffard, who commanded Eastern Army in India in 1943. Among the brigade majors were the future General Sir Miles Dempsey and the future Lieutenant-General Sir Brian Horrocks.

On 13th May, 1935, T. E. Lawrence, three months discharged from the R.A.F., rode on his powerful Brough motor-cycle from his cottage, Clouds Hill, to Bovington Camp to send a telegram to his friend Henry Williamson. On his way home he swerved in order to avoid two boys on bicycles, who had been hidden from him in a dip. The Brough crashed, and Lawrence was gravely injured. His physical vitality was such that he lay unconscious for nearly five days before he died.

A. P. Wavell to Miss Anne Wavell   *28th May, 1935*
. . . Lawrence's death was a tragic business. Some of his closest friends say that he was sad and unhappy after he left the Air Force and think he would never have done much more. He certainly had no special plans for work and was, I believe, depressed and worried, but I can't help believing that he would have found some great work to do if he had lived. He was the most impressive and attractive man I ever met.

Wavell set out his considered view of Lawrence in an essay he wrote for *T. E. Lawrence, by His Friends*, compiled by A. W. Lawrence.[19] They had discussed in talk and on paper his theory of irregular warfare and its antidotes; but on Lawrence's ideas of regular warfare and the professional soldier they touched only once, and were interrupted. Wavell had made notes on which to take up the subject with him again when he had more leisure; but the day set for its discussion was to have been a visit to Lawrence at his cottage early in June, 1935.

Wavell compared Lawrence once with Hamlet, a Hamlet who had slain his uncle neatly and efficiently at the beginning of Act II, and spent the remainder of the play in reporting his act and writing a long

175

explanation of it to Horatio, and then retired to a monastery. His final assessment of this complex being was as generous as his brief, informal tribute in his letter to his sister:

> He will always have his detractors, those who sneer at the "Lawrence legend"; who ascribe his successes with the Arabs to gold; who view the man as a charlatan in search of notoriety by seeming to seek obscurity; who regarded his descent from colonel to private as evidence of some morbid *nostalgie de la boue*. They knew not the man. Those who did, even casually and sporadically, like myself, can answer for his greatness. The complexity of his character, the "mystery" of Lawrence, on which so much has been written, seems to me to lie mainly in the fact that he transcended the ordinary heights in so many qualities: in courage, in knowledge, in self-discipline, in skill with his hands, in artistry of words, in sympathy with the common working man and with the soldier, in demanding so little from life for his body and so much —too much perhaps—for his mind. But I am not competent to analyse the man: all I can say is that he was cast in heroic but very human mould, and that it was good to know him.

Wavell had come to regard Aldershot as the citadel of orthodox soldiering. He was inside it now; and the defenders of military orthodoxy did their well-mannered but unsuccessful best to hamstring him. Nevertheless, on his own as well as others' evidence, he contrived to shake up the routine a good deal. He, who had often described himself as idle and had led others into believing that this was a just accusation, was now working harder and harder.

His concentration on training was intense. At all levels of command during exercises he strove with great ingenuity to make every officer, N.C.O. and man in his division think for himself. In the Army Exercise of 1935—always the climax of the year's training programme, and known this year as the C.I.G.S. Stakes, because three generals, Burnett-Stuart as umpire, Gathorne-Hardy of Aldershot Command and Cyril Deverell of Eastern Command as the opposing commanders, were all supposed to be competing for that appointment—Wavell was put in a fix by a blunder of Gathorne-Hardy's, against which he gave a warning while it was being made. Successfully he pulled his division out from near disaster, retreated, re-formed and withstood a strong enemy attack. When Gathorne-Hardy was severely criticised at the subsequent conference for having mishandled Wavell's division, he stood up and said, "I should like it to be known that Major-General Wavell formed an accurate appreciation of the situation and warned me of what was likely to happen."

Much of Wavell's work was still extra-curricular. He completed the revision, which was in fact a total rewriting, of Field Service Regulations, Volume III, dealing with strategy. He went on to the composition of his most ambitious R.U.S.I. lecture so far, on the Higher Commander. Not only did he combine these considerable undertakings with his ordinary work, at his desk, out visiting units, devising training schemes and putting them into operation: he kept up his golf and resumed his hunting; there was a good deal of entertaining, official and private, at home; and the family surged incessantly about him, on spring-tide after spring-tide of proprietary affection. Bernard Fergusson, who had come to him from The Black Watch as his first A.D.C., was awestruck by his powers of concentration. His writings, Fergusson said, "were all works which, one would have thought, called for complete isolation and a Trappist silence. They were in fact brought forth in a welter of daughters borrowing three-ha'penny stamps, and puppies chewing at his bootlaces, and a series of bulletins about what was happening in the stables and who couldn't come to luncheon."[20]

Wavell always had time for the young: Archie John, with his Wykehamist views on politics and on poetry; Archie John's friends from Sandhurst; Pamela's debutante acquaintances, and larky young subalterns to entertain the debutantes. His interest in and encouragement of the young officer (or N.C.O.) were unflagging—providing always that he was active and zestful, and the more unorthodox in his outlook the better.

One such was Harry Fox-Davies, a subaltern in the Durham Light Infantry, who pondered the realities of modern war as he saw them emerging, and their difference from the neat little dream-patterns which the Army (in his experience) evolved in conventional exercises at his level. He composed a paper, pointing out the importance of guerrilla troops, and basing his arguments on the incontestable—but then forgotten—principle that a handful of men striking at the head and heart of the enemy's communications can do real and lasting damage out of all proportion to their numbers. He put it up to his C.O., who sent it back to him, having none of it. Fox-Davies, taking part in the year's exercises and watching Wavell's handling of them, decided that here was someone who would understand what he was trying to say.

Lt. H. E. Fox-Davies to A. P. Wavell   *1st October, 1935*

I hope you will forgive my taking the liberty of sending you some notes that I have written with regard to the possible scientific use of guerrilla troops in future wars.

If as a junior officer I may offer any slight criticism of army doctrines, I think that the lines we work on, especially in the attack, have become terribly orthodox, and that although we talk glibly about the value of surprise, our efforts to secure it run along very formal lines.

Also we have become so wrapped up in the necessity for securing favourable ground that we lose sight of the real object of an attack, which is to destroy the enemy's army as such.

Again, our efforts to procure information about our foes all work by rule of thumb. We get a certain amount from the air, and we push out formal patrols to "establish contact" with our opponents; from these two sources we have to guess our enemy's strength and intentions.

Lastly, we have come to believe that the only way to defeat an enemy is by a formal battle which will destroy his fighting units. We seem to have lost sight of the fact that if the brains and the arteries of an army are destroyed then that army must either surrender or be defeated in detail later. In other words, is it really necessary to have a battle at all in order to overcome one's enemy?

It is my suggestion that far more attention should be paid from the outset towards destroying the "brains," that is the commanders and headquarters, from *within* rather than on wasting time, men and ammunition on a formal attack on their external lines. Destroy his supplies, cut his wires, kill his commanders, and the object is half achieved before battle is joined at all.

And how is all this to be achieved? My answer is: by employing well-trained guerrilla troops. Surprise has always been the winning card in war, but where is there any surprise at present? Gas is old, tanks are old. Surely the field is set for some new form of surprise! So why not guerrillas?

I hope you will forgive me writing to you direct like this, but

178

you seemed on manœuvres to have considerable sympathy with any originality, and I also feel that if this guerrilla idea is to come to anything, then the fewer people who know about it the better . . .

A. P. Wavell to Lt. H. E. Fox-Davies   *22nd October, 1935*

. . . I agree with very much of what you say. We are too orthodox, we do not pay sufficient attention to the factor of surprise, we neglect means of obtaining information, and we are apt to look on battles as a thing to be sought at all times instead of something to be avoided, if possible, until the odds are heavily in one's favour. All regular troops of the armies I know suffer from much the same faults! But I'm not sure that I quite agree with you that the "trained guerrilla" is the solution to all these problems. An aspect of it that you have omitted to mention is the effect on the civilian population. Where guerrilla warfare has had most effect (Spaniards in Peninsula, Boers in S. Africa, Feisal's Arabs), practically the whole population has been involved, it has in fact been a national uprising against invaders; and the country has been a sparsely inhabited and not very highly civilised one. Guerrilla warfare in a thickly populated, highly civilised country, as in Europe, is quite another problem. If the country is enemy country, every civilian's hand is against you, you are up against the language problem, and you can hardly go a yard without being given away (this was the big problem every escaper from a German prison was up against, as you will realise if you read stories of war escapes—no bad reading to stimulate ingenuity in a young soldier); if the country is friendly or neutral the enemy has in reprisals on the inhabitants a weapon that will sooner or later turn the inhabitants against the guerrillas or cause the guerrillas to hesitate to expose their countrymen to reprisals (the Prussians in 1870 dealt with the French *franc-tireurs* this way, and the Germans adopted similar methods in Belgium in 1914; we tried reprisals, farm burning, concentration camps against the Boers). Also psychologically I don't think the "trained guerrilla" is possible; the man who will put on civilian clothes and face certain death if he is caught (and he has a poorish chance of getting away) to shoot down men in cold blood behind the enemy's lines is a rarity really. I don't mean that you shouldn't make every effort to train men to be capable of carrying out enterprises behind the enemy's lines—but as soldiers in uniform. . . .

A problem I have often considered is the motor guerrilla, who may be a prominent feature of the next war. This country is unlikely to be invaded; but if it was, consider what effect a corps of young men in motors or on motor bikes with a uniform coat and a rifle or light automatic might have on the enemy's communications; and consider what the answer might be.

Guerrilla warfare is an interesting subject and well worth reading about and thinking about. There is a novel by one C. S. Forester about the guerrilla warfare in Spain that might interest you, but the name has escaped my memory.

Wavell did not forget Fox-Davies. In the following year, in the middle of a major exercise directed by Gathorne-Hardy, he sent for the young man and, without any previous warning to formation commanders, bade him carry out a raid on the rear of his opponents, in fulfilment of his own doctrines. Gathorne-Hardy thought it had ruined his neatly planned exercise, but the umpires, though confused, could not fault it, and the troops got back to barracks a day earlier than had been intended.

Six years later Wavell, then C.-in-C. in the Middle East, sent for Fox-Davies once more; and this time it was no mere exercise. He led one Long Range desert patrol, and was decorated for gallantry; as a sick man he went on another, and died on it.[21]

On Wednesday, 4th December, 1935, Wavell delivered at the R.U.S.I. his lecture, *The Higher Commander*. It crystallised a lifetime's thinking about his profession. Jock Burnett-Stuart took the chair and said laconically: "General Wavell has lectured from this platform before and requires no introduction to you. Unlike most of those who from time to time review and analyse for us the attributes of the higher commander, he does not speak from a comfortable seat in the front row of the stalls but from the arena itself."

Wavell drew a portrait of the ideal higher commander by making a list of the qualities he thought essential: first, the fundamental soldierly virtues, loyalty, straightness and simplicity; the essential, all-important will to win; a spirit of adventure, which could also be defined as a touch of the gambler; physical robustness and courage; imaginative common sense; a capacity, at once patient and practical, to understand in principle and exercise in practice the basic art of administration; a streak, whether natural or acquired, of the impresario; flexibility of outlook combined with resolution of will; and—the higher the command the more necessary this last became— an ability to understand, talk to and co-operate with statesmen, politicians, scientists and civil servants. The root of the matter, he emphasised, is an unconquerable fighting spirit. Looking back to the First World War, he realised that its great leaders, civil and military, such as Clemenceau, Foch, Lloyd George and Haig, possessed this spirit in full measure. But not even the greatest leader can stand in isolation. Wavell's final paragraph showed how mature his philosophy had become, how wisely he thought and how deeply he felt about his own profession:

The pious Greek when he had set up altars to all the great gods by name, added one more altar, "To the Unknown God." So, whenever we speak of the "great captains" and set up our military altars to Hannibal, Napoleon, Marlborough and their like, let us add one more altar: "To the Unknown Leader": that is to the good company, platoon or section leader, who carries forward his men or holds his post and often falls unknown. It is these who in the end do most to win wars. The British have been a free people and are still a comparatively free people; and though we are not, thank Heaven, a military nation, this tradition of freedom gives to our junior leaders in war a priceless gift of initiative. So long as this initiative is not cramped by too many regulations, by too much formalism, we shall, I trust, continue to win our battles—often in spite of our higher commanders.[22]

The consequences of this lecture were far-reaching. For the first time in his life Wavell found himself dealing with a "fan mail" of some size as interest spread outside purely professional into academic and general circles. However, of all the letters he received his chairman's, written after having read the final draft two months before the lecture was delivered, was perhaps the most perceptive and the most disconcerting.

Gen. Burnett-Stuart to A. P. Wavell   *3rd October, 1935*
. . . The only comment I would make is that while you have said something about the creation of an atmosphere to encourage the development of the necessary qualities in the early stages, you have said nothing about the maintenance of an atmosphere to foster those qualities in the mature stages after the High

Commander has become a High Commander. That is where our present centralised, dictatorial system fails so completely. The business man as he advances to higher things becomes a director and has an increasing say in the conduct of the business. In the Army the High Commander at home has not only no say in the conduct of the business, but is never consulted and never even knows what is going on. He is, to use an air-defence phrase, "blacked-out." And as his own particular job under present peace conditions is futile and boring to a degree, that is bad for him—and for the Army. A dangerous subject however! . . .

At the end of May, 1936, when he had commanded the 2nd Division for little more than a year, Wavell was offered the appointment of Director of Military Training at the War Office. He had no hesitation in refusing.

"The job had no attractions whatever. I knew I should not see eye to eye with the C.I.G.S. as to how the Army should be trained, and anyway the D.M.T. could exercise comparatively little influence, and there was still no money and no equipment . . . I begged to be excused, quite firmly."

Jock Burnett-Stuart commented: "You are well out of it. It consists mainly of teaching several grandmothers to suck eggs."[23]

Nineteen years had gone by since, as a youthful and newly-married lieutenant-colonel, Wavell had been British liaison officer with the Grand Duke Nicholas in the Caucasus. The Russian Revolution was an accepted fact and Bolshevik was no longer a term of abuse. Communism was the fashionable creed of a section of the English intelligentsia; the amiable Mr. Maisky was the Soviet Union's Ambassador in London, a popular guest at all progressive functions; and even in the innermost chambers of power there was, in response to a dim awareness that Nazi Germany might be a danger rather than a bulwark against European collapse, a tepid, timid flirtatiousness towards Russia. A little later in the year an invitation for British representatives to attend the Soviet Army's 1936 manœuvres was accepted. Wavell, as one of the few Russian-speaking senior serving officers, was delighted to be nominated as head of the mission. His companions were Brigadier Martel, one of the Army's foremost tank experts, who had been on the desert reconnaissance with him two years earlier, the Deputy Director of Intelligence at the Air Ministry, and a Russian-speaking G.S.O.3 from the War Office.

Wavell prepared a detailed official report of the mission; he gave a talk on it at the Imperial Defence College; and he wrote an article for *The Red Hackle*, the regimental magazine of The Black Watch, the publication of which the War Office banned on the grounds that a copy might fall into Russian hands. Wavell remarked a little irascibly that it was more likely that a copy of the War Office's secret intelligence summary would reach the Russian General Staff. What all three documents showed was that he had not lost, in two decades, his sympathy and liking for the Russian people and that he had a shrewd and realistic comprehension of their new rulers' difficulties, their shortcomings and their merits.

At the end of a long, detailed and very percipient account of the Soviet Union in 1936, and of the Red Army's performance on manœuvres—the mission saw a paratroop drop of some 1,200 men—Wavell added in his own handwriting these notes: "Political: Desire for peace. Fear of Germany," and "Russians are not ruthless Red Devils, plotting to overthrow the world, nor are they demigods organising a new heaven on earth, but a backward country, striving earnestly and with some measure of success to bring the standard up towards that of Western Europe. They have a long way to go."

On 28th May, 1937, the Prime Minister, Stanley Baldwin, resigned and was succeeded by Neville Chamberlain, until then Chancellor of the Exchequer. Among the most significant immediate changes was the appointment of Leslie Hore-Belisha, the able and ambitious Minister of Transport, to be Secretary of State for War in succession to Duff Cooper, who went across the street to be First Lord of the Admiralty. Hore-Belisha, whatever his effect on the Army, and whatever the extent of his contribution to the Army's preparedness, or lack of it, at the outbreak of war in 1939, was neither liked nor trusted by the majority of senior Regular officers—including those whose promotion he hastened. They admitted that he had drive and energy; but they were suspicious of his motives and they disapproved of his methods. "Our first encounters," Wavell wrote, "were not propitious. The first time I met him he demanded my opinion on a matter which concerned the Adjutant-General. I replied that it was for the A.G. to advise him. He said that he knew the A.G.'s view but wanted mine, since he disagreed with the A.G. I refused to give it. I said that the A.G. had the full facts, which I had not, and that it would not be fair on the A.G. for me to give my views behind his back. H-B was not very pleased and did not seem to see the objection."

Nevertheless it was during Hore-Belisha's period of office as Secretary of State for War that Wavell held, in quick succession, a series of appointments each more responsible and more prominent than the last. The first of these brought to an abrupt and early closure his long association with the Aldershot Command. He had a letter from the Military Secretary at the War Office.

Gen. Sir Charles Deedes to A. P. Wavell *1st July, 1937*
The Report of the Palestine Commission is likely to be known shortly, and the reception which it receives in Palestine will govern to a considerable extent the retention of Dill in that country. If the situation is serious it is probable that Dill will remain. If the Report is taken quietly Dill will be relieved and the C.I.G.S. . . . considers that you are the most suitable General Officer to succeed him there. Before doing anything officially he has asked me to let you know this . . . in the interests of the Country, he hopes that you will be ready to take over the Command in Palestine if you are asked to do so.

Palestine was virtually an active service command, in a country a large proportion of whose inhabitants were in open rebellion against British rule; a country, moreover, which Wavell had known and liked for nearly twenty years, in peace and war, and of whose tangled problems he had a great deal of experience.

VI

Towards High Command

Palestine had been a problem to the British almost from the day on which Wavell, T. E. Lawrence, and a handful of other officers had walked in Allenby's wake into Jerusalem. It had been for centuries a backward province of the Ottoman Empire, inhabited by a small, depressed population, partly Moslem, partly Christian, who scratched a bare living from a land whose potential they never tried to exploit. Though their racial origins were mixed, the Arab strain in them was predominant: they spoke Arabic, and they called themselves and spoke of themselves as Arabs. After the sack of Jerusalem in A.D. 70, a few indomitable and devout Jews crept back to Palestine and lived precariously and humbly in Safad, high up in the mountains of northern Galilee, and in Tiberias by the lake. This little remnant never had either the desire or the capacity to endanger Arab ownership or Turkish rule of the country. However, in Europe, in the latter half of the nineteenth century, there arose, in answer to the miserable existence of the ghettos and to generations of persecution and humiliation, the movement known as Zionism, seeking the return, on a large scale, of the Jewish people to the land that the Bible had told them was their own. There were already a few small and scattered Jewish communities, principally under the patronage of the great Baron de Rothschild, settled in Palestine; but a new dynamism was given to the movement, first by a succession of brutal pogroms in Czarist Russia and second by the emergence of two brilliant and forceful leaders: Theodor Herzl, a spell-binding journalist from Vienna, and Chaim Weizmann, a distinguished scientist, born in Russia, educated in Germany and settled in Manchester. During World War I Weizmann's skill and knowledge did much to help end the British shortage of munitions (especially high-explosive shells). His valuable scientific work brought him into close and friendly association with leading members of the Government. Weizmann's ardent and persuasive

185

advocacy of the Zionist cause accorded with a mood of idealism in various influential members of Lloyd George's wartime Administration—the Prime Minister himself, Winston Churchill, Lord Milner and Arthur Balfour—and seemed to offer a way of consolidating British interests in the Middle East. These linked themes found a practical consummation, after months of discreet negotiations, in the issue, on 2nd November, 1917, of the historic document known as the Balfour Declaration, which stated that the British Government viewed with favour the establishment in Palestine of a national home for the Jews, and would use their best endeavours to promote that object, provided that nothing was done which might prejudice the civil and religious rights of existing non-Jewish communities in Palestine.

Regarded by the Zionists as their Magna Carta, the Balfour Declaration was seen by others, including Wavell, as the major source of British trouble in the Middle East from 1918 onwards. As national consciousness developed in the Arabs of Palestine, they did not merely want their civil and religious rights protected; they wanted to rule themselves in their own country. Their claims were at least as well documented as the Zionists', since the Arab Rebellion, which had been of considerable assistance to Allenby in his victorious campaign against the Turks, had been brought about by an exchange of letters in 1915-16 between Sir Henry McMahon, the British High Commissioner in Egypt and the Sherif of Mecca, in which (so the Arabs passionately believed) Palestine was included in those parts of the dismembered Ottoman Empire which were to be put under Arab rule.

These directly contradictory promises were the subject of bitter controversy for thirty years. Britain was given the League of Nations Mandate for Palestine and Transjordan, under which the people of both countries were intended to evolve towards self-government and finally independence. Between Arabs and Jews—the numbers of both sections of the population increased steadily—there was an irreconcilable conflict of interest and aspiration. Sometimes this was latent, at other times it burst out in bitter communal fighting and resistance to the mandatory power. The British attitude throughout was bewildered and ambiguous. Strategic and moral considerations conflicted, and successive Governments, by frequent changes of direction, did not make any easier the task of those who were supposed to preserve law and order in Palestine.

Wavell's old friend, Arthur Wauchope, strove as High Commissioner to bring about a peaceful relationship between Jews and Arabs.

But one inevitable consequence of Hitler's seizure of power in Germany, inaugurating as it did the most tragic period in Jewish history, was a swift rise in Jewish immigration into Palestine. In 1936 the Arabs reacted with a full-scale rebellion—guerrilla warfare against the British Administration and savage attacks on Jewish rural settlements. The small complement of British troops stationed in the country had to be heavily reinforced, and Lieutenant-General Sir John Dill, a close friend of Wavell's, was sent out to take command.

This was an ominous end to several years of apparent tranquillity, during which the social and economic development of both communities had been rapid, and its benefits visible. It was especially saddening for Arthur Wauchope. He had held his post for five years, and had come to believe that under a just and gentle British autocracy, peace had been achieved and would be maintained between Jews and Arabs, who could share the land without harm—indeed with great advantage—to them both.

The first phase of the Arab rebellion lasted some six months, from April to October. The Jews remained on the defensive in the towns and countryside; a general Arab strike was called, under the direction of a body called the Arab Higher Committee, with the intention of forcing the British Government to suspend Jewish immigration; bands of Arab guerrillas were formed in the hill districts; attacks were launched on communications—the roads, the railways, the telegraph wires and the oil pipeline to Haifa. The British Government sought the advice of Arab rulers outside Palestine, which did not prove helpful.

The role of Dill's troops, after considerable reinforcement, began to shift from mere guarding of communications and installations to preparation for an offensive against the guerrillas. In May the British Government announced that a Royal Commission would be appointed "to investigate the causes of unrest." Throughout that summer there was a war of nerves between the Government and the Arabs, which ended with the calling off of the general strike without the dissolution of the guerrillas, who remained under arms in the hills. An unofficial truce supervened, in which all the contestants awaited the arrival—in early November—of the Royal Commission, an exceptionally strong one under the chairmanship of Lord Peel, a former Secretary of State for India.

During this eventful year Wavell had had little direct contact with or knowledge of Palestine. But after his visit to Russia he wrote to

187

Dill, giving him a full account of what his mission had seen and thought, and mentioned his old friend, Wauchope. Dill's answer was both candid and percipient.

Lt.-Gen. Sir John Dill to A. P. Wavell   *31st October, 1936*

... Arthur Wauchope, as you say, is charming. He has been kindness itself to me since I arrived and I would give a lot to be able to see eye to eye with him. He says, with some justice, that he and I should do all in our power to agree. But the risk of straining to agree is that washy compromises are arrived at.

Arthur Wauchope loves every stone of this country, he has worked himself to the bone for it—and it has let him down.

But as I see it Arthur Wauchope would never face the fact that those whom he believed to be his friends had let him down. His forbearance knew no bounds and for it he got no thanks— it was merely held to be weakness. He hated the idea of Martial Law. He felt its operation would leave a sullen people with rebellion in their hearts. He is delighted that peace has come without having had to resort to stern measures. But the peace is only an armed truce. The whole Arab organisation, under that arch-scoundrel the Mufti, remains to renew rebellion when the result of the Royal Commission's labours proves distateful to the Arab population.

The fatal error was bringing the Arab Kings into the party. From henceforth they will consider themselves entitled to a say in Palestinian affairs. Moreover they prevented the declaration of Martial Law, because we obviously could not act while the conversations, which we had encouraged, were going on. And so the Arab leaders slipped out with honour and renown instead of being scattered to the four winds.

For the present there is nothing to be done but prepare for the next opportunity.

As I see it, Arthur Wauchope loves greatly, administers with knowledge and imagination, but he does not rule.

This is all very much for your eye alone. ...

The Royal Commission did its work with exemplary despatch. Its Report[1]—a classic document in the history of the British Empire— was published six days after the Military Secretary had given his informal invitation to Wavell to succeed Dill. After a skilful and impartial survey of the whole situation, it recommended the termination of the Mandate as it then stood, and the partition of Palestine into three: An Arab State comprising those parts of the country which were predominantly Arab; a Jewish State comprising those parts predominantly Jewish; and certain areas, of particular religious or strategic importance, which were to remain under the Mandate. Independent status, it advised, should be granted almost at once to the Arab and Jewish States, subject to treaties with Britain which would provide for British control over foreign policy and defence.

Accompanying the Royal Commission's Report was a Statement of Policy[2], which declared the Government's general agreement with its arguments and conclusions, and their desire to put through a scheme of partition, based on an effective measure of consent on the part of both communities; as a corollary the Government proposed to prohibit any land transactions which might prejudice such a scheme, and to permit Jewish immigration at the rate of 1,000 persons a month during the eight months August, 1937—March 1938, "provided that the economic absorptive capacity of the country is not exceeded."

On 16th July Wavell was summoned to the War Office, and was told officially that he was to succeed Dill. The appointment was in the rank of major-general, and was to be regarded as temporary, though no limit was set on the time he might expect to be in Palestine. He was to leave England within the month.

Wavell did not share either the bewilderment or the ambiguity which afflicted many of his fellow-countrymen over Palestine. Where Wauchope was emotionally involved, he was clear-cut and unsentimental. It was perhaps as well for both of them that when Wavell arrived in the country Wauchope was at home on sick leave, and the Officer Administering the Government was the Chief Secretary, Sir William Battershill, a career colonial official with a good record as a tough and competent administrator.

Wavell had been present at the inception of British rule in Palestine, and he had no great liking for the course it had taken. He was fully aware of the considerations which had led to the issue of the Balfour Declaration, but he laid greater stress on its negative safeguards for the Arabs than on its positive provisions for the Jews. He was opposed to the idea of Jewish possession of so large a part of Palestine, and believed that by length of tenure and for other reasons the Arabs had the greater claim to the country. He believed, too, that the fulfilment of Zionist aspirations would lead to trouble in the Middle East and—since it was the one subject on which all Arabs were united—would focus antagonism against Britain throughout the region.

He could justly claim that events vindicated his view. Italy had consolidated her swift and ruthless conquest of Ethiopia, and was becoming openly more aggressive in her colonial territories bordering on Egypt. Nazi Germany and Fascist Italy had become allies, and co-operated in fomenting anti-British feeling among millions of Arabs. The historic lines of communication of the British Empire, to India, Australasia and the Far East, were seriously menaced. And now Britain was engaged, as a result of her support of Zionism, in sup-pressing an Arab uprising in Palestine when, by all the canons of her traditional strategy, she ought to be conciliating them and winning their support.

But if this dilemma was almost intolerably grievous to Wauchope and saddening to Dill, it had no such effect on Wavell who, as well as being of more robust fibre than either of his two friends, had not yet, in his own career, reached the point of national policy-making. His task was simply to maintain—if necessary to restore—law and order, as a precondition of the major decisions which he knew to be essential but which it was for others to make. But his own views were very clear.

He took over from Dill on 12th September, 1937. By this time Palestine was again seething with Arab unrest. On the Jews' side the Zionist Congress, which had met in Zürich in the previous month, had approved the principle of partition, but declared the suggested boundaries to be inadequate. On the Arab side the extremists inside the country, under the leadership of the ruthlessly ambitious Mufti of Jerusalem, Haj Amin el Husseini, were making rapid preparations for another bout of violence; while in the capitals of the various Arab countries outside Palestine, British emissaries were failing in their endeavours to procure support for a "moderate" policy of partition coupled with conciliation. The Arab rulers came out openly in support of the (Palestine) Arab Higher Committee in its rejection of partition; and at a conference outside Damascus on 8th December resolved that "we must make Great Britain understand that it must choose between our friendship and the Jews. Britain must change her policy in Pales-tine or we shall be at liberty to side with other European Powers whose policies are inimical to Britain."[3]

Wavell was confronted from the outset by a mounting wave of

rebellion. On 17th July, less than twenty-four hours after he, in London, had accepted his appointment, the Mufti, in Jerusalem, warned of his imminent arrest, had fled to the sanctuary of the Haram-es-Sharif, the Temple area, in the centre of the Old City, where he believed himself immune from capture and whence he continued to direct his campaign of subversion. From the end of August there was an increasing toll of murders, accompanied by other crimes of violence, sabotage and intimidation.

The forces at Wavell's disposal had been reduced during the lull from a maximum strength of two divisions and consisted, when he took over, of two experienced but rather weary infantry brigades. He had no artillery, no armoured fighting vehicles other than an armoured car company of the R.A.F., and no cavalry; the Palestine Police, the Arab Legion in Transjordan and the Transjordan Frontier Force maintained a close liaison, but were not under Wavell's orders. He was committed to the most difficult and perplexing of all military responsibilities, "aid to the civil power." This was his first independent command under active service conditions, and he held it for just over six months. As was to be his fate again and again in the next six years, he was in a position in which, as a result of long unpreparedness and at the behest of a Government that was vacillating, harassed and confused, he was pressed to accomplish miracles with the minimum resources. What he achieved in Palestine was not a miracle, but it was extremely worthy of notice and has passed virtually unrecognised.

A fortnight after he had assumed command, Mr. Lewis Andrews, the District Commissioner for Galilee, and his accompanying police guard were murdered by Arab terrorists in Nazareth as they were on their way to Sunday evening service.[4] Andrews had known for some time that he was a marked man, but when he met Wavell in Haifa a few days before his murder he told him that he was much easier in his mind, having heard that the terrorists were no longer after him. Wavell wrote: "Whether this belief was 'planted' on him to cause carelessness is uncertain, but he committed the fatal mistake for a threatened man of doing the same thing regularly by the same route at the same time."

The Arab Higher Committee uttered formal expressions of regret, which were not believed. On 1st October, with the agreement of the British Government, strong measures were put into operation. The Higher Committee was declared illegal; and the Mufti was deprived of his offices as President of the Supreme Moslem Council and member of the Waqf Committee.[5] Warrants were issued for the arrest of several prominent Arab leaders: those who were caught (the police did not handle the operation efficiently, and their Intelligence was lamentable) were deported to the Seychelles; those who avoided arrest fled the country. The Mufti remained in his sanctuary. Wavell was not allowed to have him arrested in the Temple area; he had several plans for kidnapping him, but was never permitted to make the attempt for fear of provoking a brawl in so holy a place, since the Mufti always had a couple of gunmen guarding him.

On the night of 14th October the Mufti escaped and was picked up by the French authorities in a small boat off the coast of Lebanon. The French refused to extradite him, and put him, nominally, into internment, whence in due course he escaped once more and made his way to Iraq and a career, lasting a quarter of a century, of exile, notoriety and intrigue. Wavell's view of him was unflattering: "A poor creature and certainly no leader."

Temporary though his appointment was, Wavell had been led to expect that he would be in Palestine for at least eighteen months. But Hore-Belisha, with the reins at the War Office firmly in his hands and with Captain Basil Liddell Hart as his adviser, was beginning the shake-up by which he hoped to transform the British Army. Wavell's first intimation of the impending changes was in this letter:

Maj.-Gen. Sir Frederick Pile to A. P. Wavell   *20th October, 1937*
. . . In the meantime a man called Belisha has arisen and is causing awful commotion. He has appointed Gort Military Secretary and if some of the rumours are true we are heading for a nice spot of bother. There is talk of a new Army Council and *not* selected from the next names on the list.

Personally I think Deverell is better than anyone in his vicinity but if we go on as we are now doing we won't last long as an army.

I myself am plumping for a man called Wavell as C.I.G.S. and the real reason for this letter is to tell him that an eruption is likely and that his name, which I have managed on several occasions to suggest to people that matter, is now being talked about. The firm hand in Palestine is doing him no harm. Belisha has one fear: that he will put in a man who has not the guts to re-

G.S.O.3, 1914

Captain A. J. Wavell
(Archie John)

Lady Wavell in 1914

form the show—your work in Palestine may just weight the scales.

As I say—Deverell is at least as good as any near him and it is only if the present Army Council decide to go that a radical change becomes essential.

This is a bit confidential and it may well be that nothing will happen at all, but on the other hand I have an itching in my palms that tells me that the New Year will see fundamental changes, and should the breeze blow in the direction I hope— you may find yourself faced with a great task. . . .

Pile's confidential information, however, proved to be wrong. Wavell recorded: "Liddell Hart told me afterwards that I should have been C.I.G.S. probably, if I had been at home. But H-B had only seen me twice, and then we had not hit it off. I think it was fortunate for me; I don't believe I should have been happy or successful with H-B."

Hore-Belisha reached the same conclusion by a different route. He decided that Lord Gort, after only two months as Military Secretary, should succeed Deverell. He wrote to Wavell, early in November, offering him the appointment, vacant in the following June, of G.O.C.-in-C. Southern Command, in succession to Jock Burnett-Stuart, who was due for retirement. These appointments were announced in a communiqué published on 3rd December.

The swift measures taken after Andrews' death had been salutary, but the rebellion was by no means broken. Wavell was urged by the Government at home and in Palestine to proclaim martial law and take over the whole administration of the country. This pressure he resisted because difficult though the situation was, these drastic steps, in his view, would not have remedied it. He had not enough troops to establish and maintain effective control, nor did he have enough experienced officers to staff a complete military government. He did however propose and was given, as a kind of half-way house to martial law, a system of military courts, linked with an enlarged and strengthened code of emergency regulations, with severe penalties for a wide range of offences, including the death sentence for carrying arms.

Wavell's old regiment, the 2nd Battalion The Black Watch, in which his son was now serving, was stationed in Jerusalem. On the evening of 5th November two Jocks, unarmed and in walking-out

dress, were shot in the back in the street. The Brigade Intelligence
Officer, Wavell's former A.D.C. Captain Fergusson, was sent for.
The police were at work; their dogs had traced a line to the village
of Silwan (Siloam), less than a mile away. The murdered men were
sons of families with a long tradition of service in the regiment; and
they now lay dead in the gutter, their white, neatly blancoed spats
stained with blood. Dusk came down swiftly; it was proposed to
surround the village with a cordon of troops during the night, and let
the police go in and search it next morning at dawn. Fergusson, whose
first experience of action this was, went off to report to Wavell.
Wavell questioned him closely about the mood of the battalion and
then gave orders that it should carry out the operation. Late in the
evening the C.O., Colonel McLeod, asked if he might see Wavell. He
said he did not think it was safe to use the battalion.

"The men were so worked up at the murder of their comrades
that they had already tried once to break out of barracks, with the
idea of beating up any Arabs they met; he feared that they might
break loose during the operation and take revenge. He was very
pessimistic. There were no other troops I could use; I was sure that
it was the right thing to surround and search the village as soon as
possible and the best chance of catching the murderers. I told McLeod
that I would trust the discipline of my old battalion, and that he was
to tell them so and to carry out the operation. But I must admit that
I spent an unhappy night, as I knew I had taken a certain risk. There
were a great number of people, both in Palestine and at home, who
were only too ready to accuse British troops of atrocities, and I did
not want my old regiment involved in what might well be a serious
incident. At about 3 or 4 a.m., when the troops were due to close in
on the village, I heard from my bedroom—the village was almost
visible from my window—the sound of several shots; and feared that
they marked the beginning of the incident. There were no more,
however, and I heard in the morning that all had gone well. The
murderers had not been found, but the behaviour of the troops had
been impeccable. The shots I had heard were due to a shot being fired
at the troops from a house as they closed in on the village; one or two
men had fired in return. One Arab was reported to have 'fallen over a
cliff' during the search, and I had a suspicion that he might have had
a helping hand, though the official version was never challenged."

In Samaria and in Galilee the Arab guerrillas strove to keep up the
offensive through the winter. The country was bare and mountainous,

and had very few roads. Wavell did not spread his forces out in small, vulnerable patrols, which the rebels could ambush and kill off whenever they wanted. He held the country's vital points, and kept his infantry battalions concentrated at centres of communication and organised into mobile columns (neither the Bren-carrier nor the jeep was yet in existence; lorries and Cypriot donkeys were used with some success). Wavell's own mobility was ensured by the friendly and efficient co-operation of the A.O.C., Air Commodore Roderic Hill, who was always ready to put an aircraft at the G.O.C.'s disposal and frequently piloted himself. Wavell wrote: "Whenever I could manage it I flew a two-seater dual-control machine, took charge of it in the air and had a flying lesson from the pilot. Roderic Hill was very good about letting me fly, and actually allowed me to land and take off by myself once."

The winter in Palestine is short, mild on the coastal plain and in the Jordan valley, cold and tempestuous in the mountains. In the operations of 1937-38, though it was not fierce and the rains came late, it undoubtedly hampered the British more than the rebels, who remained tenaciously if not very effectively on the offensive. The roads and the railways were under frequent attack; with their hideouts in countless little hill villages, the rebels were at their most active in the centre and north of the country; and there were repeated small skirmishes. Wavell kept his home authorities fully informed in a series of letters to General Haining, the D.M.O. and I. at the War Office, who in the November changes had been named as his successor in Palestine. Arthur Wauchope came back from his leave, looking ill and tired. The Jewish Agency asked for protection for Jewish technicians boring for water in the Negev, and Wavell told Haining that he did not think this was in the British soldier's contract. A retired Indian Police officer, Sir Charles Tegart, came out to improve the efficiency of the Palestine Police, was appalled by many aspects of what he saw, advised that a defensive wire system be constructed all along the northern border to keep out infiltrators, and urged the building all over the country of a series of massive (and costly) police posts—on the model of the old Royal Irish Constabulary's system—part fortress, part barracks, which survive to this day in both Israel and Jordan. Wavell thought him a resolute and attractive character, but had no hesitation in opposing his policy.

Several of the officers who served under Wavell in Palestine were later to attain high rank and responsibility in World War II and after; but none was to win a greater, stranger fame than a young G.S.O.3 (Intelligence) in his headquarters named Orde Charles Wingate. Wavell's immediate assessment of Wingate was that he was "an odd creature," but with remarkable qualities beneath and beyond the oddity which he recognised and sought to encourage. Wingate, who had served in the Sudan and spoke excellent Arabic, had espoused the Zionist cause with passion, and was enraged by what he thought to be open British partiality towards the Arabs, and by British military lethargy and "softness" in dealing with the Arab rebellion. He was in the grip of powerful emotions, and his dreams and visions were far-reaching; he was also a zealous and extremely practical professional soldier. Wavell could hardly be less sympathetic towards Wingate's unabashed Zionist sympathies; but he was quick to appreciate the military soundness of the scheme of Special Night Squads, for the protection of the isolated Jewish colonies in the countryside and the breaking up of the Arab gangs, which Wingate elaborated with ferocious eloquence. He gave it his assent; and Wingate found in Brigadier Evetts, commanding the British forces in Northern Palestine, an understanding and energetic supporter, so far as the military aspects of the scheme were concerned. The Special Night Squads were recruited from tough, courageous young *sabra* (native-born) Jews in the collective settlements; they operated ruthlessly, and with considerable success, against the Arab guerrillas. Wingate was awarded a well-earned D.S.O.; the foundations of what was to become the Israel Defence Force were firmly laid; and Wingate's name, face, aspirations and beliefs were as firmly fixed in Wavell's retentive memory.

In March, 1938, Wauchope retired, and was succeeded by Sir Harold MacMichael, a former member of the Sudan Political Service, who had just finished a successful period of office as Governor of Tanganyika. Wauchope's departure from Palestine, only a few weeks before Wavell himself was due to go, was an occasion of considerable emotion. Outside the railway station in Jerusalem The Black Watch mounted a guard of honour. Wauchope, as gently and urbanely punctilious as ever and as respectful of protocol, wore a grey frock-coat and a grey top hat. The order, "General salute, present arms!" was given; the band crashed into "God Save the King," palms hit riflebutts squarely. He was going from the land he loved, saluted by the regiment he loved. He came to attention, his arm swept up, his forefinger touched the rim of his top hat, and he stood thus to the end, giving his salute in return.

Wavell's own going was less emotional and less spectacular. He handed over to Haining in a hurried twenty-four hours, and with the family sailed from Port Said in the *Orontes* on 8th April. He said of this period:

"Dealing with the rebellion was a very unsatisfactory and intangible business, and I don't think I produced any better answers than anyone else. But I think I kept it within bounds and did as much as I could with the troops available."

Thinking and writing about the past (in his biography of Allenby), working in a present made difficult by the constant lack of equipment and manpower, and planning for a future of bleak contingencies was now an habitual combination of mental activities for Wavell. In Palestine, when the November excitements were at their height, he had composed and sent to Haining a far-sighted appreciation of the country's role in any future war with Italy. In December, after he had been told that he had been selected for high command in England, he jotted down on a single sheet of foolscap a note on the Army's principal requirements. They were twelve, which he listed haphazardly as they came into his mind: close co-operation with R.A.F.; air defence of London; C.-in-C. Home Defence; decide policy if continental war; grouping of infantry units; Mobile Division; modernising of drill, uniform and equipment; abolish promotion exams; confidential reports to include fitness for war; close touch with science; good propaganda; more brevets.

Wavell was perhaps the most notable of a few senior men in high places who were thinking along lines of this kind, but the England to which he returned was morally and intellectually divided and irresolute, materially unprepared for war, and slowly, reluctantly and belatedly getting into gear before beginning the first and most elementary preparations. The international scene had darkened swiftly and grievously during the months Wavell had been abroad. In February Anthony Eden had resigned his post as Foreign Secretary, in disagreement with Neville Chamberlain's determination to appease Fascist Italy. In March Hitler pounced on Austria, and immediately turned to put pressure on his next victim, Czechoslovakia. Every step took Europe nearer war. The Service chiefs and two of the three Service Ministers (Hore-Belisha, and Duff Cooper at the Admiralty) were aware of the growing menace; and so was the Committee of Imperial Defence. The Government however, with the support of

Parliament and a majority in the country, and with the backing of *The Times*, were apparently still determined to go to any lengths to preserve the peace, in obstinate disregard of the truth of the saying, "*Qui desiderat pacem, praeparet bellum.*"

In public there was increasing political acrimony. The Labour Party, in opposition, clamoured for a policy which would inevitably lead to war, but refused to commit themselves to the measures of military preparedness which would make it possible to fight that war effectively. Strong, well argued and constructive criticism of the Government came from a small group of independent Conservatives led by Winston Churchill. But since 1935 Churchill, with Professor F. A. Lindemann as his technical adviser, had been a member of the Committee of Imperial Defence on Air Defence Research which, in secret, was pressing on, so far as it could, with essential measures. A paradoxical situation prevailed therefore in the high official circles into which Wavell was drawn by his new appointment: a surface readiness to negotiate on any terms, however discreditable, with the dictators; and in private, under the guidance of advisers and officers more realistic than their political chiefs, a tardy, anxious effort to catch up with the Germans.

Wavell, transferred from an active service post in Palestine to an important Command in the United Kingdom, became a key man in this effort. The Army's senior generals, on the Army Council and in the principal Commands at home and overseas, were clearly the commanders-designate for war. A quarter of a century earlier Douglas Haig, like Wavell brought back from overseas to Aldershot, had gone to France immediately on the outbreak of war in command of the First Corps of the B.E.F. An appointment of similar or even greater responsibility obviously loomed ahead now for Wavell. At this very moment, however, he was confronted with the suggestion of a quite different climax to his career. The fact that he seriously considered that he had a choice may help to elucidate some of the enigmatic facets of his character. Early in May, before he had had time to settle into his new appointment, he was approached by General Sir Ernest Swinton, the pioneer of the tank, who was now Chichele Professor of Military History at the University of Oxford and was about to retire if a suitable successor could be found.

General Swinton to A. P. Wavell   *19th May, 1938*

If you were serious about our conversation of last week—or

the week before—let me have privately your record of service and qualifications for my personal use.

This will not commit you in any way because until the post is advertised and you apply for it the matter will not come up officially.

As I said, I can do nothing *directly*. I am not on the selection committee. *But that does not mean that I can do nothing.*

So, if you are thinking about it—send your record along. If you are not—let me know and I will not bark up an empty tree!

Wavell answered yes, provided a war did not occur meanwhile. He regarded the professorship as well paid and congenial, more attractive than a few more years of peacetime soldiering. He sent Swinton his qualifications, and Swinton did on his behalf the quiet lobbying at which his letter had hinted. "I should rather have liked the job," Wavell wrote. "It carried with it a Fellowship of All Souls; and the study of military history has always been a hobby of mine. I had, however, to make some of it instead."

Nineteen thirty-eight was for Wavell an arduous, eventful and frustrating year. Innovations in the Army were raining in thick and fast. All the questions he had jotted down on the piece of foolscap in Jerusalem came up rapidly for consideration, but few of them were answered satisfactorily. New weapons were being developed, but units were lucky if they caught a glimpse of a prototype, even in demonstration; new techniques were being evolved, new establishments devised. It was possible for a commander to lose himself in a welter of detail; this fate Wavell avoided by restricting his paper work to the minimum and spending as much time as he could out and about his widespread Command, looking at formations and units. The wartime role envisaged for the troops of Southern Command was that they were to be II Corps in an Expeditionary Force on the continent; and Wavell was assured that he would be their Commander. However, since recruitment, equipment, tactics and strategy were all in the melting-pot; since the most important developments (such as radar) were highly secret and hardly off the drawing-board; since the Government were confused and irresolute and had, under pressure two years earlier, appointed as their "Minister for the Co-ordination of Defence" an amiable lawyer, Sir Thomas Inskip, who was utterly ignorant of military matters; since the Secretary of State for War, though ambitious and talented, was both less influential in the Cabinet and less liked or trusted by his military subordinates than he wanted to believe; and since everything was being attempted in a hurry, there was little or no chance for imaginative or realistic training.

Wavell wrote: *"There were no manœuvres on any scale during this period and I had no practice in the art of command in the field."*[7] Large-scale exercises without troops—without even a mock-up of the fog and fear, the perplexity and the need for quick, intuitive and accurate decision— were not sufficient substitute.

During the whole summer and early autumn of 1938 military planning and preparation were overshadowed by the political crisis. Hitler was determined to conquer Czechoslovakia and was convinced that he could do it without war. France and Britain were frightened, blackmailed and hoodwinked. Conrad Henlein, Hitler's henchman in the Sudetenland, came to England. Lord Runciman took a British mission to Czechoslovakia to try to persuade the Czechs to accept their fate peaceably. It was one of the most unpleasant phases in British history.

In July, before the tension tautened to its fiercest pitch, there was one major exercise with troops—at brigade level—which Wavell attended. That it was held at all was due to the energy and imagination of the officer commanding 9th Infantry Brigade at Portsmouth, Brigadier Bernard Montgomery, and the willing help of the naval Commander-in-Chief at Portsmouth, Admiral of the Fleet Lord Cork and Orrery. The brigade put to sea from its home base, and landed at Slapton Sands, west of Dartmouth, with air support consisting of twelve Fleet Air Arm Swordfish, already obsolescent. It was a brave enough effort, but Wavell's assessment of it was caustic:

"It was a pitiful exposition of our complete neglect of landing operations. There was *one* so-called landing craft, an experimental one made many years before and dug out of some scrap-heap for this exercise, in which I rather think it sank. For the rest the troops landed in open row-boats as they had done for the last 200 years and more. A storm came on, and the troops were unable to re-embark as had been intended. I went in the Admiralty yacht *Enchantress* with the C.-in-C. Portsmouth, Ginger Boyle (now Cork and Orrery). It was rough and the yacht was lively, but I just managed to hold up the credit of the Army by sitting through and finishing dinner with the C.-in-C., while my staff had retired to their cabins."

Next morning, in an extremely choppy sea, the Admiral and the General left the yacht in a launch, whence they had to transfer to a small dinghy in order to be rowed ashore.[8] Wavell landed, to be greeted by a Montgomery who was bubbling over with enthusiasm and full of explanations of the course of the exercise. Wavell said, "I see," and stumped on up the hill to the car. The day's vicissitudes were not yet over. The 9th Brigade may have misdirected his driver or his A.D.C. may have misread a map: while Wavell snoozed the car ditched itself in a farm dung-heap. Driver and A.D.C. worked feverishly to extricate the car, and Wavell resumed his nap.

The A.D.C., Michael Fox, of the Coldstream Guards, was a man of quality, though very different from his predecessor, Fergusson— "diffident while Bernard was self-assured, slow of wit while Bernard was very quick, not such an amusing companion, but a very good and conscientious A.D.C., and a very attractive person."[9] Like Fergusson, however, Fox had his own vivid recollections of Wavell. During this exercise, or on another occasion, he was in attendance when Wavell lunched with Montgomery at Portsmouth. Montgomery was at his most loquacious, Wavell at his most taciturn. By the coffee, even Monty had been reduced to silence. As the car drove off Wavell observed, "Strange fellow, Monty; one of the most capable officers we have, but for some reason not popular with senior officers."

Michael Fox discussed this period in Wavell's life long afterwards with Archie John, who remarked that his father liked to cherish the illusion that he was a lazy man. Fox said: "He would like to have been, but he wouldn't allow himself to be. He had only one fortnight's leave in the two and a half years I was with him. He overworked himself—got himself progressively tired. He was overtired when he left Salisbury to command in Middle East."[10]

His stamina seemed inexhaustible: the work certainly was. The Secretary of State had sensibly decided that the four Army Commanders at home should be brought into close consultation with the Army Council. There were therefore frequent conferences at the War Office, and selection boards for senior appointments. Wavell liked and trusted Lord Gort, the C.I.G.S., and his Deputy, General Sir Ronald Adam, and two out of the three other Army Commanders were old and close friends, Generals Dill and Bartholomew. "We prepared for war," he wrote, "as well as we could."

From his headquarters at Salisbury he travelled about his Command indefatigably, by air as often as possible, either in an Army

Co-operation aircraft or in a small, dual-control machine which he himself flew whenever it was off the ground. Not only had he all his Regular formations and depots to visit; but a great many T.A. units, in camp and in their drill-halls, met a general who was interested in them and seemed to like them. He, for his part, thought them "keen, anxious to learn, and very hospitable," and enjoyed dealing with them.

After one of these airborne journeys he returned and announced to his family and his A.D.C. that he had had a narrow escape. Later he added casually, "Oh, the machine's a write-off." It had over-run the landing-strip and toppled to a halt in a sunken lane. Characteristically, he continued to fly as often as he could.

In July Archie John, who had stayed with the regiment in Palestine, was blown up in a truck by a landmine, and was badly wounded in one foot. He was invalided home and was on crutches for some time.

As the summer ended the political crisis came to its climax. Mr. Chamberlain made his successive visits to Germany. The A.A. units of the Territorial Army were hastily mobilised. Reservists were called up. Slit trenches were dug in the London parks. Gas-masks were issued. Wavell was despondent about the country's mood, and dourly convinced that the Prime Minister's policy was wrong. Seven years afterwards he wrote:

"I always held that we should have fought at Munich time; but I know that Barty and, I think, Jack Dill were against me, holding that we were quite unprepared. So we were, but I believe that at that time the Boches were also unready and that they made better use of the year's respite which Munich gave them than we did. It was not a soldier's decision anyway."

Wavell was deeply shocked by the final tragi-farce of the Munich "agreement"—even more so by the country's hysterical relief when Chamberlain returned, waving his scrap of paper and saying that he had brought peace with honour. A *Daily Mirror* poster, expressing this popular emotion in all its crudity, sickened him. "How can we hold our heads up again?" he asked, in an unaccustomed outburst. "We don't deserve to be great, and we'll end up as a second-rate nation."

Michael Fox asked him one evening, "Sir, what do you think will happen if war comes?"

"The British Empire," Wavell answered, "is a big thing to take on."

Fox persisted. "What shall *we* do? Shall we send an Expeditionary Force to France?"

The answer this time was a short, fierce snap. "I don't know. And if I did I shouldn't tell you."

The crisis passed. A strange, twilit semblance of normality returned. The A.A. gun crews stood down and went back to their civilian callings for a few more months. Archie John, as obsessed as the rest of his generation with politics, limped around the lobbies of Parliament and sat in the gallery listening to debates. Churchill spoke to louder and louder cheers from the Opposition, and Chamberlain's Chief Whip, Captain Margesson, with an imperious flick of his eyelids, ordered the Tory back-benchers out of the Chamber.

Wavell had his last season's hunting, going out as much as he could with his wife and daughters. In the New Year he took Felicity and Joan off to Wengen for a fortnight's ski-ing. "They took to it like ducks to water, but I found I had lost my skill and nerve, and my knee gave me trouble. In the twelve years since I had last ski-ed the pace had increased enormously, and the crowds, and it was quite a different sport."

In February he delivered the three Lees-Knowles lectures at Trinity College, Cambridge. His audiences were thin—twenty or thirty undergraduates, all members of the O.T.C.—and the lectures attracted no notice at all at the time. Not until more than a year later when, in the Middle East, he was going over some old papers, did he decide that they might be worth publishing; and only when Archie John took a hand was there any competition for them. In the end *The Times* published them as three turn-overs; Penguin Books re-issued them; and they have subsequently been published again, as the first three essays in *Soldiers and Soldiering*, under the title *Generals and Generalship*. They were translated into a number of languages, including German.

Their merit is as easy to see as the reasons for their wide and lasting popularity. They are Wavell the teacher at his best and they are without pedantry and stiffness. They read magnificently; and were it not for the fact that Wavell's delivery as a speaker did no justice at all to the content of what he had to say, it would be an indictment of Cambridge that there were not queues outside the biggest hall the University could provide.

They are steeped in wisdom, sanity and a profound understanding of what war is about and what men are like. The simplicity of the writing is deceptive: the lectures are the product of a lifetime's work and meditation; not a line is unconsidered. Though their immediate context is professional, and Wavell spoke out of the testing of his own experience, their application is universal. Anyone who has read these lectures and taken them to heart, though he never leads a platoon in battle, will be a better man by reason of what they have taught him. Those few undergraduates, who in a few months' time were to come to their testing, were far more fortunate than they could possibly have realised.

At least one very able professional soldier early perceived the quality of the lectures: Erwin Rommel, Wavell's famous and formidable opponent, acquired a copy of the German translation, read it carefully and annotated it. In his campaign in the Western Desert he carried it about with him in the field to the end.[11]

General Denis Bernard, the Commander of the 3rd Division, was appointed Governor and Commander-in-Chief of Bermuda in early 1939.

"When I was asked at the selection board whom I wanted to succeed Bernard in the 3rd Division, I replied at once—'Monty.' There was something like a sigh of relief from the other Army Commanders and instant acquiescence. Monty's name had come up several times before in front of the selection board; everyone always agreed that he ought to be promoted, but every other commander who had a vacancy for a major-general had always excellent reasons for finding someone else more suitable than Monty. I never had any doubts about his ability and also I liked him and was not afraid of his independent ideas and ways, which I could control."

In March, 1939, there was held the last major peacetime exercise in which Wavell took part. At his insistence it consisted of a careful study of the close support of land by air forces. His verdict on it was withering:

"It . . . showed conclusively that the R.A.F. had given little or no thought to the problem of close support of ground operations, that their pilots had not been trained to this form of war, and that the results on the targets provided were extremely poor in consequence. This was less than six months before the outbreak of war. I doubt whether the exercise occasioned even a ripple of thought about close support to pass over the minds of the Air Staff, but if I had remained in England and war had not come I intended to follow it up."

It was, however, no longer a matter of "if" war would come, but "when." Every week that passed men reckoned to be a week saved from the disaster that loomed. In March the last "rump" of Czechoslovakia was incorporated in a German protectorate. Nazi pressure was now put on Poland, as it had been put a year earlier on Czechoslovakia. At the end of the month the British and French Governments gave their pledge of support to Poland in the event of a German attack. A fortnight later similar guarantees were given to Roumania and Greece. Tardy and futile negotiations were entered into with Soviet Russia. The Territorial Army was redoubled in numbers. Conscription in Britain was introduced for the first time in peace. Some of the equipment, some of the guns that had been so blatantly missing in September, 1938, went out to formations. In the King's Birthday Honours a K.C.B. was awarded to Lieutenant-General A. P. Wavell. His old friend and former G.S.O.1, George Giffard, now Military Secretary at the War Office, wrote to him on 6th July on behalf of the C.I.G.S. asking him whether he would like to be considered for the appointment of General Officer Commanding-in-Chief, Middle East.

This was the most important though not the last great watershed. He had reached it in his fifty-seventh year. Of all the consequences that were to flow from it, of victory and defeat, of achievement and sorrow, he had mercifully no foreknowledge. He made his decision calmly and quickly, with no hesitation and no reluctance. War with Germany was imminent, as he was well aware, within a matter of months at most (it proved to be weeks). He knew the countries of the Middle East well and was interested in them, and to that extent believed himself as well qualified as any other senior officer in the Army. By the sheer fact of distance, it was bound to give him a degree of independence of command, which he always wanted and which (if he stopped at Salisbury) as a Corps Commander in the B.E.F. he might never attain. He knew better than anybody else what a similar transfer had done for Allenby. He accepted the C.I.G.S.'s invitation.

His successor at Southern Command was to be Alan Brooke, and it was arranged that he should sail for Egypt at the end of July, the family following later. A day or two before he handed over his command, his A.D.C., Michael Fox, conscious of the after-effects of a long, rough guest night, accompanied Wavell on what proved to be the last of his habitual rides in England. It was a bland day of high summer, and they hacked across the Wiltshire meadows to meet a staff car and spend the day visiting troops. Wavell's horse was not, in Fox's view, a great performer. He was horrified to see the General put the animal, in cold blood, at a well-hung and sturdy five-barred gate. Three times Wavell attempted it, and three times the horse refused. At last Fox said icily, "I think I'll open the gate." The silence that greeted this remark was as icy, and lasted for an hour. Neither of them ever referred to the incident thereafter.

Wavell left London on 27th July to join the P. & O. liner *Comorin* at Marseilles. He wrote in 1946:

"So ended my last year of peace and the old, pleasant, comfortable life of soldiering and sport in England. I think it is most unlikely that I shall ever hunt again in England; I shall have neither the money nor the nerve, even if hunting goes on. Nor will the shooting ever be on the same scale, or the pleasant hospitality of country houses. And I have done with soldiering."

In July, 1939, four inconceivably arduous and eventful years of soldiering lay ahead of him, with no respite, incessant toil, endless journeying, and every kind of challenge and ordeal. This was the moment to which, in the cold light of history, all his career hitherto had been only a prelude. He did not go to his fate with a light or eager heart—the season for such feelings was gone for him—but rather, like Stevenson's Lord Hermiston, "on he went up the great, bare staircase of his duty, uncheered and undepressed."

BOOK TWO

VII

Watching Brief

Wavell took up his appointment in Cairo on 2nd August, 1939. In time of peace he was to exercise general control over all British land forces in Egypt, the Sudan, Palestine and Transjordan, and Cyprus; his official instructions informed him that, if war broke out, the area of his Command would be extended to include British Somaliland, Aden, Iraq and the shores of the Persian Gulf.

Politically, it was his duty to keep in close touch with the senior officials who represented the British Government in this vast area; he was on a basis of equality with them; he was not under their authority, and they were not subordinate to him. They included the Ambassadors in Cairo and Baghdad; the High Commissioner in Palestine and Transjordan; the Governor-General in the Sudan; and the Governor of Cyprus. Some of these were responsible to the Foreign Office, others to the Colonial Office. Both departments had strong views on British policy in the Middle East, which they never hesitated to express.

Militarily, he was responsible—subject to the directions of the Chiefs of Staff and the War Office, and in conjunction with the two naval Commanders-in-Chief in the Mediterranean and the East Indies Station, and the Air Officer Commanding-in-Chief, Middle East—for co-ordinating the British war plans with those of Britain's allies in the Near and Middle East and North Africa, France, Turkey, and possibly Greece and Roumania.

He was to have from the beginning a small personal and operational staff; the Commanders-in-Chief of the three Services were to have a Joint Planning Staff, the three principal members of which would be their respective chief staff officers; and the Committee of Imperial Defence authorised the establishment in Cairo of a Middle East Intelligence Centre, whose information would be at the disposal of all three Commanders-in-Chief. There were six planners, and Wavell's own staff, as originally envisaged, was to number five, in addition to his A.D.C. "Such," he wrote, "was the start of an organisation which eventually expanded to hundreds of officers and men, and with which I handled something like a million men."

His directive gave only the barest, most skeletal indication of what his responsibilities would become. At the heart of every challenge he faced during the two years in which he held command in the Middle East was a political problem, almost always of extreme complexity; yet politically he was not, and could never expect to be, a free agent, except in the event of total disaster overwhelming the Government of which he was the loyal and obedient servant.

However, whatever internal sources of danger there might be in his Command seemed to be latent and easily containable in August, 1939. Germany did not appear to offer any immediate threat; however far-reaching the Nazis' dreams of world conquest, thousands of miles of sea and land, and the armies, air forces and navies of many nations, lay between them and fulfilment. How swiftly they could move, and how thin was the screen that their opponents could offer, history had yet to disclose. Therefore such external danger as existed was supplied by Italy, whose empire bordered on Egypt in the north and west, and on the Sudan, British Somaliland and Kenya in the south and east; and how Italy would act was by no means yet clear. Efforts made earlier in the year by Neville Chamberlain and Lord Halifax to appease Mussolini and prise Italy away from the Axis had failed; but a hope still lingered, in the Cabinet and in the Foreign Office, that they might in the end prove a success if nothing were done to "provoke" Italy.

On 31st July, 1939, Wavell wrote a short appreciation setting out for himself and for the C.I.G.S. what he believed ought to be the basis of his work in the Middle East Command, and stressing its objects and its importance:

> Our enemies have the initiative, so that consideration of their aims and intentions must be our starting point. Germany, as a step to world power, intends to dominate Eastern and S.E. Europe. Italy, her jackal, hopes with her aid to dominate the Mediterranean and North Africa. But Germany, the predominant partner of the Axis, is entirely selfish and is contemptuous of Italy except as a tool. Her aims and interests will certainly come first and will control the strategy of the Axis.

After a brief analysis of the possible courses of action open to Germany, he reached the conclusion—*before the Russo-German Pact dan before the declaration of war on Poland*—that the Nazis had realised that their next step would mean war, and that therefore they must have considered the advisability of using their superior preparedness in a swift advance south-eastwards, taking Poland and Roumania and aiming at the Dardanelles. He continued:

German strategy in the West is likely to be defensive. . . . The Eastern Mediterranean and not the Western Front will be the decisive theatre, where German plans must be countered.

What concerns us first, then, is the use Germany is likely to make of Italy in her plans. It may suit her to keep Italy neutral at the beginning; unless she really believes Italy capable of capturing Egypt or of controlling the Mediterranean. A neutral, but potentially hostile, Italy would contain just as much of our forces, would prevent us using the Mediterranean freely, and would keep open for Germany a line of supply against the blockade, so long as we allow it. It might give Germany time to complete her plans in S.E. Europe without the risk of exposing her weaker partner to defeat.

We must aim at placing ourselves in a sufficiently strong position in the Mediterranean to issue an ultimatum to Italy and force her to declare her intentions at once.

But whether Italy is openly hostile or nominally neutral, our only possible counter to the German intention to bring S.E. Europe under her power is by a domination of the Mediterranean at least as complete as in the Great War *as early as possible*. If not within the first month or two of war, it may be too late. . . .

The last war was won in the West. . . . The next war will be won or lost in the Mediterranean; and the longer it takes us to secure effective control of the Mediterranean, the harder will the winning of the war be.

The task of the Staff of the Middle East Command is therefore to plan, in conjunction with the other Services, not merely the defence of Egypt and our other interests in the Middle East, but such measures of offence as will enable us and our Allies to dominate the Mediterranean at the earliest possible moment; and thereafter to take the counter-offensive against Germany in Eastern and S.E. Europe.

Wavell went on to outline the steps necessary to achieve this highly desirable end. They were four, as he saw them. First there was the task of making certain that Egypt and the Canal, which would be the base of all the Allied effort in this theatre of war, were secure. This included: a defence of the Western Desert, along the frontier with Italian-ruled Libya, where he was even then sure that a bold, forward policy would be the best defence; air defence, both passive and active; measures to counter enemy propaganda, espionage and sabotage; and propaganda in Britain's favour in Egypt and elsewhere. Second, action to clear the Red Sea; and third, similar action to clear the Eastern Mediterranean. Fourth and finally, there was the consideration of eventual land action in S.E. Europe, Thrace, Salonika, Roumania, or in Russia. It was very possible, Wavell thought, that the war would develop into land battles on these fronts, in which British intervention might be necessary; a study of them, therefore, particularly of their lines of communication, would be required. He concluded with a paragraph or two setting out his own personal plans, and the allocation of duties to his staff.

This appreciation—in itself clear proof that Wavell was the opposite of rigid in outlook, cautious and unimaginative—was the foundation of his thinking from the first day he spent in Cairo; but he had to busy himself endlessly with make-do-and-mend and the prosaic details of housekeeping on a pitifully economical margin. His first problem, which was to harass him during all the years in which he held high command, was that of his own mobility—or rather, the lack of it. He wrote the first of many demi-official letters to the C.I.G.S.

A. P. Wavell to Lord Gort   *3rd August, 1939*
. . . I feel sure that it is essential that I should have a special machine here at my disposal to take me about, with good speed and radius, and a capacity for carrying three or four passengers and some luggage. The R.A.F. suggest a Lockheed 14. I am sending a cable home about this and hope that you will strongly urge the Air Ministry to provide it.

A week later, having been to Aden to see the naval C.-in-C. of the East Indies Station, who along with the A.O.C.-in-C. was all in favour of quick, aggressive action against the Italians in Eritrea the moment hostilities should begin, Wavell reverted to the theme of transport for himself, as he was to do again and again until he realised that it was quite useless.

A. P. Wavell to Lord Gort   *10th August, 1939*

I got back late last night from Aden. It took me 44 hours flying in an ancient Valentia to get there and back, which a modern machine could do quite easily in less than half the time. I could thus have saved two whole days, besides a great deal of discomfort. It is intolerable that I should have to go about in such an ancient machine; there were times when in a head wind we were doing under 70 m.p.h.!

I hope you will see that I am provided with a modern machine for use of myself and my staff as early as possible; it will be quite impossible to do this job properly otherwise. . . .

But during the whole time he held this command, he was not to have an aircraft of his own; he had always to travel by any troop-carrier, bomber or other service machine that happened to be available. He resigned himself to the consequent delays and difficulties; but if instead of this niggardly refusal to give him the mobility he needed he had had the lavish use of aircraft taken for granted by higher commanders later in the war, the effects on the conduct of his campaigns might have been considerable.

The triumvirate, consisting of the C.-in-C. in the Mediterranean, Admiral Sir Andrew Cunningham, Wavell, and the A.O.C.-in-C. Middle East, Air Chief Marshal Sir William Mitchell, who formed the effective High Command in this theatre, had their first official meeting on board H.M.S. *Warspite* in Alexandria harbour on 18th August. It became apparent from their discussions that all three Services were without any detailed instructions as to their action in the event of war; but they set up and gave their terms of reference to a Joint Planning Committee, who held their first meeting three days later.

Wavell's representative on the committee was his B.G.S., Arthur Smith. He described Smith as "a very fine character indeed, a charming personality and an excellent staff officer . . . very conscientious and accurate, had a delightful sense of humour, was the very soul of honour and uprightness, organised a staff well and ran an extremely happy show."[1]

Notwithstanding Wavell's correct forecast that Italy would not come into the war at once, he was faced, on two fronts, by Italian forces which, though their fighting quality was highly debatable, were in sheer numbers far more than he would be able to muster for many months.

To the west, Italy had nine divisions in Tripoli, and five in Cyrenaica, totalling, it was estimated, some 215,000 men. Against this sizeable army Wavell had the 7th Armoured Division (formerly the Mobile Division), still without enough men or vehicles, and not fully trained; twenty-one infantry battalions in Egypt and Palestine; two regiments of cavalry (still with their horses) and four of artillery, possessing between them sixty-four field guns, forty-eight anti-tank guns and eight A.A. guns. In the middle of August there arrived the welcome first of many invaluable contributions to the defence of the Middle East by India in the shape of the 11th Indian Infantry Brigade of the 4th Indian Division.[2] The rest of the division was to follow later. Even so, the Italians had on this front a potential numerical superiority of four to one, despite which there was every indication that they had neither the will nor the capacity to take the offensive.

The other great concentration of Italian force was in the south-east, in Italian East Africa (Eritrea, Italian Somaliland and the recently conquered but far from totally subjugated Ethiopia), where the Duke of Aosta, the Viceroy, had about a quarter of a million troops under his command, with some 400 field and mountain guns, 200 light tanks and 100 armoured cars. In the event of war this force could be, and ultimately was, cut off from its home base and subjected to an intensive siege. But the threat which it presented in August, 1939, to the virtually defenceless ring of Allied dependencies around it was formidable. For in the Sudan there were no more than three British infantry battalions and some twenty companies of the Sudan Defence Force; in British Somaliland there was the Sudan Camel Corps, a gendarmerie of some 500 men, mounted on camels and under the command of British officers; in French Somaliland, whose port and capital, Jibuti, was the seaward terminus of the only railway from Addis Ababa, there were some 5,000 native troops; in Kenya there were two brigades of the King's African Rifles (native troops under British officers) and two light batteries; and Aden was garrisoned by two Indian battalions.

As the final diplomatic crisis approached, the three Commanders-in-Chief took all the preliminary precautions they could, conscious that the Government were insisting on their being as non-provocative as possible. The Royal Navy had a considerable fleet assembled at

Alexandria. From 20th August this was ready for action. On 23rd August the Admiralty assumed control of merchant shipping; dawn and dusk patrols were inaugurated by the Fleet Air Arm off the port, and the channels were swept for mines. The R.A.F. mustered its ninety first-line bombers and its seventy-five fighters (which included one Egyptian Air Force squadron of Gladiators for the defence of Cairo).

By the 28th Wavell's forces were in position. Under the operational command of his close friend, General Maitland Wilson, the bulk of the infantry was in the Delta, the 7th Armoured Division was in the Western Desert between Mersa Matruh and Ma'aten Bagush, and there were some armoured cars at Sidi Barrani and Sollum. An infantry brigade was held in Palestine as a general reserve, and the patrolling of the Libyan-Egyptian frontier was almost entirely in the hands of Egyptian troops. It would have been difficult for the Italians to regard these arrangements as provocative.

A. P. Wavell to Lord Gort   *2nd September, 1939*
We seem to be making a rather pompous, long-winded, old-fashioned entry into this war, compared with Herr Hitler's summary methods. It looks from here rather like going through the old elaborate salute of the fencing school when facing a ruffian with a gangster-gun. However, I dare say it may help our cause in the end to have observed all the international courtesies and the *"tirez-vous-les-premiers-Messieurs-les-Boches"* sort of spirit.

All three Services here feel a little exercised over the attitude which it has apparently been decided to adopt towards Italy— I say "apparently" for we have no official guidance, except that we are to avoid irritating them. I do hope you will impress on the "frocks" (as Henry Wilson used to call them) the dangers from a military point of view of an undefined and unconditional neutrality for Italy. For instance: is she to be allowed to reinforce Libya *ad lib.*, so to speak; or to build up her stocks of aeroplane fuel and munitions in East Africa; and are her submarines to roam the seas unchecked, or to be sold to Germany and manned by German crews; or her bombers to threaten Cairo and Alexandria indefinitely? Is her propaganda to be unchecked? Are Italian civil air-lines to be allowed to continue to operate in Egypt? Egyptian nerves are not likely to stand the strain of waiting as well as we can. So that from our point of view the sooner Italy is asked to define where she stands and to give pledges the better. At present the Egyptians seem in good heart and very anxious to co-operate. . . .

On 3rd September Neville Chamberlain announced in the House of Commons and in a broadcast that a formal declaration of war upon Germany had been made. Italy for the time being remained a non-belligerent. So did Egypt, whose main anxiety was to get an assurance that there were enough British forces in the country to make the Italians frightened to attack. The principal strategic and political issues outside Egypt's borders which now confronted Wavell were: political and military liaison with the French; relations with Turkey; the necessity of keeping the Arabs friendly; and, across the Mediterranean, the possibility of a thrust by the Germans south-eastwards through the Balkans.

As soon as the war began Lord Gort was appointed C.-in-C. of the British Expeditionary Force in France, and General Sir Edmund Ironside became C.I.G.S.

C.I.G.S. to A. P. Wavell   *11th September, 1939*
. . . Our strategy in the Middle East must be Imperial strategy and it is important that it should never be subordinated to French command. The Suez Canal is in the centre of the British Empire, and it is the British Fleet which controls the eastern end of the Mediterranean. In the area comprising Iraq, Palestine and Egypt we can concentrate all the Regular forces which we may be able to strip from India and also any Australian, New Zealand and South African contingents which may come to our help.

There lies north of Syria—Turkey. The Turkish Army is a formidable body of troops. If Turkey comes in against the Germans there is no possibility of Turkey being overrun such as there is in a country like Roumania whose army is not of high value.

Our policy is therefore to develop our military strategy with Turkey, if possible, for the defence of her territory. Whether the defence of Turkey will require allied operations in Greece is a matter which can not yet be determined. Many political, naval, etc., factors are involved and the situation at the moment is too fluid for a decision to be reached. It is quite certain, however, that at the present time, when we are very definitely on the defensive, we must refuse to become involved in operations in Greece which have any aim beyond the direct defence of Turkey.

After the German conquest of Poland, the British Cabinet and Chiefs of Staff thought a threat to the Balkans likely to be the next move. Against it, and against the long-range danger of the whole Allied position in the Middle East, Turkey was regarded as the great bulwark. The French agreed in general with this view. However, on the advice of the veteran General Weygand, who had been appointed C.-in-C. in Syria and the Lebanon (he passed through Cairo on his way to take up his appointment, and won Wavell's admiration for his sagacity and *élan*), they considered that Salonika might well prove to be the key point and that its defence would be vital to the conduct of the war. It was therefore now necessary to co-ordinate the British and French negotiations with Turkey, which had hitherto been conducted independently. Wavell was ordered to hold himself in readiness to visit Ankara, in order to sign a treaty of mutual assistance between the United Kingdom, France and Turkey.

He sent Arthur Smith to London on the first of a number of liaison journeys. Smith achieved much that was of value for the Command as a whole, but failed to obtain from the Chiefs of Staff and the Cabinet a clear decision as to what fighting policy was to be adopted, offensive or defensive. If it was to be offensive, there were many glaring deficiencies in land and air forces, and in the administrative facilities which both needed. If defensive, Wavell thought that he could manage for the time being with what he had, provided that the worst shortages—for example, in anti-aircraft—could be made good. On 14th October the C.I.G.S. signalled him that a defensive policy was to be maintained in the Western Desert and that his demands for forces and for administrative developments were to be based on this decision.

With this instruction in mind, Wavell went to Ankara on 18th October, and there with Weygand initialled the treaty of mutual assistance. Weygand, eager for a forward policy in the Balkans, demanded two days' more military conversations. But, Wavell wrote, "as I had hardly any troops in the Middle East at that time, I could not make much of a contribution to any plans and contented myself mainly with a watching brief."

Holding a watching brief, politically and strategically, was Wavell's principal occupation in the weeks and months that followed. His aggressive inclinations and the streak of the gambler in him had to be subordinated to the painstaking and efficient administrator. A large and complicated military machine had to be built up from its foundations, in the midst of a society which was neither geared for war nor emotionally committed to the causes for which the war was to be fought. Wavell suggested to the C.I.G.S. that he should fly home on a short visit to discuss a working policy for the next six months.

The determination of the Wavell family not to be separated now asserted itself resolutely. Archie John, not yet fully recovered from his Palestine wound, was posted to a Black Watch Territorial battalion in Scotland; but Lady Wavell, her three daughters and Nannie all made their way to Cairo. General Maitland Wilson had a big, pleasant house on the edge of the race-course at Gezira which he agreed to share with the Wavells, an arrangement which persisted as long as he and Wavell held their respective appointments in this theatre of war. Lady Wavell took on the responsibility of organising a notable array of troops' amenities in and around Cairo, and the girls went to work in various branches of a rapidly growing G.H.Q., and to nurse in a base hospital.

His friendship with Jumbo Wilson was one of the most important in Wavell's career. Imposing in stature, shrewd, clear-headed and massively calm in manner, Wilson proved himself a rock of strength as a subordinate commander. Through nearly two years of changing fortunes, through great victories and harsh setbacks, the two men maintained the closest intellectual understanding and personal sympathy.

As he himself had urged, Wavell was summoned to London for consultations. He wanted to go by way of Algiers to meet General Noguès, his opposite number in French North Africa, but was ordered to go straight home. General Weygand, he was told, was to be in France at the same time, and there was to be an Allied conference on the Middle East in Paris, which both would attend. By the time he reached England on 6th December the Chiefs of Staff had completed a review of military policy in the Middle East. They held that:

in view of the weakness of the Allied air forces and anti-aircraft artillery it could not be said that British interests were secure against Italian attack. If Germany or Russia were to begin determined offensive operations in the Middle East it would be necessary to provide additional land and air forces to defend our interests and to prevent the defeat of Turkey. If Italian hostility were added to German or Russian aggression, we should have to deal with the Italian fronts before we could give any assistance to Greece or Turkey. Apart from the salutary political effect of a show of force there were therefore good reasons for building up our forces, but this ought not to be done at the expense of essential requirements in Western Europe or of the ability to defend Singapore. Moreover, it would be useless to add considerably to the forces without first developing the bases and communications which would sustain their operations. This administrative development, it was realised, would—particularly in respect of the land forces—be a more lengthy process than the actual concentration of troops and air forces. It ought therefore to be put in hand at once, so that if the strategical situation were to require the despatch of additional forces these would be able to function with the least possible delay.[3]

To Wavell, a journey of ten nights there and back, for five days in London and two in Paris, hardly seemed worth all the trouble. "I was never out of London while in England and hardly ever outside the War Office." All his working conversations were with Ironside, of whom he said: "Our relations were always friendly . . . but I do not think his judgment was sound. . . . I cannot remember that our discussions on the Middle East situation bore much fruit. But he talked to me a good deal about iron ore from Norway and the importance of denying it to Germany."

During what ought to have been a crucial visit, he met no Minister except Hore-Belisha; and the Chiefs of Staff review of policy in the Middle East was not considered and approved by the Cabinet until more than a month had elapsed. But he did accompany the Chiefs of Staff, Ironside, Admiral Pound and Air Chief Marshal Newall, and the Secretary of the Committee of Imperial Defence, General Ismay, when they went to confer with their opposite numbers, Gamelin, Darlan, Weygand and Vuillemin at the Château de Vincennes near Paris on 11th December.[4] Wavell found Weygand a valuable ally in his battle against strategic and tactical supineness. Together they advocated a forward policy in the Balkans to forestall German penetration. But the weight of opinion at the conference was against them. Nothing must be done, it was insisted, that might antagonise Italy; therefore nothing at all must be done.

Wavell argued that it was practically certain that the Allies would be called upon to defend their interests in the Balkans in 1940. They should begin by getting Turkey's support, and possibly by occupying Salonika. He added that he believed that the Germans would attack the rear and the bases from the air, and that therefore the first demand would be for fighter aircraft. His own forces, he concluded, were still immobile for lack of administrative services, and were particularly weak in artillery.[5]

Around the conference table, with the wintry light filtering into the great hall of the château, everyone was very cordial, but saw no possibility of doing anything active. Weygand spoke for Wavell as much as for himself when he summed up: "You are all prepared to be the sympathetic friends who sit by the sick man's bedside. I want to be the doctor who cures him before he gets any worse."

The following morning Wavell flew from Paris to Algiers, and next day on to Tunis, where he met Noguès, of whom he formed a favourable opinion, and was shown and impressed by the Mareth Line. He was held up because "the very haphazard British air service had gone wrong." Exasperated by the delay, he signalled to the War Office that he proposed to use the very efficient Italian service to Cairo via Tripoli. A scurry of alarm produced him an aircraft which got him back to his headquarters on 19th December.

Of this frustrating period he wrote: "I thought the policy of doing nothing whatever that could annoy the Italians—appeasement, in fact —quite misguided. I was allowed to send no agents into Italian territory, though all our territories were full of Italian agents, to do nothing to get in touch with the Abyssinian rebels, and so on. Meanwhile stores continued to pass through the Suez Canal to Italian East Africa, and we even continued under a pre-war agreement to inform the Italians of our reinforcements to Middle East. . . .

"It took six months to get sanction for the raising of an additional battalion of the Sudan Defence Force; it took two months to get permission to move a battalion from East Africa to Somaliland; and three or four months for leave to spend a few thousand pounds on defences and roads in Somaliland.

"All the Governors were obstructive in the matter of my passing agents. . . . They all suspected me of trying to stir up trouble on their borders and of making things difficult for them."

On 15th January, 1940, the War Cabinet laid down future policy for the Middle East. For Wavell's forces their directions were that only formations already under orders for this theatre should be sent: one Australian and the First Cavalry Division to Palestine, and one New Zealand division to Egypt. A base organisation was to be built in Egypt and Palestine and preparations were to be made to equip and maintain ultimately a force of nine divisions. One division, already offered by India, would defend the Anglo-Persian oilfields. Three Indian divisions should be trained and equipped in India to fight in Iraq and Persia, and Basra should be developed as their base and port. Since traffic in the Red Sea was likely to be interrupted, the overland route from Baghdad to Haifa, which Wavell himself had surveyed in the nineteen-thirties, was to be further improved. One more battalion was to be raised for the Sudan Defence Force; and two brigades of the Royal West African Frontier Force should be transferred from West Africa to Kenya.

Wavell was now to assume command of British land forces in East Africa and British Somaliland, and of any that might be sent to Turkey or the Balkans, including Greece. If major operations occurred in or near Iraq, Aden or the shores of the Persian Gulf, he was to command the land forces involved. Since he did not, at that time, possess the staff to enable him immediately to discharge all these duties, he was told that he would be "free to assume administrative control in the several areas of his Command in accordance with the situation and the means at his disposal." His title was altered to "Commander-in-Chief, Middle East."[6]

His reactions to the Cabinet directive were set out in an appreciation of 26th January. His principal conclusions, based on the premise that Italy was about to enter the war on Germany's side, were that (1) in the defence against ground attack the situation was, with the exception of British Somaliland, "remarkably satisfactory"; (2) in defence against air attack it was "very greatly to our disadvantage"; (3) so far as counter-attack was concerned, "no offensive against Libya would be possible without a long period of preparation and the allotment of considerable additional resources. It would seem advisable to leave this colony to be reduced by blockade"; (4) against Italian East Africa, "various plans have been considered with the general conclusion that a ground offensive on any large scale could only be undertaken from Jibuti in the general direction of Harar and Jijiga. Preparations for rebellion against the Italians in the west and south of Abyssinia had been put in hand; it was therefore most important that the political basis of propaganda against Italy in Abyssinia should

221

be decided; (5) the Turks were understood to have plans for capturing the Dodecanese Islands (then in Italian occupation), for which they would have to rely very largely on British help. The naval aspect of any war against Italy would be bound to be the most important, very considerable naval reinforcements would be required, and superiority in the air would be an essential for any offensive operations against Italy.

There were inconclusive discussions with both the Turks and the French at a conference in Cairo in February and another at Aleppo in March. The C.I.G.S. remained anxious about French aspirations, diplomatic as well as military, throughout the whole area, and warned Wavell against agreeing to any arrangement which might further these aspirations. Weygand and Wavell continued to keep in touch and on good terms with each other; but as their earlier shared hopes of swift, daring and co-ordinated action faded, each turned to concentrate on the increasing internal problems of his own Command.

Wavell's administrative preparations were well in hand: tele-communications, water, petrol, medical services, the expansion of ports and docks, railways, new roads, permanent base camps, training schools, vehicle repair and maintenance depots, the building of air-fields, ammunition depots, gun parks, bakeries, canteens, cinemas and mobile bath units. On the foundations of the small-scale facilities required to sustain a peacetime garrison, a great base, capable of servicing forces which were envisaged even then as ultimately totalling some 300,000 men, was built. The fighting efficiency of field forces, mechanised to an extent never previously known in the history of the country, and operating thousands of miles overseas, was entirely dependent on the adequate fuelling, replacement, repair and main-tenance of its vehicles, both A.F.V.s and lorries. To have cheese-pared would have been disastrous. In the first of his Lees-Knowles lectures Wavell said that administration and logistics were the crux of generalship. He did his best to put this dictum into practice in the Middle East; and he was fortunate in having, in his chief admini-strative officer, General Sir Balfour Hutchison, one of his most reliable and efficient subordinates.

Meanwhile he had his first reinforcements: cavalry from the United Kingdom, a British infantry battalion from the Far East, a brigade from Australia and a brigade from New Zealand. Mr. Anthony Eden, who had re-entered the Government immediately after the out-break of war and was now Secretary of State for the Dominions, flew out in mid-February to greet the Australians and New Zealanders. He and Wavell had not met before. Despite differences in age, background and temperament, the two men took to each other and became firm friends. Eden's outlook had been profoundly affected by service in the First World War; and Wavell warmed towards him as to no other politician. They went together to the training camp at Gaza, in Palestine, to see the new arrivals in a theatre of war with which their fathers and elder brothers had become very familiar a quarter of a century earlier. Wavell kept the notes of the address he made to the young Australians; five years later, when he made a collection of his wartime speeches, practically all written in haste and at short notice (he described them as "snapshots of my mind, not posed photographs"), he began with these notes. He treated his audience as intelligent participants in a joint enterprise, and sketched out for them as candidly as he would for the C.I.G.S. the various possibilities of operational use to which the force which was now building up in the Middle East might be put. The field was wide indeed and, he said, it was impossible to foretell what might happen. He concluded:

I should like to try to impress on you what this war means, not only to Great Britain, not only to the British Empire, but to the whole civilised world. You do not, perhaps, realise as we do, owing to your remoteness from Europe, what we are up against in the Nazi attempt to dominate the world. The issue of this struggle is absolutely vital to everything that we, and other democracies, hold most important: freedom of speech, freedom of thought, justice, toleration, and a decent standard of life. We are fighting a crusade which is far more important than all the crusades which were led against this country of Palestine nearly a thousand years ago.[7]

In the second week of March Wavell went to East Africa and on to South Africa to meet Smuts and to find out what contribution the Union could make, in men and material, to the defence of the Middle East. Back in Cairo, he summed up some of his impressions for Ironside, and added a reflection or two on the general course of the war.

A. P. Wavell to C.I.G.S.   *3rd April, 1940*
. . . I have never met Smuts before and was most impressed and

attracted. . . . I was impressed by what I saw of the South African Defence Forces. They seem to be making a big effort to produce a military force out of very little, and to be doing it very efficiently. . . .

How far Smuts and the Government can commit Union forces to the war I am naturally unable to say. But we should do everything possible to encourage the effort they are making. I believe that if Italy came into the war against us, South Africa would fight her "all out" anywhere in Africa. I think it is quite possible that the South African Air Force might eventually be placed at our disposal anywhere in the Middle East. But of course all depends on Smuts retaining health and power.

. . . Quite frankly, our policy seems undecided and hesitating, with the result that valuable time is being lost. . . . So long as Italy's hostility is possible we must continue to take all reasonable precautions, and to take them without undue delay. We have a lot of troops locked up in defence against Italy, but small additions to increase their security are only met, it appears to us, slowly and grudgingly when met at all. . . .

I think patience and preparation must be our watchwords for 1940; we are little better prepared for a big effort than we were in 1915. Certainly the Middle East will not be really ready for war much before the end of the year. . . .

Of two things about Russia I am certain: firstly, that her policy will be completely selfish and unscrupulous and will favour Germany only so far as her own interests are served; secondly, that it will puzzle even Germans to make Russian economy efficient and productive.

On 9th April the Chiefs of Staff told the Commander-in-Chief in the Middle East that, although relations with the Italians had become more uncertain, it was felt that no important moves by them were likely at the moment. On that same day German forces occupied Copenhagen and Oslo, Stavanger, Bergen, Trondheim and Narvik. The Danish Government capitulated; the Norwegian King and Government, though fugitives, resisted bravely and appealed to the Allies for help. The phoney war had been brought abruptly and ruthlessly to its end.

The first effect of the lamentable Norwegian campaign on the Middle East was to commit the Royal Navy to such extensive and costly operations (in ships and men) in northern waters that there were no spare forces at all for the Mediterranean, and it was suggested that the French might be asked to assume all naval responsibility in this theatre. Fortunately this came to nothing; but with Hitler's swift Scandinavian successes in mind, it was certain that Mussolini could not much longer be restrained from coming into the war.

A. P. Wavell to C.I.G.S.   *15th April, 1940*
. . . The C.-in-C. Mediterranean, A.O.C.-in-C. and myself have had a general discussion on war with Italy. . . .

It was obvious that we had little or no knowledge of the general Allied appreciation and plan for war against Italy, naval, military or air.

Some of the factors which have an essential importance for the Middle East are:

  a. To what extent air action will be taken against objectives in Italy itself. This will determine the extent to which Italian air forces are likely to be available to reinforce Libya;

  b. The plans for French action, by air and land, against Tripoli. It is understood that the French offensive, which was intended had Italy entered the war from the first, is now in abeyance;

  c. Whether action against Libya or the Dodecanese would be the primary commitment of any forces that become available for offensive action against Italy.

The C.-in-C. Mediterranean considers that from the naval point of view the reduction of Libya is of the greatest importance, to enable the route through the Mediterranean to be re-opened as early as possible.

From the military point of view, no offensive action against Libya would be possible without very extensive administrative preparations requiring many months. From the point of view of assistance to Turkey and action in the Balkans, the attack and neutralisation of the Dodecanese would be of greater value.

Action enabling the Red Sea route to be opened as soon as possible would be a primary requirement.

Military action in the Middle East with Italy hostile is bound to be mainly defensive for some time, whereas given adequate forces offensive naval and air action can be taken. It is therefore

W.   225   H essential to know what naval and air forces will be available to meet Italian hostility.

A signal from the Chiefs of Staff crossed with this letter. The three Commanders-in-Chief were given no direct or clear instructions at all. It was as difficult to get a grip on the intentions of the Chiefs of Staff as to understand the oracle at Delphi. One paragraph alone had any practical meaning, and it too was vaguely phrased: "The principle of a French offensive action against Libya would be maintained particularly in the case of an Italian attack against Egypt and an action of this nature should be combined with a rising to be stirred up in Abyssinia."

The time of preparation was running out fast, and belated efforts were now being made to inject some vigour into the administration of the war effort in London. A Military Co-ordination Committee, with the Prime Minister as chairman and consisting of a number of Cabinet Ministers and the Chiefs of Staff, had been in existence for some weeks. At the outset Chamberlain delegated the chairmanship to the First Lord of the Admiralty, Winston Churchill; but feeling that Churchill drove the Service advisers too hard in a zestful search for new moves, new methods and new men, he took over again in mid-April. At the same time he decided to double-bank the hard-pressed Chiefs of Staff by appointing Vice-Chiefs, who could act in their seniors' absence and could also shoulder some of the burden of departmental work. The new V.C.I.G.S. was General Sir John Dill, who was brought back from commanding a corps in France because the Prime Minister had long wanted to avail himself of his wisdom and judgment. Meetings of the Vice-Chiefs counted as meetings of the C.O.S. Committee; the first of them was held on Tuesday, 27th April. Next day Wavell sent Dill a signal of welcome, and added some information about his Command:

> Things are progressing quite well out here, but slowly. I am frankly alarmed at the slowness and heaviness with which our whole military machine still seems to move after nearly nine months of war. . . .
> I am also concerned with the complexity of our organisation and the size of our administrative requirements for even a comparatively small force. . . . It is a difficult matter to do much pruning; and I am always met with the argument that in nearly all

226

previous campaigns in this part of the world, our difficulties and defeats have been very largely due to the fact that the administrative requirements of the force were on an insufficient scale from the start.

I do not think personally that the Italians have really made up their minds to come in yet; but they would undoubtedly like to strengthen their position by imitating German action in the north by occupying Corfu or Crete, or by "protecting" Yugoslavia.

I have never ceased to state that the principal requirement in this part of the world is a stronger Air Force; and I have no doubt that it is realised, and will be remedied as soon as possible. Also the duality of Army and Air Force in this theatre raises all sorts of complications as regards planning . . . but I see no remedy to this at present.

At dawn on 10th May the Germans launched their assault on the Low Countries; and that evening—as the result of two days' fierce debate in the House of Commons—Neville Chamberlain resigned as Prime Minister and was succeeded by Winston Churchill. Britain's internal political crisis merged at once into the vast military challenge. Italy still teetered on the brink of war; but mobilisation orders went out for the Army, and the garrisons in Libya, Albania and the Dodecanese were all reinforced.

Within a week the magnitude of the imminent disaster in the Low Countries and France was revealed. It happened that two convoys bringing the second and third contingents of Australians and New Zealanders to the Middle East were now at sea. Both were capable of moving fast; but the Dominion Governments were worried lest hostilities with Italy should break out before they reached Suez, and the transports be caught, with little or no air cover, in the narrow waters of the Red Sea. However the first convoy, carrying the second brigade group of the 6th Australian Division, totalling some 7,000 troops, reached Suez safely on 17th May, and the men dispersed at once to their training areas. The second convoy, with some 15,000 men aboard, left Fremantle on 12th May. On the 15th it was decided by the Admiralty, in consultation with the Dominion Governments, to divert this convoy round the Cape to the United Kingdom; it eventually reached the Clyde on 16th June, the day on which German troops entered Paris.

227

On 18th May Wavell went up to Beirut to have conversations with the French and the Turks, in an atmosphere of mounting confusion. General Weygand had already departed for France to replace General Gamelin in command of all French land forces (he took up his appointment on 19th May), and his successor at the conference table, General Massuet, nominally commander of French mobile forces in the Levant, was a voluble, excitable man of inferior calibre. On Weygand's instructions he insisted that the first move to be made immediately upon the outbreak of war with Italy should be an attack on the Dodecanese by practically the whole Allied air strength. Both Wavell for the British and Marshal Cakmak for the Turks pointed out firmly that their respective air forces had other tasks of even higher priority elsewhere—in Libya and East Africa, in Thrace and the Caucasus.

Wavell, back in Cairo on the evening of 21st May, sent off an account of the discussions to Dill by the hand of one of his liaison officers, who flew next day to London.

Events in France and Flanders moved at breathtaking speed between the opening day of the Beirut conference and the liaison officer's arrival in London. The Germans, on the afternoon of 17th May, captured Brussels; during the 18th they passed swiftly through Cambrai, St. Quentin and Peronne, and thrust towards Arras and Amiens. The B.E.F. was far to the north, and by nightfall Lord Gort was considering withdrawing as large a proportion of forces as he could to Dunkirk. The Channel ports were in immediate danger. In London a new War Cabinet, galvanised by Churchill's leadership, confronted these dangers bravely; but the swift fate of Holland was to the fore in their minds. The immediate necessities of defence of the island itself were—rightly—of paramount importance to them all.

Prime Minister to General Ismay, for C.O.S.   *18th May, 1940*
I cannot feel that we have enough trustworthy troops in England, in view of the very large numbers that may be landed from air-carriers preceded by parachutists. I do not consider this danger is imminent at the present time, as the great battle in France has yet to be decided.

I wish the following moves to be considered with a view to immediate action:

    i. The transports which brought the Australians to Suez should bring home eight battalions of Regular infantry from Palestine, properly convoyed, even at some risk, by whatever route is thought best. I hope it will be possible to use the Mediterranean.

ii. The Australian fast convoy arrives early in June with 14,000 men.

iii. These ships should be immediately filled with eight battalions of Territorials and sent to India, where they should pick up eight [more] Regular battalions. The speed of this fast convoy should be accelerated. . . .[8]

A. P. Wavell to V.C.I.G.S.   *22nd May, 1940*

. . . Italy still seems to be hesitating on the brink, but I think must take the plunge soon. Musso looks to me rather like a man who has climbed up to the top diving board at a swimming pool, taken off his dressing-gown and thrown a chest to the people looking on. I think he must do something; if he cannot make a graceful dive, he will at least have to jump in somehow; he can hardly put on his dressing-gown and walk down the stairs again.

What his action against this country will be, no one can tell. I think it is quite likely that he will make no direct attack on it, at any rate at first. We can detect at present no signs of any aggressive attitude, or of Fifth Column methods. What the Egyptians will do is also doubtful. The Government has been, and is continuing to be, very helpful; but recent events in the West have undoubtedly shaken them for the time being. . . .

For a few critical weeks Wavell, with little more information than he could glean from the newspapers and the wireless, lived in a curious isolation, yet his own responsibilities loomed larger than ever before. If the war in the West continued to go as badly for the Allies as it had done since 10th May, and his temporary separation from his constitutional, political masters at home became permanent, what would be his fate and his duty?

On 24th May he set down his conclusions in his own handwriting on four sheets of foolscap. The first two pages, headed "The Worst Possible Case," read:

Germans obtain temporary air superiority in France. French collapse. B.E.F. cut off from Base and compelled to return U.K. with heavy losses.

U.K. in state of siege and subject to heavy bombing attacks.

M.E. cut off and attacked by Italy, supported perhaps by German air or troops.

Egpytians and other people of M.E. frightened, unfriendly or hostile.

We may have to maintain our position in Egypt by force, i.e. by declaring martial law and taking over country.

We might have anti-British rising in Iraq. Should we try and maintain position there or evacuate temporarily?

Should we try to hold Basra, or ask India to do so?

Palestine, Sudan, Kenya should be all right.

We might possibly have to evacuate Somaliland.

Aden must be held.

Problems at this stage.

Control of Egypt and specially of all transport.

Evacuation of women and children and if so where.

Collection of shipping and airplanes.

Egyptian army.

Whether and when to arm Jews.

Intentions of French in Syria.

Situation in India.

Then, under the heading "Worse Case Still," there followed:

German bombing makes U.K. untenable, Empire falls back to fight on line Canada—S. Africa—India—Malaya—Australia—N.Z.

Presumably it might be difficult to hold Egypt, Palestine and Cyprus and we might have to fall back on Sudan and Kenya.

Problems.

Keeping open Red Sea, this may mean combined attack on I.E.A.

Holding of Basra?

Evacuation of Palestine, by sea (possibility of using Aqaba?) by road to Egypt, to Baghdad, to Basra, to Kuwait, by rail to Egypt or Iraq.

Problem of Jews.

Evacuation of Egypt, by sea (if Red Sea open), by rail, by river.

4th Indian Divn.

Stores and munitions to be taken and left.

Belgian Congo.

Angola.

The final page was headed "Immediate Arrangements."

Plan to control Egypt.

Plan to seize all means of communication.

Census of numbers to be evacuated and capacity of means of movement.
Plan to transfer essential stores.

Information reqd.

Number of women to be evacuated.
Quantities of transport required.
Stores to be taken and left.
Time factor.

On 27th May General Dill was appointed C.I.G.S. in succession to
General Ironside, who took up the post of C.-in-C. Home Forces.
The liaison officer Wavell had sent to England was about to return.
Dill saw him and, in his presence, scribbled a short note.

My dear Archie,   *27th May, 1940*
      Very many thanks for your letter. . . . The men have been
grand but men with small arms can't stand up to tanks in their
hundreds. I have just taken over from Tiny today—but in what
conditions! No one is weakening in the slightest and I feel that
the nation will stand up to the situation when they know it as
soon they must.
      I have just got your message about being able to hold Africa.
That's splendid of you and if and when Musso tries to come the
jackal it will be a great relief to me and to all of us to know that
you are there.
      I have seen Weygand twice—a great little man!
      Bless you Archie.
                                                    Yours ever,
                                                         Jack

      By dawn of that day the greater part of the B.E.F. in northern
France had withdrawn within the perimeter of a narrow bridgehead
around the ancient port of Dunkirk. At 1 p.m. the C.I.G.S. sent a
signal to Gort telling him that his task thenceforward was "to evacuate
the maximum force possible." At 1857 hours a signal from the
Admiralty to Admiral Ramsay, commanding British naval forces at
Dover, initiated Operation Dynamo, which Churchill was later to
describe as "the Deliverance of Dunkirk."
      On that same day Wavell—not disregarding the worst possible
case but giving it the low priority it merited—wrote his own
appreciation:

THE POSITION—MAY 1940

1. Oil, shipping, air power, sea power are the keys to this war, and they are interdependent.

   Air power and naval power cannot function without oil.

   Oil, except in very limited quantities, cannot be brought to its destination without shipping.

   Shipping requires the protection of naval power and air power.

2. We have access to practically all the world's supplies of oil.

   We have most of the shipping.

   We have naval power.

   We have potentially the greatest air power, when fully developed.

   Therefore we are bound to win the war.

   Germany is very short of oil and has access only to very limited quantities.

   Germany's shipping is practically confined to the Baltic.

   Germany's naval power is small.

   Germany's air power is great but is a diminishing asset.

   Therefore Germany is bound to lose the war.

Within this strategic framework, Wavell perceived that the Allies' effort should be concentrated on (*a*) preventing the enemy from obtaining oil; (*b*) keeping the seas open to their own shipping and preventing the enemy from using them; and (*c*) building up their own air forces. The oil supplies which concerned Middle East Command were those of (*a*) South Persia and of Northern Iraq, which had to be protected for British use; (*b*) Baku, which Wavell rightly regarded as an enemy source, which might have to be attacked; and (*c*) Roumania, which was then a neutral source, which might have to be destroyed if the enemy tried to seize it. He assessed the importance (to the Allies and to the enemy) of the various sources of oil, and concluded:

The main tasks of Middle East may be: to prevent Roumanian oil reaching Germany as far as possible; and to safeguard Abadan and the South Persian oilfields.

This stresses the importance of (*a*) naval strength in the Mediterranean; (*b*) preparations in India to send a force quickly to Basra; (c) possibly, para-military operations against Roumanian oil.

As regards (b), we must have A.A. artillery to protect the refineries at Abadan, and this is not available at present.

On the following day, having heard that Dill had become C.I.G.S., Wavell wrote him a letter of congratulation and sympathy, and enclosed this appreciation. "We shall be all right," he told Dill, "but we may have some difficult moments."

Two days later the first of the many difficulties that were to cloud relations between the Prime Minister on the one hand and the C.I.G.S. and Wavell on the other, crept over the horizon. Churchill had not forgotten his request for eight Regular battalions to be sent forthwith to the United Kingdom. Dill was bidden to signal urgently to Wavell.

A. P. Wavell to C.I.G.S.   *31st May, 1940*
. . . I still hope that you may not find it necessary to take these battalions away from me, certainly not all. I have a very small margin to work on in view of possibilities out here, especially as regards the internal situation in Palestine and Egypt. . . .

If any battalions are taken, I do hope their transport, and as much of their equipment as possible, will be left here, for the Australians and others. It will also make the embarkation problem easier. . . .

C.I.G.S. to A. P. Wavell   *6th June, 1940*
. . . I have been doing my best to ride off those in the highest places who want to take those eight Bns. from you. I don't think that I shall be successful except in so far as events may come to my assistance. In any case my aim shall be to replace those Regular Bns. that we may take by T.A. units—but later. . . .

Prime Minister to Secretary of State for War   *6th June, 1940*
. . . I am very sorry indeed to find the virtual deadlock which local objections have imposed upon the battalions from Palestine. It is quite natural that General Wavell should look at the situation only from his own viewpoint. Here we have to think of building up a good army in order to make up, as far as possible, for the lamentable failure to support the French by an adequate B.E.F. during the first year of the war. . . . We are indeed the victims of a feeble and weary departmentalism.

Owing to the saving of the B.E.F., I have been willing to wait for the relief of the eight battalions from Palestine by eight native Indian battalions, provided these latter were sent at once; but you give me no time-table at all. I have not yet received any report on whether it is possible to send these British battalions and their Indian relief via Basra and the Persian Gulf. . . .[9]

Dill and Wavell had their point made for them by events; Regular battalions were brought back from India and replaced by others of lower category, and Wavell was able to retain his badly needed eight. But the Prime Minister had an exceptionally retentive memory, and the incident was neither forgotten nor forgiven.

Meanwhile disaster piled on disaster in France. Italy still bided her time to strike, but that she would and could strike as soon as she decided was now regarded as inevitable, even by the long-deluded mandarins of the Foreign Office.

In the Middle East the British Commanders-in-Chief had all three Services at the alert and ready for immediate war. On 4th June a signal in virtually identical terms was sent to each of the Commanders-in-Chief, reminding him that although the Mediterranean forces had at first to be strategically on the defensive, it was important, in view of the serious situation in the West, that local offensive action should be taken against the Italians wherever possible. In many ways it was a welcome signal. Wavell knew now that he must do the best he could with what he had. During the week-end of 8th-9th June events moved rapidly to their climax.

At 4 a.m. on June 10th, the 2nd Destroyer Flotilla, with two flying boats from No. 201 Group, left Alexandria for an anti-submarine sweep westwards. The Mediterranean Fleet was at two hours' notice; merchant ships were ordered to keep more than three miles from the coast of Malta, Cyprus and Palestine between sunset and sunrise; the lights of the Suez Canal were extinguished and navigation during darkness was suspended. In the Western Desert No. 202 Group and the Western Desert Force were preparing to get their blows in first.[10]

Wavell wrote: "The long-expected (by me at all events) Italian declaration of war was on 10th June. . . . I am sure that a more robust attitude towards Italy during the period of waiting instead of our

234

weak-kneed and apologetic attempts at appeasement would certainly not have increased the danger of war and might perhaps have lessened it. And our preparations would have been less hampered."

In spite of his arrogant gestures in public, Mussolini had as recently as 29th May told his Chiefs of Staff, "On the land front we cannot undertake anything spectacular, we shall remain on the defensive."[11] In view of the disasters that had already befallen France and her imminent collapse, and in view of the huge disparity in numbers between British and Italian forces, his decision could hardly be thought to be that of the dauntless warrior leader of a warrior people.

Wavell's total forces now numbered some 86,000 in all the scattered regions of his Command. Thirty-six thousand were in Egypt—short of equipment, artillery of all calibres, ammunition, A.F.V.s and transport. Two of the brigades of the 7th Armoured Division consisted of two regiments instead of three, and they were by no means fully equipped. There were only two brigades of the 4th Indian Division; its reconnaissance regiment and its artillery were far below strength. The New Zealand Division consisted of one infantry brigade, a cavalry regiment minus one squadron, a machine-gun battalion and a regiment of field artillery. There were also fourteen British infantry battalions and two regiments of artillery. Squadrons of the Egyptian Frontier Force patrolled the Libyan frontier. General Richard O'Connor took over command of all British forces in the Western Desert on 8th June. The 7th Armoured Division (less 7th Armoured Brigade) was near Mersa Matruh, with the Support Group of two regiments of Royal Horse Artillery and two motor battalions acting as a covering force between the main body and the frontier.

In Palestine Wavell had 27,500 troops: the 1st Cavalry Division, two more cavalry regiments (still horsed), two Australian brigades with two regiments of field artillery and some divisional troops, and a British infantry brigade and two other battalions. It was not thought that either the cavalry or the Australians were likely to be fully equipped and trained before the end of the year.

Against these, along the Egypt-Libya frontier and in depth behind it, in Cyrenaica and Tripolitania, Marshal Graziani had under his command almost a quarter of a million men. Wavell's intelligence network had laboured under the greatest difficulties, but his D.M.I.'s final estimate of enemy forces in the first week of June proved to be remarkably accurate: nine metropolitan (or regular) divisions, each numbering some 13,000 men; four (there were in fact three) Blackshirt divisions, and two Libyan native divisions, numbering 8,000 men each; a proportion of army and corps troops; and various other Libyan units and Frontier Guards. Under Graziani's North African Supreme Headquarters this huge force was organised as two armies: the 10th Army in Cyrenaica, consisting of one regular and one Black-shirt corps, each of two divisions, and a "group" of two Libyan divisions; and the rest forming 5th Army in Tripolitania.

France's forces in the region, though not destined to play any part in the conflict, were numerically impressive. In Tunisia General Noguès commanded six divisions, a fortress division, and a light cavalry division which would never have been capable of any but local operations with limited objectives. In Syria General Mittel-hauser, who had succeeded Weygand in over-all command, had an "expeditionary force" of three divisions, inadequately armed and trained, and some 4,000 troops organised for frontier duties and tribal control. They were soon to be of no account in any military calcula-tions that Wavell had to make; and Mittelhauser was to become a political and diplomatic problem.

In Italian East Africa the Duke of Aosta had at his disposal, it was estimated (and again the collection of accurate intelligence was exceptionally difficult), forces totalling not fewer than 300,000. The official figures of the *Ministero dell' Africa* on 1st June were: white, 91,203; native, 199,273; a total of 290,476.[12] Wavell's forces in this theatre were few, scattered and lightly equipped. In the Sudan, with a hostile frontier of twelve hundred miles to watch, there were three British battalions and the Sudan Defence Force, which with police and a variety of irregulars totalled some 9,000 men. There was still no artillery. In Kenya, whose frontier with Ethiopia was 850 miles long, there were two East African brigades and two light batteries, totalling some 8,500 men. In British Somaliland there were five com-panies of the Camel Corps and one battalion of the King's African Rifles—a total of 1,475. Aden was garrisoned by two infantry battalions.

The Official History justly comments: "Yet numbers were almost the least of General Wavell's anxieties: what he lacked was any com-plete formation—fully equipped and trained as such—and without this his force could not be regarded as being in a high state of pre-paredness for war."[13]

"I had given instructions," Wavell wrote, "for offensive action on the Italian frontier with Egypt to be taken immediately on the declaration of war."

There followed several days of lively and—for the Italians—disconcerting operations along and to the west of this frontier. The British made their first fighting acquaintance with a theatre of war in which, during the next two and a half years, they were to achieve some splendid victories and muddle into some disastrous defeats.

The Western Desert stretched almost exactly five hundred miles, as the crow flies, from El Alamein, on the coast of Egypt eighty miles west of Alexandria, to El Agheila on the Gulf of Sirte, on the border between Cyrenaica and Tripolitania. Such inhabited areas as existed were scattered along the coastline which, for the soldiers (though not for the sailors and the airmen), was the northern edge of the board. The only communications, road and rail, kept close to the coast. The desert itself was a plateau, which shelved steeply down to sea-level; this shelf was known, in desert-warfare terminology, as the "escarpment." Where the coastline bulged between Derna and Benghazi, the escarpment became a range of hills, cultivable and wooded. Southward, the desert stretched for many hundreds of miles, its rocky, barren wastes broken by a few widely separated oases—the ancient and famous Siwa within the Egyptian frontier, and Jarabub and Jalo in Cyrenaica. Its eastern boundary, providing a natural defence system, was the great Qattara depression, impassable for vehicles and infantry; but between the depression and the coast at El Alamein there was a small, forty-mile-wide gap of open desert. To the west the desert shaded into the cultivated, colonised lands of Tripolitania.

Over the years the desert became a single, huge battlefield, whose emptiness, so far as logistics were concerned, was absolute. If you wanted anything, you brought it with you or (if you were lucky) you captured it from the enemy. The needs of an army in World War II were numerous and diverse; but they were summed up under five main headings: ammunition, fuel, food, water and repairs.

Mussolini's declaration of war was to be effective, he said, from the middle of the night of 10th-11th June. Wavell (and O'Connor) took Il Duce at his word. On the evening of the 11th, the 7th Armoured Division, commanded by Major-General M. O'Moore Creagh, moved into action.

The 11th Hussars—less one squadron left at Sidi Barrani—crossed the frontier wire that night, completely surprised the Italians at Sidi

Omar, and in twenty-four hours' aggressive patrolling took some seventy prisoners. They headed west; a squadron of the 7th Hussars and a company of the 1st Battalion the King's Royal Rifle Corps came up to the wire. On 14th June the 7th Hussars took Fort Capuzzo and the 11th Hussars took Maddalena. On the 15th the 11th Hussars laid an ambush on the coast road between Bardia and Tobruk, the results of which next day were that twenty-one of the enemy were killed and eighty-eight taken prisoner, including General Lastucci, Engineer-in-Chief of the Tenth Army.

On the same day a squadron of the same regiment discovered an enemy force of some seventeen light tanks, four guns and 400 infantry near Nezuet Ghirba. This discovery was reported to 4th Armoured Brigade, who sent forward a cruiser squadron of 7th Hussars and a troop of J Battery, R.H.A. The squadron of the 11th Hussars had meanwhile taken action to hold the enemy. When the reinforcements arrived a concerted attack was made which routed the Italian force with the loss of more than 100 killed and captured, all their guns and light tanks and several lorries. There were no British casualties.[14]

In East and Equatorial Africa the same spirit was effectively demonstrated by the very small forces at the disposal of each of the local commanders. A G.H.Q. telegram to the War Office on 22nd June gave a summary of these operations, claiming that their general feature was the "superiority, initiative, skill and daring of our forward troops in contact." It pointed out that:

at small cost we have inflicted casualties wherever enemy forces encountered, capturing twenty-five Italian officers (including senior Engineer-General 10 Army) and 500 O.R.s . . . In the air we have repeatedly attacked and destroyed parked aircraft, petrol, ammunition dumps and workshops in Italian East Africa and Libya. Early attacks completely surprised enemy. Concentration of shipping in Tobruk harbour successfully engaged. . . . So far Italian air force has given poor account of itself, confirming inadequacy of training. By air combat and ground attack to date we have destroyed over fifty Italian aircraft. Morale of all ranks admirable.

The reaction in London was encouraging.

C.I.G.S. to A. P. Wavell   *26th June, 1940*

War Cabinet much pleased with your signal 22nd June. All these operations are of immense value at this time and publicity of your remarkable local successes has also importance.

Good news of any kind, from any quarter, was unaffectedly welcome. Almost a fortnight earlier Dill had tried to evoke for Wavell the momentous drama of those days.

C.I.G.S. to A. P. Wavell   *13th June, 1940*

. . . The French are standing on their last line and fighting against great odds. In men, I suppose, some three to one and in equipment completely outmatched.

I was in France yesterday with the P.M. and it was not exactly a cheerful meeting.

We have been backing the French in so far as our very limited resources allow us to do so. And we are taking great risks in this country. I hate to see good divisions like the Canadians going to France when one sometimes feels that one is throwing snowballs into Hell to keep down the temperature. And divisions take so long to get to France—M.T., etc.—and are apt to be used up in bits and pieces as they arrive. But help the French we must so long as they can continue to fight. I'm sure you will agree.

But if the French go out, what then? Home defence will become a very live issue—and at once. Air and the Navy must remain the first line—the second line is a bit thin: not in men but in equipment. From a secure base here we can then begin to lick the Boche—good and hard, I hope. I cannot say what will happen in your part of the world. . . . I am sorry you were so much worried about the Bns. from Palestine. I did my best to save you that worry although I knew that events would make it quite impossible to rob you of them. I am very thankful that they are still with you. We are getting you, I hope, some A.A. guns from the Far East but will they be in time? I seem to be spending my time trying to catch up events. I know I would have done no better than my predecessor but I did come into this job a bit late. . . .

On the afternoon of 17th June Wavell, playing golf at Gezira with one of his A.D.C.s, was brought the news of the signature of the French armistice. "I played the two remaining holes, doing them in three and four, I remember. I then went back to my office and wrote out a short Order of the Day."

> Our gallant French Allies have been overwhelmed after a desperate struggle and have been compelled to ask for terms. The British Empire will, of course, continue the struggle until victory has been won. There is no question of anything else. We shall again save Europe from tyranny as we have done before. Difficult times lie ahead but will, I know, be faced with the same spirit of calm confidence in which we have faced such crises before.
>
> We stand firm whatever happens.
>
> Dictators fade away—the British Empire never dies.[15]

The attitude of senior French officers and officials in their overseas territories was now of crucial importance. Few of these men, with considerable forces under their command, had either de Gaulle's clarity of vision or his driving ability; they were confused, torn in their loyalties, and deeply unhappy. In Tunisia, after several days of wavering, General Noguès decided to regard the armistice negotiated with Germany and Italy by the Government in metropolitan France as binding in the area under his control. He asserted that for the moment the integrity and the defence of French North Africa seemed to be assured, and called for calmness, unity, discipline and confidence in the future of France.

In Syria the situation was at once more taut and more complex. Wavell wrote:

"I still hoped that the French would fight on. . . . I had faith in Weygand and did not believe he would give in. During the next ten days I was engaged almost constantly in an effort to keep the French in Syria in the war. . . . I went up to Syria by air and saw General Mittelhauser, who had succeeded Weygand. He was neither very impressive nor effective, and dithered. At first it looked as if my hope might be fulfilled. . . . But it became obvious that the French in Syria were going to pack up.

"This raised another problem, how far should we try to induce individual French officers and troops to leave Syria and join us. There were quite a few who were anxious to continue fighting and might have been persuaded to cross the frontier and join us. I was at odds with our Foreign Office over our policy in this matter. They urged me to facilitate and encourage Frenchmen to cross over. I did not agree. My view was that I wanted a stable and neutral Syria on my northern flank, in view of my general weakness; and that to disrupt it by removing large numbers of the best French officers would be bad policy. It might result in disorder in Syria, which I did not want, and in Vichy sending out officers definitely hostile to the British to replace those we had removed. I did not think the gain of a certain number of French officers without units was worth the risk of this.

". . . Eventually I struck some sort of a bargain with Mittelhauser, that I would not encourage his officers or men to desert to us, if he would facilitate the Polish Brigade in Syria coming over complete with arms. I tried to include his Foreign Legion battalions who would have been quite glad to join us, but he would not consent.

"A certain number of French officers came over, including a senior staff officer, de Larminat, and almost the whole of a French battalion which was in Cyprus. . . .

"Legentilhomme in French Somaliland held out for nearly another month before he too was compelled by the French Government to give in.

"I had not realised the extent of the moral disintegration of the French since the end of the First War; nor the extent to which superiority of rank dominated the French military mind, and stifled independence, though when I thought of it later I remembered how subservient French senior officers had appeared to us on the course at Versailles in 1934."

Meanwhile Wavell pondered the magnitude of the political, diplomatic, strategic and administrative responsibilities with which he and the other Commanders-in-Chief would now be confronted, in view of the obvious and growing difficulty of obtaining prompt decisions from a Cabinet many thousands of miles away, probably under air attack, and preoccupied with the defence of the United Kingdom. In full agreement with Admiral Cunningham and Air Chief Marshal Longmore,[16] he signalled London on 18th June suggesting that, since the Middle East theatre looked like extending to cover most of Africa and a large part of western Asia, there should be set up as soon as possible a War Council, working under the War Cabinet's general directions, based probably in Kenya, consisting of representatives of South Africa, India, Australia, France (if French North Africa were to fight on) and perhaps Egypt, and assisted by Service advisers working on the same lines as the Chiefs of Staff Committee.

When he realised how long it would take to assemble such a body and get it working properly, Wavell dropped his proposal and substituted a suggestion for a Cabinet Sub-Committee in London which would keep a close watch on all problems in Africa, the Near East and India.

The C.I.G.S. rejected both ideas, and pointed out that since Middle East questions were already under constant review by the War Cabinet and the Chiefs of Staff there would be no advantage in establishing a special Cabinet Sub-Committee. However, the Prime Minister reversed this decision, and set up just such a body as Wavell had suggested, consisting of the Secretaries of State for War, India and the Colonies (Eden, Amery and Lord Lloyd), whose terms of reference were to keep the conduct of the war in the Middle East under review and to report to him, in his capacity as Minister of Defence.[17]

During the last part of June and most of July O'Connor's little force in the Western Desert remained on the offensive, and the Italians brought forward two divisions towards the frontier. A brigade occupied the ruins of Fort Capuzzo, which had been destroyed after its capture by the 7th Hussars. An Italian attempt to advance from this point to Sollum was repulsed by one squadron of light tanks; and their tenure of Fort Capuzzo itself was made extremely uncomfortable. They were under constant artillery attack; their transport bringing up supplies from Bardia was raided and shelled; and they lost heavily in men and vehicles.

Mussolini admitted to the King of Italy that affairs on the Egyptian frontier had not turned out "too brilliantly." The high hopes he pinned on Marshal Balbo, who became Commander-in-Chief in Libya at the outbreak of hostilities, were dashed when that romantic and resolute leader was shot down by his own A.A. artillery near Tobruk on 28th June. Nevertheless the Italians steadily moved their camps forward, and by the end of July they had established a force of at least four divisions within easy reach of the frontier.

The 7th Armoured Division maintained the offensive with great determination in the face of this build-up and under very arduous conditions.

There was no such thing as telephone communication in advance of Divisional Headquarters, and as, for security reasons, wireless communication was limited to urgent operational messages, all communications, including orders, had to be delivered by liaison officers in trucks—who frequently took a day to reach their destination.

Transport was reduced to the bare minimum to maintain units in their operational positions, and deliveries were necessarily limited to petrol for machines, hard rations for the troops, and water at the rate of half a gallon per head per day, which included that required for vehicles and loss in transit. For weeks, forward troops existed on biscuits, bully, limited tinned rations and a pint of tea in the morning and in the evening. With the shade temperature ranging between 80° and 100°, living conditions for the troops, who had little or no shade, were extremely severe.

Workshops were at Alexandria and Cairo, and the forward delivery point at Matruh, not less than a hundred miles from forward units—all replacements having to journey by stages and be driven by spare crews forward from Matruh. The position of the wounded was even grimmer, for until they could be got back to Sidi Barrani they, too, had to be laboriously staged from post to post.

Air support consisted of a flight of three Lysanders, which had a fighter cover of three Gladiators—until one was lost, when the remaining two were withdrawn. Instructions from G.H.Q. at Cairo restricted the use of 25-pounder ammunition to two rounds per gun per day and "other ammunition was only to be expended if a good dividend could be expected."[18]

In spite of shortages, fatigue and strain for men and vehicles alike—at the end of July, with 200 tanks out of Western Desert Force's normal complement of 306 under repair, almost every tracked vehicle in the forward area was ordered into the workshops for overhaul and refit—Wavell had established so great a moral ascendancy over the enemy that he could afford to take some calculated risks. With the bulk of the two armoured brigades withdrawn to Mersa Matruh, or even further east, he left the frontier covered by the Support Group, commanded by Brigadier W. H. E. Gott, which, distributed over a front of some sixty miles from Sollum to Fort Maddalena, continued active patrolling, puzzled the Italians by massing formations of dummy tanks, harassed and worried them, and inflicted a steady drain of casualties on them with practically no loss to itself, and was thus able to hold in check a force of four to five divisions for a further six weeks. The Italians' published list of casualties for the three months from their entry into the war until mid-September totalled 3,500; the British, in the same period, lost just over 150, despite bombing and machine-gun attacks by the *Regia Aeronautica* which, for reasons beyond the control of the R.A.F., could then operate almost unimpeded.

Towards the end of June Wavell created the first and one of the most efficient as well as best known of the "unorthodox" formations which were inseparably connected with his reputation as a commander.

Major R. A. Bagnold, who had led a series of expeditions into the Western Desert in the 1920s and 1930s, was now in G.H.Q. in Cairo. He believed that the Italians might send mechanised raiding parties from the remote interior of Libya across to the Upper Nile, to block British communications between Cairo and Khartoum, and he thought out a way of countering such a threat. He proposed to equip and train a cadre of men to undertake long-range motor patrolling through the great region of sand and rock south of the Italian encampments, stretching down into the Sahara. When Italy entered the war, Major Bagnold sought an interview with Arthur Smith and offered him this scheme, which Smith took in to the Chief. Bagnold was sent for at once, and Wavell gave him authority to order anything he wanted as an absolute priority from any department in Egypt, with no questions asked. Bagnold was to have personal access to himself at any time, and was to be ready within six weeks.

Bagnold's search for men, vehicles and equipment was resourceful and successful. Desert explorers and adventurers whom he knew and personally recommended were flown to Cairo and given immediate commissions, to enable them to lead the patrols. The first N.C.O.s and other ranks were recruited from the New Zealand Division. They were rapidly trained in the basic principles of desert navigation. From such small stocks as existed, specialised equipment and vehicles, designed to Bagnold's specifications, had to be improvised. A good deal had to be borrowed from the Egyptian Army; a theodolite was sent from Nairobi; the last light wireless set in Cairo, and the last but three of the machine guns, went to Bagnold. At the end of August Wavell himself, in conditions of great secrecy, inspected and bade God-speed to the Long Range Desert Group, consisting of three patrols, each of two officers and twenty-eight other ranks, when it set out on its first mission.

Since the Italians had not raided the Upper Nile areas Wavell now put the force he had so rapidly created on to the offensive. In addition to reconnaissance and the gathering of intelligence, it was to harass the Italians by making trouble in any part of Libya the patrol commanders might choose, and thus draw away troops and transport from the forces which Graziani was preparing in the coastal regions for the invasion of Egypt. The manner in which L.R.D.G. discharged both these tasks, and the success which attended it, were no small contribution not only to Wavell's first campaigns but to victory in the desert as a whole. The concept was Bagnold's; the tenacious interest and strong backing were Wavell's.

In Italian East Africa, Wavell's opponent, the Duke of Aosta, had formidable difficulties of his own, despite the impressive size and fighting potential of the forces he commanded. Mussolini's new empire was rickety and in grave jeopardy from within. The recent conquest of Ethiopia had been far from complete, and the Ethiopians' patriotic spirit was unbroken. The Duke's main preoccupation in Ethiopia was the maintenance of internal order, and it was for this that his forces were organised, trained, equipped and deployed in numerous garrisons scattered about the huge countryside. These garrisons, reasonably accessible by road, each contained a substantial force of colonial troops, with Italian officers and N.C.O.s, stiffened here and there by one or more Blackshirt battalions. With some irregular Frontier Force units, they added up to some twenty-nine brigades, each of three or four infantry battalions and two batteries of mountain artillery. There were in addition seventeen independent colonial battalions, sixteen Italian battalions and ten Italian artillery groups. The Duke also had a tactical reserve, located at Addis Ababa, Dessie and Adigrat, comprising one regular Italian division and one of locally enlisted Italian nationals. He had more than a hundred armoured cars (manned by Italians), about sixty medium and light tanks, 183 operational aircraft, sixty-one in reserve, and eighty-one more undergoing repairs.

On 9th June the Duke asked if he might, as soon as war should begin, attack the British by air and on the sea, but he was immediately ordered to take no offensive action. He had long known that this was his only opportunity, and that he had no hope of winning the defensive war which Mussolini's ham-handed strategy now imposed on him. He faced having to fight in complete isolation, cut off totally by air and by sea, and with the nearest Italian land forces stationed in the oasis of Uwainat, nearly a thousand miles away on the other side of the Sudan. Though he looked as if he held all the cards, in truth he held none. Wavell, by contrast, appeared to be in grave danger; but in ten months he was to accomplish the total defeat of his opponent and the destruction of the Italian empire in East Africa.

Wavell described his opening moves succinctly

In the Sudan it was obviously impossible . . . to cover the long and vulnerable frontier, but I directed that small mobile forces should occupy the principal places on the frontier until attacked by superior forces. Although these small forces could obviously not resist any attack which the greatly superior forces could make, I considered it desirable that they should fight a delaying action against the enemy rather than abandon the frontier posts without any fighting at all, as had been the previous policy.

. . . the Sudan Defence Force made several most successful raids on the Italian frontier posts in the earlier days of the war, and when finally attacked at Kassala on 4th July and at Gallabat on 6th July by greatly superior Italian forces fought successful delaying actions and inflicted heavy loss on the enemy, who did not follow up his success in spite of the great disparity in numbers.[19]

He followed a similar policy of holding the frontier posts in Kenya as long as possible.

"The Italians attacked our small post at Moyale in the middle of July. The post was held by one company of the King's African Rifles and the Italians brought up a brigade, with which they made one or two rather half-hearted attacks. When a second Italian brigade appeared, our company commander decided correctly that it was time to withdraw, and slipped away at night without loss. The Italians made such propaganda about their 'Invasion of British East Africa and capture of an important centre' that the War Cabinet sent me some very critical telegrams, and the authorities in S. Rhodesia and S. Africa showed signs of nerves! Some of these telegrams seemed to imply that I had lost a major engagement!"

What mattered in Wavell's eyes was not the capture or recapture of a desert fort or two, but the offensive which would destroy Italian power throughout East Africa. The core of his problem was the liberation of Ethiopia. As far back as September, 1939, he had, on the advice of his Intelligence staff, sent for a certain D. A. Sandford, a former gunner officer, who after service in the Sudan had settled in Ethiopia, farming and acting as an occasional adviser to the Emperor, and who was at that time treasurer of Guildford Cathedral. Sandford was convinced that the exiled Emperor Haile Selassie deserved the fullest possible support, since there were no other serious contenders for his throne and he himself commanded the devoted allegiance of his former subjects. Dismissing stories of large sections of the population being reconciled to Italian rule as empty propaganda, Sandford also believed firmly in the strength and tenacity of Ethiopian patriotism. He at once began to plan the raising of a revolt inside the country.

When Italy declared war Sandford was in Cairo. Wavell summoned him to a meeting of senior staff officers and formally instructed him to undertake the task for which he had been preparing. Sandford then went back to Khartoum, which he had made his base, and sent as many arms and as much ammunition as he could to a number of leading Ethiopian chieftains.

But on 25th June, the Emperor arrived in Egypt from England. For months Wavell had been trying to get the Foreign Office to say whether or not they wanted Haile Selassie to go back to Ethiopia. All his preparations and propaganda hinged on this one question. Suddenly an Air Ministry telegram told him that the Emperor would be arriving in Alexandria by flying-boat that afternoon, and instructed him to make all necessary arrangements for his re-entry into his own country as soon as possible. The British Ambassador in Cairo, who like Wavell had had no previous warning, said that Haile Selassie's landing in Egypt was impossible, as it would cause serious political complications. The Governors of Kenya and the Sudan took the same view.

"This was absurd, and I told the F.O. that they must have pressure brought on the Sudan to provide a suitable house for him. . . . Meanwhile the Emperor had to spend the night on his flying-boat; and next day we flew him on to Wadi Halfa till accommodation at Khartoum was arranged."

The reasons for the Emperor's unheralded appearance on the scene were fairly simple. At last, as a result of Churchill's galvanic leadership, the Foreign Office had made up its mind about Ethiopia. Within a few days it was going to be no longer possible to fly to Egypt from England. The Emperor had been given passage to Africa, in case he was needed. "The Foreign Office left any problems to be solved by the authorities on the spot. The problems proved enormous."[20]

To assist in some degree towards their solution, the Assistant Oriental Secretary at the British Embassy in Cairo was added to the Emperor's entourage. After a week of discomfort in the stifling heat of Wadi Halfa, the party moved on 2nd July—the Emperor going under the pseudonym of "Mr. Smith"—to Khartoum.

On 14th July Wavell set out on a brief visit to the Sudan and Kenya, in order to see how the commanders of these sparse garrisons were faring. He went out on each front as far as he could, to the Butana bridge over the Atbara river in the Sudan and to Wajir in the desert of Kenya. He had, for the first time, a reliable and comparatively fast-moving aircraft, and accomplished the whole trip in four days. In Khartoum he met Haile Selassie.

"The Emperor was an attractive personality, though not always easy to deal with. I found that he had been led by the F.O. to suppose that immediately on his arrival I would place at his disposal a large force, with tanks and guns, to re-enter his kingdom. . . . I had to disabuse His Imperial Majesty as well as I could. I never discovered who was the moron at the F.O. responsible for all this. Discussion with the Emperor at this and subsequent visits was always rather a complicated business. I think H.I.M. understood either French or English pretty well but he would not admit it; and he would never speak anything but Amharic. As the only interpreter of Amharic could only speak Arabic as his medium of interpretation, conversation had to filter through at least three languages—on one occasion four, when it was found that the interpreter of Arabic knew no English, only French."

In Kenya Wavell saw the advance party of the South African Brigade that had begun to disembark at Mombasa, and had a talk with their commander. The presence of these troops in the colony was shortly to cause acute controversy. In London Churchill was already beginning to cast a critical eye over dispersions of force in the Middle East, for which he held Wavell responsible. The latter returned to Cairo to discover that he was now to be subjected, more and more insistently, to Churchill's unique mixture of inquisition and energetic encouragement.

Prime Minister to General Ismay   *23rd July, 1940*
Where is the South African Union Brigade of 10,000 men? Why is it playing no part in the Middle East? We have agreed to-day to send further reinforcements of Hurricanes and other modern

aircraft to the South African Air Force. What is happening to the concert of the campaign in the Middle East? What has been done by the Committee of Ministers I recently set up? . . . Make sure I have a report about the position, which I can consider on Thursday morning.[21]

Ismay communicated the substance of this minute to the C.I.G.S., who passed it on without comment to Wavell. To a Minister less tenacious than Churchill, Wavell's answer would doubtless have seemed irrefutable.

A. P. Wavell to C.I.G.S.   *30th July, 1940*
South African Brigade is only partially trained at present and requires further training before being employed offensively. They must also become acclimatised and learn anti-malaria precautions, etc.

Conditions in East Africa necessitate crossing of 200 miles of almost roadless and waterless bush desert before offensive against Italian East Africa can be made. African native troops who have smaller requirements and are more accustomed to bush conditions are more suitable than white troops for forward role. . . .

As to use elsewhere, I understood when the brigade was offered that Smuts had given pledge in Union that South Africans would not be used north of Equator. . . .

Brigade should complete its training in Kenya and its future use can meanwhile be considered. I think it can probably be better employed in East Africa than elsewhere but will have the matter studied.

I am sure you will keep considerations of geography, climate, deserts, distances, etc., constantly in the minds of Middle East Committee. It all looks so simple to them and others on a small-scale map.

Prime Minister and Commander-in-Chief were not yet finally on a collision course, but to an eye as discerning as Dill's the danger-signals were apparent. Dill was on excellent terms with his Secretary of State, Anthony Eden; both perceived that the Prime Minister was gnawing and snapping over Kenya because his restless passion for aggressive activity—never more justified or more valuable than in these crucial months—was being frustrated over the Middle East.

Dill knew too that Wavell was as eager as the Prime Minister to go over to the offensive in any and every sector of his Command as soon as he possibly could. He gave Eden a full account of Wavell's shortages in troops, equipment and resources; this, in his turn, Eden reported to his Ministerial Committee, which recommended that the 7th Armoured Division, whose deficiencies it admitted, be brought up to its full strength, and also that a second armoured division be sent to the Middle East as soon as it could possibly be spared from the United Kingdom. The Chiefs of Staff supported these suggestions, but Dill pointed out that the moment must be chosen in relation to declining risks at home and increasing risks abroad. On 31st July Eden told the Prime Minister that it might be possible to spare some tanks in the next few weeks, and that if they were to reach the Middle East by the end of September, they and other equipment might have to be sent through the Mediterranean.

Colonel G. K. Edwards, one of the War Office's small team of liaison officers with G.H.Q. Middle East, was now in London. On 2nd August he submitted a brief paper which put Wavell's point of view cogently:

> . . . I feel that General Wavell would wish that the utmost possible stress was laid on the risks which will be run in the Middle East during the next six months if his request for a second armoured division and for at least one tank unit capable of dealing with German heavy tanks is not met. . . .
>
> I feel that the possibility of sending the second armoured division to Egypt with its 290-odd light tanks should be further investigated. The addition of these light tanks to General Wavell's command would be invaluable particularly against Italian forces. As cruiser production increases in the autumn and next year and increased numbers of cruisers reach the Middle East he could gradually build up this division on a cruiser basis. I would also suggest that the fullest consideration be given to the desirability of sending out as soon as possible one army tank battalion and that this unit should be preceded by a small token detachment of army tanks so that an early decision can be made, as to what modifications if any are required for desert employment.

One of the other aspects of the Middle East Command which caused the Ministerial Committee anxiety was the threat to Iraq. On 1st July—before the Committee was formed—the War Cabinet had decided that the 5th Indian Division, whose training and equipment were well in advance of those of most British formations, should go to Basra to be part of a composite force to defend the oil installations in Iraq and south-west Persia. In the meantime, however, before it was ready to sail, Wavell, the Viceroy and the Commander-in-Chief in India (General Sir Robert Cassels) all expressed their anxiety lest the move should do more harm than good.

They thought that it might provoke Russia and aggravate the situation in Iraq. They did not think one division strong enough to deal with these dangers, and pointed out that it could not be reinforced. Since there were no A.A. guns, even the defence of the oilfields would be impracticable. And they were all aware of the risk of having a repetition of the First War's Mesopotamian campaign. The War Cabinet accepted these arguments and admitted the obvious need to increase Wavell's forces. Early in August they changed the 5th Indian Division's destination from Basra to the Middle East, and Wavell then decided that its leading brigade group should disembark at Port Sudan.

It was thus becoming more and more apparent that it was necessary for Wavell to come home. On 1st August he was told by telegram that arrangements were being made for a Sunderland flying-boat to pick him up at Alexandria, probably on the 4th, and to fly him back immediately after his discussions with the War Cabinet, "which should not take more than two or three days."

Before Wavell left for London, however, one more of the many consequences of the French collapse began to make itself felt in Somaliland, a country at that time divided between Britain, France and Italy. The French and British territories had a short common land frontier; French Somaliland was bordered by Eritrea (an Italian colony) and Ethiopia; British Somaliland by Ethiopia and Italian Somaliland. The capital of French Somaliland, Jibuti, had a good deep-water harbour, and was the seaward terminus of the only railway leading into Ethiopia; its importance had been insisted upon by both the French and the British for fifteen months. The local French commander, General Legentilhomme, an able and patriotic soldier, resisted, for as long as he could, the enforcement of the Franco-Italian armistice. But desiring above all to avoid civil war, he resigned on 5th August and retired to Aden, leaving his successor to try to obtain the best local terms he could. This successor, General Germain, was under heavy Vichy pressure to sunder all relations with the British.

British Somaliland was now completely isolated—except from the sea. Its capital, Berbera, was its sole port, but as such it was a good deal less useful (to either side) than Jibuti, which the Italians now held. It had no protected harbour; all unloading had to be done by lighters, and a 3,000-ton ship usually took ten days to discharge. The colony's frontier with Ethiopia was long and open. Some fifty miles inland from Berbera, across a bare, featureless plain, two motorable roads and one track snaked down the hills. If the Italians decided to attack with the strong forces they now had available after the Vichy take-over, would it be worth resisting?

In Berbera a Royal Marine lieutenant-colonel, A. R. Chater, commanded a small, heterogeneous force, consisting of two African infantry battalions, two Indian battalions, an African light battery with four 3.7 howitzers, and the lightly-armed Camel Corps, which had just received a reinforcement of seventeen officers and twenty N.C.O.s from the Southern Rhodesian Regiment.

At the end of July the Italians massed the equivalent of an army corps across the border in Ethiopia, and early in August moved forward in a ponderous, two-column advance into British Somaliland. Wavell decided that it would be worth Chater's force putting up a fight if he could be given one more battalion and some guns. His last two operational instructions before he left for London were that two 3-inch A.A. guns (of the Hong Kong and Singapore Brigade of the Royal Artillery) should at once be sent from Aden to Berbera, and that the 2nd Battalion The Black Watch, which had lately moved to Aden from guard duty on the Suez Canal, should go forthwith to the threatened colony. It was not an easy moment for the Chief to be absent from his Command, but his presence in England was urgently needed. He reported at the War Office on the evening of 7th August.

VIII

Into Action

The summer of 1940 possessed, while it was being lived through in England even more than in retrospect, a quality extremely rare in the experience of any nation. Churchill was the unchallengeable leader and spokesman of a completely united people. His moral authority was, for the time being, unique and absolute. The tremendous crisis in the first weeks of May had thrust him into a preeminence and a power greater than any possessed by Lloyd George even at his zenith, equalled only perhaps by those of the elder Pitt. Every major speech he made, in Parliament or on the wireless, was a trumpet call to heroism, and the community at large responded by being heroic, individually and corporately. Goering's long-awaited and massive air attack was just developing; invasion would be bound to follow if the air assault succeeded. Though in material still ludicrously ill-equipped, the country under Churchill's fiery stimulus was every day showing itself better and better prepared morally. He described August, 1940, as Britain's finest hour; without doubt it was his own.

At this supreme moment in his personal drama Churchill met, in Wavell, a man of the highest moral and intellectual stature, with a great military reputation, holding a post whose responsibilities and challenges were similar to though not greater than his own, who for reasons which neither of them fully comprehended was incapable of playing the part in that drama that Churchill wished him to play. It need not be difficult: it was simply to be the foremost among "my commanders in the field."

It was the pronoun that stuck. Churchill did his brilliant best. The note of pained bewilderment, of a sense that something (which could not, surely, be his own fault?) went wrong, sounds through sentences written nearly a decade later.

I felt an acute need of talking over the serious events impending in the Libyan desert with General Wavell himself. I had not met this distinguished officer, on whom so much was resting. . . . While not in full agreement with General Wavell's use of the resources at his disposal, I thought it best to leave him in command. I admired his fine qualities and was impressed with the confidence so many people had in him.[1]

Their first encounter was as crucially significant—both for the climate of feeling it engendered between them and for the decisions they took—as in its circumstances it was dramatic.

Wavell, on his side, was not unaware of the extraordinary linking of the man and the hour, and was far from unresponsive to its poetic and patriotic implications. But never could he give what Churchill asked. Far more subtle and complex in character than Churchill, and far better educated, he was steeled by a lifetime of strong self-discipline. He was cool and reticent where Churchill was warm and overflowing with emotion. He obeyed orders as readily as he gave them, but always with a clear, far-sighted understanding of their full consequences. He was prepared to give advice and take advice; he was prepared, if necessary, to argue out any issue on paper, with all the relevant facts and figures. Calmly and with self-confidence he took his own decisions within the sphere of his responsibility, and in his turn accepted loyally the decisions of the Government to which he was responsible. His loyalty was to his conscience, his Sovereign and his country. No man could command it; no man could win it by flattery or bullying, by cozening or cajoling, or by charm, however magnificent. He would not—indeed he could not—surrender his own integrity and independence of judgment; and this was, in fact, what Churchill demanded, quite unconsciously but inexorably.

There were other sources of tension between the two men, latent for years but powerful when tapped. Churchill's sentiments about generals were ambivalent from his earliest youth onwards: he distrusted and despised them, yet he yearned to be himself a super-general, in emulation of his ancestor, Marlborough. Wavell for his part had a grasp of politics rare in British generals, but was suspicious of professional politicians and thought politics too serious a matter to be left in their hands. His memory was as retentive as Churchill's; just as the latter remembered the Dardanelles, so he had not forgotten the crisis of the Curragh, the blame for whose consequences he had always laid firmly on Churchill's shoulders. Churchill, contemplating the problems and chances of the Middle East Command at this time, thought in terms of Europe, and looked ultimately to the Balkans. Wavell, aware of his responsibilities in Africa and Asia, wanted to defeat Italy in Africa and preserve a hard-won, delicately poised peace in the British sphere of influence in Asia. Churchill was pro-Zionist; Wavell was acutely conscious that every response to Zionist aims and aspirations, every acceptance of Jewish offers to help in the war effort, would jab and inflame Arab resentment. On the general theme of the war, as distinct from its strategy and conduct, both held views of appropriate gravity, but these differed deeply. Churchill rightly called it "the Unnecessary War"; but as the leader of his country in an extremity of danger he responded, subjectively yet nobly, to its challenge and its glory. It is in no sense a criticism of him—indeed his country's victory and the saving of what remained of civilisation are the results—to say that he revelled in it, with a zest that knew no bounds. But Wavell, the soldier, knew this war to be, like all other wars, "deplorably dull and inefficiently run"; he saw it as a "wasteful, boring, muddled affair," and could see no reason why the human race "so inefficient in matters of peace, should suddenly become efficient in time of war."

Churchill, apt on impulse to be over-enthusiastic about a new relationship, and, to his credit, as tenacious in these sudden loyalties as in his dislikes, found it impossible to like Wavell. One who was present at the latter's first meeting with the War Cabinet and the Chiefs of Staff has described as "disastrous" the way in which the emotional temperature dropped in the face of Wavell's taciturnity. Churchill made no secret of his own disappointment, verging at times on chagrin. Wavell wrote:

"I do not think Winston quite knew what to make of me and whether I was fit to command or not. He was determined that something must be done to put the defence of Egypt on a sound basis; and in providing reinforcements of tanks and sending a convoy through the Mediterranean was bold in overriding the views both of those who wished to keep all armoured forces for home defence—invasion was very much a possibility at the time—and of the First Sea Lord, who stressed the dangers of sending merchant ships through the Mediterranean.

"On certain details the P.M. was difficult. He did his best to make me move both South African and West African troops from East

Africa to Egypt or the Sudan; and he never realised the necessity for full equipment before committing troops to battle. I remember his arguing that because a comparatively small number of mounted Boers had held up a British division in 1899 or 1900, it was unnecessary for the South African Brigade to have much more equipment than rifles before taking the field in 1940. In fact I found that Winston's tactical ideas had to some extent crystallised at the South African War, just as his ideas on India's political problems, as I discovered later, had not advanced much from his impressions as a subaltern in the nineties. His fertile brain was always inventive or receptive of new tactical ideas and weapons, but I do not think that right up to the end he ever understood the administrative side of war; he always accused commanders of organising 'all tail and no teeth.'

"In the end . . . I succeeded in convincing him that it would not be advantageous or politic to move the African troops from East Africa. At least I convinced him that I wouldn't do it. I am pretty sure that he considered my replacement by someone who was more likely to share his ideas, but could not find any good reason to do so. Winston has always disliked me personally."

Except for one night at Chequers, Wavell was in London all the time he was in England, staying at Dill's flat in Ashley Gardens. Dill's preoccupations were countless, the burden of his anxieties almost intolerable. He was a sensitive man, without Wavell's inner resources of gaiety. His judgments, on people as well as on strategy, were sound and well balanced; he had, however, as C.I.G.S., constantly to defend those judgments in cut-and-thrust verbal argument with the Prime Minister—a process which, to Churchill, was essential as well as enjoyable, but which exhausted and sickened Dill. Churchill used every weapon of aggressive debate—mordant sarcasm, prosecuting counsel's bullying, extravagant rhetorical flourishes, urchin abuse, Ciceronian irony and sledgehammer brutality—and Dill had to bear it all and suppress his anger and his anguish. He had only had three months of it in August, 1940, but he was already much harassed. He realised that the aspects of Churchill's personality and behaviour which caused him distress mattered nothing beside the white-hot flame of his leadership; but did Churchill ever concede that Dill's patriotism and selflessness in service were as great as his own? Part at least of his dislike for Wavell arose from the fact that Wavell was Dill's friend.

General Wavell and General O'Connor, 1940

Mr. Anthony Eden (Lord Avon) and General Dill

Churchill himself was, at this time, under a strain which would have broken a weaker man. On 30th July Hitler had ordered Goering to prepare "immediately and with the greatest haste" to begin "the great battle of the German Air Force against England." Goering's final directive for operation "Eagle" (which was to precede the sea-borne invasion of Southern England, operation "Sea Lion") was issued on 2nd August. The six weeks' lull after the fall of France, which Churchill's astonishing energy had been able to turn to Britain's advantage, was nearly over. However, more than a week of bad weather now intervened, and postponed the opening of the *Luftwaffe's* offensive until Monday, 12th August. But during these final days the tension in the inmost circles in London inevitably mounted.

It was against this background that Wavell's series of crucial conferences began. On 8th August he gave a long and detailed review of the situation and prospects in his Command to the C.O.S. Committee. His forecasts for the immediate future were guarded. In the Western Desert he said he thought that the Italians might advance on a front of about fifty miles, turning the defences at Matruh; he believed —and he gave his opponents credit for a greater boldness and originality than they possessed—that they would solve their maintenance problem by the use of air transport; and he reckoned that they could put into the air some 300 to 400 bombers, 300 fighters and 200 troop-carrying aircraft. In the event they proved to be much less adventurous, therefore much less formidable. Wavell stressed his own—and Longmore's—all-round deficiencies, from tanks of all kinds, bombers and fighters down to ammunition for the artillery and spare parts for the vehicles. It was this catalogue of the Middle East's extremely pressing needs which most impressed the Chiefs of Staff and the Cabinet's Middle East Committee, and to which they now devoted their immediate attention.

Anthony Eden, as chairman of the Middle East Committee, knew that the Mediterranean Fleet, whose deficiencies by now were almost as grave as those of the land and air forces in this theatre, was shortly to be reinforced by an expedition consisting of the aircraft-carrier *Illustrious*, the Queen Elizabeth class battleship *Valiant* and two anti-aircraft cruisers, which it had been planned should leave the United Kingdom on 20th August. Subsidiary operations had been arranged to cover the delivery of equipment and stores to Malta, by convoy from the east and by the *Valiant* and the anti-aircraft cruisers from the west. The enterprise (whose code name was "Hats") obviously required the concerted action of all British naval forces in the Mediterranean. During the afternoon of Thursday, 8th August, it occurred to Eden that fast merchant ships, loaded with the desperately needed army equipment, might accompany the naval expedition. The Prime Minister gave this idea his instant and weighty support. The Admiralty, however, which was staking a great deal on the operation, opposed the addition of a convoy of merchant ships—even fast merchant ships —to the naval vessels which, it was expected, might become heavily involved with the Italian fleet. The counter-proposal was put forward that a fast liner should take the army reinforcements round the Cape.

The Directorate of Military Operations had a memorandum ready for Wavell, the C.I.G.S. and the Secretary of State by five o'clock on the afternoon of Friday, 9th August. It proposed that a total of 3,000 men and 700 vehicles should be sent in one or two liners and four or five M.T. ships of the Clan type, and offered a provisional timetable by which the convoy could move off from the Mersey on 20th August in company with the naval forces going to the Mediterranean. It also rejected the Admiralty suggestion with the Ministry of Shipping's argument that liners' holds and lifting gear were unsuitable for large numbers of vehicles of the size and type that would be sent.

In the meantime the First Sea Lord had asked the C.-in-C. Mediterranean Fleet for his views. Admiral Cunningham thought that this was a problem which could only be solved by being tried out in practice. The convoy might go through unscathed, or every ship in it might be lost. The presence of the merchant ships would greatly increase the time during which the naval component would be exposed to bombing attacks, which might be heavy and continuous. But (he signalled) if the urgency was so great as to justify the risk of losing the army reinforcements and of causing serious damage to the fleet, he would undertake the operation, subject to some conditions which he named.

On Saturday the problem was no nearer solution, but the pros and cons were still being hotly debated.

C.I.G.S. to Prime Minister   *10th August, 1940*
After a full discussion this morning and taking all factors into consideration, we are arranging to send the following to the Middle East:

1 Cruiser Tank Battalion (52 tanks)
1 Light Tank Regiment (52 tanks)
1 Infantry Tank Battalion (50 tanks)
48 Anti-Tank guns
20 Bofors Light A.A. guns
48 25-pdr. Field guns
500 Bren guns
250 Anti-Tank rifles

Ammunition for the above and some Anti-Tank mines.

There are, I am afraid, only two fast M.T. ships available which are suitable to accompany the naval units through the Mediterranean. These two ships can take the cruiser and light tanks, the anti-tank and anti-aircraft guns and the small arms. There may not be room, however, for the 25-pdr. guns, and certainly not for the infantry tanks.

As regards personnel, a total of 700 can be sent, 150 in each of the M.T. ships and the balance of 400 in H.M. ships. This means in effect that the personnel of the Cruiser Tank Battalion and a few A.A. gunners only can go by the Mediterranean. Such material and personnel which cannot go through the Mediterranean must follow via the Cape as soon as possible.

Wavell can use a fair proportion of the light tanks with personnel he already has in Egypt until the men of the Light Tank Regiment (3rd Hussars) arrive by way of the Cape.

This is not ideal, but as good as is possible in the circumstances. One liner would have taken all the personnel, but the Navy cannot accept the risk, and another good M.T. ship would probably have taken the rest of the gear but is not available.

Prime Minister to Gen. Ismay, for C.O.S.   *11th August, 1940*

I cannot accept this proposal which deprives us of invaluable resources (50 Infantry Tanks) during a most critical period, without making them available for the Middle East at the moment when they are most needed there. I must ask the Admiralty to make further proposals, and overcome the difficulties. If necessary, could not the personnel be distributed among the destroyers, a larger force of destroyers being sent through from Force H. to the Eastern Mediterranean, and returned thereafter in the same way as the six destroyers are now being sent westward by Admiral Cunningham?

There is no objection to the 3rd Hussars going by the Cape, as General Wavell can make temporary arrangements for manning them in the meanwhile, so long as he gets their Light Tanks. I am prepared to risk the 50 Infantry Tanks in the Mediterranean, provided their personnel is distributed among H.M. ships; but there can be no question of them or their personnel going by the Cape, thus making sure they are out of everything for two months. The personnel sent through the Mediterranean must be cut down to essentials; the balance going round.

Pray let me have further proposals by tomorrow (Monday).[2]

At ten o'clock on the evening of Monday, 12th August, the Prime Minister held a meeting of senior Ministers and Service officers concerned with the Middle East. Wavell, who had already had another long session with the Chiefs of Staff, was present. Churchill presided as Minister of Defence; Mr. Eden, as Secretary of State for War, and Mr. A. V. Alexander, the First Lord of the Admiralty, the three Chiefs of Staff and General Ismay also attended.

The only subject for discussion was the controversy over the method of sending Wavell his reinforcements. The Chiefs of Staff submitted an *aide mémoire* as their considered, joint reply to the Prime Minister's minute. They said that they found repugnant the idea of having so many men and such vitally important equipment out of the battle for a day longer than was necessary, but they felt that "in all the circumstances it is better to accept the longer, but more sure, sea passage for the bulk of the armoured brigade via the Cape route, rather than accept the risk not only of compromising the offensive character of operation 'Hats,' but also of losing equipment which could not be replaced." They therefore made four proposals:

(1) To send 48 anti-tank guns in the *Illustrious*.
(2) To send as many of the personnel for the armoured brigade as could be accommodated in H.M. ships through the Mediterranean.
(3) To despatch the remainder of the convoy by the Cape route, embarking one of the tank units (either the cruiser tank battalion or the infantry tank battalion) in an 18-knot ship, and the remainder of the armoured brigade in two 16-knot ships.
(4) To accelerate the loading of these ships in order that they

should sail if possible before 20th August, and to expedite their passage round the Cape in every possible way.

They said that if these proposals were accepted, the whole of the armoured brigade would be in Egypt, for certain, on 29th September, twenty-five days after it would arrive if it passed unscathed through the Mediterranean, and they ended with the cautious hope that it might be possible to improve on this timing.

The Prime Minister was in no mood to accept these arguments tamely. He had a great respect and affection for the First Sea Lord, Admiral of the Fleet Sir Dudley Pound, whose capacity for taking justifiable risks was greater than that of any other naval officer with whom he had worked. But he would get his way against Pound if he possibly could.

Pound opened the discussion. He said that the presence of relatively slow M.T. ships accompanying the fleet through the Mediterranean would restrict its liberty of movement and reduce its effective speed, thereby increasing its vulnerability to attack by aircraft, submarines, motor transport boats and destroyers. Moreover, the Italians were bound to become aware that the M.T. ships were sailing along the North African coast, and could not fail to deduce their destination. They would thus have at least two days' warning, and would be able to mount a great concentration of aircraft, submarines and small surface craft for an assault on the convoy in the narrows south of Sicily. The chances of the convoy making the passage were, he thought, remote; it was quite possible that the M.T. ships would be lost and the warships sustain damage; and Admiral Cunningham, he added, was of the same opinion.

The Prime Minister spoke next. He was at his peak. The Battle of Britain (as he had already named it) had begun. Caution at that moment was an attitude of mind for which he had little liking. He said, "In the light of recent experiences of convoys passing between Malta and Egypt, the Admiralty's view of the risks involved appears to me unduly pessimistic. It is surely possible to pass a convoy of three fast ships through to Egypt without insuperable difficulty. The presence of these ships with the fleet ought indeed to be a bait. Will it not draw down upon the whole array those concentrations of Italian ships which the First Sea Lord described, and thereby give the chance he wants of inflicting serious damage on the Italian Navy?" He paused, and his tone changed. "Nevertheless I am bound to accept the opinion of the Naval Staff, though I do not agree with it."

The decision now lay with Wavell, who said, "Prime Minister, much as I should like the reinforcements to reach Egypt as soon as possible, I don't believe that the risks of losing them in passage through the Mediterranean, and the fact that if the equipment is lost it cannot be replaced for several months, justify the gain in time. But if it is decided not to send the armoured brigade at all, then I must warn you that, if German armoured forces are used to reinforce an Italian advance, the situation in Egypt will be very grave and its security may well be in jeopardy."

After further general discussion no immediate conclusion was reached, but it was agreed that the despatch of the armoured brigade to the Middle East should receive further consideration.

That further consideration lasted two more days.

Prime Minister to First Lord and First Sea Lord 13th August, 1940
... No one can see where or when the main attack on Egypt will develop. It seems however extremely likely that if the Germans are frustrated in an invasion of Great Britain or do not choose to attempt it they will have great need to press and aid the Italians to the attack of Egypt. The month of September must be regarded as critical in the extreme.

In these circumstances it is very wrong that we should attempt to send our armoured brigade round the Cape, thus making sure that during September it can play no part either in the defence of England or Egypt.

I request that the operation of passing at least two M.T. ships through with the Eastern reinforcements may be re-examined. The personnel can be distributed in the warships, and it is a lesser risk, from the point of view of the general war, to pass the M.T. ships through the Mediterranean than to have the whole armoured brigade certainly out of action going round the Cape. So long as the personnel are properly distributed among the warships, I am prepared to take the full responsibility for the possible loss of the armoured vehicles.[3]

On the afternoon of Wednesday, 14th August, the First Lord and the First Sea Lord saw the Prime Minister. Wavell was given a note of the conclusions which were reached:

(*i*) The route to be taken by the convoy depends upon developments in the Middle East situation. If our information leads us to think that Egypt will be in grave danger during the month of September, unless the reinforcements arrive by the quickest route, the Admiralty would be prepared to pass the convoy through the Mediterranean with operation "Hats." This would be all the more essential if there is reason to think that German armoured divisions are to take part in the invasion. On the other hand, if it looks as though September is not going to be a dangerous month for Egypt, the reinforcements should proceed via the Cape.

(*ii*) A final decision need not be taken until the convoy reaches Gibraltar (about 26th August), provided that the reinforcements are loaded in such a way that the voyage can be continued by either route. The Admiralty and War Office should immediately arrange accordingly.

(*iii*) It is vital that steps should be taken to ensure that we get the best possible information of Italian and German dispositions in Libya. The Air Ministry should be invited to make arrangements as soon as possible for long-range reconnaissance of Libya with special regard to the situation in Benghazi and movements to the eastward.

To this note was attached the revised plan, with the code name "Apology." It provided for the despatch of a fast convoy from the Mersey on 20th August, as proposed by the Directorate of Military Operations five days earlier. This would be composed of three M.T. ships carrying all the tanks, guns and ammunition specified by the C.I.G.S. in his minute to Churchill on 10th August, and a liner carrying 2,000 officers and men. Churchill put this plan to the Cabinet on Thursday, 15th August—a crucial day in the Battle of Britain, in the course of which every fighter squadron in the country was engaged, losing thirty-four aircraft against seventy-six German attackers brought down—and it was approved, with the essential proviso that the decision as to its final routing should not be made until it reached Gibraltar. "The decision to give this blood-transfusion while we braced ourselves to meet a mortal danger was at once awful and right. No one faltered."[4]

While this tense, yet in the end fruitful, controversy was being thrashed out, Churchill and Wavell were also arguing, in a succession of long and detailed minutes, about the proper employment of the South African and West African troops being trained and acclimatised in Kenya for the assault on Italian East Africa, and of Kenya's white settlers; about the large British garrison still held in Palestine; and about the thorny question of arming the Jews in that country for their own defence. To all of Churchill's points Wavell gave closely reasoned answers, but all courteously and firmly negative. The exchange of notes deepened the Prime Minister's displeasure and suspicion. During Wavell's last day or two in England he dropped the controversies, but he was far indeed from forgetting them.

Wavell left London on the evening of 15th August and reached Cairo twenty-four hours later. During his stay in Britain the brief campaign in British Somaliland had been brought to its inevitable but dismal conclusion. Churchill later described it as "a small but at the same time vexatious military episode."[5]

The Italians' main assault, launched on 11th August, deployed a great many infantry, a great many vehicles, and a number of medium tanks. The command of the British force passed that evening to General Godwin-Austen who, on his way to Kenya to command a division, was ordered to Berbera to take over from Chater. His was a pretty hopeless task from the outset.

For three days and nights the Italians, with their enormous superiority in manpower and guns, attacked incessantly. In spite of the most resolute defence, all that Godwin-Austen could do was steadily to pull his small force back. On 15th August he told G.H.Q. Middle East that he had two alternatives: immediate evacuation or the loss of a very large proportion of what remained of the force. Wilson, acting on Wavell's behalf, decided in favour of evacuation and signalled his decision to the Chief in London. "I have no doubt," wrote Wavell in his Despatch, "that both General Godwin-Austen's recommendation and General Wilson's decision were correct."[6]

Recalling Churchill's reaction years afterwards he said, "Winston had been following the course of the campaign with the greatest interest, and when I brought him the news of the evacuation I rather expected an outburst. But he took it very well, and said that it could not be helped, that the loss of Somaliland was of little importance and that I should have the troops withdrawn available for more important defence."

The final stages of the evacuation were skilfully conducted. The Black Watch fought a spirited rearguard action and the main body of the British force, except for a few hundred men holding the outskirts of Berbera and a few stragglers, was successfully embarked on the night of 17th August. During the 18th, H.M.A.S. *Hobart* embarked the rest, after as many vehicles and stores and as much petrol as possible had been destroyed. On the 19th she sailed out of the road-stead, having pumped as many shells as she could into the Government buildings.

The total casualties of the campaign were 260 (38 killed, 222 wounded and missing), as against 1,800 admitted by the Italians. Wavell disliked abandoning British territory—even if only temporarily—no less than did Churchill, who declared that, in terms of prestige, the only defeat inflicted on the British by the Italians "caused injury far beyond its strategic scale."[7] His displeasure at the small number of casualties was immediate and severe. He sent Wavell, by this time back in Cairo, "a red-hot cable," ordering the Commander-in-Chief to suspend Godwin-Austen (who had gone on to Kenya) and proposing to send a general from India to hold a court of inquiry.

"I sent a reply refusing to suspend Godwin-Austen . . . saying that a court of inquiry would be disastrous to morale and that the troops had fought very well and hard, as was evidenced by the 1,800 casualties admitted by the Italians (it was lucky for me that they were publishing their casualties at this period of the war); and ending with the remark that 'a big butcher's bill was not necessarily evidence of good tactics.' Jack Dill told me afterwards that this telegram and especially the last sentence roused Winston to greater anger than he had ever seen him in before. But there was no court of inquiry, Godwin-Austen continued in command, and I heard no more of the accusation that the troops had not fought. But I believe that Winston always kept a bad mark against Godwin-Austen, and I dare say against myself for defending him."

Churchill's account of this episode concluded: "In view of the great business we had together, I did not press my view further either with the War Office or with General Wavell."[8]

On 16th August, the day after Wavell left the United Kingdom, the Prime Minister addressed to the Secretary of State for War and the C.I.G.S. a document headed "General Directive for Commander-in-Chief Middle East." He had drafted it himself, and he said later that "the Cabinet approved it without amendment in accord with the Chiefs of Staff. With this," he added, "General Wavell returned to Cairo in the third week of August."[9]

The directive in fact reached Wavell late in the afternoon of 23rd August as a signal, which after deciphering covered three and a half foolscap pages of close typing. Its text differs in many places from that published by Churchill in 1949, both in additions and in omissions. Wavell wrote: "It showed clearly that Winston did not trust me to run my own show and was set on his ideas."

Detailed tactical instructions were given in the signal, down to the forward and rear disposition of battalions. The Prime Minister returned to his insistent desire that the South Africans and the West Africans should be moved from Kenya. Minutely careful and very long instructions were given about the defence of the Egyptian Delta, about rendering desert wells "depotable,"[10] and about damaging the surface of the coastal—then the one metalled—road in the desert, so that the Italians should not use it. Its first section was a protracted analysis of the situation, which did not bear much relation to the real facts, followed by an array of statistics from which the Prime Minister drew the conclusion that, by 1st October at the latest, the "Army of the Delta" (a title which was subsequently altered to "Army of the Nile"), without including any internal security troops, would consist of thirty-nine battalions totalling, together with armoured forces, 56,000 men and 212 guns. The second section of the directive was a brief and slightly disingenuous statement:

It is hoped that the armoured brigade from England of three regiments of tanks will be passed through the Mediterranean by the Admiralty. If this is impossible their arrival round the Cape may be counted upon by 3rd October. The arrival of this force by the earliest possible date must be considered so important as to justify a considerable degree of risk in their transportation.[11]

The third and last section began with meticulous and minutely detailed orders for Wavell's employment of his forces, after which there were three remarkable concluding paragraphs:

In this posture then the Army of the Delta will finally defeat the Italian invasion. It must be expected that the enemy will advance in great force, limited only, but severely, by the supply of water and petrol. He will certainly have strong armoured forces on his right hand to contain and drive back our weaker forces unless these can be reinforced in time by the armoured regiments from Great Britain. He may attempt to mask if he cannot storm Mersa

Matruh, but if the main line of the Delta is diligently fortified and resolutely held he will be forced to deploy an army whose supply of water, petrol, food and ammunition will be difficult. Once the army is deployed and seriously engaged, the action against his communications by bombardment from the sea, by descent at Mersa Matruh, Sollum or even much farther west would be a deadly blow to him.

The campaign for the defence of Egypt may therefore as a last resort resolve itself into strong defence with the left arm from Alexandria inland and a reaching out with the right hand using sea power upon his communications. At a later date it is hoped that the reinforcement of the A.A. defence of Malta and its re-occupation by the Fleet will hamper the sending of further reinforcements, Italian or German, from Europe into Africa, and that an air offensive may ultimately be developed from Malta against Italy.

All this (except Malta) might be put effectively in train by 1st October provided we are allowed the time. If not we must do what we can. All trained or Regular units, whether fully equipped or not, must be used in defence of Egypt against invasion. All armed white men and also Indian or foreign units must be used for internal security. The Egyptian Army must be made to play its part in support of the Delta front, thus leaving only riotous crowds to be dealt with in Egypt proper.[12]

Wavell wrote subsequently: "I carried out such parts of the directive as were practicable and useful, and disregarded a good deal of it." He answered it in four long telegrams spread over five days, from 23rd to 27th August. He held his ground firmly over the South and West Africans in Kenya; and he was as conciliatory as he could be about making the wells "depotable" and about damaging the coastal road west of Mersa Matruh (with regret, since he had "an inkling all the time that I might want it before the Italians"). But he stressed yet again that the successful defence of Egypt—and especially of the naval base at Alexandria—was dependent on sufficient air reinforcements being sent, and that the strongest ground forces would be in grave difficulties if the enemy were to gain control of the air. Cunningham, in a signal to the First Sea Lord, and Longmore, in one to the Chief of the Air Staff, supported Wavell strongly on this point, to which the directive had drawn no attention at all. For his own part, Wavell assured Dill: "It is material, especially artillery and anti-tank weapons, that is required rather than men. Enemy will not reach Delta with large forces of infantry, but only if he can bring up superior armoured force."[13]

The detailed composition therefore of the convoy once known as "Hats" and now as "Apology" was of unabated interest to him. If the convoy were to pass through the Mediterranean, would it include all the personnel for the armoured units? There was a lack, he thought, of indications of an impending heavy attack; the Cape route, in view of the Navy's anxieties, might prove feasible. "Date 3rd October is however ten days later than I was given in London." Firmly he corrected Churchill's statistics:

Approximate total of forces excluding Egyptian for defence of Egypt by 8th October is 38 battalions, 156 field guns, 18 medium guns, 90 anti-tank guns, 1,000 anti-tank rifles, 239 Bren-carriers, 40 A.A. guns, 12 light A.A. guns. Above includes reserves. Please note that proper proportion equipment for force of this size should be 380 field guns, 50 medium guns, 320 anti-tank guns, 2,100 anti-tank rifles, 730 carriers universal. Above does not include reserves.[14]

And he drove home once more the basic lessons: more armour was essential; even after the arrival of the reinforcements now on the way his one armoured division would still be incomplete; and a second armoured division was required as soon as possible. If the Prime Minister insisted on controlling the conduct of his campaign, these telegrams indicated, the Commander-in-Chief in his turn could be exigent. The directive, so firm and so flowery when it was first composed, dwindled under this resolute combination of criticism and requests, and lost the urgency and the authority of an order.

The convoy "Apology" reached Gibraltar safely. On 25th August the Commanders-in-Chief reported that reconnaissance had not revealed any signs of large-scale preparations in Libya and Tripolitania for an offensive in the next few weeks. On the following day the crucial decision was taken by the War Cabinet: the tanks, guns and spare parts which would bring the "Army of the Delta" up to something near the effective strength of one corps, were to make the long haul round the Cape. The purely naval operation, "Hats," was carried out successfully, between 30th August and 5th September.

Nevertheless if the Italians did advance, the situation could well become very dangerous, even in the dramatic, man-to-man. hand-to-hand combat which Churchill's directive had envisaged. This was the kind of battle which, at precisely the same time, the forces and the civilian population in the United Kingdom were expecting that they would have to fight.

A successful simultaneous invasion of England and Egypt could have defeated Britain as quickly and as cruelly as, three months earlier, France had been defeated. The potentialities of such a co-ordinated assault occurred to Mussolini, if to nobody else on the Axis side. After Balbo had been killed, command in Libya was assumed by Marshal Graziani, a soldier of considerable reputation and prolonged service overseas, including this theatre of war, who had been Chief of the Army Staff since the previous November. Like Wavell, he was short of everything: aircraft, anti-tank, A.A. and medium artillery, medium tanks, and vehicles of all kinds. His requests to Rome bore a strange similarity to Wavell's requests to London; and, just like Wavell, he never got nearly as much as he wanted.

In the middle of July Mussolini told him that he must advance against Egypt on the day the first Germans set foot in England, whether his preparations were completed or not, and wrote to Hitler: "The preparations for an attack on Egypt with vast objectives are now complete." Graziani raised no overt objection to the Duce's directive, but repeated that he thought it would be unwise to advance without the strength to carry the operations through, and gave effect to his views by postponing the date of readiness with great regularity.[15]

On 7th September the Duce issued a peremptory order: whether or not the Germans had begun to land in England, Graziani was to advance in the desert in two days' time. Reluctantly the Marshal went through the motions of obeying. "Never," wrote Count Ciano, "has a military operation been undertaken so much against the will of the Commander."[16] Graziani's caution does seem to have been excessive, since he was able to muster five divisions (admittedly he had been disappointed at not receiving the motor transport he needed for two of them); a mobile force, under a General Maletti; a tank group of one medium, two mixed and four light tank battalions; and some 300 bombers, fighters and ground-attack aircraft; not to mention two more divisions in reserve near Tobruk. Against this formidable force Wavell had the thin "screen" of Gott's Support Group, to which had been added a section of the 7th Medium Regiment, R.A.

This small force was distributed over a front extending from Sollum, on the coast to the north of the escarpment, to Fort Maddalena, sixty miles south-south-east in the desert.

The Maletti Group lost their way to their assembly point at Sidi Omar, and Graziani himself was fussed by reports that there were "massive British armoured forces" gathered to the south of the escarpment. It was not therefore until the 13th that he made any eastward move, and then there was no sweeping drive through the desert in the south but a slow, careful build-up on and near the coastal road. There was some confusion—never really cleared up—about what he intended to do thereafter; but Wavell's intentions were crystal clear:

"My plan for the defence of Egypt was to await the invaders at the defences of Matruh and counter-attack them there. If they by-passed the Matruh defences and pushed on towards the Delta, I had had further defences prepared at Nagamish Nullah and Ma'aten Bagush, covering the chief supplies of water. The troops holding these were to remain in position and not withdraw, but the Armoured Division would gradually withdraw on Egypt, keeping outside the defences. Thus the enemy would have on his flank on the coast a series of defended positions covering the water supplies and an armoured force threatening his southern flank. If he continued to press on, he would be in difficulties about water supply and would have to leave considerable forces to contain my defended positions on the coast. If he eventually reached the Delta he would find my remaining less mobile troops in prepared positions covering Alexandria and Cairo. I think it was the best I could do with my limited resources. I am not sure that Winston approved of it, but I believe it was quite a good plan. Tobruk later showed how effective a flank position could be."

This plan, however, was never put to the test. With several days' clear warning—not to mention the obligingly loud threats of the Italian radio—Gott's tiny force had made all their plans for a fighting withdrawal. On the morning of the 13th a whole Italian division, with its trucks, light tanks and motor-cycles drawn up in lines as if on a parade ground, deployed massively for its attack on the police barracks at Sollum. The defending garrison, which consisted of a single British platoon, watched this manœuvre with interest, and then slipped quietly away, leaving the track eastward mined. On the same day another large Italian column came down from the escarpment, through

Halfaya Pass, towards Sollum. Bombed by the R.A.F., shelled by artillery and harassed by mines, they left their lorries and scrambled down the escarpment on foot. For four days the slow, hesitant advance continued until, on 16th September, the Italians reached Sidi Barrani, sixty-five miles from where they had started. At Sidi Barrani, which was nothing more than a collection of a few mud huts and a landing ground, they halted and began laboriously to dig themselves in. Rome then put out a communiqué announcing Graziani's victorious advance and claiming that "all is quiet and the trams are again running in the town of Sidi Barrani."

A. P. Wavell to C.I.G.S. *19th September, 1940*
Have just returned from Western Desert where I visited H.Q. Western Desert Force and H.Q. Armoured Division. . . . Everyone in excellent spirits and full of confidence.

. . . If enemy has no surprise packet behind I feel confident we can deal with him when he comes within reach. I repeat that our only anxiety is our lack of reserves of material and equipment of all kinds, which is serious and may cause breakdown during battle. Co-operation of R.A.F. is excellent but they also have shortages of equipment. Navy is also assisting and shelled enemy at Sollum and near coast effectively late last night.

In his Despatch, dated 10th December, 1940, Wavell assessed these operations:

Although the enemy had large numbers of medium and light tanks with his forward troops and the leading infantry was in M.T., his advance was slow and unenterprising. He made little attempt to use his immensely superior numbers or his mobility to outflank and overwhelm our small force. His artillery was boldly used, even in front of the leading infantry, but their fire, though reasonably accurate, was ineffective. His tanks were mainly used for the protection of the infantry columns and only on one occasion, on 16th September, was any attempt made to use them to outflank our troops; and even on this occasion their timidity and hesitation lost them an opportunity.

The withdrawal of our small force was effected with admirable skill, and there is no doubt whatever that very serious losses were inflicted on the enemy, both by the artillery, which was boldly and effectively handled, and whenever opportunity offered, by

271

machine-gun and small-arms fire. Our own losses were under fifty men and a small number of vehicles.[17]

Wavell gave special praise to Gott's work in command of the Support Group, and that of Colonel Jock Campbell and his Gunners. These two officers were amongst the earliest of the Western Desert's legendary figures. Their small forces, as Wavell pointed out, had in over three months inflicted some 3,500 casualties on the Italians (including over 700 prisoners) and had captured or destroyed a considerable number of guns, tanks and lorries—for a total cost of just over 150 casualties.

Wavell put on record more than once his own standards of qualification for what he described as "the Sixth Form of generalship." In the draft of a lecture on Belisarius which he was preparing shortly before he died he wrote:

I would consider only one who had handled large forces in an independent command in more than one campaign; and who had shown his qualities in adversity as well as in success. I then proposed to judge him by his worth as a strategist; his skill as a tactician; his power to deal tactfully with his Government and his allies; his ability to train troops or direct their training; and his energy and driving power in planning and in battle.[18]

He now came to that phase in his career during which he himself stood to be judged by those standards. In a good-tempered argument with Liddell Hart on strategy and tactics he used the analogy of contract bridge: the calling was strategy; the play of the hand tactics. In both there was wide scope for judgment, boldness and originality.

But in the end it is the result of the manner in which the cards are played or the battle fought that is put down on the score sheets or in the pages of history. Therefore I rate the skilful tactician above the skilful strategist, especially him who plays the bad cards well.[19]

In this period in high command Wavell was involved mainly in problems of strategy; but nearly all his subordinate commanders, fighting the tactical battles, were men whom he knew well, who were thoroughly in his mind, whom he had chosen, taught or trained. And in battle, as on exercises throughout the previous decade, he himself repeatedly gave proof of his possession of two extremely valuable qualities: first, a capacity to be on hand at any difficult moment, to fortify, counsel and sustain, without formality or flamboyance, or any hint of fussy interference; and second, lacking obvious *panache* or rousing eloquence, the ability to impress, on officers and men alike, the sense of his personality, giving them confidence in him and faith in what he and they were attempting to do together.

The first steps towards his first great victory were taken while Graziani's offensive was being launched. On 11th September he addressed a note to his Chief of Staff, in which he requested that a study be made of the question of an offensive into Cyrenaica, which he should be in a position to launch by the end of the year or early in 1941, if all went well.

The advance, he thought, would have to be made in four stages: first, the capture of Sidi Barrani; next, the establishment of a sufficient force along the frontier; then, the occupation of Bardia and the Jarabub Oasis; and finally, the capture of Tobruk. Thereafter, if the operation were continued, the next move would be to Derna; but he did not propose, at that moment, to look so far ahead. He then went, in some detail, into the administrative and tactical issues this proposal would raise: the extension of the railway from Matruh to Sidi Barrani; the construction of a road from Sidi Barrani to Sollum; the question of building up a base at Bardia; the possibility of a combined operation with the Navy to capture Tobruk; and, if and when this had been accomplished, the decision on whether, when and how to take Derna. The note continued:

In planning the operation, let us avoid as far as we can the slow ponderosity which is apt to characterise British operations. At the time that we shall be in a position to take the offensive, we shall presumably have established a strong enough naval position in the Mediterranean to prevent Libya receiving much in the way of supplies. We may, therefore, hope to be dealing with a somewhat dispirited and not very formidable Italian, and to be able to take a certain degree of risk.

We must have a proper air component with our force, i.e. one that has been specially allotted to the Army, has discussed the problems of army support and has trained with the Army. This will be a very different thing from the *ad hoc* air support of a force which has been mainly concerned with air problems only . . . .

273

What preparations can we make now? At any rate the sooner we can make an outline plan, calculate our requirements and submit them to the War Office, the more likely we are to have what we want when the time comes. At a rough guess I should say that a force of two armoured divisions, a brigade of "I" tanks and two mobile divisions, well gunned and with adequate air support, including dive bombers, should be sufficient anyway for [the first three stages]. For the capture of Tobruk an additional division may be required.[20]

This directive was issued in anticipation of the safe arrival of the "Apology" convoy, and in the expectation that Graziani would try to advance at least as far as Mersa Matruh. O'Moore Creagh's Armoured Division was in position in the desert to the south, ready to harass and delay this advance west of Matruh as much as possible; and if and when it became necessary, to withdraw south and remain on the enemy's southern flank. Dumps of supplies had been secretly prepared in the desert, on which the Armoured Division could base itself.

During the last week of August and during September defence positions were constructed east of Matruh, in the Nagamish Nullah and at Ma'aten Bagush, to protect the water supply there. Farther east, in the approaches to Alexandria and to Cairo, defences were constructed against the possibility of a long-range raid either by armoured or by airborne troops. The 16th Infantry Brigade Group and an Australian brigade group from Palestine, a New Zealand brigade group from near Cairo, and the Polish Brigade which had been forming in the Middle East were made responsible for this work. Practically all the trained forces in Egypt and Palestine therefore, except for a few battalions employed on internal security, were concentrated in the Western Desert, under the command of General O'Connor.

On 21st September Wavell sent a note to Maitland Wilson, who was the operational commander of all British troops in Egypt, outlining his ideas on a vigorous counter-attack to the Italians' expected offensive, with as its aim the total destruction of their whole force. All troops, he said, must be prepared to go full out on this operation, whose success would have "an incalculable effect on the War." He dealt in detail with its strategy and its tactics, with the reconnaissance and preparation of the battlefield and with air co-operation, and he concluded: "I wish every possible precaution that our military training can suggest to be made in order to ensure that if the enemy attacks Matruh the greater part of his force shall never return from it."[21]

Wilson and O'Connor had already begun to discuss the possibility of just such a counter-stroke; they had prepared a plan for it, and their troops had studied the ground thoroughly. They had also speculated about launching an attack on a particularly wide gap in the south-eastern sector of the defensive line which the Italians had constructed along their present front.

Their principal opponent, Graziani, however, was in a very different frame of mind. He "lost no opportunity of pointing out that . . . his resources were quite inadequate for an immediate advance on Matruh."[22] His superiors in Rome, in their turn, jogged the Germans' elbows with repeated requests for equipment which they said was essential if they were to be effective allies. The Germans began to consider the possibility of using their own forces in the Eastern Mediterranean. The Army Staff proposed to send a corps—one motorised and two armoured divisions—to support the Italians in Libya; the Navy backed this idea strongly, because they regarded the Suez Canal as a most important objective, which the Italians by themselves would be unlikely to capture. General von Thoma (a Panzer expert who, two years later, was taken prisoner in the Western Desert) was sent to Cyrenaica to study the whole problem, and the 3rd Panzer Division was ordered to prepare itself for North Africa. Meanwhile, on 4th October Hitler and Mussolini met at the Brenner Pass; the Fuehrer offered to help his Italian ally with mechanised and specialist troops; and the Duce accepted the suggestion "without enthusiasm." They were not wanted for the next, the second, phase of the attack on Egypt—the capture of Matruh. But for the third phase—the advance to Alexandria—Mussolini admitted that he might need heavy tanks, armoured cars and dive bombers.[23]

Three days later, on 7th October, Wavell composed a note on the possibility of a German attack on Egypt. Until Italy's entry into the war he had had good reason to complain about the difficulty of getting reliable intelligence because of the Foreign Office's uncooperative attitude. Now he had a wealth of up-to-date and accurate information.

He began with the assumption that the Germans would soon take over or at least actively assist the Italian attack on Egypt, and went on to consider when this would happen and what form it would take. He saw no present signs of German land or air forces in Libya, and thought that the first hints of their coming would be increasing air attacks on Malta and on British convoys in the Western Mediterranean; strengthened A.A. and fighter defence over Benghazi and perhaps Tobruk; and preparations for the arrival of air reinforcements. The more vigorously the Navy and the R.A.F. could counter these preparations the better.

He thought the Germans might send fighter and bomber aircraft, perhaps parachutists, and probably a maximum of one armoured and one mobile (i.e. motorised) division. He believed that they would not be as scrupulous as the Italians had been about causing damage and loss of life to the Egyptians, and therefore air defence in the Delta, along the Canal and around Cairo and Alexandria would have to be strengthened. He foresaw simultaneous Italian offensives in East Africa and the Sudan, and trouble fomented in Syria and Palestine.

To counter these attacks, which he thought might begin in not less than four or five weeks' time, he asked for immediate R.A.F., A.A. and anti-tank reinforcements from Britain, and an increase in the armoured troops available.

A signal embodying the arguments and conclusions set forth in this note was sent to the C.I.G.S. It evoked a swift and dramatic response from Eden.

Secy. of State for War to A. P. Wavell 8th October, 1940, 2355 hrs.
In view of your telegram to the C.I.G.S. of 7th October and wide developments likely to take place affecting your Command have decided with concurrence of P.M. to pay you a flying visit and hope to arrive Alexandria 14th.

There was a number of reasons for Eden's visit at this time, the chief of which was certainly Churchill's restless anxiety about the conduct of the war in Wavell's theatre of operations. He knew nothing (as he subsequently admitted) of what he described as "the new thoughts which began to stir in staff and planning circles at the Middle East Headquarters." The Italians had moved more slowly than he had expected. The ships of the "Apology" convoy had docked at Suez on 24th September; and Maitland Wilson had (so the Prime Minister discovered) "formed a high opinion" of the Infantry tanks which had reached him. But Churchill was still "extremely dissatisfied" with Wavell's disposition of his forces; he feared greatly for Malta; and he regarded Kenya as overcrowded with troops. He and

Eden were in close agreement on these matters, and both felt the need of having their views put forward on the spot, instead of through endless telegrams. Only a personal visit would give them the opportunity of the survey of the Command and the supervision of the Commander-in-Chief which they both believed to be necessary.[24]

Eden arrived at Alexandria on 15th October, and left on 6th November. He had long talks with the Turkish mission in Cairo; he went with Wavell to Khartoum and there met both Smuts and Haile Selassie on 28th October. On that day the Italians launched a full-out offensive against Greece from Albania.

"I think," Wavell wrote, "Eden's general purpose was to inquire into our defence arrangements, and the training and equipment of the troops, etc." This was a fair conjecture. However, much as he liked the Secretary of State personally, he had no intention of disclosing even to him the plans which were beginning to crystallise in his own mind, and in the minds of one or two others, for an offensive against Graziani. But the immediate consequences of the Italian attack on Greece were that Longmore, the A.O.C.-in-C., was ordered to send three squadrons of Blenheims and one of Gladiators to help the Greeks to deal with the *Regia Aeronautica*, and that Wavell had to send two A.A. batteries to Athens and an infantry brigade to Suda Bay, in Crete, to assist in the defence of the Greek islands.

"All this meant a considerable drain on my resources, and led to my disclosing to Eden my plans for an early attack on the Italians. I had not intended to do so until the plans were further advanced, since I realised Winston's sanguine temperament and desire to have at least one finger in any military pie. I did not want to arouse premature hopes, I did not want Winston to make detailed plans for me, and I knew that absolute secrecy was the only hope of keeping my intentions from the Italians, who had so many tentacles in Cairo. But Eden was proposing to sap my strength in aircraft, A.A. guns, transport, etc., in favour of Greece, thinking I had only a defensive policy in mind, to such an extent that I had to tell him what was in my mind to prevent my being skinned to an extent that would make an offensive impossible."

The Secretary of State spent a great deal of time with Wavell and Wilson. It emerged at an early stage in their discussions that Wavell, no less than Wilson, thought highly of the Infantry tanks, that both generals were thinking aggressively, and that they were not sitting tamely waiting for the Italians to attack.

In a signal to the Prime Minister on 16th October Eden asked that Wavell should be sent a second battalion of Infantry tanks, with a Brigade Recovery Section, in order to keep them as fully in service as possible. The Prime Minister, replying on the same day, did not give a direct answer to Eden's request, but told him to continue to master the local situation.

On 20th October Wavell wrote to Maitland Wilson asking him to examine at once the possibility of an attack on the Italian positions in the Sofafi—Sidi Barrani—Buqbuq area. He rated its chances of securing a decisive success as "very great," but he said:

The operation I have in mind is a short and swift one, lasting four or five days at the most, and taking every advantage of the element of surprise. I should not propose to attempt to retain a large force in the Sidi Barrani area if the attack were successful, but to withdraw the bulk of the forces again to railhead, leaving only light covering forces in the forward areas.

The letter went into the possible conduct of the operation in great tactical detail and concluded: "I do not wish the contents of this note disclosed or the plan discussed with anyone except your Brigadier General Staff, General O'Connor and General Creagh."[25]

A copy was sent to O'Connor, who commented later: "The possibilities of exploiting local success were emphasised; but neither then, nor at any other time, was an ultimate objective given. In effect the operations were to be in the nature of a big raid which, if successful, was to be exploited as far as our meagre administrative resources permitted."[26]

The Prime Minister, though these matters were for the time being kept hidden from him, in a fashion which no other Commander-in-Chief in World War II dared to attempt, was becoming "hungry for a turn to the offensive in the Western Desert."[27]

Prime Minister to Secy. of State for War　　　　*26th October, 1940*
Before leaving you should consider searchingly with your Generals possibilities of a forestalling offensive. I cannot form any opinion about it from here, but if any other course was open it would not be sound strategy to await the concentration and deployment of overwhelming force. I thought the existing plans for repelling an attack by a defensive battle and counter-stroke very good, but what happens if the enemy do not venture until

the Germans arrive in strength? Do not send any answer to this, but examine it thoroughly and discuss it on return.

Please examine in detail the field state of the Middle Eastern Army in order to secure the largest proportion of fighting men and units for the great numbers on our ration strength. . . . All British battalions should be mobile and capable of taking part in battle. I fear that the proportion of fighting compared with ration strength is worse in the Middle East than anywhere else. Please do not be content with the stock answers. . . . Not only the best, but the second and third best, must be made to play their part.[28]

While Eden and Wavell were in Khartoum, Wilson and O'Connor thrashed out a plan for the operations which the Commander-in-Chief wanted. Its first phase was to be a concentrated attack with two divisions on the centre of the Italian line, south of Sidi Barrani, leaving the flanks to be contained by small forces; thereafter an infantry division (4th Indian) was to attack northwards towards the coast, capturing the enemy camps one after another, while the armoured division held the ring against counter-attacks from the west.[29]

A. P. Wavell to Gen. Maitland Wilson   *2nd November, 1940*
In continuation of my Personal and Most Secret letter of 20th October, I wish you to inform your *senior* commanders in the Western Desert as follows:

I have instructed Lieut.-Gen. O'Connor, through you, to prepare an offensive operation against the Italian forces in their present positions (if they do not continue their advance) to take place as soon as possible.

I realise the risks of such an operation and am fully prepared to accept them, and the possibility of considerable casualties to personnel and to A.F.V.s. I consider that the advantages of the operation entirely justify the risks run. Nor do I consider the risks excessive. In everything but numbers we are superior to the enemy. We are more highly trained, we have better equipment. We know the ground and are better accustomed to desert conditions. Above all we have stouter hearts and greater traditions and are fighting in a worthier cause.

I need hardly point out that a striking success, which I consider can well be won, will have an incalculable effect not only on the whole position in the Middle East, not only on the military

279

situation everywhere, but on the future of freedom and civilisation throughout the world. It is the best way in which we can help our Greek allies in their gallant struggle.

We have waited long in the Middle East; when our chance comes let us strike hard. We have been on the defensive; we must accustom our minds to the offensive which only can bring victory.

The Prime Minister has sent us every good wish in this battle with Italy and his assurance that "all acts and decisions of valour and violence against the enemy will, whatever their upshot, receive the resolute support of His Majesty's Government." I need not add that all commanders will have my full support in acting boldly and with determination. We have other large reinforcements on the way and can afford to take some of the risks without which battles cannot be won. I have the greatest confidence in the commanders and troops in the Western Desert and am sure that a striking success is possible, with good fortune which only boldness can bring.

One of our most powerful aids to victory will be surprise. Every means by which we can preserve secrecy and deceive the enemy must be studied. The plan and intentions must be confined till the last moment to as few persons as possible; and everyone must understand that the lives of his comrades and the success of the war may be imperilled by carelessness.[30]

These seven paragraphs were the only formal written directive for the operation which, given the code name "Compass," was to be so brilliant a victory and so far-reaching in its effects.

Anthony Eden was back in London on 8th November. That evening he went to see Churchill at his temporary underground abode in Piccadilly. The C.I.G.S. and General Ismay were summoned. Eden unfolded the plan for "Compass," which Churchill then and for ever after wished he had known earlier. Nevertheless at the moment they were all delighted. Churchill—he said so himself—"purred like six cats." Here was something he thought worth doing. It was decided, there and then, to give immediate sanction and all possible support to the enterprise; that it should take first place in all their thoughts; and that it should have, amid so many other competing needs, first claim upon the country's strained resources.[31] This was precisely the exuberant, enthusiastic response on Churchill's part which Wavell had striven to avert. The itch to supervise the operation, and to expand imaginatively on its potentialities, was uncontrollable. The Greeks' valorous stand, Admiral Cunningham's bold strike at the Italian fleet in Taranto harbour, and a successful skirmish at Gallabat on the Sudan front, combined to give the Prime Minister his first opportunity to interfere, within less than a week of being let into the secret.

Prime Minister to A. P. Wavell   *14th November, 1940*
Chiefs of Staff, Service Ministers and I have examined general situation in the light of recent events. Italian check on Greek front, British naval success against battle fleet at Taranto, poor showing Italian airmen have made over here, encouraging reports received of low morale in Italy, Gallabat, your own experiences by contact in Western Desert, above all the general political situation, make it very desirable to undertake operation of which you spoke to Secretary of State for War. It is unlikely that Germany will leave her flagging ally unsupported indefinitely.

Consequently it seems that now is the time to take risks and strike the Italians by land, sea and air. You should act accordingly in concert with other Commanders-in-Chief. We should be prepared to postpone reinforcement of Malta in order to give you more aircraft for your operation if this can be done in time. Telegraph latest date by which these should arrive in Egypt in order to be of use.[32]

This signal might have been deliberately and ingeniously devised to jab at the point at which Wavell was most sensitive to political supervision: the tactical control of a major operation. He was extremely—and justifiably—reluctant either to decide upon a date or, having decided, to make it known to anyone outside the small circle of officers to whom the knowledge was essential. He addressed his reply not to the Prime Minister but to Eden.

A. P. Wavell to Secy. of State for War   *16th November, 1940*
Operation is in preparation but not possible to execute this month as originally hoped. Now working to date about end first week December unless enemy moves meanwhile when earlier counterstroke may be possible.

Am discussing possibilities of air support with A.O.C.-in-C. Desirable that four fighter squadrons should be available. Please keep intentions entirely secret; premature disclosure is chief danger to plan.

In England the days passed, with no definite news from Cairo. The daylight onslaught had ceased. Now night after night the German bombers ranged over London and other great cities, and the A.A. guns banged and roared. As the winter came on, the likelihood of immediate invasion dwindled. But the situation in the Balkans looked ominous. What was Wavell doing? Dill manfully defended his friend, but Churchill's impatience could not be contained. If Wavell did not give clear proof of coming to heel and proceeding with "Compass" to his master's satisfaction, a touch of the stick was necessary.

C.I.G.S. to A. P. Wavell   *20th November, 1940*
Prime Minister and Secretary of State for War have authorised me to send you following:

You will have learnt from A.O.C.-in-C. strength of air forces which will be available from day to day in Egypt after approved air support to Greece has been provided. We realise how disturbing reduction of air forces must be to you, especially at this moment, but we are making every effort in our power to ensure that you have the squadrons you have estimated necessary to proceed with "Compass."

You will appreciate that developments in Greek theatre are likely to lead to further persistent demands for our assistance which will be the more difficult to resist so long as your forces are not actively engaged. Nevertheless decision as to how and when to act with regard to "Compass" must rest with you and we have full confidence in your judgment.

A. P. Wavell to C.I.G.S.   *20th November, 1940*
Have returned from two days in Western Desert. Commanders and troops in excellent health and spirits.

"Compass" in active preparation and forward depots already made. Main difficulties transport, spares for artillery and tanks, protection against air attack and secrecy. Can deal with first two locally as far as resources allow but air protection dependent on arrival Hurricanes in time. Am arranging to concentrate all A.A. artillery I can make available, taking risks elsewhere in Egypt. Shall endeavour to stage operation if air situation makes it at all possible but the less air support the larger the casualties will be and the greater the risk of failure. Will do my best to maintain secrecy here but difficulties in this country are great.

Wavell thought that this would be sufficient answer to Dill's signal. He had not seen the Prime Minister's original draft, which was far fiercer. But Dill's was merely the prelude.

Personal from Prime Minister to A. P. Wavell
21st November, 1940, 0130 hrs.
See our telegrams to Longmore. It becomes most necessary for me to know how this affects "Compass."

Personal from A. P. Wavell to Prime Minister
21st November, 1940, 1520 hrs.
I think my telegram to the C.I.G.S. of 20th November will give you what you require.

On Sunday, 22nd November, Churchill composed one of his angriest minutes.

Prime Minister to Secy. of State for War & C.I.G.S.
22nd November, 1940
General Wavell's telegram to C.I.G.S. does not answer the question I put. The last sentence but one leaves everything unsettled. I had expected to hear either that the reinforcements of aircraft were insufficient, or that when they arrived he would act. It is not clear that he has made up his mind.

... Every day's delay endangers secrecy in Egypt, which must be full of Italian spies and agents.

Evidently we must now call upon Turkey to come in, or face the consequences in the future. Turkey will reply either by refusing, or by demanding as a condition immediate assistance in arms, men, ships and air. A British victory in Libya would probably turn the scale, and then we could shift our forces to the new theatre. How long would it be before the Germans could strike at Greece through Bulgaria? There might just be time for Wavell to act in Libya before the pressure becomes decisive.

Anyhow all his troops, except the barest defensive minimum, will be drawn out of him before long.

Wavell held steadfastly to his secret and to his own right decision.

Since above all things he desired surprise for this operation, the highest degree of security was essential. He fully appreciated by this time the Italians' facilities for information in Cairo, and he was determined to outwit them. In G.H.Q. not more than half a dozen of the staff were aware of the plan at all; and similar precautions were taken in all the other headquarters involved. The impression was created that the forces in the Western Desert had been seriously weakened by the sending of reinforcements to Greece, and that there would soon be more withdrawals. Few big operations have been prepared with less paper work. Administrative services, such as medical and ordnance, were given no prior information. There was to be a final rehearsal on 26th Nobember, which was described as Training Exercise No. 1. The operation itself, fixed no more firmly than "for a day in the second week in December,"³³ was Training Exercise No. 2. The actual fighting units were not to be informed that this was to be a battle, and not an exercise, until after they had begun the approach. The building of the dumps was explained as being purely for defensive purposes. No leave was to be stopped until three days before the operation.

Training Exercise No. 1 was held on a plateau south of Matruh, using replicas of the Italians' camps at Nibeiwa and Tummar, reconstructed from air reconnaissance photographs. Though vigorously and convincingly carried out, it had about it a curiously orthodox air. Fourth Indian Division made the main assault, on the first camp, Nibeiwa, in accordance with the principles laid down in an official pamphlet, *The Division in Attack*. There was a long pause after it reached the assembly area while the artillery, in daylight, registered the parapet defences of the camp's perimeter and shattered the wire. But what would the Italians do during this three-hour pause, with the light strengthening every minute? Could not their aircraft very effectively blunt the edge of the assault? And where, on the tactical plane, would be the surprise which Wavell, on the level of strategy, had done his best to preserve? As rehearsed, the attack's chances of success were not great.

When the exercise was finished—the majority of the troops had for the first time heard the whistle and whine of real shells over their heads—there was what Jumbo Wilson described as "a pow-wow" in O'Connor's H.Q. among the sand-dunes between the Matruh-Alexandria road and the sea: Wilson himself; O'Connor; Galloway, Wilson's B.G.S.; John Harding, O'Connor's G.S.O.1, neat, small as

O'Connor himself, even of temper, courteous of manner; and Eric Dorman-Smith.[34]

They all pored again over the air reconnaissance pictures. They realised that all the vehicle tracks led into an entrance on the west side of the camp, where obviously no mines had been laid. Ought not this to be the point of assault for the tanks and for the infantry? But if they went in there, the camp would lie between them and their own guns. It was therefore decided—it was a highly unorthodox solution—that the whole operation should begin at first light; that the Infantry tanks of the 7th R.T.R. should lead the infantry and go into the assault against two points on the camp's western perimeter, the M.T. entrance and the north-west corner; that one brigade of 4th Indian Division should approach, in their vehicles, to within a few hundred yards of the perimeter, deploy at once, and dash forward in close pursuit of the tanks, which would fan out once they were through and into the camp; and that only while the tanks were advancing would there be a brief, intensive artillery bombardment of the camp area.

These vital alterations stood the text-book technique on its head. Wilson insisted that the crux of the whole plan, apart from making sure that the gunners got their range accurate at once, was that the first wave of infantry must reach the perimeter within five minutes of the moment at which the leading tank forced the entrance. The plan was then embodied in a document entitled *A Method of Attack on an Entrenched Camp in the Desert*, which was given an extremely restricted circulation.[35]

Prime Minister to A. P. Wavell　　　　　*26th November, 1940*
News from every quarter must have impressed on you the importance of "Compass" in relation to whole Middle East position . . . and generally to the whole war. Without being over-sanguine, I cannot repress strong feeling of confidence and hope, and feel convinced risks inseparable from great deeds are fully justified.

. . . If success is achieved, presume you have plans for exploiting it to the full. I am having a staff study made of possibilities open to us, if all goes well, for moving fighting troops and also reserves forward by sea in long hops along the coast, and setting up new supply bases to which pursuing armoured vehicles and units might resort. Without wishing to be informed on details,

I should like to be assured that all this has been weighed, explored, and as far as possible prepared.

It seems difficult to believe that Hitler will not be forced to come to the rescue of his partner, and obviously German plans may be far advanced for a drive through Bulgaria to Salonika. . . . One may indeed see possibility of centre of gravity in Middle East shifting suddenly from Egypt to the Balkans, and from Cairo to Constantinople. . . .

As we told you the other day, we shall stand by you and Wilson in any well-conceived action irrespective of result, because no one can guarantee success in war, but only deserve it. . . .[36]

However constructive its intentions, this signal did not seem, in the circumstances of its reception, entirely helpful to its recipient. For he too was thinking ahead strategically, but on very different lines from the Prime Minister.

Two days later, Wavell issued his last directive before the operation.

A. P. Wavell to Gen. Maitland Wilson   *28th November, 1940*
I know that you have in mind and are planning the fullest possible exploitation of any initial success of "Compass" operation. You and all Commanders in the Western Desert may rest assured that the boldest action, whatever its results, will have the support not only of myself but of the C.I.G.S. and of the War Cabinet at home.

. . . It is possible that an opportunity may offer for converting the enemy's defeat into an outstanding victory. . . .

I am not entertaining extravagant hopes of this operation, but I do wish to make certain that if a big opportunity occurs we are prepared morally, mentally and administratively to use it to the fullest.[37]

Wavell, no less than Churchill, regarded the desert offensive as a springboard for bigger operations elsewhere. But while the Prime Minister thought of succour to the Greeks, of a drive through the Balkans, and of Constantinople replacing Cairo as the centre of gravity, Wavell's vision was fixed firmly on what he could do in his own Command, with the troops and the equipment he possessed, and all the other practical limitations of which he had become conscious. He wanted finally and totally to defeat the Italians in Africa before he turned to other ventures. On 2nd December he held a meeting in Cairo at which were present General Platt from the Sudan, and from Kenya General Alan Cunningham, the brother of the naval C.-in-C., who a month earlier had succeeded General Dickinson. One of the main points in the policy then laid down by the Commander-in-Chief was that an operation was to be put in train for the recapture of Kassala, which the Italians had occupied soon after their entry into the war. This would require reinforcements from Egypt—equivalent to at least one infantry division—whose availability would depend, first, on the way in which the desert offensive worked out, and second, on the presence of shipping to support them. He told Platt that 4th Indian Division would begin to move to the Sudan about the middle of December; and he decided that he would replace them by the 6th Australian Division, one brigade group at once, and the whole division by the end of the month.

From 2nd December onwards, therefore, this was a factor which Wavell—and Wavell only—had to bear constantly in mind. He felt able to tell Maitland Wilson about it in strict secrecy; but the decision must be his only, and it would have to be made at short notice. He had a move in mind, if it should prove feasible, but he wanted as few people as possible to have a hint of it; and once again he did not take the Prime Minister into his confidence.

On 4th December there was a final conference about "Compass" at G.H.Q. O'Connor went forward with Harding, Galloway and a naval and an air liaison officer to his battle headquarters. Wilson and Air Commodore Collishaw moved into Ma'aten Bagush, and a G.H.Q. liaison officer was installed. In London, Churchill, conscious that the sense of the day's slow passage could be best remedied by attention to urgent business, did not (so he wrote later) worry unduly, because he was so pleased that "our generals" were taking the offensive. At 2030 hours on 5th December O'Connor was sent his final orders. They made no mention of any possibility that 4th Indian Division might be taken from him and replaced by the 6th Australian Division.

During the night of 5th/6th December Churchill could not conceal his impatience. At his instructions Dill sent a signal asking for the exact date on which the operation would begin. By a little after midnight no answer had come from Wavell. Dill was bidden to send a chaser. Wavell's reply, which had been sent off in the small hours of Friday, 6th December, did not reach the War Office for some seventeen hours, and it was not in Dill's hands until 11 o'clock on Saturday night. It read:

A. P. Wavell to C.I.G.S.   *6th December, 1940*
Actual date dependent on weather conditions. Will cable when firmly fixed.

A quarter of an hour later Dill signalled:

C.I.G.S. to A. P. Wavell   *7th December, 1940*
Have only this moment got your telegram. Hence my second wire. Forgive my importunity. Bless you.

Meanwhile, during Friday, Wavell had slightly amplified his previous signal. His new message was definite as to time, but otherwise extremely non-committal and cautious.

A. P. Wavell to C.I.G.S.   *6th December, 1940*
1. If weather permits preliminary move night 7th/8th December, approach march night 8th/9th December, attack morning 9th December.
    2. Feel undue hopes being placed on this operation which was designed as raid only. We are greatly outnumbered on ground and in air, have to move over 75 miles of desert and attack enemy who has fortified himself for three months. Please do not encourage optimism.
    3. Creagh is in hospital and may not be available which is unfortunate since so much depends on handling of armoured division.

This caused another major explosion in London, at least equal to that of 21st/22nd November. Dill, who thought he could by now predict some at least of Churchill's reactions, guessed that they would be ugly, and kept the signal in his own file. However, its general purport, though not its text, inevitably became known to the Prime Minister. The fuse was ignited.

C.I.G.S. to Prime Minister   *6th December, 1940*
I understand that you want a copy of this wire. I did not intend to send it to you because I was afraid that it might worry you and you have quite enough worries already.
    I beg of you not to be worried by it. It is a personal telegram intended for my eyes alone. Wavell is merely trying to "write

General Wavell and
General Carton de Wiart
(*far left*)

General Platt

General Dill, General and Lady Wavell

The Commanders-in-Chief, 1940–1

down" his intended operation to avoid disappointment. You know that the operation is in fact much more than a raid—my S. of S. has described it to you. As for Creagh being sick, that only means that some lucky man will have a chance of distinguishing himself who would otherwise have only a small part to play.[38]

There is nothing we can do now except hope for a real success and not worry.

Prime Minister to C.I.G.S.   *7th December, 1940*

Naturally I am shocked at paragraph 2, and I trust that your explanation of it will be realised. If, with the situation as it is, General Wavell is only playing small, and is not hurling on his whole available force with furious energy, he will have failed to rise to the height of circumstances. I never "worry" about action, but only about inaction.

Wavell never offered excuses. There were, however, some of his decisions and some of his actions which, he believed, merited explanation. Not long before his death he told Bernard Fergusson the title he thought he would give to any reminiscences he might set down. It was *Reasons in Writing*.[39] For the wording of the offending signal he gave this reason:

"I always meant to go as far as possible and exploit any success to the full, but I was a little apprehensive that Winston might urge me to do too much, as limitations of supply and transport never made any great appeal to him."

On the afternoon of Saturday, 7th December, Wavell, his wife and daughters, and several of his personal staff went to the races at Gezira. Cairo's cosmopolitan society saw them all strolling through the paddock; the Press photographers approached and were not shooed away. This appearance was neat and wholly characteristic. It was one of two final, completely convincing actions in the whole careful process of secrecy which (so far as it was under Wavell's control) had masked "Compass." The second was a dinner party which he gave that evening at the Turf Club for some fifteen senior officers in his Command, including the Australian and New Zealand commanders. Both in the afternoon and at dinner he looked—and probably was—extraordinarily carefree. But one intensely difficult decision was imminent: that of ordering the transfer of 4th Indian Division to the Sudan. Arthur Smith knew; so did Maitland Wilson. To O'Connor

W.   289   K

he had given no hint at all; and, needless to say, neither the division nor its commander, General Beresford-Peirse, had any idea of what was in store for them. The ships were available; the opportunity that Wavell had sought was his now, and it would not recur for a moath or more. Time, in the Sudan no less than in the desert, was vital. Bu how would the desert battle go?

IX

Desert Victory

At 0445 hours on the morning of Monday, 9th December, when all the attacking units of O'Connor's forces had been in position for over three hours, one infantry battalion of 4th Indian Division opened fire on Nibeiwa camp from the east, to attract the Italians' attention towards them. At 0715 hours the seventy-two guns of the divisional artillery began their brief, intensive bombardment, again from the east. Within ten minutes the Infantry or "I" tanks of the 7th Royal Tank Regiment swept down on the north-west corner of the camp, *en route* putting out of action some twenty-three Italian medium and light tanks which were parked outside the camp. Two squadrons of the Matildas—as the Mark I versions of the "I" tank had been nick-named in 1936—broke at once into the camp, tackling the Italian artillery and infantry at close quarters. General Maletti, the Italian divisional commander, was killed by a burst from one of the tanks' guns as he emerged from his dugout. Through the breach there followed almost immediately two battalions of infantry, mopping up with zest. It was by no means all easy; there was some hard fighting, but within two hours the camp was in British hands. The tanks rumbled northwards to their next objective, Tummar.

There were cohorts of journalists in Cairo. Wavell had them all assembled later that morning and briefly described the attack. His policy of secrecy had paid: they all said that they had had no previous inkling of an offensive.

"Then I went to Sirry, the Prime Minister, and told him. He asked me to keep him informed and when I went to see him next morning, he said to me: 'I congratulate you on being the first to keep a secret in Cairo. I have sources who keep me informed of all that goes on, I asked them all yesterday if they had any idea of this attack taking place and they all admitted that they had none'."

There was only one awkward consequence of the secrecy: no preparations had been made either to deal with a great volume of captured equipment or to accommodate many thousands of prisoners. Immediately, however, it was only the success of the onslaught that mattered. A succession of telegrams to Dill told the story of the next few days as it unfolded to Wavell hour by hour.

9th December, 1940, 1005 hrs.

"Compass." First objective Nibeiwa camp captured, no details. Armoured brigade established south-west of Barrani. Enemy reaction apparently slight so far. Weather favourable.

9th December, 1940, 1820 hrs.

Telephone report from General Wilson as follows at 1430 hrs. G.M.T.

Confirmed 500 prisoners taken at Nibeiwa and some material. Italian general in command killed and second-in-command captured. Our tanks have entered second objective (Tummar camp) which is now being mopped up, many more prisoners believed taken.

Fourth Armoured Brigade across road 12 miles east of Buqbuq, where 100 lorries and several hundred prisoners taken.

Little enemy air activity and that well under control.

10th December, 1940, 0955 hrs.

Position as reported 0330 hrs. 10th December: 7 Armoured Brigade and Support Group watching Sofafi area, not engaged. 4 Armoured Brigade between Sidi Barrani and Buqbuq. 5 Indian Inf. Bde. in Tummar, night attack on camp at Point 90 being staged. 16 Inf. Bde. and 11 Indian Inf. Bde. moving to positions south of Sidi Barrani. Matruh force watching Maktila.

Prisoners believed between 4,000 and 5,000. 28 medium tanks reported captured at Nibeiwa.

Our personnel casualties so far reported are light. Three cruiser tanks damaged, five "I" tanks damaged but repairable. "I" tanks require 24 hours overhaul and will not be ready for further action till tomorrow, this was foreseen.

Operation most effectively supported by R.A.F. who brought down many enemy machines and attacked transport and troops. Enemy air activity slight. Navy are co-operating and bombarded Maktila effectively night 8th/9th December.

It will be necessary to do some clearing up to-day and further operations cannot at present be foreseen. . . .

10th December, 1940, 1884 hrs.
Prime Minister has apparently announced in House of Commons that we have reached sea between Sidi Barrani and Buqbuq. This gives entirely wrong impression that we are in possession of Sidi Barrani which we are not. I have promised Egyptian Prime Minister first news of capture of Sidi Barrani. . . . Prime Minister's announcement will raise premature hopes and may annoy Egyptian Prime Minister when corrected. Heavy fighting is in progress in Sidi Barrani area. . . . It looks as if we may have caught enemy in process of a relief. Capture of Sidi Barrani by no means certain at present. . . . Please do not make public more than is given to Press here.

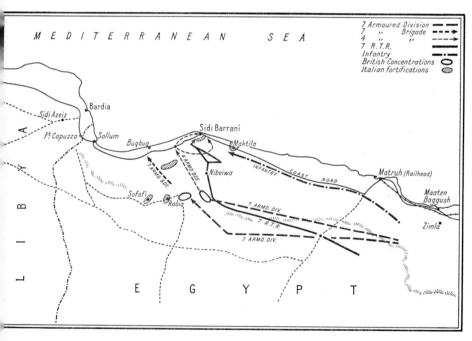

"Compass", December, 1940

293

11th December, 1940, 0815 hrs.

Situation last night still uncertain in Sidi Barrani area, which was being attacked by 4 Indian Division and 4 Armoured Brigade.

Maktila garrison withdrew west during night 9th/10th December to dig in near Sidi Barrani. Enemy still in position ... between Sidi Barrani and Buqbuq. Patrols 11 Hussars have been 15 miles west of Buqbuq.

Navy is bombarding Sollum area today.

Prisoners reported 6,000 by yesterday morning. Our own casualties apparently light, 4 Indian Division had only reported 150 wounded for evacuation by yesterday evening. . . .

11th December, 1940, 1150 hrs.

Report received successful morning drive by 3rd Coldstream Guards who captured two Libyan battalions between Maktila and Sidi Barrani. Beaters now moving to position for afternoon drive after luncheon interval.

11th December, 1940, 1400 hrs.

Report from Western Desert about noon as follows:

4 Armd. Bde. has been directed west of Buqbuq. 7 Armd. Bde. and Support Group is moving to west of Sofafi camps to cut off enemy in that area. Matruh force moving on Sidi Barrani from east and has captured two Libyan battalions (reported in my previous signal) and some guns. 4 Indian Div. moving on Sidi Barrani from south and southwest.

Situation somewhat obscure. Enemy still resisting in isolated positions. Air reports some movement from Halfway House (25 miles south-east of Sollum) towards Sollum.

11th December, 1940, 1700 hrs.

Hope you will ensure that credit for success is given in Press accounts where it is due, i.e. to Wilson and O'Connor, who planned and directed the battle, and Creagh and Beresford-Peirse, who trained and commanded the troops. Creagh unfortunately missed the battle through illness, but he was responsible for plan and efficiency of Armoured Division.

Impossible at present to judge extent of success but if all goes well we may, repeat may, carry pursuit to Egyptian frontier. Do not think even if enemy demoralised we can carry pursuit much farther. Supply difficulties are great and Bardia is strongly defended. Sollum has no water and no facilities for landing stores. We shall be beyond easy range of air support by fighter aircraft till fresh landing grounds established. If we can rush Bardia will do so but doubt it. Above is merely to show you what is in our minds.

16 Australian Brigade is on its way forward but owing shortage of transport will not be in battle area until 14th. Am continuing provisional arrangements to withdraw 4 Indian Division to Sudan.

12th December, 1940, 1654 hrs.

Visited Wilson's headquarters to-day and discussed plans with him and O'Connor. We propose to clear up enemy frontier posts south of Sollum and to occupy Jarabub Oasis at early date. . . . Meanwhile mobile column of Armoured Division will advance to Sollum—Capuzzo and endeavour to get across Tobruk road and cut off Bardia. If Bardia falls, though I think this is unlikely, I have instructed O'Connor that he can push on towards Tobruk up to the limit of endurance of vehicles and men. . . .

4 Indian Division will be withdrawn for Sudan. . . . If situation permits, New Zealand brigade group will rejoin New Zealand Division, leaving Western Desert to 7th Armoured Division and 6th Australian Division. . . .

Chief trouble at present is disposal of prisoners who may number 30,000 or more. Impossible to say what equipment captured but probably over 100 guns and 50 tanks. Our casualties believed to be well under 500.

"I" tanks fully justified their use but will require long period of overhaul. Other tank casualties believed light at present.

Sandstorm has been blowing for last three days and made visibility difficult, while swell makes supply by sea or evacuation of prisoners difficult.

The final accounting of the three days of battle from dawn on 9th December to the evening of 11th December showed that Western Desert Force had captured no fewer than 38,300 Italian and Libyan prisoners, 237 guns and 73 light and medium tanks. The total of captured vehicles was never recorded (units were notoriously reticent on this theme), but more than a thousand were at least admitted to be in British hands. O'Connor's total casualties were 624 killed, wounded and missing. His greatest shock, for which he was quite unprepared but which he took without a murmur of complaint, was the decision—finally taken, as the telegrams have revealed, on 11th December—to send 4th Indian Division to the Sudan. Churchill, recording with frank surprise the fact that Wavell took the decision "on his own direct initiative," praised it as "wise and daring."[1]

Since Major-General I. G. Mackay's 6th Australian Division replaced, brigade by brigade, the departing and exultant (but much mystified) 4th Indian Division, there was no immediate ill effect on the conduct of the campaign, for all the troops involved had been thoroughly trained in desert warfare; but the administrative consequences, on already severely strained lines of communication, were considerable; and the strategic consequence was to delay O'Connor's final victory by some six weeks.

By the evening of 12th December the only Italians (other than prisoners) left in Egypt were those blocking the immediate approaches to Sollum and a force of some strength in the neighbourhood of Sidi Omar. Churchill was now as exuberant and as full of praise as he had previously been tetchy. The horizons that had hitherto seemed dark were now rosy. Telegrams poured out of his office, to the President of the United States, to the Prime Minister of Australia, and to the Commander-in-Chief in the Middle East.

Prime Minister to A. P. Wavell   *13th December, 1940*
I send you my heartfelt congratulations on your splendid victory, which fulfils our highest hopes. The House of Commons was stirred when I explained the skilful Staff work required, and daring execution by the Army of its arduous task. The King will send you a message as soon as full results are apparent. Meanwhile pray convey my thanks and compliments to Wilson and accept the same yourself.

The poet Walt Whitman says that from every fruition of success, however full, comes forth something to make a greater struggle necessary. Naturally, pursuit will hold the first place in your thoughts. It is at the moment when the victor is most exhausted that the greatest forfeit can be exacted from the vanquished. Nothing would shake Mussolini more than a disaster in Libya itself. No doubt you have considered taking some harbour in Libyan territory to which the Fleet can bring all your stuff and which will give you a new jumping-off point to hunt them along

296

the coast until you come up against real resistance. It looks as if these people were corn ripe for the sickle. I shall be glad to hear from you your thoughts and plans at earliest. . . .

As soon as you come to a full-stop along the African coast we can take a new view of our prospects, and several attractive choices will be open.[2]

Wavell's "raid" of four to five days' duration had produced remarkable results, but he kept his aspirations on a very tight rein. By 14th December, however, he was able to tell the C.I.G.S. that leading troops of the 4th Armoured Brigade were twenty miles west of Bardia and would soon be able to harass enemy traffic along the road from Bardia to Tobruk. After having been held up by Italian bombing, until British fighters shot the attacking aircraft out of the sky, most of the Armoured Division was across the Libyan-Egyptian frontier; but the Italians were still holding out at Halfaya, Sollum, Sidi Omar and Capuzzo, and had a division in Bardia. Despite this, four complete divisions had already been destroyed, and prisoners taken numbered between 25,000 and 30,000—a considerable under-estimate, as the final count, already quoted, was to make quite clear.

Early on the morning of 16th December, exactly a week after the first attack had been launched on Nibeiwa camp, Wavell flew up to the desert again, saw O'Connor and Creagh, was back in Cairo before dusk, and reported to the C.I.G.S. that Sollum and Capuzzo had both been captured, and the road down the escarpment at Sollum destroyed. The Armoured Division, though with little more than fifty per cent of its tanks in action, was now on the rampage in the desert south of the coast road; it had had under a hundred casualties during the first three days of fighting, but about fifty more since from air attack. He estimated that Bardia, in which the remnants of various battered Italian formations had taken refuge, held now a garrison of between fifteen and twenty thousand men. In a second telegram he gave his appreciation of the situation so far and his intentions for the future.

A. P. Wavell to C.I.G.S. *16th December, 1940*
Immediate problem is how to deal with Bardia. We can (*a*) try to induce garrison to surrender, (*b*) cut it off from Tobruk and lay siege to it, (*c*) leave road to Tobruk open though under observation and if enemy withdraws by it attack him in the open.

We have had a proclamation printed to drop on garrison to

induce (*a*), and shall use it if situation seems favourable. At the moment it would not be likely to succeed.

We are not strong enough for (*b*). We are operating at the extreme limit of our resources and it will be some days before we can supply any more troops as far forward.

Course (*c*) is on whole most favourable. Bardia and its resources as a landing place and source of water supply are more valuable to us than the bodies in it and it would be easier to attack them in the open than behind the strong defences.

We are therefore leaving loophole of escape towards Tobruk, and at the same time bringing more troops forward as rapidly as transport situation permits, in case course (*b*) becomes necessary. We shall try course (*a*) whenever situation looks favourable. Meanwhile bombardment by air and sea continues.

We are considering plans if Bardia falls and I will outline them later. Meanwhile transport is my chief anxiety, these desert operations at such distances are throwing very heavy strain on all vehicles. Am already using captured Italian vehicles and have most urgent request from Greek C.-in-C. for transport.

On the following morning Wavell at last found time to write a short personal letter to Dill, full of praise for the planning and staff work of Jumbo Wilson, O'Connor, Creagh and Beresford-Peirse. The Armoured Division, he said, was "a magnificent formation." He added: "I only wish there was a bit more of it and that we had a reserve of machines." Fourth Indian Division had also earned his admiration; trained to a very high pitch, they went, he said, "extraordinarily well in the battle."

While he was writing this letter, he was handed a telegram.

Prime Minister to A. P. Wavell   *17th December, 1940, 0530 hrs.*
The Army of the Nile has rendered glorious service to the Empire and to our cause, and rewards are already being reaped by us in every quarter. We are deeply indebted to you, Wilson and other commanders whose fine professional skill and audacious leading have gained us the memorable victory of the Libyan desert.

Your first objective now must be to maul the Italian Army and rip them off the African shore to the utmost possible extent. We were very glad to learn your intentions against Bardia and Tobruk, and now to hear of the latest captures of Sollum and Capuzzo.

I feel convinced that it is only after you have made sure that you can get no farther that you will relinquish the main hope in favour of secondary action in the Sudan or Dodecanese. The Sudan is of prime importance, and eminently desirable and it may be that the two Indian brigades can be spared without prejudice to the Libyan pursuit battle. The Dodecanese will not get harder for a little waiting. But neither of them ought to detract from the supreme task of inflicting further defeats upon the main Italian Army. I cannot of course pretend to judge special conditions from here, but Napoleon's maxim, "*Frappez la masse et tout le reste vient par surcroît,*" seems to ring in one's ears.

Must recur to the suggestion made in my previous telegram about amphibious operations and landings behind the enemy's front to cut off hostile detachments and to carry forward supplies and troops by sea. . . .[3]

That same morning, the Chiefs of Staff saw the Prime Minister in London. Wavell's telegraphed appreciation was considered, along with as many operational signals as could be amassed. The appreciation had a cordial welcome. Churchill had to make a statement in the House of Commons before Christmas. It could be phrased a good deal more cheerfully than, ten days ago, he or anyone else could have dared to hope. The meeting ended in a glow of good feeling. Dill went back to the War Office and despatched a brief signal.

C.I.G.S. to A. P. Wavell　　　　　　　　　*17th December, 1940*
Thank you for your full appreciation with the conclusions of which we fully agree.

Bardia was accepted—enthusiastically—as the next objective. Churchill conscious of victory was Churchill generous.

Prime Minister to A. P. Wavell　　　　　　　*18th December, 1940*
St. Matthew, chapter 7, verse 7. "Ask, and it shall be given to you; seek, and ye shall find; knock and it shall be opened unto you."

A. P. Wavell to Prime Minister　　　　　　　*19th December, 1940*
St. James, chapter 1, verse 17, first part. More aircraft are our immediate need and these you are providing. Additional anti-aircraft also much required.

"Every good gift and every perfect gift is from above, and

299

cometh down from the Father of lights, with whom is no variable-
ness, neither shadow of turning."[4]

The 6th Australian Division was now moving up for the assault
on Bardia, and optimism ran high, but Wavell was determined not
to let it outrun his own chances of further success.

A. P. Wavell to C.I.G.S.   *19th December, 1940*
Italians have apparently decided to hold Bardia and reconnaissances have drawn fire from defences. . . .

You must not expect rapid progress at present. Defences of
Bardia are strong, supply situation is difficult and all vehicles are
showing signs of hard work. Enemy air force is still superior in
numbers, has been reinforced and remains considerable threat.
Our aircraft want time to establish themselves in advanced aerodromes.

Hunt is still going but first racing burst over, hounds brought
to their noses, huntsmen must cast and second horses badly
wanted. It may be necessary to dig this fox.

A. P. Wavell to C.I.G.S.   *20th December, 1940, 1553 hrs.*
Reference certain reports in Press and B.B.C. you realise of course
that Australian Light Horse Regiment is mechanised.

Hope that O'Connor's share in success will be given publicity
as well as Wilson's and mine. He played very large part both in
making plan and directing battle.

He had been up again to see O'Connor, but a dust-storm prevented
him from going forward to see Creagh.

A. P. Wavell to C.I.G.S.   *20th December, 1940, 1645 hrs.*
. . . Investment of Bardia proceeding. 16 Brigade and 16 Australian Brigade now grouped under 6th Australian Division.
Upwards of 100 guns should be in position against Bardia by
tomorrow morning. . . .

Transport situation still very strained owing to great distances
and difficulties of conditions. Large percentage of vehicles out of
action awaiting repair.

Defences of Bardia and spirit of garrison will be tested by raid
shortly. . . . We want Bardia as soon as possible but do not propose to risk failure and heavy casualties, especially as this is
Australians' first operation. . . .

C.I.G.S. to A. P. Wavell   *21st December, 1940*
Yes, of course I realise Australian Light Horse Regiment is
mechanised. Fear that P.M. having seen reference to Australian
cavalry . . . in moment of exuberance, and forgetting desert, distance and water, jumped to conclusion that dashing cavalry charge
had taken place and said so in the House. Feel it best to let idea
die quietly rather than attempt contradiction. Will see to
O'Connor getting credit. . . .

The question was now not whether Bardia (and Tobruk) would
be captured, but how soon. Even Churchill, for a few days, seemed
satisfied with the rate of progress, and ceased to nag. Bad weather
enforced a brief lull in the night bombing of London. In Libya,
Graziani knew perfectly well what O'Connor's pause portended. He
had given orders to the acting commander of 10th Army that both
Bardia and Tobruk must be held. Mussolini gave this decision prompt
endorsement; but Graziani was far from convinced that it was, in
fact, a justifiable decision, and on 17th December he told the Duce
that it would be difficult to reinforce Bardia and that it would only
be a matter of time before the British assembled enough strength to
overcome its defences. Would he not be wiser, he asked, to concentrate all his available forces for the defence of Tobruk, and so
gain time for the arrival of the troops and aircraft which, he hoped,
would be sent from Italy? Mussolini answered that everything possible
must be done to delay and exhaust the British, and that a prolonged
resistance at Bardia would make a useful contribution. Reluctant
though he was, Graziani assembled a formidable force to obey Mussolini's order: the equivalent of four divisions, totalling with fortress
troops and frontier guards some 45,000 men and more than 400 guns.
Wavell's Intelligence estimated them at much fewer—only about half
the true figure.[5]

A. P. Wavell to C.I.G.S.   *24th December, 1940*
We now have 88 field guns and 22 medium guns and howitzers
opposite Bardia but still require further supply of ammunition.
Enemy bombing continues to be active and is hampering use of
Sollum harbour. Transport and water are causing difficulty. Can
give no date yet for attack. Enemy resistance strong where tested.
Prisoners now number 40,000. Weather has been cold.

After Christmas Wavell paid a two-day visit to the Western

Desert and saw the Armoured Division and the Australians, who were in high spirits and making their final preparations for the attack on Bardia. He told the C.I.G.S.: "I have not tried to hurry matters too much." Seventh Armoured Division had benefited from the pause: with their forward patrols not far from Tobruk, they now had nearly seventy cruisers and 120 light tanks in action. But the "I" tank situation was difficult—twenty-five in action but all badly due for repairs; not more than eighteen could be expected to take part in the attack on Bardia, and none at all, he feared, would get to Tobruk.

O'Connor's tactical plan for the capture of Bardia dovetailed elegantly into Wavell's strategy. Bardia's perimeter, some seventeen miles in extent, defended by a continuous anti-tank ditch, numerous wire obstacles, and concrete blockhouses at intervals, covering the wire, was a far more formidable proposition than Nibeiwa, Tummar, Sollum or Fort Capuzzo. As at Sidi Barrani, O'Connor's solution lay in getting his tanks—the 7th Royal Tank Regiment once again—into the perimeter. This time he planned to send a battalion of infantry in first, in order to establish a bridgehead on the far side of the anti-tank ditch and the wire, then bridge the ditch and clear the wire and the minefields for the passage of the tanks. The tanks would then be shepherded within the perimeter and fan out in attack, with two more infantry battalions close behind them. The main point of assault was to be where O'Connor believed that the Italians least expected it: the centre of the western face of the perimeter. The 7th Armoured Division stood to the north and the north-west to block the garrison's escape routes; and the Support Group was to be ready to break through the defences in this area, if a chance to do so showed itself.

The plan worked out almost without a hitch. It was the Australians' blooding in World War II. From the outset they fought with the utmost dash and self-confidence. The tank ditch was bridged by the infantry in less than one hour. Crossing-places were quickly made and nearly a hundred mines removed, and the tanks were into the bridgehead by seven o'clock on the morning of 3rd January. By noon Italians were surrendering in scores. Off shore, the battleships *Warspite*, *Valiant* and *Barham* joined in with their heavy guns. There were two days of mopping up and on 5th January the fortress surrendered; 462 guns and 45,000 prisoners fell into British hands.

Wavell's mind was now leaping ahead of O'Connor's troops even at their most daring. On 5th January he addressed a note to Arthur

Smith in which, having taken it for granted that Tobruk would be taken within the next week or so, he set forth as the ultimate objective the capture of Benghazi. There were, he thought, two principal routes to this goal, either direct or by the west. He listed the advantages and disadvantages of each approach as he saw them from such data as was then available; and he considered the third possibility of advancing in two columns, by the direct route and along the coast. He concluded:

> Before we can make plans, much more information is required. . . .
>
> I should like the Joint Planning Staff to prepare as a matter of urgency a paper on the subject of an advance from Tobruk towards Benghazi, giving an estimate of the resistance likely to be encountered, the force we should require, the administrative difficulties and preparation of any other necessary data.

On the day he wrote this note, the Chief received a personal telegram from Dill, sent off from London late the previous night.

C.I.G.S. to A. P. Wavell   *4th January, 1941*
Important you should give us as much and as early information of battle as possible. Papers here give accounts which I can neither confirm or deny. Prime Minister anxious to give President Roosevelt heartening news in personal wire ahead of Press and if possible rosy expectations for his eye alone. This helps in encouraging President to provide those things which we desperately need. Help in this all you can.

Once again the Prime Minister was disposed to congratulate the Commander-in-Chief. There was also a very slight hint of nagging, of reprimands and reproaches to come.

Prime Minister to A. P. Wavell   *6th January, 1941*
Hearty congratulations on your second brilliant victory, so profoundly helpful at this turning point to the whole cause. You knocked and it was opened. I have now verified the Walt Whitman quotation. Authentic text as follows: "Now understand me well—it is provided in the essence of things that from every fruition of success, no matter what, shall come forth something to make a greater struggle necessary."
Time is short. I cannot believe that Hitler will not intervene soon. . . .

I am sending you in the next few days long appeals about purging rearward services. Strain of putting shipping round the Cape is definitely affecting feeding arrangements here, and transport of munitions, airplanes and pilots across the Atlantic. I am counting upon you to make every man in the Middle East row his weight in the boat. . . . Once more every good wish.

Lord Dunsany, the Anglo-Irish man of letters and poet, was at this time on a mission for the British Council in Greece. The news of victory reached him in the British Legation in Athens. He composed twelve lines of verse which he dedicated to Lady Wavell:

BARDIA

As we came by Samothrace
   Uprising sheer from Sea
My fancy found no trace
   Of the Winged Victory.

No light of evening air,
   No shadowy lingerings,
Told me that she was there
   Or hinted of her Wings.

But further on our way
   Word came, and we knew then
She was afar that day
   Among Australian men.

Early on the morning of 6th January Wavell flew to Khartoum, to see Platt and urge him—since 4th Indian Division was almost immediately to be at his disposal—to bring forward his attack on the Italians in Eritrea. Platt had not originally intended to move until the beginning of March; then the opening date of the operation had been brought forward to 9th February; now Wavell insisted that it must be within the next fortnight. He also saw the Emperor Haile Selassie, who was shortly to re-enter his own country, in which active rebellion was now well under way.

"Discussions with Haile Selassie," he wrote long after, "were always a little difficult; and when cornered His Imperial Majesty would gaze at the ceiling and maintain a dignified silence. On this occasion I asked him to formulate definite charges against two of my

officers, who he said were working against him. I can still see him
gazing pensively upwards and treating my inquiries, through two
interpreters, with imperial silence. . . . I brought him a 'going-away'
present from our Government (a gay umbrella) on his departure from
Khartoum. The next time I saw him was in Addis Ababa."

Movement about the Command was easier now than it had been
in earlier months, and Wavell was back in Cairo on 7th January.

A. P. Wavell to C.I.G.S.   *7th January, 1941*
I try to give you all I can as early as I can but dislike encouraging
hopes which may be disappointed or sending news which is not
authenticated. As you know reliable news from battlefield always
takes time especially at distances at which we are operating. Once
or twice already in anxiety to give you news have sent items
which subsequently proved inaccurate.

The Prime Minister's attempt to extract rosy forecasts was tacitly
abandoned, and was never resumed.

As Wavell approached what he himself called "the high watermark
of my military career" in the annihilation of the Italian armies
in Africa and the liquidation of Mussolini's brief and gimcrack
empire, he came also to a series of tests of unique complexity and
diversity.

On the afternoon of 6th January, the 7th Armoured Division
finally cut the westward roads out of Tobruk to Derna and Mechili;
its tanks ranged freely round the 21-mile long perimeter of the fortress,
and shot up Italian troops east of Derna and Mechili; before dusk the
Regia Aeronautica pulled out of the airfields at Gazala, Tmimi and
Bomba. When day broke on the 7th, the 19th Australian Brigade was
in position facing Tobruk's eastern defences, and the other brigades
of the 6th Australian Division, with all the artillery that Western
Desert Force could muster—two field and one medium regiment, and
one additional medium battery—and with the 7th R.T.R. extracting
every ounce of effort out of their remaining sixteen Matildas, were
moving rapidly westwards. Operationally and administratively the
capture of Tobruk was now virtually a certainty. The questions that
remained to be answered were: how soon could O'Connor do it, and
what would be the next move after he had done it?

Prime Minister to A. P. Wavell   *7th January, 1941*
I am sorry to jar the hour of your splendid victory by awkward

matters of housekeeping. If your demands for non-fighting services are maintained on the present scale the whole scope and character of our effort in the Middle East will have to be reviewed. Shipping has now become the dominant factor and will remain so certainly for six months. . . . The voyage round the Cape imposes an almost prohibitive burden. It is quite certain that all convoys will have to be severely cut.

. . . I feel I have a right to ask you to make sure that the rearward services do not trench too largely upon the effective fighting strength. . . . You have well over 350,000 troops on your ration strength and the number of units which are fighting or capable of fighting appears to me disproportionately small. It is distressing to see convoys sent by the heart's blood of the nation's effort consisting so largely of rearward services of all kinds.

. . . I beg you to convince me that you will continually comb, scrub and purge all rearward services in a hard, unrelenting manner as Kitchener did. This conviction will enable me to impose severe sacrifices required upon the British nation and to secure for the campaign of 1941 in the Middle East the opportunities which may await it under your direction.

A. P. Wavell to Prime Minister   *8th January, 1941*
Very many thanks for your telegrams. . . . Your kind congratulations are deeply appreciated and I will convey them to my subordinate commanders and troops who have more properly earned them.

I can assure you that I have always had questions of rearward services constantly in mind and have been as anxious as anyone to cut down non-fighting units. Except for anti-aircraft, demands from subordinate commanders are nearly always for more administrative units than for more fighting troops and I am continually being warned that I am working on dangerously small administrative margin.

I will again carefully examine situation to see whether we are over-insured or over-lavish in any direction and will make any possible reduction on demands for shipping. But the more I see of war, especially present-day war, the more I am impressed by part that administration plays.

I should like to thank you again for the support you have

given us and the risks you have taken to enable us to win successes here.

On Monday, 6th January, 1941, Churchill circulated to the Chiefs of Staff an appreciation of the strategic conduct of the war as a whole. A great deal of it concerned Wavell's Command; indeed, it opened with the declaration that the speedy destruction of the Italian forces in N.E. Africa must be the prime major objective of the opening months of the year. The Army of the Nile would then be free for other tasks. These he considered to include the occupation during March of Libya and Cyrenaica as far west as Benghazi by a small striking force of not more than 45,000 men, and the destruction of the Italian empire in East Africa, to be accomplished by the end of April. The successful completion of these campaigns would give Wavell, the Prime Minister calculated, a reserve of about 370,000 men, or the equivalent of twelve divisions, available for operations in the Eastern Mediterranean.

He considered in great detail the part the Germans were likely to play in the Mediterranean campaign. A heavy blow was to be expected; for example, they could come down through Italy and "establish an air-power in Sicily." Perhaps this was already happening. But the main danger, he was certain, lay in the Balkans. The vigour of the Greeks' counter-assault against the Italians on the Albanian front had seriously disturbed the Axis Powers. There was evidence of a big build-up of German troops in Roumania. What more likely than that they would press down through Bulgaria to Salonika, rather than force their way through Yugoslavia?

The moment the Greeks, the worth of whose exploits against the Italians he did not underrate, met a check, they would ask for more help from Britain; and the attitudes of Yugoslavia and Turkey were bound to be affected by the amount of such help to Greece. He declared:

It is quite clear to me that supporting Greece must have priority after the western flank of Egypt has been made secure. . . . We must so act as to make it certain that if the enemy enters Bulgaria Turkey will come into the war. If Yugoslavia stands firm and is not molested, if the Greeks . . . maintain themselves in Albania, if Turkey becomes an active ally, the attitude of Russia may be affected favourably.[6]

Much of this was extremely prescient. Its major flaw, however, was that it took far too much for granted, not in the terms of a grand strategy, but within the exigencies of reality, such as weather, distance, the breakdown of vehicles, the lack of spare parts, the dribble of petrol from ill-designed cans, and the physical and moral exhaustion of men pressed beyond endurance. To call for complex operations on a vast scale, and simultaneously to demand the wholesale reduction of the minimum administrative, supply and communication facilities needed to maintain them was—to say the least—unreasonable.

In tactical terms, the linch-pin of the whole appreciation was the destruction of all Italian forces in north-east Africa. This Churchill rightly perceived to be essential. But what he slurred over were both the means by which it must be accomplished and the fact that it must be genuinely completed before any other major offensive operation could be undertaken.

Wavell was fully committed to the advance in the Western Desert and the conquest of Cyrenaica. He was also fully committed to the advance into Abyssinia, and the liquidation of the Italian empire in East Africa. He was now to be asked, and along with him Cunningham and Longmore were to be asked, at exactly the same time and with little or no strengthening of the forces at their disposal, to launch and maintain a major expedition across hundreds of miles of sea.

Churchill was fortified in his belief that the Balkans could be held without a previous and decisive victory in Africa by the vigorous political views of Eden, now back in his old post as Foreign Secretary.

Prime Minister to Gen. Ismay, for C.O.S. Cttee.   *6th January, 1941*
Pray see the attached from the Foreign Secretary. In spite of the evident need to pursue the Italians along the Libyan coast while the going is good, we shall have to consider the despatch of four or five more squadrons of the Royal Air Force to Greece, and possibly the diversion of part of the 2nd British Armoured Division.

I cannot look beyond Benghazi at the present time, and if Tobruk is taken there will be very few Italian troops, and by no means their best, east of Benghazi. . . .

Although perhaps by luck and daring we may collect comparatively easily most delectable prizes on the Libyan shore, the massive importance of . . . keeping the Greek front in being must weigh hourly with us.[7]

Two days later Churchill had a long telegram from Smuts, containing an analysis of the situation which coincided encouragingly with his own, and making a welcome offer of an additional South African division, operating from Kenya, to assist in the rapid liquidation of the Italian empire in East Africa. There was also a meeting of the Chiefs of Staff Committee, at the conclusion of which Dill signalled to Wavell.

C.I.G.S. to A. P. Wavell   *8th January, 1941*
Greek situation causing us anxiety. Help can only come from you or Longmore. Palairet[8] is being asked whether your going to Athens would be welcomed by Greeks. If so we think it would be most valuable if you went early to discuss situation and report. If you go let us know when.

There was an immediate quickening of pace. On 9th January the Chief of the Air Staff signalled Longmore ordering him to cut air support to the Western Desert offensive far below the minimum necessary, and to send at once to Greece three squadrons of Hurricanes and one or two of Blenheims. This telegram concluded:

Fully realise that operations in Africa may be limited or even stopped by these withdrawals to Greece, but must emphasise their extreme importance and urgency and the need for making plans at once.
  Commanders-in-Chief may expect shortly to receive joint instructions from Chiefs of Staff on this subject, and this telegram is, therefore, warning only.

A. P. Wavell to C.I.G.S.   *9th January, 1941*
Longmore is arranging to send one Gladiator and one Blenheim squadron to Greece and has so informed C.A.S. This will reduce air support in Sudan but must be accepted. Am arranging to ship some captured Italian transport, guns and ammunition to Greece as early as possible and will increase such assistance as far as we can. We must however continue our advance in Cyrenaica while we have Italians on the run and this will help Greeks indirectly more than sending small additional amount of transport that

might be spared if we halted, quite apart from moral effect on our own and Italian troops of such action. . . .

On the morning of Friday, 10th January, Longmore walked into Wavell's office and showed him the signal from the Chief of the Air Staff.

A. P. Wavell to C.I.G.S.   *10th January, 1941, 1015 hrs.*
Have just seen personal telegram from C.A.S. to A.O.C.-in-C. It fills us with dismay. Our appreciation here is that German concentration is move in war of nerves designed with object of helping Italy by upsetting Greek nerves, inducing us to disperse our forces in Middle East and to stop our advance in Libya. Nothing we can do from here is likely to be in time to stop German advance if really intended, it will lead to most dangerous dispersion of force and is playing enemy's game. . . .

Within an hour the directive from the Chiefs of Staff was delivered to the three Commanders-in-Chief:

Information appears to point to an advance by the Germans through Bulgaria to attack Greece, possibly starting as early as 20th January. The probable line of German advance would be by the Struma valley on Salonika, with one armoured and two mountain divisions, supported by about 200 dive-bombers, and making use of air landings to disorganise resistance. Three or four additional divisions might be added after March. . . . It is unlikely that the Bulgarians would offer any resistance. It is also believed unlikely that the German advance would be through Yugoslavia.

His Majesty's Government have decided that it is essential to afford the Greeks the maximum possible assistance with the object of ensuring that they resist German demands by force. . . . This decision means that assistance to Greece must now take priority over all operations in the Middle East once Tobruk is taken, because help for the Greeks must, in the first instance at any rate, come almost entirely from you. This need not prevent an advance to Benghazi if the going is good, nor need the Kassala operation be abandoned.

It is not possible from here without full knowledge of Greek dispositions and plans, and without knowing the state and position of your own forces, to lay down the size of the forces which should be sent. . . . It seems likely that assistance will have to take the form of specialist and mechanised units and air forces to support the Greek divisions, and His Majesty's Government authorise the despatch of forces of the type adapted to suit the conditions which will prevail, up to the following limits:

Army   1 squadron of Infantry tanks
        1 regiment of cruiser tanks
        2 field-artillery regiments
        2 anti-tank regiments
        2 heavy A.A. regiments
        2 light A.A. regiments
        2 medium regiments, R.A.
Air   3 Hurricane squadrons
        2 Blenheim IV squadrons

together with whatever may be needed to operate and maintain these units.

The responsibilities of the Commander-in-Chief and the Air Officer Commanding-in-Chief will be extended to include the Greek theatre.

It will be realised that speed is of the greatest importance. . . . In the event of the German advance not taking place as expected, it may be found possible to utilise some of these forces to help the Greeks in Albania.

We are examining the possibility of sending a ship containing the "I" tanks, which lagged from [convoy] W.S.5, direct through the Mediterranean to Greece during the latter part of February, and would like to know whether you think this would be desirable. . . .

A. P. Wavell to C.I.G.S.   *10th January, 1941, 1226 hrs.*
Am sending comments on Chiefs of Staff cable as early as possible. Meanwhile earnestly request nothing be done to suggest to Greeks that reinforcements are being sent.[9]

The Prime Minister was displeased by more than one phrase in the telegram which Wavell, in consultation with Longmore, had composed earlier that morning, and believed it to be "far astray from the facts."[10]

During this eventful day General Heywood, the Army representative on the British military mission in Greece, flew in to Cairo.

A. P. Wavell to C.I.G.S.   *10th January, 1941, 1950 hrs.*
I have discussed [Chiefs of Staff] cable with Heywood. . . . He says Greeks consider German advance now most unlikely and in fact almost impossible owing to conditions of roads and bridges. They consider German concentration as intended to warn both ourselves and Russians off Balkans and as preparatory steps in case they are forced to intervene, but not as showing any immediate intention to do so.

He thinks that "I" tanks or cruiser tanks would be useless to Greeks at present and that they do not require field or medium artillery, which could not operate on present front. What they require immediately from army is mechanical transport, antiaircraft artillery. Some anti-tank guns and perhaps some light tanks or carriers would also be valuable. By early spring there may well be needs of units mentioned in C.O.S. cable and therefore no delay should be imposed on despatch of units from U.K.

I am examining what we can do at once about M.T., A.A. artillery, anti-tank guns and light tanks. As you know we are ourselves urgently in need of all these, especially first two, but will do all we can to help Greeks. I have already had to refuse heavy A.A. artillery to Sudan . . . and have with difficulty provided light A.A. regiment. Shall therefore have to take further risks with own troops and bases to meet Greek needs.

Am proposing to fly Athens 13th or 14th January to see Metaxas and to visit front. Will discuss with him both immediate problems of support and future arrangements for defensive front in Balkans.

A.O.C.-in-C. has already cabled C.A.S. regarding air problem. If Hurricane squadrons are withdrawn from Libya situation of our forward troops will become most dangerous and any further advance impossible.

Cunningham is at sea so cannot consult him on shipping question which is of considerable importance.

Prime Minister to A. P. Wavell & Air Marshal Longmore
                                             10th January, 1941
Our information contradicts idea that German concentration in Roumania is merely "move in war of nerves" or "bluff to cause dispersion of force." . . .

Destruction of Greece would eclipse victories you have gained in Libya and might affect decisively Turkish attitude, especially if we had shown ourselves callous of fate of allies. You must now therefore conform your plans to larger interests at stake.

Nothing must hamper capture of Tobruk but thereafter all operations in Libya are subordinated to aiding Greece. . . .

We expect and require prompt and active compliance with our decisions for which we bear full responsibility. Your joint visit to Athens will enable you to contrive the best method of giving effect to the above decisions. It should not be delayed.[11]

Wavell (Longmore followed him two days later) flew to Athens on Monday, 13th January, and spent several busy days in conference with the King of the Hellenes, who seemed to him stout-hearted and sensible; with General Metaxas, the Prime Minister and virtual dictator of the country, by whom he was impressed; and with General Papagos, nominally the Commander-in-Chief, who seemed to act really as Metaxas' Chief of Staff.

Previous political exchanges between London and Athens had raised Greek hopes sharply. Metaxas did not believe the German threat to be as imminent as did the British War Cabinet; some six weeks hence, at the least, was his estimate. In order to repel it and hold Salonika, a force of twelve divisions would be needed, of which Greece could at that time supply no more than three. Wavell gave a frank outline of the state of his forces in the Middle East, and Metaxas, with surprise but without resentment, faced the fact that help on the scale he required was quite impossible. There was a good deal of discussion at staff level about sending material rather than British units. What the Greeks wanted was aircraft, A.A. guns, transport (both M.T. and pack animals), clothing and anti-tank guns. From a cupboard already bare—though some of its shelves were being replenished by Italian booty—it was little that Wavell and Longmore could afford; but they offered the most they could.

On the main issue of direct and immediate military assistance to the Greeks there was an irreconcilable divergence of views. Wavell, under Churchill's very explicit instructions, could only offer to bolster up the Greeks' resistance to German attack, at great cost to himself. Metaxas envisaged the mounting of a large expeditionary force; and when he realised that this could not be done, he concluded that such help as Wavell could give would be enough to provoke the Germans to attack but not enough to provide real protection against the assault.

For the Albanian front, where for nearly three months the Greeks had been fighting a courageous and very successful campaign against the Italians, Metaxas wanted no help of any kind.

Chiefs of Staff to A. P. Wavell   *17th January, 1941*
. . . The refusal of the Greeks of your offer of 102 Regiment, R.H.A., and company of light tanks for the Albanian front is noted. You have made clear to General Metaxas your willingness to help on that front, and as he refused there is no question of our forcing our aid upon him.

The attitude of the Greeks towards our offer of assistance at Salonika is noted. Assume that you have fully explained to General Metaxas the information on which our desire to supply forces to meet a German invasion is based. . . . This information we still believe to be reliable. It may be that the Greeks have information which is not available to us, and which causes them to view the German preparations in a different light. If you are satisfied that the Greek refusal of our immediate assistance has been given with full knowledge of our information, then we must submit to their judgment.

You should make it clear that if we do not send now the special forces suggested in our telegram of 10th January, but wait until the German advance, these forces could not arrive in time to be effective. . . .

Before he left Athens on the morning of 17th January Wavell saw Papagos and gave him the gist of this telegram. The Greek C.-in-C., observing that the latest news was more reassuring, showed no eagerness to change his mind.

During the ten days which these discussions occupied, a new factor had emerged—important in itself, even more significant in what it portended. The *Luftwaffe* had moved into the Mediterranean theatre of operations. From about Christmas time onwards, the ground and maintenance units of *Fliegerkorps X*, which had been stationed in Norway, operating principally against shipping in the Atlantic, passed through Italy. On 10th January, by which time there were ninety-six German bombers and twenty-five twin-engined fighters established on airfields in Sicily, a heavy attack was made on a British convoy in the narrows between Pantellaria and Malta; the aircraft carrier *Illustrious* was badly damaged and had 126 of her crew killed and ninety-one wounded; but the German casualties were six aircraft destroyed and one damaged.[12] How would this development affect O'Connor's offensive and the far from satisfactory Greek situation?

A. P. Wavell to C.I.G.S.   *18th January, 1941*

My views on Salonika problem are as follows:

Present proposal is dangerous half-measure. I do not believe that troops it is proposed to send are sufficient to enable the equivalent of three Greek divisions to hold Salonika if the Germans are really determined to advance on it.

We shall almost inevitably be compelled to send further troops in haste or shall become involved in retreat or defeat. Meanwhile advance into Libya will be halted and Italians given time to recover.

Factor which may cause Germany to hesitate from move into Bulgaria is that by doing away with Bulgarian neutrality she at once exposes Roumanian oilfields to bombing attack. . . .

If we send technical troops to Salonika and Germany does not move, we have locked up valuable troops to no purpose. . . .

The most serious factor in the situation is shortage of A.A. resources and fighter aircraft in Middle East, which I have many times emphasised. If these resources are still further dispersed by Salonika commitment, we shall be weak everywhere, with none of our ports, bases or other vulnerable points properly protected. Arrival of German aircraft in Mediterranean increases seriousness of situation.

Both from naval and air point of view advance to Benghazi will give very considerable advantages both by driving back enemy air bases and by giving ports and air bases for our own use. But air protection both during advance and afterwards will be essential.

Up till recently I have been basing my arrangements and operations on understanding that force in Middle East would be rapidly and progressively increased by several divisions and that technical troops sent to Salonika would be replaced from home as early as possible. Now I find convoys being cut of drafts and units essential to keep even present force in being. If this represents change of policy and we must be prepared to live on our own leanness for some time, may I please be informed. It would of course greatly increase dangers of sending forces to Salonika.

If Greeks now accept troops proposed and War Cabinet orders their despatch, I shall of course send utmost available, but I feel it my duty to bring above considerations to notice of War Cabinet for their meeting on Monday to consider Greek problem. My conclusion is that we should accept Greek refusal but should make all necessary reconnaissances and preparations of Salonika front without giving any promises to send troops at future date. . . .

A. P. Wavell to C.I.G.S.   *19th January, 1941*
. . . Against present opposition I am prepared to continue advance towards Benghazi with present air protection . . . but effect of appearance of German aircraft in Libya remains to be seen.

In the light of these two telegrams the Chiefs of Staff for the time being—but only for the time being—gave a lower priority to the question of assistance to the Greeks, and focused their attention on the desert front.

During Wavell's absence in Greece, preparations had gone on steadily for the assault on Tobruk. O'Connor had available 7th Armoured Division, three brigades of the 6th Australian Division, two machine-gun battalions, the 7th Royal Tank Regiment, to whose sixteen "I" tanks no addition had yet been made, and a heavy concentration of artillery. For twelve days after the fall of Bardia there was constant movement around the perimeter of Tobruk: ammunition came up, gun positions were made ready, and there were aggressive patrols which continually harassed and confused the Italians.

The plan was very similar to that of the attack on Bardia, though on a bigger scale; not quite eighteen months later Rommel's plan, which resulted in Tobruk's recapture and his own promotion to Field-Marshal, was almost identical.

After a twenty-four-hour postponement caused by one of the nastiest sandstorms of the whole campaign, O'Connor's attack went in at 0830 hours on 21st January. The 16th Australian Brigade and the "I" tanks broke through the perimeter, under cover of a heavy and accurate artillery barrage; and they were followed closely by the 19th Brigade. Both brigades reached their first objectives, with few losses, by midday; but then the Italians brought their coastal and A.A. guns into action, and there were several hours of fierce fighting around and about the middle of the perimeter. By dusk, however, the Commonwealth forces were ranged along the edge of the escarpment overlooking the town, and the western and south-western portions of the perimeter—about one-third of the whole—were safely under control.

All night long the attacking troops saw fires flaring in the beleaguered town, and heard the crump and rumble of explosions. When day broke on the 22nd, they went in without resistance. There were far more troops in the town than had been estimated: nearly 30,000, including a great many specialists and a naval detachment of more than 2,000; there were, once again, so many motor vehicles that nobody bothered to count them; there were eighty-seven tanks; and there were 236 guns of a calibre of 75 mm. and over.

Prime Minister to A. P. Wavell   *23rd January, 1941*
I again send you my most heartfelt congratulations on the third of the brilliant victories which have in little more than six weeks transformed the situation in the Middle East, and have sensibly affected the movement of the whole war.

The daring and scope of the original conception, the perfection of staff work and execution have raised the reputation of the British and Australian Army and its leadership, and will long be regarded as models of the military art.

Will you please convey those expressions in which the War Cabinet and, I doubt not, Parliament would most cordially associate themselves to Air Chief Marshal Longmore and Air Commodore Collishaw and to Generals Wilson, O'Connor, Mackay and Creagh.

I shall be making a further statement on these lines before long.

Western Desert Force was now called XIII Corps. Its spirit had never been higher. Several days before Wavell received the instruction from the Chiefs of Staff about the necessity of capturing Benghazi, O'Connor was beginning to plan his next moves after the fall of Tobruk. Immense new distances, and a country hitherto untraversed by any British soldier—it was to become very familiar to thousands of them in the next two years—now opened up ahead of XIII Corps. From the seemingly endless vistas of sand and rocky desert, and the barren ravines and corries of the escarpment, the land shelved gradually into the green, cultivable region of the Jebel Akhdar. Between the Gulf of Bomba and the Gulf of Sidra the coastline bulged northwards into the Mediterranean. The bulge—and the prosperous and settled Italian colony of Western Cyrenaica—extended some 200 miles from east to west; the hills rose to a height of well over two thousand feet; there were roads; there were two small stretches of railway; there was a considerable farming population; and there was the sizeable city and harbour of Benghazi. The two principal roads from the east were of the utmost tactical importance. One kept close to the coast from Tobruk to Gazala, Tmimi, Martuba and Derna, then struck west-south-west through the Jebel to Barce, Benina and Benghazi. The other, from the junction at El Adem, due south of Tobruk, ran to Mechili on the southern ridge of the Jebel, then turned south-west to Msus, Antelat, Agedabia and El Agheila, with a branch track heading west from Msus to Solluch, and back to the main coastal road which ran due south from Benghazi to Agedabia.

On the evening of 22nd January it appeared that of all the vast army that Graziani had had at his disposal at the beginning of December there now remained: the 60th Division (less one infantry brigade group) in position just east of Derna; an armoured brigade of about 160 tanks, and the infantry brigade group from 60th Division, at or near Mechili under the command of a General Babini; and further west—whether in Cyrenaica or Tripolitania was not certain—two more divisions, the 17th and the 20th. The northern force in Cyrenaica held the coast road to Benghazi, while the southern lay at the main junction of the roads out of the desert, out of the Jebel and from the coast.

The dispersal of the enemy in two forces, the strong grounds for belief that no reinforcements had yet reached Cyrenaica, the shortening of our lines of communication by the capture of Tobruk and its harbour, and the additional motor transport and fuel, taken at Tobruk and Bardia, offered the opportunity of a rapid advance on Benghazi and a decisive victory.[13]

A. P. Wavell to C.I.G.S.   *24th January, 1941*
Returned this evening from Western Desert. Saw O'Connor, Creagh, Mackay and his brigadiers. Visited Tobruk and Bardia and reconnoitred by air country up to within short distance of Derna—Mechili. Country looks less difficult than I thought.

Tobruk less damaged than expected and should be usable as port very shortly. Pace of Australian attack probably prevented more demolitions being carried out. Prisoners estimated over 20,000 but no proper count yet made.

Tank regiments in 7th Armoured Division now reduced to four by amalgamation. 8th Hussars and 6 R.T.R. have handed over their serviceable tanks and been withdrawn. Administrative difficulties (e.g. despatch of transport to Greeks) are delaying relief by 2nd Armoured Division.

4th Armoured Brigade surrounded garrison at Mechili, about 100 miles west of Tobruk, early this morning. Garrison estimated at 300 to 400 with one battery should be captured today. Advanced reconnoitring detachment of 7th Armoured Brigade, which has now only one regiment, about 20 miles south-east of Derna in touch with enemy. Australian brigade group left Tobruk today for Derna. Unless Derna more strongly held than anticipated it should be occupied within next few days. . . .

At Mechili during the 24th there was one of the first tank versus tank battles of the campaign, in which 7th Armoured Division destroyed eight medium Italian tanks and captured one, and themselves lost one cruiser and six light tanks. O'Connor decided first to crush what remained of Italian strength in this area, while containing the 60th Division at Derna. He therefore left two brigades of the 6th Australian Division near Derna, took the third away, sent it south to join 7th Armoured Division and the Support Group, and on the 25th gave explicit orders that General Babini and his troops were not to be allowed to escape from Mechili.

Large parts of this force, however, were held up by shortage of petrol until the morning of 27th January; and during the previous night, to O'Connor's disappointment but not dismay, Babini had slipped away to the north. When air reconnaissance discovered the Italians, using a road which was shown on no map in British hands and moving as fast as they could through the wooded, ravine-slashed country, the 4th Armoured Brigade set out on a two-day pursuit, and fighters swooped down with machine-gun fire and light bombs. But by the afternoon of the 28th bad going, heavy rain, numerous mechanical breakdowns and a shortage of petrol brought the chase to a halt. O'Connor had to think again, and quickly. For the Prime Minister was becoming impatient once more.

C.I.G.S. to A. P. Wavell   *29th January, 1941, 2350 hrs.*
Please tell me urgently date when you hope to capture Benghazi. Information will be kept strictly secret but is required in connection with assistance it may be necessary to give Turkey.

This telegram was inexplicably delayed in transit and did not reach the Commander-in-Chief until 1130 hours on the following morning. He replied instantly.

A. P. Wavell to C.I.G.S.   *30th January, 1941, 1200 hrs.*
Situation in Cyrenaica obscure but owing escape of Italian troops from Mechili general plan needs adjustment. As rough forecast we may capture Benghazi about end of February, but this may be optimistic. Hope to give more accurate estimate next week when we know O'Connor's new plan.

On 29th January the Italians withdrew from Derna. It looked, for the moment, as if they might make a stand in the heights of the Jebel Akhdar. The Australians took Derna on the 30th. O'Connor had a fleeting hope that he might rest some of his officers and men and overhaul some of his battered tanks and equipment. To outflank the enemy in the Jebel, a wider movement for 7th Armoured Division than an approach march by the direct westward track from Mechili would be necessary. O'Connor knew that, on his own side, big changes were imminent. Maitland Wilson was to be Military Governor of Cyrenaica. O'Connor himself was now near the edge of exhaustion; he was to be relieved and go back to command B.T.E.; another Corps H.Q. was to replace his own; and 2nd Armoured Division, who had been brought to Middle East at so great a risk, were to relieve 7th Armoured Division. Over these tactical moves loomed the great strategic issue of aid to Greece.

What was not known on the morning of 30th January was the extent of the Italians' demoralisation; but during the next two days operations against the Australians in the north began to slacken notably, and reports came in that the *Regia Aeronautica* were abandoning their few remaining airfields. Early on 1st February these reports of withdrawal were confirmed when long columns of transport were seen moving westward to Barce and tanks were spotted being entrained at Barce station.

On the previous evening O'Connor, Creagh and John Harding had a conference at Corps Headquarters. Dorman-Smith, who had been sent up by Wavell to report on the conduct of the offensive since Sidi Barrani, was also present. O'Connor concluded, rightly, that the Italians were preparing to quit not just the coastal sector but the whole of Cyrenaica. The greatest speed in following them up was essential. He could not afford to wait for reinforcements, which could

A.P.W.

General Wavell and General de Gaulle

Ethiopian Enterprise (Colonel Sandford, Major Wingate,
H.I.H. the Emperor of Ethiopia)

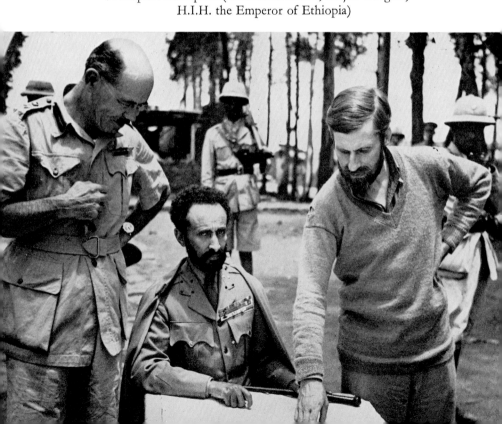

not reach him before 10th February at the earliest. The Armoured Division would have to go on as long as its vehicles could move; but it must have petrol, and O'Connor's administrative staff, after long consultation and a good deal of vigorous encouragement, declared that they could get the division to the Benghazi road with enough petrol to take it into battle.

Early next morning, at O'Connor's urgent request, Dorman-Smith flew to Cairo to see the Commander-in-Chief and get his authority for a rapid advance to intercept the Italian retreat. Wavell saw him that same evening. As Dorman-Smith told the story, all expression drained from Wavell's countenance. To marshal the pencils on his desk in a parody of parade-ground drill was his manner of doodling. He took them up in handfuls; they formed fours, they formed threes; they were ranked in close order and in open order. From time to time, when Dorman-Smith paused for breath, he observed, "Yes, Eric, I see."

At the end he looked up. "Tell Dick he can go on," he said, "and wish him luck from me. He has done well."

On that same day in London, Leopold Amery, the Secretary of State for India, wrote a secret and personal letter to the C.I.G.S. Amery, though he was one of Churchill's oldest friends and a senior Minister carrying a burden of heavy responsibility, was not one of the inner circle, guiding and controlling strategy, either military or political. However, he was aware of much that was going on, and had sturdily independent standards of judgment, sustained by experience in and close study of the South African War and World War I.

A day or two earlier he had written a note to Dill pointing out the possibilities of rapid advance, not just to Benghazi, but on to Tripoli itself. Dill had reacted with interest and had asked for a short paper on the idea. Amery now dealt with it in detail. He began with the unexceptionable proposition that the essence of success in war lies in the element of surprise, and he considered some classic instances, including Allenby's final advance to Megiddo in 1918, of surprise created by doing something that was not normally regarded as possible. He continued:

Now in the same way I would suggest that the Germans and Italians have probably ruled out a rapid advance on Tripoli as beyond Wavell's powers. They may do so all the more if, as is likely, he finds himself held up a bit in the broken country between Derna and Benghazi. On the other hand, I doubt whether there are any technical difficulties about the advance beyond Benghazi, the first few hundred miles of which are along a motor road most of it close to the sea, and through sheer desert. I doubt whether a rapid advance, even with a comparatively small mechanised force, would meet any serious resistance the greater part of the way, especially if the heavier stuff, infantry, artillery, etc., and stores came along by sea. For Wavell in his particular situation, sea transport should take the place that troop-carrying lorry transport did for the Germans last May; but with this difference—that our troop-carrying vessels can not only support the mechanised advance, but even, if necessary, go ahead of it for the purpose of out-flanking the enemy. Similarly, in our light balloon-tyred armoured fighting vehicles we have something which can move across the desert a good deal faster than the Italians can, and so should be in a position to out-flank them on the land side as well. All this taken together suggests that against a swift rush Wavell will find no serious resistance, or if he does, can envelop and mop it up as he mopped up Bardia and Tobruk.

The biggest danger facing such an advance is if the Germans are given time to establish a powerful air force in Tripoli. But this means not merely flying the planes across but somehow shipping across from Sicily all the cumbrous ground establishment required. No doubt they are thinking of doing this, but they may well be too late about it if Wavell comes along much faster than they expect.

Once we can get Tripoli there is an enormous consequential saving of troops, for sending an army across the Mediterranean in face of our command of the sea and our air force established at Tripoli is a very different proposition to strengthening a force already established in Tripoli and able to cover reinforcement by its air force and its cruisers and submarines.

On the other hand, if the Germans are given time to reinforce Tripoli heavily by air and possibly on the ground, then, even if they cannot regain Benghazi, they can certainly tie down a great part of Wavell's troops as well as of his air force, and his power to release a substantial force for polishing off Abyssinia or for subsequent operations in the Balkans is very much reduced.

The biggest issue to my mind, however, is the one which Metaxas put to Wavell only too plainly the other day, namely, that military help to Greece must be something that will really make things secure for Greece, or even turn the scale, if Germany comes in. Sending a small force, which will only afford Germany an excuse for marching down upon Salonika, is obviously from the Greek point of view worse than useless. Now, apart from what India and the Southern Dominions can spare—and in view of Japan's attitude that may not be much—the only way to send substantial reinforcements to Greece in time is to be able to send convoys through the Sicily channel. With Malta reinforced by Tripoli that might well be made a possibility. With Malta flattened out by continuous air attack and any help from us precluded by effective enemy air and sea work from Tripoli as well as from Sicily, the prospects look remote.

I need say nothing about the possibility of our presence at Tripoli encouraging Weygand to declare himself on our side in certain eventualities. With Bizerta available the whole situation would of course be immensely improved.

To sum up then, my argument is that the advance to Tripoli should not be considered merely as the exploiting of Wavell's success in North Africa, but as the key to any future operations on a serious scale against Sicily, Sardinia, or in the Balkans. It might be the Open Sesame of the whole war and as an operation of surprise might completely disorganise the enemy's plans.

There is no evidence that this document ever received the careful and detailed study, either by the Chiefs of Staff or by the War Cabinet, which it merited.

It is only fair to add that Wavell, in a postwar assessment of the chances of success of such an operation, declared unequivocally:

Our own resources were not equal to the task. Our armoured vehicles were worn out by an advance of 500 miles; we had not enough mechanised transport to maintain even a small force for an advance of another 500 miles to Tripoli; and both in the air and on the sea we were still numerically inferior to the Italians alone, without any German reinforcement. It would have been an intolerable strain on the Navy to maintain a military and air

force at Tripoli when even Benghazi could not be used as a port
for lack of A.A. artillery and other resources.[14]

The offensive galloped marvellously to its climax. On 2nd February
Dorman-Smith flew to O'Connor's headquarters. In the two days
he had been away much had happened. O'Connor had decided that
if he had Wavell's permission to go ahead he was not going to wait
for any armoured reinforcements. Seventh Armoured Division must
simply move until they could move no longer. So far as maintenance
was concerned, the first convoys loaded at Tobruk were beginning to
arrive at Mechili, and by 4th February it would be just possible for
the division to set out with their supply vehicles full; they could
be followed by a convoy containing two days' supplies, water, petrol,
food, and two refills of ammunition. They had already had their
first warning order telling them to be prepared to leave for Msus.
Early on the following morning a liaison officer set out for
Cairo. He carried a letter scribbled in pencil on the back of a signal
form.

General O'Connor to A. P. Wavell   *3rd February, 1941*
Chink[15] has returned with your heartening message. Thank you
so much. The situation has now changed, and I have determined
to go forward with what we have at present without waiting for
the other cruiser squadrons and a reserve of supplies. . . .

Next day Wavell flew up to see Wilson and O'Connor. Back in
Cairo before nightfall, he signalled the C.I.G.S. telling him that what
remained of 7th Armoured Division—one brigade with between forty
and fifty cruiser tanks, some eighty light tanks, and the Support
Group, whose vehicles were getting very worn and whose men were
getting very tired—was heading for Msus and might reach it that
evening. Meanwhile, as the Australians were following up on the
main road to Barce and Benghazi, the R.A.F. were attacking the
Italians' retreat. Unless O'Connor's information was inaccurate or
something unforeseen happened, he should therefore "be at the gates
of Benghazi in the next few days." Wavell added that he had appointed
Wilson Military Governor and C.-in-C. in Cyrenaica and left O'Connor
in command of operations until the end of this phase of the campaign.
British armoured cars occupied Msus on that day; but the battered
remnants of 7th Armoured Division found the going hard over very

324

rough country, and it was not until daybreak on 5th February that they could report that they were in position just east of Msus.

All that day the pursuit continued. A good many of the light tanks broke down. Officers and men had two days' rations, and as much ammunition as they could carry. The most perplexing question was: how long would the petrol last? By dusk O'Connor's forces were ranging deep into the south of Cyrenaica and far to the west. Fourth Armoured Brigade, indeed, was approaching Beda Fomm, where the Italians were gathering hurriedly for what might be their last stand. A column of some five thousand of them, mainly gunners with their guns, but including a good many civilians, surrendered south-west of Beda Fomm. O'Connor brought his Advanced H.Q. up to Msus, and by dawn on 6th February it was obvious that the Italians were going to make a final attempt to shoot their way out of the ring that had swiftly formed around them. They fought hard and bravely throughout that day, but when evening came their position was desperate. Seventh Armoured Division pinned down a mass of vehicles and men in complete confusion along some twenty miles of the one possible escape road from Solluch to Agedabia. In repeated attempts to break through, the Italians lost more than eighty tanks. Meanwhile O'Connor ordered the Australian 6th Division to send a fast-moving detachment—about a brigade group in strength—along the main road from Barce to Benghazi and on to Ghemines, to complete the encirclement of the Italians. The Australians pressed on as fast as they could and received the surrender of Benghazi during this eventful day.

Dawn broke cold and clear. A force of some thirty Italian tanks made a last, unavailing assault on the ring of British armour. When this broke, the surrender was immediate and unconditional.

Throughout these final days O'Connor was always where he was most needed. His determination and his energy were formidable, surpassing even Rommel's. He covered huge distances, over atrocious terrain, and was able to keep personal control of his spearhead, the 7th Armoured Division, of his own H.Q. XIII Corps, and of the Australian Division; all were kept in play though widely separated from each other. During 5th and 6th February his presence at H.Q. 7th Armoured Division at Antelat prevented any recurrence of the Babini evasion at Mechili. On the morning of the 7th he was still there when the news of the surrender at Beda Fomm was brought to him. He told Dorman-Smith to draft a signal to go to the Commander-in-Chief *en clair*. It began: "Fox killed in the open . . ."

They drove westwards and came to the battalion H.Q. of the Rifle Brigade, who had been in at the beginning, and were there at the end. The battlefield was an astonishing scene of wreckage and confusion— fifteen miles of lorries, guns and A.F.V.s, around which milled thousands upon thousands of prisoners. There were about 100 tanks, many with their crews wounded or dead inside them; there were well over 100 guns, which had also fought well and at heavy cost to their crews. General Tellera, who commanded the 10th Army, was lying in a tent, severely wounded, his life ebbing fast. General "Electric Whiskers" Bergonzoli, commander of the 13th Army, stood disconsolate with all his staff around him; there was General Babini, and more than a score of other generals. The Italians' casualties totalled 20,000 killed, wounded and captured.

O'Connor, when he was by a swift reversal of fortune himself a prisoner, wrote four months later: "I think this may be termed a complete victory, as none of the enemy escaped."[16]

A. P. Wavell to C.I.G.S.   *7th February, 1941, 0745 hrs.*
Benghazi has surrendered but no details because violent sand-storms are interfering with communications.

O'Connor began to plan his next moves. In the past three days he had succeeded beyond all expectation. Why not again? Why should he not go on, to Sirte without doubt, halt or hesitation, to Tripoli itself if possible? At the end of the day he asked Dorman-Smith to go to Cairo, by way of Maitland Wilson's H.Q. at Barce, and put the project to Wavell, just as he had done on 1st February. Four days elapsed before Dorman-Smith reached G.H.Q. in the small hours of 12th February. Wavell and the War Cabinet by now faced a crucial decision.

A. P. Wavell to C.I.G.S.   *10th February, 1941, 1900 hrs.*
Extent of Italian defeat at Benghazi makes it seem possible that Tripoli might yield to small force if despatched without undue delay. Am working out commitment involved but hesitate to advance further in view of Balkan situation unless you think capture of Tripoli might have favourable effect on attitude of French North Africa.

Further advance will also involve naval and air commitments

326

and we are already far stretched. Navy would hate having to feed us at Tripoli and Air Force to protect us. On other hand possession of this coast might be useful to both.

Will make plans for capture of Sirte which must be first step; meanwhile cable me most immediate your views as to effect on Weygand and war situation generally. Will probably go Cyrenaica discuss matter with Wilson 12th or 13th February.

C.I.G.S. to A. P. Wavell   *11th February, 1941, 1445 hrs.*
This problem has been heavily discussed by Defence Committee last two days. I put it up. General feeling is that assistance to Greece and/or Turkey must come first apart from strain on Navy and R.A.F. which advance to Tripoli would involve. Official wire will follow to-night.

On the first day of the battle of Beda Fomm, 5th February, Hitler wrote to Mussolini expressing his displeasure at the conduct of the North African campaign as a whole, and offering the assistance of a complete armoured division, on condition that what remained of the Italian Army held on and did not retreat to Tripoli. Mussolini accepted the offer on 10th February, ordered what he described as "a forward policy" for Tripolitania, and told Hitler that Graziani was about to resign and would be replaced by General Gariboldi. On 11th February the commander-designate of the *Deutsche Afrika Korps*, Lieut.-General Erwin Rommel, arrived in Rome, where he was assured that the first line of defence in Tripolitania would be at Sirte. He wasted no time. He was at Catania in Sicily that same afternoon, and was given very grave news:

> Wavell had taken Benghazi, destroyed the last Italian armoured formation south of the town and was about to advance into Tripolitania. . . . It was not impossible that the next few days would see the arrival of the leading British troops in the outer environs of Tripoli. As the first German division would not be complete in Africa until the middle of April, its help would come too late if the enemy continued his offensive. Something had to be done at once to bring the British offensive to a halt.[17]

But the British offensive had already been halted. O'Connor for his part was as little wasteful of time as Rommel. During 7th February the armoured cars of the 11th Hussars were ordered southward to

Agedabia and El Agheila. They were at El Agheila by the following evening, with patrols out some forty or fifty miles along the coast towards Sirte. No resistance whatever was encountered, but a few prisoners were taken. Other than these, of the enemy there was no sign.

At XIII Corps H.Q. O'Connor waited for permission to go on to Tripoli. In Cairo Wavell read Dill's brief signal and waited for the strategic directive whose contents that signal foreshadowed. In London on the evening of 11th February there was a War Cabinet meeting after dinner. Four days had passed since Beda Fomm. The C.I.G.S. returned to the War Office after the meeting and said to the D.M.O., Major-General Kennedy:

> I gave it as my view that all the troops in Middle East are fully employed and that none are available for Greece. The Prime Minister lost his temper with me. I could see the blood coming up his great neck and his eyes began to flash. He said: "What you need out there is a Court Martial and a firing squad. Wavell has 300,000 men, etc., etc." I should have said, Whom do you want to shoot exactly? but I did not think of it till afterwards.[18]

Wavell issued a Special Order of the Day on 14th February:

> On the capture of Benghazi, which has resulted in the occupation of the whole of Cyrenaica, I wish to express my thanks and my admiration to all those who took part in the operations—not only those at the front who have fought so gallantly and so skilfully, but also all those who by their work on the lines of communication or at the base have made possible the rapid advances which have so confounded our enemies.
>
> The Army of the Nile, as our Prime Minister has called us, has in two months advanced over 400 miles, has destroyed the large army that has gathered to invade Egypt, taking some 125,000 prisoners and well over 1,000 guns besides innumerable quantities of weapons and material of all kinds. These achievements will always be remembered.
>
> Much hard work and fighting still lies ahead of us before peace is won. The spirit of quiet resolution that during these operations has animated all ranks in all places—the combatant under fire in the fighting line, the driver making his way over bad tracks in a dust storm, the mechanic working long hours on repair

and maintenance, the pioneer unloading stores, the signaller, the engineer, the medical personnel—will continue and carry us through all dangers and difficulties.

You have done great deeds and won much glory. We are fighting for freedom and truth and kindliness against oppression and lies and cruelty, and we shall not fail.[19]

X

Succour to Greece

Dorman-Smith was ushered into Wavell's office on the morning of 12th February. Its walls had been rehung with maps of Greece and the Balkans, and the Chief's welcoming words were: "You find me busy with my spring campaign."[1]

There was to be no advance to Sirte and Tripoli. Greece, in Churchill's phrase, was to be "succoured." Behind this decision lay an explicit diplomatic undertaking. After the Italian occupation of Albania on Good Friday, 1939, Greece along with Roumania was given a joint Anglo-French guarantee of military support in the event of Axis attack. This pledge was given by Neville Chamberlain's Government; Churchill's Cabinet never repudiated it. France collapsed; Roumania declared her neutrality; but so far as Britain was concerned the guarantee to Greece was still binding. There were additional motives, which Churchill explained in a conversation in 1948:

> They said that I was wrong to go to Greece in 1940. But I didn't do it simply to save the Greeks. Of course, honour and all that came in. But I wanted to form a Balkan front. I wanted Yugoslavia, and I hoped for Turkey. That, with Greece, would have given us fifty divisions. A nut for the Germans to crack. Our intervention in Greece caused the revolution which drove out Prince "Palsy"; and delayed the German invasion of Russia by six weeks. Vital weeks. So it was worth it. If you back a winner it doesn't really matter much what your reasons were at the time. They now say that I went to Greece for the wrong reasons. How do they know? The point is that it was worth it.[2]

Wavell, within a month or two of his death, wrote in March, 1950: "I am still sure that my instinct, to fight as far forward as possible in defence of the Middle East, was correct. We did not

330

know then that the Germans would attack Russia. I believed that they were more likely to concentrate on the Middle East, and that we must gain time; we could do this best by fighting well forward."

General Metaxas died suddenly on 29th January, 1941, and was succeeded as President of the Council by M. Koryzis, a far less forceful and resolute character. He at once told General Heywood that the situation seemed to him desperate: the advance in Albania was held up by bad weather—it was one of the worst winters in living memory in the Balkans—and by lack of transport; and in two months' time there would be no artillery ammunition left. General Papagos, the C.-in-C., was almost as melancholy in his soldierly fashion. If Germany attacked Greece, which he said he did not expect, Greece would resist; but in view of the slight prospect of timely help from outside, her resistance would be little more than a protest and could not last long. On 8th February Koryzis reaffirmed his predecessor's statement that Greece would resist German aggression at all costs. He added that he would appeal for British help when the Germans entered Bulgaria, and suggested that the time had come to decide whether the size of the British force that would be sent to Greece when that happened would be sufficient, together with the Greek forces, to check the German attack and encourage Yugoslavia and Turkey to enter the conflict.[3]

Heywood passed Koryzis's inquiry on to Wavell and to the C.I.G.S., and two days later Wavell signalled to Dill giving his estimate of the assistance he could give to Greece or Turkey. At the moment he could send one armoured brigade group and two brigades of the New Zealand Division. By the middle of March he could add another armoured brigade group, and another two Australian brigades. A month later he could send a further Australian brigade, and at the end of April a complete Australian division. All these moves hinged on the arrival of convoys now *en route* to the Middle East and the progress of his operations in East Africa; but they were independent of the proposed despatch of 6th Australian Division to occupy the Dodecanese—an operation with the code name of "Mandibles." A.A. protection for these forces was bound to be on a low scale; but the biggest difficulty in the whole plan was the provision of shipping and naval escorts.

This signal and others bearing on it were considered at meetings of the Defence Committee of the War Cabinet on 10th and 11th February. Late on the night of the 11th a Chiefs of Staff telegram was despatched to Wavell. It stated that the Defence Committee, in the light of the "unexpectedly early" capture of Benghazi, the refusal by Turkey to accept immediate British military assistance, and the Greek request for information about the size and composition of any British force that might be sent to Greece, had decided that no serious operation was to be undertaken beyond Benghazi, which was to be held with the minimum forces necessary for a secure flank; and that the capture of the Dodecanese was still of the first importance and ought to be undertaken at once.

The telegram went at length into the War Cabinet's somewhat inconclusive views about the size and composition of the British expeditionary force for Greece; about the Greeks' own plans to meet a German attack through Bulgaria; about whether the British force ought to be based on Salonika or the Piraeus; and about occupying Mitylene, Lemnos and Lebinthos, with Greek permission, in order to secure British communications. The purpose of this signal, the Chiefs of Staff said, was to let Wavell know the mind of the Defence Committee, and to enable him to make all possible preparations for the move of the maximum forces to Greece at the earliest possible moment.

This signal was accompanied by another, of almost equal length, from the Prime Minister, in which congratulations on Wavell's "latest admirable victory" and its unexpected speed were followed by a disquisition on the prospects now opening out. Churchill ruled out, quite unequivocally, any serious effort against Tripoli, and reiterated his previous direction that Wavell's major effort must now be to aid Greece and/or Turkey. He glanced briefly at the hope that Turkey and Yugoslavia might join in opposing a German advance, but dismissed it with the words, "I fear they will not do this and will fool away their chances of combined resistance, as was done in the Low Countries." Since the War Cabinet's first thoughts were now for Greece, "we should try," Churchill said, "to get in a position to offer the Greeks the transfer to Greece of the fighting portion of the army which has hitherto defended Egypt and make every plan for sending and reinforcing it to the limit with men and material." The Greeks' reaction to this great offer and their plans, if any, for resisting an invasion from Bulgaria by German forces were, the Prime Minister conceded, still unknown. But, he concluded:

In order to give the very best chance of concerting all possible measures both diplomatic and military against the Germans in the Balkans we are sending the Foreign Secretary and C.I.G.S. to join you in Cairo. They will leave on 12th February and should reach you 14th or 15th. Having surveyed the whole position in Cairo and got all preparatory measures on the move, you would no doubt go to Athens with them and thereafter if convenient to Ankara. It is hoped that at least four divisions, including one armoured division, and whatever additional air forces the Greek airfields are ready for, together with all available munitions, may be offered in the best possible way and in the shortest time. . . .

In the event of it proving impossible to reach any good agreement with the Greeks and work out a practical military plan, then we must try to save as much from the wreck as possible. We must at all costs keep Crete and take any Greek islands which are of use as air bases. We could also reconsider the advance on Tripoli. But these will only be consolation prizes after the classic race has been lost. There will of course always remain the support of Turkey. . . .

Wavell's first reaction to these telegrams was: "We must get tidied up as soon as possible." In an *aide-mémoire* he summed up the tasks he had to tackle and the means at his disposal. His armoured divisions were split; part of his medium artillery was in Cyrenaica and part in the Sudan; the New Zealand Division was minus its signals component; First Cavalry Division was all over the place; and there were many other improvisations.

He decided that the minimum garrison for Cyrenaica was one division and one armoured brigade, possibly with reduced artillery, and did a good deal of paper work juggling with formations. Could an Indian division take over from an Australian? What about the South Africans? He did not want to reduce his garrison in Palestine. He had a Polish brigade; could that go to Greece instead of to the 6th Australian Division? But this would cut the division down to two brigades: for the attack on the Dodecanese could it be reinforced by another Australian division not yet equipped with artillery? Where would he find the garrisons for Mitylene, Lemnos and Lebinthos? What ports would there be for the British in Greece, and what line were they to be expected to hold? And whence would come all the shipping that would be needed?

A. P. Wavell to Prime Minister   *12th February, 1941, 1836 hrs.*
Am very grateful for your congratulations. May I say what
inspiring effect your magnificent speech has had on everyone out
here.

We have naturally been considering problem of assistance to
Greece and Turkey for some time. My telegram of 11th February
to C.I.G.S. gave estimate of available reserves but hope may be
able to improve on this, especially if Australian Government will
give me certain latitude as regards use of their troops. . . .

Am delighted that Foreign Secretary and C.I.G.S. are visiting
us, this will be most helpful.

My impression when I visited Athens was that Greek plans
for defence against Germany were decidedly sketchy, but I think
they have been considering them since.

We will do our best to frustrate German plans in the Balkans
but Greek and Turkish hesitations and Yugoslav timidity have
made our task very difficult. Owing to difficulties of shipping and
ports our arrival is bound to be somewhat piecemeal.

We are urgently considering "Mandibles" but must await
arrival Glen ships before major operation.[4]

Wednesday, 12th February, was a busy day in London as well as
in Cairo. (General Rommel, it is worth remembering, flew from
Catania to Tripoli on this same day.) Dill, who had wanted to stay
in London, in the faint but baseless hope that he might be able to
exercise a little restraining influence over the Prime Minister, was
ordered to accompany Eden. Churchill drafted, and the War Cabinet
gave formal approval to, the Foreign Secretary's instructions for his
mission, which laid down that its principal object was:

the sending of speedy succour to Greece against an attack by
Germany. It should also be Mr. Eden's object to make both the
Yugoslavs and the Turks fight at the same time or do the best
they could, bearing in mind that, while it was our duty to fight
and, if need be, suffer with Greece, the interests of Turkey in the
second stage were no less important to us than those of Greece.
. . . Mr. Eden should aim at the formation in the Delta of the
strongest and best equipped force in divisional or brigade organisations which could be despatched to Greece at the earliest possible
moment.

The Foreign Secretary was given explicit guidance about the redisposition of formations in the whole theatre of war in order that the necessary forces might be made available in Greece. In Libya, it should be determined what was the minimum garrison to hold the western frontier and Benghazi. Men and supplies were to be sent to Cyrenaica by sea instead of by the desert road. The attack against the Dodecanese should be launched as soon as possible, provided it did not impede the build-up in Greece. Eritrea must be finished up at once; and Abyssinia—though the breakdown of the Italian positions was desirable—might be left "to rot by itself" in order to bring up from it forces needed for Greece. The forces in Kenya were to be reduced, and the South African divisions there brought up to Egypt. The governing principle was to be to secure the highest form of war economy in the armies and air forces of the Middle East for all these purposes, and to make sure that the many valuable military units in that theatre fitted into a coherent scheme and were immediately pulling their weight.[5]

The vicissitudes of the weather and of air travel conspired seriously to delay the start of the mission. Held up at Plymouth, Gibraltar, Malta and Suda Bay in Crete, the Sunderland flying boat in which the Foreign Secretary, the C.I.G.S. and their staffs were travelling finally landed safely on the Nile in Cairo late on the night of 19th February, exactly a week after they had left London. There was now no chance of a reversal of the decision to concentrate on Greece and the Balkans and not to attempt to continue O'Connor's offensive in Tripoli. Events had moved fast in this week.

Maitland Wilson was now installed in Benghazi as Military Governor of Cyrenaica and O'Connor was back in Cairo to take up his new appointment as G.O.C.-in-C. British Troops in Egypt. And on 16th February German reconnaissance units at Sirte made their first contact with British patrols. On 17th February Rommel wrote to his wife: "Everything's splendid with me and mine in this glorious sunshine. I'm getting on very, very well with the Italian Command and couldn't wish for better co-operation. My lads are already at the front, which has been moved up about 350 miles to the east. As far as I'm concerned they can come now."[6]

But they did not come then, or for many a long day.

On Wednesday, 19th February, Wavell set out his views on the strategic decision which had to be taken. John Shearer, his Intelligence officer, had drawn attention, as was his duty, to the risks involved, and Wavell's reply took the form of an appreciation which he headed with General Wolfe's axiom, "War is an Option of Difficulties." He agreed that sending a force into the Balkans, and especially attempting to cover Salonika, entailed considerable risks, including military defeat, wastage of shipping, and weakening of the power to resist an enemy counter-attack in Cyrenaica. On the other hand, success in saving Salonika would put new heart into Greece and into Turkey and Yugoslavia, and might force the Germans to fight on a front where they hoped to attain their ends by peaceful penetration. It would also make it much more difficult for the Germans to exploit the corn and oil of south-east Europe which they so greatly needed.

Not to act, and to leave Germany to overrun Greece and dominate the Balkans, would lose the British almost as much prestige as a military defeat; it would put an end to any chance of Yugoslav or Turkish assistance; and it would put fresh heart into the Italians and render the whole position in the Mediterranean very difficult.

As for the enemy, Wavell regarded an offensive campaign through the Balkans at this time of year as "a difficult undertaking, even for Germany," and he thought the Germans might in fact be hoping hard that they would not have to face a British force there at present, though, he added, "in a month or two they will be strong enough to be certain of defeating us, and the climatic conditions will be more favourable."

He did not take a very serious view of the risk of an Axis counter-attack in Cyrenaica, for the enemy did not have sufficient command of the sea to pass through the considerable convoys that would be required, nor did the Germans yet have any practical experience of desert warfare. The enemy were also short of the transport they would require for the long and vulnerable advance from Tripoli to Cyrenaica. The appreciation concluded: "To sum up, we have a difficult choice, but I think we are more likely to be playing the enemy's game by remaining inactive than by taking action in the Balkans. Provided that conversations with the Greeks show that there is a good chance of establishing a front against the Germans with our assistance, I think we should take it."

Wavell certainly did not have to be persuaded against his will. The problem, as he saw it, was that of finding the means to implement the choice he had already made between two sets of difficulties.

However, in the week that had gone by since the Secretary of

State and the C.I.G.S. had set out from London, Churchill, who had taken charge of the Foreign Office in Eden's absence, had had second thoughts. Hesitation and equivocation replaced fierce resolution, and the responsibility for final decision was shifted subtly from London to Cairo. Wavell's East African campaign had begun successfully in the south, but Platt's advance in the north had been held up at Keren. The Prime Minister was again angry about the increase in ration strength in the Middle East without, as he was still convinced, a comparable increase in fighting formations. In a telegram to Eden on 20th February he dealt at some length with both these preoccupations, and concluded: "Do not consider yourselves obligated to a Greek enterprise if in your hearts you feel it will be only another Norwegian fiasco. But of course you know how valuable success would be."[7]

Eden in Cairo was not responsive to the Prime Minister's new hesitant mood. His answering signal that same day stated: "We are agreed we should do everything in our power to bring the fullest measure of help to the Greeks at the earliest possible moment."

This resolve, the Foreign Secretary made clear, was based on the belief that there was a fair chance of halting a German advance and of preventing Greece from being overrun. He then went on to a detailed analysis of the resources available to carry it out. The limitations on these, especially in the air, meant that it would be impossible to help Turkey if Greece were to be effectively supported. Longmore had a much smaller margin of modern aircraft, Eden pointed out, than they had estimated in London. Apart from the impossibility of helping Turkey, it was doubtful whether even the line covering Salonika, which the Greeks had proposed, could be held. Cunningham had said that he could give enough naval protection to enable Salonika to be used as a base, but had emphasised that his ships too would need air cover, which could prove an insuperable difficulty.

Eden then listed Wavell's proposed dispositions, and made it clear that the idea of supplying Cyrenaica entirely by sea was impracticable. Benghazi, in the view of Admiral Cunningham, was useless, because of the destruction of the port facilities and heavy air attack and minelaying. Eden assured Churchill that apart from his commitments in the Western Desert and East Africa Wavell had immediately ready for Greece one armoured brigade and the New Zealand Division, now three brigades strong; later, the Polish Brigade, two Australian divisions and another armoured brigade could be sent.

To get a force of this size to Greece would require at least fifty-three ships, which could only be taken from convoys as they arrived in the Middle East; but he believed that if this force arrived in time, it would have "a fair chance of effective resistance" to a German land attack.

He told Churchill that his own conclusion, shared by Dill and Wavell, was that in the immediate future assistance to Greece must have first call on British resources; and he intended to tell the Greeks what this help would amount to and urge them to accept it as fast as it could be shipped.[8]

There were further discussions at G.H.Q. the next day, but the lines of approach to the Greeks remained in essence those set out in Eden's telegram, and the Prime Minister signalled his approval.

A. P. Wavell to General Wilson   *21st February, 1941*

The Secretary of State and C.I.G.S. are out here and we have been discussing the question of assistance to Greece. It seems probable that a force will be sent over there as quickly as possible and the size of the force makes it essential that we should have the best and most senior commander available. You will, therefore, if the force is sent, as seems most probable, be appointed to command it. I am very sorry to have to move you again so soon but you ... with your tactical and strategical knowledge and the prestige of your recent successes are undoubtedly the man for the job and it will greatly relieve my mind to know that you are there. ...

On 22nd February Eden, Dill, Wavell, Longmore, and Captain Dick, R.N. (representing Cunningham) flew to Athens in conditions of close secrecy. As soon as they arrived they were taken to the palace of King George II of the Hellenes at Tatoi. The King at once asked Eden if he would see Koryzis alone. With some reluctance—because he wanted the discussions to be conducted on a purely military basis —Eden agreed. Koryzis immediately handed him a document describing the outcome of talks that had been held in the Greek Cabinet in the past day or two.

This statement, which Koryzis read aloud to Eden (in French), affirmed, in completely unequivocal terms, Greece's determination to continue the war until final victory at the side of Great Britain, and to resist a German invasion, if necessary alone. The King and Koryzis were both anxious that the British Government should realise that their decision had been taken before they knew whether any help would be forthcoming or not; and the King had wished to make this clear to Eden before the military conversations began. The Greeks' honour was unstained, and their courage was boundless. The nobility of their action stands out even more clearly when it is appreciated that the British decision to go to their assistance had been taken, before the mission arrived in Athens, for purely military reasons which Wavell, just as much as Eden and Dill, believed to be valid.

All the meetings were held at the Tatoi Palace. There was a plenary session at 5.30 on the afternoon of the 22nd, over which the King presided. There was then a Græco-British military discussion; the British representatives then withdrew for an informal talk among themselves; and at 10.45 that night there was a final full session. The crux of all the discussions was what Wavell described as "a clear and able statement"[9] by the Greek Commander-in-Chief, General Papagos, on the line to be held against a German attack from Bulgaria. He said that the fortified frontier line, called the Nestos line, was the strongest; but it was too extended now that all the Greek divisions except three had been withdrawn. The line of the river Struma, held by the Allies in the First World War, had the advantage of covering Salonika, but it was also too extended, unless the Yugoslavs came in as allies; if this happened, the port would be essential to supply their needs.

Wavell in his notes, made at the time in pencil on sheets of palace writing paper stamped with the Greek crown, commented: "Line to be held depends largely on Yugoslav attitude. If Germans attack, offensive operations in Albania must stop. We must therefore establish a line behind which Albanian front can withdraw. If Y.S. do not play, Aliakmon is only possible line and all troops in E. Macedonia must be withdrawn to it."

The Aliakmon line—it was named after a river which ran through it—had considerable natural strength. It would run along the northern slopes of the Olympus—Pieria mountains and then follow the line of the Vermion range northwards to the Yugoslav border—over seventy miles in a straight line. Through it there were only four major gaps: one on each side of Mount Olympus; one which formed the valley of the river Aliakmon; and the fourth, much wider, at Edessa, through which passed the road and railway from Florina to Salonika, but which Wavell believed could be easily fortified, as could the hills between it and the frontier of Yugoslavia.

The Greeks had an agreement with Turkey to hold a bridgehead about Demotika in order to enable the Turks to take the offensive into Bulgaria and turn the right of the Bulgarian line. This agreement held good only if Turkey took the offensive; should she declare war but make no attack, the obligation lapsed. If, however, the Turks declared war and promised an offensive a little later on, it would be necessary to leave the Greek forces in Thrace; they would then be maintained (except for weapons, etc., peculiar to the Greek army) by the Turks.

General Papagos realised the extreme importance of time, which made it impossible to wait for Yugoslavia and Turkey to declare themselves. He had therefore asked his Government for permission to begin the withdrawal as soon as possible, and, in any case, before a German move made the withdrawal look like a retreat. It could be made to appear that the Greek troops were being sent to reinforce the Albanian front. Troops would be withdrawn first from rear areas in Macedonia, then (if agreed with Turkey) from Thrace, and lastly from the frontier of Macedonia.[10]

At the conference Wavell noted:

No covering position in front of Aliakmon. 8 divisions reqd— + 1 in reserve. No plan of defence or work done. It would take Germans 20 days from frontier to reach Aliakmon line if demolitions effectively done. Danger of parachutists.

The security of the left flank of the line depended on the attitude of the Yugoslavs. Politically, the British and Greeks believed, they could not at the moment reckon the Yugoslavs to be their allies, though it was reasonable to suppose that they would resist any attempt by the Germans or the Bulgarians to pass through their country to attack Greece. Militarily, remembering the Serbian resistance in the First World War, they thought that the Yugoslavs would at least impose a very long delay on any enemy movement through their wild and mountainous country.

Papagos reached the conclusion—and Wavell agreed—that there was thus a good chance of holding the Aliakmon line with the forces available, provided that the Greek troops in Western Thrace and Macedonia (three good divisions) were at once withdrawn to it; that another division was brought over from Albania to support these; and that the British expedition began to move at once from Egypt. Therefore at the plenary session, late that night, the two Governments decided that the joint force, totalling seven and a half divisions (four Greek and three and a half British) and one armoured brigade, should be assembled on the Aliakmon line with all possible speed and should begin to fortify it. Since Papagos thought that the line could be held with five divisions, they thus had what appeared to be a reasonable margin of safety; they had, or thought they had, secure flanks on the sea and on Yugoslavia; and they assured themselves that if they acted at once and speedily, they could assemble their forces before the Germans could pass through Bulgaria and reach the Aliakmon line. Wavell wrote nine years later: "It seemed, therefore, an acceptable military operation. The chief danger, as we saw it, was enemy air superiority, which might even make our supply by sea hazardous. Cunningham and Longmore saw this danger, I think, more clearly than I did; but they never hesitated in supporting the general plan."[11]

Wavell's notes on this session read: "Conference 10.45 p.m.: Papagos; APW 11.10 p.m.-11.20; S of S re Y-Slavs; Proposal to send staff officer to see Prince Paul; Question of command; Final acceptance 11.50 p.m." Behind these terse phrases there lay a remarkable *accord*. The question of command was settled swiftly and without formality: the British force would come under Papagos's general control, and if their commander had any difference of opinion with him he could refer it to Wavell; if Wavell and Papagos could not settle it direct, Wavell would appeal to his own Government. The proposal to send a staff officer to see Prince Paul, the Regent of Yugoslavia, made and accepted early in the conference, was later revoked because of the security risk involved: if through leakages in the Yugoslav Government the Germans learned that the British had determined to bring forces to the aid of Greece, it would be easy for them to keep special watch for convoys, and the danger thereafter would be obvious. Instead, it was agreed that Eden should send a telegram to the Prince setting out, in cautious, general terms, the dangers inherent in German activities in the Balkans, and ask for his views.

One of the officers present described the closing scene in that long day of drama:

Finally, the Secretary of State said that he would like to be sure that the arrival of British troops in the numbers and on the conditions proposed would be sincerely welcomed by the Greek

Government. It was necessary to ask for an answer on this point, since General Wavell wished to return the following day to Cairo and at once initiate preparations for moving the force. We did not wish to give the impression that we were forcing our offer on the Greeks; we wanted to be sure that the Greeks of their own free will were anxious to accept it.

The President of the Council, without hesitation and showing some emotion, stated formally that the Greek Government accepted with deep gratitude the offer of His Majesty's Government and entirely approved the military plan on which the British and Greek military representatives had agreed. Greece would do her duty by herself and by her ally, Great Britain.[12]

These, then, were the decisive steps in the initiation of the Greek campaign. They were the joint decision of the British Empire and its ally. Its Imperial quality and significance need to be stressed. Those who took the decisions were not ashamed of the concept of the British Empire or of using its phraseology. The Greek expedition makes no sense, morally, intellectually or strategically, unless it is seen in terms of British Imperial strategy and sentiment; for those were the terms in which those who launched it thought and felt about it. This was true not only of Churchill, but of Wavell himself, of Eden, of the Australian Prime Minister, Mr. Robert Menzies, who was now in London, and of Smuts (whom Churchill was urging to go to Cairo and whose attitude, when he did, was of great importance). Their views and their feelings were rooted in recent but deep experience; and in their eyes the Empire, in spite of its diversity and its constitutional anomalies, possessed a real unity of purpose and decision. The three focal points of decision, however, during that long, anxious week-end, were in London, Cairo and Athens.

The mission and the Commanders-in-Chief flew back to Cairo on the morning of Sunday, 23rd February. The Foreign Secretary described the course of the discussions in detail in a long telegram to the Prime Minister, and added a personal message:

We are all convinced that we have chosen the right course, and as the eleventh hour has already struck felt sure that you would not wish us to delay for detailed reference home.

The risks are great, but there is a chance of success. We are

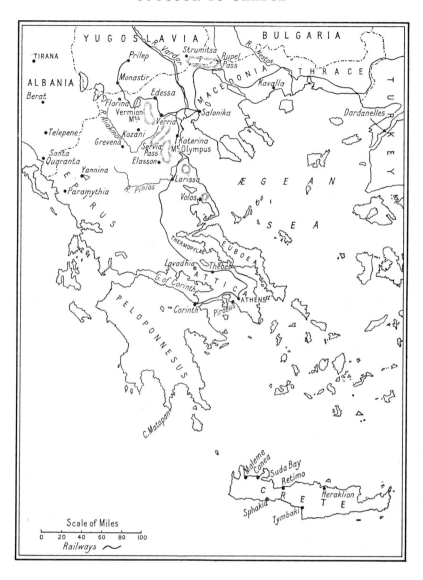

Greece and Crete

accepting difficulties which will make a heavy demand upon our resources, more particularly of fighter aircraft. . . .[13]

In London, the Chiefs of Staff considered Eden's telegram at a meeting which lasted from a quarter to five that afternoon until half past two next morning. They concluded that they should, on balance, advise that the enterprise should go forward. Kennedy, the D.M.O., thought it very wrong that the Cabinet had never asked for, or received, a purely military view from the Chiefs of Staff or from Wavell. He held that "all the service advice given on this problem had been coloured by political considerations—a very dangerous procedure." In face of opinion in favour of the project, which he conceded to be formidable, Kennedy strove without avail to press his own point of view.[14]

On Monday the War Cabinet met, and Menzies was brought into the consultations.

Prime Minister to Foreign Secretary   *24th February, 1941*
The Chiefs of Staff having endorsed action on lines proposed in your telegrams from Cairo and from Athens, I brought whole question before War Cabinet this evening, Mr. Menzies being present. Decision was unanimous in the sense you desire, but of course Mr. Menzies must telegraph home. Presume, also, you have settled with New Zealand Government about their troops. No need anticipate difficulties in either quarter. Therefore, while being under no illusions, we all send you the order "Full steam ahead."[15]

Armed with this mandate Eden, accompanied by Dill but not by Wavell, flew off to Ankara to see the Turkish Government. In the chain of decision there were now three vital but frail links: the attitude of Yugoslavia, the attitude of Turkey, and the capacity of the Greeks and the British to hold the Aliakmon line. The whole weight of the venture was thrust upon these. If one snapped, it would be jeopardised. If two? And if all three?

Eden's task now was to strengthen as far as possible the second link. He had to tell the Turks what had been decided in Athens and in London; but he had to seek their agreement for the diversion to Greece of equipment due to them; and he had to try to persuade them to support Greece by armed force in the event of a German attack.

The Ankara discussions were frank, cordial and, for all practical purposes, quite fruitless. Wavell summed them up succinctly: "The Turks entirely approved our decision to support Greece but would not agree to commit themselves to action. I suppose they were wise from their point of view and possibly also from ours in the long run. They were, in fact, in no state to undertake an offensive war, and were in some apprehension that they themselves might be attacked."[16]

The second link had not been strengthened. One assumption, therefore, had to be discounted: the British decision to help Greece had not encouraged the Turks to come into a broad, open Balkan alliance against German aggression. What about the first link, Yugo-slavia? For four days Eden had awaited an answer to the message he had addressed to Prince Paul from Athens late on the Sunday night. On the evening of 27th February, after the meetings with the Turkish leaders were ended, the Yugoslav Ambassador in Ankara delivered a communication from the Regent. It was non-committal and evasive. Yugoslavia would defend her territory and refuse passage to foreign troops across her soil; but Prince Paul would not say what line he would take if the Germans moved through Bulgaria. The Ambassador added a personal plea that the British Government should not insist on a more definite attitude for the present.

But time was running out fast. The Germans were moving in accordance with a nicely calculated plan, strategically inexorable, tactically fluid; and the initiative was now theirs. The British were compelled to react to each step taken by the Germans.

Eden and Dill left Ankara on 28th February, had to land at an air-field on the Asiatic shore of the Sea of Marmora, and were grounded for twenty-four hours by bad weather.

Prime Minister to General Smuts   *28th February, 1941*
I am so glad you are going to meet Eden and Dill. We have taken a grave and hazardous decision to sustain the Greeks and try to make a Balkan Front. I look forward to receiving your personal views upon this after your conference. This decision makes it most necessary to reinforce Egypt and Libya, and I hope you will arrange with Wavell and Dill to bring "Acanthus" [the 1st South African Division] forward to the Mediterranean at the earliest moment, asking me about shipping difficulties, which are great. Our affairs are helped by rapid successes gained in East Africa. It is only a few weeks ago they were telling us they could not

move on Kismayu till May. Now we have Mogadishu and the whole place in our hands.[17]

On 1st March—the day provided for this move in the German time-table agreed between Hitler and his Commanders-in-Chief the previous November—Bulgaria announced her public adherence to the Axis Tripartite Pact; and on the following day, with Bulgaria's connivance, elements of the German Twelfth Army began to cross the frozen Danube.

Prime Minister to Foreign Secy. (in Athens)   *1st March, 1941*
Obvious German move is to overrun Bulgaria, further to intimidate Turkey by threat of air attacks, force Greece out of the war, and then turn on Yugoslavia, compelling her to obey; after which Turkey can be attacked or not, at their hostile convenience.
    Your main appeal should now be made to Yugoslavia. A sudden move south by Yugoslavia would produce an Italian disaster of the first magnitude, possibly decisive on whole Balkan situation. If at the same moment Turkey declared war the enemy could not gather sufficient forces for many months, during which our air strength will grow. I am absolutely ready to go in on a serious hazard if there is reasonable chance of success, at any rate for a few months, and all preparations should go forward at fullest speed. But I should like you so to handle matters in Greece that if upon final consideration of all the factors, including "Manddibles" possibilities, you feel that there is not even a reasonable hope, you should still retain power to liberate Greeks from any bargain and at the same time liberate ourselves. Meanwhile all should proceed as arranged.[18]

Two of the three links in the chain of the decision reached a week earlier had already proved ineffective; what of the third link? Eden and Dill—their visit was now declared to be official—reached Athens on Sunday, 2nd March, and at once learned from General Heywood that the Greek Government had failed to carry out the agreement reached on 22nd February at Tatoi and that no order for the withdrawal of troops from Macedonia and Thrace had been given. General Papagos's reasons for this astonishing failure were first, that it had proved to be too late to begin the withdrawal, since it would take twenty days to execute and there was a danger of his troops being caught on the move by a German division; and second, that withdrawal in face of the German moves in Bulgaria would cause alarm among the Greek population of Macedonia. No troops had as yet been withdrawn from the Albanian frontier either, because Papagos feared the effect that this move would have on the morale of his own forces.

Arthur Smith, Wavell's Chief of Staff, was present when these disturbing disclosures were made. A cold wind ruffled the brightness of the spring day. Eden thought the Greeks' inaction was the result of an "unfortunate misunderstanding." Papagos himself subsequently maintained that it had been agreed at Tatoi that no final decision was to be taken until the attitudes of Turkey and Yugoslavia were determined. Wavell held, until his death, that this was certainly not the British understanding. The evidence of his own notes made at the time, as well as the Foreign Office and the War Office reports, sustain this contention; but his subsequent comment was: "It was admittedly a hard decision from the Greek political point of view to abandon Western Thrace and Macedonia without a fight; and it may be that when the point came, the decision proved too hard to take."[19]

Eden at this first meeting on 2nd March crystallised the British intention, which did not shift in the three days of arduous discussion that followed. It was, he insisted, essential to get the minimum requisite troops on to the Aliakmon line at once; and if they could not be got there by withdrawing them from Macedonia and Thrace, then they would have to be brought across from Albania. It was a tardy (and, as it was to prove, unsuccessful) effort to reconstruct the third link in the chain. British consternation now encountered Greek stubbornness and pride. During the night of 2nd/3rd March there were no fewer than four Anglo-Greek meetings, one supposedly political, the other three supposedly military. The misunderstanding was not clarified, and no progress of any kind was made. The discussion went round in circles. At one moment Koryzis, in the middle of an impassioned plea that the British should augment the forces they still proposed to send to Greece and increase their moral aid, suddenly threw out the suggestion that it would be of help if some promise were given that the question of Cyprus could be settled in accordance with Greek aspirations.[20] Eden, with the irascibility born of extreme fatigue combined with extreme disappointment, brushed aside this untimely phantasm from the future. At two in the morning —an urgent telegram having been despatched, asking Wavell to come as quickly as possible—Papagos, Dill and Arthur Smith were still talking round the misapprehension about the conditions on which the Greeks would or would not withdraw from Macedonia; the British urged a quick pull back to the Aliakmon line, and Papagos clung obstinately to the advanced Nestos line.

"If the Yugoslavs should fight," he cried out fiercely, "that is where we Greeks should stand."

Dill snapped, "General, *you* will have to fight *that* battle."[21]

Wavell was in Athens for the third time in a few weeks on 3rd March. A little later on the same day Maitland Wilson, the commander-designate of British forces in Greece, arrived at Tatoi airfield.[22] A note of bleak comedy now intruded. In an effort not to exacerbate an already thoroughly disagreeable situation, he and his staff had been requested to wear civilian clothes. For passport and visa purposes Wilson assumed the name of "Mr. Watt" and his son Patrick, who accompanied him as his security officer, called himself "Mr. Watson." If there was one general in the British Army in the Middle East at this time whom it was impossible to disguise, that general was Jumbo Wilson. However, the pretence was maintained for a week or more.

There was a series of discussions at the Legation during 3rd and 4th March, in which both the King and Koryzis took part. In the small hours of 5th March Papagos and Dill signed a joint statement on the decisions reached. It had been agreed that, while the Greeks were to leave three divisions in Macedonia holding prepared positions in the original forward line, they would concentrate their main force, two infantry and one motorised division and some seven battalions from Western Thrace then under Turkish command, along the Aliakmon line; that these formations would be put forthwith under a separate Greek commander; that the British expeditionary force would be sent as soon as possible to the Aliakmon line; and that General Wilson, "under the high command of General Papagos," would command both Greek and British armies in this line, along which it was intended that they should give battle.

Later that same morning Eden sent Churchill a long telegram describing the changed and disturbing situation, the atmosphere very different from that which they had encountered before, and the melancholy results. He compared the process by which agreement was finally reached with the haggling of an oriental bazaar, but said that while Papagos had been unaccommodating and defeatist, the King was "calm, determined and helpful." The mission, he said, had been faced with three alternatives:

a. To accept the plan of Papagos, to which he constantly returned, of attempting to dribble our forces piecemeal up to Macedonian frontier.

b. To accept three Greek divisions offered for Aliakmon line, the equivalent of about 16-23 battalions instead of 35 we had been led to expect on our previous visit, and to build up our concentration behind this. Against this we had to set the delay likely to be imposed by defence of Rupel and other passes by three divisions remaining in Macedonia.

c. To withdraw our offer of military support altogether.

They agreed, after some misgivings, to the second solution, but with the proviso that the command and organisation of the whole Aliakmon line was to be entrusted to General Wilson as soon as he was in a position to take it over. The telegram concluded:

We are all sure that we have in a very difficult situation arrived at correct decision. These two days have been indescribably anxious, but now that decision has been taken there is marked improvement in the general atmosphere on Greek side. The hard fact remains that our forces, including Dominion contingents, will be engaged in an operation more hazardous than it seemed a week ago. You will no doubt decide on any communications to be made to the Dominion Governments. . . .[23]

An immediately following signal gave details of the probable timings of the German and Allied forces' arrival at the Aliakmon line. The first British troops, it was thought, would be able to take up their positions between 16th and 19th March. The first flight of the expedition had in fact sailed from Egypt, in a convoy with the code name "Lustre," on 4th March. In the meantime Eden had tried to make a fresh approach to Belgrade, with no effective result, except that Prince Paul agreed to send an emissary to Athens, a Major Perichitch of the Yugoslav General Staff, who arrived—disguised, not very adequately, as "Mr. L. R. (Last Ray of) Hope"—more than forty-eight hours after the senior members of the mission had made their way back to Cairo.

In London, Eden's telegram had a disquieting impact. The Chiefs of Staff Committee composed a paper, which was presented to

349

Churchill on the evening of 5th March. They recorded all the factors now beginning to have an unfavourable effect on the Cabinet's Balkan policy, and particularly on the Greek enterprise. They summarised the facts set out in Eden's telegram. They then turned to the not inconsiderable difficulties which were piling up against Wavell: the unfulfilled expectation (theirs perhaps, certainly not his) that Rhodes, in operation "Mandibles," would have been captured before, or simultaneously with, the launching of the main move to Greece; the consequent lamentable effect on the R.A.F.'s gravely strained capacity to supply air cover; the fact that the Suez Canal was now blocked by mines (dropped from aircraft) and could not be cleared until 11th March, although only half the M.T.-carrying ships were in the Mediterranean, and all the personnel-carrying ships were in the Red Sea. Finally they calculated that the Germans could concentrate two divisions on the Aliakmon line by 15th March, and three more (one of which would be armoured) by 22nd March; and they concluded that, if the Greeks could delay the enemy on the Nestos line for only a short time, the best that could be hoped for was a force consisting of the New Zealand brigade and one armoured brigade in the Aliakmon line to confront the first two German divisions. "The hazards of the enterprise," they pointed out, "have considerably increased."[24]

This gloomy appreciation was signalled, *en bloc*, to Cairo early on the morning of 6th March. Churchill took a copy of it with him to Chequers, where he spent the night studying it in solitude. The results of his meditations were embodied in another telegram to Eden.

Prime Minister to Foreign Secy.   *6th March, 1941, 0300 hrs.*
Situation has indeed changed for the worse. . . . Failure of Papagos to act as agreed with you on 21st [sic] February, obvious difficulty of his extricating his army from contact in Albania and time-table of our possible movements furnished by Wavell together with other adverse factors . . . e.g. postponement of "Mandibles" and closing of the Canal, makes it difficult for the Cabinet to believe we now have any power to avert the fate of Greece unless Turkey and/or Yugoslavia come in, which seems most improbable. We have done our best to promote Balkan combination against Germany. We must be careful not to urge Greece against her better judgment into a hopeless resistance alone when we have only handfuls of troops which can reach the scene in time. Grave

Imperial issues are raised by committing New Zealand troops to an enterprise which as you say has become even more hazardous. We are bound to lay before the Dominion Governments your telegram and the Chiefs of Staff's appreciation. Cannot forecast their assent to operation. We do not see any reasons for expecting success except of course we attach great weight to opinion of Dill and Wavell.

We must . . . liberate the Greeks from feeling bound to reject German ultimatum. If on their own they resolve to fight, we must to some extent share their ordeal. But rapid German advance will probably prevent any appreciable British Imperial forces from being engaged.

Loss of Greece and Balkans by no means a major catastrophe for us provided Turkey remains honestly neutral. We could take "Mandibles" and consider plans for "Influx"[25] or Tripoli. We are advised from many quarters that our ignominious ejection from Greece would do us more harm in Spain and Vichy than the fact of submission of Balkans, which with our scanty forces alone we have never been expected to prevent.

I send you this to prepare your mind for what, in the absence of facts very different from those now before us, will probably be expressed in the Cabinet decision to-morrow.

The Prime Minister's shift of feeling greatly upset the British Minister in Athens, Sir Michael Palairet. His Air Attaché saw the King, who gave him a solemn assurance that the Greeks were determined to carry out the agreed plan of action against a German attack and had every confidence in its success, especially if, with adequate R.A.F. reinforcements, the initial German air assault could be defeated. Palairet sent two vigorous telegrams to Eden in Cairo, one of which ended curtly: "There is no question of 'liberating Greeks from feeling bound to reject ultimatum.' They have decided to fight Germany alone if necessary. The question is whether we help or abandon them."

Foreign Secretary to Prime Minister   *6th March, 1941, 1940 hrs.*
Chief of Imperial General Staff and I, in consultation with the three Commanders-in-Chief, have this afternoon re-examined the question. We are unanimously agreed that, despite the heavy commitments and grave risks which are undoubtedly involved, especially in view of our limited naval and air resources, the right

decision was taken in Athens. Palairet's telegrams to Cairo showed the position from the Greek angle.

This is merely to indicate to you how our minds are working while we await Cabinet view foreshadowed in your telegram.[26]

C.I.G.S. to Secy. of State for War   *7th March, 1941, 0205 hrs.*
General Wavell has explained to Generals Blamey and Freyberg additional risks involved in venture in Greece under existing situation. Both have expressed their willingness to undertake operations under new conditions. You will no doubt inform Prime Minister.[27]

Between the despatch of Eden's telegram to Churchill and the despatch of Dill's to the War Office much had happened in Cairo. Most important of all, General Smuts, the veteran Prime Minister of South Africa, whose friendship and advice Churchill, Eden and Wavell all valued highly, had arrived, accompanied by the Chief of the South African General Staff, General Sir Pierre Van Ryneveld. At a meeting held in the British Embassy on the night of the South Africans' arrival, attended by Eden, Lampson (the Ambassador), Dill and the three Commanders-in-Chief, Eden opened by welcoming Smuts, gratefully and gracefully, and asking for his views on the situation in the Middle East and the Balkans.

"The situation is most difficult," Smuts answered. "The gravest risks confront us whatever we do. After the recent change in our luck, I am most reluctant to see a setback. I put little faith in possible action by either Turkey or Yugoslavia. There remain the Greeks—and ourselves. The Greeks have done better than anyone could have expected. The public opinion of the world is strongly on their side. If we do not stand by them, we shall be held up to public ignominy.

"On the other hand, they have not in fact carried out the arrangements reached with them at Tatoi. Time has been lost. The question is: will our troops arrive at the Aliakmon line in time? Can the four Greek divisions on the Macedonian border hold the German advance long enough? It seems doubtful. The dilemma which faces us, therefore, is grave; but it is too late to retreat. A provisional arrangement has been made, and we have begun to carry it out. Therefore we cannot back out now. If the weather turns against the Germans and holds them up, there is a good chance that we shall be on the Aliakmon line in sufficient strength in time to hold it. It may be said that a

General Morshead   General Freyberg

General Arthur Smith   General Maitland Wilson

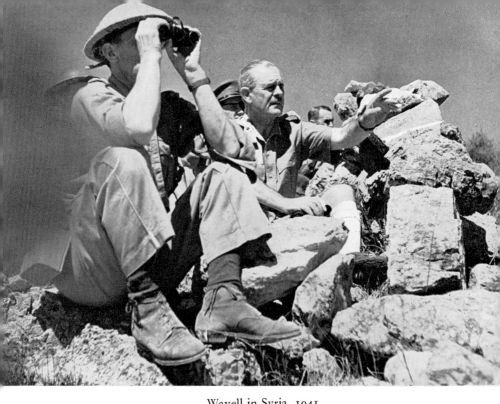

Wavell in Syria, 1941

Rommel in the Desert, 1941

German victory in the Balkans will result in a great setback to our cause; but the setback will probably be greater if we stand aside and don't help."

Wavell outlined the Greek dispositions and added: "The enemy are taking some grave risks too. They are going to have a long and indifferent line of communications through countries that aren't well disposed to Germany."

Dill broke in, "There's no doubt that we must go on with our plans. There is a reasonable chance that we shall get there in time. There's a possibility that we may provoke the Germans into showing their hands before we are committed. The formation of a Balkan front may gravely inconvenience Hitler."

Wavell reminded Smuts of the Greeks' refusal earlier of help. Cunningham made his points about the exposure of ships to air attack on the passage between Egypt and Greece, and about the effect of the mines in the Suez Canal. Longmore made it quite clear that the R.A.F. was being strained to the limit and beyond; and when Smuts observed that it was necessary to reinforce and strengthen the Balkans to the utmost, Longmore said, "I cannot send any more fighter squadrons to Greece, because I simply have not got them."

Eden said little. He had found a supporter for the Balkan front policy as stalwart as he was respected. He gave Smuts the last word.

"If Germany is sending air reinforcements to Africa and to the Balkans, she has all the less to use against the United Kingdom. I think that London must realise that a first-class front is being built up here. I very much doubt whether now the Germans intend to invade England. Isn't it better, therefore, to fight them in the Balkans? I have no doubt that the defeat of Mussolini has brought about a large-scale change in German plans. I don't think the Germans will do more in Tripoli than make a feint in order to retain our forces in North Africa and prevent them being sent to the Balkans.

"I'll sum up. The time-table is all-important. We must clear Mogadishu, we must clear the Canal, and we must take the Dodecanese."[28]

Everyone recognised the importance of the Dodecanese. The Italians had made limited use of them for offensive purposes. Once the Germans were installed, they put the islands to formidable use. Operation "Mandibles" had a high theoretical priority; but the more it was postponed, the more dangerous and costly in men and ships it was bound to be. Again and again, too, other fronts had made more urgent claims. Not till more than two years had passed was any assault to be launched against these islands. The Suez Canal, whether or not it was mined, was virtually out of use as the British Empire's chief maritime artery until the late summer of 1943. Mogadishu was cleared within a month. But on the main theme of the discussion Smut's influence had been decisive. He had expressed his views with lucidity and firmness. Blamey and Freyberg had been told about, and had accepted, the risks of the new situation. The Empire was committed. *There could now be no last-minute backing out.*

Eden reported the result of this conference to the Prime Minister in a telegram on 7th March. "While we are all conscious of the gravity of the decision," he said, "we can find no reason to vary our previous judgment."

The Prime Minister at once took the issue to the War Cabinet, at which Menzies was present. Churchill's subsequent description of this crucial meeting was dramatic and moving. The decision to go on seemed to those who took it as right and courageous as it was irrevocable. "There was," he wrote proudly, "a strong glow for action. The Cabinet was short, the decision final."[29]

Prince Paul of Yugoslavia's liaison officer, Major Perichitch, was in Athens next day and was seen by Papagos and Arthur Smith, who had stayed on after Wavell went back to Cairo. Perichitch was pessimistic and inquisitive, and the discussions were inconclusive. Arthur Smith's signalled account of them reached G.H.Q. late that night, at the end of an arduous week. Wavell and Dill, who was staying with him, had gone to bed early. They were awakened by Eden, who arrived at the house at midnight with his attendant secretaries, determined to compose a major telegram to the Prime Minister. Eden wrote a telegram as he wrote a speech: both activities required an audience, participating, advising, criticising. Wavell and Dill in their dressing-gowns sat side by side on a sofa in the drawing-room. Longmore arrived in uniform, and watched the two weary soldiers, looking like a couple of teddy-bears, trying to give the Foreign Secretary's eloquence the attention it demanded. They both went quietly to sleep, and when Eden paused for comment only their regular breathing broke the silence.

On his early ride the following morning, and in his swim afterwards at Gezira, Wavell was more than ordinarily withdrawn. An hour or two later he walked into Longmore's room and, without comment, laid a document on his desk:

MOST SECRET AND VERY PERSONAL

The Jug

(with apologies to Lewis Carroll)

In Cairo, where the Gypies are,
I sing this song to my guitar.
("Only I'm not going to sing it really," explained
   Anthony kindly.
"Thank you very much indeed," said Jacqueline.)
In Athens, when I've met the Greek,
I'll tell you what it is I seek.
("It'll be nice to know," said Jacqueline.)
In Cyprus, where I met the Turk,
I'll tell you how to set to work.
In London, when we're safely back,
I'll sing it all again to Jack.
("Who is Jack?" inquired Jacqueline, a little puzzled.
"You've heard of Jack and Jill, haven't you?" said
   Anthony severely.
"Of course," said Jacqueline, "is this he?"
"No," said Anthony pityingly, "this is Jack and Dill.
   I thought everyone knew that.")
I sent a message to the Jug,
I told him not to be a mug.
I said he must be badly cracked
To think of joining Hitler's pact.
The Jug replied, "But don't you see
How difficult it is for me."
("It's difficult for me too," said Jacqueline sadly.
"It doesn't get any easier further on," said Anthony.)
I took a pencil large and new,
I wrote a telegram or two.
Then someone came to me and said
The Generals have gone to bed.
I said it loud, I said it plain,
"Then you must wake them up again."

And I was very firm with them,
I kept them up till 2 a.m.
("Wasn't that rather unkind?" said Jacqueline.
"Not at all," said Anthony firmly." "We want Generals,
    not dormice. But don't keep interrupting.")
I took some ginger from the shelf,
I said I'd better go myself.
Our Friend replied "The door is shut,
You know I'd love to see you, but . . ."
I sent him letters once or twice
Containing all the best advice.
I put it strong, I put it hot,
A hopeless Hope was all I got.
He said, "I should be firm and stiff
And send an ultimatum if . . ."
I took red ink and fountain pen,
I wrote another wire, and then . . .
("Is that all?" said Jacqueline, after a pause.
"That's all at present. There'll be some more to-night,
    if you wait up long enough.")[30]

Churchill wrote: "I take full responsibility for the eventual decision
[to go on with the Greek campaign], because I am sure I could have
stopped it all if I had been convinced. It is so much easier to stop
than to do."[31]

Among Churchill's most valuable and most attractive qualities
were his inexhaustible thirst and capacity for action. But though
inertia is perilous, there can be times when it is wise to call a halt to
a course of action the reasons and purpose of which have been
destroyed. Now, however, the enterprise had achieved its own
momentum, and nobody could stop it. The story of the rest of March,
so far as the Balkan front was concerned, was of a series of efforts,
not to stem the onrush of events, but somehow to turn it to advantage
instead of disaster.

Eden and Dill had already been absent from London for almost a
month. After their second visit to Athens they had planned to leave
Cairo for the United Kingdom within a few days; but first of all they
were held up by bad weather, and then Churchill decided that they

should remain, since there seemed a prospect that the Prince Regent might agree to their visiting Belgrade, and there was a chance of their keeping in close touch with the situation in Turkey. They spent, therefore, another month going hither and thither, attempting to budge Turkey from her neutrality and prevent Yugoslavia, whose internal conflicts were intensifying day by day, from sliding sideways into the Axis camp. These complicated politico-diplomatic exchanges directly concerned Wavell, but his own effective part in them was small. He now had many other, even more vital, matters to deal with: East Africa, Cyrenaica, and—when it came—the fighting in Greece.

On the afternoon of 15th March a meeting was held at the Embassy in Cairo, attended by Eden, Dill, Wavell, Longmore and Lampson, to discuss policy towards Turkey. Eden said that the suggestion had been made that it would be useful to pay a second visit to the Turkish Government.

"I am opposed to this suggestion," said Wavell bluntly.

"I agree with General Wavell," said Longmore.

Wavell went on: "I believe that Turkey has so little offensive power that she would be a liability, not an asset, if she entered the war at this stage. And even if the Turks were to come in, we have nothing to spare for them. Moreover, if they are pressed to take a positive line, they'll probably raise the question of passage through Syria; and we haven't the forces to ensure that passage. I think it is undesirable to press the Turks to take any positive action—let's say, to declare war when Germany attacks Greece—which might result in provoking a German attack on Turkey. This being so, I think that a further visit to Turkey will serve no purpose."

"Don't you think, General," Eden asked, "that a somewhat stiffer attitude on the part of the Turks would be desirable?"

"Yes, I do; but surely we can best achieve this by representations made by the Ambassador. If you and the C.I.G.S. go to Ankara once more, with nothing to offer and little to ask, the Turks will be puzzled, and they'll suspect that we are desperate and clutching at straws." He paused for a moment. "But if it is essential that the Turks declare war in order to ensure that Yugoslavia stands firm, then I agree that we must urge them to do so, because it is of the greatest strategical importance that Yugoslavia is not lost to us."[32]

In these few sentences Wavell showed that he at least had no illusions. They could not now stop, turn or go back. They could only go on.

XI

End of an Empire

Wavell's East African campaign in the opening months of 1941 resulted in the total liquidation of an empire and the eradication of any enemy threat to central and southern Africa other than from attacks on shipping by long-range submarines. It was as complete a defeat of a numerically much more powerful army as any achieved during the war. Yet the Prime Minister misjudged it from the outset, and directed at it a fusillade of criticism and would-be interference which, if it had had its full desired effect, would have removed all chance of victory.

Churchill, early in his long and varied career, had travelled and fought in Africa, but this first-hand experience now proved more of a hindrance than a help. For he chose to disagree with and to distrust the Commander-in-Chief responsible for operations. Wavell described his attitude throughout as "barracking." Churchill held, from August, 1940, onwards, two *idées fixes*: the first, that it was essential to bring the South African forces, which had then just begun to arrive in Kenya, up to Egypt immediately; the second, that a defensive policy would suffice to bring the Italian empire in East Africa to an end, by a process of slow blight and economic blockade. He never abandoned these preconceptions; nor did he ever admit subsequently that they were wrong, and that had Wavell acted in accordance with them, there might have been a very different outcome to the East African campaign.

In this matter, however, Wavell resisted all Churchill's attempts to sap his strategic independence and his over-all control of his own theatre of war. At the beginning of his file about Kenya he wrote:

The P.M. always disliked Kenya force and was trying to remove troops from it. Smuts on the other hand took it very seriously from the South African point of view and always wished to reinforce. It fully justified itself in the end, after I had changed commanders (Cunningham for Dickinson) but it absorbed much transport.

This major victory was, in essence, a series of tactically well-conducted and successful operations under the strategically skilful and excellently timed direction of the Commander-in-Chief. He defined its ultimate pattern as:

> a pincer movement on the largest scale, through Eritrea and Somaliland, converging on Amba Alagi, combined with a direct thrust through Western Abyssinia by the patriot forces. It looks Teutonic in conception and execution; but this result was not foreseen in the original plan. . . . It was in fact an improvisation after the British fashion of war rather than a set piece in the German manner.[1]

It was also a highly professional, adroit and often daring improvisation. It has been well said that Wavell "conquered East Africa on two fronts with an economy and flexibility of force that ought to rank as a feat of spontaneous exploitation unsurpassed in war."[2]

When Anthony Eden, as Secretary of State for War, visited the Middle East in the late autumn of 1940, he made an important impact on the East African campaign. He and Wavell at this time were in the closest sympathy. On 28th October they flew down from Cairo to a three-day conference at Khartoum. They were joined there by Smuts, who had been inspecting South African units in Kenya, by a Foreign Office representative from the British Embassy in Cairo, and by the two generals who had been designated to command the assault on Italian East Africa, Platt from the Sudan and Alan Cunningham from Kenya; and they had a series of discussions with the Emperor Haile Selassie and his advisers, which began stormily but reached agreement before they were concluded. The points of contact between the four principal negotiators—the Emperor, Smuts, Eden and Wavell—mattered more than the points of divergence.

To the Emperor, assistance from the British Empire was of significance if it helped him to liberate his country and regain his throne; the more generous that assistance was, and the more promptly it was given, the sooner his aim would be achieved. Smuts wished for a victory which he hoped would have two consequences: first, that it would remove the diffused but real threat of Axis penetration into central and southern Africa; and second, that effective South African participation in it would consolidate his own shaky political position at home. Eden's involvement was, to a considerable degree, emotional. As a young Minister in Stanley Baldwin's Government in 1935, he had eagerly espoused the cause of Ethiopia at the League of Nations. He returned to it with zest. He "asserted Haile Selassie's right to rebellion: he persuaded the Sudan Government to look on the existing rebellion as a war of liberation."[3] Eden's approach coincided with Wavell's intended strategy. Wavell was certain that, with the resources he had, the best way of making the Italian position impossible and eventually of freeing Ethiopia was to foment as vigorously as possible a large-scale patriotic resistance within the country. It will be recalled that he had chosen Colonel Sandford for this very task. Sandford established a headquarters deep inside Abyssinia—at Faguta, some thirty-five miles south of Lake Tana—in September, 1940.

Meanwhile, between Italy's entry into the war and Sandford's departure on his mission, another officer was recruited for a similar though not precisely overlapping task. At a meeting of the War Cabinet's Middle East Committee in July, Leopold Amery suggested to the V.C.I.G.S., General Haining, that the ideal man to lead insurgent forces from within the Italian African possessions was "a certain Captain O. C. Wingate," who was, in Amery's opinion, "a much more virile and solidly balanced Lawrence, but with much the same sort of power of inspiring others."[4]

Haining passed the suggestion on to Wavell, who had not forgotten the ardent young Intelligence officer in Jerusalem in 1938, in whom he had recognised someone who might be valuable as a leader of unorthodox enterprise in war. Neither had he forgotten Wingate's single-minded, even reckless, devotion to the cause of Zionism. He signalled a request that Wingate should be sent out immediately, but attached the proviso that he must in no circumstances go to Palestine, for any reason whatever, whether on duty or on leave.[5] Wingate, who had been in the doldrums as a brigade major of an A.A. brigade in the southern suburbs of London, sailed from England to Cape Town on 19th September; he reached Cairo on 17th October, reported as ordered to a department of G.H.Q. called G(R) with a view to ultimate employment in operations against Italian East Africa, and there waited until the conference in Khartoum reached its decision.

That decision gave priority to an uprising inside Ethiopia.

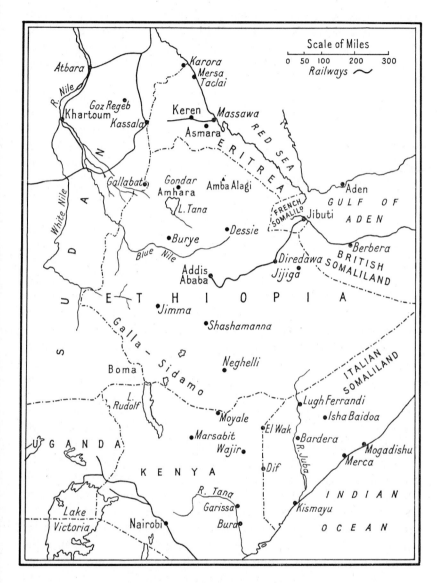

East Africa, January—May, 1941

361

Wingate was ordered to Khartoum, and arrived there on 6th November, to act as liaison between the British military authorities and the Emperor, to keep G.H.Q. informed of Ethiopian requirements, and to supervise the collection, enlistment and training of Ethiopian patriots for the rebellion.

Though Wavell was quite clear in his mind that the uprising was to be the principal operation in this theatre, he was certain that its flanks would have to be secured, north and south of the great central plateau. The frontier posts which had been lost immediately after Italy's entry into the war were to be recaptured, and thus supply postern gates through which patriots could infiltrate into the country in order to sustain and spread the revolt. Platt, it was agreed, should retake Gallabat about the middle of November, and open the frontier in that important region; then he was to move on and capture Kassala early in January. On the southern, Kenya, front Smuts was anxious for an early attack on Kismayu; Cunningham thought that transport shortage and the difficulties of maintaining a water supply across many hundreds of miles of barren desert with hardly any communications would make it impossible to launch this advance with any hope of success until after the spring rains, in May or June, 1941.

A great deal was bound to depend on very finely balanced factors, on timing and on bluff. From the outset it was anything but an orthodox campaign. The central element in it—the patriot uprising —was the most difficult to gauge. The numbers employed were, to put it mildly, as impossible to estimate as the tactical effectiveness of most of the battles they fought. In the final analysis, though the numbers engaged in any one battle were small, the sum total of their victories had a crucial effect on the campaign as a whole. But in the early stages it seemed disagreeably obvious—to the Prime Minister in London, if to nobody else—that on the flanks, explicitly relegated to a subordinate role, were big forces standing idle for weeks, lengthening into months, when they were urgently needed, to be put to far better immediate use, elsewhere. On paper and at that distance the Prime Minister had a strong case. In Kenya there were now some 75,000 men in all: 33,000 East Africans, 9,000 West Africans, and some 6,000 British serving with them; and about 27,000 South Africans. Three Divisions had been formed, the 1st South African and the 11th and 12th African. In the Sudan there were 28,000 troops, including the 5th Indian Division, made available to the Middle East in August and diverted on Wavell's orders to the Sudan; a squadron of mixed cruiser and light tanks sent from Egypt when there seemed some danger of an Italian attack on Khartoum; and the Sudan Defence Force. Churchill continued, in his own phrase, "to gird at" both the size and the apparent inactivity of these substantial forces.

Nevertheless, preparations on this front were being synchronised, delicately and secretly, with those for O'Connor's offensive in the Western Desert. Platt's first advance, launched at Gallabat on 6th November, and conducted with great resolution by an Indian Army brigadier named Slim, of whom much was to be heard later, encountered stiff Italian opposition and failed of its object. This initial setback, combined with Cunningham's decision to postpone his advance into Italian Somaliland for six months or more, made it necessary to think afresh.

A. P. Wavell to C.I.G.S.   *23rd November, 1940*
Cunningham has decided not possible to carry out bold operations this winter. He proposes to carry out series of minor operations in Northern Kenya about the middle of December, and requires both West African brigades for these. . . .[6]

When at a War Cabinet meeting two days later Churchill asked searching questions about this telegram, Dill answered that Wavell had just signalled him that he had decided to have a conference of commanders, including Cunningham and Platt, in Cairo in a few days' time, in order to consider plans for the next six months. This failed to satisfy the Prime Minister. The C.I.G.S. sent Wavell a "ginger" telegram, drawing his attention to Smuts's disappointment at the delay, bidding him prod Cunningham and Platt into hitting the Italians wherever and whenever possible, and hinting broadly that the West African brigade would be sent home if offensive operations did not begin quickly.

Wavell replied, after his conference with his commanders, that on the Sudan front there would be an attack against Kassala in February; that pressure would be maintained in the Gallabat area, but no large-scale operation would be attempted for the time being; that rebellion would be fostered inside Abyssinia by all possible means; that on the Kenya front there would be pressure towards the Abyssinian frontier through the winter months; and that after the spring rains the capture of Kismayu would be attempted. He added that reports of rebel activities in Gojjam (where Wingate was now at work) were encouraging, and that if all went well these would be on a large scale by February. He finished with a forcible request to be allowed to keep the West African brigade.

In a personal telegram to Dill on the same day he filled in the background to these decisions. The Kismayu operation, he said, was being mounted—in spite of the fact that it used up troops and transport—to give Smuts a quick success which he could exploit politically in his own country. He was determined to retain his West African brigades and had taken the trouble to discover from his old friend George Giffard, now G.O.C. in West Africa, that there was no anxiety for their return. North of Lake Rudolph, he said, he proposed to employ regular troops on irregular lines, as small, mobile columns harassing Italian communications, isolating their posts and encouraging rebels. Wingate was hopeful of a large-scale patriot rising early in 1941. But, he warned, Italian morale was still high in this theatre: rebellion might eventually bring mass desertions of native troops, but of this he saw no sign at that moment.

Less than a week after the despatch of these two telegrams the success of "Compass" was assured. On 10th December Wavell gave the order to 4th Indian Division to withdraw from the Western Desert Force. As rapidly and as secretly as possible they moved down to the Sudan by two routes, the Nile Valley and the Red Sea. They were followed by a squadron of the 4th R.T.R. with an incomplete complement of "I" tanks and a battery of 6-inch howitzers. Wavell calculated that the whole move would be complete by the middle of January.

After a lull of a month Churchill, in the course of a comprehensive *tour d'horizon* compiled for the benefit of the Chiefs of Staff, reverted to the topic of East Africa. The victories in the Western Desert were in his view no reason for any slackening of pressure in East Africa, and he demanded offensives on all fronts. The hopes of an Italian victory in Egypt had been killed, and there was now no chance of fresh supplies and men getting to Ethiopia. "It is not an unreasonable hope," he argued, "that by the end of April the Italian army in Abyssinia will have submitted or been broken up." Immediately thereafter all Wavell's forces in this area should go north; and thus, according to his somewhat optimistic calculations, there ought to be a general reserve in the Nile Valley by the end of April totalling twelve divisions.

This idea of a general reserve now began to loom large in Churchill's thinking; but all Wavell's efforts to build it up were shattered by the decision to launch another expeditionary force into the Balkans. On Churchill's insistence Dill sent a signal to Wavell on 8th January expressing his doubts about an "adequate dividend" from the East African operations, and asking whether it would not be better—political objections aside—to bring the South Africans up to join the general reserve in Egypt. Wavell replied agreeing that the dividend was unlikely to be high, but pointing out that no change of investment was possible; continuous pressure in East Africa could lead to the liquidation of this commitment in the summer or autumn of 1941, and in the long run the release of all his forces there more quickly than an immediate withdrawal which would take time and mean a relaxation of effort.

Smuts now entered the discussion, and in a signal to Churchill on 8th January urged an early liquidation of the Abyssinian situation. He proposed a two-pronged simultaneous attack from the north and from Kenya; each would require an additional division, and he offered to provide the one required for the latter operation.[7]

Churchill, delighted with the similarity between Smuts's views and his own, was eager to accept the offer at once. But Wavell, in two signals to the C.I.G.S. on 18th and 21st January, expressed his steadfast opposition to acceptance without full consideration of the transport, equipment and administrative problems it would create. Shipping, he held, since it was in such short supply, should be used for reinforcements to his main theatre; and he drew the timely moral—based on recent Western Desert experience—that small forces well equipped and well trained could achieve great results, while large numbers without full administrative resources were an embarrassment.

Events began to move fast. Throughout the winter liveliness had been maintained on the Sudan-Ethiopian border by a small and very mobile detachment from Platt's main force, consisting of Skinner's Horse and No. 1 Machine-Gun Group of the Sudan Defence Force, with a considerable amount of artillery and other units, known as Gazelle Force, under the command of Colonel Frank Messervy, a bold and cheerfully resilient Indian cavalryman. With considerable dash they harried the enemy by aggressive patrolling, and after a fortnight of almost constant battle some forty miles north of Kassala the Italians withdrew, earning a stern reproof from the Duke of Aosta himself.

The beginnings of their retreat put Platt in a difficulty: how could he follow up quickly enough? He had intended to make a renewed attack on Kassala on 8th February, and a month later advance into Eritrea. He planned to use 4th Indian Division in the north and 5th Indian Division in the south for the main assault. But the former, to which Messervy's Gazelle Force was to be attached, consisted at that moment of only one brigade, and 5th Indian Division of two, but with far too little transport for a general pursuit at short notice.

Yet a great and sudden speed-up was essential to exploit the cracking of the Italians' morale under the impact of reverses in other theatres. Platt therefore put forward the date of his attack on Kassala to 19th January. Even so, by the time he moved the Italians were already pulling back into the mountains, along the only usable roads, towards Agordat, Keren and Asmara. They could stand at Agordat; they certainly must stand at Keren, unless they could be caught before they were ready. A pursuit of this kind is one of the most difficult and tantalising of all military operations. For Wavell this was a period of knife-edge decisions. From day to day he had to improvise, adjust and readjust his plans.

A. P. Wavell to Gen. Arthur Smith   *20th January, 1941*

Sudan: The Italian withdrawal from Kassala and elsewhere makes it necessary ... to consider seriously whether an operation towards Asmara is possible or not. ...

There is also the possibility of a raid on Massawa, either along the coast or by a landing. I am sure that the Indian Motor Brigade is not sufficiently trained for this operation and we have not the troops at present to spare for a landing.

... The Joint Planning Staff might review the problem in the light of the new situation. They must, however, remember that our commitments in Libya and for aid to our allies in the Balkans are more important than the liquidation of Italian East Africa unless there is a prospect of this being done rapidly.

On this same day, 20th January, the Emperor Haile Selassie returned by air to his own country. At a little place called Um Idla, on the plain of the Blue Nile thirty miles inside the Ethiopian border, with Orde Wingate standing rigidly to attention immediately behind him, he himself raised his country's flag, while a guard of honour of his own forces presented arms.

Wavell now decided that, in spite of all the other urgent demands on his time (he had paid his first visit to Athens during this week), he must fly down to East Africa and see for himself how things stood.

Before he went he tried to settle the vexing problem created by Smuts's offer of another division, and Churchill's enthusiastic reception of it. On 25th January he sent a signal to Dill making it clear that, with maintenance, supply and signals stretched to their limits in both Kenya and the Sudan, more troops would be an embarrassment unless or until Kismayu could be captured. The telegram ended: "Could you defer any action regarding acceptance of division until my return."

Churchill acted quickly and angrily.

Prime Minister to A. P. Wavell   *26th January, 1941*

. . . I thought you wanted to have a large strategic reserve in the Delta, and this is in accordance with the directions we have given from here. Certainly there is no need to send another South African division to swell the 70,000 troops of various kinds who are now virtually out of action in Kenya. I asked General Smuts, and he has agreed, to keep the destination of the new division fluid as I thought that by the time transport, etc., could be arranged he might be willing for them to come north to join the Army of the Nile. How can you expect me to face the tremendous strain upon our shipping, affecting as it does all our food and import of munitions, in order to carry more divisions from this country to the Middle East, when you seem opposed to taking a South African division which would only have less than half the distance to come? I hope indeed that both the South African divisions now in Kenya will in a few months be moved to the Delta and that the West African Brigade will be sent as promised back to Freetown. On no account must General Smuts be discouraged from his bold and sound policy of gradually working South African forces into the main theatre. . . .[8]

A senior South African staff officer, Major-General Theron, on his way from Pretoria to Cairo to discuss this very issue with Wavell, stopped the night of Sunday, 26th January, in Nairobi. While he was there Cunningham had a signal from Arthur Smith telling him of the Commander-in-Chief's intended visit. Cunningham gave Theron a letter which, for greater secrecy, he wrote in pencil in his own hand, keeping a carbon copy.

General Cunningham to A. P. Wavell   *26th January, 1941*

I am proposing to make an attempt at the capture of Kismayu round about February 12th. The finding of water at Hagadesu has released just enough transport to make it possible, and I am hoping that the enemy morale is sufficiently shaken to make up for my lack of resources. . . .

Churchill's subsequent statements, therefore, that "under strong pressure from home Wavell eventually decided to make the effort before the rains" and that he "animated the Kenya Command" to that end, do not accord with the facts.[9] *The initiative came directly from Alan Cunningham*; and he made his proposal to Wavell (and Wavell backed it) the moment it seemed possible that his water and transport difficulties could be solved.

Cunningham also gave his view on the question of the second South African division: ". . . I am getting more and more convinced that they will not be able to keep two divisions going in manpower. I have spoken to Theron. . . . He is ex-A.G. of the Union, and I am pretty sure he thinks the same."

Wavell was in Kenya on 28th January, and on the Sudan-Eritrean border two days later. On the evening of 1st February he was back in Cairo, and at once sent a private signal to Dill telling him of Cunningham's decision and his own approval of that decision. The South African Division in the north, he said, was to move north-east in order to cut off Italian troops at Moyale on the Kenya-Ethiopia frontier. The rebellion in the centre of the country seemed to be spreading satisfactorily. In Eritrea the enemy were putting up a stiff resistance. He stressed the difficulty of the country, the inaccuracy of the maps, and the fact that the Italians' morale was still high. He was trying to bring all possible pressure from every direction in the hope that they might crack, but he feared this was unlikely. He asked Dill to regard all this as only a general forecast, liable to alteration as the situation developed.

On the following morning he sent off a second telegram in much more guarded terms which was seen by the Prime Minister, who later claimed that "thus we achieved the forward movement," that "the commanders on the spot had magnified the difficulties," and that the results showed "how right we were at home to press them to speedy action."[10] Not all the pressure from home, however, would have taken Wavell's forces across hundreds of miles of desert had water not been found at a spot so seemingly negligible that no contemporary map gave its name, and had this discovery not made it, in the view of the commanders on the spot, just possible to bring up enough supplies to maintain a rapid advance.

A. P. Wavell to General Cunningham   *3rd February, 1941*
Will see that your present operations are not hampered by any considerations regarding arrival of second South African division. Am in communication with home about it, for your private information understand it is not likely to come to Kenya anyway in near future.

On 7th February—the day of O'Connor's victory at Beda Fomm— again in pencil and again sent by the hand of a senior officer, Cunningham gave Wavell a time-table of the operation which he intended forthwith to carry out in Italian Somaliland. D-Day was to be 11th February, and Cunningham's plan envisaged with clarity the moves for the next nine days ahead.

Thus by the end of the first week in February an immensely complicated, delicate series of major operations, spread over a huge area, inhibited by every kind of administrative, communications, transport and climatic difficulty, was well in train: the patriot rising in the centre, the Kassala move in the north, and the drive on Kismayu in the south. The one sector that might give cause for anxiety was Cunningham's left flank, the troops of which had the task of pressing out of Kenya's Northern Province from Marsabit to Moyale on the southern tip of the Abyssinian escarpment. The First South African Division had worked wonders, in face of harsh and most disagreeable variations of climate, and a line of approach had been constructed. But the pagan tribal chiefs in the south of Abyssinia were no great lovers of the Amharic and Christian Emperor's feudal régime; not only was there no "patriot" activity at all, but to the west of Lake Rudolf an East African brigade made no progress against extremely hostile tribesmen. However, Alan Cunningham, who was demonstrating at this time that he shared to the full the qualities of dash and perseverance which made his brother Andrew so notable a naval commander, was more than capable of neutralising the effect of this minor, local difficulty.

On 10th and 11th February there were held in London meetings of the War Cabinet and the Chiefs of Staff Committee, the consequences of whose decisions were to be grave and far-reaching. As far as East Africa was concerned, they were not mere barracking: they were instructions with a direct bearing on the conduct of the campaign.

A. P. Wavell to Generals Cunningham & Platt   12th February, 1941
War Cabinet has decided every possible assistance to be given to Greece and Turkey in event German attack which seems imminent. Largest possible reserve to be concentrated Egypt for this purpose and preparations made for its despatch. Conference will be held here within next few days with representatives from War Office, Greece and Turkey.

Essential to continue campaign in Italian East Africa until whole northern Eritrea up to Massawa captured and until Kismayu taken. If Italian resistance still continues after these events it will be necessary to reconsider position.

It would be unnecessary and inadvisable to advance south into Abyssinia from Eritrea, especially in view approaching rainy season. Force operating from Sudan should be reduced to that necessary to garrison northern Eritrea and support efforts of patriots in Abyssinia. It is suggested that it might be possible to withdraw from Sudan two or three brigade groups and company Infantry tanks. Will Platt please cable estimate as early as possible of troops required and what formations and units might be made available. Intention is that Indian troops should garrison Cyrenaica.

In East Africa capture of Mogadishu would complete isolation of I.E.A. and hasten surrender and should be carried out after capture Kismayu provided it does not involve heavy commitment. Vital importance of support of Greece and Turkey must however be overriding consideration. Will Cunningham please answer following questions on assumption operation against Kismayu successful:

a. What would be minimum force for attempt to capture Mogadishu?

b. As operations in southern Abyssinia never likely to be decisive can South African Division be withdrawn for Egypt? How soon could this be done? Move might be made by brigades at intervals without waiting for whole division.

c. Could any East African or other formations or units be spared? M.T. companies particularly required.

Assumption for (*b*) and (*c*) above to be that after capture Kismayu no major operation required except possibly capture Mogadishu.

From 12th February onwards Dill (with Eden) was away from London for close on two months, and there was no one capable of curbing Churchill's desire to maintain absolute, if long-range, control over Wavell's strategy and tactics. Telegrams despatched as from the Chiefs of Staff were apt to be undiluted Churchill—sometimes heady, and sometimes exasperating to the point of explosion. Two such signals were sent off on the Sunday after Eden and Dill had left, while they were on their way to Cairo.

C.O.S. to Commanders-in-Chief   *16th February, 1941, 1340 hrs.*
It is essential at this moment to do everything possible to deter Japan from adopting a forward policy. We have evidence that early liquidation of Italian East Africa might have considerable effect on the Japanese in this direction. We have not the slightest doubt of the soundness of your East African plan but we think that you should be aware of the vital importance of the time factor.

The Italians had evacuated their garrison from Kismayu on the night of 13th/14th February, and on the evening of the 14th the 22nd East African Brigade was in full occupation of the port.

C.O.S. to Commanders-in-Chief   *16th February, 1941, 1820 hrs.*
Now that Kismayu has been captured without apparent difficulty do you consider quick advance on Mogadishu practicable? If so we are of opinion that it is eminently desirable.

A. P. Wavell to Chiefs of Staff   *17th February, 1941, 0840 hrs.*
I instructed General Cunningham on 12th February that he was to push on to Mogadishu after capture of Kismayu if it did not involve too heavy commitments. He is acting on these instructions.

A. P. Wavell to Chiefs of Staff   *18th February, 1941, 1140 hrs.*
Quite apart from Japan we are most anxious to liquidate East African commitment as soon as possible but we can go no faster and . . . can provide no more troops or air force.

Advance in Eritrea is at present held up at Keren where enemy

371

has concentrated greatly superior force in very strong position. Pause is necessary before we can make further effort. In view of his increasing strength enemy counter-attack possible during this period.

Have instructed G.O.C. East Africa to capture Mogadishu if possible but to be prepared to release South African Division at short notice. . . .

From the evening of 19th February, when Eden and Dill arrived in Cairo, Wavell was involved ever more deeply in great and troublesome matters. The day-to-day tactical conduct of the campaign in East Africa was not his immediate concern; but in spite of all his other commitments, he continued to exercise full strategic control. He trusted his subordinates—Platt, encountering a dour, well-planned opposition in the approaches to the great massif of Keren, which was the key to Eritrea and to all northern Ethiopia; Cunningham, in the south, making swift, unexpected progress across vast stretches of desert and semi-arid steppe; Sandford, in the interior of Ethiopia, quietly fostering the rebellion of the turbulent highland chieftains; and Wingate, with his strange, sombre and single-minded attachment to the Emperor and his ragged little army called "Gideon Force"—and they all repaid his trust with victory.

On Wednesday, 19th February, Cunningham's troops crossed the river Juba and headed towards Mogadishu. On the same day the first convoy of ships bringing supplies from Mombasa arrived at Kismayu, which became the advance base for the rest of the campaign in the south.

"General Cunningham," Wavell said in his Despatch, "pressed on his operations with the greatest vigour and was usually a little ahead of my proposals and intentions." Mogadishu fell on 25th February to the 23rd Nigerian Brigade, which had advanced 235 miles in three days. Their opponents, the Italians' 102nd Colonial Division, were, in the view of the Duke of Aosta, of no further account as a fighting formation. Great quantities of stores of all kinds were found in Mogadishu, including 350,000 gallons of motor fuel and 80,000 gallons of aviation spirit. On the airfield were the remains of twenty-one aircraft. "A particularly useful find was a handbook of every airfield and landing ground in Italian East Africa."[11]

The Prime Minister's telegrams of congratulation, warmly though they were phrased, returned to the idea of the second South African division coming "forward to the Mediterranean shore" at once, and urged Wavell to discuss it with Smuts. Churchill also pointed out that there should not be much difficulty in reclaiming British Somaliland. Wavell replied that Cunningham, as well as Smuts, was coming to Cairo on 7th March and would discuss future plans and the moving of the South African divisions; he added that he had already ordered Berbera to be reconnoitred with a view to its reoccupation.

On the northern front progress was a good deal less rapid, but the conditions and the country were very different. On 1st/2nd February Platt's forces captured Agordat and Barentu, which guarded the final approaches to Keren, and took 6,000 prisoners, some eighty guns, fifty tanks, 400 trucks and what an early official report described guardedly as "much material." Throughout the 2nd, Gazelle Force and 4th Indian Division pressed on as hard as they could into the mountains—despite a blown bridge and heavily mined stretches of road. But they were just too late to be able to go through the narrow Dongolaas Gorge, where a huge tumble of rocks, boulders and crags lay across the road leading up to the plateau on which the town of Keren stood.

The Italians, by the narrowest of narrow shaves, had shut the door on immediate disaster. Their last strategic reserve, four battalions of first-rate fighting troops, had been driven at high speed from Addis Ababa to Asmara in three days, and had reached Keren on 1st February. When the last of the fugitives from Agordat and Barentu had passed through the gorge, the cliffs at its narrowest point were blasted and the defences manned, a Colonial brigade going into the line at once with the strategic reserve. Behind this rampart two more divisions were forming up hastily for action.

There seems to be little doubt now that the timely arrival of those four battalions saved the badly shaken troops from being overrun at Keren by our initial attacks. Even so these attacks came within an ace of success and were only stopped on the very crests through the paucity of our numbers and the physical difficulties of the high precipitous slopes that had to be climbed.[12]

Keren was a formidable natural fortress, in many aspects not unlike Cassino; and at Keren, as at Cassino, one of the principal formations engaged was the 4th Indian Division. Indeed, Keren was 4th Indian Division's battle. For this they had been snatched away from O'Connor's advance in the Western Desert. The battle had great personal significance for Wavell. When he became an earl, he took as his second title the viscountcy of Keren and Winchester, and Archie John was known as Lord Keren until he succeeded his father.

The town of Keren, which was also a strategically important road and rail junction, lay over four thousand feet above sea level, protected by a ring of gaunt, grey-green mountains, which was broken only to the east. The Dongolaas Gorge, where Platt's forces were held, was dominated on the left by the towering mass of Mount Sanchil, on whose long, saddle-like summit there was a cluster of crags set out like the crown and stars of a brigadier's shoulder badge, and therefore known as Brig's Peak. On the other side the way up the gorge was commanded by the bastion of Mount Zeban and Mount Falestoh, on which stood Fort Dologorodoc. Here General Luigi Frusci, Governor of Eritrea and Commander-in-Chief of the Italian Northern Army, decided to concentrate the bulk of his forces in one final effort to hold Eritrea, and he believed that he could hold it till the British broke. But they did not break.

The Battle of Keren began on 3rd February. It proved to be a protracted and bloody siege. On 10th February 4th Indian Division launched a two-battalion attack on the heights east of the gorge. Both sides fought with stubborn gallantry; Brig's Peak was taken twice and lost twice; two other fiercely held features were taken and given up. Subadar Richpal Ram, of the 4/6 Rajputana Rifles, was awarded a posthumous V.C.; his battalion suffered 123 casualties and the other, the 4/11 Sikhs, lost more than 100 men. With Platt's agreement the Divisional Commander, General Beresford-Peirse, called off the attack after five days' stern fighting.

Platt then decided that he would have to bring in 5th Indian Division for a major assault after careful preparation which, because the front was 180 miles from the nearest railhead, would be bound to take several weeks. Meanwhile 4th Indian Division had to hold grimly on to the forward positions they had occupied. "It is going to be a bloody battle," Platt said, "against both enemy and ground. It will be won by the side which lasts longest."[13] He planned the opening of his offensive for the night of 15th/16th March.

This time the main assault was made to the right of the road, at Fort Dologorodoc, which was taken at 6.30 on the morning of 16th March. The fighting which followed was close and bitter in the

374

extreme. Between counter-attacks—the Italians launched no fewer than eight, all immensely determined, all fruitless—shells and mortar bombs rained on the 2nd Bn. the West Yorkshire Regiment, who held on with a courage and resolution beyond praise. In these counter-attacks the Savoia battalions, Alpini, Bersaglieri and Grenadiers, were decimated: five days' fighting cost them nearly 5,000 casualties, 1,135 of them killed, including their commander, the young and stout-hearted General Lorenzini.

"Keren was as hard a soldiers' battle as was ever fought."[14] To Churchill the battle seemed "rather evenly balanced," and in a telegram to Eden he raised the question of reinforcements.[15]

A. P. Wavell to Prime Minister   *23rd March, 1941*
Your telegram to Mr. Eden. Reinforcement of Keren is constantly under consideration, but time and supply are ruling factors. There is still hope that enemy resistance will crack under pressure. Their losses are undoubtedly heavy.

Platt was authorised to go on, and Wavell flew down to spend two days with him. On 25th March, just before the final assault went in, the two generals went as far forward as they could.

"As soon as I had had a good look at the position, I said to Platt that it looked to me as if the way through was straight up the main road, neglecting the high peaks to north and south. He replied that this was his plan, and it succeeded. I wonder whether it would have come off if he had tried it earlier instead of his attempts on the peaks to right and left."

This time, at any rate, it came off. The advance in the mountains on the first day was as strongly contested as ever; but under its cover the Sapper and Miner Companies of 5th Indian Division, though subjected to constant mortar and shell fire, worked steadily to clear a passage through the road-block in the gorge. By the afternoon of Wednesday, 26th March, General Frusci had decided that the situation was critical, and that it would no longer be possible to halt the British "I" tanks. That night he withdrew the bulk of his troops and guns, leaving only a screen. At dawn next morning, as the first British tanks gingerly picked their way through the remains of the road-block, a white flag was seen flying from the impregnable Mount Sanchil, and a little later others appeared on Brig's Peak and the adjoining crags. The tanks and Bren carriers passed through to the town unhindered.

Thus, after fifty-three days of siege, Keren fell. During the battle the Italians employed a total of thirty-nine battalions and thirty-six batteries, comprising some 30,000 men and 144 guns. According to General Frusci's own situation reports they had 3,000 killed. The British casualties were 536 killed and 3,229 wounded. At this cost —by no means trifling—the road into Eritrea was opened, and the end of Italian power and influence in East Africa brought within sight.

After the capture of Mogadishu, Cunningham had pushed on with all the speed he could muster towards Harar, the second city of Ethiopia, and to all intents and purposes the capital of the southern region. His first important objective was Jijiga, the junction of the roads from Harar and Berbera. Of the 660 miles of road to Mogadishu, one-third was very good and the remainder very rough, while north and south of Dagabur there were two stretches where there was no road at all. Supply and administration were, without doubt, Cunningham's principal problems in this phase of the campaign, and he solved them admirably.

On 11th March he put the 1st South African Brigade Group and the 22nd East African Brigade under the command of the 11th African Division, which already contained South African field and medium artillery, South African signals, transport, etc., and the 23rd Nigerian Brigade. On 16th March Berbera was reoccupied by two battalions and supporting units from Aden, and the next day patrols of the Nigerian Brigade entered Jijiga.

General Cunningham to A. P. Wavell   *28th March, 1941*
. . . The Nigerian Brigade have carried out a very remarkable achievement, commencing from the time they left the Juba, and culminating with the fall of Harar. . . . They have covered a distance of nearly 1,100 miles of road since 23rd February, i.e., in 31 days. Parts of the road have been good, but for large sections of it they have been driving over the open bush forming the dust pans which are an unpleasant feature of the whole of Italian Somaliland and the southern part of Abyssinia. . . .

It has all been very exciting and sometimes rather hair-raising, particularly from the administrative point of view. The opening of new ports and the collection of transport from distances nearly 1,000 miles away, to enable the attenuated lines of communication to be kept going, have caused some anxious moments, but in these respects matters are now rapidly improving and one sees clearer the weather ahead.

Churchill sent Wavell the Defence Committee's cordial congratulations on "the double success" of Keren and Harar, and their thanks to the commanders for the continued rapid execution of their memorable campaign. The Italians in East Africa were now in a desperate situation. In addition to the troops there were thousands of civilians whose security looked like becoming a major problem, on which Churchill had firm views.

Prime Minister to Foreign Secy. & A. P. Wavell   *31st March, 1941*
Now that our forces are advancing on Asmara and Massawa, we should inform Duke of Aosta that if ships in Massawa harbour of which there are reported to be 25 are scuttled, we shall consider ourselves relieved of all responsibility for either feeding Italian population of Eritrea and Abyssinia or removing them from these countries, in view of great shortage of shipping in the world and our own requirements.

On 1st April Asmara was captured.

A. P. Wavell to Prime Minister   *1st April, 1941*
Have given instructions for message about shipping at Massawa to be dropped. Events are moving rapidly and now that Asmara has surrendered question of Massawa should be soon decided. We will do our best to save shipping. . . .

On 8th April Massawa was in Platt's hands. The ships had not been scuttled, and the harbour had not been sabotaged and was in use at once. This was fortunate, for Wavell's difficulties in Cyrenaica were becoming grave. After the fall of Keren, 4th Indian Division was ordered to return to Egypt as soon as possible. There also began the northward movement of air forces, since the *Regia Aeronautica* had been eliminated as a fighting component. Meanwhile, during a dark and eventful week elsewhere, Wavell had to decide whether or not he should authorise Cunningham to go on to Addis Ababa. It had been originally intended that he should halt after the reoccupation of British Somaliland and the capture of Diredawa, on the Jibuti-Addis Ababa railway, since Wavell urgently needed the 1st South African Division and the use of the large quantities of transport which the operations demanded. Also, Wavell wrote, "it seemed to me that the occupation of Addis Ababa would confront us with an embarrassment of very large numbers of Italian civilians and would have no very great strategical object."[16]

However, Cunningham was quite confident of capturing Addis Ababa and of dealing with the civilian problem. Wavell decided to let him go ahead, and his forces entered the Ethiopian capital on 6th April. Henceforth the requirements of a vast mopping-up operation in East Africa, combined with the pacification of tribal unrest and the establishment of a measure of law and order, had to be balanced in Wavell's mind against the grim necessities which thrust themselves upon him from every other quarter of his Command. Now, for example, Cunningham (who in a two months' campaign had taken more than 50,000 prisoners and occupied some 360,000 square miles of territory at a cost of 500 casualties, of whom fewer than 150 were killed) wanted to employ his forces to the west and south-west of Addis Ababa, reduce an Italian stronghold at Gimma, and secure his lines of communication in the Lakes area. But Wavell, as every day passed, needed more and more urgently in Egypt the men and the trucks that would be dispersed over immense stretches of the Abyssinian highlands. He therefore ordered Cunningham to go north to secure the main road from Addis Ababa to Asmara, in order that the troops in southern Abyssinia might reach Egypt by embarking at Massawa or Port Sudan or by the Nile Valley route. On 13th April the 1st South African Brigade set out from Addis Ababa on this task.

Meanwhile the Duke of Aosta, with quiet fortitude, faced the consequences of shattering defeat. A few days after the fall of Keren he saw that he had no hope of holding Eritrea. On 30th March he telegraphed to the Duce that the very rapid crumbling, long foreseen, had now set in. "It only remains," he added, "for us to resist wherever we can and for as long as we can for the honour of the flag."[17] He ordered the remnants of General Frusci's Eritrean Army to withdraw south down the Asmara-Addis Ababa road to another natural stronghold 230 miles away at Amba Alagi; and he himself joined them there on 3rd April, with the remainder of his reserve troops. Platt's only remaining sizeable formation, 5th Indian Division, was ordered in to the pursuit from the north, as Cunningham's South African closed in from the south. Though Amba Alagi was a strong defensive position, and had a certain amount of water, and food for three months, it was clear that the end could not be long delayed.

In the meantime, through a series of hard-fought engagements,

Wingate's Sudanese battalion and a growing number of Ethiopian patrots advanced steadily and drove some 12,000 Italians from Gojjam into Debra Markos; half were captured, and the rest fled north into the wild highlands of Gondar. The Emperor re-entered his capital on 5th May, with Wingate, riding a white charger, in the van of the procession.[18]

At Amba Alagi the final, two-pronged attack began on 13th May. Of all the great army that, four brief months earlier, had held the Italian empire in East Africa, some 5,000 survivors remained under General Frusci's command. For two days they resisted; but on 16th May opposition on both fronts petered out, and negotiations were opened for an armistice.[19] Major-General Mayne, the commander of the 5th Indian Division, conducted them on behalf of General Platt. He arranged, at the suggestion of the Duke of Aosta, a "surrender with honour," by whose terms the garrison were allowed to march out in military formation and hand over their arms, not on the battle-field, but a couple of miles away. Mayne for his part secured, by this arrangement, two valuable advantages: he got, as he hoped, a clean and complete hand-over of valuable equipment and stores; and booby-traps, mines and the like were all pointed out before the final parade and rendered harmless, with considerable saving of life and limb. On 19th May the garrison duly marched out past a guard of honour, while the pipers of the 1st Transvaal Scottish played "Flowers of the Forest"; and on the following day the Duke and his personal staff made their formal surrender to General Mayne before being conducted to General Platt.

Prime Minister to A. P. Wavell   *18th May, 1941*
Following for Generals Cunningham and Platt. I send you and your gallant armies my heartfelt congratulations and those of H.M. Government upon this timely and brilliant culmination of your memorable and strenuous campaign. Pray make this known to your troops if you desire.

At the time, the East African campaign was lost sight of in the welter of bitter misfortune that now enveloped Wavell's Command. In the perspective of history, however, it takes on another and far from transient significance.

Wavell was well served by his two immediately subordinate commanders; they in their turn had excellent officers under them, many of them products of the Indian Army. No other theatre of operations was a better or more fertile training and testing ground for those who were to hold high command later in the war. At some time or another, between 1941 and 1945, the names of Bill Slim, Frank Messervy, "Pasha" Russell, Denys Reid, Pete Rees and Reg Savory were to become deservedly famous[20]; and there were many others. The record of 4th and 5th Indian Divisions was especially notable.

"Has any campaign in history lasting two months produced from two divisions a fighting army commander, two fighting corps commanders, and seven fighting divisional commanders within four years? It may be doubted."[21] These officers and the men they led—British, Indian, South African, East and West African, Sudanese and Cypriot— were a purely Imperial force, of a character never to be seen again. They fought and defeated a huge, well-trained, well-equipped army containing some of the most resolute, skilled and valorous troops encountered by the Allies anywhere in the world throughout the war. After four months of campaigning, a quarter of a million men were either dead or prisoners of war, and their equipment had been either ceded or destroyed; and a million square miles of territory had been overrun. The Italian colonial empire in East Africa was at an end, and Haile Selassie was restored to his throne. The East African campaign was Britain's first complete victory in the Second World War, and it must be realised that it set in train a course of events in Africa whose consequences—for good and for evil—were to stretch far ahead into the future, long after the ancient, fierce silence and solitude habitual to that high wilderness had returned to the jagged, granite peaks and crags of Keren.

In its strategic completeness, the victory was Wavell's. His was the vision that created it, by careful planning, in the face of all the barrage of long-range adjurations and criticism; and his was the hand that steadied and guided this astonishing campaign, through every vicissitude, to that final ceremony at Amba Alagi which he was by then far too preoccupied to be able to attend.

XII

The German Onslaught

On 14th February, 1941, a German reconnaissance battalion and an anti-tank battalion arrived at Tripoli. On the same day, at Rommel's insistence, an Italian division was put on the march for Sirte. On the 16th the first German patrols joined the Italians, and Rommel himself took command at the front. On the 17th British patrols were very active, and Rommel feared that the advance towards Tripoli was to be renewed. He had, however, no cause for anxiety. On the 24th the first clash occurred between British and German troops in Africa, and the British patrol was the loser: two scout cars, a lorry and a car were destroyed; one officer and two other ranks were taken prisoner. The Germans suffered no casualties.[1]

In answer to a request for a short appreciation of the effect of this development on defence commitments in Egypt and Cyrenaica, Wavell signalled the Chiefs of Staff on 2nd March. He said that the recent enemy reinforcements in Tripolitania were two Italian infantry divisions, two Italian motorised artillery regiments and one German armoured brigade group. He had no evidence of more mechanical transport having been landed, and though air reconnaissance had shown an increase in traffic on the Tripoli-Sirte road, the enemy must still be short of transport. Tripoli to Agheila was 471 miles, to Benghazi 646—a single road and inadequate water for 410 miles of this distance. These factors limited the threat. The enemy could possibly maintain up to one infantry division and one armoured brigade along the coast road in about three weeks. If they had a second armoured brigade they might send it across the desert to attack the British flank. They might do some offensive patrolling at Agheila, and if they found the British screen weak, push on to Agedabia. "I do not think," he said, "that with this force he will attempt to recover Benghazi."

Wavell predicted that eventually two German divisions, with one or two infantry divisions, might launch a large-scale attack. He emphasised the enemy's shipping difficulties, and pointed out that while the Italian air threat was negligible, the *Luftwaffe* were now well established in the Central Mediterranean. Nevertheless, he thought an attack by German airborne forces unlikely.[2]

Churchill subsequently stated that this telegram was accepted in London "as the basis of our action."[3] He also said that the Desert Flank was the peg on which all else hung, and there was no idea in any quarter of losing or risking that for the sake of Greece or anything in the Balkans.[4] The telegrams despatched from 6th January onwards and the decisions reached in the meetings in the Tatoi Palace and the British Embassy in Cairo hardly substantiate this claim. The effort to succour Greece, on the scale which the Prime Minister and the Foreign Secretary demanded and which Wavell agreed to make it, could only have been achieved at the sacrifice of the Desert Flank. There were not enough troops, there was by no means enough equipment, to go round. If Greece got men, aircraft, tanks, trucks, field guns, A.A. guns, radar and signal equipment, the Western Desert went without. One soldier could, for a time, do the duty of two; one radar set could be overworked till it fell apart; but neither man nor radar set could do the same job at the same time in two different theatres of operations many hundreds of miles apart. In this simple axiom, which Wavell understood but from which Churchill always shied away, lies the explanation of the happenings of the next two months.

The Axis forces in Tripolitania were being reinforced quickly, troops disembarking, stores being unloaded by lamplight at night, if necessary, in disregard of British air attack. Most of the German equipment was better than the Italian; some of it proved better than the British. These factors were important, but not crucial. What mattered most was the morale of the Germans and their commander. Rommel, his officers and his men all glistened with self-confidence and bristled with energy. He was to learn much in four eventful years; but caution, to the end, was not a word he understood.

The men who had to pit their wits against Rommel's were Wavell's subordinate commanders. His responsibility was that of choosing them, and of giving them strategic direction, finally of replacing them if necessary. Shortly after Beda Fomm he set up Cyrenaica Command, with Maitland Wilson as Military Governor and G.O.C.-in-C.; both of them thought that the major part of this Command's work would be the administration of occupied enemy territory. O'Connor took over Wilson's appointment in Cairo and went off for a badly needed spell of leave in Palestine; and XIII Corps Headquarters was replaced by the 1st Australian Corps Headquarters under General Blamey. But then came the insistent demands of the Greek enterprise: Wilson went to Athens on 4th March, and Blamey followed, with his headquarters.

To succeed Wilson, Wavell chose Lieut.-General Philip Neame, v.c. He wrote: "I did not know him well; he had had the 4th Indian Division and had then gone to Palestine to replace George Giffard. He was a Sapper, and had been an instructor at the Staff College, and was the author of a book on strategy, so I accepted him as a skilful and educated soldier; and his V.C. was a guarantee of his fighting qualities. He was at this time a great friend of Dick O'Connor's for whose judgment I had much respect."

The 2nd Armoured Division, which was intended to replace 7th Armoured Division in Cyrenaica, had been brought out from England under the command of Major-General J. Tilly, who died suddenly at Bardia in January, before the division had completed its training—"a great loss in every sense."[5] In his place Wavell appointed Major-General M. D. Gambier-Parry, a cheerful and energetic tank officer whom he had known from the days of the first Armoured Force on Salisbury Plain.

Neame and Gambier-Parry were given difficult, perhaps impossible, tasks. Neame's Command consisted, in name, of two Divisions: the 2nd Armoured and the 9th Australian, whose commander, General Leslie Morshead, was a soldier of high calibre. Two of his brigades, however, had gone to Greece in place of two from the less well-equipped 7th Australian Division; his staff was incomplete and only partially trained; and he was short of transport, Bren guns, anti-tank weapons and signal equipment. Gambier-Parry's formation, though described as the 2nd Armoured Division, was in fact nothing of the sort, being untrained for desert warfare, under-equipped and under-manned. In the words of the official historian: ". . . this so-called division amounted to barely one weak armoured brigade, not fully mobile, and likely to waste away altogether if it did much fighting, and an incomplete Support Group."[6]

These formations were to be controlled, in the event of battle, by Neame's Cyrenaica Command, which was to all intents and purposes static, and which lacked the trained staff and the signal equipment required to handle mobile operations over large distances.

Wavell accused himself of committing serious mistakes:

Eden and Dill arrived immediately after the Benghazi battle, and kept me fully occupied, and I never had time to go out till, I think, about the middle of March, when it was rather too late. I remember that I got from a report from Jumbo Wilson an entirely erroneous idea of the escarpment south of Benghazi; I imagined that it was an escarpment similar to that running east from Sollum, with only a very few passages fit for vehicles. I therefore imagined that if we had a mobile force on the escarpment, holding these passages, it would be impossible for an enemy to advance across the open plain below towards Benghazi; and what I had continually in mind for the defence of Benghazi was a mobile force operating on the escarpment and able to attack the flank or rear of any force which attempted to move on Benghazi. When I actually went out and saw the escarpment, I realised that it could be ascended almost anywhere and was no protection. The second topographical feature which I failed to realise was the Salt Marshes near Agheila. If I had gone out there and seen for myself what a formidable defensive barrier they could be made, I think I should certainly have insisted on our pushing our force down to these marshes, whatever the supply difficulties were. As it was we stopped short of them, and allowed the Germans passage through them.

My next great error was that I made up my mind that the enemy could not put in any effective counter-stroke before May at the earliest. I had some warning from my Intelligence of enemy convoys to Tripoli, but the information was so poor and vague that I largely discounted it. I also thought that the Germans could never build up a supply system over the distance between Tripoli and the frontier of Cyrenaica in the time that they did.[7]

This second error was all the more puzzling (though its explanation may have lain in the sheer volume of work, as well as the weight of responsibility, that was Wavell's at this time) in view of the fact that on 6th March Shearer put up an "Appreciation of the Situation on 5th March, 1941, by General 'X', General-Officer-Commanding German Troops in Libya," which was an assessment of Rommel's intentions and chances of fulfilling them, from Rommel's point of view but with no knowledge of Rommel's character. It contained these prophetic sentences:

As a striking force I have full confidence in my own Command. Subject to administrative preparations, I believe that the German Armoured Corps, after a few weeks' training and experience in desert warfare conditions, and unless the British substantially reinforce their present forces in Libya, could successfully undertake the reoccupation of Cyrenaica.

Wavell, however, disagreed with his Director of Intelligence and concluded that there was no real danger of a counter-attack before May; but he was not unduly complacent. On 6th March he compiled a note headed "Defence of Cyrenaica":

In view of the arrival of German forces in Tripoli as well as Italian reinforcements, it is obvious that we have thinned out the defence of Cyrenaica prematurely and too much. We shall have to reinforce it, especially with armoured troops and means of defence against armoured troops, also probably with aircraft and anti-aircraft. . . .

Any troops that we employ must be mobile, and the defence must be elastic. We must not allow ourselves to be forced into static defence as the Italians were.

The immediate requirements seem to be to see what reinforcements we can make available of armoured troops, anti-tank guns, artillery, anti-aircraft; to build up properly distributed reserves; to see that we have sufficient means of defence such as anti-tank mines and explosive for demolition, and a well-prepared scheme for using them; and that we have a well worked out scheme of defence against any force that the enemy may bring.

It should not be difficult to produce a perfectly adequate answer to the German threat but we must take action at once in order to avoid an initial reverse, which might allow the enemy to get on top.

At noon on Sunday, 16th March, Wavell, with Dill, left Heliopolis airfield on his long delayed visit to Cyrenaica. He wrote afterwards:
"I found Neame pessimistic and asking for all kinds of reinforcements which I hadn't got. And his tactical dispositions were just

crazy; he had put a brigade of Morshead's 9th Australian Division out into the middle of the plain between Agheila and Benghazi, with both flanks exposed, immobile with no transport, completely useless and an obvious prey to any armoured vehicles that broke through at Agheila. I ordered it to be moved back to the heights above (east of) Benghazi, where there was at least a defensible position, and thus saved it from annihilation when Rommel's attack did come. I told Neame that if his advanced troops were driven back, he was not to attempt the direct defence of Benghazi, but to pull his Armoured Brigade back on to the left flank of the Australians on the escarpment above Benghazi. I think this was sound in principle if it could have been executed.

"But the really alarming feature was the state of the cruiser tanks of the 2nd Armoured Division, which were the core of the whole force. Out of fifty-two tanks, half were already in workshops and the remainder kept breaking down at intervals. I was also appalled at the size and unwieldiness of the 2nd Armoured Division head-quarters. Gambier-Parry, though he had only one brigade to handle, had brought forward the whole of his headquarters, with the idea of getting them exercised in the field. All right if they were not attacked but a dangerous encumbrance if they were.

"I came back anxious and depressed from this visit, but there was nothing much I could do about it. The movement to Greece was in full swing and I had nothing left in the bag. But I had forebodings and my confidence in Neame was shaken."

Next day he dictated a directive which set out Neame's task in detail for him. He defined this as the defence of Cyrenaica against possible counter-attack, in which the enemy would have local superiority both on the ground and in the air. For Neame, therefore, the safeguarding of his forces from a serious reverse and the infliction of losses and ultimate defeat of the enemy were of much greater importance than the retention of ground. It was not, Wavell said firmly, worth risking defeat to hold Benghazi. He asked Neame to consider the possible improvement of his Agheila defence positions by a forward, westward move to the salt marshes; but whatever Neame's decision, the front was to be covered by light, mobile forces, committed to nothing more than offensive patrolling. If and when these had to be withdrawn, their task would be to delay the enemy's advance and inflict losses on him without becoming seriously engaged. Wavell considered the alternative routes by which the enemy might advance, and advised Neame to keep his armour on the flank near Antelat, always flexible and ready to oppose and harass, to catch the enemy in the rear and to manœuvre him, whenever possible, on to concealed minefields. He envisaged a fighting and strictly limited withdrawal in face of a cautious and equally limited advance, during which Neame could, if he employed the tactics outlined for him, retain both freedom of manœuvre and initiative. He counselled Neame to remember that:

the enemy's supply and maintenance problem will be a most difficult and precarious one, and do everything in your power to render it more so. Forward dumps of stores are likely to be the surest indication of the offensive intentions of the enemy and should be attacked by air action as far as possible. Similarly, during the advance, attack on his maintenance system will be one of the best methods of bringing him to a standstill.

He concluded with an explicit warning: "Time is pressing and you must put all necessary moves and work in hand without the least delay."

Rommel on this same day, Wednesday, 19th March, flew to Hitler's headquarters to report and to obtain fresh instructions. Field-Marshal von Brauchitsch told him that there was no intention of striking a decisive blow in Africa in the near future, and he could expect no reinforcements. After the arrival of the 15th Panzer Division at the end of May, he was to attack and destroy the British units around Agedabia. Benghazi "might perhaps be taken." Rommel pointed out that he could not just take Benghazi, but would have to occupy the whole of Cyrenaica. Before he left for Europe he had instructed the 5th Light Division to prepare an attack on El Agheila for 24th March, with the object of taking the airfield and driving out the garrison of the small fort. He returned to Africa with the clearest and most cautious directive from Hitler's headquarters, and proceeded instantly and methodically to disregard it. On the 24th the attack on El Agheila duly went in, and succeeded. He recorded: "The garrison, which consisted only of a weak force, had strongly mined the whole place and withdrew skilfully in face of our attack."[8]

Prime Minister to A. P. Wavell   *26th March, 1941*
We are naturally concerned at rapid German advance to Agheila. It is their habit to push on whenever they are not resisted. I pre-

sume you are only waiting for the tortoise to stick his head out far enough before chopping it off.

It seems extremely important to give them an early taste of our quality. What is the state and location of 7th Armoured Division? Pray give me your appreciation. I cordially approve your request to General Smuts for a brigade of 1st South African Division. Everything must be done to accelerate movements of 2nd South African Division. . . .[9]

Wavell had left for the Sudan the previous afternoon. Eden and Dill had also set off by flying-boat for London, thinking that their mission in the Middle East had been completed. Wavell was back in Cairo at 5 p.m. on 27th March.

A. P. Wavell to Prime Minister 27th March, 1941, 1905 hrs.
No evidence yet that there are many Germans at Agheila, probably mainly Italians with small stiffening of Germans.

I have to admit to having taken considerable risk in Cyrenaica after capture of Benghazi in order to provide maximum support for Greece. My estimate at that time was that Italians in Tripolitania could be disregarded and that Germans were unlikely to accept risk of sending large bodies of armoured troops to Africa in view of inefficiency of Italian Navy. I therefore made arrangements to leave only small armoured force and one partly trained Australian division in Cyrenaica.

After we had accepted Greek liability evidence began to accumulate of German reinforcements to Tripoli which were coupled with attacks on Malta which prevented bombing of Tripoli from there on which I had counted. German air attacks on Benghazi which prevented supply ships using harbour also increased our difficulties.

Result is I am weak in Cyrenaica at present and no reinforcements of armoured troops which are chief requirement are at present available. I have one brigade of 2nd Armoured Division in Cyrenaica and one in Greece. 7th Armoured Division is refitting and as no reserve tanks were available is dependent on repair which takes time. Next month or two will be anxious but enemy has extremely difficult problem and am sure his numbers have been much exaggerated. I cannot however at present afford to use my small armoured force as boldly as I should like.

Steps to reinforce Cyrenaica are in hand. I hope fall of Keren will release some troops from Sudan before long and that I shall also get some South African troops from East Africa.

You know our difficulties about aircraft. Longmore and his people give me magnificent support everywhere but there is never quite enough of them. My own chief difficulty is transport. . . .[10]

Meanwhile the Nazi pot was coming swiftly to the boil in the Balkans. All the British Government's efforts to build up a strong defensive alliance had failed. Turkey remained watchful but stubbornly neutral; British troops were arriving in a steady stream in the Piraeus, the port of Athens, under the eyes of German agents; and in Yugoslavia a fierce and tragic drama was about to be enacted. The hapless Regent, Prince Paul, had been summoned to see Hitler at Berchtesgaden in the first week of March, and had given a verbal undertaking—extracted under severe pressure—that Yugoslavia would adhere to the Tripartite Pact, the treaty of alliance between Germany, Italy and Japan which had been signed in Berlin the previous September, and to which all the Axis satellites were compelled to adhere. Three Ministers resigned, but on 25th March the pact was formally signed in Vienna.

There followed a rapid and bloodless *coup d'état*. On the morning of 27th March a number of officers under the leadership of the commander of the Yugoslav Air Force seized control of the Government and rallied round the person of the young King, Peter II; the Council of Regency was dissolved; Prince Paul and his family departed to Greece. There was a great upsurge of Serbian national pride: crowds thronged the streets of Belgrade chanting "Rather war than the pact, rather death than slavery." The new Government had not even time to go through the motions of denouncing the hated pact. Hitler, enraged by this defiance of his will, ordered immediate preparations to destroy Yugoslavia militarily and as a national unit. His generals worked until four o'clock on the morning of 28th March drafting the new operational orders, which threw out of gear all the arrangements so far made for Germany's spring campaign.

The news of the revolution in Belgrade gave great satisfaction in London. Churchill was eager to seize the opportunity it offered. Eden and Dill were now in Malta, held up by bad weather. The Prime Minister signalled Eden on 27th March urging him to go back to Cairo with Dill, to form a joint front in the Balkans. He suggested a meeting of all concerned in Cyprus or Athens; and thereafter Eden, he thought, should go to Belgrade.

Early on the morning of 28th March Dill and Eden arrived back in Athens, and began at once to make strenuous efforts to get in touch with the new Yugoslav Government. These developments coincided with the new round of battle on the desert flank; and Wavell, during the succeeding weeks, had to keep three theatres of war constantly in mind (the number was soon to be increased to five): the final phase in East Africa, Rommel's aggressiveness in the Western Desert, and confusion, collapse and disaster in the Balkans. No other British general in the war was subjected to so testing and so complex an ordeal.

The Germans were now at El Agheila—not in great strength, it was true. That had been the place to hold them, but now Neame's forward formation—2nd Armoured Division's Support Group—lay in the Mersa Brega defile, some forty miles to the north on the coastal road to Benghazi, with the 3rd Armoured Brigade on the flank and slightly behind. The 9th Australian Division had two brigades near Benghazi and one in Tobruk. All the formations had little transport and too little petrol; and they had had no collective training.

The Mersa Brega position was similar to that at El Agheila, with salt marshes stretching inland from the sea to the foothills. Rommel thought it stronger than it was; while he was in Europe his field commander, General Streich, planned a reconnaissance in force to test out these defences. After the capture of El Agheila Rommel approved Streich's plan, and on 30th March gave orders that it was to be carried out on the following day.

On 30th March Wavell signalled Neame. He told him of reports—perhaps planted and certainly exaggerated—of large German forces landing at Tripoli, and warned that if the enemy saw a chance of scoring a success against Neame's advanced formations he would certainly take it. "But I do not believe," he added, "that he can make any big effort for at least another month." At the moment he himself could spare Neame no more troops than he had already been promised. The signal ended:

> Your task for the next two months is to keep enemy from crossing the 150 miles between Agheila and Benghazi without heavy loss to your armoured and mobile troops. This ground and even Benghazi itself has no military value except so far as it [would] enable enemy to push forward his air forces within closer range

of Egypt and of our shipping in the Mediterranean. You should give ground rather than risk defeat but the less you give the better.

I know I am giving you difficult and dangerous task. On other hand enemy's difficulties are greater with so long and exposed line of communications which we will do all we can to threaten. Good hunting. I will come and see you again soon.

General Neame to A. P. Wavell   *31st March, 1941, 1400 hrs.*
Am quite clear as to my task. . . . Enemy commenced advance from Agheila early this morning apparently only by coastal route. . . . This may be only local advance like that to Agheila but German tanks and armoured cars are reported. . . . At 1230 hours enemy aircraft dive-bombing heavily our forward posts which believed still held. Signs of enemy withdrawal reported 1400 hours. . . .

Four hours before this telegram was despatched the German Fifth Light Division made a deliberate and rather cautious attack on the main defences; the Support Group of 2nd Armoured Division put up a stout resistance. "Our advance came to a halt," Rommel recorded. He had been up in the forward area the whole day, and in the afternoon reconnoitred the possibility of attacking north of the coast road. He then ordered a dive-bomb assault by Stukas. This was followed at half past five in the afternoon by a machine-gun battalion attack through the sand hills. Rommel claimed that "this succeeded in throwing the enemy back to the east," and that the Mersa Brega defile was taken.[11] The British Official History's account laid the stress differently: "The Support Group held its delaying positions all day, and only when it was clear that it might be cut off did it withdraw to the south-west of Agedabia. The 3rd Armoured Brigade conformed."[12]

Wavell wrote: "It would have been better if the 3rd Armoured Brigade had made an immediate counter-attack, their tanks would then at least have done some damage to the enemy before breaking down, as most of them did in the withdrawal. But Gambier-Parry was quite right in carrying out his instructions to withdraw to the escarpment above Benghazi if heavily attacked. Everything seems to have gone wrong, tanks broke down and communications broke down, the enemy air making a dead set at all W.T. vehicles. Gambier-Parry was not a sufficiently experienced commander to cope with such a situation; and Neame remained at his H.Q. in Barce and tried to control a hopelessly confused situation by telegrams instead of personal action."

Throughout 1st April the 2nd Armoured Division continued its withdrawal to Agedabia. This movement was closely watched by German reconnaissance aircraft and ground patrol; but there was no fighting throughout this confused All Fools' Day. By nightfall Rommel had come to a very bold decision: "It was a chance I could not resist and I gave orders for Agedabia to be attacked and taken, in spite of the fact that our instructions were not to undertake any such operation before the end of May."[13]

On the morning of 2nd April an advance party of eight German tanks cut off a section of the Support Group, and in the afternoon the main body of the 3rd Panzer Regiment, moving along the coastal road, overtook the main body of Gambier-Parry's 3rd Armoured Brigade. The 5th R.T.R. lost five tanks in the fight, and two more broke down shortly afterwards, leaving a total of twelve still in action. Gambier-Parry then ordered a general retreat to Antelat, which was some ninety miles north-north-east of Mersa Brega. Neame, meanwhile, ordered the Support Group to continue to block the Benghazi road as long as possible without risking being overrun. Instructions from higher headquarters became meaningless when they reached formations that were actually fighting. Confusion deepened rapidly. In Cairo, Wavell became extremely uneasy.

A. P. Wavell to Chiefs of Staff   *2nd April, 1941*
. . . Some forward posts were overrun yesterday. . . . Losses not serious at present, but the mechanical condition of the Armoured Brigade is causing Neame much concern, and there seem to be many breakdowns. As I can produce no more armoured units for at least three or four weeks, I have warned him to keep three brigades in being, even if it involves considerable withdrawal, possibly even from Benghazi.[14]

At his ten o'clock conference at G.H.Q. Wavell decided that he must go out to Cyrenaica at once to see for himself what was happening.

"I soon realised that Neame had lost control and was making no effort to regain it by the only possible means, going forward personally. I wanted to go forward myself but no suitable aircraft was available, and no one seemed to have much idea where our own troops or the enemy were. I sent in a message for Dick O'Connor to come out and take over from Neame."

392

The message was in fact two signals, the first of which Arthur Smith gave to O'Connor on the telephone at his house after dinner. This said that the situation seemed somewhat critical, and that the Chief wanted O'Connor to go up at once to Barce and give his advice, as he knew the country and had had considerable experience in desert fighting. An hour or two later there was a second signal, in which Wavell asked O'Connor to take over command from Neame. Later O'Connor wrote: "I cannot pretend I was happy at the thought of taking over command in the middle of a battle, which was already lost."[15]

The story of 3rd April was, in grim truth, one of "increasing misfortune and confusion,"[16] not least at the command level. O'Connor flew up early in the morning, taking with him Brigadier J. F. L. Combe, whose knowledge of the country and of desert tactics was as good as his own, and on whose judgment he felt he could rely. They reached Barce at three in the afternoon, and after a brief word with Neame, O'Connor was ushered in to see Wavell, who looked, he thought, "worn and depressed."

Neame had lost his grip and his tactical handling was at fault. He had originally intended the Armoured Brigade to fall back east of the escarpment, which ran parallel to the road from Agedabia to Benghazi, in order to be able to counter any German thrust across the desert to Mechili. O'Connor commented, "This seemed to me to be eminently sound." Wavell, however, would have none of it, because it laid Benghazi open, and "thereupon took control of the operations himself and issued orders for the Armoured Brigade to fall back towards Benghazi, west of and below the escarpment."

To O'Connor the resulting situation seemed "most confused"; nobody knew where either the Armoured Brigade or Gambier-Parry's Divisional H.Q. was; but the Australian Division was known to be holding the escarpment between Abiar and Regima. Wavell, still doubtful of the enemy's intention, continued to hope that his ultimate objective was no further east than Benghazi; "but I think," O'Connor wrote, "the wish was father to the thought." O'Connor's narrative continued:

It seemed to me the situation was definitely more serious than the Chief believed, and that one of the most important things to do was to get our defences organised much further east than the Benghazi area. And I felt that I should be employed on this task,

W.   393   N2 as soon as it was possible. I felt also that changing horses in mid-stream would not really help matters. Our troops were definitely committed to a certain line of action, and I had to carry on with it. It was not possible, therefore, at this stage, to introduce new tactics. In addition I did not know the 2nd Armoured Division or the 9th Australian Division and they did not know me, and my taking over would not have given them any renewed confidence. And finally, I thought that the Chief was misjudging Neame. I had known him in the past and had always considered him first class. I therefore decided that I would ask the Chief to reconsider my replacing Neame, and to consider, as an alternative, my remaining with him for a few days, but ultimately returning to organise the defence of Egypt.

The Chief agreed to this proposal provided I remained until the situation had stabilised. He then sent for Neame and told him his decision. Before he left he said we were to do whatever we judged best in the circumstances, and he told me personally that if the Germans did threaten our flanks by moving across the desert, I was to retire right out of the coastal sector if I thought fit. He then left, saying he must return to Cairo at once, to arrange about reinforcements, and he also told me he would stop any further troops going to Greece. So evidently he had begun to think that the situation was very serious.[17]

Wavell was back in Cairo at eight o'clock that evening. For several hours a signal from London had been waiting for him.

Prime Minister to A. P. Wavell　　　*2nd April, 1941, 2340 hrs.*
It seems most desirable to chop German advance against Cyrenaica. Any rebuff to Germans would have far-reaching prestige effect. It would be all right to give up ground for the purpose of manœuvre but any serious withdrawal from Benghazi would appear most melancholy. I cannot understand how the enemy can have developed any considerable force at end of this long waterless coast road. From most secret message sent you, you will see that a squadron of Ju. 88s was stopped going to Tripoli because operational focus had shifted. Therefore cannot feel there is at the moment a persistent weight behind German attack on Cyrenaica. If this blob which has come forward against you could be cut off you might have prolonged easement. Of course if they succeed in wandering onward they will gradually destroy

the effect of your victories. Have you got a man like O'Connor
or Creagh dealing with this frontier problem?[18]

Attached to this was the copy of an outgoing telegram.

General Arthur Smith to Prime Minister 3rd April, 1941, 0730 hrs.
General Wavell flew Cyrenaica yesterday. All points you mention
had received his consideration.

At lower levels in the battle area 3rd April was, for the British, a
day of unmitigated disaster; but it was for Rommel a day of destiny
and of sudden, unlooked-for opportunities that he seized with relentless vigour. In the same setting as Beda Fomm, two short months
later, the positions of the opposing forces were completely reversed.
Of what really happened it was possible, in the aftermath, to build
up only a fragmentary picture. All official documents, war diaries,
signals and other records of both Cyrenaica Command and H.Q. 2nd
Armoured Brigade were destroyed. It took little time to comprehend
the magnitude of the catastrophe, but it was to take months, stretching
into years, to understand how and why it happened.

There was hardly any ground fighting at all. It was a day of movement
and decision: woefully muddled and mistaken decisions, and movement which can only be described as almost panicky, on the part of
the British; brilliant, if improvised, decisions and swift, bold movements on the part of the Germans.

During the morning, the Support Group moved to Sceleidima,
and 3rd Armoured Brigade to an area just south of it. By 1215 hours
Gambier-Parry's large, unwieldy headquarters (both tactical and rear)
and the headquarters of the Support Group and 3rd Armoured
Brigade were all at Sceleidima. Gambier-Parry himself, however, had
set off for Msus, to have a conference with Neame which was never
held, because Wavell had taken charge at Barce, and he and Neame
were waiting there for O'Connor to arrive.

While Gambier-Parry was absent there arrived Wavell's orders,
which were understood to mean that the whole division was to take
up a position on the Sceleidima escarpment, covering the approaches
to Sceleidima itself and overlooking Benghazi. Since the northern
sector of this new position was allotted to the Support Group and the
southern to 3rd Armoured Brigade, there had to be a hurried regroup-
ing of units between the two. Third Armoured Brigade, having
arrived first, moved out to take up its new positions. At 1400

hours back came Gambier-Parry, and at once held a conference to give out his detailed orders.

Rommel meanwhile moved his forward H.Q. up to Agedabia, and had the British movements watched closely from the air and by ground patrols. There was a brief false alarm that a force of twenty British tanks had been spotted some twenty miles north of Agedabia; Rommel sent a liaison officer up the Benghazi road as far as El Magrun, past all the wreckage of Beda Fomm; the "enemy force" was identified as a tumble of abandoned Italian tanks. Rommel now concluded that "the British intended to avoid, in any circumstances, fighting a decisive action." He decided "to stay on the heels of the retreating enemy and make a bid to seize the whole of Cyrenaica in one stroke."[19]

False alarms on both sides were of the utmost significance. At exactly the time that Rommel was reaching his crucial decision, Gambier-Parry's conference began to break up; as it did so (some witnesses said that it was just after it dispersed), a tactical reconnaissance report was received that a large German armoured force was moving towards Msus, where the division's main supply and petrol dumps were. Had this been true, the threat not only to Msus, but to the main desert track north-east to Mechili, would have been grave. But the "large enemy force of A.F.V.s" was in fact a patrol of Long Range Desert Group and 3rd Armoured Brigade's Recovery Section; this, however, was not realised until twenty-four hours later. New orders were hurriedly issued: it was vital to hold Msus; the Support Group, with two squadrons of the 6th R.T.R., using captured Italian tanks, was to take over the whole line of the escarpment; and 3rd Armoured Brigade, with a number of sub-units, was to move to Msus as quickly as possible. Before it could get there, the detachment guarding the dump destroyed all the petrol because they heard that the enemy were approaching. "From now onwards the movements of the 3rd Armoured Brigade were almost entirely dictated by lack of petrol."[20]

Thus, on the British side, a single false report set in motion a great train of misfortunes. On the German side, Rommel, having discarded a false report, proceeded vigorously to exploit his real and rapidly growing advantage. His blood was up; he lashed his formations into rapid movement. Streich had misgivings about the state of his vehicles; Rommel brushed them aside: "One cannot permit unique opportunities to slip by for the sake of trifles."[21] An Italian general said that the track westwards from Agedabia, by which Rommel proposed to send part of his Fifth Light Division on a wide outflanking movement, was a death-trap; Rommel went and reconnoitred it himself for twelve miles or so, found it "quite good for driving," and confirmed his order. The commander of 5th Light protested—it was now four o'clock in the afternoon—that he needed four days' pause in which to replenish his petrol. Rommel told him that every vehicle was to be unloaded and sent back to the divisional dump with orders to bring up, within twenty-four hours, enough petrol, rations and ammunition for the advance through Cyrenaica. Rommel then dashed off northwards up the Benghazi road; at El Magrun he encountered the forward patrols of his 3rd Reconnaissance Battalion, and was informed that an Italian priest had come out from Benghazi to report that the British had already left the town. Immediately (and at its C.O.'s request) he ordered the battalion forward to Benghazi.

Back at his headquarters, and with darkness falling, Rommel found the Italian Commander-in-Chief, General Gariboldi (nominally his superior officer), who was in a very bad temper and beside himself with anxiety. Rommel must discontinue all action and undertake no further moves without his express authority, which—he made quite clear— would only be exercised with Rome's explicit permission. "I would not stand for it, and said that I intended to go on doing what I felt I had to in whatever situation might arise. This brought the argument to a climax. At that very moment, a signal arrived—*deus ex machina*— from the German High Command, giving me complete freedom of action, and settling the argument exactly as I wanted it."[22]

As for the British, the night of 3rd/4th April found Cyrenaica Command in process of swift and total dissolution, and 2nd Armoured Division in completely inextricable confusion and useless as a fighting formation. At Barce, Neame was still in command; O'Connor's position as "adviser" was, even if it was a consequence of his own selfless gesture, hourly growing more and more invidious. Somehow John Harding, Neame's B.G.S. (as he had been O'Connor's in February), managed to extract some coherence out of deepening chaos. Decisions were made, orders were given, and the complete catastrophe which had overtaken the Italians two months earlier was averted, but only very narrowly. The following signal, however, revealed the extent of the day's calamities:

General Neame to A. P. Wavell   *4th April, 1941, 0043 hrs.*
Enemy armoured and mobile forces advanced north and north-

east from Agedabia to-day and air reconnaissance . . . confirmed presence of enemy force estimated at 100 tanks and M.T. at Msus.

Weak effective strength 2nd Armoured Division made it impossible to check enemy advance or prevent occupation Msus. . . .

Benghazi was evacuated and demolitions completed without loss or interference. . . . Position 9th Australian Division untenable. Intention therefore is to withdraw to general line Wadi Derna—Mechili but lack of A.F.V.s makes it impossible to guarantee that further withdrawal may not be necessary. . . . 3rd Indian Motor Brigade . . . on move to Mechili to stop any enemy advance by desert route from Msus. 2nd Armoured Division will continue withdrawal and join 3rd Motor Brigade in Mechili area.

9th Australian Division . . . will withdraw to position covered by Wadi Derna. . . . Enemy force Msus will be kept under observation by armoured car patrols. H.Q. Cyrenaica closing 0300 hours 4th April opening Marawa same hour and moving later to Tmimi. No estimate of casualties day's fighting yet available. . . . Maximum effective A.F.V.s strength reported 1120 hours 3rd April, 12 cruisers, 26 M13s and 18 light tanks.

The British, from daybreak on 4th April, were in full, precipitate retreat. If any Western Desert force at all were to be kept in being they must, until they could reach a defensive position that they could hold, withdraw more quickly than Rommel could advance. His aim, on the other hand, was to force them to battle before they could reorganise; his chance, as he perceived, was as dazzling as it was sudden. It was not to be granted to him to grasp it to the full, but he had six dramatic, swift-moving and very successful days. In the first four of them he achieved the complete reconquest of Cyrenaica. He flung every formation he had into the advance; and his primary object (in which he succeeded) was to destroy the hapless remnants of 2nd Armoured Division. He sent his own principal armoured formations on two convergent north-westerly arcs: the bigger from Agedabia towards Mechili, the smaller by way of Antelat and Msus to Mechili. These were all in the Mechili area by the afternoon of 6th or the morning of 7th April. A third formation drove due west from Benghazi by way of Charruba; this too was at Mechili on 7th April. A fourth group took the north-westerly coastal road out of Benghazi, by Maddalena towards Derna.

Mechili, therefore, was the key point. As Rommel was drawn towards it, so was 2nd Armoured Division, and so was the 3rd Indian Motor Brigade, ill-equipped, only half trained, and new to the country. The only sizeable proportion of Neame's forces not thus committed to disaster was the 9th Australian Division which, as Wavell said in his Despatch,

> after repulsing an enemy attack at Regima, withdrew without particular incident and in good order. It was found impossible, in view of the development of events to the south, to maintain a position on the Wadi Derna, and the Division was finally withdrawn to Tobruk, where one of its brigades already was. It had established itself west of the Tobruk defences by 7th April.

Second Armoured Division's fate was very different. From 4th April onwards, with its communications severed and its petrol reserves lost, its headquarters was never properly in touch with the forces it was supposed to command. The *Luftwaffe* attacked again and again, dive-bombing especially petrol and signal lorries. The Divisional Headquarters straggled into Mechili on the evening of 6th April. Third Armoured Brigade ought to have followed, but shortage of petrol made its commander decide to go to Derna. There, with his headquarters and most of the remains of his brigade, he was cut off and captured. The King's Dragoon Guards, in their armoured cars, had also gone with the Support Group to Derna; but the majority of this unit got back to Tobruk. The Support Group fought a skilful and determined action on the eastern outskirts of Derna and put some German tanks out of action.

At Mechili by 7th April there were, besides the Divisional H.Q. with its assemblage of unarmoured vehicles, the 3rd Indian Motor Brigade, some of the 1st R.H.A., and remnants of other scattered units. Rommel's motorised infantry and some field guns had reached Mechili the previous afternoon, to be seen off effectively by 3rd Indian Motor Brigade, who took some prisoners. Demands for surrender were treated with contempt. The whole force could and ought to have withdrawn during 7th April; but because they waited vainly for 3rd Armoured Brigade, it was not until the evening that they had their orders from Force H.Q. to withdraw to El Adem.

At dawn on the 8th they attempted to break out of Mechili. Rommel had brought his armour up in strength. A few small parties, with determination and resource, escaped: the detachment of the 1st

R.H.A., accompanied by some Indian infantry, broke away to the south and reached Sollum on the 11th; another group from the 18th Indian Cavalry Regiment and some Australian anti-tank gunners also fought their way out; but the remainder of the force, including Gambier-Parry and practically the whole of his H.Q., was captured.

As if this were not trouble enough, on the night of 6th/7th April one more cruel calamity befell the British in this theatre in general, and Wavell in particular, both as a man and as a commander.

On the evening of Friday, 6th April, O'Connor was in the fast emptying "advance" headquarters of Cyrenaica Command at Marawa, waiting for Neame. The latter had spent all day in a fruitless attempt to find Gambier-Parry, who had moved his H.Q. to Mechili, but had been unable to inform Neame or O'Connor. Neame was back before nightfall. The two generals decided that they must close down the headquarters and move off before it was too late. An R.A.F. group captain looked in and told O'Connor that he was taking every aircraft he had eastwards from Marawa and Derna to Tmimi. With him went a G.H.Q. liaison officer, who was able to take two letters from O'Connor, one to his wife, the other to Wavell explaining what had happened so far. O'Connor, having come up so hurriedly and still holding no official appointment, had no staff car; Neame offered to take him and John Combe in his, while his A.D.C. went with John Harding.

Neame took the wheel, because his driver was very tired. He drove in the column until it debouched into the desert at Marawa, and then decided to fall behind to avoid the dust. This resulted in his losing the way and turning north towards Martuba. Although the error was at length recognised, it was decided to keep on to Derna, as no enemy had been reported anywhere in that area and it was known that another British column was moving south-east on the Derna-Martuba road. Neame now handed over to his driver, with orders to press on. He, O'Connor and Combe all fell into a doze, from which they were abruptly awakened by loud orders—in German—to hold up their hands and get out of the car. They had driven into the middle of a strong German reconnaissance unit, which had moved round behind the British lines during the late afternoon and was bivouacked for the night.[23]

O'Connor gave his considered verdict on the whole disastrous episode more than four years later, when he was G.O.C.-in-C. Eastern Command in India and Wavell was Viceroy:

... As you did have confidence in me I am sure you were right in having me up. On the other hand, it was no good having two of us up at the same time. So if you wanted me up, it would have been better for Neame to go. The trouble was everything was already committed to a certain line of action. I did not see that I could alter anything very much. I doubt if I could have done much better than he did with the Armd. Div. flagrantly disobeying their orders, as they did. I should certainly not have been captured but might have been killed!

... I don't suppose you realise quite how much your presence meant to me. I could have accomplished anything under you with you to guide me, and not to serve under you again was quite the worst part of being a prisoner. Please don't think I ever blamed you for my being taken.[24]

In the ruin and the retreat of these days there was one important strategic fact: Wavell had Tobruk. He was determined to hold on to it. Meanwhile, the extent of the defeat began to be appreciated in Cairo and in London. Churchill became magnanimous, constructive and helpful. He was suddenly at his best. Recrimination could wait. The situation must be held and defeat converted into victory. On the afternoon of 5th April a flying-boat brought Eden and Dill back to Cairo after their final, fruitless excursion to the Balkans. At dawn next morning the Germans launched their assault on Greece and Yugoslavia.

The first of the day's telegrams from London was from the Chiefs of Staff to the Commanders-in-Chief. It began: "We have considered the new situation in Cyrenaica with a view to seeing how we can help you." The Chiefs of Staff went on to accept the fact that the re-establishment of the Desert front must have first priority. The 7th Australian Division therefore would not move, and the invasion of the Dodecanese was postponed. Big reinforcements of armour were promised in convoys now about to sail from Britain, and one armoured brigade would be sent on ahead in fast ships to reach the Middle East by 10th June. Cunningham was offered five destroyers from the Indian Ocean and a couple of submarines from the Western Mediterranean, and Longmore thirty-eight Wellingtons for the Desert and six Beauforts for Malta.

The Chiefs of Staff suggested attacks by commandos and special assault craft on the enemy's ever-lengthening communications, reminded the Middle East commanders once again that the South

Africans and Indians ought to be brought north from East Africa, and requested a brief description of Tobruk's defences.

Andrew Cunningham came down to Cairo from Alexandria. On the afternoon of 6th April a full conference of the Commanders-in-Chief was held, which Eden and Dill also attended. The reply they composed to the Chiefs of Staff began with a grateful acknowledgement of the help that was being provided. Wavell for his part asked for more cruiser tanks and if necessary fewer "I" tanks. His greatest need was for armoured mobility. He wanted more A.A. and anti-tank guns, and some ordnance personnel to speed up tank repairs, to be sent through the Mediterranean in a cruiser or a submarine. More lorries were also needed. Longmore gave details of the way he proposed to use his Beauforts and Wellingtons, and Cunningham pointed out that seaborne attacks on communications between Benghazi and Tripoli would mean that the ships would be bombed and sunk. The signal ended: "Tobruk defences are as Italians left them. Defence will be put in hand. Secretary of State and C.I.G.S. agree. . . ."

Wavell gave out his intention calmly. He would hold Tobruk as a fortress; he would hold the frontier about Sollum as a threat to any enemy attempt to eliminate Tobruk; and he would rebuild and re-man the defences of Egypt at Mersa Matruh. The Middle East, despite what was happening in the Balkans, was not to be allowed to crumble. He made no effort, however, to minimise the gravity of the crisis.

Next day, Monday, 7th April, Eden and Dill were due to go by flying-boat, via Gibraltar, back to the United Kingdom.

Foreign Secretary to Prime Minister   *7th April, 1941, 1045 hrs.*
Situation in Western Desert is serious and Germans are advancing in much greater strength and much more rapidly than we anticipated. Wavell is doing all in his power to arrest German advance at Tobruk but it is a race against time. We hope to reach you on 9th April.

During 7th April the remnants of Neame's "rear" H.Q. reached Tobruk. In the fortress there was one brigade of 9th Australian Division; the rest of the division was still stretched in good order along the northern road out of Cyrenaica, and prepared to fight a rear-guard action if required. Late in the afternoon John Harding got through on the telephone to the Commander-in-Chief and told him that all the generals had disappeared. Wavell answered that he himself would come out at once.

It proved to be an extremely narrow shave. A combination of vast distances (over which he had been unable to attempt to reconnoitre), logistics and his own impetuosity now robbed Rommel of the opportunity which had so suddenly beckoned him. Only on the morning of 8th April did the hapless Gambier-Parry, and Vaughan of the 3rd Indian Motor Brigade, surrender at Mechili; and during that day, while some of Rommel's desert columns were still stranded around Tengeder without fuel or water, the first of his northern formations reached the Derna area. Their commander had been wounded, but Rommel ordered Major-General von Prittwitz, commander of the 15th Panzer Division, to take command and at once follow up the British to Tobruk. He wrote: "It still seemed to me very important to remain on the enemy's heels, and, by keeping the pressure up, persuade him to continue his retreat."[25]

Wavell was the last man to be hustled or unnerved in this manner. He was off from Heliopolis at seven o'clock on the morning of 8th April in a battered and not very reliable old Hudson. He took with him Major-General J. D. Lavarack, the commander of the 7th Australian Division, who was for the time being his only spare commander. They had a disagreeable and bumpy flight; there was a strong wind whipping up the sand and making visibility bad and patchy at or near ground level. Between squalls the pilot got the aircraft down safely at Tobruk. On the airfield to meet him were Major-General Morshead and his G.S.O.1, Colonel Loyd. They were dog-tired, unshaven, and conscious that they looked and smelt of the desert, of defeat and of retreat. Wavell's presence gave them back their confidence—in him and in themselves. Tobruk, he said, was to be held; he had merely come to settle the method by which this was to be done. The party went into the town, and a conference was held round a glass-topped table in the loggia of Tobruk's principal hotel. Wavell noted with approval Morshead's quiet and soldierly demeanour, and decided that he was the right man to command the 9th Australian Division. He appointed Lavarack for the time being commander of all troops in Cyrenaica and Libya, with the task of holding Rommel's advance at Tobruk to procure time for the assembly of reinforcements —especially of armour—for the defence of Egypt. Then they studied the defences of the town in detail.

Wavell did not know until late the following day that early that morning Arthur Smith, in his office in G.H.Q., had read and dealt with a telegram from London.

Prime Minister to A. P. Wavell   *7th April, 1941, 2340 hrs.*
                                          (received 8th April, 0305 hrs.)
You should surely be able to hold Tobruk with its permanent Italian defences at least until or unless the enemy brings up strong artillery forces. It seems difficult to believe he can do this for some weeks. He would run great risks in masking Tobruk and advancing upon Egypt observing that we can reinforce from the sea and would menace his communications. Tobruk therefore seems to be a place to be held to the death without thought of retirement. Should be glad to hear your intentions. . . .

Gen. Arthur Smith to Prime Minister   *8th April, 1941, 1040 hrs.*
General Wavell is visiting Tobruk and will telegraph on his return.

The Italian defences of Tobruk, such as they were, were not entirely appropriate for the new garrison's needs at that moment. The most important of them faced eastwards. The full perimeter was between twenty-eight and thirty miles in circumference, far too big for the troops that the defenders would have available. Many of the trenches had sanded up; the anti-tank ditch was not a particularly formidable obstacle, especially to a Panzer battalion on the attack. The minefields were either unknown or had been cleared. There were a few "I" tanks already in the town, and Wavell immediately ordered some recently overhauled and slightly less antiquated tanks to be sent up by sea. His inspection was as thorough as his instructions were explicit.

He wrote: "I have been praised for my decision to hold Tobruk, but I doubt whether I really had much option. There was not sufficient transport to mount the Australian Division, and marching troops would have been at the mercy of an armoured force. Also it would have been disastrous to abandon all the stores, workshops, etc., which had accumulated there. But I was anxious about the defence, remembering the enormous perimeter and the ease with which we had overcome the Italian resistance a few months earlier."

It was late in the afternoon before he was ready to fly back to Cairo. At the airfield the storm was blowing harder than ever. As the Hudson was about to take off, a wheel brake seized up. While this was being mended—the job took an hour—Wavell took refuge in a small hut on the edge of the airfield. A party of young Lysander pilots who had just flown in from the battle area came into the hut to find the Commander-in-Chief sitting on the floor composedly reading a book. From their aircraft they produced four bottles of tepid beer, and Wavell gladly accepted one and sat talking to them until the repair was finished. A few days later the Lysander squadron received a case of champagne with his compliments and thanks.

After a quarter of an hour in the air the oil pressure failed on one engine, and the pilot turned back to El Adem—by now abandoned and likely to be overrun by enemy patrols at any moment. As the sun was setting they took off once more, but within twenty minutes the oil gauge was back to zero again. After trying to fly on with a single engine, which rapidly overheated, the pilot had to make a forced landing. He did it with great skill, but the faulty wheel brake swung the aircraft violently over to port. The port wing was shattered and the tail came off. Everyone scrambled out unhurt. They had come down south of the Tobruk-Sollum road and a good many miles west of Sollum. Wavell decided that they should stay where they were until dawn.

A fire was lit, a brew-up was begun. "Just then some motor-vehicles approached; it seemed quite possible they were hostile; and I took cover in a *wadi* and destroyed a specially secret document I had with me."

Some fifty yards from the wrecked aircraft the first car stopped. A gigantic figure, carrying a rifle and a bayonet, emerged, and covered by the slowly-moving vehicle approached the little party. When he challenged them his voice was foreign. He came forward slowly. He grinned, and his teeth gleamed white in a black face. It was a patrol of Sudanese troops heading for Sollum. The Chief and his party bundled into the cars.

"Somewhere about midnight I managed to get through to G.H.Q. in Cairo, where consternation reigned at my disappearance, since I had been due back early in the afternoon.

"I stupidly omitted to inform my C.G.S. of the secret document I had destroyed, and he did not know I had taken it with me, so that there was more consternation when it was found missing, and much frantic searching by the staff. Finally Arthur Smith came to me with a long face and confessed its loss. I don't know whether his relief or annoyance was greater, when I in my turn confessed what had happened."

There was a brief, crucial pause. Throughout 9th April the generals on both sides were making some radical administrative changes as quickly as they could. On 10th April Rommel told his staff and subordinates that the British were collapsing and must be vigorously pursued, that his objective was now the Suez Canal, but that Tobruk must be attacked and taken as soon as possible, before Wavell had a chance to reorganise its defence. Wavell knew that Tobruk and the frontier defences must be held, and he now also understood the quality of his enemy. Eden and Dill reached London that afternoon, and in the evening Wavell received one of the most magnanimous signals that Churchill ever sent.

Prime Minister to A. P. Wavell   *10th April, 1941, 2330 hrs.*
We all cordially endorse your decision to hold Tobruk and will do all in our power to bring you aid.

By this time 9th Australian Division—having fought a brisk, tough rearguard action at Derna—was safely gathered in at Tobruk. The preparations for the siege went ahead at relentless speed under frequent and often viciously accurate dive-bombing.

On Friday, 12th April, Wavell left at seven in the morning for Athens, and was not back in Cairo until lunch-time on the Sunday. While he was away, his opponent in the Western Desert was striving, with almost demoniac energy, to bring about a decisive battle. But he had stretched his forces to the utmost. Tobruk was invested on 11th April. Rommel wrote: "Stukas attacked the defence works, the layout of which was still completely unknown to us. More troops arrived on the 12th April and it was decided to open the first major attack on the stronghold that afternoon. Bardia was taken that day by 3rd Reconnaissance Battalion."[26]

However, Rommel's first major attack on Tobruk, launched as he had ordered on the afternoon of the 12th, was a failure. Morshead, whom Wavell had made directly responsible to himself, was from the outset determined to maintain an aggressive defence. He reported that there was a total of some 36,000 souls in Tobruk, but these included, besides combatant troops, the personnel of base units, Italian P.O.W.s and Libyan refugees. They were to be thinned out to fighting units only as soon as possible.

"There'll be no Dunkirk here," Morshead said to his commanders. "If we should have to get out, we shall fight our way out. There is to be no surrender and no retreat."[27]

Rommel renewed his attack from the south on Sunday, 13th April. By this time Morshead had six brigades of infantry at his disposal, each with one anti-tank company; four regiments of field artillery armed with 25-pounders; two anti-tank regiments, one British and one Australian, each less one battery; sixteen heavy A.A. and fifty-nine light (Bofors) A.A. guns; and the hastily forming 3rd Armoured Brigade, which consisted in all of twenty-six cruiser, fifteen light and four "I" tanks.

On the night of 13th/14th April Rommel's 5th Light Division, making the fiercest attack on the fortress so far, met its heaviest reverse, losing sixteen tanks out of thirty-eight. The garrison's losses were twenty-six killed, sixty-four wounded, and two tanks and one 25-pounder gun disabled. After this unmistakable setback (which infuriated Rommel), the Axis forces abandoned for the time being their attack on Tobruk's southern front.

When Wavell returned from Greece the crisis in the Western Desert was over. Though much remained to be done, the moment of acute danger had passed. This fact was not so clear to those watching in London as it was in Egypt. The Prime Minister was by now thoroughly roused. He assured President Roosevelt that Tobruk was going to be held "not as a defensive position but as an invaluable bridgehead on the flank of any serious by-pass advance on Egypt."[28] He deluged Dill's overworked staff with advice, criticisms and "prodding" minutes. Some at least of his ideas were embodied in this signal:

C.I.G.S. to A. P. Wavell   *12th April, 1941, 1820 hrs.*
Have been studying your Western Desert problem and am convinced that enemy's supply difficulties must be immense. If his communications can be attacked by naval (bombardment and possible blocking of Tripoli and Sirte) by air (bombing and machine-gunning columns as well as bombing of ports) and by land forces (desert patrols cutting in and destroying supply and petrol convoys) his advance must be checked till you can assemble enough tanks to strike back. This is a time when great daring is needed and great losses accepted. Know you will not in this anxious time think I am trying to interfere with your

conduct of battle by sending you above thoughts.   Good luck.

Eden and Dill were summoned to Chequers, and at the end of a long, long evening the Prime Minister dictated a telegram.

Prime Minister to A. P. Wavell   *13th April, 1941, 0315 hrs.*
We are working night and day here to aid you especially by navy and air action on Tripoli and communications. Hope signal you to-morrow large-scale decisions.

Following is personal from me. Tobruk seems an invaluable bridgehead for offensive punches against all by-passers; one has the hope that our fellows will establish unit ascendancy in minor combats and that incursion of small raiding parties will not be allowed to deflect the general layout. Foreign Secretary and C.I.G.S. are with me here and we all send you our assurance of complete confidence and every wish for good fortune. This is one of the crucial fights in the history of the British Army.

This, with the Prime Minister's brief signal of 10th April, was awaiting Wavell when he walked into his office on the Sunday afternoon. He answered them together, in a short telegram that was as courteous as it was cautious.

A. P. Wavell to Prime Minister   *13th April, 1941, 1712 hrs.*
Thank you for your [two telegrams]. Tobruk now isolated and may be hard pressed. Garrison in good spirits and have beaten off at least two attacks. Just back from Greece where morale of our forces high but general situation of Greek Army on their left dangerous. Will wire appreciation situation here to C.I.G.S. to-night.

With great decisiveness and rapidity Wavell gathered all the threads of his now infinitely more complicated task into his hands. First he sent a private telegram to Dill, conceding the point about Rommel's supply difficulties but pointing out that he continued to advance at great speed and was supplying his forward formations by air and at night. The Germans' armoured cars, he said, were doing most of the damage, disorganising communications and command. "We will stop him in time," he declared, "but the situation is most anxious."

Then he signalled Lavarack at Tobruk, warning him that he would be, for the time being, isolated by land, but that the defence of Egypt now depended largely on the Tobruk garrison. "I know I can count on you to hold Tobruk to the end," he wrote. "My best wishes to you all."

Finally, in a little over an hour and a half, he composed an 800-word appraisal of the situation in the Western Desert as it had crystallised within the past forty-eight hours. He set out in detail the steps he had taken to reorganise the system of command in the battle area, to prepare Tobruk for siege, and to strengthen the defences of Egypt. He concluded:

> I can see no hope of being able to relieve Tobruk for at least several months. Whether garrison can hold out long enough will remain to be seen, it depends mainly on whether port can be kept open. At least it should inflict heavy losses on enemy and cripple his effort for some time. . . .
>
> Situation is ugly at the moment but enemy's difficulties are great and provided we keep going, receive reinforcements of material and men, and Egyptians do not stab us in the back we shall recover and in due course counter-attack. But next few months will be very difficult, quite apart from what has happened in Greece.

"So there we were," he wrote afterwards, "by the middle of April back to much the same position as in December before I started the offensive, except that we, not the Italians, now held Tobruk."

This was a fundamental fact which Rommel was extremely loth to accept. He developed, and he preserved until his final defeat in this theatre, a fierce obsession about Tobruk. Now he goaded his tired troops into repeated, extravagant and vain attempts to capture the citadel which had also become a symbol. Before dawn on 14th April one more strong attack was launched in the southern sector. Tanks, infantry and gunners alike were hurled back with a ferocity on the part of the Australians and the British 1st Royal Horse Artillery such as hardly any German soldier had yet encountered in all Hitler's years of conquest. They lost sixteen tanks out of thirty-eight under the concentrated fire of the R.H.A.'s 25-pounders, fired over open sights. By half past seven the survivors were fighting desperately to flee from what one German described as "a witches' cauldron," and the Nazi war correspondents called "the hell of Tobruk." Throughout the morning the Australians mopped up the mess. Some 250 dazed and bewildered Germans, many of them weeping, were marched back to the prisoners' cage. Wavell reported this fact to the C.I.G.S. and added: "Their morale is definitely low." Churchill commented: "Perhaps it was because their morale and expectations had been so high that they wept!"[29]

On 16th/17th April Rommel made one more effort. This time the attack was from the west. He used the Italian Ariete Division with an infantry regiment of the Trento Division under command. He led the assault in person. The Ariete had never yet been in action; but out of the 100-odd tanks with which they had started the advance, all but ten had broken down. Rommel and his staff drove to put some fire into them, but they were obviously reluctant to fight. "It made one's hair stand on end," said Rommel, "to see the sort of equipment with which the Duce had sent his troops into battle."[30] They lost five of their tanks, and twenty-six officers and men surrendered. Rommel, angry, weary and disappointed, decided to halt the offensive until he had more and better troops, and much more and much better equipment.

Prime Minister to A. P. Wavell　　　　*7th April, 1941, 2040 hrs.*
I like the look of your situation very much. . . . Tobruk is your offensive hook and has called their bluff to some purpose already. . . . They are frightfully short of everything. It would be a fine thing to cop the lot. . . .

But Wavell had suffered a severe reverse, and almost all that had been gained by the winter offensive was lost. There were even graver events happening elsewhere. On 14th April he signalled Dill suggesting that an offer be made to the Italians to exchange any six of their captured generals for O'Connor. It took the Defence Committee almost a fortnight to meditate on this extremely unorthodox, but by no means frivolous, suggestion.

C.I.G.S. to A. P. Wavell　　　　*29th April, 1941*
Regret that C.O.S. have considered your proposals for exchange of O'Connor and decided we cannot discriminate in favour of generals.

Early on the morning of 6th April the Germans attacked Greece and Yugoslavia simultaneously. The Commander-in-Chief of the *Reichswehr*, Field-Marshal von Brauchitsch, took personal charge of the whole operation from his headquarters in Vienna. He had at his disposal thirty divisions (out of a grand total, in the army as a whole, of 154); he deployed in the Balkan campaign twenty of them, including the majority of his mountain divisions and six out of the fourteen Panzer divisions which the *Reichswehr* then possessed.

In face of this immense numerical superiority, the British campaign on the mainland of Greece, which lasted three weeks in all, could only be from first to last a fighting retreat. Wavell bore strategic responsibility; but the great tactical burden fell on Maitland Wilson. The speed and size of the German onslaught, the distance, and the severe strain on very sparse communications, combined to make it impossible for the Commander-in-Chief to exercise more than a nominal supervision over the day-to-day—let alone hour-to-hour—conduct of the campaign; and he was only able to pay two visits to Greece during its course.

When the Germans attacked, Wilson's formations, known collectively as W Force, were disposed as follows: the New Zealand Division and the 12th and 20th Greek Divisions were on the Aliakmon line, and the British 1st Armoured Brigade was about twenty miles forward, along the Vardar river in the plain of Salonika, as a covering force. The 6th Australian Division was in the process of arriving in Greece. The 7th Australian Division, which had been due to embark, Wavell had held for use in the Western Desert when he realised the extent of Rommel's threat; this action had brought an immediate and vigorous protest from Blamey, the Australian Corps Commander, which—since he had no knowledge of the magnitude of the desert disaster—was quite justified. Wilson took over command of the Aliakmon positions on 5th April, and found that Papagos had taken the third Greek division he had been promised, the "mechanised" 19th, and had sent it forward to strengthen the three Greek divisions and frontier troops described as the Eastern Macedonian Army. The remainder of the Greek Army—by far the greater part—was still on the Albanian front.

Since Salonika had been ruled out, and was in the event immediately captured by the Germans, Wilson's only major supply port was at Piraeus, more than 300 miles from his front line, and connected to it by one railway and a road so narrow in places that it could only carry a single line of traffic. To coincide with the opening of their land advance the Germans launched a very strong air assault on the Piraeus on 6th April. The port was crowded with British and Greek ships, carrying supplies and munitions of all kinds. One of these, the *Clan*

Fraser, berthed at a quay in the inner harbour, had deep in her hold a cargo of 350 tons of T.N.T. During a day of incessant bombing, work went on strenuously to clear this dangerous vessel. But because of delay at a quay where there was no railway track, and everything had to be manhandled out of her, at nightfall there were still some 250 tons of high explosive aboard. Soon after ten o'clock she was hit by three bombs in quick succession. It was impossible to move her, because the Germans had sown the whole harbour with magnetic mines. The fire aboard her blazed for two hours before she blew up. The whole port of Piraeus was destroyed, and eleven ships, with a total tonnage of nearly 42,000 tons, were lost. *"From that fateful night Piraeus virtually ceased to exist as a port."*[31]

The events of this grim Sunday followed the final failure of the Eden-Dill mission to create a Balkan front. The news of the Yugoslav *coup d'état* had brought the Foreign Secretary and the C.I.G.S. back in haste from Malta to the Eastern Mediterranean. They reached Athens early on 28th March, where neither Maitland Wilson nor the Greeks had any knowledge of the intentions of the new Yugoslav régime. Papagos was striving without success to establish contact with the Yugoslav commanders; he talked about a common front to defend Salonika, and suggested that he might move his Greek divisions up to the Bulgarian frontier and leave the British forces alone on the Aliakmon line. Eden, Dill and Wilson sensibly urged that it might be as well first to make certain of Yugoslavia's attitude. Eden got a message through to the British Legation in Belgrade to the effect that he and Dill attached the utmost importance to meeting a representative of the new Yugoslav Government as soon as possible. On Saturday, 29th March, the Counsellor of the Legation, Mr. Terence Shone, arrived in Athens with the information that General Simovich, President of the Council in Belgrade, would welcome a visit from Eden and Dill. But on Sunday Mr. Ronald Campbell, the British Minister to Yugoslavia, telephoned to say that Simovich had decided that he could not agree to a visit by a British representative. On the Monday the General changed his mind once more: word came that, although he could not see Eden, he was prepared to receive Dill very secretly in Belgrade.

Dill arrived in the Yugoslav capital by air on 31st March. He spent two fruitless days trying to persuade Simovich to come to some kind of an agreement. Simovich and his colleagues were preoccupied with the internal state of Yugoslavia and the general mobilisation of their forces. They frequently changed their minds; they were elusive and vague, and in the end the most they would accept was a proposal for staff talks with the British and the Greeks, with no obligations on either side. It was arranged that these should be held forthwith at Florina, on the Greek-Yugoslav frontier.

> During these discussions General Simovich and General Ilich [the Minister of War] gave personal and emphatic assurances of Yugoslavia's determination to resist the Germans if attacked, but their liberty of manœuvre was clearly limited by doubts about the Croat minority and fears lest any binding obligations should become known and thus result in dividing the country.[32]

Dill was back in Athens on 2nd April; and on the following morning a special train set out for Florina, carrying British and Greek military representatives, the Foreign Secretary, the C.I.G.S., and their staffs. The Yugoslav representatives' train broke down. The meeting which was to have been held at noon began at ten o'clock at night. Eden and Dill sat in their compartment and took no part in the discussions, which were just as inconclusive and just as valueless as all the other negotiations which had preceded them. The Yugoslavs were not empowered . . . they could not commit themselves . . . they knew nothing of British or Greek dispositions and intentions . . . they had no authority to permit any reconnaissance across the frontier . . . they might be persuaded to send staff officers to Athens to continue these exchanges. . . .

The trains rumbled off on their separate ways into the night. In the meantime, attempts had been made, by telegram, by representation by the Ambassadors in Ankara, and by the Military Mission, to persuade the Turks to take measures which might "inspire the Yugoslav Government with confidence in Turkish determination to stand up to Germany and readiness to collaborate with Yugoslavia and Greece." All kinds of ingenious ideas were hopefully put forward. The reaction of the Turkish Government to all these suggestions was negative.

On 5th April Eden and Dill—prompted by a vehemently anxious telegram from Churchill about the Western Desert—returned to Cairo. Two days later they flew back to London; the German onslaught in the Balkans was in full swing, and Belgrade and Piraeus were smoking ruins. There is a story that just as Dill boarded the aircraft Wavell said to him, half laughing, half sadly, "Jack, I hope when this action is reviewed, you will be elected to sit on my court martial."[33]

A. P. Wavell to Prime Minister   *10th April, 1941*
Am going Greece to-morrow to see Wilson. Probably return morning 13th April and will report.

In Greece Wilson's forces were already engaging the enemy. The first contact was made on 8th April, when detachments of the 1st Armoured Brigade encountered German advance patrols. On the evening of 10th April the Australians holding the left sector of the front, near Amynteion, were under heavy attack. This battle lasted for two days. Although the Germans were held, and suffered a number of casualties, it was obvious that the line was much too long for the number of troops available: there had been no time to consolidate its defences properly. The left flank was protected by a single Greek cavalry division on a very extended front; and beyond it there yawned the Monastir gap, with no troops and no defences at all between this cavalry division's left and the right flank of the main Greek forces in Albania. A new line was therefore decided on, running from Mount Olympus along the valley of the river Aliakmon. This was a strong position, provided that the Yugoslavs and the Greeks were able to close the roads by which the line could be turned. The withdrawal thither began on the night of 11th/12th April.

It was at this phase in the campaign that Wavell paid his first visit to the battle area. He spent the night at Wilson's headquarters north of Larissa. Blamey came in to see the Commander-in-Chief, who had the difficult task of explaining what had happened in the Western Desert, and his reasons for holding up the embarkation of the 7th Australian Division. Blamey not unnaturally was angry, but recovered quickly enough. The whole situation was so bleak that it was obviously useless to spend time and effort in argument.

While Wavell was in Greece he took, in agreement with Blamey and Freyberg, an imaginative and decorous decision. He renamed the 6th Australian Division and the New Zealand Division (hitherto called the 1st Australian Corps), the Anzac Corps, reviving for a new generation the memory of their predecessors' greatness.

Wavell now had his back to the wall. The most immediate and the most serious danger came from that part of his Command which, a fortnight earlier, had seemed the most secure, and where he had scored his finest victory: the Western Desert. On 15th April he took out the "Worst Possible Case" file, which he had opened in June, 1940, and composed a new appreciation, based on the assumption that he would be unable to check the German advance in the Western Desert. The consequence would be that Egypt would become untenable under heavy air attack, Alexandria would fall, and the enemy would advance on Cairo. The loss of Egypt would mean the loss of the forces in Greece, Crete and Cyprus. This would not mean the loss of the war, though the Suez Canal and the Mediterranean would cease to be of much value. "We shall have to fall back on Africa south of Egypt and Libya, and perhaps assist Smuts and the Union to form an African Empire of Sudan, East Africa, Portuguese East Africa, Belgian Congo, Angola, the Rhodesias, etc."

He then assessed, in some detail, the methods by which the personnel and material surviving in Palestine could be saved. The question of the civilian population was "most difficult": with an obvious shortage of shipping, were they to take precedence over the troops or be ordered to stay put? How long would Palestine hold out after the evacuation of Egypt? How could the forces there be evacuated when necessary? What about the Jews? Would there have to be an expedition from India into Iraq? The data for answering these questions must be collected and kept up to date.

By 14th April Wilson's withdrawal of W Force to the line stretching westwards from Mount Olympus to the Servia Pass and then turning north-westwards, begun while Wavell himself was in Greece, had been completed. But the Germans shattered the southern Yugoslav Army, and poured through the Monastir Gap and across the mountains on Wilson's left flank. On the afternoon of the 16th Wilson signalled Wavell, following a conference with Papagos, that his present line was untenable, as the Germans were thrusting towards Grevena, far to the south, and turning his flank once again. Papagos, whose own difficulties were increasing just as swiftly, since his army in Albania was in danger of being cut off, agreed that W Force should pull back to Thermopylae, where the peninsula was only some thirty miles wide. He also suggested that the British troops should be re-embarked to save Greece from devastation, and asked Wilson's advice on whether or not his Government should leave the mainland and go to Crete. Wilson said that this should be done at once, and himself put in motion his second big retreat, across the Thessalian plain, which meant abandoning the principal airfields.

Wavell, reporting these decisions in a telegram to the C.I.G.S., said that he had ordered all ships *en route* to Greece to turn back, ships in Greek ports not yet unloaded to go back to Egypt with full loads, and no more ships to be loaded. He asked for instructions on Papagos's suggestion of a British re-embarkation and added: "Propose however to make all arrangements with this in view. Am assuming Crete will be held. . . ."

His answer came from the Prime Minister himself in the small hours of the following morning. After an abrupt "We have no news from you of what has happened on Imperial front in Greece," Churchill authorised all preparations for the evacuation of the mainland, and insisted that Crete must be held in force.

Wavell replied: "I send you all I get. My reports from Wilson lately have been most scanty due to intercommunication difficulties." Such secret reports as he had, mostly by way of London, showed that Wilson's forces were in an increasingly dangerous position. He could give Churchill one piece of good news: things were brighter in the Western Desert, thanks to the offensive spirit of the Tobruk garrison and of Gott's force at Sollum, and constant attacks by the R.A.F.

On 18th April Churchill issued a directive on the Mediterranean situation. The extrication of Wilson's forces from Greece, he said, affected the whole Empire. The Commanders-in-Chief were to divide their efforts between protecting the evacuation from Greece and sustaining the battle in Libya; but if these clashed, a victory in Libya counted first. Crete initially would only be "a receptacle of whatever can get there from Greece," and its fuller defence would have to be organised later. The shipping of supplies to Tobruk must be fitted in as convenient.

At seven o'clock on the morning of Saturday, 19th April, Wavell set off on his last visit to Athens. He found the situation extremely confused. The King, though full of fight, had failed to find a Government or any outstanding and inspiring personality, either civil or military, to whom he could turn. Papagos painted a gloomy picture of the Greek Army's isolated position in Epirus, and repeated the suggestion he had made to Wilson that the British forces should re-embark to save Greece from devastation by the *Luftwaffe*.

Wavell answered that he and Wilson hoped to consolidate and hold the Thermopylae line, covering Athens, so long as the Greeks wished them to do so, and so long as the Greek Army continued to fight. The decision about re-embarkation was postponed. Compared with the King, Papagos was a beaten man; but Wavell realised that with this mercurial people, the conclusion was still in the balance. While he was weighing up the effects of evacuating or of staying and fighting, there came a thunderbolt from Churchill.

Prime Minister to A. P. Wavell, repeated to General Wilson
19th April, 1941, 1205 hrs.

So far H.M. Government have not received from General Wilson or from you any account of the fighting in Greece although heavy and prolonged actions have been in progress for several days and lengthy newspaper reports of a confused character have been telegraphed home. This is not the way H.M. Government should be treated. It is also detrimental to the service as many decisions have to be taken here and we are in constant relations with the Dominions and with foreign countries. I wish you to make sure that this state of things ends at once and that a short daily report of what is happening on the front of the British and Imperial Army is sent direct from our H.Q. in Greece at least every 24 hours.

Wavell sent off his answer to Churchill late that night. He agreed that the reports of the operations had been unsatisfactory. Signals had been faulty; two of Wilson's three liaison officers had been wounded; it was not possible to visit forward headquarters by air; movement by road was blocked by refugees and withdrawing vehicles and also subject to bombing. Army co-operation aircraft had nearly all been out of action since the second day of the battle; the weather had been bad; and staffs of forward units, not all highly trained, had neglected reports while they were fighting. The situation as he understood it then was that two New Zealand brigades and one Australian had got back to Thermopylae, and the 1st Armoured Brigade, all of whose cruiser tanks had broken down and were out of action. W Force's rearguard, another Australian brigade, had been pressed out of the Vale of Tempe by German armour. Wavell said he had instructed Wilson to cable a full narrative of the fighting and an estimate of the casualties, and to send more detailed reports as soon as possible. He concluded: "General impression is that troops have acquitted themselves very well in difficult manœuvre and have inflicted heavy loss on enemy whenever he gave opportunity. Our artillery fire seems to have been most effective."

It was nearly ten o'clock by the time he signed this telegram. He then set off for Blamey's headquarters. After a long, difficult drive in the dark he found the Australian general at two o'clock in the morning in a tent at Levadhia, near Thebes. Wavell asked whether Blamey had any feeling that Dominion troops had been mishandled from above in these operations, or that things might have been handled differently, leaving aside the original decision to send troops to Greece. Blamey said emphatically that the situation was caused by the collapse of the Yugoslavs and the Greeks, and that nothing else could have been done by Wilson and his staff. "I hope," he added, "that no political trouble will be made out of what has happened."

Wavell was not back in Athens until daybreak. There he saw the King again, accompanied this time by the new President of the Council, M. Tsouderos. During the course of the day it became clear that the German ground forces were ranging deep into Greece, and that the *Luftwaffe* had established air supremacy. The surrender of the Greek army in Epirus was accepted by the Chief of Staff of the German 12th Army. Wavell told the King that, in view of all this, it was his duty to prepare at once to embark as much of his force as he could. The King apologised deeply for having put the British forces in such a position, and promised all the help he could. Early next morning Wavell set off for Egypt in the middle of an air-raid alert. There were no fighters available to provide an escort. His flying-boat flew as low over the sea as possible; luckily no ranging German aircraft attacked it, and he reached Cairo in the late afternoon.

Early on the following morning he signalled Dill an account of his meeting with Blamey, who had shown himself a fine fighting commander, well fitted for high command. He therefore recommended that, as soon as he could be spared from Greece, Blamey be appointed Deputy Commander-in-Chief, Middle East, and added that he himself would continue to maintain the closest co-operation with both the Australians and the New Zealanders and would have their liaison officers at his headquarters.

During the afternoon of 22nd April he drafted a communiqué intended to prepare the public for the collapse in Greece which he knew to be imminent. In view of its effect on world opinion he was convinced that it should be issued in London, where its various implications could be assessed at their full value; he therefore embodied it in a telegram to Churchill. The communiqué gave an outline of the story in terms as favourable as possible to the Greeks and to the

Anzac forces engaged in the campaign, and Wavell ended his signal: "Do not wish anything yet said about possibility of re-embarkation."

Two days later the Greeks capitulated. By this time the King, with a small personal staff, had escaped to Crete. Various Ministers of the Greek Government were on their way to Crete or Cairo. On the night of 24th April, while the first British troops were being evacuated from the Greek mainland, Wavell reassessed his whole strategic and tactical situation.

He realised that he was vulnerable everywhere in the Mediterranean sector of his Command. He foresaw a series of heavy assaults, including one by airborne troops, subversion and Fifth Column activities in Egypt and Palestine, and incitement of the Iraq Army to attack the British, with perhaps support by German aircraft and paratroops. To meet these attacks he had a considerable number of troops, but the majority were not battle-worthy. "There is not at present in the Middle East," he noted, "a single formation complete in organisation and equipment."

His principal problems were: the defence of the western frontier of Egypt; the internal security of Egypt; the defence of Palestine, Crete and Cyprus; and the organisation of a central reserve. On Crete he wrote:

> It seems unlikely that the enemy will attempt a landing in force in Crete from the sea. An airborne landing is possible but not probable, since the landing force would be isolated without sea support. Scale of air attack on Crete will, however, undoubtedly be heavy, especially in view of presence in island of King of Greece and Government.

The evacuation of the British expeditionary force from Greece was accomplished in five successive nights, in an operation of remarkable skill, conducted with exemplary courage by the Royal Navy, and in accordance with a scheme worked out by a Joint Planning Staff which had been sent to Greece for that very purpose, on Wavell's instructions, as soon as the campaign began. However, at Nauplion some 1,700 men had to be left behind, because one of the transports, sunk by *Luftwaffe* bombs, blocked the channel; and two destroyers which picked up survivors from another bombed ship were both subsequently sunk, with the loss of some 700 more soldiers. At Kalamata, by a misunderstanding between the Royal Navy and the Army, some

8,000 troops, including unfortunately the first reinforcements for the New Zealand Division, were also left behind.

The total number of troops sent to Greece was 58,364 (including 5,000 Cypriot and Palestinian Pioneers). Of these 50,732 were re-embarked.[34] All guns, transport and equipment, other than that which each man could carry, were lost. Of the troops evacuated, 26,000 were landed in Crete and the remainder (nearly all wounded) were taken back to Egypt. The motive for taking so many to Crete was to shorten the sea journey, and to make possible quicker and more frequent round trips.

Blamey reached Cairo on 25th April, and stayed in Wavell's house. Wilson was taken to Suda Bay in Crete, in a Sunderland flying-boat which somehow managed to pack 55 passengers into its roomy hull, on the night of 26th/27th April. Wavell summed up in his Despatch:

The expedition to Greece was ill-starred from the first. The change of plan by the Greek Commander-in-Chief after the first decision to despatch a force resulted in the position on which the Imperial forces were to concentrate being held by a very inadequate Greek force instead of the five organised divisions which General Papagos had promised. The uncertainties of the Yugoslav attitude seriously affected the plans both of ourselves and of the Greeks, while the complete collapse of their armies on the German invasion exposed the flank of what was an otherwise extremely strong position. The German attack took place while the Imperial force was still in process of concentration and before it had time to get properly settled down. That the Greek Army which had fought so heroically against the Italians disintegrated so rapidly under the German attack is not surprising. They had already been strained to the uttermost and neither their organisation nor equipment were sufficiently up to date to enable them to face the German Army. Finally the enemy bombing attacks on the Piraeus closed the only good port, deprived us of any chance of removing any of our heavy equipment, and made the re-embarkation of the personnel of the force an extremely hazardous operation. Thus, while the whole expedition was something in the nature of a gamble, the dice were loaded against it from the first. It was not really such a forlorn hope from the military point of view as it may seem from its results.[35]

Meanwhile the affair of the worst possible case was carried a stage or two further—not in the Middle East but in England. As the situation worsened in Greece and in the Western Desert, Dill re-read a copy of "The Worst Possible Case" which had been sent to him in great secrecy on 14th June, 1940, and given the code name "Mongoose"; he showed it to the D.M.O., Major-General Kennedy, and on 21st April sent Wavell a very cautious telegram saying that, although he hoped there would be no necessity for this scheme, he would like to know if it still held and if there was anything which, at his end, he could do to help, such as building up stores elsewhere.

A. P. Wavell to C.I.G.S.   *27th April, 1941*
Conditions have obviously changed since my paper of June 1940 and matter is under active reconsideration by my staff.

Copy of my note of 15th April on the subject will be brought to you by liaison officer who will explain situation.

Kennedy, in company with Ismay, spent the night of Sunday, 27th April, at Chequers. Others present were Captain Margesson, the Secretary of State for War, Professor Lindemann, General Alan Brooke (then C.-in-C. Home Forces) and Mrs. Randolph Churchill. During dinner Churchill engaged Brooke and Kennedy—but particularly the latter—in a discussion about the Middle East. At Kennedy's suggestion that it might not be possible to hold Egypt, the Prime Minister lost his temper. After he had proclaimed that, if Wavell lost Egypt, blood would flow, and that he would have firing parties "to shoot the generals," he accused Kennedy of defeatism for even mentioning the possibility of losing Egypt.

Kennedy sought to refute the accusation with the argument that to consider the worst case as well as other possibilities was a normal function of any commander and his staff. Surely the Prime Minister knew that Wavell had a plan for withdrawal from Egypt should it be forced upon him, and that even retreat would not mean defeat, since there were other lines on which Wavell's forces could stand to prevent the Germans breaking through to the Indian Ocean or the Persian Gulf.

"This," exclaimed the Prime Minister, "comes like a flash of lightning to me. I never heard such ideas. War is a contest of wills. It is pure defeatism to speak as you have done."

Kennedy continued to argue stubbornly. Churchill grew more and more furious. Brooke and the others sat silent. The discussion then veered, but more than once throughout a long and difficult evening the Prime Minister reverted to the theme of defeatism, which had aroused his deepest, most pugnacious instincts. Kennedy, not fully aware of the complexity and tenacity of the anger he had provoked, went back to London the following day, and told Dill what had happened.[36]

Prime Minister to C.I.G.S.   *28th April, 1941*
The D.M.O. yesterday spoke of plans which had been prepared in certain eventualities for the evacuation of Egypt.
    Let me see these plans, and any material bearing upon them.

C.I.G.S. to Prime Minister   *28th April, 1941*
This is an old and now quite out of date plan for withdrawal from Egypt should the worst happen. I know Wavell is working on a revised plan as an insurance but of course only the most limited number of people will know anything about it.

Later in the day Dill went to a meeting of the War Cabinet; when he returned to the War Office he sent for Kennedy and said, "My word, you have raised a terrific storm, and it was made worse by Menzies—he spoke in the Cabinet on the same lines as you did at Chequers."[37]

It was perhaps as well that, if the mere mention of an out-of-date scheme could cause so formidable an outburst of indignation, the liaison officer had not yet arrived in London with Wavell's new, much more radical and far-reaching assessment of the worst possible case. But the knowledge that Wavell's thought was moving along these lines served only to deepen the Prime Minister's misunderstanding and distrust of the Commander-in-Chief. More and more relentlessly Churchill sought for adequate grounds on which he could relieve Wavell of his appointment, and for a successor who would be both amenable to his views and instantly victorious in all sections of the Command.

A. P. Wavell to C.I.G.S.   *30th April, 1941, 2005 hrs.*
Evacuation now complete. . . . Troops in good heart and brought away personal equipment, etc., as far as possible. No doubt that our troops were completely on top whenever they met Germans under reasonable conditions and inflicted heavy losses on them in personnel and material. Great numerical superiority in the air

and numbers of A.F.V.s were the only factors in which enemy had advantage.

Prime Minister to A. P. Wavell   *1st May, 1941, 2040 hrs.*
I congratulate you upon successful evacuation. We have paid our debt of honour with far less loss than I feared. Feel sure you are waiting to strike a blow. Enemy's difficulties must be immense. Am looking forward to hear from you but best of all by events. . . .

Thus the Greek enterprise was brought to its conclusion. Within less than a month there was to be a final, ferocious postscript in Crete.

XIII

Under Great Strain

From the middle of April onwards Wavell's anxieties deepened; his weight of responsibility grew heavier; and even he, with all his resilience, could not overcome his mounting sense of strain. His commitments increased and his resources to meet them were, in proportion though not in actual numbers, smaller than they had ever been. Action after action was demanded of him; and he had the greatest difficulty in finding the formations he needed to hold, let alone launch an attack from, his most vital front, the Western Desert. Yet as he and the War Cabinet both fully appreciated, on a secure grip on this front all else depended.

On 17th April Rommel had called a temporary halt to his assaults on Tobruk. On 18th April, the day before he went off to Athens, Wavell sent two telegrams to Dill setting out the details of his principal problem in the desert, the shortage of tanks. To confront an estimated enemy total of at least 150 tanks in the fighting line, he had one weak unit in Tobruk of mixed cruisers, "I" tanks and light tanks, and in the Matruh area one squadron of cruisers. Looking ahead, the best he could hope for by the end of the month was one cruiser regiment less one squadron, and one "I" tank regiment less one squadron, to assist in the defence of Matruh. During May he might get some 30 or 40 cruisers out of the workshops to make up another weak unit, and some "I" tanks which would probably be needed for the close defence of Alexandria. He could not count on getting any tanks back from Greece. To this signal he added a "Stop press" message:

I have just received disquieting intelligence. I was expecting another German Colonial division (18th Division) which disembarked at Tripoli early this month to appear in fighting line about end of month. Certain units have already been identified. I have just been informed that latest evidence indicates this is not

Colonial but armoured repeat armoured division. If so, situation is indeed serious since armoured division contains over 400 tanks of which 138 are medium. If enemy can supply it, it will take a lot of stopping. I will cable again when I have digested this unwelcome news.[1]

The second signal concluded:

> . . . there are only two regiments of cruiser tanks in sight from Egypt by end of May and no reserves to replace casualties, whereas there are now in Egypt trained and excellent personnel for six tank regiments.
>
> Consider provision of cruiser repeat cruiser tanks vital addition to Infantry tanks which lack speed and radius of action for desert operations.
>
> C.I.G.S. please give your personal assistance.

Copies of these messages reached Churchill on 20th April at a country house where he was spending the week-end. He reacted promptly and helpfully. He resolved not to be governed any longer by the Navy's natural reluctance to allow merchant ships through the Mediterranean, and to send a convoy, carrying large-scale armoured reinforcements, direct from Gibraltar to Alexandria, accepting the risks implicit in the decision. When the Defence Committee met on Monday, 21st April, the First Sea Lord rallied to the Prime Minister's support, and the Chief of the Air Staff said he would try to give the ships the air cover of a Beaufighter squadron from Malta eastwards.

Prime Minister to A. P. Wavell   *22nd April, 1941, 0235 hrs.*
I have been working hard for you in the last few days and you will, I am sure, be glad to know that we are sending 307 of our best tanks through the Mediterranean, hoping they will reach you around 10th May. Of these 99 are cruisers Mark IV and Mark VI with the necessary spare parts for the latter and 180 "I" tanks. . . .

You should furnish us with your plan for bringing these vehicles into action at very earliest. If this consignment gets through the hazards of the passage . . . no German should remain in Cyrenaica by the end of the month of June.

In making your preparations for bringing these vehicles into action you should pretend that they are coming round the

Cape. . . . Thus when you get them the chance of surprise may be offered. . . .²

This signal brought a glimmer of light into the bleakness of a gruelling week.

A. P. Wavell to Prime Minister   *23rd April, 1941, 0916 hrs.*
Most grateful for your great effort. All preparations will be made to place tanks in action at earliest possible date after arrival and plans will be submitted.

You will like to know that South Africa had already offered us invaluable aid in technical personnel for our workshops.

Garrison Tobruk, our force in Sollum and air force are inflicting severe casualties on enemy in Western Desert. Enemy air force has however sunk three ships in Tobruk harbour and we shall have difficulty there. . . .

This was the most testing phase so far of Wavell's whole time as a fighting commander; but his opponent Rommel too was extended to his utmost. He had embarrassed his High Command, who thought he had gone too far, far too fast; they could offer him little or no substantial help to go further; the most they could or would do was to try to save him from retreat and defeat. On 27th April their emissary, General Paulus, arrived at Rommel's headquarters, sent, as General Halder noted in his diary, because he was "perhaps the only man with enough influence to head off this soldier gone stark mad."³ His task was to send back a clear picture of the situation, assess the chances of a successful defensive should Sollum be lost, try to discover Rommel's intentions, and make him understand that there were very few resources from which he could be sent any further help.⁴ On the same day Wavell ended a signal to the C.I.G.S. with these words: "I must confess that German performance so often exceeds calculations that I am not confident that Germans will not improve on our estimate of their abilities. They began an advance yesterday evening from Sollum area which would not be justified by what we believe to be their supply situation."

Wavell's assessment coincided closely with that of the German High Command. The Italian High Command, for its part, was both scared and angry. Paulus, arriving in the middle of the Sollum advance (which Gott's scratch force dealt with firmly), found that an attack on Tobruk was planned for 30th April, and flatly refused to sanction it until he had investigated the whole situation for himself. Two days later he gave it his approval, as did General Gariboldi, the Italian who was nominally C.-in-C. of all Axis forces in North Africa.

The attack was launched on the night of 30th April/1st May, and the fighting, which was fierce and dogged, lasted until the small hours of 4th May. Paulus watched the course of the battle with concern; when it was called off, various important positions in the Tobruk perimeter had changed hands more than once; Rommel had captured one excellent observation point, and penetrated the perimeter on a three-mile front to a depth of something under two miles. The Germans had about 650 casualties, the Italians 500. Paulus described the battle as "an important success"; but he ordered that the attack was not to be renewed unless the garrison evacuated the fortress of their own accord. *Afrika Korps'* principal task, he said, was now to hold Cyrenaica, regardless of who held Sollum, Bardia, or even Tobruk. He communicated these decisions to the High Command, in a cipher which had lately been broken in London.

Prime Minister to A. P. Wavell　　　　　*5th May, 1941, 0405 hrs.*
Have you read my telegram of 4th inst? Presume you realise the highly secret and authoritative character of this information? Actual text is more impressive than paraphrase showing enemy "thoroughly exhausted" unable pending arrival of 15th Panzer Division and of reinforcements to do more than hold ground gained at Tobruk and assigning as main task of Africa Corps retention of Cyrenaica with or without Tobruk, Sollum, Bardia. Also definite forbidding of any advance beyond Sollum except for reconnaissance without permission.

This condition of enemy only bears out what you believed would be brought upon him by supply difficulties and his premature audacious advance. Severe fighting which has attended his attacks on Tobruk imposes utmost strain on troops in this plight. It would seem to me judging from here important not to allow fighting round Tobruk to die down, but to compel enemy to fire his ammunition and use up his strength by counter-attacks. For this purpose trust you will consider reinforcing Tobruk as well as harrying enemy about Sollum. It seems to me that if you leave him quiet he will gather supplies and strength for a [forward?] move but if he is continuously engaged now, his recovery will be delayed and perhaps prevented.

This was only the first part of a most important signal. The convoy which had been ordered to go through the Mediterranean bore the code name "Tiger," and consisted of five 15-knot cargo ships, escorted by Admiral Somerville's "Force H" (*Renown*, *Malaya*, the aircarft carrier *Ark Royal* and the cruiser *Sheffield*). It was due to pass Gibraltar on 6th May. A smaller convoy, with the code name "Jaguar," was also taking vital supplies to Malta. The Prime Minister was sharply conscious of the administrative battle he had had to fight to get these convoys on the move, and of the risks that were being run. Though he was generous in praise of the way in which Tobruk was being held, and eager that Rommel should be given no respite there, he was anxious to know how soon the precious supplies which "Tiger" was bringing would be brought into action, and pressed Wavell for detailed information about his plans. He reminded him that he had close on half a million men under his command, and asserted that there could not be more than 25,000 Germans in Africa. If Wavell delayed until he was quite ready, Rommel might be ready too, and victory, "now not far off," might recede indefinitely. He concluded with a message for Morshead in Tobruk: "The whole Empire is watching your steadfast and spirited defence of this important outpost Egypt with gratitude and admiration."

A. P. Wavell to Prime Minister   *5th May, 1941, 1405 hrs.*

I saw the secret message yesterday and at once ordered Creagh to visit Beresford-Peirse and discuss possibility using all available tanks for offensive operation. He will return this evening and report. Possibility depends largely on air support available.

Have lately reinforced Tobruk with some "I" tanks. Have sent special message Commander to inform him of enemy situation. Reinforcement of Tobruk not easy owing constant attacks on harbour. Attack in Sollum area may be more effective if it can be staged.

I have already issued orders for offensive in Western Desert at earliest possible date to be prepared on assumption "Tiger" successful.

Iraq commitment is worrying me more than anything at present and I have gravest doubts about this and about its effect on Egypt and Palestine. Crete, Cyprus and Syria are also potential dangers.

My numbers may be impressive on paper but equipment still

very short, particularly A.F.V.s, A.A. guns and transport. . . .

Prime Minister to A. P. Wavell   *7th May, 1941, 2340 hrs.*
I told them to send by the most secret method the actual text of
message to which I referred in my telegram of 4th May. You
and your generals alone can judge the tactical possibilities whether
at Sollum or Tobruk. But if "Tiger" comes through it will be a
moment to do and dare. I am asking for a rapid transfer from
Malta of Hurricanes to your Command once the "Tiger's" tail is
clear. The Hun people are far less dangerous once they lose the
initiative. All our thoughts are with you. . . .

Wavell wrote: "I always disliked Iraq—the country, the people and
the military commitment. . . . It blew up at the worst possible time
for me, when I had the Western Desert, Crete, East Africa and
Syria on my hands, and no troops."

Iraq was a country of major strategic importance, which since
1930 had been an independent and sovereign Arab State, linked to
Great Britain by a treaty ensuring to the latter a number of important
military facilities: the maintenance of a large air base at Habbaniya,
some fifty miles west of Baghdad, and in the event of an emergency
the use of ports, railways, roads, airfields and all means of communication to ensure the passage of troops across the country.

At the beginning of 1941 the only Iraqi elder statesman who
was liked and trusted by the British, Nuri Pasha es Said, was losing
influence steadily. The King, Feisal II, was a little boy whose powers
were exercised by a Regent, his uncle Prince Abdulillah, also a steadfast friend of the British. But the dominant politician in Baghdad at
this time, one Rashid Ali el Gailani, was in close and frequent touch
with Axis agents, and was deeply under the influence of the former
leader of the Palestine Rebellion, Haj Amin el Husseini, who had
taken refuge in Iraq, and had there set up a centre of anti-British
intrigue and propaganda.

The R.A.F. had their base at Habbaniya, its hangars housing a
handful of elderly training aircraft; and there were no British troops
at all in the country. There was in existence, however, a plan, called
"Sabine," for the occupation of the port of Basra in order to protect
the oilfields and installations of south-west Persia and the Gulf, to be
carried out by an expeditionary force of three Indian divisions under

the control, initially, of Army Headquarters (India). The operational role of this force, as part of Wavell's Command, was left undecided.

When General Auchinleck became Commander-in-Chief in India at the beginning of 1941, he at once appreciated that the fate of Iraq, of Persia and of the sheikhdoms of the Persian Gulf was his first and most pressing concern. Wavell, for his part, made no secret of his willingness to be rid of the commitment. He had no forces available to handle any threat militarily, and therefore got the Chiefs of Staff to agree that the worsening political situation should be dealt with by strong diplomatic action, supported by financial and economic pressure and propaganda.

Sir Kinahan Cornwallis, an able senior official with fifteen years' experience of Iraq, then doing routine work at the Foreign Office, was appointed Ambassador, but the vicissitudes of wartime travel prevented him from arriving in Baghdad until the beginning of April. By then much had happened. In March Rashid Ali, who had been out of office for some time but was in German pay, entered into an anti-British and anti-Regent conspiracy with three senior army officers—two divisional commanders and the commander of Iraq's mechanised troops—an association which became notorious as the "Golden Square." Axis pressure on the Iraqi Government increased rapidly, and so did the Golden Square's influence and appetite for power. Rashid Ali and the Foreign Minister, Tewfiq Suwaidi, were uncertain whether they should come out openly on the side of the Axis or keep some sort of relationship with the British. Axis offers of help became more insistent and more extravagant. There was a proposal that Germany should buy wool from Iraq and in return give the Iraqis arms and rolling stock. These approaches did not go unnoticed in Cairo, whither Auchinleck had sent for a conference on 15th March his own C.G.S., General Hutton, and the commander-designate of "Sabine," Major-General Quinan. These officers remained in Cairo until the end of the month.

On 31st March the Regent, forewarned of a plot to arrest him, escaped from Baghdad to Habbaniya; the R.A.F. flew him to Basra and he was given refuge in H.M.S. *Cockchafer*. On the night of 1st/2nd April the Golden Square mobilised their troops and compelled the Prime Minister, Taha el Hashimi, to resign. In the midst of this turmoil Sir Kinahan Cornwallis arrived to take up his post. On 3rd April Rashid Ali seized power in Baghdad and proclaimed himself chief of a Government of National Defence. The Chiefs of Staff in

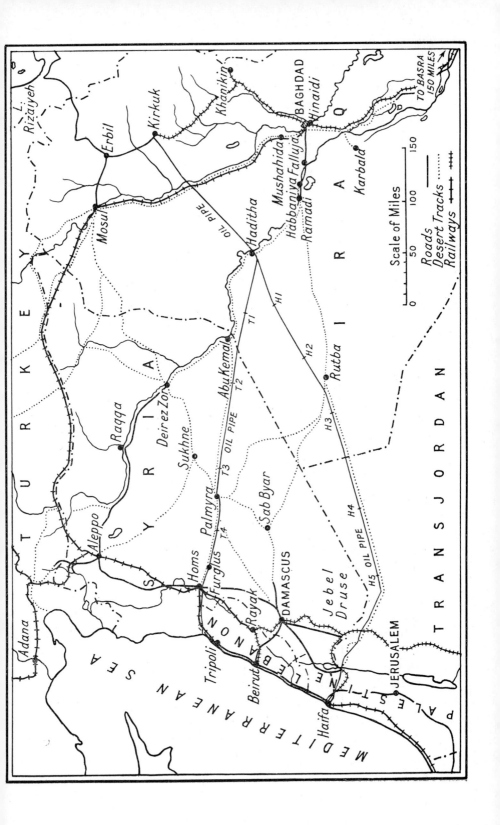

London were in favour of rapid armed intervention; so, from their Indian standpoint, were the Viceroy, Lord Linlithgow, and Auchinleck. But London insisted that the intervention should be made by Middle East Command, and under Wavell's tactical as well as strategic control, despite the fact that this was the week in which Rommel made his lightning advance, Generals O'Connor, Neame and Gambier-Parry were taken prisoner, and the Germans launched their attack on Greece and Yugoslavia.

On 8th April Auchinleck sent a private and personal signal to Wavell telling him, unofficially, of proposals devised by the Viceroy and himself which the Secretary of State for India was to put to the War Cabinet on the following day. They were: first, to send at once to Basra a force of an infantry brigade and a field regiment of artillery, at that moment in ships in Karachi destined for Malaya; second, to send off, within three weeks, two more brigades and all the base troops needed to bring the force in Basra up to the strength of one division; third, to send some 400 British infantry, with twelve light machine guns and six Vickers guns, by air to Shaiba, in a move that would begin on 13th April and take seven to eleven days to complete.

The War Cabinet gratefully accepted India's offer on 10th April, and asked that the force should go at once to Basra and Shaiba. On the same day Wavell signalled Auchinleck: "This proposal involves critical decision. It is just probable that this force might suffice to swing scale in Iraq. I am fully committed in Cyrenaica and in Greece and can spare nothing for Iraq. Longmore could spare squadron Wellingtons temporarily to support landing at Basra in addition to air force already in Iraq."

In Baghdad Rashid Ali played for time, and so did Cornwallis. When Rashid Ali made a speech in the Iraqi Senate, declaring that he intended to honour international law and obligations and to abide by the Anglo-Iraqi Treaty in both letter and spirit, Cornwallis advised that the move of the forces from Karachi should be held up. In London too there were plenty of second thoughts. On 11th April the Chiefs of Staff asked Wavell to send "a sizeable force" from Palestine across the desert to Habbaniya, and the India Office signalled the Viceroy the Cabinet's acceptance of Cornwallis's advice.

From India Linlithgow retorted with vigour that to delay going to Basra would mean that the port would not be taken at all, and urged that the convoy should be allowed to move at once. In Cairo, Arthur Smith had to answer the Chiefs' of Staff signal, because Wavell had gone up to the Desert. He told London that the Palestine garrison —one battalion of infantry and the partially equipped Cavalry Division —was now so weak that it was impossible to send a sizeable force across the desert to Iraq as suggested.

During 12th April the Indian convoy sailed from Karachi, although the Chiefs of Staff did not signal their permission until the following day. On the 17th the first airborne troops (a detachment of the 1st King's Own Royal Regiment) and on the 18th the first sea-borne units—totalling one brigade group—made unopposed landings in Basra. Rashid Ali and the military clique who had kept him in office had been, for the moment, taken by surprise; and for the moment the British had the initiative. But when Cornwallis told Rashid Ali on 28th April that the second convoy from India was due to arrive at Basra the following day, he precipitated a major explosion. Rashid Ali had, three days earlier, signed a secret treaty with Italian and German representatives in Baghdad, guaranteeing him large-scale financial aid in a war against the British Empire, and the recognition of a United Kingdom of Syria and Iraq under the King of Iraq; he was therefore adamant in his refusal to permit the disembarkation of the troops in this convoy. Cornwallis warned him of the serious consequences of his attitude, but without any marked effect.

R.A.F. headquarters at Habbaniya sent out an ominous report on 29th April:

> Situation grave . . . Ambassador under impression Iraqi attitude is not bluff and may mean definite promise Axis support. Unmistakable signs treaty may be repudiated. Ambassador asking Rashid Ali this morning for safe conduct women and children from Baghdad to Habbaniya with further evacuation by air to Basra and thence by air to India. Three D.C.2 aircraft now transporting troops Habbaniya are being retained for this purpose.[5]

During that afternoon about 240 British women and children were sent to Habbaniya by road, under safe conduct. Then the road was closed because there were large-scale Iraqi troop movements along it. Tempers rose in Baghdad itself; some 350 British subjects, of many races, took refuge in the British Embassy, and the American Legation gave shelter to about 150 more. Rashid Ali had decided to make life as difficult as possible for the Embassy, which was put virtually under siege, and to deliver an outright attack on Habbaniya. The total number in the R.A.F. station and cantonment there was just over 2,200 fighting men and some 9,000 civilians. The A.O.C., Air Vice-Marshal H. G. Smart, had no artillery at his disposal; of his 82 aircraft all were either obsolete or of a purely training type, with the exception of six Gladiators which had arrived as a reinforcement earlier in the month. He had 12 R.A.F. armoured cars; and on 27th April three hundred of the K.O.R.R. were flown up from Shaiba. Command of the ground forces was assumed by Colonel Ouvry Roberts, of the staff of 10th Indian Division, who flew up from Basra to examine the situation and decided to remain.

On 30th April the plateau overlooking the airfield and the camp was occupied by Iraqi forces; by midday these numbered some 9,000 men, with 50 guns. The next two days "were spent in fruitless parleys, and at dawn on 2nd May fighting began."[6] On this same day, General Quinan arrived in Basra to take over command of project "Sabine." He brought with him a directive from Auchinleck, whose first two sentences read: "You will command all British Empire land forces in Iraq from the time of your arrival. You will be under my orders." London's reaction was swift.

Chiefs of Staff to A. P. Wavell   *2nd May, 1941, 2215 hrs.*
(Repeated to C.-in-C. in India)
In view of situation in Iraq which is not that which we visualised when India took responsibility it seems operational command should now pass temporarily to Mideast whence alone immediate assistance can be given. This will take place forthwith unless you see strong objections. . . .

Thus the control of a crucial operation was precipitately transferred from the commander who had both the will and the forces (though not all the weapons and equipment) to exercise it effectively to one who was most evidently reluctant to assume it, whose forces on several other fronts were strained to the limit, and who was himself extremely tired. Auchinleck's assessment of the situation, and his proposals for grappling with it, approximated much more closely to those of the War Cabinet and the Chiefs of Staff than did Wavell's. Yet they clung to Wavell and loaded him with a burden he did not want to bear.

C.-in-C. in India to Chiefs of Staff   *2nd May, 1941*
We concur with the temporary transfer of operational command

but request higher operational control by Middle East so far as it affects situation at Basra may be exercised through this head-quarters. No objection however to direct communication Middle East to Basra.[7]

Wavell's answer was by no means so amenable. He was out in the Western Desert during the morning of 2nd May, and was keenly aware of the weight and ferocity of Rommel's latest attempt to storm Tobruk, which was in full progress.

A. P. Wavell to Chiefs of Staff   *3rd May, 1941*
I have consistently warned you that no assistance could be given to Iraq from Palestine in present circumstances and have always advised that commitment in Iraq should be avoided.

Nothing short of immediate action by at least a brigade group with strong support of artillery and A.F.V.s could restore situation. There are no guns or A.F.V.s in Palestine and to send forward weak and unsupported forces of cavalry or infantry seems merely asking for further trouble.

My forces are stretched to limit everywhere and I simply cannot afford to risk part of forces on what cannot produce any effect.

I do not see how I can possibly accept military responsibility for force at Basra of whose disposition and strength I am unaware, and consider this must be controlled from India.

I can only advise negotiation with Iraqis on basis of liquidation of regrettable incident by mutual agreement with alternative of war with British Empire, complete blockade and ruthless air action.

Longmore has seen this cable and agrees there is no alternative to above.

Three hours later, having thought it all over, and having talked to Arthur Smith, Wavell sent off another signal, setting out his ideas on accomplishing the impossible. He said he would do what he could to impress the Iraqi Government with apparent preparations for large-scale action from Palestine; he would try to improvise a force consisting of a mechanised brigade out of the Cavalry Division, a field artillery regiment less one troop, and not available for another six days, and an infantry battalion lifted in trucks. The headquarters and three mechanised squadrons of the Transjordan Frontier Force were also available; but their loyalty in an attack on their Iraqi Moslem brethren was something of a gamble. The force would have no armoured cars or tanks, and very few anti-aircraft or anti-tank guns; its departure would leave Palestine, where there was already incitement to rebellion, dangerously weak; and in his opinion it would be both inadequate and too late. He therefore suggested that a Turkish offer to mediate should be accepted and the co-operation of the U.S.A. be obtained.

The impact of these telegrams in London was ineffaceable. Dill's reaction was concern; the Prime Minister's was anger, all the deeper for having to be bottled up for the moment. An agitated week-end passed slowly.

A. P. Wavell to C.I.G.S.   *4th May, 1941, 1724 hrs.*
MOST IMMEDIATE—CLEAR THE LINE
No reply yet received to my [first signal to the C.O.S.], and am not clear as to intentions of War Cabinet. Is it proposed to accept Turkish or Egyptian mediation?

Chiefs of Staff (No. 88) to A. P. Wavell   *4th May, 1941, 1935 hrs.*
1. We much deplore extra burden thrown upon you at this critical time by events in Iraq. A commitment in Iraq was however inevitable. It was essential for us to establish a base at Basra and to put ourselves in control of port of Basra and to be ready to safeguard Iranian oil in case of need. . . . Had we sent no forces to Basra the present situation at Habbaniya might still have arisen under Axis direction. . . .
2. With reference to your reluctance to assume responsibility for operations in Basra, the Iraq problem is admittedly divided by geography into (*a*) Basra and (*b*) Habbaniya and oil. Control of operations in northern area must be in your hands as help can only come from Mideast. . . . This responsibility cannot be divided and orders will therefore be given by C.-in-C. direct to General Basra, C.-in-C. India being kept informed.
3. There can be no question of accepting Turkish offer of mediation. For reasons in para. 1 above we can make no concessions. . . . Essential that we should do all in our power (*a*) to restore situation at Habbaniya and (*b*) to place ourselves in a position to control pipeline to Mediterranean. Nothing in way of a demonstration is likely to be effective, and positive action as soon as forces can be made available will be necessary.

4. Your actions will therefore now be directed to implement the following policy:

(a) The active defence of Habbaniya must be maintained by all possible means.

(b) Preparations for sending a force to restore situation as given in para. 3 above must be pressed on. . . .

(c) Our Ambassador in Iraq is being instructed to continue to exercise all possible pressure on Iraqi Government. For this purpose he can threaten the following action should situation develop into active war:

(1) Air bombardment of Baghdad.
(2) Destruction of Akrutiyah dam (we are advised this is possible by air action).
(3) Destruction of oil pumping stations.
(4) Complete blockade of Basra. . . .

This signal reached Cairo in the small hours of 5th May. It did not take Wavell long to digest its meaning. He and the War Cabinet and the Chiefs of Staff were dangerously near being at loggerheads. His answer revealed a sense of strain almost too great to be borne.

A. P. Wavell to Chiefs of Staff   *5th May, 1941, 1018 hrs.*
Your 88 takes little account of realities. You must face facts.

I am arranging to assemble at H.4,[8] near Transjordan—Iraq frontier, force consisting of following: mechanised cavalry brigade (incomplete), one field regiment (less one troop), R.A.F. armoured cars (15), three squadrons Transjordan Frontier Force, 1st Essex Regiment. It cannot be assembled before 10th May at earliest and could not reach Habbaniya till two days later even if no resistance met at Rutbah or elsewhere.

Very doubtful whether above force strong enough to relieve Habbaniya or whether Habbaniya can prolong resistance till its arrival. I am afraid I can only regard it as outside chance.

I feel it my duty to warn you in gravest possible terms that I consider prolongation of fighting in Iraq will seriously endanger defence of Palestine and Egypt. Apart from the weakening of strength by detachments such as above, political repercussions will be incalculable and may result in what I have spent nearly two years trying to avoid, serious internal trouble in our bases.

I therefore urge again most strongly that settlement should be negotiated as early as possible. . . .

As regards para. 4 (c), I feel that particular threats are most unwise unless they can be carried out in decisive fashion. Surely threat of war with British Empire is most effective.

Will do my best to control Basra situation, where fighting appears to have broken out, and am sending liaison officer to ascertain situation as soon as possible. I still feel that India, where reinforcement possibilities are known and whence force is maintained, is better place to exercise effective control.

This telegram arrived in London at much the same time as one from Auchinleck offering reinforcements up to a total of five infantry brigades and ancillary troops by 10th June if shipping could be provided. Churchill was "not content" with Wavell's, but "gratified" by Auchinleck's. The signs of a swift switch of favour began to be ominous; they were to multiply rapidly in the next few weeks. Meanwhile Wavell girded himself for his unwelcome, thankless task.

A. P. Wavell to C.I.G.S.   *5th May, 1941, 1725 hrs.*
Nice baby you have handed me on my fifty-eighth birthday. Have always hated babies and Iraqis but will do my best for the little blighter. Am hatching minor offensive in Western Desert but not sure yet can bring it off.

In the War Office on the morning of 6th May, when Kennedy went in to see Dill the C.I.G.S. said, "There is a serious matter to be settled to-day. The Prime Minister wants to sack Wavell and put Auchinleck into the Middle East." Dill told Kennedy that he intended to say that, since Churchill had obviously lost confidence in Wavell, it would be right to get rid of him; that he himself had not lost confidence, but that it was Churchill whose opinion mattered.[9]

However, before this issue came up for discussion, the Chiefs of Staff had in front of them a minute from the Prime Minister, demanding that the telegrams from Wavell and Auchinleck be considered and reported upon forthwith. Churchill was scornful of all Wavell's arguments—"Fancy having kept the Cavalry Division in Palestine all this time without having the rudiments of a mobile column organised!" —and declared that he seemed to have been taken as much by surprise on his eastern as on his western flank and that, in spite of the enormous number of men at his disposal and the great convoys reaching him, he seemed to be hard up for battalions and companies. While Auchin-leck's proposals for reinforcing Basra deserved most favourable consideration, Wavell "gives me the impression of being tired out."[10]

At noon that day Churchill brought the question of Iraq before the War Cabinet. The following orders were sent:

C.O.S. to A. P. Wavell and others concerned   *6th May, 1941*
Your telegram of yesterday has been considered by Defence Committee. Settlement by negotiation cannot be entertained except on the basis of a climb down by Iraqis, with safeguard against future Axis designs on Iraq.

Realities of the situation are that Rashid Ali has all along been hand in glove with Axis Powers, and . . . was merely waiting until they could support him before exposing his hand. Our arrival at Basra forced him to go off at half-cock before the Axis were ready. Thus there is an excellent chance of restoring the situation by bold action if it is not delayed.

Chiefs of Staff have therefore advised Defence Committee that they are prepared to accept responsibility for despatch of the force specified in your telegram at the earliest possible moment. They would like to see some light tanks and Bofors added if possible but there should be no delay on this account. Telegraph Command arrangements.

Defence Committee direct that A.O.C. Iraq should be informed that he will be given assistance and in the meanwhile it is his duty to defend Habbaniya to the last.

Subject to security of Egypt being maintained, maximum air support possible should be given to operation in Iraq. . . .[11]

The tone of a simultaneous signal to the Commander-in-Chief in India was far more cordial, and was yet another indication of the change in Churchill's feelings.

C.O.S. to C.-in-C. in India   *6th May, 1941*
Your bold and generous offer greatly appreciated. Please prepare forces as a matter of urgency. Notify dates by which they will be ready to sail and we will confirm before despatch.

Wavell had no inkling of the Prime Minister's intentions so far as he himself was concerned, though a shrewd comprehension of his general sentiments. But two telegrams which he despatched in the course of this stormy Monday brought the temperature down when they were received in London.

A. P. Wavell to C.I.G.S.   *6th May, 1941*
Concentration of Habforce for relief of Habbaniya proceeding as rapidly as possible. Have ordered immediate occupation of Rutbah to be attempted, it seems to be only lightly held. Situation at Habbaniya apparently stable and signs that enemy may be short of gun ammunition and waiting Axis aid. . . .

A. P. Wavell to C.O.S.   *6th May, 1941*
Now that Iraqi force appears to have withdrawn from Habbaniya require urgently guide to policy. Is R.A.F. to continue attacking military objectives throughout Iraq? Have no knowledge situation Baghdad, is Rashid's Government still in power and is there any sign of change of attitude? A.O.C.-in-C.[12] is issuing instructions to confine air action to Iraqi aerodromes and troops in immediate neighbourhood Habbaniya, Shaiba or Basra.

Habforce will advance to Habbaniya as soon as assembled. H.3 already in our hands.[13]

And at the end of the day Dill responded to his friend's birthday signal.

C.I.G.S. to A. P. Wavell   *6th May, 1941, 2000 hrs.*
What a birthday present. Sincerely hope that you will be able to kill the little brute. Many happy returns of birthday but not of baby.

Meanwhile, the defenders of Habbaniya, with a great display of courage, initiative and resourcefulness, had supplied the War Cabinet, as well as the headquarters in Cairo and in Delhi, with the intensely welcome surprise to which Wavell's telegrams referred. Their action without doubt turned the tide in Iraq and prevented the country, its oil resources, and its access to the Persian Gulf, from falling under Axis control. It was an important little battle.

At 0245 hours on the morning of 2nd May Air Vice-Marshal Smart, the Air Officer Commanding in Iraq, informed the local Iraqi commander that if his forces were not withdrawn forthwith, air action would be taken immediately. There was no response to this ultimatum. So:

In the half-light which preceded the dawn ... every aircraft which could be coaxed into the air taxied out to the runways and took off to attack the Iraqi positions. ... Orders were to drive the Iraqi forces beyond artillery range of the cantonment, and targets were given the following priority: guns, tanks, armoured cars, transport, troops.[14]

Thirty-two of the quaintly assorted aircraft from Habbaniya were joined by eight Wellingtons from Shaiba. At 0500 hours they began to bomb the Iraqis on the plateau; and less than a minute later the first Iraqi shells hit the cantonment. The battle continued throughout that day and for three days thereafter. On the first day there were 193 R.A.F. sorties; five of the Flying School's aircraft were destroyed and several others put out of action. During the morning Iraqi Air Force fighters joined in, without much effect. Inside the cantonment the artillery bombardment killed thirteen and wounded twenty-nine, of whom nine were civilians. Unpleasant as this was, it was a good deal less effective than had been anticipated. But the well-camouflaged Iraqi guns on the plateau did not appear to have suffered much damage, and their infantry, though they had "sat in their trenches keeping their heads well down," [15] had not shown any signs of withdrawing and were now up to brigade strength.

However, Smart went boldly on with his offensive next day and directed a proportion of his effort against the Iraqi Air Force and the Army's line of communication. Rashid airfield, outside Baghdad, and the Baghdad-Falluja road were bombed; and there were renewed attacks on the Iraqi guns and vehicles on the plateau. After forty-eight hours more of this aggressive defence—in the course of which Blenheims and Hurricanes, newly arrived from Egypt, made low-level machine-gun attacks on the airfield at Mosul, where the *Luftwaffe* (coming from the Balkans and the Dodecanese through Aleppo in Syria) had established a small detachment—the Iraqis had had enough. The Axis support for which they had asked had not been given; there was discouragement in Baghdad; and during the night of 5th/6th May, after a raid on their trenches by patrols of the K.O.R.R., the ground troops withdrew from the plateau at Habbaniya, leaving large quantities of badly needed arms and equipment. During the morning the R.A.F. armoured cars, the levies and the K.O.R.R. went into action, with effective close support by aircraft of the Flying School, against the Iraqi forces on the Falluja road. The Iraqis fled in disorder;

twelve of their officers and three hundred other ranks were taken prisoner. In the afternoon a new column was observed moving up from Falluja; it was "met with a low bombing and machine-gunning attack by forty aircraft. A welter of exploding ammunition and burning lorries was left behind and many more prisoners were taken. This was the end of the siege."[16]

Prime Minister to A.O.C.-in-C. Iraq   *7th May, 1941*
Your vigorous and splendid action has largely restored the situation. We are all watching the grand fight you are making. All possible aid will be sent. Keep it up.[17]

Churchill wrote: "Although I realised his cares and his devotion, I continued to press General Wavell hard."[18]

During Wednesday, 7th May, no fewer than four imperative telegrams, all marked "Most Immediate," three of them (of considerable length) from the Chiefs of Staff and one (much shorter) from Churchill himself, were sent to Wavell, giving him explicit instructions which he simply had not the means to follow.

In India, the course of events was watched with increasing concern. There ensued a triangular telegraphic debate between London, Cairo and Simla. A series of long signals was exchanged, which made it clear that the War Cabinet, though determined to avoid a repetition of the Mesopotamia campaign of World War I, liked and sympathised with Auchinleck's vigorous outlook; that Wavell fully shared the War Cabinet's sentiments about Mesopotamia and, aware of his military weakness, strove to discover a political solution to the Iraq issue; and that the desire for a political solution was shared and energetically canvassed by civilian and military Middle East experts both in London and in Cairo. A workable compromise between this mixture of ideas and aims had to be evolved, and it was apparent that a big step towards achieving that compromise would be an early meeting between Wavell and Auchinleck, if possible at Basra.

Prime Minister to A. P. Wavell   *13th May, 1941, 0205 hrs.*
About Iraq—you do not need to bother too much about long future. Your immediate task is to get a friendly Government set up in Baghdad and to beat down Rashid Ali's forces with utmost vigour. . . . What matters is action, namely the swift advance mobile column to establish effective contact between Baghdad and Palestine. Every day counts, for Germans may not be long. We

hoped . . . that column would be ready to move 10th and would reach Habbaniya 12th, assuming Habbaniya could hold out, which they have done and a good deal more. We trust that you will do your utmost to accelerate this movement.[19]

A. P. Wavell to Prime Minister   *13th May, 1941, 1740 hrs.*
We will do our best to liquidate this tiresome Iraq business quickly. Shortage of transport is causing difficulty. Flying column should reach Ramadie and Falluja which may make it difficult to approach Baghdad. German Air Force now about to take hand, hope R.A.F. can arrange to deal with them. Am sending my C.G.S. to Basra tomorrow to see G.O.C. Will try to meet Auchinleck later but do not like leaving here at present.

Meanwhile the situation in Iraq looked uglier. German aircraft, with Aleppo as their staging-post, had begun to operate more freely. They made more than one attack on Habforce, which had begun its eastward march on 12th May. On the following day an advance party of the *Luftwaffe*, headed by Major Axel von Blomberg, the son of the German field-marshal, flew to Baghdad. Rashid Ali, his Ministers and a number of other notables waited on the airfield to welcome the Major. As his Heinkel came in to land, some Iraqi police levies, who had been posted as airfield defence troops but whom nobody had bothered to brief, opened fire on it. One chance shot killed von Blomberg. The result was that the Germans did not establish themselves in Baghdad, but operated only from Mosul, and then in no great strength. The R.A.F. dealt more than adequately with the task of attacking them and preventing their being supplied by rail from Syria. The advance guard of Habforce reached Habbaniya on 18th May. On the next day they and the ground forces of the Habbaniya garrison sallied out to attack Falluja, around which the Iraqis had done extensive flooding. There was a day of hard fighting, at the end of which the Iraqis withdrew, leaving a number of casualties; some 300 prisoners were taken.

On 14th May Arthur Smith flew to Basra and saw Quinan. Wavell signalled the C.I.G.S. on the 16th that Quinan saw quite clearly that his first task was to secure Basra as a base, and that any premature move northwards would be dangerous, and he added that in any case extensive flooding in the Tigris plain made it impracticable during the next three months.

A week after Arthur Smith's visit, Wavell himself went to Basra to his first meeting with Auchinleck—of only a few hours' duration, but friendly and fruitful. They agreed on the text of a telegram which he sent as soon as he got back to Cairo.

A. P. Wavell to C.I.G.S.   *25th May, 1941, 0902 hrs.*
From discussion with Auchinleck it is obvious that we regard Iraq from somewhat different angles. My main task, defence of Egypt and Palestine, would be made more difficult but would not be greatly jeopardised by hostile control of Iraq, whereas hostile control of Syria would affect me much more closely and danger-ously. So long as my resources are inadequate I am bound to be influenced by the closer and more threatening danger. India on the other hand regard Iraq as absolutely vital outpost of their de-fence since they consider that hostile Iraq would mean hostile Iran and Afghanistan and compromise whole defence of Indian Empire. From point of view of greater interest it seems there-fore desirable that India should control operations in Iraq.

Middle East is already fully occupied with Western Desert campaign, defence of Crete, danger to Syria and Cyprus, besides East Africa campaign.

Troops in Iraq are mainly Indian, maintenance must be from India and administration can more easily be done from India.

In theory there is advantage in allotment of equipment being controlled by Mideast but at present there is difficulty and waste of time since Mideast itself is so short of equipment and there is no means of sending equipment to Indian troops in Iraq except by sea from Suez to Basra, possibly via India.

From political point of view it is better that all Arab affairs should be under one control, which can only be Mideast, also if Iraq becomes line of communication to Turkey there are advan-tages in Mideast, which must be closely concerned with Turkish operations, exercising control. By good liaison, however, both above difficulties could probably be overcome if India took over Iraq.

To sum up, it seems that in view of her greater interest and greater stake in Iraq operations, India should resume control as soon as possible. This seems to be when force at Basra is in position to control and maintain operations from Habbaniya against Baghdad, and this can presumably only be when communications can be established between Basra and Habbaniya.

On the night of 27th May the advance on Baghdad from Falluja—only 25 miles away—began, but made slow progress, being impeded by extensive inundations and blown-up bridges over the many irrigation canals. The R.A.F. destroyed the remnants of the *Luftwaffe* at Mosul and elsewhere in the north. Quinan, obeying the instructions issued to him after the Commanders-in-Chief had their meeting, moved quickly northwards up the Tigris to the capital.

Rashid Ali's nerve collapsed. Even the Axis money—a milliard lire of which (under the terms of the secret treaty) would have gone straight into his own pocket—had turned out to be fairy gold, and he had been denied the Axis military advice and aid on which he had relied. On the night of 29th/30th May a party of fugitives crossed the frontier into Persia; they included Rashid Ali, thirty of his closest associates, the German and Italian Ministers, and the ex-Mufti of Jerusalem. The Mayor of Baghdad took over the Administration and sued for an immediate armistice. At six o'clock on the morning of 31st May an Iraqi deputation bearing a flag of truce was met in the outskirts of the city by the commander of Habforce, Major-General Clark, Smart's successor, Air Vice-Marshal D'Albiac, and Major Glubb, the commander of the Arab Legion, a detachment of which had joined Habforce. A car was sent to fetch Sir Kinahan Cornwallis; the siege of the Embassy was lifted. An armistice was signed at three o'clock that afternoon. A new Administration took office, under a pro-British Prime Minister, and the Regent returned. The episode was over.

It would be facile to dismiss the Iraq campaign as a simple case of all's well that ends well. Disaster would have resulted if it had not ended well: Egypt and Palestine, whose defence Wavell maintained as his first priority, would have been outflanked; and the Axis Powers would have had control of the main sources of British and Commonwealth oil. Churchill wrote: "Hitler certainly cast away the opportunity of taking a great prize for little cost in the Middle East. We in Britain, although pressed to the extreme, managed with scant forces to save ourselves from far-reaching and lasting injury."[20]

Hitler, however, had his mind elsewhere.

445

Chiefs of Staff to C.s-in-C. Middle East 31st May, 1941, 2245 hrs.
We have had firm indication that Germans are now concentrating large army and air forces against Russia.

Under this threat they will probably demand concessions most injurious to us. If the Russians refuse the Germans will march.

Russian resistance may be strongly influenced if they think that should they submit to Germans we shall attack Baku oil.

If we are to use this threat to exert pressure on Russians we must control Mosul before Russians and/or Germans can forestall us.

Most energetic action should therefore be taken to get control in Mosul. Can you devise method to achieve this? Small airborne force might suffice.

Wavell's final verdict on the Iraq episode fully agreed with Churchill's:

"I was inclined to accept the Turkish offer of mediation. But Winston quite rightly refused to have anything to do with it and said we must deal with the matter by our own military force. . . . I told Winston that I was doubtful whether the force ordered across to Habbaniya was strong enough to effect its purpose, and it would leave me without any reserve whatsoever for any eventuality in Syria. He ordered me to send it, a bold and correct decision, which I always felt I really ought to have taken myself."

The real lessons which the Iraqi episode ought to have driven home were those of strategy and high policy, which the Prime Minister disregarded, making instead important but mistaken judgments about personalities. A chance had dissuaded him, at the outset of the affair, from relieving Wavell of his command forthwith; but such transient confidence as he had ever possessed in the officer from whom he had demanded so much, and who had given of his best again and again, was lost and irrecoverable. He wrote in after years:

Although no one was more pleased and relieved than Wavell himself, the episode could not pass without leaving impressions in his mind and in ours. At the same time General Auchinleck's forthcoming attitude in sending, at our desire, and with the Viceroy's cordial assent, the Indian division to Basra so promptly, and the readiness with which Indian reinforcements were supplied, gave us the feeling of a fresh mind and a hitherto untaxed personal energy.[21]

Churchill combined insatiable intellectual curiosity and energy with great initiative and powerful, often highly undisciplined emotions; once an emotional impulse had become fixed in him, it was extremely unlikely to be either changed or deflected. His emotions and his intuition led him now to certain quite firm but very wrong conclusions.

While Wavell was being harassed by the Iraq episode, he was also involved in the defence of Crete. This was the inevitable postscript to the Greek expedition; it was the last stand made by British and Commonwealth troops on European soil until they returned, more than two years later, by way of Sicily; and it was the first time that airborne troops were employed on any scale by either side.

The British code name for the Cretan campaign was "Scorcher," the German "*Merkür*" (Mercury). For it the German Command assembled, with great speed, immediately after the surrender of the Greek mainland, what proved to be their total airborne component. British Intelligence, excellently informed about many aspects of Germany's war objectives and fighting capacity, knew curiously little about the enemy's airborne formations. It was believed that the force assembled for "*Merkür*" might be one of half a dozen such units, and not until some months later was it known to be the only one—as Churchill said, "The spear-point of the German lance."[22]

It comprised the two *Fliegerkorps*, VIII and XI. The former provided most of the reconnaissance, and the fighter and bomber aircraft; the latter contained all the troops who were to be landed, whether by parachute, glider or transport aircraft, or from boats. These troops were the Assault Regiment (three battalions of parachute and one of glider troops) and the 7th Air Division of three parachute rifle regiments and divisional troops. Attached were three rifle regiments, specially trained for mountain warfare, and a number of other units including a Panzer battalion, a motor-cyclist battalion, and some A.A. detachments. They totalled some 22,000 men—"the flower of German manhood," Churchill called them, fanatical Nazis many of them, fiercely brave, and with their training tuned up to its highest pitch.

447

Prime Minister to A. P. Wavell   *28th April, 1941*

It seems clear from our information that a heavy airborne attack by German troops and bombers will soon be made on Crete. Let me know what forces you have in the island and what your plans are. It ought to be a fine opportunity for killing the parachute troops. The island must be stubbornly defended.

From the outset of the Middle East campaigns it had been recognised that Crete must be defended; but in a long list of urgent requirements it took a low priority. The Greeks, though cautious about British assistance on the mainland, were willing to be helped in the defence of Crete; and they admitted the importance of Suda Bay as a haven and fuelling base for the Royal Navy.

The Royal Marines were in process of building up a formation for this precise task, called the Mobile Naval Base Defence Organisation (M.N.B.D.O.), but it was still in England at the end of 1940, and the 14th Brigade of the still embryo 6th British Division was the only force stationed in the island. It was impossible to secure a senior commander, of the level of brigadier or above, to take permanent charge of the island's defences; several officers held the appointment for a few weeks and then were posted elsewhere. The more important the Greek expedition became, from the beginning of March onwards, the more difficult it was to give Crete the men, the guns and the equipment it needed.

It was true that the island presented formidable problems to any invader, and the Italians prudently confined themselves to air attack from the Dodecanese and one small, enterprising seaborne raid on Suda Bay. Crete is a lozenge-shaped island, 160 miles long and 40 miles across at its widest point. Its mountainous spine, with peaks rising to 7,000 feet, runs the entire length of the island; the northward slopes are gradual, but the southern face is steep and precipitous. The only ports fit for cargo ships are all on the north coast; in 1941, Suda could only handle two small ships at a time, and Heraklion, the chief commercial port, little more; at Canea and Retimo, ships had to discharge into lighters. The island as a whole was undeveloped. There were no railways; telecommunications were almost non-existent; the island's one main road, linking its ports, ran along the north coast, close to the sea almost the whole way. Its one airfield—Heraklion—and two landing grounds—Maleme and Retimo—were all near the road. One or two unmetalled cart tracks led across the

448

mountains to the high villages and down to the few fishing havens on the windswept, inhospitable southern shore. The Cretans are courageous, likeable and hardy, combining the characteristics of highlanders and islanders—volatile yet loyal, fierce in battle, kind and immensely hospitable. They numbered in 1941 some 400,000 souls; but the majority of their able-bodied men were in the Greek Army fighting in Albania.

Churchill said that the Middle East Command's preparations for the defence of Crete lacked plan and drive. Any amount of planning, any amount of drive could not have replaced the men who were training or fighting elsewhere, or the guns, the transport and the equipment which did not exist. "The responsibility for the defective study of the problem and for the feeble execution of the directions given," said Churchill, "must be shared between Cairo and Whitehall."[23] It may be added that nobody in authority in Whitehall knew anything about the problem; that nobody in Cairo had the time, in the huge onrush of events, to give it the careful and detailed attention and reflection it needed; and that, energetic as they were, the directions issued were for the most part impracticable. As late as 18th April, the Chiefs of Staff told the Commanders-in-Chief that Crete rated below the extrication of British and Imperial forces from Greece, the retention of Tobruk and the battle in Libya, and that the island was to be regarded primarily as a receptacle of whatever could be got there from Greece. Its fuller defences were to be organised later, and in the meantime all the forces that were there were bidden to protect themselves from bombing by dispersion and to use their bayonets against parachutists or airborne intruders, if any.

The Greek expeditionary force was rapidly evacuated. The King of Greece and a small staff were ferried to Crete. Some 26,000 of the men brought away from Greece were landed in the island, and swamped the 14th Infantry Brigade. Most of them had retained their own small arms and as much ammunition as they could carry; but there were a good many from administrative units with no arms and no equipment at all. There were no guns, but a good many gunners. There were R.A.S.C. drivers and maintenance men with no vehicles. Tools and signal equipment were very scarce. "In spite of competing claims in all directions the Middle East Command tried hard at the eleventh hour to make good the worst deficiencies, but here they were unlucky, for the ever-increasing air attacks caused the loss of some valuable cargoes, more especially in Suda Bay."[24] Fairly sizeable quantities of food were, however, safely carried to the large body of troops that had assembled in the island by the last days of April.

The M.N.B.D.O., after a long, circuitous passage from the United Kingdom, made a timely arrival at Suez on 21st April. Its commander, Major-General E. C. Weston, who had flown out in advance, was already in Crete; his force, which was to supply the hard core of the island's defence system, was hastily put on a combat footing. Maitland Wilson and Freyberg, evacuated from Greece, were both in the island. On 29th April, just twenty-four hours after Churchill's order to Wavell that Crete must be stubbornly defended, the Chiefs of Staff told him to instruct General Weston to signal his appreciation for its defence against airborne attack; they asked when M.N.B.D.O. would arrive and how soon the defences would be installed, and they requested a report on the state of the troops from Greece and of their arms.

Wavell gave an immediate, brief answer: Crete had been warned on 18th April of the possibility of airborne attack. The permanent garrison—three infantry battalions, two heavy and three light A.A. batteries and coast defence artillery—had now been augmented by at least 30,000 of all ranks evacuated from Greece; these were being organised to defend Suda Bay, Canea, Retimo and Heraklion; their morale was said to be good. The Mobile Naval Base Defence Organisation was due to reach the island during the first fortnight in May.

Wavell was in Crete on the morning of 30th April, and while he was conferring with Maitland Wilson, Freyberg and Weston in Canea, he was handed a signal, relayed from G.H.Q. The C.I.G.S., who had had doubts about Weston's fitness for this difficult command, suggested that Freyberg be appointed—a proposal which Wavell instantly accepted. He ordered Freyberg to take command forthwith of all troops in the island, including (at the request of the Greek Government) the Greeks.

He flew back to Egypt and spent the night in Alexandria with Admiral Cunningham. Freyberg meanwhile made a rapid survey of his new responsibility. On 1st May he signalled Wavell:

Forces at my disposal are totally inadequate to meet attack envisaged. Unless fighter aircraft are greatly increased and naval forces made available to deal with seaborne attack I cannot hope to hold out with land forces alone, which as result of campaign in Greece are now devoid of any artillery, have insufficient tools for digging, very little transport, and inadequate war reserves of equipment and ammunition. Force here can and will fight, but without full support from Navy and Air Force cannot hope to repel invasion. If for other reasons these cannot be made available at once, urge that question of holding Crete should be reconsidered. I feel that under terms of my charter it is my duty to inform New Zealand Government of situation in which greater part of my division is now placed.[25]

This warning, which it was Freyberg's constitutional duty to give, not unnaturally made the New Zealand Government profoundly anxious: was a Cretan catastrophe to follow immediately after the adventure on the Greek mainland? Mr. Peter Fraser, the Prime Minister, happened to be on his way to London via Cairo. Churchill sent him a long telegram on 3rd May intended to allay his and his Government's anxieties; and on the same day, having received from Wavell the assurance that, though the enemy's air superiority made the defence of Crete a problem for all three Services, "difficulties are being dealt with and will be overcome if we get time," he sent a personal signal to Freyberg: "Congratulate you on your vitally important Command. Feel confident your fine troops will destroy parachutists man to man at close quarters. Every good wish. Winston."

Two days passed in which Freyberg reached a fresh assessment of his situation.

General Freyberg to Prime Minister, United Kingdom   5th May, 1941
Cannot understand nervousness; am not in the least anxious about airborne attack; have made my dispositions and feel can cope adequately with troops at my disposal. Combination of seaborne and airborne attack is different. If that comes before I can get the guns and transport here the situation will be difficult. Even so, provided Navy can help, trust all will be well.

When we get our equipment and transport, and with a few extra fighter aircraft, it should be possible to hold Crete. Meanwhile there will be a period here during which we shall be vulnerable.

Everybody in great form and most anxious to renew battle with our enemy, whom we hammered whenever we met him in Greece.[26]

The Germans now began in earnest to assemble their forces for the assault on Crete. *Fliegerkorps VIII* had 228 bombers, 205 dive-bombers, 114 twin-engined and 119 single-engined fighters, and 50 reconnaissance aircraft—a total of 716. *Fliegerkorps XI* had more than 500 transport aircraft and 72 gliders. British Intelligence in London had detailed information about both the extent and the rapidity of these preparations. The Prime Minister was aflame with martial excitement: the more they came, the more there would be to kill.

C.O.S. to Commander-in-Chief   *9th May, 1941, 1635 hrs.*
Reference "Scorcher." So complete is our information that it appears to present heaven-sent opportunity of dealing enemy heavy blow. . . .

They followed this signal, ten hours later, by another which, while admitting ignorance of local conditions, put forward a number of detailed suggestions for implementing any plan that would inflict the maximum losses on the Germans. It crossed a telegram from Cairo, setting out the appreciation which had been demanded a week earlier.

Commanders-in-Chief to C.O.S.   *10th May, 1941, 0806 hrs.*
. . . Main threat comes from air. Enemy has ample strength . . . to maintain very heavy scale air attack on Crete, at same time continuing operations in strength against Malta, Cyrenaica, Egypt. . . . Adequate degree fighter protection Crete impracticable until further reinforcements arrive, and during this period use naval and air bases Crete liable to serious interruption. Heavy casualty rate aircraft Crete inevitable. Landing enemy airborne division and of seaborne expedition up to one division (supported by heavy air attack) is possibility which we are preparing to counter.

Estimated minimum land garrison three infantry brigade groups. . . . Propose eventually relieve Anzacs by British formations. Equipment being despatched Crete includes four 3.7 howitzers and number 75-mm. guns, 18 light and 6 Infantry tanks. A.A. defence will require eventually three heavy and two light batteries addition to present 16 heavy, 36 light guns and M.N. B.D.O. . . . Consider reasonable chance Suda Bay being sufficiently usable by Navy with one squadron Hurricanes with 100 per cent reserve pilots and replacement rate aircraft 100 per cent per month, but if enemy really concentrated on problem seems little doubt harbour could be rendered untenable. . . . Present air garrison for defence purposes is one fighter squadron Gladiators, a few Hurricanes and Fleet Air Arm fighters.

The total number of troops in Crete was now about 28,600. Those evacuated from Greece were in need of rest and reorganisation; their glaring shortages in arms and equipment have been noted. Mixed units were formed, armed and equipped with what was available. G.H.Q. hoped to be able to evacuate from the island before the Germans attacked as many men as could not usefully be employed in the defence; but shortage of shipping and of Royal Navy escorts seriously cut down the numbers lifted. There were also some 16,000 Italian prisoners of war, captured by the Greeks, under guard on the island.

Freyberg, in his subsequent report on the campaign to the New Zealand Government, stressed the fact that Wavell "did everything that was humanly possible to get us every available bit of equipment, artillery and defence stores."[27] By the time the attack came there were 32 heavy and 36 light A.A. guns on Crete, and 24 searchlights; and Middle East had no more A.A. reserves at all. Two more British infantry battalions were sent from Egypt; one reached the island on the day before the Germans attacked. After the evacuation of Greece some 15,000 tons of stores were put ashore, mostly by night. But half the guns and half the engineering material needed for defence works went down in ships bombed by the *Luftwaffe*. For the same reason only 3,000 tons of ammunition, out of 27,000 shipped, got through. And there was a glaring shortage of tanks.

Freyberg's own defence plan was a straightforward, hasty and simple improvisation, making the best of a very bad job. He organised four sectors, in an attempt to deny the Germans access to the air-fields, the adjacent beaches and the road, all on the north side of the island. The sectors were Heraklion, held by two British and three Greek battalions, 300 Australian riflemen, and 250 gunners armed as infantry; Retimo, with the H.Q. of the 19th Australian Infantry Brigade, four Australian battalions, and six Greek battalions; Suda Bay, with two improvised Australian battalions, 1,200 British riflemen from a variety of units, 106 Battery R.H.A. armed as infantry, and two Greek battalions; and Maleme, with two New Zealand brigades, an improvised brigade of New Zealanders and Greeks, and one Greek battalion. There were anti-aircraft guns at Suda Bay,

Maleme and Heraklion. The field artillery consisted of Italian guns intended for static defence only. There were two "I" tanks at each of the three airfields; three more "I" tanks were also sent to the island. From the outset, it was obvious to Freyberg, each of the three main groups, at Heraklion, at Retimo, and in the Suda Bay—Maleme area, would have to fight as a separate force.

On 11th May he handed a G.H.Q. liaison officer a staunchly cheerful letter to the Chief:

> . . . Given a little more time I am certain that we could make our position here a relatively strong one. I am certain that everybody will do their best and the morale is now high. If they come as an airborne attack against our aerodromes I feel sure we should be able to stop him if he attacks after the 16th.
>
> If however he makes a combined operation of it with a beach landing with tanks, then we shall not be in a strong position. . . . I know you will do all you can. . . .
>
> I am glad you think I inspire confidence. I appear at any rate to have a fatal habit of backing into the limelight. . . .

Churchill's strategic ideas may have been amateurish, his judgment on people and events often mercurial, and his attitude towards senior commanders ambivalent; but his courage and his zest in a dark time were matchless. On the night of 10th May London was heavily bombed; the House of Commons was completely shattered; Liverpool and other ports were savagely attacked. The immediate prospects were almost as bad as they had been a year earlier when he became Prime Minister. Yet in the middle of such a week he could send this signal bursting with gusto:

> *Prime Minister to A. P. Wavell*　　　　　　　*14th May, 1941*
> All my information points to "Scorcher" any day after 17th. Everything seems to be moving in concert for that and with great elaboration. Hope you have got enough in Colorado[28] and that those there have the needful in cannon, machine guns and A.F.V.s. . . . I should particularly welcome chance for our high-class troops to come to close grips with those people under conditions where enemy has not got his usual mechanical advantages and where we can surely reinforce much easier than he can. . . .

A. P. Wavell to Prime Minister   *15th May, 1941*
Have done best to equip Colorado against beetle pest. . . .

Not easy commitment and German blitzes usually take some stopping. But we have stout-hearted troops keen and ready for fight under stout-hearted commander and I hope enemy will find "Scorcher" red-hot proposition.

During 15th May Mr. Peter Fraser arrived in Cairo, but it was not until the morning of the 17th that he could see the Commander-in-Chief officially. The effect of his visit was immediate.

A. P. Wavell to General Freyberg   *17th May, 1941, 1225 hrs.*
Fraser insists on seeing you and is prepared to wait till opportunity offers. A.O.C.-in-C. considering ways and means, might send in Sunderland during dark or wait till after attack.

Think you should nominate successor if you become casualty (which Heaven forbid) and inform Greek Government. Let me know your recommendation. . . .

General Freyberg to A. P. Wavell   *17th May, 1941, 2335 hrs.*
Although I know he will insist, Mr. Fraser could not come here without undue risk and I am strongly of opinion it would be wrong to allow it. . . .

If I become casualty General Weston is best successor pending somebody being sent from Middle East. Will inform Greek Government. . . .

A. P. Wavell to Prime Minister   *17th May, 1941*
Have just received following from Freyberg:

"Have completed plan for defence of Crete and have just returned from final tour of defences. . . . I do not wish to be over-confident but I feel that at least we will give excellent account of ourselves. With help of Royal Navy I trust Crete will be held."

A. P. Wavell to General Freyberg   *19th May, 1941, 0625 hrs.*
Following for you from Prime Minister U.K.:

"All our thoughts are with you in these fateful days. We are glad to hear of reinforcements which have reached you and strong dispositions you have made. We are sure that you and your brave troops will perform a deed of lasting fame. Victory where you are would powerfully affect world situation. Navy will do its utmost." . . .

Most Secret. There are some indications which point to delay in attack on you or even possible diversion elsewhere.

These indications were not fulfilled.

The only solid victory now left to Wavell was in East Africa. As the moment of crisis approached in Crete he was ordered to invade and occupy Syria and the Lebanon.

These two countries, with an Alsatian High Commissioner, General Dentz, in command, were Vichyist. But units of General de Gaulle's Free French movement had been in action, under British command, in the Western Desert; and de Gaulle himself, after a stay in Cairo, was now in Brazzaville consolidating Free French authority over the whole of French Equatorial Africa, and was represented in Cairo by the senior and much respected General Catroux. Nevertheless, by a curious anomaly, normal diplomatic relations were also being maintained with the representatives of the Vichy authorities in the Middle East. There were French consuls in Palestine and British consuls in Syria and the Lebanon, and the frontiers were open; but there were hotbeds of Vichyist, pro-Axis and anti-British propaganda and under-cover effort throughout the Levant.

At the beginning of April, while de Gaulle was in Cairo, he was preoccupied with the maintenance of a full blockade to break the Vichy Government's hold on French Somaliland. In a telegram from London dealing principally with de Gaulle's objections to what he considered a "soft" local policy, the question of Syria cropped up, almost as an aside.

Prime Minister to A. P. Wavell   *1st April, 1941*
. . . I hope that on this [French Somaliland] and similar matters you will feel able to give full weight to the views of General de Gaulle to whom His Majesty's Government have given solemn engagements and who has their full backing as leader of the Free French movement.

There are indications that Syria may soon be ripe to come across but for the present it should be allowed to simmer. . . .

A. P. Wavell to Prime Minister   *2nd April, 1941*
Had already discussed matters with de Gaulle and agreed generally

UNDER GREAT STRAIN

on lines of your telegram, i.e. initial approach will be made by Free French and blockade will be maintained. Details will now be settled. We also agreed on Syria, to maintain propaganda but take no action at present. We will collect French troops into formations as they become available and can be fully equipped.

The "indications" that Syria might come across were, as Wavell knew perfectly well, hopelessly inaccurate, and were manifestations of the gallant but misplaced optimism which sustained many Free French at this time. However, the threat of German penetration remained latent rather than active for three more weeks. On 23rd April, that black day in Wavell's fortunes, he was able to signal Dill, without any particular urgency in the statement: "Catroux has asked me on behalf of de Gaulle to assemble Free French forces in Palestine rather than Egypt both for operational and disciplinary reasons."

But four days later London became alert to the approach of danger.

C.I.G.S. to A. P. Wavell   *27th April, 1941*
In view of danger of German airborne attack on Syria, Foreign Office are instructing Mr. Havard Beirut[29] . . . to warn General Dentz and ask what preparations he is taking to defend Syria. Dentz will probably reply that he will resist but will not ask us for aid. This will however give us the opportunity of offering to help him if Syria will fight. . . . If Germans land in Syria and French can be induced to resist it would be greatly to our advantage to stiffen them to prevent advance on Palestine or Iraq. Will you say what you could spare to assist Syria in these circumstances to enable a firm offer to be made to Dentz. Inadvisable under these conditions to employ Free French forces unless asked for.

Dentz's attitude had been correctly diagnosed. After a lapse of several days he replied that any attempt by the Germans to penetrate into Syria would be contrary to the terms of the Franco-German armistice of 1940, and that he would accordingly be prepared to resist it, but that he himself would obey whatever instructions he might receive from Vichy.

Then on 2nd May Rashid Ali appealed to Hitler for armed support for his rising in Iraq, and on the following day the German Embassy in Paris was instructed to obtain the French Government's permission

w.   457   P2 to send aircraft and war material across Syria to the Iraqi rebels. Admiral Darlan negotiated a preliminary agreement with the Germans on 5th and 6th May by which three-quarters of the war material assembled in Syria under the control of the Italian Armistice Commission was to be transferred to Iraq and the *Luftwaffe* granted landing facilities in Syria. General Dentz received the appropriate instructions and complied with them; between 9th May and the end of the month about a hundred German and twenty Italian aircraft made use of Syrian airfields.[30]

Churchill was strongly in favour of instant and vigorous action in Syria. The Foreign Office, however, feared—as over Iraq—any step which might in any way antagonise any Arab anywhere in the Middle East. Wavell was prepared to consider the project on military grounds; but he was believed, in London, to be as reluctant to be involved as he had been over Iraq. Churchill did not bother to conceal his impatience with the Commander-in-Chief. Wavell offered a brigade group (cavalry or infantry) and a mobile group, if he could find the men: he was told testily that these must be got in readiness at once and held on the Palestine border, with an implied rebuke for his lack of zest. Churchill told the Chiefs of Staff on 8th May that "a supreme effort" had to be made to prevent the Germans using Syria as a jumping-off ground for the air domination of Iraq and Persia. Next day he signalled Wavell that in face of his feeling of lack of resources, the only course would be "to furnish General Catroux with the necessary transport and let him and his Free French do their best" when they deemed it suitable, with the R.A.F. acting against German landings.[31]

On 12th May the "Tiger" convoy, carrying its precious load of tanks, on which Churchill's hopes had been set, reached Alexandria in spite of repeated German dive-bombing attacks by moonlight as well as by day. Six of the new "I" tanks and fifteen light tanks Wavell had already arranged to send to Crete. "Tiger" certainly brought valuable and timely reinforcements; but to Churchill's eager and thrusting imagination it seemed that all Wavell's problems were now solved.

The Commanders-in-Chief sought, and were immediately granted, permission to act against the German aircraft on Syrian airfields, irrespective of the effect on relations with Vichy and the Free French. But the Prime Minister wanted action by ground troops as well. He knew that a brigade of Poles, who had reached the Middle East by a variety of routes, was being trained and equipped in the Nile Delta.

Since "Tiger" had now arrived, could not the Poles go up to the Palestine-Syria frontier? The C.I.G.S. signalled this suggestion to Wavell, who replied on 15th May: "Considered Poles but would prefer to keep them for Crete if necessary. Am moving one brigade group 4th Indian Division to Transjordan and am considering another."

As Wavell remarked in a letter to Maitland Wilson, it was "as usual, spreading the butter very thin." It was clearly more sensible to keep the Poles for Crete, where they could fight the Germans they hated, than to embroil them in a confused conflict of Frenchman versus Frenchman, Arab versus Arab, and old friends and allies trying to kill one another.

A brigade group of 4th Indian Division, Wavell's indomitable maid-of-all-work, was duly impressed for one more improvisation. There was only one other formation he could employ, the 7th Australian Division which—less one brigade—would have to be relieved in the Mersa Matruh defences by the remainder of 4th Indian Division. On Saturday, 17th May, after he had seen the New Zealand Prime Minister, he sat in his office wrestling with this new jigsaw puzzle, which was like all its predecessors only in the fact that, as always, there were far too few pieces and the pattern must be completed forthwith.

Perhaps there was a solution. For the first time in many months he gave his imagination rein. He began to think of this particular task not as one more dismally difficult commitment, another set-piece and orthodox campaign doomed to failure from the outset, but as an adventure, as unconventional as it could possibly be. If he must have an addition to the family of strange babies fathered on him at short notice, let it at least be a lively one: speed and secrecy, with the plan known to no more than a couple of officers; a night thrust across the frontier, and the sudden seizure of Beirut, so that the whole town— government offices, railway station, posts and telegraphs and the airfield—would be in British hands by dawn; then a swift drive onwards to Rayak, seizing the airfield there and the road and railway line to Damascus, and to Tripoli for the oil refinery.

This bold, hazardous scheme was doomed from the outset. The Prime Minister was on the rampage in London. De Gaulle was hastening up from Equatorial Africa. Catroux was filled with optimism. General Spears, a parliamentary associate and friend of Churchill, who had played a crucial role as the latter's special liaison officer in

WAVELL

France in May/June, 1940, had arrived in Cairo at the head of a mission
to the Free French forces in the Middle East, and had established his
own lines of communication with the War Cabinet; his views seldom
coincided with Wavell's. And now the Arabists muscled in on the
enterprise, insisting that if Free French troops went in, unless they
were accompanied by and subordinate to British forces, and preceded
by a proclamation announcing that independence would be granted to
Syria and the Lebanon, the whole Arab world would be set on fire.
Orthodoxy quickly gained the upper hand. Wavell sent for his
Deputy C.-in-C., Blamey, and talked it all over with him. That evening
he signalled Dill.

A. P. Wavell to C.I.G.S. *17th May, 1941*
. . . I feel strongly that Free French without strong British
support would be ineffective and likely to aggravate situation
and that original action must be British, to be followed by Free
French if successful. . . .

Hope I shall not be landed with Syria commitment unless
absolutely essential. Any force I could send now would be
painfully reminiscent of Jameson Raid and might suffer similar
fate. . . .

The week-end passed with no answer to this important telegram.
In London on Monday, 19th May, Churchill asked Dill to go across
to Downing Street after luncheon for a cup of coffee and a cigar. In
the course of their conversation the Prime Minister told the C.I.G.S.
that he had decided to send Wavell to India as Commander-in-Chief,
and to replace him in the Middle East by Auchinleck. His reasons for
sending Wavell to India were, he said, that he could not have him
hanging around London living in a room in his club, and that in India
he could "enjoy sitting under the pagoda tree."[32]

The Chiefs of Staff refused to accept Wavell's arguments, and in a
signal sent off later that day told him firmly: ". . . there is no option
but to improvise the largest force that you can manage without prejudice to security Western Desert and be prepared move into Syria at
the earliest possible date. . . ."

This telegram crossed with one to the C.I.G.S. from Wavell,
summarising the discussion at a conference held in G.H.Q. that
morning as a result of a request made by General Catroux the previous
evening that the Commander-in-Chief should order an immediate
advance into Syria with strong forces. Catroux's information was, said

Wavell, that all French troops in Syria would withdraw into the Lebanon, the independence of Syria under Axis auspices would be declared, and the German occupation would begin as soon as possible. He then gave an account of Catroux's optimistic appreciation of the consequent military and political situation, and reported that he himself had stated categorically that the move which the Free French demanded was entirely beyond his resources. Catroux had then formally requested that the Free French forces be moved to the frontier opposite Deraa, to test Vichy French and Arab reactions, and to be available to take advantage of the situation, should it appear favourable.

"I dislike the proposal," Wavell told the C.I.G.S., and set out his objections: the political effects on the Arab population, and the administrative and tactical difficulties he foresaw. Himself greatly preferring his own idea of a daring, secret attack on Beirut and Rayak, he considered Damascus a military liability rather than an asset. All agreed, he said, on the dangers of a German occupation of Syria; but hasty action with weak forces would only bring further difficulties. Since de Gaulle was expected to arrive on the following Saturday and a blank refusal of Catroux's request would involve a definite break with the Free French, he asked for an immediate decision: should he accede to it despite his own objections? If the answer were affirmative, he asked that an immediate Free French declaration of independence for Syria, backed by the British Government, should precede any action.

In another signal to the Prime Minister and the C.I.G.S. despatched early on the morning of 20th May, Wavell explained: ". . . Advance into Syria is major operation which could only be done by taking considerable risks in Western Desert and elsewhere and must take some time to stage. Possibilities are being examined."

That afternoon the Cabinet's Defence Committee sent him a directive: Catroux's request was to be granted; the Free French were to be given not only the transport they wanted but as much military and air support as possible; an immediate Free French declaration of independence for Syria and the Lebanon would be backed by Britain. The opportunity was too good to miss, and entering these two territories was to be regarded as a political coup rather than a military operation, and timing was all-important.

Wavell, despite the fact that his resources in manpower and equipment were stretched to the limit, was aware of the strategic and political difficulties implicit in these peremptory instructions. He was not prepared to see his own preparations for a combined British and Free French operation under Wilson's command thrust aside, and was stung into a brusque retort.

A. P. Wavell to C.I.G.S.   *21st May, 1941, 1255 hrs.*
. . . All reports from trustworthy sources including Arab and Syrian agree that effect of action by Free French alone likely to be failure. . . . You must trust my judgment in this matter or relieve me of my command. I am not willing to accept that Catroux, de Gaulle or Spears should dictate action that is bound seriously to affect militarily situation in Middle East.

Prime Minister to A. P. Wavell   *21st May, 1941, 1935 hrs.*
To be handed personally to C.-in-C.
. . . Nothing in Syria must detract at this moment from winning the battle of Crete or in Western Desert. . . .

There is no objection your mingling British troops with Free French who are to enter Syria, but as you have clearly shown you have not the means to mount a regular military operation and as you were instructed yesterday all that can be done at present is to give best possible chances to . . . armed political inroad.

You are wrong in supposing that policy arose out of any representations made by Free French leaders or General Spears. It arises entirely from view taken here by those who have the supreme direction of the war and policy in all theatres. Our view is that if Germans can pick up Syria and Iraq with petty forces, tourists and local revolts we must not shrink from running equal small-scale military risks and facing the possible aggravation of political dangers from failure. For this decision we are of course taking full responsibility, and should you find yourself unwilling to give effect to it arrangements will be made to meet any wish you may express to be relieved of your command.

Late in the evening of 21st May Dill, alone in his room at the War Office, wrote two letters. One was to Auchinleck, warning him to be ready to succeed Wavell when the latter was relieved of his command. The other was to Wavell:

What a time you are having. How I wish that I could be of more help to you. I do not know whether or not you will pack up on receiving the telegram from the Defence Committee—or rather from the P.M.—which has just been drafted about Syria. . . .

From your own personal point of view you will be sorely tempted to hand in your portfolio—you could hardly go on a better wicket—but from a national point of view it would I feel be a disaster. And yet I feel that the P.M. has only two alternatives—to trust or to replace. But even if he does not trust it would, I feel, be disastrous for you to go *at this moment* when you are handling so many difficult, if not critical situations.

My attitude has always been that if the P.M. has lost confidence in you he should at once replace you. I have told him this several times because I felt that he was losing confidence in you; and yet in spite of that I am sure, as I have already said twice, it would be disastrous for you to go now. It is odd how difficult it is to apply simple principles, such as trust or sack. Ll. G. didn't trust Haig and couldn't sack him. At least I don't think he could. Too many people had complete confidence in him. Is history going to repeat itself? If I thought you could get this letter in time I would be tempted to offer you some wise advice on your immediate situation but as you won't I will just leave what I have said for you to think over after the event. . . .[33]

XIV

Change of Command

For the time being the matter of Wavell's resignation or dismissal was pressed no further. He retained his control over four operational fronts: the Western Desert, Crete, Iraq and Syria; on each he had to husband his resources with the utmost nicety of judgment; and on all he was being vehemently urged by Churchill to take the offensive and achieve instant victory. By the end of the month, however, Iraq had ceased to be a burden. The Western Desert and Syria both held hazards still to be faced. During the latter part of May attention was concentrated almost entirely on Crete.

From the 14th onwards there were repeated attacks on the island—particularly its three airfields—by waves of German bombers and fighters, to soften up the garrison before the main onslaught. This was planned with great speed (Hitler's directive authorising it was issued as late as 25th April) but with less than the usual German thoroughness. The enemy's Intelligence seriously under-estimated both the number and the quality of the British forces in the island, and believed that the civilian population would be friendly to the invaders.

Fliegerkorps XI, under the command of General Student, a soldier of high calibre with a bold and unconventional outlook and a cool yet resolute temper, delivered the principal airborne assault some two hours after dawn on 20th May. First the gliders swooped in west of Maleme airfield and on both sides of the town of Canea. Then came the paratroops, and in the haze of dust and smoke that had followed earlier bombing it seemed that, for minutes at a time, the sky was black with them. In and around Maleme both they and the glider detachments—who had brought 20-mm. guns with them, motor-bicycles, trench-mortars and flame-throwers—ran immediately into fierce resistance from the New Zealanders and the Greeks who were brigaded with them. There were many hours of close and stubborn fighting. The Germans sent their aircraft in again and again, pinning

464

the defenders down with low-level and dive-bombing attacks. Signal communications broke down; runners seldom got through; attackers and defenders fought one another savagely in small, isolated groups. During this first day, in spite of very severe casualties, some 5,000 Germans established themselves in the Maleme and Canea area.

In the afternoon six more German assault battalions were launched into the battle at Retimo and Heraklion. There was equally ferocious fighting here, in which the Australians and a British brigade, which included Wavell's battalion of The Black Watch, successfully held every German attack.

By the end of the day the German casualties were greater than the total number of the *Wehrmacht* hitherto killed in the war, and General Student in his headquarters in Athens was aware that there had been extravagant losses among his senior commanders and their staffs, and that "his men were everywhere, as in some terrible frustrated offensive of the first World War, at their starting point." Just before midnight his Intelligence officer asked him if he should begin to study the problem of breaking off the engagement if this should prove advisable.[1]

Student's answer was to decide to concentrate all his remaining forces in the island, and such reinforcements as he could throw in next day, on one spot, Maleme, because there he thought he could see a glimmer of light. It was a crucial decision. Some three hours earlier the commander of the New Zealand battalion at Maleme had withdrawn all his forces to a compact position south-east of the airfield; and when dawn came the airfield was a no-man's-land, which gave the Germans their opportunity.

Meanwhile Freyberg had signalled Wavell at 2200 hours: "To-day has been a hard one. We have been hard pressed. So far, I believe, we hold aerodromes at Retimo, Heraklion and Maleme, and the two harbours. Margin by which we hold them is a bare one, and it would be wrong of me to paint an optimistic picture."[2]

On 21st May the Germans, still at a heavy cost in men and aircraft, retained and extended their hold on Maleme, and were able by this means to continue their build-up. By the third day they had made it an effective operational airfield, on which troop-carriers arrived at the rate of more than one every three minutes. Those that did not crash took off at once and came back with reinforcements.

A counter-attack was attempted by the now very weary New Zealanders on the morning of the 22nd; it failed and they were forced to withdraw, so that by that evening they were nearly ten miles from the airfield. While at Canea and Retimo Freyberg's forces were still in control, it was at Maleme that the Germans won Crete.

It was some time before this bleak fact was understood in Cairo or in London. On the morning of 23rd May, in answer to an urgent request from the Chiefs of Staff for an appreciation of the situation in Crete, Arthur Smith reported that matters were well in hand at Heraklion, Retimo and Canea, but that the Germans were in control at Maleme, where British casualties had been fairly heavy; the R.A.F. were making determined attacks there, and that evening two Special Service battalions would be sent to the south-west corner of the island, to march over the hills and reinforce Maleme.

Later that day Churchill signalled to Wavell, who had gone, by way of Jerusalem, to Basra to meet Auchinleck.

Prime Minister to A. P. Wavell (0.30)   *23rd May, 1941*

. . . These are very hard times and we must all do our best to help each other.

Crete battle must be won. Even if enemy secure good lodgments fight must be maintained indefinitely in island, thus keeping enemy main striking force tied down to task. This will at least give you time to mobilise Tiger cubs and raise situation of Western Desert. While it lasts it also protects Cyprus. Hope you will reinforce Crete every night to fullest extent. Is it not possible to send more tanks and thus reconquer any captured aerodromes? Enemy's exertions and losses in highest class troops must be very severe. He cannot keep it up for ever. . . .

Following for General Freyberg from me: "The whole world is watching your splendid battle on which great events turn."

On the evening of 24th May Arthur Smith set out the situation as it was understood in Cairo in a telegram to the C.I.G.S. Freyberg's immediate object, he said, was to secure Suda Bay, his main base. The Germans were estimated to have upwards of 10,000 men operating around Canea and Suda; Freyberg had about the same; but the Germans had the big advantage of air supremacy, and Freyberg's men, under the strain of continuous and heavy bombing, were very tired. He described in detail Freyberg's administrative difficulties, with shortages of food, ammunition, entrenching tools and medical supplies caused by the German bombing attacks on ships trying to service Crete. He thought Student's situation equally unpleasant:

Undoubtedly he has not attained the success he expected and is having to fight hard with no hope of withdrawal if he fails. . . . It appears that, provided we can prevent him from securing the use of Suda Bay, his position may become critical.

If we are forced to give up Suda it will still be possible to withdraw on Retimo and Heraklion, but since Suda is our main base it would only be a matter of time before shortage of supplies and ammunition would compel us to evacuate the island, a difficult and dangerous operation.

In a second appreciation by all three Commanders-in-Chief, Admiral Cunningham pointed out that the scale of the Germans' air attack had made it no longer possible for the Navy to operate in the Aegean or in the vicinity of Crete by day. He could not guarantee the prevention of German seaborne landings, and the Navy was unable either to reinforce or to supply Freyberg's forces, except by using fast warships at night. There seemed little prospect of the R.A.F. being able to stop the movement of enemy ships, which could now take place "piecemeal and under strong air protection." Nevertheless they assured London: "We appreciate vital importance of holding Crete and consider that we are justified in diverting forces available from other fronts including Western Desert."

Chiefs of Staff to Commanders-in-Chief   24th May, 1941, 1440 hrs.
. . . If we stick it out enemy's efforts may peter out. It seems to us imperative that reinforcements in greatest strength possible should be sent as soon as possible to island to ensure destruction enemy already landed before they can be seriously reinforced. . . . Great risks must be accepted to ensure our success.

Wavell returned to Cairo on the morning of Sunday, 25th May. Among his early callers were Generals de Gaulle and Catroux. De Gaulle had himself arrived that morning from Brazzaville, buoyed up by a telegram from Churchill telling him that action in Syria was imminent. He knew that the British Prime Minister had ordered Wavell to launch this offensive, and found him "resigned to do so." He added, in his account of this meeting, the comment that "the loss of Crete and the disappearance of the Greek front lightened, for the moment, the burden of the Commander-in-Chief."[3]

Wavell saw General Spears at noon, and de Gaulle again in the afternoon, but without either Spears or Catroux present. Wavell and de Gaulle trusted and respected one another. They spoke frankly. At their morning interview de Gaulle had made imperious demands which were impossible to fulfil; he had urged Wavell to operate with four divisions, one of them armoured, and "to deploy a large section of the Royal Air Force in the Syrian sky"; and he had "*insisted*" that the Free French troops who were to take part should be given what they chiefly lacked—means of transport and artillery support. De Gaulle found that these requests met with "a negative courtesy," and ascribed Wavell's attitude to Churchill's "comminatory telegrams."[4]

After de Gaulle had departed Wavell drafted a telegram to the C.I.G.S. setting out his plans for the Syrian operation, to which he gave the code name "Exporter." The earliest date by which he could move would be the first week in June; Wilson would advance on a broad front, stretching from the Lebanon coast to the road to Damascus, using the 7th Australian Division, minus a brigade, the Free French troops, part of the 1st Cavalry Division and certain other units—a smaller force, in Wavell's view, than that needed to occupy the whole country. The furthest he could hope to get would be the line from Damascus by Rayak to Beirut, with possible raids on Tripoli and Homs. Aleppo he could not reach, but perhaps the Turks would deal with this city.

He told the C.I.G.S. that he had given an outline of these plans in strict secrecy to de Gaulle, whose estimate of the force required (four divisions, one of them armoured) was higher than his own. De Gaulle had accepted the idea of the Turks occupying Aleppo, but gave a sensible warning of the possibility that they might do it in collaboration with the Germans. He ended the signal by quoting the answer to the British Ambassador in Ankara, who had asked for the views of the Commanders-in-Chief on Turkey's position: "In circumstances there is no alternative to accepting Turkish policy as always being ready to die in next ditch but one. We sincerely hope however that the passage of troops through Turkey will not be granted and that Turkey will not accept without action German occupation of Syria."

Then Wavell turned to Churchill's signal of two days before and as he read and re-read it he weighed his own task against that of the Prime Minister and the War Cabinet.

A. P. Wavell to Prime Minister　　　　　*25th May, 1941, 1800 hrs.*
Many thanks for your o.30. We realise our burdens and re-

sponsibilities here, though heavy, are nothing to those you shoulder so gallantly.

We are doing our best to reinforce Crete and keep it going. I sent your message to Freyberg; he is putting up wonderful fight.

Syria. . . . Had satisfactory interview with de Gaulle this afternoon; he goes Palestine to-morrow and sees Wilson and I will see him again on return. . . .

Weaning of Tiger cubs proceeding satisfactorily but even tigers have teething troubles.

But Churchill's anxieties were once more fretted with anger. Arthur Smith's appreciation of 24th May, prepared during Wavell's visit to Basra, did not meet with his approval. Late on the Sunday night the three Chiefs of Staff were summoned to a conference with the Prime Minister, and a telegram was drafted.

Dill went back to the War Office and sent for Kennedy. "Do you realise," he said bleakly, "that we are fighting for our lives now?" The Chiefs' of Staff signal was a reflection of this sombre mood.

Chiefs of Staff to Commanders-in-Chief   25th May, 1941, 2330 hrs. If the situation is allowed to drag on the enemy will have the advantage because unless more drastic naval action is taken than is suggested in your appreciation, the enemy will be able to reinforce the island to a considerable extent with men and stores.

It is essential therefore that Commanders-in-Chief should concert measures for clearing up the situation without delay. In doing so the Fleet and the R.A.F. must accept whatever risk is entailed in preventing any considerable reinforcements of men and material from reaching the island by sea either by night or by day.

Should air reconnaissance show any movement by sea or any collection of craft at Milos it will be essential for the Fleet to operate north of the island by day. It is probable that the losses incurred in so doing will be considerable and only experience will show for how many days this situation can be maintained. This confirms that time is the dominating factor.

During the morning of Monday, 26th May, a Commanders'-in-Chief conference was held at Alexandria to discuss the Crete situation in the light of this new and urgent directive. Tedder and Blamey joined Wavell and Cunningham aboard the Admiral's flagship. The

Prime Minister of New Zealand was also present. They were confronted by a bleak prospect. The Germans were, as Cunningham put it, "so prolific" in the air that, unchecked by any British air action, they could reinforce and supply their forces in Crete at will, and the constant procession of the Ju.52 transport aircraft to and from the island was, of itself, bad for British morale. The Navy was continuing to do its utmost, but the loss in ships was heavy—the cruisers *Gloucester* and *Fiji* and the destroyers *Kelly*, *Kashmir* and *Greyhound* were all sunk between 22nd and 24th May, and the *Valiant* and the *Warspite* badly damaged—and officers and men were strained almost to breaking point. Yet each night the surviving cruisers and destroyers went back to sweep the waters north of Crete. No transports, however, could venture on this side of the island; the only reinforcements that Wavell could possibly put in had to go either by destroyer to Suda by night or by merchant ship to the small harbour of Tymbaki in the south. At most they would number three battalions, since neither could the ships be risked further nor could any more troops be spared from the Western Desert.

Wavell went back to Cairo, to report these facts to the C.I.G.S.

General Freyberg to A. P. Wavell   *26th May, 1941*
I regret to have to report that in my opinion limit of endurance has been reached by troops under my command here at Suda Bay. No matter what decision is taken by C.-in-C. from military point of view our situation here is hopeless. A small, ill-equipped and immobile force such as ours cannot stand up against the concentrated bombing with which we have been faced during the last seven days. I feel I should tell you that from an administrative point of view difficulties of extricating this force in full are now insuperable. Provided a decision is taken at once a certain proportion of force might be embarked. Once this sector has been reduced the reduction of Retimo and Heraklion by same method will be only a matter of time. Troops we have at Suda Bay with the exception of Welch Regiment and Commando are past offensive action. If you decide in view of whole Middle East position that hours help, we will carry on. I would have to consider how this could be best achieved. Suda Bay may be under enemy fire within twenty-four hours.

A. P. Wavell to General Freyberg   *26th May, 1941*
Your force has accomplished great feat in holding attack so far.
Longer we can hold on in Crete the greater effect on whole
Middle East position. With two Special Service battalions,
remainder of which reach you to-night, and Welch Regiment cannot you drive back enemy or relieve most threatened sector? If
you cannot retain Suda Bay position after to-morrow, you should
use freshest troops to cover withdrawal inland to-morrow night,
joining up if practicable with troops in Retimo area and barring
further progress eastward of enemy, who must be very weary and
has only limited offensive power. It should thus be possible to
hold enemy for some time.
        Cable me your outline proposals and will do best to help you.

A. P. Wavell to C.I.G.S.   *26th May, 1941*
. . . Matter is in balance and doubtful whether we can retain
permanent hold.

Prime Minister to Commanders-in-Chief   *26th May, 1941*
Victory in Crete essential at this turning point in the war. Keep
hurling in all aid you can.

Prime Minister to General Freyberg   *26th May, 1941*
Your glorious defence commands admiration in every land.
We know the enemy is hard pressed. All aid in our power is being
sent.

    Adjurations of this kind, however well meant and however
stirring, were now of no use. Courage itself—and the troops in Crete
had fought and endured very bravely indeed—could not prevail against
the now overwhelming weight of attack.

A. P. Wavell to Prime Minister   *27th May, 1941*
Fear that situation in Crete most serious. Canea front has collapsed and Suda Bay only likely to be covered for another twenty-
four hours if as long. There is no possibility of hurling in reinforcements. . . . Yesterday ship taking battalion to Tymbaki
was bombed and badly damaged and had to turn back, while
store ship at Heraklion was also hit. . . . Reinforcement has
steadily become more difficult on account increasing enemy air
force and may now be considered impossible.

On island itself our troops, majority of whom had most severe trial in Greece from overwhelming air attack, have been subjected to same conditions on steadily increasing scale in Crete. Such continuous and unopposed air attack must drive stoutest troops from positions sooner or later and makes administration practically impossible.

Telegram just received from Freyberg states only chance of survival of force in Suda area is to withdraw to beaches in south of island, hiding by day and moving by night. Force at Retimo reported cut off and short of supplies. Force at Heraklion also apparently almost surrounded.

Fear we must recognise that Crete is no longer tenable and that troops must be withdrawn as far as possible. . . .

This telegram reached London just as the day's work was beginning on the morning of Tuesday, 27th May. Dill had hardly sat down at his desk before he was summoned by the Prime Minister to discuss it. But many hours went by before it was answered, hours of bitter and unavailing battle in Crete and in the waters around the island, hours of increasing anxiety in G.H.Q. in Cairo.

A. P. Wavell to C.I.G.S.   *27th May, 1941, 1500 hrs.*
Have ordered evacuation troops from Crete as opportunity offers.

He followed this some two and a half hours later with a fuller explanation of his decision and the factors which had, in his view, made it essential.

A. P. Wavell to C.I.G.S.   *27th May, 1941, 1726 hrs.*
I deeply regret failure to hold Crete and fully realise grave effect loss of it will have on other problems in Middle East. . . . But it has become quite obvious that attempt to prolong defence will not only be useless but is likely so to exhaust navy, army and air resources as to compromise defence position in Middle East even more gravely than loss of Crete.

Result due to overwhelming enemy air superiority. He has been able to establish what practically amounts to box barrage of bombing aircraft round island. . . .

Enemy losses have undoubtedly been very heavy but ours have not been light and proportion which can be safely evacuated remains to be seen.

Fear that troops at Heraklion may have considerable difficulty in holding out and evacuation of remainder will not be easy. . . .

It was close on midnight when Wavell received London's reply to his earlier telegram, giving belated sanction to a decision already taken.

Chiefs of Staff to Commanders-in-Chief   *27th May, 1941, 1935 hrs.*
. . . You should evacuate Crete forthwith saving as many men as possible without regard to material and take whatever measures you think best whether by reinforcements or otherwise.

C.-in-C. Mediterranean should take any steps to prevent seaborne landings which would interfere with evacuation. . . .

There were now between 30,000 and 35,000 German troops in Crete. In addition to some 10,000 Greek troops, the total number of British of all services and contingents, including those that arrived during the battle, was just over 32,000. Of these, the majority had already been evacuated from Greece. They all now faced yet another evacuation, in even worse conditions. Only two ports were usable by the Royal Navy, and both of these merely for a few hours at night. Heraklion, on the north coast, was already under heavy air attack, and its sea approaches were vigilantly watched by the enemy. Sphakia, on the south coast, chosen for evacuation rather than Tymbaki, was nothing more than a small strip of beach. It was approached from the north by a stony mountain track which it was a gross exaggeration to describe as a road. From Suda it wound upwards through olive groves high into the mountains, bare and rocky or dotted with thin, prickly scrub. Then, with the sea in sight, there was a series of steep, scrambling descents to crumbling cliffs and the beach. When the Commander-in-Chief's order to evacuate was made known, this became the one road to release from an ordeal which many of those engaged had found too hard to bear. Evacuation, it was learned, was to begin on the night of 28th/29th May. An Australian detachment at Retimo was cut off from all the other forces on the island, and fought stubbornly on, increasingly short of ammunition as well as food, until the 30th. Elsewhere scratch formations, hastily assembled in the past four weeks, without coherence and without unity, dissolved into small huddles of individuals. But units which had retained their identity now preserved their discipline. It was to Sphakia that the great majority of them made their way. Every now and again—though less frequently than many had feared—a German fighter came low over the peaks and sprayed the track with machine-gun fire. The more soldierly and experienced parties of men rested by day under the olive trees; the stragglers trudged on in weary despair. Parched throats, blistered feet, bursting boots, and the miserable mixture of fear and fatigue made that road indeed, as Freyberg said in his report, a *via dolorosa*. At the final descent to the beach, military police imposed a stern control. For three nights, from 29th May to 1st June, the evacuation continued, at increasingly heavy cost to the Royal Navy in ships and men. On the night of 30th/31st May, Freyberg, at Wavell's direct order, left Sphakia by Sunderland flying-boat, leaving the Marine General, Weston, in command of the remainder of the troops on the island.

Next morning Wavell held a meeting in Cairo; the New Zealand Prime Minister and General Blamey agreed with him that they could not ask the Navy to do anything more. They flew down to Alexandria to tell Admiral Cunningham.

"We met him and his staff at a conference hut on the airfield, and I gave him our decision and absolution from further effort on behalf of the Army. I saw the faces of his staff light up with relief. I heard afterwards that they had been trying to impress on him that any further losses by the Navy, and even the Italians could not help being masters of the Eastern Mediterranean. Then Andrew C. spoke briefly. He thanked us for our effort to relieve him of responsibility but said that the Navy had never yet failed the Army in such a situation, and was not going to do so now; he was going in again that night with everything he had which would float and could bring off troops."

Wavell described Cunningham's as "a very gallant decision."

As soon as it was dark the ships stood in for the last time. A Sunderland arrived to take off Weston. A small rearguard covered the evacuation for as long as possible, and before dawn made their way to the beach. Some four thousand men were taken off during that last night. It was an unforgettable achievement by the Royal Navy.

The troops at Heraklion had been less fortunate. During 28th May the Navy sent the cruisers *Ajax*, *Orion* and *Dido* and six destroyers to their rescue. From late afternoon onwards Stukas bombed them all again and again; so fierce were the attacks and so resolute the Navy's response that half the force's A.A. ammunition was spent before it arrived off Heraklion. Half an hour before midnight the ships came as close inshore as they could. A little after three in the morning they moved off with 4,000 troops on board, opening up as soon as possible to a maximum speed of 29 knots. The steering gear of one of the destroyers suddenly failed; another took off her troops and crew and sank her, and the speed of the rest of the force was reduced to 15 knots to give this destroyer a chance to catch up. At sunrise the Stukas came out again and wreaked havoc. For nine hours they attacked incessantly. One destroyer had to beach on the Cretan shore, and all those on board who survived were taken prisoner. One of three direct hits on the *Orion* burst in her crowded mess decks and killed 260 soldiers and wounded 280 more. In a single direct hit on the *Dido*, out of 240 officers and men of Wavell's old battalion, the 2nd Black Watch, 103 were killed.

When the battered ships sailed into Alexandria harbour at eight o'clock on that hot summer night, of the four thousand troops that had been embarked, 800 were now either dead, wounded or prisoners of war. Thereafter no further attempts could be or were made to go to the north of the island.[5]

Nevertheless, in the three nights of the evacuation some 18,000 men, including 1,500 wounded, out of the 32,000 sent to Crete were brought away to Egypt. The naval casualties during the battle were: in men, 1,828 killed and 183 wounded; in ships, one aircraft carrier and three battleships damaged, three cruisers and six destroyers sunk, six cruisers and seven destroyers damaged. All this was accomplished by shore-based German aircraft; the Italian Navy was unaffected, and its numerical strength was considerably greater than that of the British at the end of the battle. The R.A.F. lost seven Wellingtons, 16 medium bombers and 23 fighters; while the Germans reckoned their losses in aircraft to be 147 destroyed and 67 damaged by British action, and 73 destroyed and 84 damaged "by other causes."[6]

But the crucial test of Crete, from the British standpoint, lay in the German losses in manpower in this, the first completely airborne invasion the world had ever seen, and in the long-term consequences of those losses. According to the most reliable German records they lost 1,990 killed, 1,995 missing (of whom the greater proportion must be accounted killed) and 2,131 wounded, a total of 6,116; the casualties among officers and N.C.O.s was particularly high.

The short and in many aspects tragic conflict in Crete can only be judged fairly, so far as Wavell's responsibility and reputation are concerned, in relation to the Greek expedition to which it was the unavoidable sequel, and in relation to the Mediterranean and Middle Eastern campaign as a whole.

The Germans' casualties were so severe that they were never again able to assemble spearhead airborne assault forces even remotely rivalling, in training, equipment and morale, those whom General Student had hurled into the first two days of the battle. In spite of the air supremacy which they established, they came very near to failure and, as the British Official History has pointed out, "never tried anything of the sort again." This rough consolation at least the surviving defenders of Crete could extract from their bitter, apparently hopeless, ordeal. But it is too much to argue—and Wavell himself never argued—that "it may be that the loss of Crete at such a high cost to the Germans was almost the best thing that could have happened."[7] In June, 1941, in a personal letter to the commanders of all formations and units that had served in Crete, Wavell said merely that for strategical reasons it was necessary to hold the island if this could reasonably be done; "as Commander-in-Chief I accept the responsibility."[8]

At no time during these critical weeks did the Prime Minister have to prod a reluctant and defence-minded Commander-in-Chief about action in the Western Desert. Churchill himself has emphasised that Wavell believed that a victory there "would make amends for all," and acknowledged that, realising what risks had been run to get him back the armour lost in March, he had loyalty to "Tiger." Churchill added: "His spirit was buoyant, and he did not overlook the broad principle that in war as in life everything is relative. Our united strategic conception may be claimed to be correct."[9]

Well in advance of any promptings, Wavell on 1st May issued to Beresford-Peirse, whom he had appointed G.O.C. Western Desert, a directive which began, "It is my intention that we should take the offensive in the Western Desert as soon as our resources permit." He requested the new desert commander to examine in detail the prospects of fulfilling this intention and told him that he would have O'Moore Creagh to help him in his planning.

On 4th May, in a note like that which had initiated "Compass," Wavell said: "Provided we are not compelled to fritter away our resources on the ground and in the air, to meet attacks on Crete, Palestine, Iraq, Cyprus, etc., I see no reason why we should not be able to stage a really effective counter-offensive by the end of this month or early in June."

Intelligence reports both in London and in Cairo gave clear indications of Rommel's weakness. On 7th May Churchill sent

Wavell details of Paulus's secret reports and gave him the choice of attacking either in the Tobruk or in the Sollum area (see chapter XIII, p. 429 *supra*).

A. P. Wavell to Prime Minister   *9th May, 1941*
On seeing original secret message I ordered all available tanks to be placed at disposal of Gott's force for offensive action in Sollum area. This is now in active preparation and should take place soon. I shall only cancel it if complete disaster overtakes "Tiger."

The "Tiger" convoy, bringing 82 cruisers, 135 "I" and 21 light tanks, reached Alexandria on 12th May; but Wavell now had no intention of waiting until these tanks, welcome as they undoubtedly were, had been unloaded and made desert-worthy.

A. P. Wavell to Prime Minister   *13th May, 1941*
Without waiting "Tiger" I ordered available tanks to join Gott's force to attack enemy in Sollum area. Action should take place in next day or two and think Gott should be able to deal with forward enemy troops. If successful will consider immediate combined action by Gott's force and Tobruk garrison to drive enemy west of Tobruk. It may be necessary to wait for some of "Tiger" to do this but am anxious to act as quickly as possible before enemy can be reinforced.

Two days later Gott put in his attack. A mixed force of infantry, field gunners and "I" tanks took Sollum and Capuzzo, and the 7th Armoured Brigade Group went forward to Sidi Azeiz, with under thirty cruiser tanks and three columns of the Support Group. But the Germans, whose strength of some seventy tanks was a good deal greater than reports had suggested, counter-attacked strongly and retook Capuzzo that same afternoon, inflicting heavy casualties on the infantry battalion which tried to retain it.

In conjunction with this operation there was a sally by the Tobruk garrison which, at the cost of some 150 casualties, brought in 60 prisoners, some German and some Italian, and killed about 200 of the enemy.

Gott held Sollum that night; but on the following day, 16th May, he withdrew almost his whole force, leaving garrisons on the pass over the escarpment at Halfaya and Sidi Suleiman.

Prime Minister to A. P. Wavell   *17th May, 1941*
Results of action seem to us satisfactory. Without using Tiger
cubs you have taken offensive, have advanced 30 miles, have
captured Halfaya and Sollum, have taken 500 German prisoners
and inflicted heavy losses in men and A.F.V.s upon the enemy.
For these, 20 "I" tanks and 1,000 or 1,500 casualties do not seem
to be at all too heavy. . . .

News from Tobruk is also good, especially as enemy loss is
greater than ours. . . . It seems of utmost importance to keep on
fighting at Tobruk.

The enemy is bringing up "awful reinforcements" and is seeking to re-establish the situation. We should surely welcome this
as he may not be in a condition to stand severe continuous fight.
C.I.G.S. and I both feel confident of good results of sustained
pressure. . . . You should keep at it both at Sollum and Tobruk. . .

What are your dates for bringing Tiger cubs into action?

Little more than twenty-four hours later the Prime Minister sent
off another telegram about the "Tiger" convoy, setting out in detail
the dates of the ships' arrival and unloading schedules, and demanding
a definite time-table of the mobilisation of all the A.F.V.s they had
carried. Why, he asked, did it take a fortnight to bring them into
action? And he warned that Wavell would by that time face a very
different enemy. "Of course I understand," Churchill remarked,
"that we must not fritter Tiger cubs away piecemeal." This signal,
reaching Cairo in the middle of the morning of 20th May, coincided
with the news of the first German landings on Crete. A copy was on
Dill's desk when he went to the War Office. On the previous day,
as described earlier, Churchill had sent for Dill and had told him that
he proposed to get rid of Wavell and put Auchinleck in his place. Dill
then saw Leopold Amery, who said that he did not wish Wavell to go
to India, because it would be thought that India was being saddled
with a cast-off, whether because of failure or mere fatigue; neither
reason, in Amery's view, made a good background for a new Commander-in-Chief in India in time of war. Dill, for his part, regarded
Wavell as the one big figure in the Services, trusted by public and
soldier alike; and he was convinced—mistakenly—that Wavell's
removal would rock the Government. [10]

Though he took another month to fulfil it, Churchill did not
deviate from the decision he made on 19th May. Meanwhile he strove

478

to exercise closer and closer control over the conduct of the war. And nothing that Wavell did (or did not do) about the Tiger cubs really satisfied him. On 21st May Wavell reported that the unloading of three of the ships had been up to schedule, despite the tightness of their loading. The fourth ship had caused difficulties; but the whole job ought to be finished by the 25th. He gave a meticulous schedule for the delivery of the tanks to units in the Matruh area over a period from then until 14th June. He pointed out that, in spite of every preliminary effort to avoid delay, all the tanks had to go into the workshops for desert modifications, including camouflage. In addition to other troubles, there were wireless sets packed in unmarked containers which had to be sorted. The cruiser tank Mark VI, he pointed out, was an entirely new type in the Middle East, and a period of training was necessary before its crews could use it.

Until the following Sunday night—in a week in which there was a mass of signals over Crete, Syria and Iraq—there was no more mention of the Tiger cubs, or indeed of the Western Desert. But on Sunday evening such small restraints as the C.I.G.S. could impose on Churchill's exuberance were briefly removed. On 26th May, a little before midnight, his thoughts and his emotions swirled back to the Western Desert.

Prime Minister to A. P. Wavell   *27th May, 1941, 0045 hrs.*
Hope you are preparing your desert stroke and that Tobruk will not be idle.

A. P. Wavell to Prime Minister   *27th May, 1941, 1320 hrs.*
Am most anxious to launch desert stroke earliest possible and events in Crete have increased urgency, since if enemy transfers large force dive-bombers to Western Desert before we can join up with Tobruk or get fighter force within closer range, fear same fate for Tobruk force sooner or later as that at Canea. Liaison officer just returned from Tobruk reports that already enemy unopposed bombing is having some effect on morale. Hope to give approximate date for attack shortly, provision of transport is causing difficulty. Meanwhile enemy has attacked in Sollum area and driven our advanced forces back, but do not think this is likely to be large-scale effort.

By this time the Germans had three battalions of tanks—some 160 in all—on the Egyptian frontier, but shortage of fuel sharply re-stricted the distances at which they could operate. However, on 26th May Rommel's subordinate commander in the most forward area—a certain Colonel Herff—began an operation whose intention was to bluff the British by a display of force into giving up the plateau above the escarpment. This was garrisoned, after Gott's abortive offensive towards Capuzzo and Sollum, by the Support Group on the Southern flank; and the 3rd Bn. the Coldstream Guards, with detachments of "I" tanks and field, anti-tank and A.A. artillery, held the Halfaya Pass.

Colonel Herff's probe developed into a serious attack, maintained throughout a blazingly hot Sunday and with greatly superior force, on the Coldstream Guards and their supporting detachments. The Germans could not be driven off a superior position which they seized early in the day, and by dusk there was a danger of the British garrison being completely surrounded. But before dawn on 27th May Gott authorised a withdrawal; the force was extricated with some skill, but suffered 173 casualties and lost four field guns, eight anti-tank guns and five "I" tanks. It was not an auspicious prelude to the offensive which Wavell—no less than Churchill—was eager to see launched in the Western Desert.

On the night of 27th May the War Cabinet and the Chiefs of Staff drafted a new directive, which declared that the first object was a de-cisive victory in the Western Desert, which would "destroy the enemy armed forces in a battle fought with our whole available strength." Wavell's general plan for Syria, outlined in his telegram of three days earlier, was approved, but no Free Frenchman except de Gaulle was to be taken into the C.-in-C.'s confidence. Syria was far more import-ant than Cyprus, for which nothing could be done until after the Syrian campaign, except that a small garrison should be kept there to make sure that the Germans did not get it for a song. Wavell's views on and proposals for giving effect to these decisions were re-quested.

Wavell responded the next afternoon with a personal telegram to Dill. He declared at the outset that he was putting all his available armour into the Western Desert operation, and that this would be the deciding factor. But the reconstitution of 7th Armoured Division was taking time, and the earliest possible date for his attack was 7th June, and might be later. He added: "I think it right to inform you that the measure of success which will attend this operation is in my opinion doubtful." He hoped it would drive Rommel west of Tobruk, and re-open the road to the port. If possible, he would exploit the success further. But he set out with some care the mechanical troubles that were afflicting his armour, and several tactical disadvantages under which the desert force now laboured.

"We shall not be able to accept battle with perfect confidence in spite of numerical inferiority as we could against Italians," he told the C.I.G.S., but went on to make it clear that over the Syrian campaign and the decision about Cyprus he conformed completely with the directive.

Meanwhile, the Prime Minister had been brooding throughout the day. He composed a personal signal to Wavell, which blended blandishment, expostulation and exhortation in a characteristic and quite inimitable manner.

Prime Minister to A. P. Wavell   *28th May, 1941*
... Everything must now be centred upon destroying the German forces in the Western Desert, only by this deed will you gain the security on your western flank which will enable you to keep the Germans out of Syria and yourself gain contact with Turkey. I hope therefore that the maximum possible forces will be thrown into what unless you have a better name may be called "Tiger-cubs." For the first time it seems to me that you have a definite superiority in numbers of A.F.V.s especially heavier types as well as in mechanised infantry, artillery and supplies. The Tobruk sallyport also presents strategic opportunities of the highest order. In spite of Cretan losses the air position in Libya has improved. Now, before the enemy has recovered from the violent exertions and heavy losses involved in his onslaught upon Crete, is the time to fight a decisive battle in Libya and go on day after day facing all necessary losses until you have beaten the life out of General Rommel's army. In this way the loss of Crete will be more than repaired and the future of the whole campaign in the Middle East will be opened out.

We were all very much puzzled when you sent Wilson to Palestine and appointed Beresford-Peirse to the Western Desert. Although the latter is a good divisional commander it is difficult to believe that he can compare with Wilson in military stature, reputation or experience of high command in desert warfare. As so much of our fortune hangs upon this impending battle

I ask you to consider whether there is still time for Wilson to be given the command.

As I try to support you and your army in every way and especially in adversity, I feel sure that you will not resent these observations which I feel it my duty to make.

When Dill saw the draft of this signal he sent at once by hand to the Prime Minister's office the following letter:

My dear Prime Minister,
I have of course despatched your telegram of to-day to Wavell. At the same time I feel that I should let you know that there is much in it that I do not like.

In the first place it really adds nothing to the directive the Chiefs of Staff sent yesterday in accordance with your orders. Then I would say that the "Tobruk sallyport" does not present strategic opportunities of the highest order. It has great tactical value in containing enemy forces and using them up and it may have even greater tactical value if the garrison can strike at the enemy's communications when he is hard pressed. My fear for Tobruk now is that it may come in for very severe bombing—something much more than it has known before, and that this may so affect the garrison that it will become a beleaguered garrison and not a sallyport.

Again, I do not consider it sound to tell a General "to go on day after day facing all necessary losses until you have beaten the life out of General Rommel's army." I think that that will probably be the right answer but with so many commitments Wavell may not wish to risk great losses and "all necessary losses" seems to me to imply facing great losses. Lastly I do not like the suggestion that Wilson should now take command in the Western Desert. Wavell may feel that if he does not do this and things go wrong he will be blamed. In fact it may tend to shake Wavell in a decision he has, rightly or wrongly, taken. And Wilson really has big things to do in Iraq and Syria.

Forgive this letter but I know that you will like me to speak my mind.

Yours very sincerely,
J. G. Dill

When this appeal failed to change Churchill's mind, the C.I.G.S.

hurried across to Downing Street to speak to him. The Prime Minister was adamant.[11]

That same day Wavell issued his formal instructions to Beresford-Peirse for his offensive, which then bore the code name "Bruiser" (and was referred to as such in telegrams to and from London) but came to be known, more resoundingly, as "Battleaxe."

It was essential, Wavell declared, that the enemy should be defeated and driven west of Tobruk, with which land communications must be re-established, as soon as possible. The time factor was of the greatest importance in order to forestall the arrival of enemy ground and air reinforcements, and to get fighter protection to Tobruk before the enemy could attack it in overwhelming strength. Therefore as soon as 7th Armoured Division was ready and Beresford-Peirse's other preparations were complete he was to attack, in a three-stage operation: first, the defeat of the Axis forward forces and an advance to the area Bardia—Capuzzo—Sidi Omar—Sidi Azeiz; second, the advance to Tobruk and El Adem and the defeat of the enemy in that area; and third, the exploitation of the success up to Derna and Mechili, and if possible beyond. It was for Beresford-Peirse to lay down the role that the garrison of Tobruk should play in each of the three stages. The instructions ended: "The success of these operations is of vital importance to the defence of Egypt. The sooner they can be staged the greater the success likely to be achieved."

Next morning Wavell replied to the Prime Minister's signal, the draft of which had aroused such distress and anxiety in Dill's mind. There was no trace of resentment or irritation in the telegram. He repeated to Churchill his warning to Dill that his strength in A.F.V.s, aircraft and transport might not be sufficient for a decisive victory. He explained that when he had had to appoint a commander in the Western Desert, Wilson was fully occupied, first in Greece and then in Palestine. He described Beresford-Peirse as a good fighting soldier with good local knowledge, who would, he believed, do well; to make a change now, when both the Desert and the Syrian operations were in the final stages of planning, would be most unwise.

Churchill's interest in the Tiger cubs was that of a jealous father, as Wavell understood; and despite his own burdens and difficulties, he could sympathise with the Prime Minister's affectionate sentiments. But like many other spoiled children they were an infernal nuisance to everyone except their progenitor.

A. P. Wavell to C.I.G.S.   *30th May, 1941*
State of Tiger cubs on arrival Egypt.

Light tanks Mark VI. Eight out of the 21 require complete overhaul.

Cruiser Mark IVA 15, average mileage 700 or half their life.
Cruiser Mark VI 67, in good order.

Infantry tanks, first 69 ready on 28th May required average 48 man-hours each in shops. Examples of heavier repairs are: two gear boxes, cracked and faulty required exchange, broken sprockets, rackham clutches slipping, unserviceable tracks, one left-hand engine seized, top rollers seized, two engines over-heating and lacking power required top overhaul.

Had cubs only required to be fitted with desert equipment and camouflage painted, all would have been ready for operations by 31st May.

Churchill could not bring himself, either at the time or afterwards, to make any direct reference to this brief, withering indictment of his treasures. He recorded that: "on May 31st General Wavell reported the technical difficulties which he was having with the re-formation of the 7th Armoured Division."[12]

In a very long telegram to the C.I.G.S. on 31st May Wavell did indeed set out all the technical difficulties that had manifested themselves, and he followed it with another in which he analysed Beresford-Peirse's and Creagh's tactical problems that had arisen of course out of the mechanical and technical difficulties he had already recorded. He told Dill that having discussed these with his generals, he had authorised the postponement of the offensive until 15th June. In view of the Prime Minister's violent antipathy towards postponing any operation, he was taking a calculated but heavy risk. However, since Churchill's mind was already set on a change of command, the new date was received with calm in London. The only notable reaction was a personal telegram from Dill.

C.I.G.S. to A. P. Wavell   *2nd June, 1941*
In view of postponement of "Bruiser" to 15th June have you considered possibility of getting some more "I" tanks into Tobruk? This might be an effective move if it can be done.

Wavell spent all that day in the desert. The mechanical defects of his armoured fighting vehicles were giving him constant concern.

What use were the Tiger cubs—to say nothing of the battered remnants of his original force of tanks—if they could not move out of the workshops? The strategist and the tactician alike were powerless in the oil-blackened hands of the garage mechanic; and this was a factor whose effect Winston Churchill—who had, as a younger man, done so much to bring about the mechanical and technical revolution in war—admitted too seldom in the years 1940-5. He replied a little tartly: "I have already reinforced Tobruk with four "I" tanks, three on 25th May and one on 28th May. Do not consider further reinforcement advisable."

The gulf that yawned between the desires and needs of commanders in the field in the Middle East and the designing and productive capacity of the factories in England and elsewhere was never bridged in Wavell's time, nor in his successor's. The cause of these countless deficiencies lay in the decades of neglect before the war. Now, on day and night shifts, on short rations and long hours, and under the constant threat of bombing, men and women laboured to remedy in a few months the shortcomings of years; and on the vast sand-table of the desert the dead, stained flesh of their sons, brothers and lovers rotted from their bones.

The plans for "Battleaxe" (the Western Desert offensive) and for "Exporter" (the attack on Syria and the Lebanon) became more and more closely entangled as the dates for their launching approached. Had both been instantaneous and unequivocal successes, Churchill might have found it difficult to replace Wavell by Auchinleck. No hint, however, was conveyed to Wavell that, to this extent, his personal future was in question. But London's interest in the two operations was relentless, and the appetite for information insatiable.

C.I.G.S. to A. P. Wavell   *5th June, 1941*
We are still somewhat in dark regarding scope and timings of "Exporter" and "Battleaxe." A little appreciation in a personal telegram would help me a lot. Head your telegram *Most Secret* and to have *Most Limited Circulation.*

A. P. Wavell to C.I.G.S.   *5th June, 1941*
Date "Exporter" 8th June. Sending appreciation "Exporter" and "Battleaxe" separate cable.

In two long and copiously detailed telegrams on 5th and 6th June,

Wavell gave every scrap of information about the two offensives that the Defence Committee could conceivably desire. He gave full appreciations of both operations; the background, political, tactical and logistical, to his decisions; his objectives; the orders he had issued to subordinate commanders; his difficulties and his hopes. He named the formations designated to take part, and in his "Battle-axe" telegram gave a comparative assessment of his and the enemy's strength in tanks and artillery; and with care and clarity he described the risks entailed in failure.

For the time being the Defence Committee could hardly complain. They now had the fullest and most detailed picture possible of the way in which each offensive was meant to be carried out. Both had been hurriedly planned; as these telegrams were studied, some comprehension emerged of the magnitude of the tasks Wavell had assumed with the minimum of resources. There followed a short spasm of anxiety lest one or other should fail. The Prime Minister's itch to interfere, even at this late stage, could not be resisted.

The most sensitive point of disagreement hitherto had been tanks; now it suddenly became air support. In London all—including the Prime Minister, the Chief of the Air Staff and the C.I.G.S.—were convinced that the British and Commonwealth forces in the Middle East had great air superiority: Wavell knew they had not. Longmore, his trusted friend, had been summoned back to London a month earlier and had been replaced by his deputy, Air Marshal Tedder (see note 12, chapter XIII, p. 534). At first Wavell's relations with Tedder were nothing like as close, but the experiences of the next few days brought them much nearer together. The dispute began with a Chiefs of Staff signal to them both on 6th June, which made the somewhat obvious point that if "Exporter" was to have a reasonable chance of success it should be allotted a larger temporary concentration of air forces than had recent operations, and added that the loss of position and prestige if the Vichy French held Syria would be serious. The Chiefs of Staff then suggested that as the aircraft needed for the Western Desert operation must not be drained away, those made available for "Exporter" need not be based in Palestine but could operate from there on a day-to-day basis.

Wavell and Tedder replied that two squadrons of Hurricanes, one of Tomahawks, one of Blenheims and a flight of Gladiators had been allotted to "Exporter," and additional air action against Aleppo would be taken from Mosul. They explained that a day-to-day allocation of aircraft to the operation was not feasible, since aircraft were needed at that moment in the desert for preparatory action against Rommel's communications and supplies.

On a half-sheet of scribbling paper Tedder gave Wavell his assessment of the R.A.F.'s targets in support of "Battleaxe," both before and after Beresford-Peirse launched his offensive, and of the squadrons available. It read:

> Now to 10th June: Ships in Benghazi. Now to 12th June: Convoys road Benghazi—Derna. 12th to 14th June: Transport between Tobruk and frontier. Aerodromes.
>
> Expect—up to 20th June: 2 Hurricane squadrons, 2 Tomahawk, 2 Blenheim, 2 Glen Martin, 1 Army Co-operation.

Four of these squadrons had just come up from East Africa; they were new to the desert and had no experience of fighting Germans. The losses in Greece and Crete had brought the strength of the other squadrons down far below their proper establishment, and aircrews were trickling out for them from the United Kingdom.

Many years later the Official History gave the comparable British and Axis figures of serviceable aircraft in the desert at this time. The British had 105 heavy and medium bombers, and 98 single and twin-engine fighters; the Germans had 59 bombers and dive-bombers, and 60 single and twin-engine fighters; and the Italians had 25 bombers and 75 fighters.[13] In June, 1941, Middle East Intelligence was therefore much nearer the truth than its optimistic counterpart in London. But London was in no mood to accept the Middle East's view. The Chiefs of Staff pored over Wavell's "Battleaxe" appreciation. It was agreed that Dill should signal him informally.

C.I.G.S. to A. P. Wavell   *7th June, 1941*
But Archie your greatly superior air force is surely your greatest asset and you don't mention it. I hope that Tedder will see that his lads play their part in closest possible support.

A. P. Wavell to C.I.G.S.   *8th June, 1941*
Did not include air since knew Tedder was cabling. . . . His figures show no superiority and at moment we have certainly none. In fact Beresford-Peirse very concerned about air though Tedder keeps assuring me he realises importance and that it will be all right on the night.

There, for the moment, this controversy was allowed to rest.

However, like the Tiger cub imbroglio, this question of "air superiority" was merely a symptom of a deeply-rooted and widespread *malaise* in the whole relationship, or rather the complex accumulation of relationships on many levels, between the Supreme Command in the United Kingdom and Middle East Command. The Prime Minister now made a herculean effort to find a simple panacea, which he proposed to apply at once, whether or not he dismissed Wavell.

On 3rd June he set out his conclusions and his decision in a telegram to the Commander-in-Chief. The intention, he stated at the outset, was to lighten his burden of administration in the conduct of four different campaigns, as well as much "quasi-political and diplomatic business." He then gave in detail his estimate of the number of men, guns and vehicles in the Command; he pointed out that General Alan Brooke (then C.-in-C. Home Command) had the help of the Ministry of Supply and of the War Office, and argued that something like this separation of function must be established in the Middle East, which would leave Wavell free to give his fullest thought to policy and operations. The Prime Minister calculated that by the autumn or early winter there would be 600,000 men—the equivalent of 15 divisions—under G.H.Q. Middle East, and that in addition India would be supplying six or seven divisions, "with apparatus." The development and maintenance of such an army would require "organisation and workshops on a far larger scale than you have yet enjoyed."

The Prime Minister therefore proposed to set up, under the C.-in-C.'s general authority, an organisation commanded by an officer of high rank, styled "Intendant-General of the Army in the Middle East." With an ample staff drawn largely from Wavell's own, and with a powerful and growing civilian element, he would be able to discharge many of the services rendered by the War Office and the Ministry of Supply to the C.-in-C. Home Forces. There would arrive forthwith by air in Cairo to take up the appointment General Haining, previously V.C.I.G.S. He would be accompanied by Mr. T. C. L. Westbrook of the Ministry of Aircraft Production who, under Haining, would take charge of the development of ports and transportation facilities and the reception, maintenance and repair of all motor transport and armoured fighting vehicles. The Intendant-General's first duties were:

to examine on the spot and to discuss with you the implementing and precise definition of the general directive and policy set forth in the preceding paragraphs, which must be accepted as a decision of His Majesty's Government.

After not more than a fortnight from the date of his arrival the report must be telegraphed home. I hope it may be agreed, but any points of difference will be settled promptly by me. Moreover I shall not allow the scheme to lose any of its force and scope in the detailed application which must now be given to it.

In addition to this fundamental change in the structure of the Middle East Command, the telegram gave the news of the beginning of that vast flood of American supplies which, even before the United States' entry into the war, was to have so profound an influence on its course and conduct. Some 74 ships, the Prime Minister told Wavell, were being sent across the Atlantic, at President Roosevelt's orders, carrying 200 light tanks "and many other important items of which I shall furnish you a list." In order to help Wavell in his reception and distribution of what Churchill foresaw as increasing quantities of American supplies, Mr. Averell Harriman, the President's special envoy, would be coming at once to Cairo, accompanied by one or two of his assistants who had shown "great aptitude and ardour" in London. Churchill commended Harriman to Wavell's most attentive consideration, and informed him that the American would report back both to his own Government "and to me as Minister of Defence."[14]

Wavell replied four days later:

I welcome the appointments of General Haining and Mr. Westbrook which will be most valuable in dealing with the very complex administrative problems of the Middle East. My D.Q.M.G., General Hutchison, has shown remarkable ability in coping with all these problems, but the additional experience and fresh view of the officers named will be most welcome.

He then went on to a detailed rejoinder to the Prime Minister's array of figures which was accurate but perhaps hardly tactful; and he made no mention at all of American supplies or Mr. Harriman's mission, which was certainly not tactful.

Wavell at this time gave little outward indication of the long, fierce strain to which he had been and still was being subjected. In Cairo he rode every morning and had his swim in the pool at Gezira. His eye gleamed as appreciatively as always if a pretty and intelligent young woman was put to sit beside him at luncheon or dinner. He wrote as regularly and as affectionately as he could to his sisters and his friends, though the mails from home were in a chaotic condition, and three or four months could go by (for the Commander-in-Chief as much as for a private) without the delivery of a single personal letter. In the extraordinary swirl of Cairo at that time the Chief was rock-like in his fortitude, his wisdom, his seeming serenity. But though he showed little or no outward trace of it, he was himself aware of fatigue and staleness of spirit.

A. P. Wavell to C.I.G.S.   *6th June, 1941*
If "Exporter" and "Battleaxe" go well there may be partial lull in Middle East till autumn. If so should like some weeks' rest and possibly you might like me home part of time to report.

Dill, unable to respond to this appeal at the moment, kept it in his mind.

Wavell had bowed to Churchill's insistence on the Syrian adventure; but his own later verdict was:

I was not very sympathetically treated by the War Cabinet over this. I warned them, and they knew well, that I had not sufficient troops to make a quick job of the invasion; yet they continually grumbled at its slowness. De Gaulle and the Free French were in high favour at the time, and I was told to comply with their views, though I warned them that their information was unreliable and optimistic and that the French in Syria would undoubtedly fight the Free French. I was preparing an offensive in the Western Desert which I was told was to have absolute priority over Syria, yet I was constantly being urged to take air squadrons and troops away from the Western Desert for Syria.

These are justifiable criticisms. But though the Syrian campaign was an unhappy one, strategically and politically it was necessary; and, as Wavell himself admitted, "it came out all right in the end," though after he himself had left the Middle East. De Gaulle, as he made clear in his *War Memoirs*,[15] suspected more perfidy and chicanery than in fact existed: he did not trust Churchill, to whom he owed much, but he trusted Wavell, whom he liked; and there his trust was not misplaced. At lower levels however, on the staff, in the Embassy in Cairo, and in the accretions of cloak-and-dagger and political warfare organisations which were fast expanding in both Cairo and Jerusalem, there were men who were eager to establish what they thought of as British leadership in the Arab world, and who had no scruples about replacing French influence and French authority in the Levant. The Free French, not least de Gaulle himself, wanted to re-establish every ounce of that authority and that influence, and to extend them if possible. On this they were in complete agreement with the Vichyists whom they had to fight.

Despite the fact that a joint proclamation had been prepared declaring that Free France would grant independence to Syria and the Lebanon, and that this promise had been guaranteed by the British, the Free French, three days before the launching of the operation, took a step which (in British eyes) was both reckless and unscrupulous.

A. P. Wavell to Prime Minister   *5th June, 1941*
Have just received telegram from Wilson to effect that use of term High Commissioner by Catroux will cause grave trouble and will create doubt as to our intentions towards inhabitants. Efforts by Spears to move de Gaulle at this end have failed.

Prime Minister to A. P. Wavell   *5th June, 1941*
Please convey following personal message to General de Gaulle from Prime Minister:
  "I must ask you in this grave hour not to insist on declaring Catroux High Commissioner of Syria."

The joint British—Free French advance into Syria and the Lebanon began early on the morning of 8th June. The aim was to reach Damascus and Beirut on the first day, with Rayak as the next objective, and then if possible an advance to Tripoli. The advantages of swiftness and secrecy for which Wavell had hoped were completely absent; and since Churchill, the War Cabinet and the Chiefs of Staff, overruling his own view, had ordered him to launch the operation, it was inevitable that it was watched in London with the keenest interest. Therefore disappointment sharpened quickly into indignation when, for close on twenty-four hours, there was a disconcerting silence from the front, from Wilson's headquarters in Jerusalem and from Cairo. Just before midnight the C.I.G.S. sent a sharp signal to Wavell saying that the news from Syria was coming in in Press flashes, and requesting him to report at once and make better arrangements for prompt reports thereafter.

Next morning Wavell went up to the Western Desert to see Beresford-Peirse and Creagh, and stayed the night. In London the whole day went by without the information for which Churchill was now clamouring.

C.I.G.S. to A. P. Wavell   *9th June, 1941, 2020 hrs.*
Essential that Prime Minister should have fuller report Syrian operation for his statement to House at noon to-morrow 10th, particularly regarding attitude French and Arabs. Please cable urgently all possible news.

A. P. Wavell to C.I.G.S.   *11th June, 1941, 1041 hrs.*
Sorry about lack of information from Syria, my almost hourly requests produce nothing. Have sent up several liaison officers without result. Communications are poor and forward troops especially Free French are apparently not reporting. Am going to Palestine myself to-morrow and will try to improve matters.

The enterprise proved to be anything but a walk-over. The Vichyist High Commissioner for Syria and the Lebanon, General Dentz, had under his command a force of some 35,000 men, of whom about 8,000 were Frenchmen, whose loyalties were grievously torn. It became apparent early in the campaign that their bitterest hostility was reserved for the Free French fighting alongside the British, Australians and Indians. The Germans made it clear that they regarded it as a purely Anglo-French matter, but announced that they would give the Vichy forces their "full co-operation." Thereafter they discreetly avoided involvement of any kind, and withdrew from the conflict and the country. The Free French hope that officers and men would flock to serve under the Cross of Lorraine ought now to have been fulfilled; but the atmosphere of unreality in which the operation began was rapidly dispelled by the fierceness of the resistance offered by the Vichy forces.

On the left of the advance, up the coastal road in the Lebanon and through the high tangle of mountains, the Australians in some very hard fighting took the hill town of Merj Ayoun on 8th June and crossed the river Litani near the coast. On the right flank, the Free French by 12th June were still some ten miles from Damascus, which took them, supported by a brigade of 4th Indian Division, another nine days to capture.

The Vichy French now began a series of counter-attacks, using medium tanks with considerable effectiveness. Although all these were driven back, the advance was brought almost to a standstill and Wavell had to send reinforcements. Towards the end of June Wilson took several formations from Iraq under his command. Even with their help, and after a good deal of hard fighting, it was not until 11th July that Dentz was compelled to sue for an armistice, which he signed at Acre three days later.

The occupation of Syria, despite the hazards of its launching, despite the political difficulties which inevitably it brought in its train, despite the stress to which it subjected Wavell, despite the deficiencies in the equipment of the formations which undertook it, and despite the vicissitudes they encountered, greatly improved Britain's strategical position in the Middle East. Wavell, in view of the paucity of his resources, was justified in his reluctance to accept this latest burden thrust upon him by the War Cabinet and the Chiefs of Staff; and they on their side were justified in imposing their will upon him. "There is always much to be said for not attempting more than you can do and for making a certainty of what you try. But this principle, like others in life and war, has its exceptions."[16]

A. P. Wavell to C.I.G.S.   *9th June, 1941, 0825 hrs.*
Am visiting Western Desert this afternoon returning to-morrow. Tedder also out there to-day. Will give you more information about "Battleaxe" on return. . . .
Haining has arrived Alexandria, should be Cairo this morning.

Wavell was back in Cairo early on the afternoon of 10th June. De Gaulle was due to call on him at seven o'clock. Before this appointment the Chief composed a telegram to Dill setting out, as he had promised, the final plan for "Battleaxe."

The advance, he said, was to be made in three columns. The coastal column, consisting of a brigade of 4th Indian Division, the Central India Horse, a field regiment and a field company, would advance between the sea and the escarpment to the area of Sollum barracks, and would help the second, escarpment, column to capture Halfaya. The second column, consisting of the main body of 4th Indian Division and the 4th Armoured Brigade Group, was to advance just south of the escarpment to capture Halfaya, Musaid, Bir Wair and the Capuzzo area. The third column, consisting of 7th Armoured Division less the 4th Armoured Brigade Group, now had one regiment with the new cruiser tanks, called Crusaders, and had the task of advancing south of the escarpment on the general axis Bir Habata—Sidi Suleiman—Bir Azeiz, to protect the escarpment column's left flank and to attack the enemy's tank force wherever encountered.

The first and second columns would deal with the enemy's principal defended area; 7th Armoured Division would threaten their rear and their supplies. Wavell believed that this would lead to a tank battle, either east of the frontier while Halfaya was under attack or in the Capuzzo—Bir Azeiz area during or after the attack on Capuzzo.

What would happen next must depend on the result of this first phase of the battle. The intention was to mask Bardia, if the Axis forces withdrew into it, and move on to El Adem with 7th Armoured Division, two field regiments and part or all of the 22nd Guards Brigade as soon as possible. If there had been a heavy tank battle on the first day, a day's pause might be necessary to overhaul the vehicles and reorganise, but light covering detachments would meanwhile be pushed forward.

The advance to El Adem, he pointed out, would take two days, because the "I" tanks lacked range and mobility. The garrison of Tobruk would keep the enemy pinned by minor offensive action but were not to make their main effort until 7th Armoured Division was within striking distance. The signal ended:

> Particularly request that Press and B.B.C. are made to treat this operation in initial stages as continuation of minor activity on frontier which has been going on for some time past and not as large-scale counter-offensive.

The Commander-in-Chief spent less than forty-eight hours in Cairo. On 12th June, at 7.30 in the morning, he was off from Heliopolis to Palestine, to see for himself how the Syrian expedition was going. He returned to Cairo on the following morning, and dined that evening with the Egyptian Prime Minister. On the morning of Saturday, 14th June, a private telegram from the C.I.G.S. was on his desk. Dill strove hard to strengthen his friend's self-confidence. He assured Wavell that he was the right man for handling "our present immense difficulties." Close support from Tedder in the air, and the ability in Beresford-Peirse "to drive on when there is no drive left in anyone," were what he asked for. The battle would not be won without heavy losses, and Wavell's inspiring presence might be necessary before the end. "I feel that 'Battleaxe' is going to be a close-run thing," he said, "but believe that you are likely to get a greater and more important success than you ever dreamed of."

That afternoon Wavell played a round of golf with Blamey, and won it. Earlier in the day he had sent a signal to Beresford-Peirse which illustrated the magnitude of the hopes that now attached to "Battleaxe."

A. P. Wavell to General Beresford-Peirse   *14th June, 1941*

"Battleaxe" is most important operation yet undertaken in Middle East, success will bring incalculable results. First decisive defeat of German troops on land will be outstanding event. Impress on all that attacks must be pressed with utmost boldness and resolution and losses accepted. You have air resources on scale that we have not had before and I know Collishaw[17] will give you closest possible support. Use any troops at your disposal and confirm and exploit success and do not worry about rear defences. Am confident you will gain decisive victory and send you and your troops my very best wishes.

"Battleaxe," the last major battle fought under Wavell's command in the Middle East, failed in its purpose, and the hopes that had been pinned on it were not fulfilled.

Rommel, himself forbidden to attack and unable to retreat, had been expecting a British offensive for some weeks. His intelligence was good, but he over-estimated the British tank strength almost as much as the British over-estimated his. He thought that Wavell had more than 300, while Wavell believed that his opponent "could concentrate 300 against our total of approximately 200." In fact Rommel had fewer than 200 German tanks, half in the forward area with the tank regiment of the 15th Panzer Division and the rest with the 5th Light Division in reserve near Tobruk. No Italian tanks were engaged in the battle at any time.

Beresford-Peirse's forces began their approach march from Sofafi and Buqbuq on the late afternoon of 14th June. Rommel alerted the whole of what he called "the Sollum front" at 2100 hours that evening. The British approach march was completed by moonlight in the early hours of 15th June. The R.A.F. had carried out their preliminary attacks successfully; they gave the approach march fighter cover, and it was executed without any interference from the enemy. On the 15th, when the ground attack opened, the R.A.F. quickly established a local air superiority, and there were only six air attacks, all light, during the day.

The first day, though the Official History described it as one "of varying fortunes," went on the whole much better for the Germans than for the British. Of the three columns that went into the attack, the one on the coastal, right, flank made no headway towards Sollum or at Halfaya. The centre column took Capuzzo during the morning, and then moved on to Halfaya Pass, guarding the eastern end of the escarpment and one of the primary objectives of the whole attack. At the top of the Pass the Germans had dug in four 88-mm. guns, using them for the first time in the desert as anti-tank weapons. As the British "I" tanks, each armed with a two-pounder (whose effective range was 800 yards at most), moved slowly forward, they were torn to pieces in a matter of moments by the Germans' 20-pound shells, which were deadly at a range of one mile. In the Pass eleven out of twelve Matildas were burned out instantly, and below the escarpment four more, in the second wave of six, were trapped by mines.

Seventh Armoured Brigade, the spearhead of the inland column, came up from the south through a thickening haze, and at Hafid Ridge encountered four more 88-mm. guns, emplaced with similar skill; by nightfall they had only 48 cruiser tanks still fit to fight.

> The British armour had been reduced to less than half its initial strength, whereas Rommel's had not yet been seriously engaged, and his losses were very light in comparison. His orders to the 15th Panzer Division had been to keep its panzer regiment in hand until the situation had clarified, so the tank counter-attack did not begin until the evening. Meanwhile the 5th Light Division was driving to the scene, by relays, from Tobruk.[18]

General Rommel to Frau Rommel   *16th June, 1941*

Dearest Lu,

There was heavy fighting in our eastern sector all day yesterday, as you will have seen long ago from *Wehrmacht* communiqués. To-day—it's 2.30 a.m.—will see the decision. It's going to be a hard fight, so you'll understand that I can't sleep. These

lines in haste will show you that I'm thinking of you both. More
soon—when it's all over. [19]

The British plan for 16th June was that the 4th Indian Division,
whose new commander was General Frank Messervy (who had won
fame earlier in the year with Gazelle Force), should renew its attack on
the Halfaya Pass, consolidate its hold on the Capuzzo area, and try
to exploit any enemy weakness by driving towards Bardia. The 4th
Armoured Brigade was to join 7th Armoured Division; and their task
would be to destroy Rommel's armour in the Hafid area and secure the
desert flank.

But Rommel's plan, prepared late on the night of 15th/16th June,
after a careful analysis of British wireless intercepts and captured
documents, was destined to play havoc with the British force's
movements. He decided that the main component of his 5th Light
Division should launch an attack early on the morning of the 16th
from a point west of Sidi Azeiz towards Sidi Suleiman, with the
object of getting through to the Halfaya Pass; and that the 15th
Panzer Division should move south at first light on either side of
Capuzzo in order to pin down the considerable British force holding
out there. "I planned," Rommel wrote, "to concentrate both armoured
divisions suddenly into one focus and thus deal the enemy an unexpected blow in his most sensitive spot." [20]

Early on the morning of the 16th, the 15th Panzer Division
launched its attack on Capuzzo as ordered. A violent and heavy tank
battle developed; the Germans' onslaught was held and shattered
by the 4th Armoured Brigade, the 31st Field Regiment R.A. and the
Buffs. The Scots Guards took Musaid in the small hours and went on
to drive the enemy out of Sollum barracks. At about 1030 hours the
15th Panzer Division reported that it had been forced to break off its
attack on Capuzzo. British morale at this moment was very high.
Of the 80 tanks which the 15th Panzer Division had taken into battle,
only 30 remained; the others were either burned-out hulks on the
battlefield or were awaiting recovery and repair. Nevertheless,
Messervy thought the situation too tense to allow 4th Armoured
Brigade to join the 7th Armoured Division, as had been arranged the
night before.

A. P. Wavell to C.I.G.S.   *16th June, 1941, 1230 hrs.*
"Battleaxe." We are sending you all information as it comes in.
General impression heavy fighting and close-run battle. Position

appears not unsatisfactory but obviously losses are considerable and there will have to be pause and reinforcement before second stage can be attempted. Am just off to Western Desert, probably return to-morrow.

While Wavell's aircraft was on its way to Bagush, Rommel's 5th Light Division, moving from just west of Sidi Azeiz, ran into the British 7th Armoured Brigade and two columns of the Support Group some six miles west of Sidi Omar. A fierce tank versus tank battle ensued which, Rommel wrote,

> was soon decided in our favour and the division succeeded in fighting its way through to the area north-east of Sidi Omar and continuing its advance on Sidi Suleiman. This was the turning point of the battle. I immediately ordered the 15th Panzer Division to disengage all its mobile forces as quickly as possible and, leaving only the essential minimum to hold the position north of Capuzzo, to go forward on the northern flank of the victorious 5th Light Division towards Sidi Suleiman. . . .
> The enemy seemed unwilling to relinquish the initiative so easily, and concentrated the bulk of his armour north of Capuzzo in order to launch a heavy attack early next morning against the element of 15th Panzer Division still left in the north, with the object of forcing a break-through. To impose my plans on the enemy from the outset, I ordered the 5th Light and 15th Panzer Divisions to get their attack on Sidi Suleiman moving at 4.30 a.m., i.e. before the probable start time of the enemy attack.[21]

When Wavell's Hudson reached Bagush at five o'clock on the afternoon of the 16th, he found that Beresford-Peirse had gone up to his advanced headquarters at Sidi Barrani. The R.A.F. sent him on in a small Proctor with an escort of three Hurricanes; he reached Sidi Barrani just as Beresford-Peirse returned from seeing his divisional commanders, to whom the position had seemed fairly satisfactory when he left them at four o'clock.

The 22nd Guards Brigade, with two field-gunner regiments, a medium battery and some anti-tank guns, appeared to be firmly installed at Capuzzo, Musaid and Bir Wair, and was extending its right flank towards Sollum. Fourth Armoured Brigade was in support and had repulsed several counter-attacks. Some seven to eight hundred prisoners and a number of guns had been taken. The tank battle to the south-east was described, not at all accurately, as "a successful engagement."

But Wavell was uneasy. Rommel's hold on Halfaya had not been loosened, despite heavy casualties in repeated assaults up the escarpment throughout the day by the 11th Indian Infantry Brigade. His air activity was increasing, and the R.A.F. had had some losses. It was far more disturbing, however, that while Beresford-Peirse's total of armour now in action amounted to 40 cruisers and 30 "I" tanks, Rommel was estimated to have many more still battleworthy.

Rommel's tank losses, as a matter of fact, were serious, in the 5th Light as well as the 15th Panzer Division; but he was at his most decisive and resilient, and had a far quicker grasp of the tactical opportunities and dangers of this fast-moving and complicated battle than his opponents. Out of their confusion he made his own kind of sense.

That evening Messervy and Creagh agreed that, with the 22nd Guards Brigade still holding firmly on to Capuzzo, 4th Armoured Brigade was to join 7th Armoured Division next morning and make a concerted attempt to shatter Rommel's armour. But during the night British wireless communications broke down, and it was not till the morning was far advanced that they were restored. Meanwhile Rommel's attack came in at dawn. Fifth Light was at Sidi Suleiman by six o'clock in the morning; Messervy's headquarters was almost overrun by a great wave of German tanks of the 15th Panzer Division, which proceeded to wreak havoc amongst 4th Armoured Brigade.

At 9.30 a corrupt and incomprehensible signal came through to Sidi Barrani from 7th Armoured Division's headquarters. When it was repeated Creagh explained to Beresford-Peirse, and to Wavell standing alongside his subordinate commander, that the situation was very serious: he now had left only 22 cruisers and 17 "I" tanks, and Rommel was excellently placed to cut off all the British forces remaining at Capuzzo and Halfaya. Would Beresford-Peirse come up at once by air, because an important decision would have to be made? Beresford-Peirse agreed, and added that he had a distinguished visitor with him.

This radio-telephone conversation was overheard by the Germans' interception service, and Rommel concluded that Creagh no longer found himself capable of handling the situation. "It being now obvious that in their bewildered state the British would not start anything for the time being, I decided to pull the net tight by going on to Halfaya."[22]

Wavell realised that he would have to make the vital decision himself. With a strong fighter escort he and Beresford-Peirse flew up to Creagh's headquarters near Halfway House. By the time they arrived the matter had been taken summarily out of his hands. Messervy, believing that only an instant decision could save 22nd Guards Brigade and the formations still grimly fighting to get up to Halfaya, had ordered a withdrawal along the narrow corridor still open to Halfway House, and had told Creagh on the radio-telephone, in Hindustani, what he intended. The movement had begun at eleven o'clock; it was now close on noon and too late for Wavell to counter-mand Messervy's order even if he wanted to. He listened to Creagh's report, abandoned any idea that 7th Armoured Division should counter-attack at Sidi Suleiman, ordered that the operation should be broken off and formations withdraw and refit, collecting as many crippled tanks as possible, and asked that Messervy should come to see him.

When Messervy arrived at the airstrip Wavell's face was grim, but all he said was: "I think you were right to withdraw in the circumstances, but orders should have come from Western Desert Force."[23]

He flew back at once to Cairo, and that afternoon signalled Dill a full account of the battle from the time of his arrival at Sidi Barrani. Its opening words were: "I regret to report failure of 'Battleaxe'."

Churchill, that usually gregarious but complicated being, was overborne with a desire for solitude while he waited for the reports of "Battleaxe," which had for him so personal an emotional significance. He went, quite alone, to his own home, Chartwell, shuttered and sheeted, silent, beloved. There they brought him the news. "I wandered about the valley disconsolately for some hours."[24]

"Battleaxe" was a sharp setback, but not a calamitous defeat. Rommel was extended to his limit, and although he exulted in his victory, he had no hope whatever, as he made clear in his letters to his wife, of exploiting it or of advancing towards the Delta; the best that he could say, optimist though he was by temperament, was: "Now the enemy can come, he'll get an even bigger beating." Churchill, however, felt it deeply, and he mourned the frustration of his hopes as keenly as the destruction of his Tiger cubs. Wavell, immediately and without any complaint, took all the responsibility—despite the shortcomings of his tanks and his guns, despite the breakdown in communications, and despite Messervy's impetuous order to withdraw—and it was on Wavell's shoulders that the punishment was bound to fall. Yet Rommel, not in the first aftermath of battle but when he was compiling his memoirs, said:

Wavell's strategic planning of this offensive had been excellent. What distinguished him from other British army commanders was his great and well-balanced strategic courage, which permitted him to concentrate his forces regardless of his opponent's possible moves. He knew very well the necessity of avoiding any operation which would enable his opponent to fight on interior lines and destroy his formations one by one with locally superior concentrations. But he was put at a great disadvantage by the slow speed of his heavy infantry tanks, which prevented him from reacting quickly enough to the moves of our faster vehicles. Hence the slow speed of the bulk of his armour was his soft spot, which we could seek to exploit tactically.[25]

In "Battleaxe" the Western Desert Force lost 122 officers and men killed, 588 wounded and 259 missing. Four guns were lost. Of the 90 cruiser and roughly 100 "I" tanks which began the battle, 27 cruisers and 64 "I" tanks were lost through enemy action or breakdown. The R.A.F. lost 33 fighters and three bombers. On the German side, 93 officers and men were killed, 350 wounded and 235 missing. They began the battle with 190 tanks, of which 107 were gun tanks; twelve in all were destroyed by British action; and the number of those that broke down was uncertain, but was probably about 50 in all, apart from those that were repaired during the battle. Ten German aircraft were destroyed. The Italians—with infantry only—played a small part in the battle. The British claimed to have taken 350 prisoners and to have turned most of them loose before withdrawing.[26]

A. P. Wavell to C.I.G.S.   *19th June, 1941*
Very sorry about "Battleaxe." Main trouble was that 7th Armoured Division hastily re-equipped was not fit for battle tactically or technically. Infantry tank without transporter is definitely not weapon for desert warfare. Tank crews were not sufficiently trained, hence shooting not good and too many mechanical breakdowns. Think troops fought all right but enemy

was waiting for us with carefully prepared counter-attack and was too strong.

C.I.G.S. to A. P. Wavell   *20th June, 1941*
Don't worry too much about "Battleaxe." I am sure you are right about main trouble. Of course Infantry tanks were never intended for desert warfare. Original ones were sent because I thought they would be useful in the Delta. Being wise after event would it have been better to get enemy committed at Tobruk by a really hearty prick and chance the losses just before attacking or just as attack was made on Sollum? This is alas only of academic interest now.

A. P. Wavell to Prime Minister   *21st June, 1941*
Am very sorry for failure of "Battleaxe" and loss of so many Tiger cubs, especially since I have realised from figures produced by liaison officer how short we are of requirements at home. Fear this failure must add much to your anxieties. I was over-optimistic and should have advised you that 7th Armoured Division required more training before going into battle. Feel I should also have deferred "Exporter" till we could have put in larger force, but in both places I was impressed by apparent need for immediate action.

Wavell pondered the hard lessons of the past four or five months. He drafted, for discussion with Andrew Cunningham and Tedder, a short note on future policy in the Middle East. A liaison officer was due to leave for London the following morning, Sunday, 22nd June; by the hand of this officer Wavell sent a copy of the draft, with a personal line to Dill, so that the War Cabinet and the Chiefs of Staff might be aware of the lines on which his mind was working.

Hitherto we have been living a somewhat hand-to-mouth existence in the Middle East with no definite policy for more than a few weeks ahead at the best. I suggest that the time has now come when we can take a somewhat longer view and direct all our preparations towards a certain date and a certain thing.

It seems probable that the German concentration against Russia has given us a breathing space in the Middle East. The length of this respite will depend on the result of the negotiations or of the conflict between Germany and Russia. It is impossible to forecast this, but I propose that we assume that it may be some seven or eight weeks before Germany is ready to begin offensive operations against the Middle East. I suggest that we assume 1st September as our zero date and that by that date we must be ready to resist the most intensive attack on our positions in the Middle East.

As early as possible, and certainly before that date, we must carry out the following:

    a. Complete our defences and defensive preparations in the Western Desert.

    b. Complete the occupation of Syria and make our defensive arrangement.

    c. Complete the defences of Cyprus and place the necessary garrison in it.

    d. Concert a common plan of action with India for the defence of Syria and Iraq.

    e. Be prepared to meet an intensive air attack on Egypt. I suggest that if we are agreed on this we should lay down a general project and then work intensively at carrying it out.

But by the time the liaison officer's aircraft left Cairo, certain decisions had been taken in London which were to make the note he carried, and indeed all Wavell's views on the future policy for the Middle East, of indirect and historical interest only. The Prime Minister shrank from the abrupt course of dismissing the Commander-in-Chief, which held, he believed, a real degree of political risk. During the Iraq campaign the alternative of making Wavell and Auchinleck exchange posts began to appeal to him more and more, in spite of the opposition shown by both Amery and Dill. As has been seen, he put it aside for a time, while Crete, Syria, and finally "Battleaxe" engaged everyone's attention and energies. The swift failure of "Battleaxe" confirmed the Prime Minister's determination to hesitate no longer. He was convinced that he had found the right solution, and he would brook no opposition and consider no compromise.

On Saturday, 21st June, Kennedy, the D.M.O., returned to the War Office from a week's leave. When he reported to Dill, the C.I.G.S. said: "I suppose you realise we shall lose the Middle East?"[27] This view was by no means shared in the Middle East, as Wavell's note composed that same day made quite clear.

Late that afternoon the Prime Minister sent over to the War

Office copies of two telegrams he had decided to send, one to Wavell and the other to Lord Linlithgow, the Viceroy of India. There had been a brief preliminary exchange between the Prime Minister and the Viceroy; Linlithgow, after evincing considerable reluctance to agree to the change, finally conceded that "on the P.M.'s judgment of the necessities of the situation, he must express his readiness to make any sacrifice."[28]

Dill made one more valiant, if unavailing, effort to avert some at least of the consequences of the step. He at once composed a minute to the Prime Minister setting out a number of cogent arguments against the proposal to send Wavell to India, and recommending that he be brought back to the United Kingdom to report and then have the rest that two years of incessant strain had earned him. He took the document across to Downing Street himself. Churchill, with Margesson, the Secretary of State for War, sitting beside him, read it through without comment, and sent off his two telegrams unaltered.

Prime Minister to A. P. Wavell   *21st June, 1941*

I have come to conclusion that public interest will best be served by appointment of General Auchinleck to relieve you in command of armies of Middle East. I have greatly admired your command and conduct of these armies both in success and adversity, and victories which are associated with your name will be famous in the story of the British Army and are an important contribution to our final success in this obstinate war. I feel however that after the long strain you have borne a new eye and a new hand are required in this most seriously menaced theatre. I am sure that you are incomparably the best man and most distinguished officer to fill the vacancy of Commander-in-Chief in India. I have consulted the Viceroy upon subject and he assures me that your assumption of this great office and task will be warmly welcomed in India, and adds that he himself will be proud to work with one who bears, in his own words, so shining a record. I propose therefore to submit your name to His Majesty accordingly.

General Auchinleck is being ordered to proceed at once to Cairo where you will make him acquainted with the whole situation and concert with him the future measures which you and he will take in common to meet the German drive to East now clearly impending. I trust he may arrive by air within the next four or five days at latest. After you have settled everything up with him you should proceed at your earliest convenience to India. No announcement will be made and matter must be kept strictly secret until you are both at your posts.

Prime Minister to Viceroy   *21st June, 1941*
Will you kindly pass following to General Auchinleck. I have already telegraphed to General Wavell.

After very careful consideration of all circumstances I have decided to submit your name to King for command of His Majesty's armies in the Middle East. You should proceed forthwith to Cairo and relieve General Wavell. General Wavell will succeed you as Commander-in-Chief in India. You should confer with him upon whole situation and should also concert with him the measures you will take in common to arrest eastward movement of German armies which is clearly impending. Pray let me know when you will arrive. The change is to be kept absolutely secret until you are installed in your new post.[29]

These signals reached their destinations in the small hours of Sunday, 22nd June. At almost exactly the same time, with German aircraft and German ground forces already invading the Soviet Union, Ribbentrop, Hitler's Foreign Minister, delivered a formal declaration of war to the Russian Ambassador in Berlin. In Cairo Churchill's signal was delivered to Arthur Smith. A little after daybreak the C.G.S. dressed and went to the Chief's house. He found Wavell shaving, his face covered with lather and his razor poised. He read out the signal. Wavell showed no emotion. He merely said, "The Prime Minister's quite right. This job needs a new eye and a new hand," and went on shaving.[30] He then went out into the crisp Cairene morning; he had his ride, and his swim at the Sporting Club, and talked genially, if a trifle inscrutably, in the dressing-room to his A.D.C. and some of the A.D.C.'s young friends about the German attack on Russia.

From the Prime Minister's viewpoint it was a neat and relatively painless operation. Wavell, he recorded, received the decision "with poise and dignity."[31] What its ultimate consequences—for good or ill—would be, no one at that time could predict.

C.I.G.S. to A. P. Wavell   *21st June, 1941*
I shall miss you in command of Middle East more than I can say.

I have rejoiced in your wonderful successes and have felt an understanding sympathy in your failures. In India our association will still be very close and as *Drang nach Osten* develops, your task may well transcend in importance that which you have performed in Egypt with so much distinction and success. May all good fortune attend you.

A. P. Wavell to Prime Minister   *22nd June, 1941*

I think you are wise to make change and get new ideas and action on the many problems in Middle East and am sure Auchinleck will be successful choice. I appreciate your generous references to my work and am honoured that you should consider me fitted to fill post of C.-in-C. in India. If at all possible would like short period at home before proceeding India to see my son and settle some business and I should probably be better for some rest and change before taking up new command. Fully recognise however that public interest may require my immediate departure for India.

The change of Commanders-in-Chief was accomplished with courtesy and friendliness. The public announcement on 2nd July was accompanied by a number of photographs of the two generals posed together. There was no interregnum. Arthur Smith stayed on as C.G.S., to give as loyal and efficient service to Auchinleck as to Wavell. So did his Intelligence chief, Shearer. An able young major-general named Neil Ritchie, who had been an officer in The Black Watch, was flown out to take up the post of D.C.G.S. It was also announced that the King had approved the appointment of the Rt. Hon. Oliver Lyttelton, D.S.O., M.C., M.P., as Minister of State and member of the War Cabinet resident in the Middle East, charged with the responsibility of representing the War Cabinet in that theatre and concerting on their behalf measures necessary for the prosecution of the war other than the conduct of military operations. General Haining, the Intendant-General, took up his appointment, in which he was supposed to relieve the new Commander-in-Chief of administrative chores. Wavell reflected, without rancour, that there were now three high-powered authorities to tackle the work that he had done single-handed for the past two years.

Churchill thus found a fairly dignified, if temporary, escape from, but not a solution to, a painful dilemma. As anyone who has served in a war knows, its verdicts are always rough justice. But from the beginning there were tensions between Churchill and Wavell. If the latter had been granted an unbroken succession of victories from February, 1941, onwards, instead of having to face increasing difficulties and severe setbacks, these tensions might have been ignored on both sides; but in the end the break had to be made.

The truth was known to few. Dill said in his minute of protest on 21st June that Wavell would not add to Churchill's burdens by suggesting, or encouraging others to suggest, that he had been badly treated. This undertaking was completely fulfilled. "After the war," Dill added, "he may write—he writes well—and goodness knows what he may say, but who cares?"

The roughest and the least magnanimous part of the decision was the way in which Wavell's repeated requests for leave in the United Kingdom, and Dill's formal support for those requests, were disregarded. Churchill would not take a risk, which in fact was nonexistent. The greatest of statesmen can be cruel, and the most illustrious of generals can be tired and homesick. Wavell made no complaint: like the men he commanded, he soldiered on. Five days after he had handed over to Auchinleck, he flew off to Delhi. India had given him much happiness and adventure in his youth. Now he in return was to give India service of no small value in her most perilous and most challenging epoch.

CHRONOLOGICAL
TABLE

1940	Egypt, Libya and Cyrenaica	East Africa	Iraq and Syria
May 10th			
27th-28th	Wavell assures Dill he can hold Africa		
June 10th-11th	Immediate frontier offensive activity by Wavell's forces. Offensive maintained during June and July	Frontier activity on Sudan and Kenya borders	
17th			
July 4th		Italians take Kassala and Gallabat	
15th		Italians take Moyale	
August 5th-19th		Italians take British Somaliland	
7th-15th			
September 13th-18th	Italians advance into Egypt		
October 16th	Mr. Eden (S. of S. for War) in Middle East		
28th			
29th			
November 2nd	Wavell issues directive for "Compass"		
4th			
8th			
18th			
December 9th	O'Connor launches "Compass"		

Greece and Crete	*United Kingdom and other theatres of war*	1940
		May
	Germans attack in the West	10th
	Mr. Churchill becomes Prime Minister	
	Sir John Dill C.I.G.S.	27th-28th
	Dunkirk begins	
		June
	Italy declares war on Great Britain	10th-11th
	Franco-German armistice	17th
		July
	Battle of Britain begins	4th
		August
	Wavell in London to report to War Cabinet	7th-15th
		September
		October
Italians invade Greece		28th
First British troops in Crete		29th
		November
R.A.F. begins to operate in Greece		4th
Greeks break Italian advance		8th
Greeks counter-attack Italians		18th
		December

1940	Egypt, Libya and Cyrenaica	East Africa	Iraq and Syria
December			
11th	Wavell withdraws 4th Indian Div. for use in E. Africa		
16th	Sollum and Capuzzo captured		

1941			
January			
4th	Bardia captured		
6th		Wavell flies to Khartoum, advances date of East African offensive	
11th			
13th			
18th-19th		Platt captures Kassala Cunningham advances in Kenya	
22nd	Tobruk captured		
29th			

February			
3rd		Battle of Keren begins	
6th	Benghazi captured		
7th	Battle of Beda Fomm Limit of O'Connor's advance		
12th	Rommel arrives in Tripoli		
14th		Kismayu captured	
16th	Rommel at front		
19th	Eden-Dill mission in Cairo (Eden now Foreign Secy.)		
22nd			
25th		Cunningham takes Mogadishu	

Greece and Crete	United Kingdom and other theatres of war	1940
		December
		1941
		January
	Luftwaffe begins to operate from Sicily	11th
Wavell flies to Greece Offer of British troops refused by Metaxas		13th
Death of Metaxas		29th
		February
Eden, Dill and Wavell in Athens		22nd
	Bulgaria joins Axis	25th

1941	Egypt, Libya and Cyrenaica	East Africa	Iraq and Syria
March			
1st		Worsening political situation in Iraq	
4th			
5th			
24th	Rommel takes El Agheila		
25th			
27th		Keren captured	
31st			Regent of Iraq quits Baghdad
April			
1st	Rommel takes Mersa Brega	Asmara captured	
3rd	Benghazi falls		Rashid Ali seizes power
5th		Addis Ababa captured	
6th			
7th	Gens. Neame and O'Connor taken prisoner		
8th	Wavell flies to Tobruk Rommel takes Mechili	Massawa captured	
10th-11th	Rommel takes Bardia and Sollum		
11th-14th			
13th	Tobruk besieged		
15th-19th	Rommel attempts unsuccessfully to capture Tobruk		British and Free French negotiations over Syria
19th			
21st			
24th-30th			
30th			Habbaniya besieged
May			
4th	Rommel's renewed attack on Tobruk fails		
5th		Haile Selassie enters Addis Ababa	*Luftwaffe* granted landing facilities in Syria Wavell given operational command in Iraq

514

Greece and Crete	United Kingdom and other theatres of war	1941
		March
Final Athens conference		4th
British troops sail for Greece		5th
	Yugoslavia signs Tripartite Pact	25th
	Coup d'état (pro-Allied) in Yugoslavia	31st
		April
Germans invade Greece and Yugoslavia		6th
Wilson withdraws to Olympus-Servia line		11th-14th
	Germans occupy Belgrade	13th
Wilson withdraws to Thermopylae		15th-19th
Wavell flies to Greece		19th
Decision to evacuate Greece		21st
British withdrawal from Greece		24th-30th
Wavell in Crete, appoints Freyberg to command defence of the island		30th
		May

1941	Egypt, Libya and Cyrenaica	East Africa	Iraq and Syria
May			
5th-12th	"Tiger" convoy passes through Mediterranean to Alexandria		
6th			Siege of Habbaniya lifted
15th-17th	British attack on Halfaya-Sollum-Capuzzo		
16th		Final Italian surrender at Amba Alagi	
19th	Longmore replaced by Tedder	Patriot operations continue in central Ethiopia	Decision to invade Syria and Lebanon ("Exporter") Falluja captured
20th			
21st			
27th	Germans recapture Halfaya Pass		British advance on Baghdad
28th-31st			
31st			Armistice in Iraq
June			
3rd			British forces occupy Mosul
8th			British forces enter Syria and Lebanon
15th-17th	Wavell's last Desert offensive ("Battleaxe") fails		
20th			Damascus captured
21st	Churchill replaces Wavell by Auchinleck		
22nd			

Greece and Crete	United Kingdom and other theatres of war	1941 May
German airborne invasion of Crete		20th
Loss of Maleme airfield		21st
Decision to evacuate Crete	*Bismarck* sunk	27th
Evacuation of Crete		28th-31st

		June
	Germans invade Russia	22nd

●

517

NOTES

Notes

Chapter I

page   note

29   1   *The Times*, 15th March, 1941, quoted in *Ronald Knox* by Evelyn Waugh, p. 49. Among Wavell's contemporaries or near-contemporaries at Summer Fields were Lord Simonds, Sir Maurice Hallett, Sir Basil Gould, Gen. Sir Kenneth Buchanan, Sir Evelyn Wrench, Sir Hubert Young and Mr. Christopher Stone.

29   2   R. H. Dundas: Emeritus Student of Christ Church, Oxford, 1910-57, lecturer in Greek history; served in The Black Watch, 3rd Bn., attached 2nd Bn. 1915-19.

31   3   *Other Men's Flowers*, Memorial Edition (1952), p. 373.

33   4   ibid., p. 243.

34   5   Sir Duncan Mackenzie, K.C.I.E. (Indian Civil Service, 1907-38).

34   6   *Other Men's Flowers*, p. 243.

36   7   Speech by A.P.W. on being made a Freeman of Winchester, *Hampshire Chronicle*, 25th September, 1943.

37   8   *The Boer War* by Edgar Holt, p. 144.

40   9   "Government Houses," article by A.P.W. in *House and Garden*, 1950.

42   10   *The Scotsman*, 30th September, 1901.

48   11   *The Pathans* by Olaf Caroe, p. xiii.

51   12   Col. Maxwell's son, in a letter to Major the Earl Wavell (hereafter referred to as A.J.W.), while not objecting to the publication of these stories, made the point that it would be unkind and inaccurate to give the impression that the Colonel was not interested in the regiment: there was no one who, all his life, retained a greater affection for and interest in The Black Watch.

52   13   *Other Men's Flowers*, p. 234.

52   14   ibid., pp. 201-2.

53   15   Col. the Hon. Malise Hore-Ruthven, C.M.G., D.S.O., to A.J.W.

Afterwards Air Vice-Marshal A. E. Borton, C.B., C.M.G., D.S.O., A.F.C.

Later Sir George Roos-Keppel, Chief Commissioner, N.W. Frontier Province, 1910-19. See *The Guardians* by Philip Woodruff, pp. 294-5, and Olaf Caroe, op. cit., pp. 423-5.

Chapter II

Other Men's Flowers, p. 25. These sentences, biographically among the most illuminating Wavell ever wrote, must be read in conjunction with some equally perceptive observations of his son's, in his Introduction to this Memorial Edition of the anthology: "My father unconsciously revealed some facets of his personality to the public at large in the only way his nature allowed"; and ". . . best of all, his book was a new sesame to the hearts of his oldest and dearest friends."

Everard Calthrop Wavell described as "the most attractive of my friends at the Staff College. He was the son of an artist and was himself artistic to the finger-tips. I always wondered why he chose the Army as a profession, but he was a good soldier. He had spent several years in Japan as a language student, and was a great admirer of Japanese artistry and of their simplicity of life. He himself reduced the baggage of life to a minimum. I think he never had more than one suit and one pair of boots at a time. I remember his coming to stay at Cranborne for a week-end and arriving on a bicycle with a small package containing his washing kit and one shirt which he considered ample equipment. It shook my very conventional mother to the core. He had the most original and independent mind of our term at the Staff College; but the Directing Staff considered him too unorthodox and he did not make the impression his abilities deserved. I don't think he had much military ambition and was more interested in art and ideas outside soldiering. He had charm and he had sincerity. He was killed as a battery commander near Ypres, in 1915 I think."

Gen. Sir Ivo Vesey, whom Wavell described as "the star turn of our term, the perfect staff officer, hard-working, accurate, sensible."

Maj-Gen. Cuthbert Fuller was a Sapper; nine years older than Wavell, he retired in 1935. Wavell's view of his Staff College contemporaries was that "we were not on the whole a very distinguished lot." His standards were high: they included one field-marshal, two full generals, one lieutenant-general and four major-generals.

66 5 Mme. Ertel's daughter, Mrs. Duddington, commented to A.J.W.: "A friend of Tolstoy. . . . Well, not really—he knew Tolstoy, was received at his house, and once had a visit from Tolstoy himself, but they weren't friends in the true sense, as my father and Chekov were. Father did not share Tolstoy's ideas, much as he admired him as an artist."

66 6 Forty years later Mrs. Duddington explained the relationships to A.J.W.: " 'A cousin of sorts' refers to Lenochka, our adopted sister. She was not related to us but we grew up together. The *babushki* were our grandmother, great-aunt and Lenochka's aunt. No, no—they did not do most of the housework; we had very good servants. Grandmother was nearly blind and spent her time knitting, and the aunts looked after the housekeeping. I think your father got the wrong impression owing to my great-aunt's extremely active character."

68 7 Football was a by-product of the Industrial Revolution, for the Russians as much as for the British. Textile mills, developed by British concessionaires in the Moscow suburbs, brought hundreds of peasants crowding in to work in unfamiliar conditions; they also brought, under contract, a number of British skilled craftsmen as supervisory staff. These men had Rugby kick-abouts on waste land near the factories; soon the Russian hands clamoured to be taught this fascinating pastime. The scrums turned into fierce rough-houses; the police stepped in, thinking the game was a cover for a new kind of revolutionary movement; and the British changed to Association football, for which the mill-hands had just as much enthusiasm, but which the police were prepared to tolerate. By 1911 there was a league in existence, consisting of eight to ten clubs.

71 8 The Grenadier Corps ranked immediately after the Guard Corps of the old Czarist Army, but it did not distinguish itself greatly in World War I.

72 9 Wavell thought that a possible explanation for this singular piece of misinformation was that Queen Victoria had sent a present of chocolate to her brave Tommies in South Africa.

74 10 Maj.-Gen. C. G. Fuller wrote to A.J.W.: "You might have had a Russian mother. Your father was fond of a girl—the daughter of a man who owned the Arbatski property. Her father would not approve it. She was going on the Volga

trip with myself and Churchill as chaperons, but her father forbade it."

74	11	*History of the British Army* by the Hon. J. W. Fortescue.
76	12	*France and Belgium 1914* by Brig.-Gen. Sir John Edmonds, p. 18.
84	13	*Mutiny at the Curragh* by A. P. Ryan, p. 124.
84	14	ibid., p. 132. Ryan adds that "permitted to disappear" was the exact phrase used by the War Office.
84	15	Gen. Fergusson's younger son, Lieut. Bernard Fergusson, was to be Wavell's A.D.C. when the latter commanded the 2nd Infantry Division in 1935.
84	16	Later Gen. Sir Hubert Gough, G.C.B., G.C.M.G., K.C.V.O.
84	17	Ryan, op. cit., p. 127.
85	18	ibid.

Chapter III

98	1	Maj.-Gen. R. J. Collins, in his book *Lord Wavell, A Military Biography*, wrote of this episode (p. 67): "It was typical of Wavell that . . . he at once offered to serve as a G.S.O.3, under the author as G.S.O.2." C. B. Thomson, who had been at the Staff College with Wavell, as Lord Thomson was Secretary of State for Air from 1929 to 1930 and was killed in the R101 disaster.
99	2	ibid.
105	3	Lady Edward Churchill was Eugénie Quirk's godmother.
106	4	*Allenby: Soldier and Statesman* by A. P. Wavell, p. 126.

Chapter IV

121	1	*The Supreme Command 1914-1918*, vol. II, p. 637.
122	2	*Allenby: Soldier and Statesman*, pp. 48-9.
122	3	ibid., p. 154.
124	4	*The Anvil of War* by F. S. Oliver, quoted in *Allenby*, p. 153.
124	5	op. cit., p. 255.
125	6	*The Australian Official History*, quoted by Wavell, op. cit., p. 158.
125	7	*Other Men's Flowers*, p. 442.
126	8	*Allenby*, pp. 168-70.
128	9	*Army Diary 1899-1926* by Col. Richard Meinertzhagen, p. 222.
128	10	*Allenby*, p. 169.
129	11, 12	ibid., p 179.

| 131 | 13 | ibid., pp. 182-3. |

131 13   ibid., pp. 182-3.
132 14   *Seven Pillars of Wisdom*, ch. LXXX.
132 15   ibid., p. 453.
135 16   Hankey, op. cit., vol. II, p. 767.
136 17   A.P.W. to W.C. Garcia, 29th January, 1939.
137 18   *Allenby*, p. 215. Wavell opens this section of his book with a sardonic quotation from the official Intelligence handbook on the Jordan Valley: "Nothing is known of the climate in summertime, since no civilised human being has yet been found to spend summer there."
139 19   ibid., pp. 224-5.
140 20   ibid., p. 229.
141 21   Wavell took a lasting pride in this raid, and recorded it in detail in an article in *The Army Quarterly* in July, 1930, under the title "Night Attacks—Ancient and Modern." Reproduced in *Soldiers and Soldiering* by A. P. Wavell, pp. 159-74.
143 22   op. cit., vol. II, p. 839.
144 23   *Allenby*, pp. 245-6.

Chapter V

146 1   *Other Men's Flowers*, p. 16.
151 2   *Trenchard, Man of Vision*, by Andrew Boyle, p. 551.
153 3   The articles were: Army; Seven Weeks War; Palestine Operations; Russian Campaigns in 1914-18. These last comprised: Caucasus Campaigns; Battles of Brest-Litovsk, Carpathians, Dunajee-San, Lemberg, Lodz, Narew, Lake Narocz, and Vistula-San; Sieges of Przemysl.
154 4   Later Field-Marshal Sir Francis Festing (C.I.G.S. 1958-61).
155 5   Quoted by B. H. Liddell Hart in *The Tanks*, vol. 1, p. 244.
156 6   Lieut.-Col. (later General) Sir Frederick Pile and Maj. (later Lieut.-Gen. Sir) Gifford le Q. Martel.
157 7   Liddell Hart, op. cit., vol. 1, p. 261.
158 8   Collins, op. cit., p. 131.
160 9   *The Palestine Campaigns* by A. P. Wavell.
162 10   A summary of lectures delivered to Staff College candidates of the Aldershot Command at various dates between 1930 and 1935.
162 11   R.U.S.I. Journal, No. 510, May 1933, pp. 254-73.
164 12   Subsequently Maj.-Gen. Dorman-Smith (now Dorman O'Gowan).
165 13   R.U.S.I. Journal, No. 510, p. 268.
167 14   Mr. John Carden, a brilliant engineer, was the manager of a

London garage owned by a Mr. Loyd. Immediately after World War I, in an attempt to make motoring inexpensive, he invented the Carden cycle-car; adapting it to military use, with the idea of making the infantryman mobile, he designed a tiny car moving on tracks. Through various vicissitudes, described in Liddell Hart's *The Tanks* (vol. I, p. 240), Carden went on improving and enlarging his designs, and in 1928 produced his Mark VI vehicle, "which showed a remarkable advance both in cross-country performance and in reliability." This became the standard British machine-gun carrier. Liddell Hart described Carden as "a man of genius," and his death in an air crash in 1935 as "a disaster from which British tank progress never recovered."

167 15 Collins, op. cit., p. 144.

170 16 Maj.-Gen. Dorman O'Gowan to the author.

170 17 Gen. Sir Thomas Riddell-Webster, Lieut.-Gen. Sir Gifford Martel and Air Marshal Sir Lawrence Pendred.

172 18 Joint Report on the *Cycle d'Information des Généraux et des Colonels* by Maj.-Gens. Wavell, Freyberg and Marshall-Cornwall.

175 19 Reproduced in *Soldiers and Soldiering*, pp. 95-100.

177 20 *Wavell: Portrait of a Soldier*, p. 38.

180 21 ibid., pp. 26-7.

181 22 R.U.S.I. Journal, February, 1936.

182 23 The man appointed to the post was Brigadier Alan Brooke later Field-Marshal Lord Alanbrooke.

Chapter VI

188 1 Cmd. 5749 of 1937.

189 2 Cmd. 5513 of 1937.

190 3 *The Seat of Pilate* by John Marlowe, pp. 145-6.

191 4 Lewis Andrews "was an Australian and had been a member of the Administration since its beginning. He spoke Arabic and Hebrew and knew the country in detail. He was generally accounted the ablest man in the Palestine Service. Fatally for him, the Jews considered him to be a friend." *Orde Wingate* by Christopher Sykes, p. 136.

192 5 The first appointment was honorary; the second gave the Mufti control of the Waqf—Moslem charitable funds, obtained from the subscriptions of the faithful—which he used for subversion and terrorism.

192 6 Field-Marshal Sir Cyril Deverell was then C.I.G.S.

200	7	Author's italics.
201	8	Collins, op. cit., p. 183.
201	9	Of the change-over of A.D.C.s Fergusson himself wrote: "It pleased Wavell's fancy that Fox should relieve me on precisely the second anniversary of Wavell taking over the 2nd Division, the 11th March [1937]; and I still have in my scrapbook my receipt for One Major-General, complete with Division, signed for by Michael Fox on that date." *Wavell*, p. 40. Fox's duplicate is in the scrapbook of the 2nd Bn. the Coldstream Guards.
201	10	To A. J. W.'s record of the conversation a note is appended by Lady Wavell: "I disagree here." This is a conflict of first-hand evidence and opinion, and is of crucial importance.
204	11	Many years later Frau Rommel presented the battered and historic little volume to Lady Wavell.

Chapter VII

213	1	Arthur Smith commented on this passage (after A.P.W.'s death): "I find such praise from a man like Wavell very humbling. I may be permitted to say that I often wondered why he was apparently satisfied with me as a C.G.S. I really did, for I had no 'originality' and disliked tanks and aeroplanes and all the mechanical things of modern warfare! I know of no [other] man who made all his staff want to do their utmost for him, our chief concern often being that he sometimes told us so little that we had (I believe successfully) to find out by intuition and understanding. I remember once saying to him, 'Can't we get on the offensive?' and he quietly replied, 'Arthur, I have been thinking of that for weeks.' This was prior to the first Cyrenaica offensive. He taught us all to look well ahead."
214	2	*History of the Second World War* (hereafter referred to as the *Official History*), *The Mediterranean and Middle East* by Maj.-Gen. I. S. O. Playfair, vol. 1, p. 38.
219	3	ibid., p. 61.
219	4	General Gamelin was Commander-in-Chief of the Franco-British forces in France, 1939-40, Admiral Darlan was C.-in-C. of the French Navy, and General Vuillemin was Chief of the French Air Staff.
220	5	*The Business of War* by Maj.-Gen. Sir John Kennedy, pp. 43-4.
221	6	A.P.W. commented to his sister: "It makes little difference, if any, being a C.-in-C. instead of G.O.C.-in-C., but puts me

on a level with Gort in France and the C.-in-C. India, I suppose."

223   7   *Speaking Generally* by A. P. Wavell, p. 7.

229   8   *The Second World War* by Winston S. Churchill (hereafter referred to as "Churchill"), vol. II, p. 49. Gen. Ismay was Chief of Staff to Churchill in his capacity as Minister of Defence, and was his principal liaison with the Chiefs of Staff.

234   9   ibid., p. 145.

234   10   *The Mediterranean and Middle East*, vol. I, pp. 99-100.

235   11   *Official History, Grand Strategy*, vol. II, by J. R. M. Butler, p. 298.

236   12   *The Mediterranean and Middle East*, vol. I, p. 93. The day before, it appears, Mussolini told Hitler that there were 350,000 troops of all arms in East Africa.

236   13   ibid., p. 94.

238   14   ibid., pp. 118-19.

240   15   *Speaking Generally*, p. 11.

241   16   Air Chief Marshal Sir Arthur Longmore had succeeded Sir William Mitchell as A.O.C.-in-C. in May.

242   17   *Grand Strategy*, vol. II, p. 303.

243   18   Note by Lieut.-Col. (later Maj.-Gen.) H. L. Birks, the G.S.O.I of 7th Armd. Div., quoted by Liddell Hart, op. cit., vol. II, p. 40.

246   19   Despatch: *Operations in the Middle East from August 1939 to November 1940*.

247   20   Christopher Sykes, op. cit., p. 242.

249   21   Churchill, vol. II, p. 375.

Chapter VIII

254   1   Churchill, vol. II, p. 376.

260   2   Wavell Papers. Also quoted in Churchill, vol. II, pp. 396-7. Force H: a naval task force, formed in June 1940, to work in the Atlantic and the approaches to the Western Mediterranean, based on Gibraltar. It comprised the battleships *Hood, Resolution* and *Valiant*, the aircraft carrier *Ark Royal*, two cruisers, and eleven destroyers.

262   3   Churchill, vol. II, p. 397. Churchill gives the whole of this long minute; the argument of the first three paragraphs is solely naval.

263   4   ibid., p. 379.

264   5   ibid., p. 383.

264	6	*Operations in the Somaliland Protectorate, 1939-1940.*
265	7	Churchill, vol. II, p. 383.
265	8	ibid., p. 384. The *Official History* (*The Mediterranean and Middle East*, vol. I, p. 179) gave a balanced verdict. Wavell, it said, after weighing a series of unknown and intangible factors, had justifiably concluded that in British Somaliland he could take a risk without endangering his decisive front in Egypt. The Italians, on the other hand, though they had ample forces and a good plan, had supply difficulties and overcame them, and won the battle, were unable to follow up in sufficient strength to interfere with the embarkation, "and paid for their success with 2,052 casualties and an expenditure of material that they could ill afford."
265	9	Churchill, vol. II, pp. 379-82.
266	10	Churchill himself noted (ibid., p. 381): "This was the wretched word used at this time for 'undrinkable.' I am sorry."
266	11	Wavell Papers. The version quoted by Churchill gave the estimated date of arrival, if by way of the Cape, as "during the first fortnight in October." Even the more precise amendment was queried by Wavell, who in London on 14th August had been given the date as 26th September.
267	12	Wavell Papers. Compare text in Churchill, vol. II, p. 382.
268	13	A.P.W. to C.I.G.S., 23rd August, 1940.
268	14	A.P.W. to C.I.G.S., 24th August, 1940.
269	15	*The Mediterranean and Middle East*, vol. I, p. 208.
269	16	ibid., note, p. 209.
272	17	*Despatch on Middle East Operations, August, 1939-November, 1940.*
272	18	*Soldiers and Soldiering*, p. 72.
272	19	*The Times*, 23rd October, 1942. Reproduced in *Soldiers and Soldiering*, pp. 45-56.
274	20	Wavell Papers, Note on genesis of "Compass," appendix A.
275	21	ibid., appendix B.
275	22	*The Mediterranean and Middle East*, vol. I, p. 258.
275	23	ibid., p. 257.
277	24	See Churchill, vol. II, pp. 441-3.
278	25	Note on genesis of "Compass," appendix C.
278	26	From an unpublished report compiled by Gen. O'Connor while a P.O.W. in Sulmona, in Italy, in the summer of 1941, and smuggled out to the U.K. Large extracts from this report are quoted in *Against Great Odds* by Brig. C. N. Barclay.
278	27	Churchill, vol. II, p. 447.

279	28	ibid., pp. 447-8.
279	29	*Eight Years Overseas* by Field-Marshal Lord Wilson of Libya, p. 47.
280	30	Note on genesis of "Compass," appendix D.
280	31	Churchill, vol. II, pp. 479-80.
281	32	Wavell Papers. This telegram is also quoted in Churchill, vol. II, p. 483, but the last two sentences are omitted.
284	33	General O'Connor's report. See Barclay, op. cit., p. 24.
285	34	Brig. (later Lieut.-Gen. Sir Alexander) Galloway; Col. John Harding (later Field-Marshal Lord Harding of Petherton). Dorman-Smith was now a brigadier and Commandant of the Middle East Staff School at Haifa; he had come up to Ma'aten Bagush on 25th November on the secret and personal instructions of Wavell himself.
285	35	Note on genesis of "Compass," appendix E.
286	36	Churchill, vol. II, pp. 483-4.
286	37	Note on genesis of "Compass," appendix F.
289	38	In Creagh's absence his division was commanded with great skill by Brig. J. A. C. Caunter.
289	39	*Wavell* by Bernard Fergusson, p. 11. Arthur Smith recalls that when he once asked A.P.W. why Churchill did not like him, the Chief said, "Perhaps because I don't talk enough."

Chapter IX

296	1	Churchill, vol. II, p. 540.
297	2	ibid., pp. 541-2.
299	3	Wavell Papers; also quoted in Churchill, vol. II, pp. 542-3.
300	4	Wavell Papers. This exchange is also given in Churchill, vol. II, p. 543, but Wavell's practical requests are omitted.
301	5	*The Mediterranean and Middle East*, vol. I, pp. 281-2.
307	6	See Churchill, vol. III, pp. 5-10.
309	7	ibid., p. 14.
309	8	Sir Michael Palairet was British Minister in Athens.
311	9	None of this series of telegrams from 8th-10th January is quoted by Churchill.
311	10	Churchill, vol. III, p. 16.
313	11	Wavell Papers; also quoted in Churchill, vol. III, pp. 16-17.
315	12	*The Mediterranean and Middle East*, vol. I, p. 319.
318	13	Despatch: *Operations in the Western Desert from 7th December, 1940, to 7th February, 1940*.

324	14	*The British Expedition to Greece, 1941*, published in *The Army Quarterly*, January, 1950, vol. 59, No. 2.
324	15	"Chink" was Brig. Dorman-Smith's nickname.
326	16	Gen. O'Connor's report. See Barclay, op. cit., p. 69.
327	17	*The Rommel Papers*, edited by B. H. Liddell Hart, pp. 99-100.
328	18	Kennedy, op. cit., p. 75.
329	19	*Speaking Generally*, p. 23

Chapter X

330	1	Maj.-Gen. Dorman O'Gowan to the author.
330	2	Churchill to Lord Boothby; from the latter's *My Yesterday, Your To-morrow*.
331	3	*The Mediterranean and Middle East*, vol. 1, p. 371, and *Grand Strategy*, vol. 11, p. 384.
334	4	The "Glen" ships were three liners converted for use as Infantry Assault Landing Ships.
335	5	Wavell Papers. The instructions are quoted in full in Churchill, vol. iii, pp. 60-2.
335	6	*The Rommel Papers*, p. 103.
337	7	Churchill, vol. iii, p. 63.
338	8	Wavell Papers; see also Churchill, vol. ii, pp. 63-5.
339	9	*The British Expedition to Greece, 1941*.
340	10	ibid.
341	11	ibid.
342	12	Wavell Papers.
344	13	Churchill, vol. iii, p. 68.
344	14	Kennedy, op. cit., p. 84.
344	15	Churchill, vol. iii, pp. 68-9.
345	16	*The British Expedition to Greece, 1941*.
346	17	Churchill, vol. iii, p. 85. For East African campaign, see chapter xi below.
346	18	ibid.
347	19	*The British Expedition to Greece, 1941*.
347	20	Wavell Papers.
348	21	ibid.
348	22	Lord Wilson, in *Eight Years Overseas*, says that he arrived on 4th March; but his name is given in the Wavell records as being present at the meeting held at the Legation at 1830 hrs. on 3rd March.
349	23	Wavell Papers; see also Churchill, vol. iii, pp. 87-8.
350	24	Churchill, vol. iii, p. 89.
351	25	"Influx" was the code name for an airborne assault on Sicily.

352	26	Wavell Papers; see also Churchill, vol. III, pp. 90-2.
352	27	Lieut.-Gen. Blamey was now the commander of the Australian contingent in M.E.F., and Freyberg was commander of the New Zealand contingent. They were both under the C.-in-C.'s operational orders, but possessed—and used—the right of direct consultation with their respective Governments.
353	28	Wavell Papers.
354	29	Churchill, vol. III, p. 94.
356	30	Wavell Papers, and Air Chief Marshal Sir Arthur Longmore in a communication to the author. "Jacqueline" was Lady Lampson, the wife of the British Ambassador in Cairo.
356	31	Churchill, vol. III, p. 90.
357	32	Wavell Papers.

Chapter XI

359	1	Despatch: *Operations in East Africa, November, 1940, to July, 1941.*
359	2	*The Campaigns of Wavell, 1939-1943*, by Robert Woollcombe, p. 42.
360	3	Christopher Sykes, op. cit., p. 244.
360	4	ibid., p. 230.
360	5	ibid., p. 232. Mr. Sykes adds that Wingate never knew that the prohibition was Wavell's, but believed that it was imposed by "people in the War Office who wished to revenge themselves on him." This was clearly not Wavell's motive. He disapproved of Zionism, and he wanted as little truck with it as possible; and he had no doubt that Wingate would bring trouble in his train if he set foot in Palestine.
363	6	Churchill, vol. III, pp. 73-4.
365	7	ibid., p. 15.
367	8	Wavell Papers; also quoted in Churchill, vol. III, pp. 74-5.
368	9	See Churchill, vol. III, p. 75.
368	10	ibid.
372	11	*The Mediterranean and Middle East*, vol. I, p. 416.
373	12	Weekly Review of the Military Situation, G.H.Q., M.E.F., 23rd June, 1941.
374	13	*The Mediterranean and Middle East*, vol. I, p. 439.
375	14	*Eastern Epic* by Compton Mackenzie, p. 60.
375	15	Churchill, vol. III, p. 79.
378	16	Despatch: *Operations in East Africa, November, 1940, to July, 1941.*

378   17   *The Mediterranean and Middle East*, vol. I, p. 442.
379   18   A full and detailed account of Wingate's campaign is to be found in Christopher Sykes's biography, chapters XII and XIII.
379   19   A full account of the Italians' last stand at Amba Alagi is given by Compton Mackenzie, op. cit., pp. 65-70.
380   20   Field-Marshal the Viscount Slim, Gen. Sir Frank Messervy, Lieut.-Gen. Sir Dudley Russell, Maj.-Gen. D. W. Reid, Maj.-Gen. P. W. Rees and Lieut.-Gen. Sir Reginald Savory.
380   21   Compton Mackenzie, op. cit., p. 63.

Chapter XII

381   1   *The Rommel Papers*, pp. 102-3.
382   2   Churchill, vol. III, pp. 174-5.
382   3   ibid., p. 177.
382   4   ibid., p. 173.
383   5   Liddell Hart, op. cit., vol. II, p. 67.
383   6   *The Mediterranean and Middle East*, vol. II, pp. 3-4.
384   7   Letter from A.P.W. to Gen. O'Connor, 17th June, 1945.
387   8   *The Rommel Papers*, p. 106.
388   9   Wavell Papers; also quoted in Churchill, vol. II, pp. 178-9.
389   10   ibid.; also quoted in Churchill, vol. III, p. 179.
391   11   *The Rommel Papers*, p. 107.
391   12   *The Mediterranean and Middle East*, vol. II, p. 19.
392   13   *The Rommel Papers*, p. 109.
392   14   Churchill, vol. III, p. 180.
393   15   Gen. O'Connor's report.
393   16   *The Mediterranean and Middle East*, vol. II, p. 21.
394   17   Gen. O'Connor's report. Wavell commented in his Recollections: "I think I should have done better to insist on Neame coming back with me, but in the circumstances I agreed [to O'Connor's suggestion]."
395   18   Wavell Papers; also quoted in Churchill, vol. III, p. 180, but Churchill does not make it clear (1) that it was despatched from London shortly before midnight on 2nd/3rd April, (2) that Wavell could not and did not see it until he himself returned from Cyrenaica on the evening of the 3rd and (3) that Wavell had already taken the action suggested in the final sentence.
396   19   *The Rommel Papers*, p. 109.
396   20   Despatch: *Operations in the Middle East from 7th February, 1941, to 15th July, 1941.*

396	21	*The Rommel Papers*, p. 110.
397	22	ibid., p. 111.
400	23	Gen. O'Connor's report.
401	24	Letter from Gen. O'Connor to A.P.W., 28th June, 1945.
403	25	*The Rommel Papers*, p. 118.
406	26	ibid., p. 123.
407	27	*Tobruk* by Anthony Heckstall-Smith, p. 47.
407	28	Churchill, vol. III, p. 185.
410	29	ibid., p. 186.
410	30	*The Rommel Papers*, p. 127.
412	31	*Greek Tragedy* by Anthony Heckstall-Smith and Vice-Admiral H. T. Baillie-Grohman, p. 49. Author's italics.
413	32	Wavell Papers.
414	33	*Letter from Grosvenor Square* by John G. Winant, reproduced by Kennedy, op. cit., p. 87, footnote 1.
420	34	*The Mediterranean and Middle East*, vol. II, p. 105.
420	35	*Operations in the Middle East from 7th February, 1941, to 15th July, 1941.*
422	36	Kennedy, op. cit., pp. 106-8.
422	37	ibid., p. 108.

Chapter XIII

425	1	Wavell Papers; also quoted in Churchill, vol. III, p. 217.
426	2	ibid.; also quoted in Churchill, vol. III, p. 220.
426	3	Quoted in *The Mediterranean and Middle East*, vol. II, p. 153.
426	4	ibid.
433	5	*Auchinleck* by John Connell, p. 210.
434	6	Churchill, vol. III, p. 226.
435	7	John Connell, op. cit., p. 215.
437	8	H.4 was a pumping station on the Kirkuk-Haifa oil pipeline across the Syrian desert.
438	9	Kennedy, op. cit., p. 116.
439	10	Churchill, vol. III, pp. 228-9.
439	11	Wavell Papers; also quoted in Churchill, vol. III, p. 229.
440	12	On 3rd May Air Chief Marshal Longmore had been summoned to London for consultations. His deputy, Air Marshal Tedder, was acting A.O.C.-in-C. Longmore was never allowed to return to the Middle East, and Tedder was appointed to succeed him on 19th May.
440	13	H.3 was another pumping station on the oil pipeline to Haifa.
441	14, 15	*Five Ventures* by Christopher Buckley, p. 13.

442	16	*The Mediterranean and Middle East*, vol. II, p. 184.
442	17	Churchill, vol. III, p. 230.
442	18	ibid., p. 231.
443	19	Wavell Papers; also in Churchill, vol. III, p. 231.
445	20	Churchill, vol. III, p. 236.
447	21	ibid., p. 237.
447	22	ibid., p. 253.
449	23	ibid., p. 239.
449	24	*The Mediterranean and Middle East*, vol. II, p. 123.
451	25	Churchill, vol. III, p. 243.
451	26	ibid., p. 246.
453	27	Robert Woollcombe, op. cit., p. 127.
454	28	"Colorado" was the code name for Crete.
457	29	Mr. Godfrey Havard was Consul-General in Beirut.
458	30	Churchill, vol. III, p. 288
458	31	ibid., p. 289.
460	32	Kennedy, op. cit., p. 119.
463	33	There is no indication as to when Wavell received this letter; it was almost certainly after 21st June, 1941.

Chapter XIV

465	1	*The Fall of Crete* by Alan Clark, p. 101.
465	2	Churchill, vol. III, p. 254
467	3	*War Memoirs, The Call to Honour*, by Charles de Gaulle, p. 183.
468	4	ibid.
475	5	*The Mediterranean and Middle East*, vol. II, pp. 142-3.
475	6	ibid., p. 147. The wide discrepancies in the estimated numbers of British troops must be noted. It has proved impossible to make these figures, gleaned variously from contemporary telegrams and situation reports, from the *Official History*, and from Churchill, vol. III, either accurate or consistent. It can only be established that between 28,000 and 32,000 British (or Imperial) troops of all services and all contingents took part in the Battle of Crete. The confusion of retreat and defeat is the practical if not the statistical explanation of the variation of 4,000.
476	7	ibid., p. 148.
476	8	Reproduced in full in *Speaking Generally*, p. 24.
476	9	Churchill, vol. III, pp. 298-9.
478	10	Kennedy, op. cit., pp. 119-20.
483	11	ibid., p. 127.
484	12	Churchill, vol. III, p. 304.

487	13	*The Mediterranean and Middle East,* vol. II, p. 166.
489	14	This telegram is dated 3rd June; its time of origin was 0100 hrs., 4th June. It was only therefore on 4th June that Wavell had any knowledge of this important new appointment. There is, however, a considerable confusion of evidence as to the exact date on which the decision to send out Gen. Haining was taken. Churchill himself says only, discussing the subsequent replacement of Wavell by Auchinleck and the appointment of a Minister of State resident in the Middle East: "I had already on June 4 appointed General Haining. . . ." (op. cit., vol. III, p. 311). One *Official History* states: "On 19th May General Sir Robert Haining . . . was, at the Prime Minister's direction, appointed Intendant-General of the Army of the Middle East," and goes on to give a detailed account of the instructions he received on 21st and 30th May. (*The Mediterranean and Middle East,* vol. II, pp. 237-8.) On the other hand, Prof. J. R. M. Butler says that the Prime Minister "proposed early in June to strengthen the command on the administrative side by sending out" Gen. Haining and Mr. Westbrook. (*Grand Strategy,* vol. II, p. 528.) What is clear is that Wavell and his staff were neither consulted nor informed until *after* the decision had been taken.
490	15	op. cit., p. 188.
493	16	Churchill, vol. III, p. 297.
495	17	Air Commodore R. Collishaw, commanding No. 204 Group, R.A.F., in the Western Desert.
496	18	Liddell Hart, op. cit., vol. II, p. 87.
497	19, 20	*The Rommel Papers,* p. 144.
498	21	ibid., pp. 144-5.
500	22	ibid., p. 145.
500	23	*Spearhead General* by Henry Maule, p. 123.
500	24	Churchill, vol. III, p. 308.
501	25	*The Rommel Papers,* p. 146.
501	26	*The Mediterranean and Middle East,* vol. II, p. 171.
503	27	Kennedy, op. cit., p. 133
504	28	John Connell, op. cit., p. 241.
505	29	ibid.
505	30	Gen. Arthur Smith to the author; see also *Wavell* by Bernard Fergusson, p. 59.
505	31	Churchill, vol. III, p. 310.

GLOSSARY
CODE NAMES
BIBLIOGRAPHY

Glossary

A.A.	Anti-aircraft
A.D.C.	Aide-de-camp
A.F.V.	Armoured fighting vehicle: tank
A.G.	Adjutant-General
A.O.C.	Air Officer Commanding
A.O.C.-in-C.	Air Officer Commanding-in-Chief
Bde.	Brigade
B.E.F.	British Expeditionary Force (1914-18 and 1939-40)
B.G.G.S.	Brigadier-General General Staff (1914-18)
B.G.S.	Brigadier General Staff (1939-45)
Bn.	Battalion
B.R.A.	Brigadier Royal Artillery (commanding all artillery in a division)
Brevet	Promotion awarded to a Regular officer, granting him permanent tenure of the rank achieved without regard to pay, appointment or placing in his regimental list
B.T.E.	British Troops in Egypt
C.A.S.	Chief of the Air Staff
C.C.F.	Combined Cadet Force
C.G.S.	Chief of the General Staff
C.I.G.S.	Chief of the Imperial General Staff
C.-in-C.	Commander-in-Chief
C.O.	Commanding Officer
C.O.S.	Chiefs of Staff
C.R.A.	Commander Royal Artillery (directly responsible to the Commander-in-Chief)
C.R.E.	Commander Royal Engineers (directly responsible to the Commander-in-Chief)
D.A.Q.M.G.	Deputy Assistant Quartermaster-General
D.C.G.S.	Deputy Chief of the General Staff
Deutsche Afrika Korps	The German formation, consisting of the 5th Light Division and the 15th Panzer Division, commanded by Rommel in Africa from February to June, 1941

Div.	Division
D.M.I.	Director of Military Intelligence
D.M.O.	Director of Military Operations
D.M.O. & I.	Director of Military Operations and Intelligence
D.M.T.	Director of Military Training
D.S.O.	Distinguished Service Order
E.E.F.	Egyptian Expeditionary Force (1914-18)
Fliegerkorps VIII, X and *XI*	Formations of the German Air Force deployed in Crete and Sicily
F.S.R.	Field Service Regulations
G.H.Q.	General Headquarters (e.g. in B.E.F., M.E.F. and India Command)
G.M.T.	Greenwich Mean Time
G.S.	General Staff
G.O.C.	General Officer Commanding
G.O.C.-in-C.	General Officer Commanding-in-Chief
G.S.O. 1, 2 & 3	Grades of General Staff Officer.
Habforce	The force deployed for the relief of Habbaniya in the Iraq campaign
H.A.C.	Honourable Artillery Company
H.M. ship	Ship of the Royal Navy (used in telegrams)
H.M.A.S.	Ship of the Royal Australian Navy
H.M.G.	His Majesty's Government
"I" tank	Infantry tank ("Matilda")
I.D.C.	Imperial Defence College
I.E.A.	Italian East Africa
Inf. Bde.	Infantry Brigade
Ju.	*Junkers*—type of German aircraft
K.A.R.	King's African Rifles
K.C.B.	Knight Commander of the Order of the Bath
K.O.R.R.	King's Own Royal Regiment
Ll. G.	Mr. David (later Earl) Lloyd George
L.R.D.G.	Long Range Desert Group
Luftwaffe	German Air Force
M.C.	Military Cross
M.E.	Middle East
M.E.F.	Middle East Force
M.F.H.	Master of Foxhounds
M.G.	Machine gun
M.N.B.D.O.	Mobile Naval Base Defence Organisation
M.O.1 & 5	Sections of Military Operations, a department of the General Staff in the War Office
M.T.	Motor Transport

N.Z.	New Zealand
O.E.T.A.	Occupied Enemy Territory Administration
O.R.	Other Ranks
O.T.C.	Officers' Training Corps
Panzer	Generic German term for a tank
P.O.W.	Prisoner of War
Q	Abbreviation applied throughout the British Army to the Quartermaster-General's department
R.A.	Royal Artillery
R.A.S.C.	Royal Army Service Corps
Regia Aeronautica	Italian Air Force
Reichswehr	German Regular Army
R.F.C.	Royal Flying Corps (1914-18)
R.H.A.	Royal Horse Artillery
R.I.R.	Royal Irish Rifles
R.T.R.	Royal Tank Regiment
R.U.S.I.	Royal United Service Institution
S.A.S.O.	Senior Air Staff Officer, R.A.F.
S.S.	*Schutzstaffeln* (Protection squads): Elite Nazi formations, which grew up during Hitler's rise to power and were embodied in the armed forces at the outbreak of war, but retained a great degree of organisational and operational independence
T.A.	Territorial Army
T.E.W.T.	Tactical Exercise without Troops
T.J.F.F.	Transjordan Frontier Force
V.C.I.G.S.	Vice-Chief of the Imperial General Staff
Wehrmacht	The German armed forces
W.O.	War Office
W.O.1, 2	Grades of warrant officer in the British Army
W.T.	Wireless telegraphy

Code Names

Acanthus	1st South African Division
Apology	Fast convoy from U.K. to Middle East, August-September, 1940
Barbarossa	German attack on Russia, June, 1941
Battleaxe	Operation in the Western Desert, June, 1941
Brevity	Probing attack in the Western Desert, May, 1941
Bruiser	Original name for Battleaxe
Colorado	Crete
Compass	General O'Connor's advance in the Western Desert, December, 1940
Eagle	German name for *Luftwaffe's* offensive against U.K., August, 1940
Exporter	Operation against Syria and the Lebanon, June, 1941
Hats	Passage of naval reinforcements into the Mediterranean, September, 1940
Influx	Projected British operation against Sicily
Jaguar	Small convoy to Malta, May, 1941
Lustre	Transport of British forces to Greece, March, 1941
Mandibles	Projected British operation against the Dodecanese
Mercury	German name for Cretan campaign, May, 1941
Sabine	Landing of Indian forces in Basra, April, 1941
Scorcher	Cretan campaign, May, 1941
Sea Lion	German name for proposed seaborne invasion of U.K., 1940
Tiger	Convoy of fast merchant ships carrying A.F.V.s and aircraft to Egypt, May, 1941

Bibliography

ALEXANDER OF TUNIS, FIELD-MARSHAL EARL, *Memoirs 1940-1945*, Cassell, 1962

AMERY, LEOPOLD, *My Political Life*, 3 vols., Hutchinson, 1953-5.

BARCLAY, BRIGADIER C. N., *Against Great Odds*, Sifton Praed, 1956

BARNETT, CORRELLI, *The Desert Generals*, William Kimber, 1960

BEAVERBROOK, LORD, *Men and Power 1917-1918*, Hutchinson, 1956

BLAKE, ROBERT, *The Private Papers of Douglas Haig 1914-1918*, Eyre & Spottiswoode, 1952

BOYLE, ANDREW, *Trenchard: Man of Vision*, Collins, 1962

BRETT-JAMES, ANTONY, *Ball of Fire: The Fifth Indian Division in the Second World War*, Gale and Polden, 1951

BUCKLEY, CHRISTOPHER, *Five Ventures*, H.M.S.O., 1954

BUTLER, J. R. M., *History of the Second World War: Grand Strategy*, vol. II, H.M.S.O., 1957

CAROE, OLAF, *The Pathans*, Macmillan, 1958

CHANDOS, LORD, *Memoirs*, Bodley Head, 1962

CHURCHILL, WINSTON S., *The Second World War*, vols. I, II and III, Cassell, 1948-50

CLARK, ALAN, *The Fall of Crete*, Blond, 1962

CLIFTON, BRIGADIER GEORGE, *The Happy Hunted*, Cassell, 1952

COLLINS, MAJOR-GENERAL R. J., *Lord Wavell: A Military Biography*, Hodder & Stoughton, 1947

DE GAULLE, GENERAL CHARLES, *War Memoirs: The Call to Honour, 1940-1942*, Collins, 1955

DE GUINGAND, MAJOR-GENERAL SIR FRANCIS, *Generals at War*, Hodder & Stoughton, 1964

Operation Victory, Hodder & Stoughton, 1955

EDMONDS, BRIGADIER-GENERAL SIR JOHN, *History of the Great War: Military Operations France and Belgium*, 8 vols., H.M.S.O., 1922-49

EVANS, LIEUTENANT-GENERAL SIR GEOFFREY, *The Desert and the Jungle*, William Kimber, 1959

FALLS, CYRIL, *The First World War*, Longmans, 1960

FERGUSSON, BERNARD, *The Black Watch and the King's Enemies*, Collins, 1950

Wavell: Portrait of a Soldier, Collins, 1961

FIRTH, J. D'E., *Rendall of Winchester*, Oxford, 1954

FLOWER, DESMOND, and REEVES, JAMES, *The War 1935-1945*, Cassell, 1960

GARNETT, DAVID (selected by), *The Essential T. E. Lawrence*, Cape, 1951

HANKEY, LORD, *The Supreme Command, 1914-1918*, vols. I and II, Allen & Unwin, 1961

HASTINGS, MAJOR R. H. W. S. (and others), *The Rifle Brigade in the Second World War 1939-1945*, Gale & Polden, 1950

HECKSTALL-SMITH, ANTHONY, *Tobruk*, Blond, 1959

HECKSTALL-SMITH, ANTHONY, and BAILLIE-GROHMAN, VICE-ADMIRAL H. T., *Greek Tragedy*, Blond, 1961

HOLT, EDGAR, *The Boer War*, Putnam, 1958

HORROCKS, LIEUTENANT-GENERAL SIR BRIAN, *A Full Life*, Collins, 1960

ISMAY, GENERAL THE LORD, *Memoirs*, Heinemann, 1960

JOHNSON, PROFESSOR FRANKLYN A., *Defence by Committee*, Oxford, 1960

KENNEDY, MAJOR-GENERAL SIR JOHN, *The Business of War*, Hutchinson, 1957

KESSELRING, FIELD-MARSHAL, *Memoirs*, William Kimber, 1953

KIPPENBERGER, MAJOR-GENERAL SIR HOWARD, *Infantry Brigadier*, Oxford, 1949

KIRK, GEORGE, *The Middle East in the War*, Oxford, 1952.

LAWRENCE, T. E., *Seven Pillars of Wisdom*, Cape, 1935

LEASOR, JAMES, and HOLLIS, GENERAL SIR LESLIE, *War at the Top*, Michael Joseph, 1959

LIDDELL HART, B. H., *Strategy: The Indirect Approach*, Faber, 1925, and (revised) 1954

The Tanks, Cassell, 1959

(edited by) *The Rommel Papers*, Collins, 1953

LINKLATER, ERIC, *A Year of Space*, Macmillan, 1953

MACKENZIE, COMPTON, *All Over the Place*, Chatto & Windus, 1949

Eastern Epic, vol. I: *Defence*, Chatto & Windus, 1951

MAGNUS, PHILIP, *Kitchener, Portrait of an Imperialist*, John Murray, 1958

MARLOWE, JOHN, *The Seat of Pilate*, Cresset Press, 1959

MAULE, HENRY, *Spearhead General*, Odhams, 1962

MEINERTZHAGEN, COLONEL RICHARD, *Army Diary 1899-1926*, Oliver & Boyd, 1960

MINNEY, R. J., *The Private Papers of Hore-Belisha*, Collins, 1960

MONTGOMERY, FIELD-MARSHAL THE VISCOUNT, *Memoirs*, Collins, 1958

MOOREHEAD, ALAN, *The Russian Revolution*, Hamish Hamilton & Collins, 1958

NICOLSON, HAROLD, *King George V, his Life and Reign*, Constable, 1952

OWEN, FRANK, *Tempestuous Journey*, Hutchinson, 1954

PLAYFAIR, I. S. O., *History of the Second World War: The Mediterranean and Middle East*, vols. I and II, H.M.S.O., 1957 and 1962

RYAN, A. P., *Mutiny at the Curragh*, Macmillan, 1956

SMYTH, BRIGADIER SIR JOHN, V.C., *Before the Dawn*, Cassell, 1957

SYKES, CHRISTOPHER, *Orde Wingate*, Collins, 1959

TERRAINE, JOHN, *Douglas Haig: The Educated Soldier*, Hutchinson, 1963

USBORNE, RICHARD (edited by), *A Century of Summer Fields*, Methuen, 1964

VERNEY, JOHN, *Going to the Wars*, Collins, 1955

WAUGH, EVELYN, *Ronald Knox*, Chapman & Hall, 1959

WAVELL, A. P., *Allenby: Soldier and Statesman*, Harrap, 1946

   Other Men's Flowers, Memorial Edition, Cape, 1952

   The Palestine Campaigns, Constable, 1931

   Soldiers and Soldiering, Cape, 1953

   Speaking Generally, Macmillan, 1946

WEIZMANN, CHAIM, *Trial and Error*, Hamish Hamilton, 1949

WEYGAND, GENERAL MAXIME, *Recalled to Service*, Heinemann, 1952

WILSON, FIELD-MARSHAL LORD, *Eight Years Overseas*, Hutchinson, 1950

WOODRUFF, PHILIP, *The Guardians*, Cape, 1954

WOODWARD, E. L., *History of the Second World War: British Foreign Policy in the Second World War*, H.M.S.O., 1962

WOOLLCOMBE, ROBERT, *The Campaigns of Wavell, 1939-1943*, Cassell, 1959

YOUNG, DESMOND, *Rommel*, Collins, 1950

INDEX

Index

of signals with A.P.W. on policy in Iraq, 436-40, 442; concern over possible German attack on Russia, 446; disagreement with A.P.W. on policy in Syria, 460-1, 493; insistence on every effort to save Crete, 467-9; sanction evacuation of Crete, 473; directives on Western Desert and Syria, 480, 486
Chitral Relief Column, 54-5
Churchill, Lady Edward, 105, 108, 111
Churchill, Captain G. Spencer, 111
Churchill, Mrs. Randolph, 421
Churchill, Sir Winston S., in political battle over Home Rule in Ireland, 82-3; Chancellor of the Exchequer, 150; supports the Balfour Declaration, 186; against policy of appeasement, 198, 203; Chairman of Military Co-ordination Committee, 226; becomes Prime Minister, 227-8; brush with A.P.W. over bringing back troops to U.K., 228, 233-5; sets up Middle East Committee, 242; critical over disposition of the S. African Brigade, 248-9, 255-6; leadership of, summer 1940, 253, 257; difference in temperament from A.P.W., 254-5; relations with Dill, 256; in planning of operation "Hats," 258-63; on the loss of British Somaliland, 264; drafts directive to A.P.W., Aug. 1940, 265-8; anxious on conduct of war in Middle East, 276, 278-9; informed of "Compass" and enthusiasm for it, 280-1; signals to A.P.W. on "Compass," 282-5; impatience over start of "Compass," 287-9; announcement in House of Commons on success of "Compass,"

293; congratulates A.P.W. on successes, 296, 303, 317; plans for future operations, 298; signals to A.P.W. on rearward services, 306; appreciation of strategic conduct of the war, 307-8; on necessity for aid for Greece, 312-13; anger with C.I.G.S. on availability of troops for Greece, 328; desire to form a Balkan front, 330, 334, 389; signals A.P.W. that aid to Greece and Turkey must be major effort, 332-4; signals to Eden on final decision of aid to Greece, 337, 344-6; signals exchanged with Eden on grave risks of Greek aid, 350-2; final decision on Greek expedition, 354, 356, 382; pressure on A.P.W. over East African operations, 358, 362-5; on Smuts's offer of a second S. African Division, 365-6, 372-3; congratulates A.P.W. on victories, 377, 379; concern on German advance in Cyrenaica, 387-8; magnanimous on defeat in Cyrenaica, 401; on necessity to hold Tobruk, 404, 406-7; exchange of signals with A.P.W. on situation in Greece, 407-10, 413-14; demands more information on fighting in Greece, 416-17; misunderstanding and distrust of A.P.W. deepens, 421-3; exchange of signals with A.P.W. on sending more tanks and policy for Tobruk, 425-9; loses confidence in A.P.W. on Iraq question, 438-9; on loss of opportunity by Germans in Iraq, 445; orders Crete to be defended, 450-1, 454; policy for occupation of Syria, clashes with A.P.W., 456-63; decides to replace A.P.W. in

350, 352, 354; Rommel's objective, 406
Summer Fields School, 28-30, 99, 158
Supreme War Council, 133-6
Swinton, General Sir E., 198
Syria, partly under French administration after World War I, 147; French forces in, June 1940, 236; complex situation in, on fall of France, 240-1; preparations for British occupation of, 456-62, 479-80; operation "Exporter," 485-6, 490-3

Taha el Hashimi, 430
Tanks, *British*, great amount of wear and tear on, 245; A.P.W. wants more in Middle East, 250, 257; numbers sent to Middle East in operation "Hats," 259; high opinion of newly arrived tanks, 276-7; "I" tanks (Matilda's) in "Compass," 291, 295; difficulty of repairs, 302; alarming state of cruiser tanks, 386; shortage of tanks in Crete, 453; A.P.W. signals for urgent replacement of losses, 424-6; "Tiger" convoy planned, taking tanks to Middle East, 428-9; "Tiger" arrives with, 458, 477; A.P.W.'s exchanges with Churchill on use of new tanks (Tiger cubs), 469, 478-9, 481, 483-5; in "Battleaxe," 495-502
German: at Mersa Brega, 391; in Rommel's advance, 398-9; losses in attack on Tobruk in April, 407, 409; A.P.W.'s estimate of total in Western Desert, 424-5; in Crete, 447; strength at Sollum, mid-May, 477; strength on Egyptian frontier, end May, 479-80; in

"Battleaxe": strength, 495; counterattack by, 496; tank battles, 497, 498, 499; total losses in operation, 501
Italian: in Italian East Africa, 214, 215, 373; in Western Desert; near Nezuet Ghirba, 15th June, 1940; in September operation, 269, 270, 271; in Nibeiwa camp attack, 9th December, 291-2; numbers captured to 11th December, 295; losses at Tobruk, Jan. 1941, 317; strength in Cyrenaica, 318; tank battle at Mechili, 319; in battle of Beda Fomm, 325-6; in assault on Tobruk, 410
Taranto, 281
Tedder, Marshal of the R.A.F. Lord, A.O.C.-in-C. Middle East, 469, 486-7, 493-4, 502
Tegart, Sir C., 195
Tellera, General, 326
Tewfiq Suwaidi, 430
Theron, Major-Gen. F. H., 367-8
Thompson, Francis, 60
Thomson, Major C. B. (later Lord Thomson), 97
Tiflis, 113-19
"Tiger" operation, convoy to Egypt, May 1941, 425-6, 428-9, 458-9, 477
Tilly, Major-Gen. J., 383
Times, The, 152, 198, 203
Tobruk, air attack on, June 1940, 238; mentioned, 273, 297-8, 301-3, 305, 308, 313; capture of, 316-17, 324; withdrawal to, 399, 402-3, 406; determination to hold, 401-3; invested, 406-10, 424; sally from, 477; part it should play in "Battleaxe," 481-3, 494
Transjordan Frontier Force, 435, 437
Trenchard, Marshal of the R.A.F.

INDEX

B.G.G.S. to Allenby, 147-8; returns to regimental duty in 1920,
149; appointed Assistant Adjutant
General and promoted to Colonel,
149; appointed G.S.O.1 in M.O.I,
150; literary activities, 152-3; appointed G.S.O.1 in 3rd Div. in
1926, 154; association with the
Experimental Armoured Force,
155; views on use of armoured
forces, 156-7; appointed to command 6th Infantry Brigade, 158;
views on mobility and training,
159-60; views on value of military
history, 160-2; lectures on training
to Staff College and R.U.S.I., 162-
4; unorthodox training exercises,
163-8; on value of Aldershot
Tattoo, 169; promoted to Major-
General and appointed to
command 2nd Division, 170;
attends French Army course,
comments on its complacency,
171-2; death of his father, 173:
qualities of and standing in the
Army, 173-4; on death of T. E.
Lawrence, 175-6; on guerrilla warfare, 177; re-writes Field Service
Regulations, 177; *The Higher
Commander*, 177, 180-2; refuses
appointment of Director of Military Training, 182; attends Soviet
Army's 1936 manœuvres, 182-3;
commands British troops in Palestine in 1937, 184, 188-96; transferred to command Southern
Command in U.K., 197-8; considers applying for post of Chichele Professor of Military History, 198-9; pre-war exercises,
200-1; despondent over Munich
agreement, 202; delivers Lees-
Knowles lectures, 203-4, 222;

critical of R.A.F. close support
in peacetime operations, 204;
awarded K.C.B., 205
Middle East Command: appointed
G.O.C.-in-C. Middle East, 205,
209; writes appreciation of situation in event of war with Axis,
210-12; presses for personal aircraft, 213; forces at his disposal, 213-14; signals to C.I.G.S.
on Middle East strategy on outbreak of war, 215-16; initials treaty
of mutual assistance with Turkey,
217; visit to London and conference in Paris, 218-20; War
Cabinet lays down policy for
Middle East, 220-1; writes appreciation based on above policy,
221-2; administrative preparations,
222; addresses newly arrived reinforcements, 223; visit to South
Africa, 223-4; signals to C.I.G.S.
on situation, April 1940, 225; conference with French and Turks
at Beirut, 228; conclusions on
over-running of France, "The
Worst Possible Case," 229-31,
415, 421; appreciation of position
in May 1940, 232; signals exchanged with C.I.G.S. over sending eight battalions to U.K., 232-
4; disposition of his forces and
the enemy's, 235-6; initial successes, 238; signals from C.I.G.S.,
June 1940, 239; dealings with the
French after fall of France, 240-1;
suggests setting up of a Cabinet
sub-committee to deal with problems in Middle East, 241-2;
creates Long Range Desert Group,
244-5; strategy against Italian
East Africa, 246; meeting with
Haile Selassie, 247-8; answers

571

M E D I T E R R

Derna

Jebel Akhdar

Barce

Bomba

Benghazi

Mechili

Gazala
TRIGH CAPUZZO

Tobruk

El Adem

Sidi
Azeiz

Solluch

Tengeder

TRIGH EL ABD

Msus

Bir Hacheim

C Y R E N A I C A

TRIGH EL ABD

Fort
Maddalena

Agedabia

Mersa Brega

El Agheila

L I B Y A

Scale of Miles

0   20   40   60   80   100   200